Urgent Advice and Probing Questions

Publication of this volume is made possible
by a generous grant from the
John and Mary Franklin Foundation, Atlanta, Georgia

Urgent Advice and Probing Questions

Collected Writings on Old Testament Wisdom

by
James L. Crenshaw

Mercer
·1995·

ISBN 0-86554-483-2   MUP/H379

BS
1455
.C66
1995

Urgent Advice and Probing Questions.
Collected Writings on Old Testament Wisdom.
Copyright ©1995
Mercer University Press, Macon, Georgia 31210-3960
All rights reserved
Printed in the United States of America

Essays in this collection were published previously and are reproduced here by permission. Copyrights for the individual essays in
their original publication forms are reserved by the original publishers as indicated in the preface below. The acknowledgments statement in the preface is hereby made part of this copyright notice.

The paper used in this publication meets the minimum requirements
of American National Standard for Information Sciences—
Permanence of Paper for Printed Library Materials, ANSI Z39.48–1984.

Library of Congress Cataloging-in-Publication Data

Crenshaw, James L.
Urgent advice and probing questions.
Collected writings on Old Testament Wisdom.
xiv+606 pages. 6"x9" (15x23 cm.).
Includes bibliographical references and indexes.
ISBN 0-86554-483-2 (alk. paper).
1. Wisdom Literature.   2. Wisdom—biblical teaching.
3. Bible. O.T.—criticism, interpretation, etc.
I. Mercer University.   II. Title.
BS1455.C66   1995
223'.06—dc20   95-13926   **CIP**

Contents

The Wisdom Books
A. Proverbs

B. Job

C. Qoheleth

Abbreviations

1. General

ET	English translation	MT	Masoretic text
EVV	English versions	orig.	original(ly)
H	Hebrew (text or versification)	repr.	reprint(ed)
LXX	Septuagint	v / vv	verse / verses

2. Journals, reference works, serials

ÄA	Ägyptologische Abhandlungen
AB	Anchor Bible
AcOr	*Acta Orientalia* (Copenhagen)
ÄF	Ägyptologische Forschungen
AfO	*Archiv für Orientforschung*
AJSL	*American Journal of Semitic Languages and Literature*
AnBib	Analecta biblica
ANET	*Ancient Near Eastern Texts*
AnGreg	Analecta gregoriana
AnOr	Analecta orientalia
ANQ	*Andover Newton Quarterly*
AO	Der alte Orient
AOAT	Alter Orient und Altes Testament
APOT	*Apocrypha and Pseudepigrapha of the Old Testament* (Charles)
ATAbh	Alttestamentliche Abhandlungen
ATD	Das Alte Testament Deutsch
AzT	Arbeiten zur Theologie
BA	*Biblical Archaeologist*
BASOR	*Bulletin of the American Schools of Oriental Research*
BAT	*Die Botschaft des AT* (Stuttgart)
BBB	Bonner biblische Beiträge
BeO	*Biblia e oriente*
BETL	Bibliotheca ephemeridum theologicarum lovaniensium
BEvT	Beiträge zur evangelischen Theologie
BHT	Beiträge zur historischen Theologie
Bib	*Biblica*
BibOr	Biblica et orientalia
BibS(F)	Biblische Studien (Freiburg)
BibS(N)	Biblische Studien (Neukirchen)
BJRL	*Bulletin of the John Rylands University Library of Manchester*
BKAT	Biblischer Kommentar: Altes Testament
BLS	Bible and Literature series

BO   *Bibliotheca orientalis*
BSac   *Bibliotheca Sacra*
BTB   *Biblical Theology Bulletin*
BWANT   Beiträge zur Wissenschaft vom Alten und Neuen Testament
BZ   *Biblische Zeitschrift*
BZAW   Beihefte zur ZAW
BzEATuAJ *Beiträge zur Erforschung des Alten Testament und der antiken Judentums*
CalTM   Calwer Theologische Monographien
CB   *Cultura bíblica*
CBQ   *Catholic Biblical Quarterly*
CBQMS   CBQ monograph series
CBSC   Cambridge Bible for Schools and Colleges
CJT   *Canadian Journal of Theology*
ConBOT   Coniectanea biblica, Old Testament
EB   Echter Bibel
EF   Erträge der Forschung
EHAT   Exegetisches Handbuch zum AT
ET   English translation
ETL   *Ephemerides theologicae lovanienses*
EvT   *Evangelische Theologie*
ExpTim   *Expository Times*
FFC   Folklore Fellows Communications
FRLANT   Forschungen zur Religion und Literatur des Alten und Neuen Testaments
FTS   Freiburger Theologische Studien
HAR   *Hebrew Annual Review*
HAT   Handbuch zum Alten Testament
HKAT   Handkommentar zum Alten Testament
HLW   Handbuch der Literaturwissenschaft
HO   Handbuch der Orientalistik
HSAT   *Die heilige Schrift des ATs*
HTR   *Harvard Theological Review*
HUCA   *Hebrew Union College Annual*
HUCM   Hebrew Union College monographs
IRT   Issues in Religion and Theology
ICC   International Critical Commentary
IDB   *Interpreter's Dictionary of the Bible*
IDBSup   IDB supplementary volume
Int   *Interpretation*
ITQ   *Irish Theological Quarterly*
JAAR   *Journal of the American Academy of Religion*
JAOS   *Journal of the American Oriental Society*
JBL   *Journal of Biblical Literature*
JBR   *Journal of Bible and Religion*
JCS   *Journal of Cuneiform Studies*
JEA   *Journal of Egyptian Archaeology*
JEnc   *The Jewish Encyclopedia*
JEOL   *Jaarbericht Vooraziatisch-Egyptisch Gezelschap "Ex Oriente Lux"*
JNES   *Journal of Near Eastern Studies*
JQR   *Jewish Quarterly Review*
JSJ   *Journal for the Study of Judaism in the Persian, Hellenistic, and Roman Period*
JSNT   *Journal for the Study of the New Testament*
JSOR   *Journal of the Society of Oriental Research*

JSOT	*Journal for the Study of the Old Testament*
JSOTSup	JSOT supplements
JSS	*Journal of Semitic Studies*
JTS	*Journal of Theological Studies*
Jud	*Judaica. Beiträge zum Verständnis des jüdischen Schicksals in Vergangenheit und Gegenwart*
KAI	Kanaanäische und aramäische Inschriften
KAT	Kommentar zum Alten Testament
KHAT	*Kurzgefasstes exegetisches Handbuch zum Alten Testament*
KHC	Kurzer Handcommentar zum AT
KKANT	Kurzgefasster Kommentar zu den heiligen Schriften Alten und Neuen Testaments sowie zu den Apocryphen
LD	Lectio divina
LUÅ	Lunds universitets årsskrift
MDOG	Mitteilungen der deutschen Orient-Gesellschaft
MGWJ	*Monatsschrift für Geschichte und Wissenschaft des Judentums*
MVAG	Mitteilungen der vorderasiatisch-ägyptischen Gesellschaft
NEBib	Neue Echter Bibel
NorTT	*Norsk Teologisk Tidsskrift*
OBO	Orbis biblicus et orientalis
OBT	Overtures to Biblical Theology
OLZ	*Orientalische Literaturzeitung*
OrAnt	*Oriens antiquus*
OTL	The Old Testament Library
OTRG	Old Testament Reading Guide
OTS	*Oudtestamentische Studiën*
OTWSA	Die Ou Testamentiese Werkgemeenskap in Suid-Afrika (Pretoria)
PAAJR	*Proceedings of the American Academy of Jewish Research*
PTMS	Pittsburgh Theological Monograph series
RB	*Revue biblique*
RevExp	*Review and Expositor*
RGG	*Religion in Geschichte und Gegenwart*
RHPR	*Revue d'histoire et de philosophie religieuses*
RHR	*Revue de l'histoire des religions*
RS	*Ras Shamra*
RSR	*Recherches de science religieuse*
SAIW	*Studies in Ancient Israelite Wisdom* (ed. James L. Crenshaw, 1976)
SAK	*Studien zur Altägyptischen Kultur*
SANT	Studien zum Alten und Neuen Testament
SAT	*Die Schriften des AT in Auswahl*
SB	Sources bibliques
SBL	Society of Biblical Literature
SBLDS	SBL dissertation series
SBLMS	SBL monograph series
SBLSP	SBL seminar papers
SBS	Stuttgarter Bibelstudien
SBT	Studies in Biblical Theology
ScEccl	*Sciences ecclésiastiques*
Sem	*Semitica*
SGV	Sammlung gemeinverständlicher Vorträge aus dem Gebiet der Theologie und Religionsgeschichte
SJT	*Scottish Journal of Theology*

SNVAO   *Skrifter utgitt av det Norske Videnskaps-Akademi i Oslo*
SOTS   Society for Old Testament Study
SOTSMS SOTS monograph series
SQAW   Schriften und Quellen der Alten Welt
SPOA   *Les sagesses du Proche-Orient Ancien, Colloque de Strassbourg*
SQAW   Schriften und Quellen der alten Welt
SR   *Studies in Religion / Sciences religieuses*
SRSup   SR supplements
ST   *Studie theologica*
StMiss *Studia Missionalia*
STU   *Schweizerische Theologische Umschau*
SUNT   Studien zur Umwelt des Neuen Testament
TBü   Theologische Bücherei
TD   *Theology Digest*
TDNT   *Theological Dictionary of the NT*
TDOT   *Theological Dictionary of the OT*
TGl   *Theologie und Glaube*
TGUOS   *Transactions of the Glasgow University Oriental Society*
ThArb   *Theologische Arbeiten*
ThStud Theologische Studien
ThW   *Theologische Wissenschaft*
TLZ   *Theologische Literaturzeitung*
TRu   *Theologische Rundschau*
TSK   *Theologische Studien und Kritiken*
TToday *Theology Today*
TUMSR   Trinity University Monograph Series in Religion
TWNT   *Theologisches Wörterbuch zum NT*
TynNTC Tyndale New Testament Commentary
TynOTC Tyndale Old Testament Commentary
TZ   *Theologische Zeitschrift*
UF   *Ugarit-Forschungen*
VF   *Verkündigung und Forschung*
VS   Verbum salutis
VT   *Vetus Testamentum*
VTSup   VT supplements
WF   Wege der Forschung
WMANT Wissenschaftliche Monographien zum Alten und Neuen Testament
WUNT   Wissenschaftliche Untersuchungen zum NT
WZ   *Wissenschaftliche Zeitschrift* (Halle)
YJS   Yale Judaica series
ZAW   *Zeitschrift für die alttestamentliche Wissenschaft*
ZÄS   *Zeitschrift für Ägyptische Sprache und Altertumskunde*
ZDMG   *Zeitschrift der deutschen morgenländischen Gesellschaft*
ZST   *Zeitschrift für systematische Theologie*
ZTK   *Zeitschrift für Theologie und Kirche*

Preface

The essays in this collection were written over a period of thirty years. The oldest one appeared in print in 1969, and the latest, unpublished until now, was presented as the plenary address at the Southwestern meeting of AAR/SBL/ASSR/ASOR in Dallas, on 10 March 1995. Although this book does not constitute the complete corpus of my published articles on wisdom literature, it does include the vast majority of them and thus provides insight into my thoughts over the years. To some extent, the essays also exemplify the shifting trends within scholarship itself during the last quarter of a century.

I have not attempted to revise the articles in any way, although I would naturally express things somewhat differently now than years ago. Nowhere do I detect any compelling reason for radically altering the arguments or conclusions contained in these essays. Nor have I tried to improve the style of the essays, although at times I have been sorely tempted to do so. Believing these essays still contain much valuable information, I have devoted considerable energy to making them available in a single volume.

The topics under which the articles have been grouped suggest my special interests: identifying the extent of wisdom literature; theodicy; education; method; individual books (Proverbs, Job, and Qoheleth). My eclectic approach combines insights from form and tradition history, literary and theological perspectives, with emphases from traditional historical criticism.

In preparing these essays for publication, I have received extraordinary assistance from Anthony N. Whitley, who supervised the manuscript from the beginning, proofread it more than once, checked the Hebrew, and prepared the index, and from Anita Gail Chappell, whose remarkable skill in typing made publication possible. Both Tony and Gail have earned my lasting gratitude.

I am also grateful to my publishers, who generously gave me permission to reproduce these essays. The names of these publishers, together with pertinent publication information, follow.

1. "Wisdom Literature, Biblical Books," 401-409 in vol. 15 of *The Encyclopedia of Religion*, ed. Mircea Eliade et al. (New York: Free Press, 1987).
2. "The Wisdom Literature," 369-407 in *The Hebrew Bible and Its Modern Interpreters*, ed. D. A. Knight and G. Tucker (Chico CA: Scholars Press, 1985).
3. "Wisdom," 225-64 in *Old Testament Form Criticism*, ed. J. Hayes (San Antonio: Trinity University Press, 1974).

4. "Wisdom Literature: Retrospect and Prospect," 161-78 in *Of Prophets' Visions and the Wisdom of Sages*, ed. H. A. McKay and D. J. A. Clines (Sheffield: JSOT Press, 1993).

5. "Prolegomenon," 1-60 in *Studies in Ancient Israelite Wisdom*, ed. J. L. Crenshaw (New York: Ktav, 1976).

6. "The Shift from Theodicy to Anthropodicy," 1-16 in *Theodicy in the Old Testament*, ed. J. L. Crenshaw (Philadelphia: Fortress Press; London: SPCK, 1983).

7. "The Problem of Theodicy in Sirach," *JBL* 94 (1975): 49-64.

8. "Popular Questioning of the Justice of God in Ancient Israel," *ZAW* 83 (1970): 380-95.

9. "The Concept of God in Old Testament Wisdom," 1-18 in *In Search of Wisdom*, ed. L. G. Perdue, B. B. Scott, and W. J. Wiseman (Louisville: Westminster/John Knox, 1993).

10. "The Restraint of Reason, the Humility of Prayer," forthcoming in Brown Judaic Studies.

11. "The Contest of Darius's Guards in 1 Esdras 3:1-5:3," 74-88 and 119-20 in *Images of Man and God: The Old Testament Short Story in Literary Focus*, ed. B. O. Long (Sheffield: Almond Press, 1981).

12. "Education in Ancient Israel," *JBL* 104 (1985): 601-15.

13. "The Contemplative Life," appearing in *Civilizations of the Ancient Near East*, ed. J. Sasson (New York: Scribners, 1995).

14. "Impossible Questions, Sayings, and Tasks," 19-34 in *Gnomic Wisdom*, ed. J. D. Crossan (Chico CA: Scholars Press, 1980).

15. "The Expression *mî yôdēa'* in the Hebrew Bible," *VT* 36 (1986): 274-88.

16. "The Acquisition of Knowledge in Israelite Wisdom Literature," *Word & World* 7 (1987): 245-52. Copyright ©1987 by *Word & World*, Luther Northwestern Theological Seminary.

17. Review: "*Wisdom in Israel*, by Gerhard von Rad," in *RSR* 2 (1976): 6-12.

18. "Method in Determining Wisdom Influence upon 'Historical' Literature," *JBL* 88 (1969): 129-42.

19. "Wisdom and Authority: Sapiential Rhetoric and Its Warrants," *VTS 32, Congress Volume, Vienna, 1980* (Leiden: E. J. Brill, 1982): 10-29.

20. "Murphy's Axiom: Every Gnomic Saying Needs a Balancing Corrective," 1-17 in *The Listening Heart*, ed. K. G. Hoglund et al. (Sheffield: JSOT Press, 1987).

21. "Proverbs, Book of," 513-20 in volume 5 of *The Anchor Bible Dictionary*, 6 volumes, ed. David Noel Freedman et al. (New York: Doubleday, 1992). Copyright ©1992 by Doubleday, a division of Bantam Doubleday Dell Publishing Group, Inc. Used by permission of Doubleday, a division of Bantam Doubleday Dell Publishing Group, Inc.

22. "Clanging Symbols," 51-64 in *Justice and the Holy*, ed. D. A. Knight and P. J. Paris (Philadelphia: Fortress Press, 1989).

23. "A Mother's Instruction to Her Son (Proverbs 31:1-9)," 9-22 in *Perspectives on the Hebrew Bible*, ed. James L. Crenshaw (Macon GA: Mercer University

Press, 1988).

24. "Poverty and Punishment in the Book of Proverbs," *Quarterly Review* 9 (1989): 30-43.

25. "The Sage in Proverbs," 205-16 in *The Sage in Israel and the Ancient Near East*, ed. L. G. Perdue and J. Gammie (Winona Lake: Eisenbrauns, 1990).

26. "Prohibitions in Proverbs and Qoheleth," 115-24 in *Priests, Prophets, and Scribes*, ed. E. Ulrich et al. (Sheffield: JSOT Press, 1992).

27. "Job, Book of," 858-68 in volume 3 of *The Anchor Bible Dictionary*, 6 volumes, ed. David Noel Freedman et al. (New York: Doubleday, 1992). Copyright ©1992 by Doubleday, a division of Bantam Doubleday Dell Publishing Group, Inc. Used by permission of Doubleday, a division of Bantam Doubleday Dell Publishing Group, Inc.

28. Review: *"Job the Silent: A Study in Historical Counterpoint*, by Bruce Zuckerman," in *Hebrew Studies* 33 (1992): 174-81.

29. "When Form and Content Clash: The Theology of Job 38:1–40:5," 70-84 in *Creation in the Biblical Tradition*, ed. R. J. Clifford and J. J. Collins, CBQMS 24 (Washington DC: Catholic Biblical Association, 1992).

30. "The High Cost of Preserving God's Honor," *The World and I* (December 1987): 375-82. This article appeared in the December 1987 issue and is reprinted with permission from *The World & I*, a publication of the Washington Times Corporation, copyright ©1987.

31. "Job as Drama: A Response to Louis Alonso-Schökel," *Semeia* 7 (1977): 64-69.

32. "In Search of Divine Presence," *Review and Expositor* 74 (1977): 353-69.

33. "Ecclesiastes, Book of," 271-80 in volume 2 of *The Anchor Bible Dictionary*, ed. David Noel Freedman et al. (New York: Doubleday, 1992). Copyright ©1992 by Doubleday, a division of Bantam Doubleday Dell Publishing Group, Inc. Used by permission of Doubleday, a division of Bantam‚Doubleday Dell Publishing Group, Inc.

34. "Qoheleth in Current Research," *HAR* 7 (1984): 41-56.

35. "Youth and Old Age in Qoheleth," *HAR* 10 (1986): 1-13.

36. "The Eternal Gospel (Ecclesiastes 3:11)," 23-55 in *Essays in Old Testament Ethics*, ed. J. L. Crenshaw and J. T. Willis (New York: Ktav, 1974).

37. "The Shadow of Death in Qoheleth," 205-16 in *Israelite Wisdom* (Philadelphia: Fortress Press, 1979).

Finally, Cecil Staton and Edd Rowell of Mercer University Press deserve a word of appreciation, as does the John and Mary Franklin Foundation.

1 (1987)

Wisdom Literature: Biblical Books

Certain books within the Hebrew scriptures stand out as significantly different from the narrative and legal material comprising the Pentateuch as well as from prophetic and apocalyptic literature. This "alien corpus" is altogether silent with regard to the dominant themes found in the rest of the Bible, for example the promise to the patriarchs, the deliverance from Egypt, the Mosaic covenant, the centrality of Jerusalem and the Davidic dynasty, the prophetic word, and so forth. In the place of such emphases one finds ideas and literary forms that are closer to certain Egyptian and Mesopotamian works. That literary corpus contains a rational principle of the cosmic order that is worthy of study (חָכְמָה in ancient Israel, *ma'at* in Egypt, *me* in Mesopotamia) and expresses a belief that conduct in accord with this principle brings well-being. Or the literature gives voice to various levels of doubt about the validity of this understanding of reality, a skepticism spawned by life's inequities. Since study of the underlying principle of the universe rather than proclamation of the divine word comes to prominence here, modern scholars designate these texts as wisdom literature.

Characteristics of Wisdom Literature. Decisive differences do exist between Israel's sapiential literature, on the one hand, and certain texts written in Egypt and Mesopotamia on the other. Egyptian wisdom functioned almost exclusively at the royal court. Its aim was to provide proper education for future bureaucrats in the pharaoh's court. Accordingly, this literature largely assumed the form of instruction (e.g., the *Instruction of Ptahhotep*, the *Instruction of King Amenemhet to His Son Sesostris*, and the *Instruction for Merikare*) and its setting was usually the scribal school (praise of which occurs in Papyrus Sallier, Papyrus Anastasi, and the *Instruction of a Man for His Son*). In Mesopotamia the study of school texts also played an important role, but the fundamental feature of wisdom was cultic, indeed, magical, and the goal of wisdom was to manipulate the paraphernalia of the cult in order to ensure one's existence.

Israelite wisdom finds primary expression in the books of Proverbs, Job, and Ecclesiastes within the Palestinian (Masoretic) canon and in Ben Sira (Ecclesiasticus) and the Wisdom of Solomon in the Alexandrian canon (the Septuagint). Its influence extends beyond these texts to Psalms (Pss 1, 19, 33, 39, 49, 127) and various other books. The precise extent of this influence is the subject of considerable discussion; scholars have claimed much of the Hebrew scriptures for the sages (Genesis 1–11, the Joseph story, Deuteronomy, Amos, Isaiah, Micah, Jonah, Habakkuk, Esther, the succession narrative in 2 Sam 9–20, 1 Kgs 1–2, and more). While such claims appear to be exaggerated, they do serve as a reminder that the sages did not dwell in isolation from the prophets, priests, and raconteurs in ancient Israel.

With the exception of Job, these Israelite wisdom books are pseudonymous. There is no historical basis for the attribution of the older collections within Proverbs to Solomon or for Solomonic authorship of Ecclesiastes and Wisdom of Solomon; in Egyptian wisdom literature pseudonymity and literary fiction of royal authorship also play a significant role. The unique example of pride of authorship is Yehoshua ben Sira, the author of Ben Sira, who claims to have run a school about 190 B.C.E. during the high priesthood of Shimon II. Confirmation of this date comes from information provided by Ben Sira's grandson, who translated the Hebrew text into Greek around 132 B.C.E., and from the hymn in praise of Shimon. Proverbs contains several different collections from various times, some of which may be preexilic. Ecclesiastes probably comes from the end of the third century B.C.E., while Wisdom of Solomon is known to be considerably later, because it was written in Greek and because its thought patterns and rhetoric are thoroughly hellenized. In dating Ecclesiastes, grammar and syntax seem conclusive. Job is particularly hard to date, but a combination of things, including both language and thought, suggest the sixth century B.C.E. or slightly later.

Themes, Literary Type, and Function. In general, wisdom literature comprises two quite distinct types: brief observations about the nature of reality and instructions deriving from experience or extensive reflection on the deeper meaning of life. The former are formulated in parallel half lines for the most part; one statement is thus balanced by another, either synonymously or antithetically. Three variants are "Better is this than that" (e.g., Prov 15:16); a graded numerical proverb, such as "Three things . . . yea, four" (e.g., Prov 30:18-19); and "There is . . . " (e.g., Prov 20:15). Most of these brief aphorisms are complete in themselves, although larger paragraphs appear in the latest collection in Proverbs 1–9, Ecclesiastes, and, especially, Ben Sira, constituting paragraphs that resemble brief essays on a specific topic. Speculative wisdom literature (Job and Ecclesiastes) prefers dialogue and monologue as its peculiar mode of expression.

Another way of categorizing various types of wisdom literature derives from the four uses to which the texts were put: juridical, experiential, theological, and natural. Since the king was the final court of appeal, and since society relied on royal power to implement justice, the judicial ability to ferret out the truth amid competing claims was greatly prized, as the widely disseminated story about Solomon's royal verdict in the case of two harlots' dispute over a surviving infant suggests (1 Kgs 3:16-28). Experiential wisdom encompasses the overwhelming majority of biblical proverbs. These represent conclusions based on experience, and they endeavor to assist others in the difficult task of coping. Some are content with stating the way things are; others engage the pedagogic enterprise with zeal, offering warnings and motivations for following a particular path of conduct. Theological wisdom is concerned with the first principle of knowledge in religious devotion, the fear of the Lord. It speculates on the presence or absence on earth of the divine rational principle (personified wisdom), and sometimes equates revelation of Torah and human reasoning. Natural wisdom refers to encyclopedic data about heavenly bodies, atmospheric conditions, wild animals, and so forth. Although prominent in Egypt and Mesopotamia, such noun lists (onomastica) did not survive in biblical wisdom, although the divine speeches in the Book of Job resemble them in some ways.

The function of Israelite wisdom literature is by no means clear, partly because of the difficulty in tracing the history of this sort of thinking. At least three distinct stages seem likely. Wisdom's earliest phase seems to have coincided with early clan existence, when parents instructed their children in the ways of the world. The vast majority of proverbs attributed to Solomon may well have arisen in this early period because they rarely reflect the situation of the royal court. In the second phase, with Solomon perhaps, and certainly with Hezekiah, wisdom makes itself at home in the court. This phase placed a distinct mark on only a few proverbs, although it did evoke a tradition about "men of Hezekiah" who transmitted the collection in Proverbs 25–29. With Ben Sira the third phase comes to light, school wisdom. Precisely when this phenomenon first surfaced remains hidden. Certainly, the first epilogue to Ecclesiastes (12:9-12) identifies the unknown author of that book as a "wise man" who taught "the people," and the strange pen name Qohelet has often been interpreted as one who summoned people to a place of worship and study. (It is more likely that the word alludes to his assembling of proverbs about life's absurdity.)

School Texts. For various reasons, several scholars have proposed that biblical wisdom literature originated in Israel in monarchic or premonarchic times as texts for study in schools. This theory is based on analogy with schools in the pharaoh's court and in the Mesopotamian temple precincts. Israel's familiarity with international wisdom cannot be denied; witness Solomon's relations with Egypt, the incorporation of a portion of the *Instruction of Amenemope* in Proverbs 22:17–23:33, and the *Sayings of Agur* and *of Lemuel's Mother* in Proverbs 30:1-4 and 31:1-9. Corroborative evidence has come from the nature of canonical wisdom—its exceptional literary quality, its conscious rhetoric and pedagogic thrust. To these have recently been added data from Palestinian inscriptions (alphabetic series, drawings, inaccurate spellings, transposed letters, large and poorly formed consonants, and so forth). None of this evidence is altogether compelling, although its cumulative force merits consideration. The preservation of wisdom literature implies such a group of individuals, whether they attended a formal institution or not. At least one scholar has simply called this phenomenon "Israel's intellectual tradition."

Internal evidence suggests that the Book of Proverbs was written for the instruction of young men. That conclusion seems inevitable for at least two reasons: the direct address to "my son" and the extensive warning against the foreign woman,

Dame Folly, together with the erotic language about Dame Wisdom, which is appropriate only if the audience is male. This erotic language becomes fully evident in the Wisdom of Solomon where readers are invited to strive for marriage with Sophia ("wisdom"), here a divine attribute. Male dominance also explains the misogyny within canonical wisdom, particularly in Ben Sira but also in Ecclesiastes (although this explanation has been disputed). If the author of the epilogue to Ecclesiastes is trustworthy, a democratization may have taken place under this collector of sayings who taught "the people."

Wisdom as a Way of Thinking. Just what did the teachers wish to communicate to their students? The sages endeavored to discover ways to secure one's existence and to enrich it, as in Ecclesiastes' question "What is good for humans?" Their ultimate goal was to achieve life's good things: a good name, longevity, wealth, wise children. Believing that the creator had implanted within the universe the secrets to success, these sages looked for analogies that unlocked the doors to such insight. Observation of nature and human nature, the study of animals and insects—these were the ways in which they obtained information that was then applied to their own concrete situation. They also moved beyond the visible universe to speculate about God's nature and activity, and even their quest for pleasure was grounded in religious conviction. Since order in society, like cosmic order, is divinely ordained, the wise individual is not disruptive of society. Entirely missing, therefore, is the prophetic sense of social revolution. In its place prudence reigns, and a calculated use of bribes, silence, and the concealment of real thoughts and feelings. Self-control and the right word were their aim. The seekers of wisdom sought to know the appropriate word or proper deed for a given occasion, the one that would confirm their membership in the company of the wise and therefore the righteous.

A Crisis of the Intellect. Experience was sometimes ambiguous, forcing the wise to question their own hardened dogmas. That was especially the case with regard to the conviction that virtue flourished and vice resulted in calamity. Belief in reward and retribution evoked powerful protests from the authors of Job and Ecclesiastes. In Mesopotamia a similar crisis of faith produced such works as the Sumerian *A Man and His God*, *I Will Praise the Lord of Wisdom*, the *Babylonian Theodicy*, and the *Dialogue of a Master and Slave*. Furthermore, to the biblical sages life was infinitely more complex than their proverbial formulations might suggest. They therefore ventured to speculate about things that could not be verified in experience. Religion thus emerged into prominence, both as the essential ingredient of all knowledge and as a faith claim. Whereas Yahwism tended to ground its claims in history, the wise took creation as their starting point. They even posited a feminine principle (חָכְמָה) as active in the process of creation (Prov 8:22-31), eventually identifying it with the Torah of Moses (Sir 24:23). In general, creation faith functions to undergird belief in divine justice; only the creator has sufficient power and knowledge to assure justice on earth. As long as sages believed in the power of the human intellect to secure their existence, grace remained in the background. In time, loss of faith in the power of wisdom creates a vacuum into which competing forces come. These opposing responses are pessimism and divine mercy, and their spokesmen are Ecclesiastes and Ben Sira, respectively.

Skepticism's roots go back a long way prior to the time of Ecclesiastes (e.g., Jdgs 6:13, Prov 14:1, 13; 16:9, 33). Integral to the earliest sapiential expression is the concession that human ingenuity has its definite limits. Those who devise plans for battle must ultimately acquiesce before an incalculable divine will. Life has its mystery, which cannot be penetrated. Even instances of injustice cropped up now and then. In time, those cracks in the fundamental conviction of the sages became more frequent, and the idea of wisdom's hiddenness suddenly emerged as a viable epistemological option. The poem, probably by another author, that has been inserted into the Book of Job (28) marvels at the remarkable achievements humans have to their credit but expresses the opinion that wisdom is accessible to God alone. The author of Ecclesiastes admits that wisdom is very deep, so much so that it cannot be fathomed. Ben Sira cannot endorse such skepticism, although he does advise against trying to understand that which is too difficult. In a sense, the nature of human knowledge has been greatly qualified as a consequence of man's limited powers.

Sometimes an inability to comprehend life's mysteries ends in awe rather than skepticism. That is the insight put forth with poetic brilliance in the Book of Job. The decisive issue here is whether faith can transcend self-interest. To be sure, the book offers counsel on how to respond when trouble strikes innocent victims, but even more central is the issue of whether anyone will serve God for nothing. Job's final submission before a self-manifesting deity points to a wholly different response from that of skepticism or banality: a bowed knee and silenced protest, a seeing with the eye of faith. A similar response occurs in Psalm 73, which is often included in discussions of wisdom literature, where the believer comes close to abandoning the faith because of the prosperity of the wicked but in the end recognizes God's presence as the highest good.

Wisdom as a Tradition. Such shifts in perspective indicate that the wise were very much aware of history even if they did not ground their teachings in it. Indeed, a decisive transition takes place in the early second century with Ben Sira. In part a result of the Hellenistic environment within which he wrote, this borrowing of various features from Yahwism, for example, references to the primeval history, patriarchs, and prophets, was Ben Sira's way of salvaging the ancient teaching in a changing society. By means of mythological speculation he was able to identify earlier revelation with divine wisdom (Sir 24:23) and locate its residence in Jerusalem (Sir 24:1-12). Again and again Ben Sira alludes to biblical stories, until finally he compiles a hymn in praise of ancient heroes of the faith (Sir 44:50).

The unknown author of Wisdom of Solomon continued Ben Sira's reliance on canonical tradition as a framework, particularly the account of Egyptian bondage and divine deliverance. This Exodus material generated unusual interest for the Jews who resided in Alexandria a millennium later. In this instance the author reflects on the events of the Exodus in Midrashic style; the running comments on scripture are designed to evoke psychological factors such as dread even though the central focus is a frontal attack on idolatry. Nevertheless, the Hebraic tradition shares equal billing with the Hellenic, and this is entirely new for the wisdom literature. The Greek influence is considerable: the style is replete with Greek rhetoric, and the content is equally Greek in origin, including the four cardinal virtues, the notion of immortality, the twenty-two attributes of deity, the description of the curriculum in a local school, the rhetorical device called *sorites*, and much more.

Personified Wisdom. The change within wisdom thinking from the sixth to the first century B.C.E. is nowhere clearer than in the notion of personified wisdom. In the latest collection of Proverbs (1–9) Wisdom appears in the guise of a teacher; here she invites and threatens young men, seeking to deliver them from Dame Folly. In Proverbs 8 Dame Wisdom is a celestial figure who assists God in creation; she is the manifestation of divine thought, depicted in veiled erotic language. Interpreters have often compared this theologoumenon to the Isis myth and to the teachings about the Egyptian goddess *Ma'at*. Elsewhere in Proverbs (3:16), Wisdom holds life in her right hand, riches and honor in her left hand, just as Ma'at is depicted as holding in each hand emblems that symbolize these qualities. In the Book of Job there is mention of an impenetrable wisdom who is known to the underworld by rumor but to whom only God has direct access (Job 28:20-28).

In contrast, Ben Sira writes that wisdom existed in heaven but searched the whole earth for a place of residence and finally chose Jerusalem as a permanent abode. This celestial figure then loses her enigmatic character, however, and becomes identical with the Mosaic law. Divine wisdom is thereby domesticated on earth, and Greek philosophy and the Hebraic tradition become equal in this aspect. In Wisdom of Solomon this heavenly figure is a divine attribute that guides the chosen people to their destiny. Those who desire to succeed in life must win her favor, and she is therefore to be courted like a bride.

To sum up, poetic imagery in Proverbs has by the time of Wisdom of Solomon become an actual figure who functions to bring well-being to God's people. By way of Ben Sira this imagery was particularized to refer to an actual body of literature, the Mosaic law. From first to last, however, wisdom's role in the initial act of creation was an active one. The intention was to give a name to the order that governs reality itself and thus to suggest a universe in which right thinking and acting would prosper. The author of Ecclesiastes, who did not endorse such faith, maintained silence with regard to personified wisdom. Instead, he echoes one feature of the poem in Job 28: the profundity of wisdom and, therefore, its hiddenness (Eccl 7:23-29).

A Corpus of Literature. The thesis of a shift in wisdom thinking that took place with Ben Sira and Wisdom of Solomon does not imply monolithic thought prior to the second century, but it does assume that certain essentials held the literature together despite individual characteristics. A closer look at the actual contents of this literature may illustrate this point.

Proverbs. The Book of Proverbs comprises at least nine separate collections, four major ones—(I) 1–9, (II) 10:1–22:16, (III) 22:17–24:22, (IV) 25–29—and five minor ones—(V) 24:23-34, (VI) 30:1-9, (VII) 30:10-33, (VIII) 1:1-9, (IX) 31:10-31. Two (VI and VIII) are attributed to foreign authors (Agur and King Lemuel's mother, respectively), and another (III) makes extensive use of an Egyptian source (Amenemope). Three (I, III, and IV) are credited to King Solomon, and one (V; cf. III) is simply called "More Sayings of the Wise." Only two brief collections (VII and IX) have no superscriptions. The probable order of dating is IV, II, III, and V, from oldest to most recent; the relative ordering of the others is uncertain. The initial collection is probably the latest one, with the possible exception of IX. Affinities with Canaanite literature suggest an early date for VI and VIII, but their religious content renders the issue unclear. In any event, much of the material probably arose in preexilic times.

In the older collections the dominant form is a single verse parallel with another. The parallel verse may be synonymous, antithetical, or ascending (climactic). Each brief aphorism registers an observation that compels assent; therefore, the sentence argues from what is presumed to be a general consensus. The other major proverb type is the instruction, which urges a particular course of action and reinforces it with threats of punishment or promises of reward. Instruction pervades the latest collection, but the decision about the date of composition is not based on form. In Egypt "instructions" (a form that has its own genre identification, and covers a wide spectrum of texts) date from very early times, while the late *Teaching of 'Onkhsheshonqy* resembles the brief aphorisms in the earliest collections of Proverbs. Thus we see that dating from form is tricky. In the later biblical material single proverbs give way to brief essays, some of which make their point by citing a proverb and developing it. Ben Sira develops this trend so that paragraph units result. In Proverbs one finds extended treatments of such themes as the relative value of various professions (38:24–39:11), the place of physicians in society since God punishes the wicked by sending illness (38:1-15), duty to parents, drunkenness (19:1-3), headstrong daughters (42:9-11), dreams, discipline (30:7-13), passions (40:1-11) and shame (41:16–42:8). The different form in Proverbs 1–9 is accompanied by a more self-conscious theology. Whereas wisdom literature throughout the ancient Near East prefers the general name for God, these chapters use the name Yahweh quite freely. Furthermore, they insist that the fear of the Lord is the *sine qua non* of true intelligence. It is possible that one passage (6:20-35) draws on language from Deuteronomy in juxtaposing the fire of lust and the lamp of parental instruction. In these chapters, too, personified wisdom functions to mediate divine presence. Accordingly, she addresses the people in the manner of a prophet or a prophetic depiction of God, and she offers life itself.

There are some brief sayings elsewhere in the Book of Proverbs that are wholly secular in tone. That does not necessarily indicate an early date. It is more likely that religious and secular proverbs existed simultaneously but that they served different constituencies. Some of these secular sayings call attention to social inequities without any indication that such situations should be rectified. Other proverbs identify areas in which humans confront their limits. Those who wage war can make careful plans, but the battle's outcome rests in divine hands. This awareness of finitude crops up in Egyptian wisdom as well, where royal wisdom abounds. The attribution of wisdom to Solomon is therefore an interesting parallel, although it cannot be known whether this tradition of Solomonic authorship has any basis in history. One thing appears certain: the supposed Solomonic enlightenment never existed, and the type of wisdom credited to that king in 1 Kings 4:29-34 (English version) does not correspond with sayings in the collections bearing his name. Nevertheless, Solomon may have sponsored a group of sages in his court, as Hezekiah did in the late eighth century. These sages may have shown their appreciation by attaching the king's name to their compositions. Unfortunately, these collections do not require an assumption of courtly provenance, although they do contain an occasional reference to royalty. The same is true of Proverbs 25:2, which states that God's glory consists in concealing things, whereas a king's glory lies in searching them out.

In general, the thrust of the sayings in the Book of Proverbs has a universal quality. Similar aphorisms exist in Egyptian wisdom and, to a lesser extent, in Mesopotamian. The biblical proverbs contrast the wise and the foolish (called the silent and the heated in Egyptian wisdom literature), offer advice on table manners, warn against laziness and sexual debauchery, endorse eloquence, observe human foibles for what they are, talk about responsibilities in given vocations, compare human conduct to that of animals or insects, encourage strict discipline of children, inculcate respect for parents and persons in authority, and treat social relations in all their complexity. Extended treatises occur outside the initial collection on significant issues, for instance, the dangers of strong drink and the virtues of a good wife.

The Book of Job. The fundamental presupposition underlying virtually all these proverbs is a belief in reward and retribution. The universal creator oversees the governance of the universe and makes certain that those who merit life's good things receive them. The author of the Book of Job questions this principle, although at first the argument set forth by his hero rests on the very premise it refuses to acknowledge. Were it not for this principle, Job would have no basis on which to complain, since there would be no anticipated correlation between conduct and life situation. The author of Ecclesiastes is much more thorough in rejecting this dogma, for in his view time and chance strike everyone without respect to behavior. In both cases, later tampering with the author's final product has radically altered its meaning.

The Book of Job resembles disputes in Mesopotamian wisdom (such as *I Will Praise the Lord of Wisdom*), but it also has elements of a lament (one critic has called the book a paradigm of an answered lament). An old folk tale in epic prose sets the stage for the poetic dispute: a patient Job loses everything and praises God nonetheless until God rewards him by doubling his original possessions. Apart from this narrative framework, Job consists of a dispute between Job and his three friends and a second dispute between God and Job. Speeches by the youthful Elihu interrupt these two disputes; like the poem in Job 28, these speeches (Job 32–37) are probably secondary. The hero of the poetic speeches is far from patient. Instead, he complains bitterly because God has become a stranger to him for no discernible reason. Although his three friends encourage him to pray for forgiveness, Job insists that he has done nothing to deserve such harsh treatment. His bitterness arises from a sense of an oppressive divine presence and an awareness that the deity he once knew can no longer be found. Now and again Job entertains the notion that a vindicator will set things right and establish his innocence. At last, despairing of assistance from his friends, Job utters an oath of innocence highly reminiscent of Egyptian cultic practice and challenges God to slay him or confirm his oath of purity (Job 31). God responds to the challenge but hardly in the way Job expected (Job 38–41). In a style similar to school questions in Egyptian texts, the deity addresses Job with a host of questions that force him to look beyond his own situation and survey the vast scope of creation. The shift in focus corrects Job's anthropocentricity while acknowledging divine solicitude for wild creatures beyond the parameters of human habitation. The divine speeches evoke a feeling of unworthiness in Job, who confesses that this new insight about God overshadows his former knowledge as immediate information does secondhand information. The resolution comes through repentance, if that is the true meaning of Job's final response to God. The Mesopotamian parallels to Job find their answer in the cultic realm, and proper ritual plays a significant role.

Ecclesiastes. Israel's contribution to skeptical literature, the Book of Ecclesiastes, presents reflections on life's vanity and concludes that everything is empty, like breath itself. Purporting to be written by the wisest and wealthiest king in Israel, it claims that all pursuits achieve no lasting results. For this book's author, wisdom no longer possesses the power to guarantee success; all human endeavors amount to a senseless "chasing after wind." He feels that even though some sages claim to know the truth about reality, they do not really penetrate to the heart of things (8:17). The great shadow hanging over life is death, which makes no distinctions between good and bad people or between animals and humans. The universe is out of kilter, and God is indifferent to what takes place on earth (9:11-12). As a consequence humans are advised to follow a path of moderation, to be neither overly righteous (like Job) nor excessively wicked (7:15-18). Such dark thoughts eventuate in hatred for life (2:17), and stillborns are considered more fortunate than the living (6:1-6). To be sure, wisdom does bestow a relative advantage over folly, as light is usually superior to darkness. But oppression runs rampant, and there is no comforter. The positive advice given is to enjoy life during one's youth, before death wields its awesome power. The book closes with a poem about old age and death (comparable texts have been found in ancient Sumer and Egypt). Unhappy with the negative note on which the book ends, someone added an epilogue that characterizes the teacher and his work (12:9-12), to which yet another epilogue has been attached

(12:13-14). This final word neutralizes the entire book by summing up its contents as fearing God (piety) and keeping the commandments (praxis).

Ben Sira. The author of Ben Sira strives mightily to combine traditional religious belief and the wisdom tradition. Although capable of soaring to lofty heights in poetic verse, his heart is especially stirred when priestly interests and prerogatives come to mind. This fact has led some critics to the view that religion (the "fear of the Lord"), not wisdom, was central to Ben Sira. The same emphasis occurs in the long poem celebrating heroes of the past, a poem that concludes with a lavish description of the high priest in attendance at the altar (44–50). Competing traditions are held in check in Ben Sira. This accounts for the acceptance of old belief in the functioning of reward and retribution, along with special attention to divine mercy.

In some respects Ben Sira resembles Proverbs, even with regard to the subject matter. Nevertheless, whereas Proverbs for the most part couches its teaching in succinct observations, Ben Sira systematically elaborates upon one topic after another. In so doing Ben Sira occasions a decisive stylistic change: refrains occur with regularity. The same phenomenon is typical of Egyptian instructions; in fact, Egyptian influence in Ben Sira is likely (cf. *The Satire on the Trades* and Papyrus Insinger).

One important concern in Ben Sira is theodicy, the defense of divine justice. Ben Sira employs an ancient form of debate to achieve the defense and adds two distinct answers, one metaphysical and the other psychological, to the problem of theodicy: that the universe itself fights on the side of virtue and punishes wickedness, and that reward or punishment may be inner states of tranquillity or anxiety. Furthermore, God will set things right in a moment, so that one cannot be adjudged righteous or sinful until death; a similar expectation of future divine action furnishes comfort to the author of Psalm 73. Such faith finds appropriate expression in prayer and in hymnic praise; both modes of worship characterize Ben Sira the teacher. Wisdom has now become an integral fact of Yahwistic faith.

Wisdom of Solomon. The combination of piety and practical ethics continues in Wisdom of Solomon, which presents Hebraic ideas in Hellenistic dress. In this Hellenistic setting religious syncretism poses a problem of grave proportions; to combat the attractiveness of idols as an expression of devotion to the gods, the author ridicules this type of worship mercilessly. A similar attitude pervades the author's references to Egyptian rulers; like the earlier sages, this unknown author deals with only two categories of people, wise and foolish, who are, respectively, good and evil. The new element is an identification of good and evil along ethnic lines, a precedent for which occurs in Ben Sira. The earlier universalism that was an identifying mark of wisdom has faded under the mighty impact of national religious tradition.

Perhaps the single most radical departure from older sapiential teachings is the elevation of the erotic dimension as the dominant metaphor for the educational enterprise. Knowledge is a highly desirable bride of the one who is favored by the deity. The paradigm that functions effectively in this respect is grounded in the legend about King Solomon, wisest of men. But such intellectual superiority came as a divine gift in response to humble prayer. The power of wisdom transcends the personal inasmuch as it governs the affairs of a nation. In fact, wisdom functions in the same way that the holy spirit is described as functioning in the rest of the Hebrew Bible: as a personification guiding the prophets and leaders of Israel. Once again, an earlier characteristic of wisdom literature, its individualism, gives way to the nation of Israel.

With increased stress on divine activity come two further transformations of ancient wisdom: humanism bows before revelation, and eudaemonism bows before duty. Belief in immortality relieves the human finitude of its tragedy, because pleasures may be delayed until the next life.

Later Developments. The Jewish Alexandrian philosopher Philo Judaeus, who was born about 20 B.C.E., avails himself of Logos speculation from Greek and Jewish thinkers to present wisdom as the ordering principle of the universe and an expression of the divine will. Comparison with the Stoic Logos principle was almost inevitable, because this similarity in the two intellectual systems served as a bridge to bring them closer together. Like the author of Wisdom of Solomon, Philo was steeped in Hellenistic thought and expression. Nevertheless, the content of his thought is often thoroughly Judaic. Scholars cannot decide whether the language of mystery religions belongs to the heart of his message or is mere window dressing.

Philo does not borrow exclusively from Israelite wisdom literature but makes free use of the patriarchal stories. His elaborate allegorical exegesis of biblical texts is largely Greek, although certain writings from Qumran also employ a complex kind of hermeneutics (cf. the *Habakkuk Commentary*). This ancient sect in the region of the Dead Sea largely ignored the wisdom literature, with one possible exception—the erotic dimension of knowledge.

Late Jewish narratives—Tobit, for example—make occasional use of motifs and data from canonical and noncanonical wisdom. Certain affinities between older wisdom and *Pirqei abot* (Sayings of the Fathers) have often been cited, but these seldom extend beyond surface resemblances. Within the Apocrypha, 2 Esdras (4 Ezra) wrestles with the difficult problem of theodicy, and the pseudepigraphic *Testaments of the Twelve Patriarchs* contains ethical teachings that resemble wisdom texts.

The New Testament. The wisdom tradition seems to have influenced the unknown author of the earliest source for the Gospels, known as Q. Jesus is credited with a number of gnomic sayings, most of which function to orient by disorientation: they challenge listeners by forcing them to rethink their own presuppositions about a given situation. One noteworthy feature of these sayings attributed to Jesus is their unusual attitude toward women. Whereas aphorisms concerning women in the first-century Greco-Roman world and in Jewish literature contain a strong misogynistic element, the brief sayings placed in Jesus' mouth are remarkably free of this sentiment.

The prologue to the Gospel of John utilizes Logos speculation to express the belief that Jesus was an earthly incarnation of the deity, and the Gospel of Matthew dares to identify Jesus with divine wisdom, the embodiment of Torah (Matt 11:25-30). Outside the Gospels, Paul's letters rely on Judaic speculation about wisdom to express Jesus' role in creation itself. Furthermore, just as the sages had developed a theory in opposition to theodicy as an extreme response to evil (that is, the very wish to defend God's honor is blasphemous, since the deity is by definition just), Paul ridicules human wisdom and proclaims that God's love and power are demonstrated by Jesus' death on the cross. It is conceivable that Paul's opponents were witnessing the birth of Christian gnosticism, perhaps even performing midwife service. One other New Testament text is strongly influenced by Hebrew wisdom, the short Letter of James, which draws freely upon brief aphorisms to inculcate certain teachings in the minds of listeners.

Gnosticism. The influence of the wisdom tradition in gnosticism is somewhat anomalous. In Jewish tradition wisdom played a vital role during the creation of the world. For the gnostics the present material universe is the product of demiurges, inferior divine beings. Nevertheless, wisdom speculation was too appealing for gnostics to ignore, although they soon found ways to overlook wisdom's role in creating the universe. Three documents deserve consideration here: the *Gospel of Thomas*, the *Sentences of Sextus*, and a nongnostic text from Nag Hammadi, the *Teachings of Silvanus*. The influence of the wisdom tradition on Thomas may explain why instead of a passion story one finds a collection of sayings. The *Sentences of Sextus* (second century) contains over four hundred maxims of non-Jewish origin whose purpose is to describe the ideal Christian. The *Teachings of Silvanus* is a text that manifests typical Jewish stylistic forms: the address to "my son," which is reminiscent of the Book of Proverbs; poetic parallelism; and certain subjects and expressions that correspond to canonical ones. All this indicates that early Christians may have been drawn to some features of Hebrew wisdom and that they agree with their predecessors who believed that the intellect was a sufficient means of coping with reality and achieving the good life.

Bibliography

The most comprehensive discussions are James L. Crenshaw's in *Old Testament Wisdom* (Atlanta, 1981) and Gerhard von Rad's in *Wisdom in Israel*, trans. James D. Martin (Nashville, 1972). Three older treatments contain much valuable material: Johannes Fichtner's *Die altorientalische Weisheit in ihrer israelitisch-jüdischen Ausprägung*, BZAW 62 (Giessen, 1933); Oliver S. Rankin's *Israel's Wisdom Literature* (Edinburgh, 1936); and Hilaire Duesberg and Irénée Fransen's *Les scribes inspirés*, 2nd ed. (Maredsous, Belgium, 1966). Three colloquiums have illuminated many disputed points. These are *Les sagesses du Proche Orient ancien*, ed. Francois Wendel (Paris, 1963); *La sagesse de l'Ancien Testament*, ed. Maurice Gilbert (Gembloux, 1979); and *Sagesse et religion*, ed. Edmond Jacob (Paris, 1979). Three additional collected works are highly informative: *Studies in Ancient Israelite Wisdom*, ed. James L. Crenshaw (New York, 1976); *Israelite Wisdom: Theological and Literary Essays in Honor of Samuel Terrien*, ed. John G. Gammie et al. (Missoula MT, 1978); and *Aspects of Wisdom in Judaism and Early Christianity*, ed. Robert L. Wilkin (Notre Dame IN, 1975).

The finest survey of current research on Egyptian wisdom is R. J. Williams's "The Sages of ancient Egypt in the Light of Recent Scholarship," JAOS 101 (1981): 1-19, while Glendon E. Bryce's *A Legacy of Wisdom* (Lewisberg PA, 1979) is an update of Paul Humbert's pioneer study of Egyptian influence on Israelite wisdom, *Recherches sur les sources égyptiennes de la littérature sapientiale d'Israël*, Mémoires de l'Université de Neuchâtel 7 (Neuchâtel, 1929). For Mesopotamian wisdom three references are noteworthy: W. G. Lambert's *Babylonian Wisdom Literature* (Oxford, 1960); Giorgio Buccellati's "Wisdom and Not: The Case of Mesopotamia," JAOS 101 (1981): 35-47; and Bendt Alster's *Studies in Sumerian Proverbs*, Mesopotamia 3 (Copenhagen, 1975). Leo G. Perdue's *Wisdom and Cult* (Missoula MT, 1977) remains the fullest discussion of that issue, and the related matter of royal wisdom has been studied by Leonidas Kalugila in *The Wise King*, ConBOT 15 (Lund, 1980).

Several examinations of school wisdom have appeared: Roger N. Whybray, in *The Intellectual Tradition in the Old Testament*, BZAW 135 (New York, 1974), opposes such a view, while Hans-Jürgen Hermisson, in *Studien zur israelitischen Spruchweisheit*, WMANT 28 (Neukirchen-Vluyn, 1968), Bernhard Lang, in *Frau Weisheit* (Düsseldorf, 1975), and André Lemaire, in *Les écoles et la formation de la Bible dans l'ancien Israël*, OBO 39 (Göttingen, 1981), defend the existence of a school in Israel.

Heinrich Schmid, in *Wesen und Geschichte der Weisheit*, BZAW 101 (Berlin, 1966), has documented the crisis throughout the ancient Near East that resulted from a collapse in the dogma of reward and punishment. The pervasive presence of sapiential themes and theology has been examined by Donn F. Morgan, *Wisdom in the Old Testament Traditions* (Atlanta, 1981); Gerald T. Sheppard, *Wisdom as a Hermeneutical Construct: A Study in the Sapientializing of the Old Testament*, BZAW 151 (New York, 1980); and Max Küchler, *Frühjüdische Weisheitstraditionen*, OBO 26 (Göttingen, 1979). The problem of theodicy is discussed in an anthology ed. James L. Crenshaw, *Theodicy in the Old Testament* (Philadelphia, 1983). Burton L. Mack, in *Wisdom and the Hebrew Epic* (Chicago, 1985), discusses Ben Sira's hymn in praise of the fathers.

2 (1985)

The Wisdom Literature

I. The Elusive Quest

Identification. Reflection upon wisdom's inaccessibility prompted Ben Sira to utter an enigmatic truism that, *like her name*, חָכְמָה is not accessible to many (6:22). For ancient sages like Ben Sira, Job (chap. 28), and Qoheleth, wisdom remained an elusive creature. Modern lovers of wisdom have also found her to be a slippery word (Whybray 1978). One by one, they pronounce her name, only to have her essence slip away like oil through one's fingers. "She is humanistic, international, nonhistorical, eudaemonistic," they have claimed, but each term has required qualification. The eudaemonism has a theological foundation, for God created an orderly universe that rewards virtue and punishes vice. The sayings have their own history and are altered according to new social realities. The teachings of sages represent a special tradition that is known to a limited group, and their language constitutes "in-house" speech. Face to face with ultimate mystery, humanism acknowledges its own limits arising from finitude itself.

In the same way, increasing qualification characterizes all attempts to define wisdom: the art of steering one's life successfully into harbor; practical knowledge of laws governing the world, based on experience; the total experience transmitted as a spiritual testament by a father to his son; the right deed or word for the moment; an intellectual tradition; a body of literature, a way of thinking, and a tradition. Each definition captures a significant feature of wisdom, but none of them succeeds in isolating the total phenomenon that gave birth to wisdom literature (Crenshaw 1976a, 3-5).

Extrabiblical Parallels. Israel's wisdom belonged to a larger context; her teachers seem drawn to acknowledge familiarity with truth as it had been grasped by foreign sages (the sayings of Agur; the teachings of Lemuel's mother; Job). Such openness led to actual borrowing (eleven sayings from *The Instruction of Amenemopet*) without directly identifying the Egyptian source (Bryce 1979). This reliance upon foreign wisdom, together with great similarity of the literature in general, has encouraged current scholars to search for a definition of Israelite wisdom in terms of Egyptian and Mesopotamian parallels.

The central feature of Egyptian wisdom, the principle of *Ma'at* (Volten; Gese 1958, 11-21; Schmid 1966, 17-22), has influenced Israel's understanding of Dame Wisdom, particularly the cosmological speculation in Proverbs 8 (Gilbert 1979;

Kayatz), and provides the underlying presupposition of all sapiential texts. That assumption of a harmonious universe explains the optimism that characterizes early wisdom. In time, historical events brought this belief into question, and a serious crisis exploded throughout the ancient world (Schmid 1966). In Egypt, the failure of nerve gave rise to discussion literature (in which sages expostulated with deities) and stimulated reflection upon life's futility (Otto). Noteworthy shifts within the thinking of the sages occurred: reward and punishment ceased to be automatic, and the gods interceded in the nexus of cause and effect. As a result, piety came to characterize sages, and the former optimism faded. Israel's share of Egyptian wisdom represents, for the most part, the commingling of piety and old wisdom: the weighing of the heart, righteousness as the foundation of the royal throne, the satire of professions, the royal confession, and possibly the garland of honor (Kayatz). Decisive differences between Egyptian and Israelite wisdom exist despite these resemblances. The essential distinction concerns the setting: Egyptian wisdom literature arose in connection with the royal court and its particular goals (Kalugila). That is, sapiential literature functioned in Pharaoh's palace to ensure a successful political regime (Brunner 1952).

Mesopotamian wisdom also belonged to an entirely different social milieu from the Israelite corollary (Lambert; van Dijk; Buccellati). Both Sumerian and Akkadian wisdom arose in schools and served as texts for scholarly instruction, particularly with regard to correct ritual and proper divinatory technique. In essence, wisdom meant mastery of magical arts in connection with the cult. Lacking an assumption of an orderly cosmos, Mesopotamian sages endeavored to determine the fate of their affluent clients by enabling them to act in accord with heavenly bodies and natural signs. Here too a crisis emerged quite early, and sages composed powerful dialogues about innocent suffering, divine injustice, and suicide's attraction. Israel's sages virtually ignored encyclopedic lists and omen wisdom, despite claims to the contrary by two critics (von Rad 1960; Bryce 1975), but joined their Eastern neighbors in asking about human misery and in challenging God's justice.

Canaanite wisdom (Albright; Khanjian) undoubtedly thrived alongside the Israelite, Egyptian, and Mesopotamian. Like the Edomite, which Old Testament texts acknowledge, it has not survived—except in the form of some fatherly advice to a son who is about to leave on a journey, which symbolizes life itself (Nougay-rol, 47-50). Other features of Canaanite thought are hardly wisdom's exclusive domain: myths about primal human beings, royal terminology concerning obligations to ensure justice for all, and divine epithets that allude to wisdom. Ebla's contribution in this regard has not yet been determined, although sapiential texts are said to exist in this recent discovery (Pettinato, 45).

Comparisons between Israelite wisdom and that of her neighbors rely upon the labor of specialists in those disciplines. An immense wealth of information has poured forth from these circles. Reliable translations of relevant texts (ANET; Simpson; Lambert; Lichtheim), explanatory commentaries (Zaba; Brunner 1944), interpretative clarification of the literary corpus in toto (Lambert; van Dijk; Brunner 1952), and specific monographs on particular problems have greatly enriched our knowledge and opened up these texts to biblical scholars. Rare indeed are the biblical critics who make themselves at home in this alien world (Gemser 1960; Gese 1958; Cazelles). Occasional congresses devoted to comparisons among the several sapiential collections have fostered further insight at the expense of some over-simplification (Wendel; Kraeling and Adams).

Perhaps more debate has raged over divine freedom than over any other topic. Some biblical scholars insist that Yahweh exercised control over the ordering principle of the universe (Gese 1958), while others claim that a given human action sets a force into motion that works itself out for good or ill apart from divine intervention (Koch 1955). Varying attempts to understand retribution in ancient sapiential thought have therefore arisen, many of which now appear in a single volume (Koch 1972). Such endeavors assist in clarifying a world view and suggest that belief in retribution scarcely belongs to wisdom's distinctive characteristic, since all ancient peoples shared this conception of reality (Schmid 1974).

Intracanonical Relationship. For the most part, caution has characterized recent search for ancient Near Eastern parallels to canonical wisdom. This cannot be said for attempts to ascertain wisdom influence in the Hebrew Bible. The effort to broaden the Israelite sapiential impact threatens to sweep a substantial portion of the Bible into its path. The result may render the term wisdom so diffuse as to be utterly worthless in scholarly discussion. At the same time, this desire to relate wisdom to other traditions in the Hebrew scriptures arises from a correct intuition: the sages did not operate in complete isolation. Ironically, the case for sapiential influence often rests upon an assumption of exclusive vocabulary employed only by the sages. More often than not these words belong to the semantic field of universal discourse (good and bad, wise and foolish, knowledge, understanding, and the like).

Prophetic literature was the first to come under the sweeping claim of wisdom influence. Isaiah first (Fichtner; Whedbee 1971; Jensen) and then Amos (Terrien 1962; Wolff 1964) were viewed as former sages or students of the teachers. Then came Habakkuk (Gowan), Jonah (Trible; Fretheim), and Micah (Wolff 1978) as well as scattered passages throughout the prophetic canon. Narrative texts were viewed in the same fashion, especially the Joseph story (von Rad 1953), the succession narrative (Whybray 1968), Esther (Talmon) the primeval history (McKenzie; Alonso-Schökel 1962), the lost "Acts of Solomon" (Liver), and the wooing of Rebekah (Roth). Even the book of Deuteronomy succumbed to this bold endeavor (Weinfeld), and similarities between Deutero-Isaiah and hymnic texts in Job called forth a thesis of direct relationship (Terrien 1965). To be sure, earlier scholars had perceived many of these affinities between wisdom literature and the remaining portions of the Hebrew Bible, but they explained them as later glosses or anthological composition, largely because of an assumption that wisdom represented, for the most part, a late development.

In the light of this trend toward transforming wisdom into a kind of insatiable "Sheol figure" who swallows the rest of the Hebrew canon, a call for self-conscious methodological reflection was issued (Crenshaw 1969). This summons included three test cases (the Joseph story, the succession narrative, and Esther) and registered a negative judgment in each instance. Another treatment of this problem focused upon the circular reasoning required in such efforts to establish influence, especially linguistic studies, although reaching more positive conclusions (Whybray 1974). Some subsequent research has indicated an awareness of the issues (Coats), but reluctance to abandon the effort altogether seems to prevail (Morgan).

Certain assumptions have become problematic as a result of this restless search for wisdom influence. Possibly the single most important issue concerns the development of wisdom thinking in ancient Israel (Cazelles). The crucial stage is the middle one—court wisdom (Humphreys). Did clan wisdom evolve into court instruction, and did a virtual enlightenment occur during Solomon's era (von Rad 1953; Galling 1952)? If this putative fresh burst of humanism stands between all subsequent scholars and early wisdom, how has that new world view affected older texts? Several attempts to trace a theologization of older secular wisdom have arisen, with modest success (Whybray 1965; McKane). As yet, no compelling description of wisdom's evolution has appeared. Three distinct stages seem likely: clan, court, and scribal wisdom (Lemaire). Even though the canonical proverbs probably derive from the first of these, a definitive analysis of clan wisdom is lacking. Its kinship with apodictic legal texts has been emphasized (Gerstenberger 1965).

The most disconcerting feature of this drive to discern wisdom's presence outside Proverbs, Job, and Qoheleth is the assumption that certain words constitute technical vocabulary. Naturally, חָכָם in its various forms does yeoman's service for such a theory, despite the ambiguity of the evidence (Whybray 1974). A single example suffices, since it has led to considerable speculation. The adjective "wise," which describes the woman of Tekoa (2 Sam 14:2), may simply mean intelligent; if so, it would provide no support for elaborate theories about Tekoa as a center for sapiential instruction and the role of women in Israelite wisdom (Camp). One additional difficulty merits comment. Sometimes technical vocabulary may function differently in Israel from the way it functions in its Egyptian counterpart. David's two counselors (יוֹעֲצִים) in 2 Sam 16:20–17:23 may have nothing to do with the wisdom enterprise as it manifested itself in Israel.

Distinctive Tradition. It follows that the goal of wisdom research is to understand what was distinctive about Israelite wisdom with regard to ancient Near Eastern parallels and other canonical material. Israel's sages thought in different categories; as a result, they developed a unique tradition. In a word, they believed in the sufficiency of human virtue to achieve well-being in this life, apart from divine assistance. That unbridled optimism was grounded in a theological conviction about the goodness of creation. The pathos of the wisdom literature arose from a consuming passion to maintain this belief in human sufficiency in the face of unjust suffering and divine despotism. Little by little this distinctive viewpoint collapsed—first with the emergence of a heavenly messenger, Dame Wisdom, then with theophany as the resolution of a grievous spiritual problem, and finally with

Ben Sira's wholesale embracing of sacral traditions which breathed the atmosphere of God's gracious dealings with a chosen race (Rylaarsdam).

Appropriation by Modern Interpreters

Ethics and Theology. Considerable attention has centered upon religious pragmatism, both in Egypt and Israel, as the singular ingredient of sapiential ethics. The adjective that modifies pragmatism has become increasingly significant as clarification of the underlying premise of all wisdom is achieved. This cosmostatic quality inherent in every human deed bestows immense gravity upon ethical action (Schmid 1966, 22-24) and justifies hostile language which was directed at hotheaded fools who undermined the universe itself. Since divine action took place at the moment of creation rather than in the living present, the sages in Israel concentrated upon the implications of creation for human conduct. Naturally, their theology presupposed the existence of one deity, the universal creator (Zimmerli 1963; Hermisson 1978). Even when the special name Yahweh occurs, it connotes the Lord of heaven and earth.

Aesthetics. In the area of sapiential aesthetics, virtual neglect has prevailed until now. We do not know what ancient sages thought about beauty, either visual or auditory. Certain clues have survived, nonetheless, that may enable sensitive critics to grasp this important aspect of sapiential thought (von Rad 1972). These include, among other things, the exquisite poetic images (especially in Job and Sirach) that sear the imagination of contemporary readers and the polished rhetoric that demonstrates profound understanding concerning the art of persuasion (Crenshaw 1981b; 1981c).

II. The Book of Proverbs

Growth of Individual Collections

"Nuclear" Sayings and "Brief Essays." A decisive shift has taken place in the theory concerning an evolutionary development from the short, one-line saying to longer essays, and with this change came a tendency to view the initial collection (Proverbs 1-9) as much earlier than had otherwise been thought possible (Skladny; Kayatz). The Egyptian *Instruction of 'Onchsheshonqy* has played a decisive role in this shift, for that relatively late demotic text resembles the putative early collections in that it uses short, pithy sayings (Gemser 1960). The formal evidence for a developing complexity of sayings was thereby negated, and this new insight corresponded to a growing conservative trend in dating ancient texts. Older attempts (Schmidt) to show how brief sayings later took on motivation and result clauses and became increasingly theological were questioned. This rejection of earlier hypotheses also applied to the assumption that stylistic niceties arose at a later stage when sages became much more self-consciously literate (Hermisson 1968).

As a result, the entire proverbial collection is thought to have arisen before or during the monarchical period, and emphasis falls upon different contexts within which the separate units developed. This trend appears to be on target, provided that it does not sacrifice the gains that have accrued to various attempts to show how simple proverbs achieved complexity in form. One can retain these insights while accepting the view that brief essays existed simultaneously with succinct sayings. Besides, the evidence for gradual adaptation of originally "secular" sayings, even within collections that use the short form altogether, seems conclusive. Furthermore, some of the short essays are actually constructed around a simple proverb, which they quote as the decisive argument supporting the point of the essay (Crenshaw 1979).

The Sociological Context. If the several collections arose in different contexts, what characterized each one? On the assumption that sages expressed their special interests, interpreters have searched for evidence pointing to the sociological milieu in which individual sayings arose (Kovacs). Two opposing views have arisen: the proverbs reflect a clan ethos (Gerstenberger 1965), particularly in the negative employed, or they point to a school setting (Hermisson 1968). The special kind of negative has led one critic to argue for a group ethos (W. Richter). The existence of folk proverbs has been denied (Hermisson 1968), largely because conscious literary artistry appears in nearly all Israelite sayings. The dubious assumption that only schools prized stylistic artistry renders this argument tenuous and strengthens the position of those who endorse popular proverbs (Scott 1972) and traditional sayings (Fontaine).

Most scholars have assumed that the intellectual tradition depended upon ample leisure to permit reflection (Gordis 1943/44; Whybray 1974), a view that finds support in *The Satire of the Trades* and in Sirach, as well as in the scribal tradition in postcanonical Jewish circles (Urbach). Thus, a theory that sages were wealthy landowners has experienced general acceptance, and confirmation has seemed to come above all from Qoheleth, who writes like one lacking power to redress human grievances while escaping those ills that characteristically befall the poor.

Structural Unity. Although some signs of editorial intention manifest themselves, particularly in the introduction to the book (1:1-7), the general structure of Proverbs has defied analysis. Various theories have arisen to explain the structural unity of important segments within the book. One approach relies upon numerical equivalents for the Hebrew characters in the superscriptions and envisions the entire work in the shape of a house built upon seven columns (Skehan, 9-45). Another perspective distinguishes four main sections in the "Solomonic" proverbs which manifest an architectonic unity. These include (1) chaps. 10-15, the contrast between righteousness and wickedness; (2) 16:1–22:16, Yahweh and the king; (3) chaps. 25-27, nature and agriculture; and (4) chaps. 28-29, the king or potential rulers (Skladny). The third approach focuses upon the entire book and divides it into two basic forms: (1) the sentence (Prov 10:1–22:16; 24:23-34; 25–29); and (2) instruction (Prov 1–9; 22:17–24:22; 31:1-9) (McKane). If in fact a single editor was responsible for the final form of the book, the teacher's openness to diverse viewpoints has allowed remarkable diversity to characterize the collected sayings.

Precisely what principle governed the clustering of proverbs remains an unresolved issue even if a single editor is granted (Plöger; Conrad), for only a few small units seem to be joined on the basis of similar consonants, a common word, or the same sounds.

Ancient Near Eastern Parallels. Proverb collections existed in Egypt and Mesopotamia (ANET; Lambert; Gemser 1960); in addition, a few isolated proverbs or proverblike sayings have been discovered at Mari (Marzal), in the Amarna letters (Albright), and in Ahiqar (ANET, 427-30). Sumerian proverbs (Alster; Gordon) and Babylonian sentences and instructions (Lambert) differ greatly in content from those preserved in the Hebrew canon, whereas striking similarities between Israelite and Egyptian proverbs occur (Gemser 1960), even apart from the actual adaptation of one instruction in Prov 22:17–24:22 (Bryce 1979; Würthwein). Apparent differences often vanish upon closer examination. For example, the opposites "wise/fool" appear in Egypt under "silent one/hotheaded one." Affinities become especially close with regard to language about hearing, although Egyptian sages were more likely to coin technical terms than their Israelite colleagues.

Theological Analysis

Themes. The lion's share of attention has gone to the theological meaning of a single phrase—"the fear of Yahweh." Its use approximates the contemporary word "religion," in all its richness. According to one modern exegete, this awareness that faith frees the intellect for maximum achievement offers a cogent corrective to twentieth-century scientific dogmatism (von Rad 1972, 53-73). Precisely what is implied by the motto, "The fear of Yahweh is the רֵאשִׁית of knowledge," remains unclear, but both "essence" and "beginning" have their champions.

Equally ambiguous is the referent for the foreign woman who posed such a threat to Israel's youth. The older theory that she represented a cultic fertility goddess (Boström) has been found wanting, for the most part, and explanations from closer to home have prevailed. Accordingly, the foreign woman is usually viewed as an adulteress, although her enticement has certainly been enhanced by use of elements from fertility worship (Whybray 1965; McKane). The personification of Dames Wisdom and Folly has also made free use of that cultic language (Lang; Bonnard).

In one sense, it is hardly accurate to speak of theological analysis of Proverbs, since most observations in this regard belong to the category of ethics. Some attention has fallen upon the "kerygma" in Proverbs (Murphy 1966), as well as the place such a work must have occupied in Israel's total theological scheme. Such discussions have emphasized an openness to the world (Murphy 1970), fundamental trust in men and women (Brueggemann), and symbolic language (Habel 1972). The conservative nature of wisdom produced an appeal to ancient tradition (Habel 1973), resulting in remarkable continuity with the past. For at least one scholar, wisdom's lack of sacred traditions places sapiential texts alongside pagan materials as devoid of revelatory content or redemptive power (Preuss 1970).

Authority. One reason for this denial of revelatory authority grows out of the sages' way of expressing themselves. On the surface, "Listen, my son, to your dad's advice," hardly compares with the prophetic oracular formula, "Thus hath Yahweh spoken." Once this mode of expression is examined (Bühlmann), it becomes clear that sapiential sayings carried considerable authority beyond their own internal logic. Behind each bit of advice stood the weight of tradition, the authority of parents, the accumulated ethos, and the divine intention as it had penetrated reality at creation (Crenshaw 1971, 116-23; Gemser 1968).

III. Qoheleth

The Composition of the Book

Literary Forms. Reflection upon the composition of Qoheleth arose already within those circles which endeavored to understand the work during the author's own lifetime or shortly afterward. According to this editorial gloss (12:9-14), Qoheleth sought earnestly to combine truth with literary artistry. If the result baffled his contemporaries, how much more puzzled must modern interpreters be. Obscurity reigns in the effort to determine the precise form of the book, whether a collection of sentences, a tract (Zimmerli 1974), or even a diary. Consensus seems to have formed on the actual pedagogic use of these pleasing—yet trying—observations about life's emptiness (Gordis 1951; Kroeber; Lauha 1978; Scott 1965).

As ancient rabbis surmised, the fiction of Solomonic authorship seems to be an effort to reinforce the weight of the claim that life had no real advantage over death. The Egyptian royal testament (instructions in the name of the pharaoh) lies behind the section in which Qoheleth reports the conclusions he drew from careful experimentation (1:12–2:26). Making generous use of autobiographical language, he shows a decided preference for stereotypical expressions (Wright; Loretz) and polar structures (Loader). Other literary forms (Crenshaw 1974a) Qoheleth uses with considerable power include proverb and allegory, the latter of which characterizes the ravages of old age in a manner reminiscent of the opening lines in Ptahhotep's maxims and a recently discovered Sumerian text (Alster 1975, 93). Although several kinds of proverbs occur, a preference for "excluding" ones is apparent, largely because they reinforced the negative impact of Qoheleth's thought (Müller 1968). At least two didactic poems emphasize the monotony of existence under the sun and assert that everything belongs to its own particular moment (1:4-9; 3:1-9). The special character of the work derives in part from the strong emphasis upon deductions from experience, which form the basis for personal advice. Therefore, exhortation appears as the mode of address when positive counsel breaks free from the shadow cast by death's ominous presence (Crenshaw 1978b).

Integrity. The inconsistency that stands out within the book does not necessarily indicate multiple authorship. The element of contradiction has been exaggerated, although attempts to deny it altogether (Kidner) have proved unsuccessful. Two possibly complementary explanations for those opposing viewpoints have been brought forward. The first assumes that Qoheleth quoted generally acknowledged truisms as a foil for his opposing message (Gordis 1951; Whybray 1981). Considerable supporting evidence from ancient Near Eastern texts strengthens the case greatly. This thesis is further bolstered by awareness that Qoheleth had a tendency to juxtapose a *bonum* and a *malum* (Müller 1968); the good is stated so as to demonstrate its basic falsity. When God is the subject, this exposure of real truth achieves intense pathos. The other solution to the presence of contradiction has its basis in psychology: Qoheleth lacked consistency because he recognized the impossibility of being dogmatic when discussing matters like punishment for sin and reward for virtue. The complexity of such issues forced him to view them from several different perspectives (J. Williams 1981).

While both arguments carry a certain amount of persuasive power, they do not rule out the likelihood that a few actual glosses have been added to the text, especially to counter the impact of Qoheleth's denial that God rewarded and punished individuals according to their actions. This thesis of editorial additions grows stronger when one takes into account the undeniable fact that the final section of the book (12:9-14) comes from a sage other than Qoheleth (Sheppard 1977). Furthermore, the author of this epilogue launches a mild attack against the book, while acknowledging its essential truth. The attempt to sum up Qoheleth's teaching in 12:13-14 misses the point entirely, and this bold piety hardly grew out of inability to understand what the gentle cynic had written. Instead, the epilogist offered advice that was intended to replace Qoheleth's counsel.

Thematic Unity. To be sure, one theme runs through the entire book: Vanity of vanities, all is vanity." The word הֶבֶל may occur here in the sense of "profitless," like יִתְרוֹן, which was used in daily commerce and referred to a ledger on which life's credits and debits appear, the latter naturally prevailing. But הֶבֶל must surely carry its original meaning as well; everything is as empty as breath itself, which remains outside our control. Like all God's gifts, it comes and goes according to divine time schedules (Galling 1961) and thus constantly reminds creatures of their finitude (Gese 1963).

Another theme which unites much of the book also points to the limits imposed upon human knowledge. This emphasis upon an inability to find out desired data or to know everything presses beyond mere denial of ultimate knowledge to outright attack on anyone who thinks otherwise. Dissent from traditional teachings assumes many forms: explicit rejection, implicit correction, alteration of language, and omission (Crenshaw 1977b). One example demonstrates Qoheleth's skill in dealing with school tradition. In 3:11 he alludes to the Priestly creation narrative's refrain that every created thing was especially good, but Qoheleth varies the language appreciably and turns the original affirmation into an expression that approaches despair. Shunning the pregnant words בָּרָא or טוֹב, he used instead עָשָׂה and יָפֶה and thus divested the text of rich theological meaning. Not satisfied with this neutralization of heavily laden vocabulary, Qoheleth further qualifies the divine gift, bestowed at creation, and turns it into a burden. He very nearly accuses God of teasing human beings by giving them a valuable yearning for the hidden realities of life but rendering men and women incapable of discovering precious truth (Crenshaw 1974b).

These two refrains ("Vanity of vanities, all is vanity" and "He cannot find it out") seem to provide structural unity to the book (Wright). In addition, several other formulas mark transitional points within the larger units. Among others, these include the concluding summary that encouraged the enjoyment of life during youthful vigor, the "contemplative" observations that referred to self-examination and the resulting personal action, and the allusions to chasing after the wind, toil, and lot. Qoheleth shows decided preference for certain words and phrases that seem to catch the monotony characterizing life under the sun (Loretz). In addition, he seems to use words in a double sense, almost playfully. This richness of meaning may explain the unusual form בּוֹרְאֶיךָ, which alludes to one's *bonum* (his wife) and *malum* (the grave).

Thematic unity is achieved by other means as well, chief of which are mood and idea. A single atmosphere almost suppresses the written word itself; that oppressive mood arose from awareness that death cancels all supposed gain under heaven. No relief from this burden presented itself as an acceptable response to the aching cry for permanence—not even the hope of life beyond the grave. Alongside this ominous atmosphere exists a central conception that signifies an awareness of being alone in the universe (von Rad 1972, 232-33). The crisis of the spirit prevented Qoheleth from deciding whether God was a despot or not, although the sage comes perilously close to answering in the affirmative.

Foreign Infuence. Older theories of pervasive Greek influence upon Qoheleth's thought have given way to alternative claims, particularly the attempt to demonstrate affinities with Phoenician (Dahood) and Mesopotamian literature (Loretz, 90-134). One interpreter has gone further afield in an effort to compare Qoheleth's concept of opposites with Taoist views (Horton). The pendulum has begun to swing back once again to its earlier position, although this time the thesis of Greek influence depends, for the most part, upon similarities with the teachings of popular Hellenistic philosophers (Braun; Whitley). This analysis of the environment within which Qoheleth worked has made significant advance toward clarifying the transition within wisdom thinking that a Hellenistic context must have precipitated (Marböck; Hengel; Middendorp). Nevertheless, attempts to show that Aramaic was the original language of Qoheleth continue (Zimmermann).

The Appropriation of Meaning

Pre-Christian and Early Christian Endeavors. The controversial views of Qoheleth and the dissent from established opinions could hardly be ignored, especially when such thinking supplied the justification for immoral behavior. The author of Wisdom of Solomon almost certainly has Qoheleth in mind when attacking conduct that seems to have arisen from a thorough misunderstanding of Qoheleth's counsel regarding enjoyment while one can still taste life's nectar (contra

Skehan, 172-236). Rabbinic debate about books that defile the hands indicates further alarm over Qoheleth's teaching but bears strong witness to the power of tradition in the canonization process. Christian response differed little from the Jewish; the process of neutralizing Qoheleth's language, which began in the translation activity behind the LXX rendering of the book, gained impetus until grand claims surfaced (Holm-Nielsen). Qoheleth was understood as a splendid example of a person without Christ or of one caught in law's bondage. The Church Fathers seem never to have tired of comparing the Christian's promise of resurrection with the dismal fate facing this Old Testament sage. In this sense, Qoheleth was viewed as a messianic prophecy (Hertzberg, 238).

Contemporary Theological Approaches. Perhaps the most appropriate word to characterize Qoheleth's thought is crisis (Gese 1963). For him, the givens of human existence no longer compelled assent; the result amounted to discovery of human existence *in tormentis* (Galling 1961, 1). Dialogue with eternity as it occurred in the world had vanished, and in its place sprang up a self-centered monologue (von Rad 1972, 233, 237). The personal pronouns throw the spotlight on Qoheleth alone; the sense of isolation from God and other humans mounts as again and again the author exposes human misery and obtains momentary relief in awareness that a companion assists during danger and keeps one warm. Obviously, even here Qoheleth has not escaped self-centeredness, since others exist for his sake. The heart of the spiritual crisis concerns God's justice; for Qoheleth, arbitrariness characterizes divine action. It follows that the fundamental presupposition of wisdom collapses, since one cannot be sure what will greet a given act.

This recognition of God's freedom has been seen as a restoration of authentic Yahwism rather than as a departure from genuine wisdom (Zimmerli 1963, 135). To be sure, Israel's sages had always perceived an element of mystery beyond which they could not pass, but such limits did not become oppressive because both Yahweh and the world were thought to be trustworthy. Neither God nor the universe gave comfort to Qoheleth, who resented having to rely upon another for gifts dispensed in God's own good time. Naturally, the thesis that Qoheleth functioned as a guardian of authentic Yahwism depends upon an assumption that wisdom thinking hardened into a dogma of retribution. At least one interpreter rejects that hypothesis entirely (von Rad 1972).

Since both Qoheleth and Job wrestle with existential concerns, comparison between the two thinkers is inevitable. In these assessments of two radical positions, Qoheleth invariably loses. One critic has labeled him an example of a secular individual as opposed to Job, a *homo religiosus* (Lauha 1960). Perhaps the scales tipped against Qoheleth because of his unrelieved skepticism, although not all critics think Qoheleth's message lacked vigorous optimism (Whybray 1982). After all, he did observe that light is sweet to behold (Miskotte, 450-60; J. G. Williams 1971a; Witzenrath).

The emergence of skepticism in ancient Israel (Klopfenstein; Priest) owes much to a combination of factors: the crisis of tradition and ancient pedagogy (Crenshaw

1980). In short, historical circumstances alone fail to offer an adequate explanation for the rise of skepticism. Alongside the element of a collapsing ethos stood an emphasis upon imponderables within the teaching enterprise. Certain things lay outside the scope of human knowledge, and these "intellectual teasers" assumed the form of riddle and impossible question (Crenshaw 1978a, 1979). In Qoheleth, rhetorical questions achieved this end, especially the haunting "Who knows?"

Such skepticism tempers traditional affirmation and hallowed language. For example, the fear of God functions in Qoheleth as sheer terror in the presence of divine tyranny (Pfeiffer). Of course, the phrase occurs in its normal sense of religious devotion as well, but evidence seems to suggest that this traditional use belongs to the epilogist or represents school teaching which Qoheleth proceeds to attack (Murphy 1979).

Current Nontheological Interpretations. The powerful influence of Freudian psychology upon contemporary thought has led one critic to undertake a thoroughgoing analysis of Qoheleth from this particular perspective (Zimmermann). Seizing clues in their most fragile form, Zimmermann thinks Qoheleth suffered from all the classical symptoms that Freud exposed so tellingly: impotency, incest, Oedipus complex, inferiority complex, and so forth. Such flights of fantasy possess more entertainment value than truth. Scholars have often admired Qoheleth for the timeless quality of his message. Comparisons with existential philosophy have acknowledged this unusual modernity while recognizing essential differences (Gordis 1951, 112-21). Naturally many philosophers have found in Qoheleth a kindred spirit.

IV. The Book of Job

The Emergence of the Book

Prose and Poetry. Whereas older critics usually viewed the framing narrative and the poetry in isolation, the current trend is to link the two more closely. An old popular story with an epic substratum (Sarna) about a faithful just man who suffers without complaining seems to have been adapted for pedagogic ends by the author of the dialogue, but tensions remain nevertheless between the prose and the poetry (Fohrer 1963). One way to neutralize the different viewpoints is to understand the divine commendation of Job as irony. One could even view Job's response in the same way; repentance would then be simple manipulation of a deity (J. G. Williams 1971b). Regardless, the story moves in an entirely different environment from the poetry. As a result, many cries ignore the story altogether when interpreting the dialogue.

Within the dialogue, the poem on wisdom's inaccessibility (chap. 28) (Zerafa) and the Elihu speeches (32-37) present special problems. Sufficient stylistic similarities between these texts and the rest of the dialogue give some weight to theories about common authorship, especially when coupled with a thesis that several years separate them. Thus at least one interpreter thinks the same author who had earlier written the poem on wisdom later tried his hand at another answer to the problem of innocent suffering. The result was the Elihu speeches, which reflect the subsequent scribal solution (Gordis 1978). The third cycle of speeches has suffered disarrangement; some think the poem in chap. 28 is also out of place since it anticipates the divine response in the theophany. Naturally, attempts to relocate 24-27 rely upon an assumption of logical consistency (Tournay). One could imagine other reasons for Job's contradictory remarks, especially in the light of his extra-ordinary psychological and physical state.

Literary Form. On one claim most scholars can agree: Job is sui generis. Beyond that consensus, considerable diversity in viewpoint prevails, largely because no single genre suffices in describing such a complex composition, which contains elements borrowed from prophecy (Bardtke), wisdom (Fohrer 1963), and psalms (Westermann). The most appropriate category would seem to be disputation, if one takes into account the prose and poetry. Accordingly, one can distinguish a mythological prologue and epilogue, a debate, and the divine resolution of the dispute. Disregarding the prose, the category of lament seems apt, either a lament proper (Westermann) or a paradigm of an answered lament (Gese 1958). Legal terminology certainly occurs, justifying attempts to distinguish a pre-judicial stage, a judicial process, and a verdict from the divine judge (H. Richter 1959). The purification oath in chap. 31 strengthens this argument (Fohrer 1974), although one need not see this act as forcing God's hand (contra Robertson; Good). Perhaps dialogue is the one term that comes closest to characterizing the poetry, but this word may assume more amicability between Job and the friends than is actually present. In any case, neither Elihu's observations nor God's speeches move beyond monologue, since both speak past Job.

Extrabiblical Sources. The Egyptian Book of the Dead offers a striking parallel to the negative confession in chap. 31 (Murtagh), but most parallels for Job are Mesopotamian in origin. Several studies of innocent suffering in Babylonian and Sumerian texts have called attention to similarities between Job and these earlier texts, even to the combination of prose and poetry (von Soden, Müller 1978). Research into the problem of theodicy has also pointed to the Sumerian and Babylonian literature as the closest link with Job, although Egypt also wrestled with this issue (R. J. Williams). In the land of the Nile the seriousness of divine injustice was tempered by belief in life after death and by the conviction that justice was a gift of God rather than one's right. The remarkable affinity between Job and Mesopotamian texts is broken at one point; only the former understands suffering as God's way of educating a person.

Although formal connections between Job and Mesopotamia can hardly be denied, certain links with Ugaritic texts have also been postulated (Irwin). The putative parallels with Dan'el lack cogency, and the explanation of the divine vindicator as Baal seems superfluous, given the Israelite concept of blood revenge. Still, numerous linguistic affinities between Job and Northwest Semitic are powerful testimony to the influence Canaanite culture exercised upon the author of Job (Pope). One need not assume a line of traditional wisdom at Canaanite city states

(Gray) to explain this similarity in language and motifs, but some explanation for such common ideas seems called for (Cazelles).

Postcanonical Tradition. Discovery at Qumran of a variant tradition to Job (Fitzmyer; van der Ploeg and van der Woude) has illuminated the early postcanonical understanding of the book. That information has now been extended in two directions: (1) Job in Arabic and early Jewish tradition (Müller 1970), and (2) Job in Jewish interpretation from the Middle Ages to the present (Glatzer 1966). Such motif analyses have greatly enriched our sense of the presuppositions that control what we see in a particular text. A recent study of Job in French literature shows how intellectual moods change, and with each shift comes another way of viewing religious problems (Hausen). The profundity of the book of Job may be measured partly by the fascination it holds for intellectuals in many different disciplines, as exemplified by two recent anthologies on twentieth-century interpretations of Job (P. Sanders; Glatzer 1969).

Theological Mystification

The Problem of Suffering. The suffering of innocent victims constitutes the fundamental problem addressed by the book of Job. It offers several explanations for undeserved suffering (J. Sanders) but fails to reach an adequate justification for it. Nevertheless, the author does not flinch from placing the blame upon God, although the divine speeches qualify that concession by drawing attention to the vast universe that lies under God's control. In ordinary human experience one cannot discover proof of God's justice; instead, an act of faith is called for despite the absence of convincing demonstration that God acts justly (Tsevat). Suffering may be disciplinary, educative, retributive, or redemptive. It follows that God may use innocent suffering to build character, hence, the way an individual reacts to discipline demonstrates true character. For this reason, one could even say that conduct during suffering is the real theme of the book (Fohrer 1963). Thus the existential problem of suffering and the moral issue of correct response to innocent suffering comprise the basic themes of the book. The many answers to proper conduct range from outright Titanism to abject humility, and it is difficult to tell which one the author endorses.

Theodicy. A strong desire to justify God's ways (von Soden) occupies the thoughts of Job's erstwhile comforters and underlies the divine speeches, although in an oblique manner. Several features of Israelite and Mesopotamian religion exacerbated the issue of theodicy. The moral understanding of God and its correlate, a high degree of ethical demand placed on individuals, contributed most in this struggle to defend God's ways, since divine conduct did not always appear to accord with belief in an ethical deity. Conviction that reward and punishment accrued during this life made the problem of inappropriate fruits for conduct especially painful. So, too, did an individualizing of religious devotion and a suspicion of the cult, which received its share of criticism. The Babylonian Theodicy and Ludlul offer close parallels to Job in language and form, but a theory of direct literary dependence remains problematic.

Evidence seems to support the thesis of considerable popular wrestling with the problem of theodicy in Israelite texts other than the book of Job (Crenshaw 1970; 1971; 1976b; 1983). While this struggle in Job and elsewhere may be illuminated through terms drawn from Thomas Aquinas (Scaltriti) or even Kantian philosophy (Faur), these discussions bear eloquent testimony to the persistence of the problem of divine injustice in modern times. That debate between two opposing sides in ancient Israel gave rise to a formula which can be found in Qoheleth and Sirach ("Do not say . . . ") and shows how serious the dissenters understood the problem to be. The furor that typifies "imagined speech" issuing from the mouths of those who challenged God's justice can hardly be missed; in this respect, Job's literary heirs retained an authentic element of his speech (Crenshaw 1975).

Theophany. It seems likely that the divine speeches offer the poet's real solution to the problems of innocent suffering and divine injustice. In God's presence, all previous understandings explode, paving the way for genuine knowledge. One achievement of the theophany is the crushing of the illusion that men and women occupy the central position (Neiman), a delusion that permits them to assume that the universe exists for their sakes alone. God's speeches, which seem to ignore the aching questions Job has raised, force the accuser to glance backward in time to the beginning when no humans roamed the earth (Sekine) and far enough in space to perceive the habitat of wild animals whose ways are wholly unknown to people. Once Job focuses his thoughts on others, he has opened the way for a new vision of God. In truth the divine speeches necessitate the three fundamental intellectual stances: *Ignoramus*, *Ignorabimus*, and *Gaudeamus* (Gordis 1965, 134). The positive function of nature wisdom in shaping religious views, particularly the divine speeches in Job, emerges as the divine speeches become better understood (H. Richter 1958; Keel; Kubina).

Naturally, Job's difficulty in the face of a blustering deity has prompted considerable contempt for the God described in the book. The speeches from the whirlwind have been labeled sublime irrelevance and categories like humor, comedy, and irony have been applied freely to these passages (Robertson; Miles; Whedbee 1977; J. G. Williams 1977). The two divine speeches and human repentances still puzzle scholars although most retain them while conceding that minor additions have occurred (the descriptions of the wild ostrich, horse, and hippopotamus).

Existential categories have illuminated the problem of Job's response to the theophany (Terrien 1957; Cox). Job represents a person in dialectical tension between hopeless suffering and trust regardless of the circumstances. His suffering leads him into alienation so that he confronts God as enemy, only to discover at last that he is redeemer as well (Pope, lxxxiii). Others apply the categories of faith and grace, arguing that faith awakens through God's action and assures Job that suffering belongs to the divine economy. Whatever else the theophany accomplishes, it forces Job to acknowledge his creatureliness. Presumably, forgiveness and comfort accompany submission to God's will. In this case, a true dialogue of love and silence finally occurs (Leveque, 532).

Nontheological Interpretations

Psychological. From the leader of one branch of modern psychology has come a particularly stringent critique of God for the answer given to Job (Jung). This provocative outburst of emotion has been criticized from different perspectives (Hedinger; J. G. Williams 1971b), but the causes for the outrage are too substantial to ignore. Two other ventures to understand Job in the light of psychological studies have concluded that the biblical hero needed therapy above all else (Taylor) and that Job passed through the various stages of loss, grief, and integration (Kahn).

Literary. Of course, the modernization of Job in the play *J.B.* deserves special recognition (MacLeish), particularly because of its impact upon many intellectuals. This play, which had quite a long run on Broadway and stimulated lively discussion, succeeds remarkably well in showing how Job stands for everyone. Nevertheless, it departs from the biblical book in significant ways (Terrien 1959) and ultimately opts for unrelieved humanism. A god who does not love but "is" cannot be the biblical deity, even if this passage actually refers to the revelation to Moses that God is appropriately identified as "I Am that I Am." Still, *J.B.* represents a powerful resurgence of an ancient message concerning divine injustice. In this regard, it towers high above the latest attempt to take up the Joban theme once again. The ironic title of that work, *God's Favorite* (Simon), and the tone capture the blasphemous mood of Job's speeches, although they hardly participate in the spirit of the biblical work.

Two recent attempts to capture the literary merit in the book of Job deserve some attention, particularly since historical norms still dominate much discussion of wisdom literature, where such a category is surely out of place (Roberts). The first, written by a specialist in comparative literature (Cook), applies standards of classical literary criticism (Barr) in a fruitful manner. The second endeavor in this realm consists of a number of essays by several scholars which have been published in a single issue of *Semeia*. The articles concentrate on the genre of comedy as the correct way of viewing the book of Job (Whedbee 1977; Robertson), offer an analysis of the book in terms of drama (Alonso-Schökel 1977; Crenshaw 1977a) and treat humor and irony as they apply to Job (Miles; J. G. Williams 1977). Perhaps one should include under this heading the comparison of Job and Faust (Zhitlowsky), which offers numerous insights into the meaning of the biblical figure, as well as discussions of William Blake's artistic representations of the book of Job (Damon).

Political. The revolutionary mood of much contemporary political thought has led one critic to analyze Job in terms of the political struggle to overcome the strong tendency to maintain the status quo (Bloch). In this interpretation, Job abandons the status quo in the defiant appeal to another God. Reaction to this view has insisted that Job cannot be understood properly apart from faith in Yahweh, which gave birth to the book in the first place (Gerbracht).

V. The Wider Quest

The means of determining precisely which psalms belong to the category of wisdom is by no means clear (Murphy 1962; Gerstenberger 1974; Crenshaw 1974a). The basic criteria fall into one of three categories: (1) vocabulary (wise and foolish, understanding, knowledge); (2) themes (fear of God, innocent suffering); and (3) rhetorical devices (אַשְׁרֵי sayings, better speeches, ascending numbers). At best, such features only permit a conjecture of wisdom influence, inasmuch as they could also derive from other sources. Certain Psalms (49, 73) wrestle with the problem of innocent suffering, and this kinship with Job naturally draws attention to them (Perdue 1974; Ross; Luyten). Conscious didactic intention has also prompted a claim that sages composed Psalm 34 (Kuntz).

The problem of theodicy elicited untraditional answers from Ben Sira as he endeavored to draw upon Hellenistic resources in addition to Hebraic ones (von Rad 1972; Crenshaw 1975; Prato). Naturally, this new combination of intellectual streams gave pride of place to the Israelite but allowed considerable Greek influence to infiltrate Ben Sira's teaching (Middendorp; Hengel). Furthermore, his openness to new theological traditions resulted in a remarkable combination of sapiential and sacral themes, so much so that wisdom entered a transitional stage (Marböck 1971; Sheppard 1980). The Yahwistic traditions threatened to subsume the wisdom ones, if the emphasis upon the fear of God provides a proper clue (Haspecker; contra von Rad 1972). Still, Ben Sira emphasized the special profession of sages (Marböck 1979) and reflected upon the dignity of human beings in a manner reminiscent of traditional wisdom thinking (Alonso-Schökel 1978). New discoveries with regard to the text of Sirach (Yadin; Rüger; Riekenbacher) may enrich attempts to assess Ben Sira's thought (Jacob).

The Hellenistic background of the Wisdom of Solomon is firmly established (Reese 1970), although the exact date of this work may be considerably later than earlier assumed, if the first century C.E. date recently postulated holds up (Winston). Similarities to Philo's thought are striking (Mack; Sandmel), and the Greek rhetoric employed by both suggests that their ideas, even when Hebraic, are clothed in Hellenistic forms. Even the lengthy critique of idolatry, which draws heavily upon biblical material, differs little from comparable Greek texts (Gilbert 1973). Since Wisdom of Solomon is written in language that derives from Greek thought, perhaps a biblical hermeneutic based on contemporary philosophy (specifically, Paul Ricoeur's) offers a helpful way to interpret the ancient text (Reese 1979).

VI. Conclusion: The Unfinished Task

Trends in Research

The preceding discussion, which carries on the work of earlier interpreters (Scott 1970; 1971a; Kegler; Clements; Emerton; R. J. Williams 1981; Murphy 1981a; 1981b), calls attention to numerous unresolved issues that await satisfactory answers, but it also celebrates many significant responses to difficult questions. So far in this essay, little attention has fallen upon recent comprehensive attempts to interpret ancient wisdom, the impact of which is by no means negligible. The central thrust of each current analysis would seem to be that:

(1) Wisdom is a primordial revelation which God implanted in the universe and which actively woos men and women. Faith therefore makes knowledge possible, for wisdom is essentially another form of Yahwism (von Rad 1972; Scott 1971b).

(2) Biblical wisdom provides a valuable corrective to the modern Protestant burden of guilt, which arises from excessive emphasis upon the law and God's grace. That ancient literary corpus announces the joyous news that God trusts men and women to steer their lives successfully without fear of consequences. The creation narrative and Davidic history function as normative for Israelite wisdom in this analysis (Brueggemann).

(3) Nothing demands a theory of sages as an institution in ancient Israel; instead, the canonical texts suggest that an intellectual tradition existed among upper classes. These elite thinkers composed and treasured the wisdom corpus, which has its own distinctive vocabulary, but use of חָכָם in its various forms does not constitute a technical term (Whybray 1974).

(4) Beginning with the Egyptian principle of *Ma'at*, this analysis focuses upon the world view of sages and postulates an evolution from genuine belief in an order governing the universe to a crisis in that belief and resultant frozen dogma. According to this approach, creation functions as the central theological concept in the entire Hebrew scriptures (Schmid).

(5) The stylistic niceties that characterize biblical proverbs imply self-conscious literary artistry, which invalidates the hypothesis of popular composition. Israelite wisdom had its center, origin, and places of cultivation in a school (Hermisson 1968).

(6) Early wisdom possessed strong self-confidence, thereby lacking any sense of divine grace. In time, that optimism faded and grace came to play an increasing role in sapiential thought (Rylaarsdam).

(7) Research into wisdom literature has advanced along the lines of affinities with related texts, form, and structure. The importance of creation theology derives from the fact that it undergirds belief in divine justice, the presupposition of old wisdom (Crenshaw 1976a; 1981a).

(8) Close examination of wisdom texts in which the cult is mentioned or implied shows a positive attitude, for the most part, despite the usual assumption that Israel's sages had little interest in cultic matters (Perdue 1977).

(9) The literary dimensions of aphoristic thinking (the establishing of order by counterorder, orientation by disorientation, especially in Qoheleth and in Jesus' brief sayings) are clarified in the light of the Western gnomic tradition (J. G. Williams 1981).

To be sure, space does not permit discussion of many significant monographs in the area of sapiential studies, particularly commentaries. Two recent collections of essays (*Israelite Wisdom: Theological and Literary Essays in Honor of Samuel Terrien*, and *La Sagesse de l'Ancien Testament*) and the forthcoming monographs by Donn F. Morgan (*Wisdom in the Old Testament Traditions*) and Roland E. Murphy (*Wisdom Literature*) demonstrate the vigor that characterizes the study of wisdom today.

Fruitful Avenues for Investigation

Since research has a certain cumulative character, it might be possible to predict the general direction in which the scholarly enterprise will move, but such conjecture would serve no real purpose. Instead, this survey of recent trends in wisdom scholarship will close by noting some significant areas that will reward further study.

(1) The current interest in aesthetics—that is, literary artistry—throughout the Hebrew scriptures will naturally extend to wisdom literature. Some progress has already occurred in this area, but much remains to be done. There is no more appropriate endeavor, since such analysis takes its cue from ancient sages who labored to master the art of speaking and writing. Perhaps we shall soon understand, among other things, the dynamics of sapiential dialogue.

(2) This study of the art of persuasion will inevitably encounter the problem of authority. Precisely what constituted the ground upon which sages stood when offering their valuable counsel? Previous responses to this important question stand in need of revision.

(3) The book of Job shows that the obvious authority that prophets and priests assumed tempted certain sages as they searched for means to legitimate their words. This conscious use of prophetic and psalmic motifs raises the issue of influence, which has as yet defied adequate resolution for the entire wisdom corpus.

(4) In the light of the sages' fondness for correct speech and artful composition, one can assume that collections of proverbs and wise sayings were not thrown together haphazardly. It follows that further research in the area of structure in Job, Proverbs, and Qoheleth cannot be off target.

(5) Current research outside the wisdom corpus threatens operative assumptions concerning the dating of various literary complexes. Reassessment of the entire Hebrew scriptures will become necessary, and fresh thinking will have to be given to the wisdom texts in particular. In this endeavor, we shall have occasion to discard some dominant hypotheses regarding the evolution of sapiential thought. In doing so, we may come closer to understanding the social milieu within which sages moved.

Bibliography and Reference List*

Albright, William F.
1960   "Some Canaanite-Phoenician Sources of Hebrew Wisdom." In *Wisdom in Israel and in the Ancient Near East*, 1-15. VTSup 3. Leiden: E. J. Brill.

Alonso-Schökel, Luis
1962   "Motivos sapienciales y de alianza en Gn. 2-3. *Bib* 43:295-316. ET: *TD* 13 (1965): 3-10. Repr: Crenshaw 1976a, 468-80.
1977   "Toward a Dramatic Reading of the Book of Job." *Semeia* 7:45-61.
1978   "The Vision of Man in Sirach 16:24-17:14." In *Israelite Wisdom*, 235-45. Ed. J. G. Gammie et al. Missoula MT: Scholars Press.

Alster, Bendt
1974   *The Instructions of Suruppak: A Sumerian Proverb Collection*. Mesopotamia 2. Copenhagen: Akademisk Forlag.
1975   *Studies in Sumerian Proverbs*. Mesopotamia 3. Copenhagen: Akademisk Forlag.

Bardtke, Hans
1967   "Prophetische Zuge im Buche Hiob." In *Das Ferne und Nahe Wort: Festschrift Leonhard Rost zur Vollendung seines 70 Lebensjahres am 30. November 1966 gewidmet*, 1-10. BZAW 105. Berlin A. Töpelmann.

Barr, James
1971   "The Book of Job and Its Modern Interpreters." *BJRL* 54:28-46.

Bloch, Ernst
1972   *Atheism in Christianity*. New York: Herder and Herder.

Bonnard, P. E.
1979   "De la Sagesse personifiée dans l'Ancien Testament à la Sagesse en personne dans le Nouveau." In *La Sagesse de l'Ancien Testament*, 117-49. Ed. M. Gilbert. BETL 51. Gembloux: J. Duculot.

Boström, Gustav
1935   *Proverbiastudien. Die Weisheit und das fremde Weib in Spr. 1-9*. LUÅ 30:3. Lund: C. W. K. Gleerup.

Braun, Rainer
1973   *Kohelet und die frühhellenistiche Popular philosophie*. BZAW 130. Berlin and New York: Walter de Gruyter.

Brueggemann, Walter A.
1972   *In Man We Trust*. Richmond: John Knox.

Brunner, Hellmut
1944   "Die Lehre des Cheti, Sohnes des Duauf." *ÄF* 13.
1952   "Die Weisheitsliteratur." *HO* 1. Ägyptologie 2:90-110.

---

*The JAOS volume on Oriental Wisdom (101/1 [1981]) arrived too late to be consulted in this essay. The articles on Egyptian wisdom (R. J. Williams), Israelite (Murphy), and Mesopotamian (G. Buccellati) are complemented by discussions of Arabic (D. Gutas), Asian (R. Dankoff), and Indian wisdom (L. Sternbach).

Bryce, Glendon E.
1975   "Omen-Wisdom in Ancient Israel." *JBL* 94:19-37.
1979   *A Legacy of Wisdom: The Egyptian Contribution to the Wisdom of Israel.* Lewisburg and London: Bucknell University and Associated University Presses.

Buccellati, Giorgio
1981   "Wisdom and Not: The Case of Mesopotamia." *JAOS* 101:35-47.

Bühlmann, Walter
1976   *Vom Rechten Reden und Schweigen.* OBO 12. Göttingen: Vandenhoeck & Ruprecht.

Camp, Claudia V.
1981   "The Wise Women of 2 Samuel: A Role Model for Women in Early Israel." *CBQ* 43:14-29.

Cazelles, Henri
1963   "Les debuts de la sagesse en Israel." In *Les sagesses du Proche-Orient ancien*, 27-39. Paris: Presses Universitaires de France.

Clements, Ronald E.
1976   *One Hundred Years of Old Testament Interpretation.* Philadelphia: Westminster Press.

Coats, George W.
1973   "The Joseph Story and Ancient Wisdom: A Reappraisal." *CBQ* 35:285-97.
1976   *From Canaan to Egypt.* CBQMS 4. Washington: Catholic Biblical Association of America.

Conrad, Joachim
1967   "Die innere Gliederung der Proverbien." *ZAW* 79:67-76.

Cook, Albert
1968   *The Root of the Thing.* Bloomington: Indiana University Press.

Cox, Dermont
1978   *The Triumph of Impotence: Job and the Tradition of the Absurd.* Analecta Gregoriana 212. Rome: Universita Gregoriana Editrice.

Crenshaw, James L.
1969   "Method in Determining Wisdom Influence upon 'Historical' Literature." *JBL* 88:129-42. Repr: Crenshaw 1976, 481-94.
1970   "Popular Questioning of the Justice of God in Ancient Israel." *ZAW* 82:380-95. Repr: Crenshaw 1976a, 289-304.
1971   *Prophetic Conflict.* BZAW 124. Berlin and New York: Walter de Gruyter.
1974a   "Wisdom." In *Old Testament Form Criticism*, 226-64. Ed. John H. Hayes. San Antonio: Trinity University Press.
1974b   "The Eternal Gospel (Eccl. 3:11)." In *Essays in Old Testament Ethics*, 23-55. Ed. J. L. Crenshaw and J. T. Willis. New York: Ktav.
1975   "The Problem of Theodicy in Sirach." *JBL* 94: 47-64.
1976a   Editor. *Studies in Ancient Israelite Wisdom.* New York: Ktav.
1976b   "Theodicy." In *IDBSup*, 895-96.
1977b   "The Human Dilemma and Literature of Dissent." In *Tradition and Theology in the Old Testament*, 235-58. Ed. Douglas A. Knight. Philadelphia: Fortress Press.
1978A   *Samson: A Secret Betrayed, a Vow Ignored.* Atlanta: John Knox; London: S.P.C.K. (Dist. by Mercer UP.)

1978b   "The Shadow of Death in Qoheleth. In *Israelite Wisdom*, 105-16. Ed. John G. Gammie et al. Missoula MT: Scholars Press.

1979   "Questions, dictons et épreuves impossibles." In *La Sagesse de l'Ancien Testament*, 96-111. Ed. M. Gilbert. BETL 51. Gembloux: J. Duculot.

1980   "The Birth of Skepticism in Ancient Israel." In *The Divine Helmsman: Studies on God's Control of Human Events, Presented to Lou H. Silberman*, 1-19. Ed. J. L. Crenshaw and Samuel Sandmel. New York: Ktav.

1981a   *Old Testament Wisdom, an Introduction*. Atlanta: John Knox.

1981b   "The Conquest of Darius's Guards." In *Images of Man and God*, 74-88. Ed. Burke O. Long. Sheffield: Almond.

1981c   "Wisdom and Authority: Sapiential Rhetoric and its Warrants." In *Congress Volume: Vienna 1980*, 10-29. VTSup 32. Leiden: E. J. Brill.

1983   *Theodicy in the Old Testament*. Philadelphia: Fortress Press.

Dahood, Mitchell

1952   "Canaanite-Phoenician Influence in Qoheleth." *Bib* 33:30-52, 292-332.

Damon, S. Foster

1969   *Blake's Job*. New York: E. P. Dutton.

Dijk, J. J. A. van

1953   *La sagesse sumero-accadienne*. Leiden: E. J. Brill.

Emerton, J. A.

1979   "Wisdom." In *Tradition and Interpretation*, 214-37. Ed. G. W. Anderson. Oxford: Clarendon.

Faur, Jose

1970   "Reflections on Job and Situation-Morality." *Judaism* 19:219-25.

Fichtner, Johannes

1949   "Jesaja unter den Weisen." *TLZ* 74:75-80. Repr: *Gottes Weisheit*, 18-26. Stuttgart: Calwer, 1967. ET: Crenshaw 1976a, 429-38.

Fitzmyer, Joseph A.

1979   "The First-Century Targum of Job from Qumran Cave XI." In *A Wandering Aramean*, 161-82. SBLMS 25. Missoula MT: Scholars Press.

Fohrer, Georg

1963   *Das Buch Hiob*. KAT 16. Gütersloh: Gerd Mohn.

1974   "The Righteous Man in Job 31." In *Essays in Old Testament Ethics*, 1-22. Ed. J. L. Crenshaw and J. T. Willis. New York: Ktav.

Fontaine, Carol Rader

1979   "The Use of the Traditional Saying in the Old Testament." Ph.D. dissertation. Duke University.

Fretheim, Terence E.

1977   *The Message of Jonah: A Theological Commentary*. Minneapolis: Augsburg.

Galling, Kurt

1952   *Die Krise der Aufklärung in Israel*. Mainz: Johannes Gutenberg-Buchhandlung.

1961   "Die Rätsel der Zeit im Urteil Kohelets (Koh 3:1-15)." *ZTK* 58:1-15.

Gemser, Berend

1960   "The Instructions of 'Onchsheshonqy and Biblical Wisdom Literature'." In *Congress Volume. Oxford 1959*, 102-28. VTSup 7. Leiden: E. J. Brill. Repr: Crenshaw 1976a, 102-28.

1968   "The Spiritual Structure of Biblical Aphoristic Wisdom." In *Adhuc Loquitur. Collected Essays of Dr. B. Gemser*, 138-49. Ed. A. van Selms and A. S. van der Woude. Leiden: E. J. Brill. Repr: Crenshaw 1976a, 208-19.

Gerbracht, Diether
1975   "Aufbruch zu sittlichen Atheismus. Die Hiob-Deutung Ernst Blochs." *EvT* 35:223-37.

Gese, Hartmut
1958   *Lehre und Wirklichkeit in der alten Weisheit.* Tübingen: J. C. B. Mohr (Paul Siebeck).
1963   "Die Krisis der Weisheit bei Koheleth." In *Les Sagesses du Proche-Orient ancien*, 139-51. Paris: Presses Universitaires de France.

Gilbert, Maurice
1973   *La critique des dieux dans Livre de la Sagesse (Sg 13-15).* AnBib 53. Rome: Pontifical Biblical Institute.
1979   "Le discours de la Sagesse en Proverbes, 8, Structure et cohérence." In *La Sagesse de l'Ancien Testament*, 202-18. Ed. M. Gilbert. BETL 51. Gembloux: Duculot.

Glatzer, Nahum N.
1966   "The Book of Job and its Interpreters." In *Biblical Motifs*, 197-220. Ed. A. Altmann. Cambridge MA: Harvard University Press.
1969   *The Dimensions of Job.* New York: Schocken Books.

Good, Edwin M.
1973   "Job and the Literary Task: A Response." *Soundings* 56:470-84.

Gordis, Robert
1943/1944 "The Social Background of Wisdom Literature," *HUCA* 18:77-118.
1951   *Koheleth—the Man and his World.* New York: Schocken Books.
1965   *The Book of God and Man.* Chicago and London: University of Chicago Press.
1978   *The Book of Job: Commentary, New Translation and Special Studies.* New York: Jewish Theological Seminary of America.

Gordon, Edmund I.
1957   "Sumerian Proverbs: Collection Four." *JAOS* 77:67-79.
1958   "Sumerian Proverbs and Fables." *JCS* 12:1-21, 43-75.
1959   *Sumerian Proverbs. Glimpses of Every Day Life in Ancient Mesopotamia.* Philadelphia: Westminster.
1960   "A New Look at the Wisdom of Sumer and Akkad." *BO* 17:122-52.

Gowan, Donald
1968   "Habakkuk and Wisdom." *Perspective* 9:157-66.

Gray, John
1970   "The Book of Job in the Context of Near Eastern Literature." *ZAW* 82:251-69.

Habel, Norman
1972   "The Symbolism of Wisdom in Proverbs 1-9." *Int* 26:131-56.
1973   "Appeal to Ancient Tradition as a Literary Form." SBLSP (1973), 1:34-54. Ed. George W. MacRae. Cambridge MA: Society of Biblical Literature.

Haspecker, Josef
1967   *Gottesfurcht bei Jesus Sirach.* AnBib 30. Rome: Pontifical Biblical Institute.

Hausen, Adelheid
1972   *Hiob in der französischen Literatur.* Bern and Frankfurt: Herbert and Peter Lang.

Hedinger, Ulric
    1967   "Reflexion über C. G. Jungs Hiobinterpretation." *TZ* 23:340-52.
Hengel, Martin
    1974   *Judaism and Hellenism: Studies in Their Encounter in Palestine during the Early Hellenistic Period.* Two volumes. Philadelphia: Fortress Press.
Hermisson, Hans-Jürgen
    1968   *Studien zur israelitischen Spruchweisheit.* WMANT 28. Neukirchen: Neukirchener Verlag.
    1978   "Observations on the Creation Theology in Wisdom." In *Israelite Wisdom,* 43-57. Ed. J. G. Gammie et al. Missoula MT: Scholars Press.
Hertzberg, Hans Wilhelm
    1963   *Der Prediger.* KAT 17. Gütersloh: Mohn.
Holm-Nielsen, Svend
    1974   "On the Interpretation of Qoheleth in Early Christianity." *VT* 24:168-77.
Horton, Ernest, Jr.
    1972   "Koheleth's Concept of Opposites." *Numen* 19:1-21.
Humphreys, W. Lee
    1978   "The Motif of the Wise Courtier in the Book of Proverbs." In *Israelite Wisdom,* 161-75. Ed. J. G. Gammie et al. Missoula MT: Scholars Press.
Irwin, William S.
    1962   "Job's Redeemer." *JBL* 81:217-29.
Jacob, Edmond
    1978   "Wisdom and Religion in Sirach." In *Israelite Wisdom,* 247-60. Ed. J. G. Gammie et al. Missoula MT: Scholars Press.
Jensen, Joseph
    1973   *The Use of Torah by Isaiah.* CBQMS 3. Washington: Catholic Biblical Association of America. Repr: *JAOS* 101/1 (1981).
Jung, Carl G.
    1970   *Answer to Job.* Cleveland and New York: World.
Kahn, Jack H.
    1975   *Job's Illness: Loss, Grief, and Integration.* Oxford and New York: Pergamon.
Kalugila, Leonidas
    1980   *The Wise King.* ConBOT 15. Lund: Gleerup.
Kayatz, Christa
    1966   *Studien zu Proverbien 1-9.* WMANT 22. Neurkirchen-Vluyn: Neukirchener Verlag.
Keel, Othmar
    1978   *Jahwes Entgegnung an Hiob.* FRLANT 121. Göttingen: Vandenhoeck & Ruprecht.
Kegler, Jürgen
    1977   "Hauptlinien der Hiobforschung seit 1956." In Claus Westermann, *Der Aufbau des Buches Hiob,* 9-25. Stuttgart: Calwer.
Khanjian, J.
    1975   "Wisdom." In *Ras Shamra Parallels,* 2:371-400. AnOr 50. Rome: Pontifical Biblical Institute.
Kidner, Derek
    1964   *Proverbs.* Downers Grove: InterVarsity Press.
Klopfenstein, Martin
    1972   "Die Skepsis des Qohelet." *TZ* 28:97-109.

Koch, Klaus
  1955   "Gibt es ein Vergeltungsdogma im Alten Testament?" *ZTK* 52:1-42.
  1972   *Um das Prinzip der Vergeltung in Religion und Recht des Alten Testaments.* WF 125. Darmstadt: Wissenschaftliche Buchgesellschaft.
Kovacs, Brian W.
  1974   "Is There a Class-Ethic in Proverbs?" In *Essays in Old Testament Ethics*, 171-89. Ed. J. L. Crenshaw and J. T. Willis. New York: Ktav.
  1978   "Sociological-Structural Constraints upon Wisdom: The Spatial and Temporal Matrix of Proverbs 15:28-22:16." Ph.D. dissertation. Vanderbilt University.
Kraeling, Carl H., and Robert Adams, eds.
  1960   *City Invincible: A Symposium on Urbanization and Cultural Development in the Ancient Near East.* Chicago: University of Chicago Press.
Kroeber, Rudi
  1963   *Der Prediger.* SQAW 13. Berlin: Akademie-Verlag.
Kubina, Veronika
  1979   *Die Gottesreden im Buche Hiob.* FTS 115. Freiburg/Basel/Vienna: Herder.
Kuntz, J. Kenneth
  1974   "The Canonical Wisdom Psalms of Ancient Israel—Their Rhetorical, Thematic and Formal Dimensions." In *Rhetorical Criticism*, 186-222. Ed. Jared Jackson and Martin Kessler. Pittsburg: Pickwick.
Lambert, William G.
  1960   *Babylonian Wisdom Literature.* Oxford: Clarendon.
Lang, Bernhard
  1975   *Frau Weisheit: Deutung einer biblischen Gestalt.* Düsseldorf: Patmos.
Lauha, Aarre
  1960   "Die Krise des religiösen Glaubens bei Kohelet." In *Wisdom in Israel and the Ancient Near East*, 183-91. VTSup 3.
  1978   *Kohelet.* BKAT 19. Neukirchen-Vluyn: Neukirchener Verlag.
Lemaire, André
  1981   *Les écoles et la formation de la Bible dans l'ancien Israel.* OBO 39. Göttingen: Vandenhoeck & Ruprecht.
Leveque, Jean
  1970   *Job et son Dieu.* Paris: Gabalda.
Lichtheim, Miriam
  1973,1976,1980   *Ancient Egyptian Literature.* I-III. Berkeley: University of California Press.
Liver, J.
  1967   "The Book of the Acts of Solomon." *Bib* 48:71-101.
Loader, J. A.
  1979   *Polar Structures in the Book of Qohelet.* BZAW 152. Berlin and New York: Walter de Gruyter.
Lohfink, Norbert
  1980   *Kohelet.* NEBib. Würzburg: Echter Verlag.
Loretz, Oswald
  1964   *Kohelet und der Alte Orient.* Freiburg/Basel/Vienna: Herder.
Luyten, J.
  1979   "Psalm 73 and Wisdom." In *La Sagesse de l'Ancien Testament*, 59-82. Ed. M. Gilbert. BETL 51. Gembloux: Duculot.

Mack, Burton L.
1973 *Logos und Sophia: Untersuchungen zur Weisheitstheologie im hellenistischen Judentum.* SUNT 10. Göttingen: Vandenhoeck & Ruprecht.
McKane, William
1970 *Proverbs.* Philadelphia: Westminster.
McKenzie, J. L.
1967 "Reflections on Wisdom." *JBL* 86:1-9.
MacLeish, Archibald
1967 *J.B.* Boston: Houghton Mifflin.
Marböck, Johann
1971 *Weisheit im Wandel: Untersuchungen zur Weisheitstheologie bei Ben Sira.* BBB 37. Bonn: Peter Hanstein.
1979 "Sir., 38:24-39:11: Der Schrift-gelehrte Weise. Ein Beitrag zu Gestalt und Werk Ben Siras." In *La Sagesse de l'Ancien Testament*, 293-316. Ed. M. Gilbert. BETL 51. Gembloux: Duculot.
Marzal, Angel
1967 *Gleanings from the Wisdom of Mari.* Studia Pohl 11. Rome: Pontifical Biblical Institute.
Middendorp, Th.
1973 *Die Stellung Jesu ben Siras zwischen Judentum und Hellenismus.* Leiden: E. J. Brill.
Miles, John A.
1977 "Gagging on Job, or, The Comedy of Religious Exhaustion." *Semeia* 7:71-126.
Miskotte, Kornelis H.
1967 *When the Gods Are Silent.* New York and Evanston: Harper & Row.
Morgan, Donn F.
1981 *Wisdom in the Old Testament Traditions.* Atlanta: John Knox.
Müller, Hans Peter
1968 "Wie Sprach Qohälät von Gott?" *VT* 18:507-21.
1970 *Hiob und seine Freunde.* ThStud 103. Zurich: EVZ Verlag.
1978 *Das Hiobproblem.* EF 84. Darmstadt: Wissenschaftliche Buchgesellschaft.
Murphy, Roland E.
1962 "A Consideration of the Classification 'Wisdom Psalms'." In *Congress Volume: Bonn 1962*, 156-67. VTSup 9. Leiden: E. J. Brill. Repr: Crenshaw 1976a, 456-67.
1966 "The Kerygma of the Book of Proverbs." *Int* 20:3-14.
1970 "The Hebrew Sage and Openness to the World." In *Christian Action and Openness to the World*, 219-44. Villanova University Symposium II, III. Villanova PA: Villanova University Press.
1979 "Qohelet's 'Quarrel' with the Fathers." In *From Faith to Faith*, 235-45. Pittsburgh: Pickwick.
1981a "Hebrew Wisdom." *JAOS* 101:21-34.
1981b *Wisdom Literature: Job, Proverbs, Ruth, Canticles, Ecclesiastes, Esther.* Grand Rapids: Eerdmans.
Murtagh, J.
1968 "The Book of Job and the Book of Dead." *ITQ* 35:166-73.
Neiman, David
1972 *The Book of Job.* Jerusalem: Massada.

Nougayrol, Jean
    1963   "Les sagesses babyloneinnes. Études recentes et textes inédits." In *Les sagesses du Proche-Orient ancien*, 41-50. Paris: Presses Universitaires de France.

Otto, Eberhard
    1951   *Der Vorwurf an Gott: Zur Entstehung der ägyptischen Auseinandersetzungsliteratur.* Vorträge der orientalistischen Tagung in Marburg 1950. Hildesheim: n.p.

Perdue, Leo G.
    1974   "The Riddles of Psalm 49." *JBL* 93:533-42.
    1977   *Wisdom and Cult.* SBLDS 30. Missoula MT: Scholars Press.

Pettinato, Giovanni
    1976   "The Royal Archives of Tell Mardikh, Ebla." *BA* 39:44-52.

Pfeiffer, Egon
    1965   "Die Gottesfurcht im Buche Kohelet." In *Gottes Wort und Gottes Land: Hans-Wilhelm Hertzberg. Zum 70. Geburtstag*, 133-58. Ed. H. G. Reventlow. Göttingen: Vandenhoeck & Ruprecht.

Ploeg, J. P. M. van der, and A. S. van der Woude, eds.
    1972   *Le Targum de Job de la Grotte XI de Qumran.* Leiden: E. J. Brill.

Plöger, Otto
    1971   "Zur Auslegung der Sentenzen-sammlungen des Proverbienbuches." In *Probleme biblischer Theologie*, 402-16. Ed. H. W. Wolff. Munich: Kaiser.

Pope, Marvin H.
    1973   *Job.* AB 15. Garden City NY: Doubleday.

Prato, Gian Luig
    1975   *Il problema della teodicea in Ben Sira. Composizione dei contrari e richiamo alle origini.* AnBib 65. Rome: Pontifical Biblical Institute.

Preuss, Horst Dietrich
    1970   "Erwägungen zum theologischen Ort alttestamentlicher Weisheitsliteratur." *EvT* 30:393-417.
    1972   "Das Gottesbild der alteren Weisheit Israels." In *Studies in the Religion of Ancient Israel*, 117-45. VTSup 23. Leiden: E. J. Brill.

Priest, John F.
    1968   "Humanism, Skepticism, and Pessimism in Israel." *JAAR* 36:311-26.

Pritchard, James B., ed.
    1969   *Ancient Near Eastern Texts Relating to the Old Testament* (ANET). Third edition. Princeton: Princeton University Press.

Rad, Gerhard von
    1953   "Josephsgeschichte und ältere Chokma." In *Congress Volume: Copenhagen 1953*, 120-27. Leiden: E. J. Brill. ET: Crenshaw 1976a, 439-47.
    1960   "Hiob XXXVIII und die altägyptische Weisheit." In *Wisdom in Israel and the Ancient Near East*, 293-301. VTSup 3. Leiden: E. J. Brill. ET: Crenshaw 1976a, 267-77.
    1972   *Wisdom in Israel.* Nashville and New York: Abingdon.

Reese, J. M.
    1970   *Hellenistic Influence on the Book of Wisdom and its Consequences.* Rome: Pontifical Biblical Institute.

1979 "Can Paul Ricoeur's Method Contribute to Interpreting the Book of Wisdom?" In *La Sagesse de l'Ancien Testament*, 384-96. Ed. M. Gilbert. BETL 51. Gembloux: Duculot.

Richter, Heinz
1958 "Die Naturweisheit des Alten Testaments im Buch Hiob." *ZAW* 70:1-20.
1959 *Studien zu Hiob.* ThArb 11. Berlin: Evangelische Verlagsanstalt.

Richter, Wolfgang
1966 *Recht und Ethos: Versuch einer Ortung des weisheitlichen Mahnspruches.* SANT 15. Munich: Kösel.

Rickenbacher, Otto
1973 *Weisheits Perikopen bei Ben Sira.* OBO 1. Göttingen: Vandenhoeck & Ruprecht; Frieburg/Schweiz: Universitätsverlag.

Roberts. J. J. M.
1977 "Job and the Israelite Religious Tradition." *ZAW* 89:107-14.

Robertson, David
1973 "The Book of Job: A Literary Study." *Soundings* 56:446-69.
1977 "The Comedy of Job: A Response." *Semeia* 7:41-44.

Ross, James F.
1978 "Psalm 73." In *Israelite Wisdom*, 161-75. Ed. J. G. Gammie et al. Missoula MT: Scholars Press.

Roth, Wolfgang M. W.
1972 "The Wooing of Rebekah: A Tradition-Critical Study of Genesis 24." *CBQ* 34:177-87.

Rüger, H. P.
1970 *Text und Textform im hebräischen Sirach.* BZAW 112. Berlin and New York: Walter de Gruyter.

Rylaarsdam, J. Coert
1946 *Revelation in Jewish Wisdom Literature.* Chicago: University of Chicago Press.

Sanders, Jim Alvin
1955 *Suffering as Divine Discipline in the Old Testament and Post-Biblical Judaism.* Rochester: Colgate Rochester Divinity School.

Sanders, Paul S.
1955 *Twentieth Century Interpretations of the Book of Job.* Englewood Cliffs NJ: Prentice Hall.

Sandmel, Samuel
1979 *Philo of Alexandria.* New York and Oxford: Oxford University Press.

Sarna, Nahum M.
1957 "Epic Substratum in the Prose of Job." *JBL* 76:13-25.

Scaltriti, G.
1955 "Giobbe tra Cristo e Zaratustra." *Palestra del Clero* 34:673-82, 721-28.

Schmid, Hans Heinrich
1966 *Wesen und Geschichte der Weisheit.* BZAW 101. Berlin: A. Töpelmann.
1974 *Altorientalische Welt in der alttestamentlichen Theologie.* Zurich: Theologischer Verlag.

Schmidt, Johannes
1936 *Studien zur Stilistik der alttestamentlichen Spruchliteratur.* ATAbh 13/1. Münster: Aschendorffsche Verlagsbuchhandlung.

Scott, R. B. Y.
    1961   "Folk Proverbs of the Ancient Near East." *Transactions of the Royal Society of Canada* 15:447-56. Repr: Crenshaw 1976a, 417-26.
    1965   *Proverbs. Ecclesiastes.* AB 18. Garden City NY: Doubleday.
    1970   "The Study of Wisdom Literature," *Int* 24:20-45.
    1971a   "Wisdom. Wisdom Literature." *EncJud* 16:557-63.
    1971b   *The Way of Wisdom in the Old Testament.* New York: Macmillan.
    1972   "Wise and Foolish, Righteous and Wicked." In *Studies in the Religion of Ancient Israel,* 146-65. VTSup 23. Leiden: E. J. Brill.

Sekine, Masao
    1958   "Schöpfung und Erlösung im Buche Hiob." In *Von Ugarit nach Qumran,* 213-23. BZAW 77. Berlin: A. Töpelmann.

Sheppard, Gerry T.
    1977   "The Epilogue to Qohelet as Theological Commentary." *CBQ* 39:182-89.
    1980   *Wisdom as a Hermeneutical Construct.* BZAW 151. Berlin and New York: Walter de Gruyter.

Simon, Neil
    1975   *God's Favorite, a Comedy by Neil Simon.* New York: Random House.

Simpson, William Kelly, ed.
    1973   *The Literature of Ancient Egypt.* New Haven and London: Yale University Press.

Skehan, Patrick W.
    1971   *Studies in Israelite Poetry and Wisdom.* CBQMS 1. Washington: Catholic Biblical Association of America.

Skladny, Udo
    1962   *Die ältesten Spruchsammlungen in Israel.* Göttingen: Vandenhoeck & Ruprecht.

Smith, D. E.
    1975   "Wisdom." In *Ras Shamra Parallels,* 2:215-47. Ed. Loren Fisher. AnOr 50. Rome: Pontifical Biblical Institute.

Soden, W. von
    1955   "Die Frage nach der Gerechtigkeit Gottes im Alten Orient." MDOG 96:41-59.

Talmon, Shemaryahu
    1963   "'Wisdom' in the Book of Esther." *VT* 13:419-55.

Taylor, W. S.
    1956   "Theology and Therapy in Job." *TToday* 12:451-62.

Terrien, Samuel
    1957   *Job: Poet of Existence.* New York: Bobbs Merrill.
    1959   "*J.B.* and Job." *The Christian Century* 76/1 (7 January): 9-11.
    1962   "Amos and Wisdom." In *Israel's Prophetic Heritage,* 108-15. Ed. B. W. Anderson and Walter Harrelson. New York: Harper & Row. Repr: Crenshaw 1976a, 448-55.
    1965   "Quelques remarques sur les affinites de Job avec la Deutéro-Ésaïe." In *Volume du Congres: Geneve 1965,* 295-310. VTSup 15. Leiden: E. J. Brill.

Tournay, R.
    1957   "L'ordre primitif des chapitres XXIV-XXVII du livre de Job." *RB* 64:321-34.

Trible, Phyllis
    1963   "Studies in the Book of Jonah." Ph.D. dissertation. Columbia University.

Tsevat, Matitiahu
   1966   "The Meaning of the Book of Job." *HUCA* 37:73-106. Repr: Crenshaw 1976a, 341-74.
Urbach, Ephraim E.
   1975   *The Sages: Their Concepts and Beliefs*. I-II. Jerusalem: Magnes.
Vawter, Bruce
   1980   "Prov. 8:22: Wisdom and Creation." *JBL* 99: 205-16.
Volten, Aksel
   1963   "Der Begriff der Ma'at in den Ägyptischen Weisheitstexten." In *Les sagesses du Proche-Orient ancien*, 73-99. Paris: Presses Universitaires de France.
Weinfeld, Moshe
   1960   "The Dependence of Deuteronomy upon the Wisdom Literature." In *Yehezkel Kaufman Jubilee Volume*, 89-108. Jerusalem: Magnes.
   1967   "The Origin of Humanism in Deuteronomy." *JBL* 80: 241-47.
   1972   *Deuteronomy and the Deuteronomic School*. Oxford: Oxford University Press.
Wendel, Francois
   1963   *Les Sagesses du Proche-Orient ancien*. Paris: Presses Universitaires de France.
Westermann, Claus
   1977   Repr: *Der Aufbau des Buches Hiob*. Stuttgart: Calwer. Original edition, 1956.
Whedbee, J. William
   1971   *Isaiah and Wisdom*. Nashville: Abingdon.
   1977   "The Comedy of Job." *Semeia* 7:1-39.
Whitley, Charles
   1979   *Koheleth*. BZAW 148. Berlin and New York: Walter de Gruyter.
Whybray, Roger N.
   1965   *Wisdom in Proverbs*. SBT 45. London: SCM.
   1968   *The Succession Narrative*. SBT 9. London: SCM.
   1974   *The Intellectual Tradition in the Old Testament*. BZAW 135. Berlin and New York: Walter de Gruyter.
   1978   "Slippery Words. IV. Wisdom." *ExpTim* 89:359-62.
   1981   "The Identification and Use of Quotations in Ecclesiastes." In *Congress Volume: Vienna 1980*, 435-51. VTSup 32. Leiden: E. J. Brill.
Williams, James G.
   1971a   "What Does It Profit a Man?: The Wisdom of Koheleth." *Judaism* 20:179-93. Repr: Crenshaw 1976a, 379-89.
   1971b   "'You Have not Spoken Truth of Me': Mystery and Irony in Job." *ZAW* 83:231-55.
   1977   "Comedy, Irony, Intercession: A Few Notes in Response." *Semeia* 7:135-45.
   1981   *Those Who Ponder Proverbs: Aphoritic Thinking and Biblical Literature*. Sheffield: Almond.
Williams, R. J.
   1956   "Theodicy in the Ancient Near East." *CJT* 2:14-26.
   1981   "The Sages of Ancient Egypt in the Light of Recent Scholarship." *JAOS* 101:1-19.
Winston, David
   1979   *The Wisdom of Solomon*. AB 43. Garden City, NY: Doubleday.
Witzenrath, Hagia
   1979   *Süss ist das Licht . . .* ArzTu Sprache 11. St. Ottilien: Eos Verlag.

Wolff, Hans Walter
  1964   *Amos' geistige Heimat.* WMANT 18. Neukirchen-Vluyn: Neukirchener Verlag. ET: *Amos the Prophet.* Philadelphia: Fortress, 1973.
  1978   "Micha the Moreshite—The Prophet and his Background." In *Israelite Wisdom*, 77-84. Ed. J. G. Gammie et al. Missoula MT: Scholars Press.

Wright, Addison D. G.
  1968   "The Riddle of the Sphinx: The Structure of the Book of Qoheleth." *CBQ* 30:313-34. Repr: Crenshaw 1976a, 245-66.

Würthwein, Ernst
  1970   "Die Weisheit Ägyptens und das Alte Testament." In *Wort und Existenz, Studien zum Alten Testament*, 197-216. Göttingen: Vandenhoeck & Ruprecht. ET: Crenshaw 1976a, 113-33.

Yadin, Yigael
  1965   *The Ben Sira Scroll from Masada.* Jerusalem: Israel Exploration Society and Shrine of the Book.

Zaba, Z.
  1956   *Les Maximes de Ptahhotep.* Prague: Ed. de l'Academie tchecoslovaque des Ceiences.

Zerafa, Peter Paul
  1978   *The Wisdom of God in the Book of Job.* Rome: Herder.

Zhitlowsky, Chaim
  1968   "Job and Faust." Pp. 90-162 in *Two Studies in Yiddish Culture.* Ed. P. Matenko. Leiden: E. J. Brill.

Zimmerli, Walther
  1963   "Ort und Grenze der Weisheit im Rahmen der Alttestamentlichen Theologie." In *Les sagesses du Proche-Orient ancien*, 121-36. Paris: Presses Universitaires de France. ET: "The Place and Limit of the Wisdom in the Framework of the Old Testament Theology." *SJT* 17 (1964) 146-58. Repr: Crenshaw 1976a, 314-26.
  1976   "Concerning the Structure of Old Testament Wisdom." *ZAW* 51:177-204. Repr: Crenshaw 1976a, 175-207.
  1978   *Old Testament Theology in Outline.* Atlanta: John Knox.

Zimmermann, Frank
  1973   *The Inner World of Qohelet.* New York: Ktav.

3 (1974)

Wisdom

Walter Baumgartner, "The Wisdom Literature," in *The Old Testament and Modern Study*, ed. H. H. Rowley (London: Oxford University Press, 1951) 210-37; Sheldon H. Blank, "Wisdom," *IDB* R-Z:852-61; James L. Crenshaw, "Method in Determining Wisdom Influence upon 'Historical' Literature," *JBL* 88 (1969): 129-42; Johannes Fichtner, *Die altorientalische Weisheit in ihrer israelitischjüdischen Ausprägung*, BZAW 62 (Giessen: A. Töpelmann, 1933); idem, *Gottes Weisheit*, ATh 11/3 (Stuttgart: Calwer Verlag, 1965); Ernst Sellin and Georg Fohrer, *Einleitung in das Alte Testament* (Heidelberg: Quelle & Meyer, [10]1965) 331-73 = ET: *Introduction to the Old Testament*, trans. David E. Green (Nashville: Abingdon Press, 1965) 304-41; Erhard S. Gerstenberger, "Zur alttestamentlichen Weisheit," *VF* 14 (1969): 28-44; William A. Irwin, "The Wisdom Literature," *IB* A-D:212-19; Christa Bauer-Kayatz, *Einführung in die alttestamentliche Weisheit*, BibS(N) 55 (Neukirchen: Neukirchener Verlag, 1969); W. G. Lambert, *Babylonian Wisdom Literature* (London: Oxford University Press, 1960); *Les Sagesses du Proche-Orient ancien* (Paris: Presses Universitaires de France, 1963); William McKane, *Prophets and Wise Men*, SBT 44 (London: SCM Press, 1965); John L. McKenzie, "Reflections on Wisdom," *JBL* 86 (1967): 1-9; Roland Murphy, "Form Criticism and Wisdom Literature," *CBQ* 31 (1969): 475-83; idem, "The Interpretation of Old Testament Wisdom Literature," *Int* (1969): 289-301; Martin Noth and D. Winton Thomas, eds., *Wisdom in Israel and in the Ancient Near East*, VTSup 3 (Leiden: E. J. Brill, 1960); Horst Dietrich Preuss, "Erwägungen zum theologischen Ort alttestamentlicher Weisheitsliteratur," *EvT* 30 (1970): 393-417; Gerhard von Rad, *Weisheit in Israel* (Neukirchen: Neukirchener Verlag, 1970); O. S. Rankin, *Israel's Wisdom Literature* (Edinburgh: T.&T. Clark, 1936); Hans Heinrich Schmid, *Gerechtigkeit als Weltordnung*, BHT 40 (Tübingen: J. C. B. Mohr, 1968); idem, "Hauptprobleme der altorientalischen und alttestamentlichen Weisheitsliteratur," *ST* 35 (1965): 68-74; idem, *Wesen und Geschichte der Weisheit*, BZAW 101 (Berlin: A. Töpelmann, 1966); R. B. Y. Scott, "The Study of the Wisdom Literature," *Int* 24 (1970): 20-45; idem, *The Way of Wisdom in the Old Testament* (New York: Macmillan, 1971); Patrick William Skehan, *Studies in Israelite Poetry and Wisdom*, CBQMS 1 (1971); Walther Zimmerli, "Zur Struktur der alttestamentlichen Weisheit," *ZAW* 51 (1933): 177-204.

I. Introduction

Form critical investigation of wisdom literature advances only to the degree that it gives adequate answers to the following questions: (1) What is the scope of the literature? (2) What are the literary forms making up this body of literature? (3) What precise setting in life did these forms occupy? (4) What function did they perform in the life of ancient Israel? The significance of the definitional question cannot be overestimated, for solutions to the other three questions will be greatly affected by this decision. For example, if one assumes that historiography is by its very nature a product of the sages, then the literary genres which would demand attention would be wholly different from what is usually the case in studies of wisdom literature. Our primary task, then, is to determine at the outset what is to be the basis for all that follows.

The question of the assessment of Israelite literature in terms of wisdom thought can be answered, as is to be expected, from two extremes and several mediating positions. At one extreme is the critic who seeks to define wisdom literature as broadly as possible, specifically as nonrevelatory speech. Accordingly, anything that does not fall under the category of divine speech is fair game for the interpreter of wisdom literature. This means that all historiography is the product of the wise man, who by use of reason attempts to make sense of the course of human events (cf. McKenzie). When the nonrevelatory argument is coupled with the psychological one, namely that wisdom thinking is anthropocentric in the sense of laying bare the deepest feelings and aspirations of man, much of the Old Testament suddenly falls within the category of wisdom (cf. von Rad). I have reference to the Primeval History (Gen 1–11), the Joseph Narrative (Gen 37–50), the Succession Narrative (2 Sam 9–20, 1 Kings 1–2), and Esther. Furthermore, once a didactic tendency is recognized as clear evidence that a sage has been at work, additional literature enters the discussion, especially Tobit, Judith, 1 Esdras 3–4, and Ahiqar. Even a humanitarian concern has been viewed as evidence of wisdom origin; thus, Deuteronomy is seen as the legal expression of the sages (cf. Moshe Weinfeld, "The Origin of the Humanism in Deuteronomy," *JBL* 80 [1961]: 241-47). Still others have used a concatenation of factors as proof that various literary works are wisdom in orientation (Amos, Hab 3, Deut 32, Exod 34, and specific texts in Isa, Jer, and Hos). The kinship of wisdom thinking and apocalyptic has led some to the view that Daniel is wisdom literature, particularly since the hero of the book that bears his name is a wise man. Finally, reflection on the problem of innocent suffering has been used as a basis for inclusion of a number of psalms in the wisdom corpus.

At the other end of the spectrum is the interpreter who chooses to define wisdom literature as narrowly as possible so as to retain the distinctiveness of that body of texts. Accordingly, the minimal literary works are emphasized, specifically Job, Qoheleth, Proverbs, Sirach, and Wisdom of Solomon. I shall adopt this position for the following discussion, inasmuch as there is general agreement that the above-mentioned are, to a degree at least, normative for wisdom thought.

On the basis of this literature it can be stated that wisdom literature is of four kinds: (1) juridical, (2) nature, (3) practical, and (4) theological. Distinction must be made between wisdom literature, wisdom tradition, and wisdom thinking. Similarly, there exist (1) family/clan wisdom, the goal of which is the mastering of life, the stance hortatory and the style proverbial; (2) court wisdom, with the goal of education for a select group, the stance secular, and method didactic; and (3) scribal wisdom, with the aim of providing education for everyone, a stance that is dogmatico-religious, and a dialogico-admonitory method. It would be a mistake to assume that these differences in style are chronological, although they correspond roughly to the three stages through which the wisdom movement passed.

Wisdom literature has its origins in the family, and from the period of the clan ethos derive many of the proverbs whose purpose was to equip one for the mastery of life regardless of circumstance. To this period belong also the onomastica, in rudimentary form, or lists of character traits and experiences of nature. From the family ethos arose the terms for teacher and student (father/son), as well as the emphasis upon domestic illustrations for emulation or shunning. With the emergence of court wisdom, in the Solomonic era perhaps, came a decisive shift in the interests of the sage, who now found himself in the employ of the state and commissioned to see to its welfare. An elite group, these counsellors were soon at odds with representatives of the prophetic movement and more and more apart from the common man and his concerns. Religious interests increasingly come under the wings of the wisdom movement, possibly at the impetus of Hezekiah, but certainly in the person of Sirach and the unknown author of Wisdom of Solomon (Fichtner). Similarly, the religious quest for meaning in the midst of the suffering of the innocent elicits from the fringes of wisdom thought the poetic masterpieces Job and Qoheleth. The diversity of literature and its concomitant emphases would lead one to expect a multiplicity of literary forms, and one is not disappointed in such anticipation.

Delineation of literary genres, while still in its infancy, has made considerable progress. Job has posed the most difficult problem, and some scholars have been willing to consider the book sui generis. Others have seen the poetry as a variant of the philosophical dialogue, a *Streitgespräch*, a Paradigm of the Answered Lament, or a Lawsuit. The dominant characteristic of Qoheleth, the confession, is recognized as a *Gattung* of Egyptian wisdom literature, while most of the final chapter is clearly an allegory (12:1-8; cf. Prov 9:1-6, 13-18). The book of Proverbs is composed of sentences (aphorisms) and admonitions, while the riddle may be hidden behind certain numerical proverbs. Additional categories present in one (or all) of these books are the hymn, which appears frequently in Sirach and Wisdom of Solomon, the prayer (likewise dominant in these two late works), didactic poetry and narrative (for lack of a better term), and lists. Apparently, no particular form is limited to one period of the wisdom movement or to any type of wise man. On the contrary, the forms are in use at every period in the history of the movement and in all facets of wisdom thinking.

Little precision is possible in specifying settings within which each literary genre functioned, that is, beyond the general category of didactic. Still this function is capable of a number of locales, including the home, school (cf. Hans-Jürgen Hermisson, *Studien zur israelitischen Spruchweisheit*, WMANT 28 [Neukirchen: Neukirchener Verlag, 1968] 192: "Israelite wisdom has its center, its locus of origin, and its nurture in the Israelite school"), court and possibly the temple (if the Mesopotamian parallel of a temple school has any importance for Israel, and if the hymns and prayers in Sirach may be in any way normative). But even these settings provide little clarity, for there is room for diversity within each. The school, for example, may have served totally different purposes, perhaps simultaneously, depending on whether the welfare of the state or of the individual was uppermost. The latter aim would be religious in distinction from the purely secular emphases of the counsellor to the king (if such extreme secularity ever existed, as McKane thinks).

Finally, there is evidence of multiverse structuring of various proverbs, as well as acrostic and categorizing sequence of larger paragraphs. This means that the individual sentence or admonition exists within a context that is didactic, hence has received a new *Sitz*. It may be, too, that the total book is the product of intentional arrangement, so that one must speak of a unit larger than verse or paragraph. I have reference to Skehan's hypothesis about Wisdom's House as the conscious architectonic construct of the final editor of Proverbs, as well as to the book of Job.

After these preliminary remarks about the scope of wisdom and the genres, both as to form and function, I now turn to an analysis of the forms within wisdom literature. Eight categories will be discussed: proverb, riddle, fable and allegory, hymn and prayer, *Streitgespräch* or dialogue, confession, lists, didactic poetry and narrative.

II. The Forms

A. Proverb (מָשָׁל)

André Barucq, *Le Livre des Proverbes*, SB (Paris: J. Gabalda, 1964); A. Bea, "Der Zahlenspruch im Hebräischen und Ugaritischen," *Bib* 21 (1940): 196-98; G. Boström, *Proverbiastudien. Die Weisheit und das fremde Weib in Spr. 1–9*, LUÅ NF 1.30.3 (Lund: C. W. K. Gleerup, 1935); Otto Eissfeldt, *Der Maschal im Alten Testament*, BZAW 24 (Giessen: Töpelmann, 1913); Erhard S. Gerstenberger, *Wesen und Herkunft des sogenannten "apodiktischen Rechts" im Alten Testament*, WMANT 20 (Neukirchen: Neukirchener Verlag, 1965); A. H. Godbey, "The Hebrew *Māšāl*," *AJSL* 39 (1922/1923): 89-108; A. S. Herbert, "The 'Parable' (*Māšāl*) in the Old Testament," *SJT* 7 (1954): 180-96; Hans-Jürgen Hermisson, *Studien zur israelitischen Spruchweisheit*, WMANT 28 (Neukirchen: Neukirchener Verlag, 1968); Aubrey R. Johnson, "*Māšāl*," VTSup 3 (1955): 162-69; Christa Bauer-Kayatz, *Studien zu Proverbien 1–9*, WMANT 22 (Neukirchen: Neukirchener Verlag, 1966); William McKane, *Proverbs* (Philadelphia: Westminster, 1970); Wolfgang Richter, *Recht und Ethos: Versuch einer Ortung des weisheitlichen Mahnspruches*, SANT 15 (Munich: Kösel-Verlag, 1966); Helmer Ringgren, *Word and Wisdom* (Lund: H. Ohlssons, 1947); Wolfgang M. W. Roth, *Numerical Sayings in the Old Testament*, VTSup 13 (Leiden: E. J. Brill, 1965); idem, "The Numerical Sequence X/X+1 in the Old Testament," *VT* 12 (1962): 300-11; Georg Sauer, *Die Spruche Agurs*, BWANT 4/4 (Stuttgart: W. Kohlhammer, 1963); R. B. Y. Scott, *Proverbs, Ecclesiastes*, AB 18 (Garden City NY: Doubleday, 1965); U. Skladny, *Die ältesten Spruchsammlungen in Israel* (Göttingen: Vandenhoeck & Ruprecht, 1962); W. B. Stevenson, "A Mnemonic Use of Numbers in Proverbs and Ben Sira," *TGUOS* 9 (1938/1939): 26-38; W. A. van der Weiden, *Le Livre des Proverbes*, BibOr 23 (Rome: Biblical Institute Press, 1970); Roger N. Whybray, *Wisdom in Proverbs*, SBT 45 (London: SCM Press 1965); Hans Walter Wolff, *Amos's geistige Heimat*, WMANT 18 (Neukirchen: Neukirchener Verlag, 1964) 24-29; A. Wünsche, "Die Zahlenspruche in Talmud und Midrasch," *ZDMG* 65 (1911): 57-100.

"One must possess discernment in order to grasp its meaning, and emotion to feel the beauty of its expression" (J. G. Herder, *Spruch und Bild insonderheit bei den Morgenländern*, Suphan 16 [1887]: 9-10, quoted by Gerhard von Rad, 49). The precise sense of מָשָׁל is not known, although "similitude" and "ruling word" appear to cover the broad spectrum of usage. Both meanings are possible etymologically; the former focuses on the sense of likeness, representativeness, hence similitude (Eissfeldt, Godbey), while the latter takes its departure from the root meaning "to rule, have dominion, reign," thus a word spoken by a ruler or a word bearing special power (Boström). Hylmö's definition of מָשָׁל as "a winged word, outliving the fleeting moment" (see Aage Bentzen, *Introduction to the Old Testament*, vol. 1 [Copenhagen: G. E. C. Gad, 1948] 168) is an interesting variant that has found a recent champion in William McKane (22-33), for whom the timeless, paradigmatic character of the proverb is decisive. Accordingly McKane translates מָשָׁל by "paradigm, model, exemplar" and judges a saying on the basis of its universal character.

Such diversity of meaning derives from the fact that מָשָׁל not only refers to similitudes (Ezek 16:44; Gen 10:9; 1 Sam 10:11), but also to popular sayings (Jer 23:28; 31:29; 1 Sam 24:13; Isa 32:6; 1 Kings 20:11), literary aphorisms (Prov 10:1–22:16, 25-29; Qoh 9:17–10:20), taunt songs (Isa 14:4; Mic 2:4; Hab 2:6-8; Ezek 12:22-23; 18:2-3), bywords (Deut 28:37; 1 Kings 9:7; Jer 24:9; Ezek 14:8), allegories (Ezek 17:1-10; 20:45-49; 24:3-14), and discourses (Num 23:7, 18; 24:3-24; Job 27:1; 29:1; Ps 49:4; 78:2).

A further complication is the multiplicity of forms of מְשָׁלִים in the book of Proverbs. At least five types are discernible, namely sentence (*Spruch* or *Aussage*), instruction, exhortation or admonition (*Mahnrede, Mahnwort, Mahnspruch, Rat*), numerical (*Zahlenspruch*), comparison or excluding, to use H. H. Schmid's descriptive term, and antithetic proverb. Biblical proverbial patterns are likewise disparate and in their variety are at one with nonbiblical parallels. Scott's delineation of both isolates seven patterns (1) identity, equivalence, invariable association; (2) non-identity, contrast, paradox; (3) similarity, analogy, type; (4) contrary to right order, futile, absurd; (5) classification and clarification; (6) value, relative value or priority, proportion or degree; (7) consequences of human character and behavior (5-7).

The basic unit of gnomic apperception is the saying, either proverb or aphorism. The simplest form of *Sprichwort* is the popular proverb, a number of which have been preserved in the narrative literature of the Old Testament. While most of these brief *Volksprüche* are in prose, on occasion they are clothed in metrical garb (Jer 31:29; Ezek 18:2, "The fathers have eaten sour grapes, and the children's teeth are set on edge") and make use of consonantal and vocalic assonance (Prov 11:2; 13:3). Studies of popular proverbs have singled out such passages as Gen 10:9 ("Like Nimrod a mighty hunter before the Lord"), 1 Sam 10:12 ("Is Saul also among the prophets?" cf. 19:24), 2 Sam 5:8 ("The blind and the lame shall not come into the house"), 1 Kings 20:11 ("Let not him that girds on his armor boast himself as he that puts it off"), Prov 10:6, 11 ("The mouth of the wicked conceals violence" to which should be compared 1 Sam 24:13 "Out of the wicked comes forth wickedness"), Jer 13:23 ("Can the Ethiopian change his skin, or the leopard his spots?"), 23:28 ("What has straw in common with wheat?"), Ezek 16:44 ("Like mother, like daughter"; cf. Hos 4:9, Sir 10:2), as well as the above-mentioned poetic popular proverbs (Eissfeldt; Scott, xxvi–xxiv). By nature secular and nondidactic, these popular proverbs were occasionally enlisted in the service of morality and consequently assumed a religious tenor.

The proverb is bilinear and registers a conclusion based on experience; as such it must be self-confirming, commending itself to empirical validation or to disconfirmation. Since the saying is a result of the collective experience of mankind, it has a retrospective character, and because of its nature as an observation of how things are, it lacks the imperative. Hence any didactic intent is secondary to the proverb, and the style is succinct, epigrammatic, and highly metaphorical. However, even the literary proverb may be set within a didactic context, as in the case of the folk proverb. This pedagogic function of the aphorism was abetted by the addition of motivation clauses, which led to a disintegration of the form of the proverb, as well as by the attaching of consequences of conduct. Certain stylistic features give evidence of serious reflection in the service of teaching, for example the parallels of comparison (parabolic parallelism) that express evaluative judgments ("as . . . so," "better is . . . than"), and the frequent use of paranomasia, assonance, alliteration, puns, listing, repetition, synonymy, rhyme (Fohrer, *Introduction*, 313). In synonymous parallelism the second line emphasizes the moral of the first, whereas in synthetic parallelism it frequently resolves the image. In a didactic setting the interrogative form, particularly rhetorical questions, comes into prominence.

The relative chronology of the popular and literary proverbs, that is, the development of the unilinear and bilinear proverb, has been the subject of much discussion. Eissfeldt's study of the מָשָׁל led him to the conclusion that the popular proverb was anterior to the literary proverb, which was the result of artistic refinement. Similarly J. Schmidt contended that the proverb developed from a brief one-line popular saying to a poetic, two-line *Kunstspruch*, and ultimately, on analogy with the development of multiverses, into larger units by the addition of motivation clauses and reasons for conduct, attached syntactically to the original proverb by dependent clauses (*Studien zur Stilistik der alttestamentlichen Spruchliteratur*, ATA 13/1 [Münster: Aschendorffsche Verlagsbuchhandlung, 1936]). This assumption of a development from the simpler form to the more complex came to serve as an axiom of form criticism, so that the date of proverb collections was determined largely on the basis of complexity of sayings contained therein, despite the possibility that the short saying may be fragmentary, a corruption of an original two-line proverb. This procedure has come under attack from several quarters recently, both on literary and sociological grounds.

In every instance comparison with Egyptian wisdom literature has forced a reexamination of the assumption of development from simple to complex sentence structure. R. N. Whybray based his analysis of Prov 1–9 on the Egyptian instruction genre and called into question the lateness of these chapters. In dating them early Whybray took up a major conclusion of U. Skladny, who emphasized the architectonic nature of the collection of biblical proverbs and claimed to have discovered four major sections with thematic coherence: (1) 10–15, contrast between righteousness and wickedness; (2) 16:1–22:16, Yahweh and the king; (3) 25–27, nature and agriculture; (4) 28–29, the king, or potential rulers. Kayatz examined Prov 1–9 in terms of a formal analysis of the instruction genre in Egypt, concluding that the prototype of the personification of wisdom may be the divine speeches in Egyptian wisdom literature. A thoroughgoing analysis of the instruction genre has been undertaken by McKane, who argues for two types of proverb: (1) Instruction, Prov 1–9; 22:17–24:22; 31:1-9; and (2) Sentence, Prov 10:1–22:16; 24:23-34; 25-29.

The very existence of folk proverbs (with rare exceptions) has been challenged by H.-J. Hermisson, who submits Eissfeldt's conclusions to exhaustive analysis, both as to the definition of proverb and criteria employed for distinguishing a folk proverb from a literary proverb. But Hermisson goes further than the mere rejection of form critical arguments based on a temporal priority of the simplest form; rather he postulates a fundamentally different community that is responsible for creating and collecting biblical proverbs. In this regard he gives confirmation to Bentzen's observation that the popular proverb could not be the origin of wisdom poetry, which was *literature by scholars for scholars* (so Hylmö; see Bentzen, *Introduction* 1:168, 173) and encourages the view that folk proverbs and artistic sayings existed simultaneously as is the case in extrabiblical literature.

The presuppositions of the community that expressed its observations about reality in succinct proverbs are difficult to ascertain, although much can be known (see especially von Rad, *Weisheit in Israel*, and Kayatz, *Einführung in die alttestamentliche Weisheit*). A distinction between *Erfahrungsweisheit* (the wisdom of experience) and *theologische Weisheit* (theological wisdom) is essential, the former embracing both clan and court wisdom. The proverb is an elementary quest for order, comparisons, and contrasts, as well as numerical speech serving to assure the Israelite of regularity and dependability in the universe. The concerns of the clan were encapsulated in proverbs, specifically the contrast between rich and poor, good and bad, hate and love, wisdom and folly. By means of comparative speech, direct admonition, questions, riddles, and numerical speech the concept of retribution was promulgated, and Yahweh's role as guarantor of order was emphasized.

Inasmuch as all knowledge leads to self-knowledge, experiential and nature wisdom were recognized as complementary rather than contradictory. Since the order of the universe was fundamental, there was no room for the heroic individual, yet both Proverbs and Sirach have examples of ethical radicalization. The wise man is the just man, and the fool is the practical atheist, not the ignorant. This implies the necessity for obedience, since the word is empty unless it is given a hearing. In the process of listening, however, the word is submitted to new personal and communal experience, is subjected to occasional disconfirmation. Out of this struggle between the claims of the past and the reality of the present, ambiguity emerges, and the riddle of the world changes, resulting in contradictory statements. Such ambiguity forces upon the community an awareness of the limits of human wisdom; these limitations were also the result of the Israelite view of God, who always retained sovereign freedom to dispose of man's best-laid plans. (See H. Brunner, "Der freie Wille Gottes in der ägyptischen Weisheitstexten," *Les Sagesses du Proche-Orient ancien*, 103-20, for the Egyptian scene; W. Zimmerli, "Ort und Grenze der Weisheit in Rahmen der alttestamentliche Theologie," ibid., 121-38 = Zimmerli's *Gottes Offenbarung*, TBü 19 [Munich: Chr. Kaiser, 1963] 300-15 = "The Place and Limit of the Wisdom in the Framework of Old Testament Theology," *SJT* 28 [1964]: 146-58, and H. Gese, *Lehre und Wirklichkeit in der alten Weisheit* [Tübingen: J. C. B. Mohr, 1958] 45-50, for the Israelite.) The mystery of God was, nevertheless, a source of comfort, a basis for joy, and all creation was thought to sing his praises. Hence there was no possibility for a tragic view of life, and the ancient Israelite was remarkably at home in the world, which was God's great secret, worthy of trust and punishing false trust.

Court wisdom focused on the king and his responsibilities, both as guarantor of justice and as one whose throne is established on righteousness, an Egyptian concept (H. Brunner, "Gerechtigkeit als Fundament des Throns," *VT* 8 [1958]: 426-28; H. Schmid, *Gerechtigkeit als Weltordnung*, 23). Other prominent themes were the education of potential rulers and court personnel, the limitations of wisdom, and the fear of the Lord. Here one finds a commingling of urban and agricultural concerns, particularly those of the wealthy plantation owner (R. Gordis, "The Social Background of Wisdom Literature," *HUCA* 18 [1943/1944]: 77-118). The humanization of man is evident in the concern for the welfare of the poor, the art of eloquence and cultivation of the proper silence, warnings about the wiles of the adulteress and the deleterious effect of excessive drinking, together with the enumeration of obstacles to the mastery of the tongue (cf. Prov 23:29-35, which may originally have been a riddle).

Theologische Weisheit, on the other hand, consists of long poems of theological reflection on the relation of Yahweh to wisdom and creation. The personification of wisdom is the means of maintaining an intimate relationship between the creator and the created order where revelation is not assumed; such hypostatization, if the term is applicable (von Rad would deny its appropriateness except for Wisdom of Solomon; see *Weisheit in Israel*, 193), may have emerged into prominence as a response to the problem of theodicy (see B. L. Mack, "Wisdom Myth and Mythology," *Int* 24 [1970]: 46-60). The influence of prophetic speech, however, is felt in the manner of Dame Wisdom's call to obedience, although she goes beyond the prophetic oracle by inviting men to *come to her* for life.

It has been said that the proverb is self-validating, that it cannot appeal to any authority other than that of human experience (Zimmerli, "Zur Struktur der alttestamentlichen Weisheit"). This understanding of עֵצָה as advice devoid of compelling authority came to be normative until recently, when syntactical, thematic, and contextual arguments were mustered against it (see James L. Crenshaw, "'*ēsâ and dābār*: The Problem of Authority/Certitude in Wisdom and Prophetic Literature," in *Prophetic Conflict, Its Effect upon Israelite Religion*, BZAW 124 (Berlin: Walter de Gruyter, 1971] 116-23).

The didactic character of the proverb is heightened in the admonition, which seeks to inculcate a desired behavior pattern and right thinking. To accomplish this end the admonition makes use of motive clauses, positive commands, and grounds for conduct. The whole weight of tradition undergirds the exhortation and warning, for the *Mahnrede* purports to embody the findings of generations of experience. Furthermore, the authority of the instructor, either as father, clan leader, counsellor, scribe or teacher in a school, stands behind every word. But an even greater authority is assumed, namely that of the creator and sustainer of order. Since God is the ultimate source of all justice, the fear of the Lord is indeed the beginning of wisdom. Given the authoritative character of the admonition, one can understand the wise man's contempt for the fool, the man too stubborn to act on what everyone knew to be right.

The admonition may also be negative. This phenomenon has been the subject of much discussion recently, particularly as to the *Sitz* indicated by the form of negative employed. W. Richter views the negative admonitions as the product of *Gruppenethos* in schools responsible for the education of public officials, hence associated with the royal court and probably the temple. For him the distinction between a vetitive and prohibitive is fundamental. The vetitive uses the jussive with אל and is a negation of the imperative, usually with a motive clause. It seldom occurs in legal codes. On the other hand, the prohibitive uses the negative particle לא with the imperfect; it appears mostly in legal corpora. The life setting of both is said to be the *Gruppenethos* of the school (Richter, *Recht und Ethos*).

A different understanding of the prohibition is offered by E. Gerstenberger, for whom the occurrence of אל in legal codes without any diminution of seriousness constitues a refutation of Richter's thesis. Gerstenberger attempts to locate the prohibitions in the *Sippenethos* (clan ethos), which is for him a milieu in which law and wisdom coincide.

The absence of any correspondence in wisdom literature between form and setting renders a decision between these theses virtually impossible; a further complication is the fact that the prehistory of the legal admonition is the everyday intercourse of human activity. In addition, there is in court wisdom an intermingling of agricultural imagery and other concerns of the *Sippenethos* with the more office-oriented interests of the *Gruppenethos*. It is thus not possible to limit agricultural metaphors to folk wisdom, royal to court wisdom; accordingly, the precise origin of any passage is open to question. As a criticism of Richter's contention that the two forms of negative admonitions, vetitive and prohibitive, constitute distinct *Gattungen*, R. Murphy's stricture that only one basic form is present here, namely negative admonition, appears to be justified ("Form Criticism and Wisdom Literature," 481).

The numerical proverb moves one step further in the direction of didacticism; despite its probable origin in connection with the riddle, the *Zahlenspruch* gives the impression of a mnemonic device in schools. It is at home, however, in the earliest stage of wisdom and represents an elementary need of man seeking order. Fohrer has surmised that its origin is Canaanite, appealing to RS 51.3.17-21 (*Introduction*, 312); in any case G. Sauer emphasizes the kinship between the numerical proverbs and Ugaritic literature (70-112). The favorite scheme is three/four, although one/two (Job 33:14-15; cf. Ps 62:12; Sir 50:25-26), two/three (Job 13:20-22; Sir 26:28), six/seven (Prov 6:16-19; Job 5:19-22, cf. "Dispute between the Tamarisk and the Date Palm," *ANET* 592-93), and nine/ten (Sir 25:7-11) are also attested (perhaps even four/five in Prov 30:24-28, if Sauer is correct [103-104]). In some instances, only one fact is mentioned, despite the formula calling for three/four; this is particular]y striking in the prophetic use of the stylistic device (Amos 1:3–2:8), where the expression appears to represent the totality of offenses, that is, stands for comprehensiveness. In still other passages the demand for parallelism, if that is the actual explanation for the formula, does not necessitate an ascending scale, but is content with an elaboration of the things making up the number (Prov 30:7-9, 24-28; Sir 25:1-2). The usual form, however, is x/x plus one, with emphasis being placed on the larger number as if the answer to a "riddle" (Prov 6:16-19; 30:15b-16, 18-19, 21-23, 29-31; Sir 25:7-11; 26:5-6, 28). As Torczyner perceived, Prov 30:18-19 may originally have existed in question, that is, riddle form: "What three or four things move without leaving any trace?" ("The Riddle in the Bible," *HUCA* 1 [1924]: 125-49, see 135-36). Another variant is a moralistic addition to the last-mentioned component, which amounts to an admission that further clarification of the reason for including it within such a nexus of relationships was necessary (Sir 26:5-6, 28). This appendage calls attention to the fact that the emphasis in numerical proverbs is most often to be found on the final element, the previous ones merely serving to heighten the wonder or disgust over the point at issue.

Each of these variants may be illustrated from Proverbs or Sirach, there being no numerical proverbs in Qoheleth (11:2?) or Wisdom of Solomon. First, the simple number without any heightening:

> Two things I ask of thee;
> do not withold them from me before I die.
> Put fraud and lying far from me;
> give me neither poverty nor wealth,
> provide me only with the food I need.
> If I have too much, I shall deny thee
> and say, "Who is the Lord?"
> If I am reduced to poverty, I shall steal
> and blacken the name of my God.   (Prov 30:7-9 NEB; cf. Job 13:20-27)

Again:

There are three sights which warm my heart
and are beautiful in the eyes of the Lord and of men:
concord among brothers, friendship among neighbors,
and a man and wife who are inseparable.
There are three kinds of men who arouse my hatred,
who disgust me by their manner of life:
a poor man who boasts, a rich man who lies,
and an old fool who commits adultery.   (Sir 25:1-2 NEB).

In this example there is the additional stylistic device of contrast, to be discussed below. The usual form occurs often in Prov 30, but also in 6:16-19, where one reads:

Six things the LORD hates,
seven things are detestable to him:
a proud eye, a false tongue,
hands that shed innocent blood,
a heart that forges thoughts of mischief,
and feet that run swiftly to do evil,
a false witness telling a pack of lies,
and one who stirs up quarrels between brothers.   (NEB)

Here the attempt was made to use parts of the body as illustrative of evil conduct, although the author was unable to maintain the analogy throughout. Possibly Prov 6:12-15 was also a numerical proverb, as K. Budde suggested (*Geschichte der alt-hebräischen Literatur* [Leipzig: Amelang, 1906] 301). The third type is evidence of the use of the numerical proverb in religious instruction. "Two things grieve my heart, and a third excites my anger: a soldier in distress through poverty, wise men treated with contempt, and a man deserting right conduct for wrong—the Lord will bring him to the scaffold" (Sir 26:28 NEB). The frequent use of numerical proverbs to refer to sexuality, both its wonder (Prov 30:18-19) and the *Angst* of a bad marriage, may further attest to the kinship of this form with the riddle, in which sexual themes abound. In this regard Sir 26:5-6 is instructive: "Three things there are that alarm me, and a fourth I am afraid to face: the scandal of the town, the gathering of a mob, and calumny—all harder to bear than death; but it is heartache and grief when a wife is jealous of a rival, and everyone alike feels the lash of her tongue" (NEB). While it is impossible to trace the history of the form, the numerical proverb changed drastically from the time of Prov 30:18-19 to Sirach's use in 25:7-11, which stands apart both in style and content (use of the interrogative, the אַשְׁרֵי formula, the comparative, and the religious motif of the fear of Yahweh as the most excellent gift), as von Rad has observed (*Weisheit in Israel*, 55).

Less debate has taken place over the form or function of the comparison and antithetic proverb. The comparative aphorism occurs frequently in wisdom literature, its purpose being to single out certain kinds of character or conduct as superior to others. Its origin was in clan wisdom, but the comparison was also a favorite of later sages. In Proverbs the majority of occurrences are in the oldest collections: 12:9; 15:16-17; 16:8, 16, 19; 17:1; 19:1; 21:9, 19; 25:24; 27:10c; 28:6; cf. 17:12; 21:3; 22:1. The didactic intent is given religious overtones in 15:16-17:

> Better is a little with the fear of the LORD
> than great treasure and trouble with it.
> Better is a dinner of herbs where love is
> than a fatted ox and hatred with it. (RSV)

Domestic problems gave rise to the following comparison, which appears twice in Proverbs:

> It is better to live in a corner of the housetop
> than in a house shared with a contentious woman.
> (21:9; 25:24 RSV; cf. Sir 25:16)

A variant is found in Prov 21:19:

> It is better to live in a desert land
> than with a contentious and fretful woman. (RSV)

The comparison is used frequently in Qoheleth, where it calls attention to the limits of human wisdom. Here one finds a poem with the comparison as its motivating force (7:1-12), as well as excluding sayings that sum up Qoheleth's despair (2:24; 3:22; 9:16). But the more common form of the comparison also appears (4:6, 9, 13; 5:5; 6:9; 9:4). It is used in Wis 4:1, where the Greek attitude to progeny has made an impact ("Better than this is childlessness with virtue, for in the memory of virtue is immortality, because it is known both by God and by men"). To this may be compared Sir 16:3 ("Do not trust in their survival and do not rely on their multitude; for one is better than a thousand, and to die childless is better than to have ungodly children"). "Better" sayings abound in Sirach (11:3; 19:24; 20:2, 18, 25, 31; 25:16; 30:14-17; 41:15; 42:14, for example). The last, a clear expression of misogyny ("Better is the wickedness of a man than a woman who does good; and it is a woman who brings shame and disgrace") witnesses to the emerging speculation about woman's role in man's fall (cf. 2 Esdras, 2 Enoch).

Antithetical proverbs make up the gist of the collection in Prov 10–15. Their purpose is to expose folly at its worst by contrasting it sharply with its opposite. Their subject matter ranges from parental guidance to the control of the tongue and takes up anything worthy of discussion (false balances, laziness, gossip, anxiety, hope deferred, sacrifice of the wicked, and so forth). These proverbs are found throughout wisdom literature and require no documentation. Even Qoheleth makes use of the antithetic maxim to describe the orientation of a fool in contrast to that of a wise man ("A wise man's heart inclines him toward the right, but a fool's heart toward the left," 10:2).

B. Riddle (חִידָה)

T. Andrae, "Rätsel," *RGG²* 4:1685; Sheldon H. Blank, "Riddle," *IDB* R-Z:78-79; Otto Eissfeldt, "Die Rätsel in Jud 14," *ZAW* 30 (1910): 132-35; Hermann Gunkel, "Dictung, profane, im Alten Testament," *RGG²* 1:56; M. Hain, *Rätsel* (Stuttgart: Metzler, 1966); H. Hepding, "Zwei biblische Rätsel," *Humaniora, Archer Taylor Festschrift* (Locust Valley: Augustin, 1960) 270-76; V. E. Hull and Archer Taylor, *A Collection of Welsh Riddles* (Berkeley: University of California Press, 1942); J. Jacobs, "Riddle," *JEnc* (1905) 10:408-409; A. Jolles, *Einfache Formen* (Halle: Max Niemeyer, ²1956); Hans-Peter Müller, "Der Begriff 'Rätsel' im Alten Testament," *VT* 20 (1970): 465-89; J. Roy Porter, "Samson's Riddle: Judges XIV, 18," *JTS* 13 (1962): 106-109; L. Röhrich, "Rätsel," *RGG³* 5:767; S. Schechter, "The Riddles of Solomon in Rabbinic Literature," *Folklore I* (1890) 349-58; A. Taylor, *A Bibliography of Riddles*, FFC 126 (Helsinki: Academia scientarum fennica, 1939); idem, *The Literary Riddle before 1600* (Berkeley: University of California Press, 1948); Harry Torczyner (Tur Sinai), "The Riddle in the Bible," *HUCA* 1 (1924): 125-49; A. Wünsche, *Die Rätselweisheit bei den Hebräern mit Hinblick auf andere alte Völker* (Leipzig: Otto Schultze, 1883).

"Whoever wishes to understand the world discovers it as a riddle." (W. Porzig, "Das Rätsel im Rigveda. Ein Beitrag zum Kapital 'Sondersprache'," *Germanica* [Sievers Festschrift] 1925, 660). Porzig's striking observation is fully in accord with that of Wünsche, for whom the entire universe and human nature itself are alive with riddles (7). In such a context the riddle functions as a paradox that is paradigmatic of the paradox of reality, and the propounder of riddles, namely the wise man, takes as his elementary function the formulating of analogies descriptive of the structure of reality. Hence there is a close relationship between riddle and myth, described aptly by A. Jolles as follows: "Myth is an answer in which a question is presupposed; riddle is a question that conceals an answer" (106). Jolles goes on to point out decisive differences in regard to the polarities of freedom and bondage, activity and passivity, and to establish a connection between riddle and divination, a thesis championed subsequently by E. Peuckert (*Deutsches Volkstum in Märchen und Sage* [Berlin: de Gruyter, 1938]). Since every riddle is a judgment situation in which the ambiguities of the riddle stand between the one who seeks to conceal and him who strives to unveil the secret "watchword," a measure of *Angst* is generated. Whenever the questioner is divine, an element of the demonic surfaces; such a contest necessarily assumes grave proportions, becomes a struggle for life, against death. Fundamentally, all riddles are *Halsrätsel*—a matter of life or death—if Jolles is to be trusted (110), although riddles come to function in festive occasions once the burden of mythology and divination eases. Since knowledge of another is power over him, the riddle functions as a defensive mechanism; the contest therefore becomes one to establish worthiness, or, in other words, it determines the one who possesses magical power rather than the superior intelligence of the contestants (so Tor Andrae). Although missing from the Old Testament, the *Halsrätsel* is not far removed from the *Streitgespräch*, hence makes itself felt both in wisdom and prophetic literature.

Basic to the riddle is the ambiguity of language; it can only operate where words bear meanings that are common knowledge and at the same time conceal special connotations for an exclusive group. This movement from *Gemeinsprache* to *Sondersprache* is essential to the riddle; for example, in the expressions "foot of the mountain" or "lamp of the body" the words "foot" and "lamp" are used in a special, symbolic sense. Once such ambiguity is possible, riddles can be formulated by use of ambivalent language interrogatively: "What has a foot but cannot walk?" Inasmuch as there is ambiguity in the symbolism of the riddle, there is often no final, sole solution, for the answer can itself be a riddle, hence ambiguous. Besides the use of metaphor and cipher, other stylistic features of the riddle are paranomasia, onomatopoeia, description, personification, narrative debate, and the like. Nor is the riddle necessarily poetic; on the contrary, it varies from popular prose to strict parallelism and strophic formulation (Röhrich). Such stylistic devices as those mentioned above originally served as mnemonic aids and without a doubt point to a didactic setting for the artistic riddle. But the life setting of the riddle was diverse, ranging from initiation ceremonies to courtship and marriage, as well as the political contests between kings and their courtiers, ritual questions in catechetical form, banquets (as, for example, in Plutarch's "The Feast of the Seven Wise Men" and the Epistle of Aristeas, 187-300), children at play, and in the schools (Hain, 1).

Strictly speaking, the riddle is rare in the Old Testament, occurring in pure form only in Judg 14:10-18. A number of passages suggest, however, that the riddle was far more prominent in ancient Israel than the scarcity of examples would lead one to believe. In Num 12:8 there is a tradition that Yahweh spoke with Moses "mouth to mouth, clearly, and not in dark speech" (בְּחִידֹת). Furthermore, this statement implies that normal oracular utterance was in riddle form, an exception being made in Moses' case. In Prov 1:6 there is a practical equation between חִידָה and מָשָׁל, and this parallelism is by no means unique (cf. Ps 78:2; Wis 8:8; Sir 39:3, and with מְלִיצָה, Hab 2:6; Sir 47:17). Besides this linguistic evidence for the important role of the riddle in ancient Israel, there is the "historical" tradition of Solomon's mastery of the art of riddle solving (1 Kings 10:1-5 and 2 Chron 9:1-4), a tradition elaborated upon in Josephus (*Antiquities* 8.5.3), who mentions a riddle contest between Solomon and envoys sent by Hiram, king of Tyre. While the Solomonic tradition cannot be accepted at face value, Alt's thesis about this king's sponsorship of sages whose task was to gather onomastica (*Naturweisheit*) has merit (see his "Die Weisheit Salomos," *TLZ* 76 (1951): 139-44 = Alt's *Kleine Schriften zur Geschichte des Volkes Israel II* [Munich: Beck, 1953] 90-99).

The presence of only one riddle in the Old Testament, despite impressive evidence for the popularity of the form, suggests that we may be able to discover additional riddles now in disintegrated form. Such attempts have been made as early as Herder, who believed that riddles lurked behind the numerical proverbs in Prov 30:15-33, and Gunkel, who claimed the same for Prov 6:16-19, Sir 25:7-11, as well as for Prov 30:15-31. So far the search for riddles has been limited to numerical sayings, which are generally thought to be derived from or integrally related to the riddle. Recently, however, Müller has mustered strong arguments against the putative bond between riddle and numerical proverb. These have to do with the attitude toward paradox, nature of the solution, and specificity of the answer. Whereas the riddle is concerned to call attention to the paradox of reality, the numerical proverb displays little interest in the paradox as such, but rather seeks to identify it in various situations. Again, he who gives a riddle knows its solution; by way of contrast, the numerical proverb expresses the astonishment of *discovery*. While for the riddle many answers are possible, the numerical proverb is capable of only one solution. In any case, it may be possible to identify still other broken riddles by means of a careful investigation of figures of speech, particularly sexual imagery, in the Old Testament (what Wünsche has referred to by the rabbinic phrase לְשׁוֹן הַכְמָה). As a start I would suggest the following passages as possible bearers of disintegrated riddles: Prov 23:29-35; 23:27; 16:15; 20:27; 25:2-3; 27:20; 5:1-6; 5:15-23; 6:23-24.

The riddle in Judg 14:10-18 appears to antedate its context; its appropriateness for a wedding celebration, however, tempers the intrusive nature. As H. Gressmann perceived, the answers to the two riddles ("Out of the eater came something to eat. Out of the strong came something sweet" and "What is stronger than a lion," 14:14,18) may be "vomit" and "love" respectively (Gressmann, *Die Anfänge Israels*, SAT 1/2 [1922] 243; see also Blank, 79). The first alludes to the aftermath of a round of debauchery during the wedding festivities, when even the strong man is unable to retain the unaccustomed delicacies, while the other refers to the power of love (cf. Cant 8:6, כִּי־עַזָּה כַמָּוֶת אַהֲבָה, a theme taken up at length in the contest between the court pages recorded in 1 Esd 3:1–4:47. Even the final response of Samson may echo a standard riddle ("If you had not plowed with my heifer, you would not have found out my riddle," or in riddle form, "What is plowed, but not with oxen?"). As is well known, the wife is frequently likened to a field, cultivated or uncultivated depending upon whether it is positive or a curse of barrenness, and sexual intercourse is thought of in terms of "plowing." ("As for me, my vulva is a . . . hillock—for me, I, the maid, who will be its plower? My vulva is . . . wet ground for me, I, the queen, who will station there the ox? Lady, the king will plow it for you, Dumuzi, the king, will plow it for you. 'Plow my vulva, my sweet-heart?'" ANET 643.)

Only one of the riddles is in interrogative form, while the other(s) is narration. The poetic form of the riddles belies their popular origin; each is composed of 3+3 meter, while the letter "m" begins four words in the first and five in the second (it begins one and terminates two in the "third," while "l" and "h" introduce two words each). Within the first stand four cipher words—אֹכֵל signifies the lion, that is, the bridegroom; מַאֲכָל represents honey, that is, the sperm; while עַז and מָתוֹק are indicators for the quality of love. As has already been pointed out, עֶגְלָה is a symbol for the bride. The technical term for solving a riddle appears to be נגד in the hiphil, as Müller has recognized (465, 477, 481). The malicious character of the riddle, here on the human level, stands out with unforgettable pathos, even though permeated with a touch of humor ("You only hate me, you do not love me. . . . And Samson's wife was given to his companion, who had been his best man." —Judg 14:16, 20 RSV).

The close relationship between riddle and divination, together with the fact that oracular utterance had an enigmatic character, raises a question about the narrow definition of riddle functioning above. Müller's thoroughgoing analysis of riddle in the Old Testament operates on the broadest possible basis; he distinguishes four types: (1) the popular riddle, namely Judg 14:10-18; (2) the symbolic dream and enigmatic oracle, as found in Gen 37:40-41; Dan 2, 4 (the dream); Dan 5; Ez 17:1-10; Dan 12:7-10 ("The dream unveils a special *reality* which the peculiar *language* unfolds in the dream narrative for the first time," 475-76); (3) royal contests, alluded to in 1 Kings 10, the intention of which is to drain the opponent of all strength (it is said of the Queen of Sheba: וְלֹא־הָיָה בָהּ עוֹד רוּחַ, 10:5), and in Dan 8:23; and (4) court-school wisdom. While one can agree with Müller that the symbolic dream and enigmatic oracle concern themselves with the "peculiar speech of a transcendental world," it seems better to consider these passages under the *Gattungen* of dream and oracle, while at the same time being conscious of the considerable interpenetration of three genres. The riddle is related to the simile/parable on the one hand and allegory on the other. Accordingly Wünsche treated Ezek 17:1-10 as a symbolic riddle, following the lead of the text, which designates the oracle as a חִידָה. The line of demarcation between this passage and allegory, Qoh 12:1-7, for example, is virtually nonexistent, so that one hesitates to classify it as a riddle, even though it makes use of ciphers. It must be admitted, however, that a comparable "riddle" is found in *Bereshit Rabba* 67, according to which Judah the Patriarch gives political advice to envoys of Marcus Aurelius by uprooting mature plants in his garden and replacing them with younger ones. In light of the loose use of חִידָה in the Old Testament, some diversity in interpretation is to be expected; regardless of whether one operates with a narrow definition, or a broad one, any discussion of riddle inevitably moves into the area of mantic oracle, symbolic dream, and allegory (see Hans-Peter Müller, "Magisch-Mantische Weisheit und die Gestalt Daniels," *UF* 1 [1969]: 79-94).

A note on postbiblical riddles is in order, particularly since they make extensive use of the bible. In rabbinic literature there is considerable speculation about the nature of the riddles put to Solomon by the Queen of Sheba. The subjects of these riddles placed in the mouth of the royal visitor include, among others, pregnancy and nursing, the unique relationship between Lot's daughters and their father and sons, male and female characteristics, antimony (used for cosmetic purposes), flax and naphtha. There is also an account of a riddle contest between the children of Jerusalem and men of Athens, where the answer is obtained from a rabbi familiar with Jewish practice in regard to circumcision and with the number of months required for pregnancy, nursing, and weaning. The reply of the children indicates the relevance of this riddle to our discussion: "If you had not plowed with my heifer, you would not have found out my riddle" (*Echa Rabbati* 1:1). Finally, the contest literature gave rise to catechetical texts, both in Jewish and Christian settings; worthy of mention are the Pesach haggadah where the refrain מִי יוֹדֵעַ אֶחָד is used to lead up to the number thirteen ("One, who knows it? One, I know it. One is our Lord in heaven and earth. Two, who knows it? Two, I know it. Two are the covenants of the law. One is. . . . Thirteen are the qualities of divine compassion . . . ") and the "Jocha Monachorum," which makes use of the Adam/Eve, Noah, Lot, and Jonah narratives for catechetical purposes.

C. Fable and Allegory

H. Gressmann, *Israels Spruchweisheit in Zusammenhang der Weltliteratur*, KA 6 (Berlin: K. Curtis, 1925); Hermann Gunkel, *Das Märchen im Alten Testament* (Tübingen: J. C. B. Mohr, 1921); W. Lambert, *Babylonian Wisdom Literature*, 150-212; K. Mueli, "Herkunft und Wesen der Fabel" *SAVK* L (1954) 65-93; R. J. Williams, "The Fable in the Ancient Near East," in *A Stubborn Faith*, ed. E. C. Hobbs (Dallas: Southern Methodist University Press, 1956) 3-26; A. Wünsche, *Die Pflanzenfabel in der Weltliteratur* (Leipzig: Akademischer Verlag fur Kunst und Wissenschaft, 1905).

Closely kin to the riddle are the fable and allegory, both of which make use of metaphors or ciphers. Ancient Near Eastern fables abound, particularly in Mesopotamian wisdom literature (cf. "Dispute between the Tamarisk and the Date Palm, *ANET* 592-93), in sharp contrast to the Israelite wisdom corpus. It is possible that the reference in 1 Kings 4:32-34 to Solomon's three thousand proverbs and one thousand and five songs, the content of which was "trees, from the cedar that is in Lebanon to the hyssop that grows out of the wall" and "also of beasts, and of birds, and of reptiles, and of fish," should be taken to mean that the son of David was remembered as a master of coining fables. If that is the case, the absence of fables in the collection of wisdom texts that survived is difficult to comprehend; however the same difficulty adheres to the alternative explanation of this passage in terms of lists or onomastica, for this genre is likewise scantily represented in the final collection of Israelite wisdom. Little weight can be given to the argument that Solomon must have learned fables from Nathan, in whose charge he was placed by David, for Nathan's well-known indictment of the king is actually a parable and appears to antedate its context (2 Sam 12:1-4). Despite the inapplicabilty of some of the elements of the story to the relationship among David, Bathsheba, and Uriah, the parable has been placed within a didactic setting rather successfully. The same may be said of the Jotham fable (Judg 9:8-15) and of the fable in truncated form preserved in 2 Kings 14:9 ("A thistle on Lebanon sent to a cedar on Lebanon, saying, 'Give your daughter to my son for a wife'; and a wild beast of Lebanon passed by and trampled down the thistle").

The fable is characterized by "dramatis personae" which are animals or plants; hence, it bears an element of the comic. However, it is often used to underscore the horror of a situation, even when half comical (Num 22:21-35; Gen 3; 37:5-11; 41). Originally the fable was amoral, but it soon came to function in didactic contexts; it is particularly useful for an ability to call attention to the obvious, which because of its everyday character is often overlooked. Essentially, however, the fable was at home in political settings, and found ready acceptance by those with appreciation for the satirical. In time it disintegrated into pure allegory, particularly in prophetic hands (Ezek 17:1-10; 19:1-14; von Rad, *Weisheit in Israel*, 65: "Here the form of the fable is completely dismantled by the prophet for his purposes").

Two allegories have been preserved in wisdom literature, namely Prov 5:15-23 and Qoh 12:1-6. Each of these texts may originally have been a riddle; nevertheless, the present form is that of an admonition with an allegorical key. In Prov 5:15-23 the metaphorical significance of "cistern" is explained, so that none can read the text without recognizing the allusion to one's wife. Furthermore, the common reference to woman as a fountain from which man drinks becomes an occasion for warning against foul water, specifically, the loose woman. The text is as follows:

> Drink water from your own cistern,
>   flowing water from your own well.
> Should your springs be scattered abroad,
>   streams of water in the streets?
> Let them be for yourself alone,
>   and not for strangers with you.
> Let your fountain be blessed,
>   and rejoice in the wife of your youth,
>   a lovely hind, a graceful doe.   (RSV)

The allegory of Qoh 12:1-6 takes up the metaphor of a wife as a fountain or cistern (cf. *ANET* 642), and juxtaposes it against an exquisite description of old age. The allusion to בּוֹרְאֶיךָ is a *double entendre*; by this means the author recalls both the positive and negative assessment of reality in the preceding pages of his work, namely "the wife whom you love" and the grim reaper, death (on this unusual form, בּוֹרְאֶיךָ, see P. Humbert, "Emploi et portée du verbe bara [créer] dans l'Ancien Testament," *TZ* 3 [1947]: 402, where it is argued that the root is בָּרָא, "to split"). The passage is susceptible to two interpretations, intentionally so: before crippling old age sets in, enjoy the woman whom you love, but at the same time keep in mind that the ancient sentence stands—"you shall die" (cf. Sir 14:17). Although some of the metaphors are difficult, the following appear to be self-evident: the keepers of the house are the arms, the strong men are the legs, the grinders are the teeth, those that look through the windows are the eyes, the doors on the street are the ears, the daughters of song is the voice, the almond tree is the gray hair, the grasshopper is the creaking bone or sluggish movement, the snapped silver cord, broken golden bowl, shattered pitcher and broken wheel are death.

D. Hymn and Prayer

Walther Baumgartner, "Die literarischen Gattungen in der Weisheit des Jesus Sirach," *ZAW* 34 (1914): 161-98; Frank Crüsemann, *Studien zur Formgeschichte von Hymnus und Danklied in Israel*, WMANT 32 (Neukirchen: Neukirchener Verlag, 1969); H. L. Jansen, *Die Spätjüdische Psalmendichtung. Ihr Entstehungskreis und ihr "Sitz im*

Leben," SNVAO 2/3 (Oslo: Jacob Dybwad, 1937); J. Kenneth Kuntz, "Considerations of Form and Intention in the Canonical Wisdom Psalms with Special Reference to Psalm 34" (privately circulated, 1970); Burton Lee Mack, "Wisdom Myth and Mythology," *Int* 24 (1970): 46-60; Sigmund Mowinckel, "Psalms and Wisdom," in *Wisdom in Israel and in the Ancient Near East*, 205-24; idem, "The Learned Psalmography" in his *The Psalms in Israel's Worship*, trans. D. R. Ap-Thomas (Nashville: Abingdon Press, 1962) 2:104-25; P. A. Munch, "Die jüdischen 'Weisheits-psalmen' und ihr Platz im Leben," *AfO* 15 (1937): 112-40; Roland Murphy, "A Consideration of the Classification 'Wisdom Psalms'," VTSup 9 (1962): 156-67; Helmer Ringgren, *Word and Wisdom* (Lund: Ohlssons, 1947); Gerhard von Rad, *Weisheit in Israel*, 189-228.

Baumgartner's distinction between a *sage*, whose task was to describe things exactly as they are, and a *poet*, for whom hyperbole is an indispensable tool, suggests that one should expect little, if any hymnic material in wisdom literature (193-94, 198). Nevertheless, this observation did not blind him to the presence of hymns and hymnic themes in Sirach, namely, 42:15–43:33; 39:12-35; 24:1-22; 1:1-10; 10:14-18; 16:18-19; 16:26–17:24; 17:29-30; 18:1-7; 23:19-20 and 44-50 (a *profanen Hymnus* since it praises men rather than God). Baumgartner also identified a *Danklied* or thanksgiving song (51:1-12) and three *Klagelieder* or lamentations (51:10-11; 33:1-13a; 36:16b-22), as well as themes belonging to the lament (14:17-19; 17:27; 18:8-10; 22:27–23:6).

In this regard Sirach is typical, for hymns and hymnic motifs appear in Job (5:9-16; 9:5-12; 12:13-25; 26:5-14; 28), Proverbs (8), and Wisdom of Solomon (11:21–12:22). However, the presence of hymns in wisdom texts does not make them wisdom genres, as Murphy has noted (160-61). Rather these texts are hymns, thanksgiving songs, and laments and are to be compared with similar passages from nonwisdom literature. Most of these wisdom texts make use of the participial style and frequently praise God as creator and redeemer, even when including rhetorical questions and concluding warnings. Likewise, the thanksgiving song is made up of introduction, a reference to the deliverance, a description of the plight from which rescue was a deliverance, a plea, vow, and confession of confidence. The lament, too, bears the customary invocation, request and vow, so that there is no justification for speaking of wisdom genres.

The case is different with a series of hymns dealing with the relationship between Yahweh and creation, each of which praises Wisdom as the point of contact between the two (Prov 1:20-33; 8; Job 28; Sir 24:1-22; Wis 6:12-20; 7:22–8:21). The Egyptian background for these hymns is virtually certain, as has recently been perceived (cf. Kayatz, *Einführung in die alttestamentliche Weisheit*, 70-78), but the accuracy of the term "hypostasis" is subject to question for all texts except Wisdom of Solomon (von Rad, 193, 200). In Job 28, which is probably an addition to the book, man's amazing success at extracting precious metals from the deep recesses of the earth is contrasted with his miserable failure at laying hold of wisdom, whose price is far above that of the ores. Even Abaddon and Death have only heard a rumor of wisdom, and man's efforts at finding her are futile. Yet God knows her place and has searched her out. The text closes with an identification of wisdom with the fear of the Lord (יִרְאַת אֲדֹנָי).

In Prov 1:20-33 wisdom stands in the busy streets and cries aloud in the style of a prophetic indictment; even the language is that of the divine oracle in prophecy: the hand stretched out in invitation, the summons that was spurned, the threat that they will seek her but not be able to find her, and the rather harsh description of the results of a refusal to hear. Chapter 8 again takes up the motif of wisdom calling beside the gates; this time she describes her wares and defends their high value, particularly for ruling officials. But wisdom also identifies herself as the first of God's acts, hence as one who existed before the creation of the universe (cf. H. Grapow, "Die Welt vor der Schöpfung," ZÄS 67 [1931]: 34-38; the Egyptian background for this series of metaphors is incontrovertible). Despite the danger to Yahwism created by the presence of a female deity alongside God, wisdom is characterized as his daily delight and master workman (or little child; for a discussion of the meaning of the difficult אָמוֹן, see R. B. Y. Scott, "Wisdom in Creation: The אָמוֹן of Proverbs viii 30," VT 10 [1960]: 213-23).

The identification of wisdom and torah is the hidden theme of Sir 24:1-22, explicitly stated by Sirach in 24:23. In this text wisdom's source is said to be the mouth of the Most High, an epithet preferred by Sirach, and her availability in some measure to all mankind is proclaimed. However, the creator commanded her to make a dwelling in Israel, at Zion; having taken root there, she is likened to trees and plants of the land and invites all to eat and drink from her with promise that one taste or sip will create greater thirst or hunger. An appendix to the hymn concludes with a reference to the mystery inherent within wisdom, which makes mastery of her an impossibility.

Augustine's comment that Wisdom of Solomon stinks of Greek rhetoric is particularly apropos to 6:12-20, 7:22–8:21 (note the *sorites* in 6:17-20, as well as the list of attributes in 7:22-23). Here the easy access to wisdom is highlighted, in contrast to earlier texts. She is called the breath of the power of God, "a pure emanation of the glory of the Almighty," who in every generation passes into holy souls, and who orders all things well. Striking is the statement that she teaches the four cardinal virtues: self-control, prudence, justice, courage.

These hymns are distinctive both in subject matter and form, so that one may legitimately refer to them as a wisdom genre, the praise of wisdom. Their style is strongly influenced by Egyptian wisdom and Israelite prophetic texts, as well as Greek rhetoric. The occasion for borrowing an Egyptian concept (*Ma'at*) may have been a crisis of confidence, so that the function of the idea of personified wisdom was to soften the problem of theodicy, although one gets the impression that these texts are less polemical than would be the case if this thesis of Mack's were accurate. In any case, the hypostatization of wisdom serves as a means of relating God to his universe in a nonrevelatory wisdom tradition and addresses itself to the problem of authority (see J. Coert Rylaarsdam, *Revelation in Jewish Wisdom Litera-*

ture [Chicago: University of Chicago Press, 1946] and J. Marböck, *Weisheit im Wandel*, BBB 37 [Bonn: Peter Hanstein Verlag, 1971]).

Certain stylistic and thematic characteristics distinguish a small group of psalms, to which has been given the title "wisdom psalms," from the rest of the Psalter. Unfortunately there is little agreement as to which psalms belong to this category; indeed, its very existence has been denied by Engnell. Most critics, however, would find themselves somewhere between the position of Bentzen, for whom only 1, 112, 127 are de rigueur wisdom psalms, and that of Castellino, who views Pss 1, 9–10, 12, 14–15, 17, 36–37, 49, 52, 73, 91, 94, 112, 119, 127–128, 139 from this perspective. Two of the more prominent psalms interpreters, Gunkel and Mowinckel, reject the title "wisdom psalms" but not their existence; to these psalms Gunkel gives the name *Weisheitsdichtung* but insists that no *Gattung* is involved, while Mowinckel writes (somewhat derogatively on stylistic grounds) of "Learned Psalmography," the purposes of which are to praise the deity and to instruct the youth. Likewise Munch discerns a dual purpose *within the cult* for these psalms, which are to him *school texts*, namely devotional and instructional. The school setting for the wisdom psalms is also defended by Jansen, although he does not feel confident of any ability to describe the setting precisely. Murphy's delineation of wisdom psalms, based on careful methodological considerations, gives prominence to Pss 1, 32, 34, 37, 49, 112, 128 but recognizes wisdom influence elsewhere, for example, in 25:8-10, 12-14; 31:24-25; 39:5-7; 40:5-6; 62:9-11; 92:7-9; 94:8-15.

Stylistic features that have been decisive in identifying wisdom psalms are: אַשְׁרֵי formulas, numerical sayings, "better" sayings, an address of a teacher to a "son," alphabetic structure, simple comparisons and admonitions, and rhetorical questions. Thematic considerations are: a contrast between the רָשָׁע and the צַדִּיק, the two ways, preoccupation with the problem of retribution, practical advice about conduct, fear of the Lord, and special wisdom vocabulary, such as מָשָׁל, בִּינָה, חִידָה, and חָכְמָה. While Murphy discerns the significance of life setting as a criterion for distinguishing wisdom psalms, in the end he has to admit that by and large the *Sitz* eludes scholarly research, although he thinks the didactic character of the testimony points to the cult, quoting with approval Mand's claim that "Aus dem Beter ist ein Lehrer geworden" ("The worshiper has become a teacher," 167).

Even with the use of such criteria, however, identification of wisdom psalms is no simple matter. The presence of any one of these characteristics is not sufficient to classify a psalm; a good example is Ps 111, which employs the wisdom motto, "The fear of the Lord is the beginning of wisdom" but is still not a wisdom psalm. Rather, it is only as several of these traits appear that the psalm assumes the "tone" of wisdom. Particular care has to be taken lest a concern for retribution lead one astray into a hasty conclusion that wisdom is at work here (cf. von Rad, 171); the same may the said of אַשְׁרֵי formulas and the idea of the fear of the Lord, both of which occur frequently in the Psalter.

Inasmuch as the list of wisdom psalms in Murphy's definitive article has much to commend it, I shall use it as the point of departure for discussion. The use of the figure of a flourishing tree to describe a sage in Egyptian wisdom literature strengthens the argument for the inclusion of Ps 1 in the wisdom group (but see 52:8 and 92:14). As for 32, Murphy rightly notes that the crucial factor is a matter of emphasis but opts for a *sapiential structure* as decisive. This decision, while admittedly subjective, may be an accurate assessment of the situation, although I would be more inclined to view the psalm under Murphy's second category of wisdom influence. Accordingly, I would find wisdom influence only in verses 8-9. In any case, the mood of the entire psalm does not strike me as sapiential. The use of the style of Dame Wisdom in Ps 49 is not conclusive proof of a wisdom origin, for Prov 6 is imitative of *prophetic preaching*; one could just as readily argue for prophetic influence here. Nevertheless, other factors such as vocabulary, theme, and the use of a summary appraisal give some force to the contention that a wisdom psalm is under consideration. Ps 128 is less certain; its form is that of a benediction, and the putative wisdom traits are precisely the ones that are least reliable, namely the oft-used אַשְׁרֵי formulas and the idea of the fear of the Lord.

Murphy's intriguing suggestion that Book One of the Psalter (1-41) has been subjected to redaction at the hands of the sages merits closer scrutiny. A strong case can be made for the inclusion of Pss 19, 33, and 39 in the wisdom category. In 19 one finds instruction, special language of wisdom, creation theology, fear of the Lord, and comparatives ("more than . . . sweeter than"), none of which is exclusively wisdom thought but the whole of which permits a suspicion of sapiential impact. Psalm 33 mentions counsel, fear of the Lord, divine plans, *creation of all men alike*, salvation by means other than weapons, and makes use of the אַשְׁרֵי formula. Furthermore, Ps 39 gives the impression of schooling at the feet of Qoheleth; the description of life as phantom existence, as a puff of wind, and the emphasis on the vanity of wealth since man *cannot know* who will inherit it echo many of the themes of the skeptical genius who saw life as "vanity of vanities."

Other psalms outside Book One also give the impression of wisdom influence, especially 94:8-11 and 127. The first draws on a hymn that is apparently a product of the sages used to attack those who deny the justice of God (cf. Ps 10). The accusation of divine blindness is found frequently in wisdom literature, though not exclusively there. In any case, I would suggest a possible origin of this hymn in wisdom, particularly in its emphasis upon the all-seeing eye of the Judge of all mankind (cf. 33:13-15; 34: 15). Again, the theme and language of Ps 127 is that of Qoheleth, Prov and Sir. This includes the idea of the vanity of human effort, as well as the corrective from the more optimistic strain of wisdom that Yahweh is the guarantee of all that is good, and the image of sons as arrows in a quiver, which Sirach takes over for a different image, though still sexual. A word should also be said about Ps 104, particularly verses 13-18, which are strikingly similar to onomastica both in Egypt and in Israel. A wisdom milieu for the Egyptian Hymn to the Sun (*ANET* 369-71), the ultimate source for Ps 104, is highly likely.

A word of caution needs to be registered, however, lest the problematic character of the above arguments be overlooked and excessive confidence in our ability to identify influence, whether sapiential, prophetic, or priestly, be spawned. The evidence does nevertheless, permit one to conclude that the closest parallels to the above-mentioned "wisdom psalms" are found in sapiential literature.

While one cannot speak of a fixed *Gattung* of wisdom prayer, it is possible to distinguish common language and themes (von Rad, 70). The wisdom psalms and prayer are closely related, as has been pointed out above. Evidently the wise men coined prayers for instruction in schools, but in any case they are pure prayer rather than didactic instruction; in post-canonical wisdom literature the didactic element prevails, as in PsSol 15 (von Rad, 70). Normally the prayer is expressed in hymnic form, as Tob 13:1 illustrates clearly.

From Sirach the following prayers deserve mention: 22:27-23:6, 36:1-17, and 51:1-12, while Wis 9:1-18 is a distinct prayer and 11:21–12:27 is in broken prayer form. In Sir 22:27–23:6 there are two indirect requests (22:27; 23:2) and an additional two direct requests preceded by the vocative address ("O Lord, Father and Ruler of my life," "O Lord, Father and God of my life"). The prayer is for protection, as well as for deliverance from gluttony and lust. Chapter 36:1-17 is a lament familiar from the Psalter, while 51:1-12 is a typical thanksgiving song. The influence of the well-known Solomonic prayer in 1 Kings 8 is discernible in Wis 9, even though alien concepts appear (man's reasoning is worthless since "a perishable body weighs down the soul, and this earthly tent burdens the thoughtful mind," vv. 14-18).

Von Rad has called attention to the *Gerichtsdoxologie* (judgment doxology) (Ps 49, 73, 139) as a special prayer form in wisdom texts; he recognizes, however, the original sacral-legal context for these passages (71, 263-66). The similarity of these texts to the prose prayers of narrative cultic texts (Dan 9, Ezra 9, Neh 9, 1 Kings 8, Jer 32) demands that caution be used in treating them as special wisdom prayers (see my discussion in "*YHWH Ṣᵉbā'ôt Šmô*: A Form-Critical Analysis," *ZAW* 81 [1969]: 171-74).

It is difficult to determine the precise setting of these prayers within Sirach and Wisdom of Solomon. One can surmise that the wise man came to recognize a need to instruct the student in prayer and made use of the Psalter as a model. A didactic setting, then, is probable, although little more can be said.

E. *Streitgespräch* or Dialogue

James L. Crenshaw, "Popular Questioning of the Justice of God in Ancient Israel," *ZAW* 82 (1970): 380-95; H. Gese, *Lehre und Wirklichkeit in der alten Weisheit* (Tübingen: J. C. B. Mohr, 1958) 51-78; J. Gray, "The Book of Job in the Context of Near Eastern Literature," *ZAW* 82 (1970): 251-69; W. Lambert, *Babylonian Wisdom Literature*, 21-117; H. Richter, "*Erwägungen zum Hiobproblem*," *EvT* 18 (1958): 302-24; idem, *Studien zu Hiob. Der Aufbau des Hiobbuches, dargestellt an den Gattungen des Rechtsleben*, AT 2/11 (Stuttgart: Calwer, 1959); Norman Snaith, *The Book of Job*, SBT 2nd ser. 11 (London: SCM Press, 1968); J. J. Stamm, "Die Theodizee in Babylon und Israel," *JEOL*

9 (1944): 99-107; von Rad, *Weisheit in Israel*, 267-91; Claus Westermann, *Der Aufbau des Buches Hiob*, BHT 23 (Tübingen: J. C. B. Mohr, 1956); J. G. Williams, "'You Have Not Spoken Truth of Me': Mystery and Irony in Job," *ZAW* 83 (1971): 231-54; R. J. Williams, "Theodicy in the Ancient Near East," *CJT* 2 (1956): 14-26.

At the outset it should be stated that Job is *sui generis*, so that what is written below is an attempt to discern the components that make up this masterpiece. No single genre can explain all the facets of the book, and several have certainly contributed to it. There are traces of the רִיב (lawsuit) within Job, and much of the book can be successfully illuminated from this perspective (Stamm, 104). The speeches of Job often make use of the language of litigation, Job accusing God of a breach of contract. Legal terminology, therefore, is at home in the accusations, and there is a full-fledged oath of innocence (chap. 31) that has its closest parallels in the negative confession within Babylonian literature. Furthermore, the intimate relationship between law and wisdom, particularly during the period of the *Sippenethos* (clan ethos), strengthens the thesis that Job is a covenant lawsuit (Gerstenberger, *Wesen und Herkunft des sogenannten "apodiktischen Rechts,"* and "Covenant and Commandment," *JBL* 84 [1965]: 38-51. According to this view of Job as a secular lawsuit chapters 4–14 comprise a preliminary attempt at reconciliation; 15–31, a formal legal effort at reconciling Job and his friends; 32–37, Elihu's appeal of the case; 38–41, God's judgment in the form of a secular lawsuit between God and Job, resulting in Job's withdrawal of the accusation (Richter).

Others interpret the book of Job as a lament, either dramatized or a paradigm of an answered lament (so Westermann and Gese). The components of the lament are: (1) the lament proper, (2) complaint, and (3) an indictment of the enemies. There can be no question about the similarity of the laments and sections of Job; however, the narrative framework and the character of the poetic dialogue suggest another answer to the form of the book.

The closest parallels to Job are the disputations within Egyptian and especially Babylonian literature. These controversy dialogues are composed of a mythological introduction, a debate between two friends, and a divine resolution of the issue (see Lambert, 150-212). Job makes use of the form of the *Streitgespräch*, although influenced by its function within prophetic literature as self-vindication. Whereas the Mesopotamian disputations are calm treatises on the relative worth of things, animals, or professions, Job employs the *Streitgespräch* as a weapon of warfare, his own vindication being at stake. The key to Job, according to this interpretation, is 13:16 ("This will be my salvation, that a godless man will not come before him"). The mythological introduction and legendary conclusion (the prose prologue and epilogue) are probably of popular origin and antedate the dispute, which utilizes three formal traditions (wisdom disputational material, legal terminology associated with the lawsuit, and cultic laments).

Von Rad has objected to viewing Job as a *Streitgespräch* on the grounds that the *dialogue* is between friends with God present from the beginning as a third party

(270-72). He rejects the understanding of Job as a biography of the soul and emphasizes the difference between the main character and his friends as theological: they stress *the order* of the universe, whereas Job is concerned about the *relationship* between him and God. The new feature of the book, from this perspective, is the recognition that God is Job's *personal enemy*, that the wrath of God singles out one individual who according to the prologue was God's glory and pride (Herder). The single issue of Job, von Rad argues, is *Yahweh pro me*. Nevertheless, he is obliged to admit that the dissent between Job and his friends was greater at the end than in the beginning, so that his refusal to recognize the intensity of strife, the basis for rejecting the *Streitgespräch* as descriptive of the book, carries little weight. The same must be said of his claim that the dogma of retribution is more accurately a dogma of interpreters, indeed, that the impact of Job and Qoheleth was minimal. For however much truth there is in his charge that the dogma has been overemphasized, the fact is that a cause-effect theory was operative and precipitated a crisis in ancient Israel comparable to the failure of dogma to accord with reality in Egypt and Babylon (Schmid, *Wesen und Geschichte der Weisheit*, 74-78; Crenshaw, *Prophetic Conflict*, 23-38, 103-109, and "Popular Questioning of the Justice of God in Ancient Israel").

A variant of the *Streitgespräch*, namely, the "Imagined Speech," appears in Wis 2:1-20 and 5:3-13. Here again the similarity to prophetic texts is noteworthy. In each case the musings of wicked men are brought to light, together with the warning that such reasoning leads to destruction. The subject of the imagined speech is usually the contradiction between promise and fulfillment, expectation and reality, as intensified by the transitoriness of life. In 2:1-20 the pessimism of Qoheleth has left its mark, the similarity of language being rather noticeable (chance, fleetingness, finality of death, man's portion). "Come, therefore, let us enjoy the good things that exist, and make use of the creation to the full as in youth" (v. 6) reads like a restatement of Qoh 12:1; 9:7. However, the mild "hedonism" of Qoheleth has given way to violence in search of pleasure regardless of the cost, as well as to malicious persecution of the devout man. The error of this evil way is confessed in 5:3-13, this time utilizing an older proverb or perhaps a riddle (Prov 30:18-19). Here the serpent on the rock has been replaced by an arrow, and the climactic way of a man with a maiden has been omitted. Furthermore, this passage interprets the original in terms of movement without leaving a trace (cf. the gloss in Prov 30:20; note the imagined speech!), which does not appear to be the intent of the proverb in its earliest form (Murphy, "The Interpretation of Old Testament Wisdom Literature," 295-97, emphasizes דֶּרֶךְ in these verses and suggests that the impossibility of recovering a trace of movement is the original point of the proverb).

The "imagined speech" is found frequently in Proverbs, for example, in 1:11-14, 22-33; 3:28; 5:12-14; 7:14-20; 8:4-36; 9:4a-6, 16a-17; 20:9, 14a, 22a, 25a; 22:13; 23:7b, 35; 24:12a, 24a, 29; 25:7; 26:13, 19b; 28:24b; 30:9b, 20c; 31:29. It functions both as stimulus for correct thinking (31:29) and as a critique of false reasoning (30:20), which it holds up to ridicule. Often the malicious words prompt a strong admonition or even a pronouncement of judgment upon those who so think (cf. 1:19, "Such are the ways of all who get gain by violence; it takes away the life of its possessors"; see also 7:21-27; 24:12, 24). On occasion the whole imagined speech is given over to a castigation of those who stubbornly stick to their own way (1:22-33).

F. Confession (Autobiographical Narrative)

Robert Gordis, *Koheleth—The Man and His World* (New York: Schocken, 1951); Gerhard von Rad, *Weisheit in Israel*; Roger N. Whybray, *The Succession Narrative*, SBT 2nd ser. 9 (London: SCM Press, 1968).

Wisdom's rootedness in experience led to a confessional style in which the aged sage gave his pupils the advantages of his varied experience. When the wise man was at the same time a king the authority of such retrospection was increased, as in the "Instruction for Merikare" (*ANET* 414-18) and the "Instruction of Amenemhet" (*ANET* 418-19), as well as the fiction of Solomonic authorship of Qoheleth. The Egyptian origin of the autobiographical style is generally acknowledged. In the Egyptian context not only kings and prominent officials left their confessions for the benefit of progeny, however, for the tomb inscriptions describe the experiences of ordinary individuals and laud their examplary lives (Whybray, 74). It is possible that the form of the cultic thanksgiving song has influenced the confession in Israel, although such affinity is not necessarily an indication of direct borrowing (Whybray, 74, appeals to Pss 18; 34; 40:9-10). The formula for the autobiographical narrative is generally רָאִיתִי . . . וָאֶרְאֶה ("I saw . . . and I have seen"), together with the verb עָבַר ("pass by"), while the moral of the story usually is spelled out at the end. What is not certain, however, is the extent of this genre; should it include observations about other persons' experiences? Despite the positive response to this question by Whybray (75), I have chosen to limit this discussion to first person confessions, treating the third person narratives under the category of didactic poetry and narrative.

From Proverbs two examples of autobiographical narrative are instructive: 4:3-9; 24:30-34. The first of these appears to be modeled on Egyptian prototypes; in any case it includes the Egyptian motif of a garland to be placed around the wise man's neck (Kayatz, *Einführung in die alttestamentliche Weisheit*, 47). In Prov 24:30-34 the observation (vv. 30-31) prompts reflection (v. 32), the result of which is a moral lesson (vv. 33-34). To this may be compared Ps 37:25, 35-36, a wisdom psalm. In verse 25 there appears what I have elsewhere called "the creed of the blind man" ("I have been young, and now am old; yet I have not seen the righteous forsaken or his children begging bread"; see "Popular Questioning of the Justice of God in Ancient Israel," 395). The other verses (35-36) make use of רָאִיתִי and עָבַר, together with the customary וְהִנֵּה ("and behold").

The confession is used in Qoh 1:12–2:26 with great impact; here the affinity with the royal *Bekenntnis* (confession) of Egypt is undeniable. Emphasis is placed on the fact that the author has been "king over Israel in Jerusalem" (v. 12). Here again רָאִיתִי (v. 14) points to the ground of Qoheleth's conclusions: he has applied his mind to all that is done and has seen with his own eyes everything under the sun, thus arriving at the conclusion that all is vanity and a striving after wind. Qoheleth has tried every possible avenue to purpose in life, in each instance despairing of any meaning. Wisdom (note יָדַעְתִּי ["I know"] rather than רָאִיתִי ["I saw"] in v. 17), pleasure (עַד אֲשֶׁר־אֶרְאֶה, v. 3), madness and folly (וְיָדַעְתִּי, v. 14), despair, all lead to the same conclusion and force upon Qoheleth a hatred of life, the opposite of everything wisdom literature stands for (Zimmerli, "Zur Struktur der alttestamentlichen Weisheit," 201). The same style occurs in Qoh 3:10; 4:8; 5:18; 8:9–9:1; 9:11, 13, 16; 10:5, 7 (Gordis, 109, 385).

Sirach 33:16-18 makes use of confessional language to invite people to the בֵּית מִדְרָשׁ ("the house of instruction"), the author comparing himself to the last watchman and grape gleaner who has excelled despite the obstacles to knowledge. Sirach cannot resist the temptation to call attention to his altruism: "Consider that I have not labored for myself alone, but for all who seek instruction," v. 17). Similarly, 51:13-22 employs autobiographical narrative, although set within a thanksgiving song, which has colored the language considerably, and is again followed by an invitation to the house of learning (51:23-30). In this passage emphasis is placed on wisdom as the answer to fervent prayer, and the heartfelt gratitude to God for answering the request for knowledge. The transition to devotional confession is complete in Wis 7–9, where the great patron of wisdom praises God for the gift of understanding. Here, however, the confession alternates with prayer and lists, and priase of wisdom has, indeed, disintegrated.

The two invitations to the school in Sirach suggest a probable *Sitz* for the confession; the autobiographical narrative serves as a certificate of credentials for the head of a school. Whether such a setting can be posited for the origin of the form is impossible to determine, but the principle that prompted these accounts is the value of recording for posterity the lessons learned from life itself by one who is trained to reflect on experience and to sift its teachings for the benefit of those less gifted.

G. Lists (Onomastica)

Albrecht Alt, "Syrien und Palastina im Onomastikon des Amenemope," *STU* 20 (1950): 58-17 = Alt's *Kleine Schriften des Volkes Israel*, vol. 1 (Munich: C. H. Beck, 1953) 231-45; Heinz Richter, "Die Naturweisheit des Alten Testaments," *ZAW* 70 (1958): 1-20; Gerhard von Rad, "Hiob xxxviii und die altägyptische Weisheit," *Wisdom in Israel and in the Ancient Near East*, 293-301 = von Rad's *Gesammelte Studien zum Alten Testament*, TBü 8 (Munich: Chr. Kaiser, 1958) 262-71 = ET: *The Problem of the Hexateuch and Other Essays*, trans. E. W. T. Dicken (New York: McGraw-Hill, 1966) 281-91.

The presence of onomastica or lists (*Naturweisheit*) in Egypt and Mesopotamia suggests that Israelite wisdom literature may have comparable material. The epoch making study of Job 38 and Egyptian wisdom by von Rad recognized this fact and attempted to comprehend the unusual juxtaposition of onomastica and rhetorical questions addressed to Job.

While it might be argued that anyone wishing to enumerate the marvels of nature would have just so many phenomena to work with—hence the remarkable similarity between Amenemope (*ANET* 421-25), Sir 43, Ps 148, the "Song of the Three Hebrews," and Job 38 could be accidental—it seems more plausible to follow von Rad in postulating geographical, cosmological, and meterological "catechisms" within the repertoire of the sages of Israel. That being the case, a number of passages in Job, Sirach and Wisdom of Solomon become more comprehensible: Job 28; 36:27–37:13; 38:4–39:30; 40:15–41:34; Sir 43; Wis 7:17-20, 22-23; 14:25-26 (cf. 2 Esd 7:39-42; Ps 104; and Gen 1; 10). In Wis 7:17-20 the author alludes to the entire curriculum of the wise man:

> For it is he who gave me unerring
> knowledge of what exists,
> to know the structure of the world
> and the activity of the elements;
> the beginning and end and middle
> of times,
> the alternations of the solstices
> and the changes of the seasons,
> the cycles of the year
> and the constellations of the stars,
> the natures of animals
> and the tempers of wild beasts,
> the powers of spirits
> and the reasonings of men,
> the varieties of plants
> and the virtues of roots; . . .   (RSV)

There is reference in this passage to philosophy, cosmology, chronology, astronomy, zoology, demonology, botany, and medicine. The other examples from this author consist of a list of virtues and vices, the Greek style of which is quite pronounced.

Sirach 43, like Wis 7:17-20, uses the *Naturweisheit* for the glory of God; the majestic hymn describes the wonders of nature as those especially fashioned to assure the prosperity of the righteous and to make certain the downfall of the wicked. Sirach's response to the burning problem of theodicy grows out of the dilemma forced upon him by rigid adherence to the dogma of retribution and tenacious refusal to opt for Hellenism's easy way out (the belief in immortality). However, Job and Qoheleth had made their point, forcing Sirach into a twofold retreat, namely into psychology (the wicked man has excessive nightmares) and metaphysics (nature itself fights for the good man and against the sinner).

Another passage from Sirach may be viewed from the perspective of onomastica, namely, 38:24–39:11 (although "character portrayal" has been suggested as a better description of this text). Here the wise man describes various trades, as in the Egyptian "The Instruction of Duauf" (*ANET* 432-34), and contrasts the leisurely life of the sage. However, Sirach has a genuine appreciation for the farmer, craftsman, smith, and potter:

> Without them a city
>   cannot be established,
> and men can neither sojourn
>   nor live there. . . .
> But they keep stable
>   the fabric of the world,
> and their prayer
>   is in the practice of their trade.   (38:32, 34 RSV)

Nevertheless, the emphasis is placed upon the attributes of a wise man, who "devotes himself to the study of the law of the Most High," seeks out the wisdom of all the ancients, concerns himself with prophecies, preserves the discourse of notable men, penetrates the subtleties of parables, searches out the hidden meaning of proverbs, and is at home with the obscurities of parables (39:1-3).

H. Didactic Poetry and Narrative

Brevard Childs, *Isaiah and the Assyrian Crisis*, SBT 2nd ser. 3 (London: SCM Press, 1967); James L. Crenshaw, "A Liturgy of Wasted Opportunity (Am. 4:6-12; Isa. 9:7–10:4; 5:25-29)," *Sem* 1 (1970): 27-37; Gerhard von Rad, *Weisheit in Israel*; J. William Whedbee, *Isaiah and Wisdom* (Nashville: Abingdon Press, 1970); and Roger N. Whybray, *The Succession Narrative.*

In his form-critical study of *Isaiah and the Assyrian Crisis*, Childs came across a literary form to which he gave the name "Summary-Appraisal" and which he attributed to the wisdom tradition. Specimens of this genre are said to occur in Isa 14:26-27; 17:14b; and 28:29, the function of which is to summarize an oracle and evaluate it. The character of the statement as summary necessitates its appearing at the end of an oracle, and each time a demonstrative pronoun or similar word establishes a reference and serves as an indication of an independent appraisal. The summary appraisal is differentiated from concluding hortatory sentences, confessions, divine judgment or popular word, and is not connected syntactically in a causal relationship to a main oracle, but serves an independent role. Childs is unable to discover close parallels in other prophets (despite Isa 54:17; Jer 13:25; Isa 47:14-15); the didactic flavor and analogies from nature provide for him the clue, namely, wisdom. The reflective tone supports such an identification, as does the vocabulary, Childs argues. Accordingly he finds close parallels in Prov 1:19 (cf 6:29); Ps 49:13 [14]; Job 5:27; 8:13; 18:21; 20:29; 27:13, Qoh 4:8 and passim; and Sir 43:27. In spite of his belief that the summary appraisal form is probably employed in the wisdom literature of the ancient Near East in general, Childs is obliged to write that "a close parallel in the extrabiblical material to the summary-appraisal form does not appear" (129-36, esp. 136).

The arguments of Childs have been accepted, with some reservation, by Whedbee, who adds Sir 16:23 and 39:27, while rejecting Isa 17:14b as doubtful inasmuch as it uses the first person plural and bears the marks of cultic interests (76-79). Von Rad, on the other hand, is not entirely convinced that the form appears only in summary or concluding position; accordingly he adds to Childs's list two texts with the formula in the middle (Job 8:13 and Wis 2:9) and one, perhaps two, at the beginning (Job 27:13; Jer 13:25; *Weisheit in Israel*, 58).

While Childs has illuminated a form that occurs in wisdom literature, he has not, in my opinion, demonstrated that it is a *wisdom form*. On the contrary, the evidence points to its use both in prophetic and wisdom texts, the differences between Isa 54:17; 47:14-15; and Jer 13:25, on the one hand and Isa 14:26-27; 17:14b; and 28:29, on the other, being less decisive than Childs thinks. When one recognizes the didactic character of legal and cultic texts, indeed of some prophetic ones, as well as the reflection upon nature's lessons for mankind, which also appears in texts other than wisdom, it becomes hazardous to argue for a wisdom origin of the summary-appraisal, particularly in view of the absence of ancient Near Eastern parallels. The summary-appraisal is nonetheless present in wisdom literature, and Childs has gone a long way in elucidating its form and function.

Another form of didactic poetry is the *Auseinandersetzungsliteratur* or problem poetry (Pss 37; 49; 73; 139), Egyptian parallels of which are well known (E. Otto, *Der Vorwurf an Gott: Zur Entstehgeschichte der ägyptische Auseinändersetzungsliteratur* [Hildesheim: Gerstenberg, 1951]). This literature concerns itself with the fate of the wicked in light of their apparent prosperity, urging the just man to bide his time and trust in Yahweh's ability to enforce ultimate justice. Often the theme of the all-seeing eye of God is appealed to in contexts dealing with the fate of the wicked (37:13, 18; cf. 73:11, which questions God's vision; 139:1-18). It is even said that God knows man before he is born and writes down the life span allotted to each creature.

> I praise thee, for thou art fearful and wonderful.
>> Wonderful are thy works!
> Thou knowest me right well;
>> my frame was not hidden from thee,
> when I was being made in secret,
>> intricately wrought in the depths of the earth.
> Thy eyes beheld my unformed substance;
>> in thy book were written, every one of them,
> the days that were formed for me,
>> when as yet there was none of them.　　(Ps 139:14-16 RSV)

Related to the autobiographical narrative (confession) discussed above is the didactic narrative (Prov 7:6-23). In this instance the narrator describes a typical happening, giving the minutest details and livening the account with superb dialogue. The event is a common seduction scene, which the narrator had viewed from his window, and which the adulterous wife whose husband had gone on a long journey played with perfection. The metaphors descriptive of the obedient compliance of the foolish young man are intended to suggest that his conduct is animalic.

> With much seductive speech she persuades him;
>> with her smooth talk she compels him.
> All at once he follows her,
>> as an ox goes to the slaughter,
> or as a stag is caught fast
>> till an arrow pierces its entrails;
> as a bird rushes into a snare;
>> he does not know that it will cost him his life.   (Prov 7:21-23 RSV)

The didactic narrative was not the exclusive domain of the wise men, for it is found throughout the Old Testament (the Joseph narrative, the succession narrative, Esther, Dan 1:3-6, Tobit, Judith). All attempts to trace each of these to wisdom circles must be judged a failure, if the term *wisdom literature* is to have any meaning at all (cf. my "Method in Determining Wisdom Influence upon 'Historical' Literature").

Another type of didactic narrative is the historical summary (or historical retrospect); Sir 44–50 and Wis 10–19 fall into this category. The former is a "hymn" in praise of famous men and, indirectly, of God who poured out his spirit upon each. Cultic interests surface in the selection of heroes of the faith; there can be no question but that Sirach's heart throbs at the mention of Aaron, David the founder of the Jerusalem cult, Josiah, Hezekiah, and Simon the high priest. The entire second part of Wisdom of Solomon is devoted to illustrating God's control of historical events to encourage virtue and to punish the wicked, in this instance, the Egyptians. This material has the characteristics of a midrash (but see J. Reese, *Hellenistic Influence on the Book of Wisdom*, AnBib 41 [Rome: Pontifical Biblical Institute, 1970]), the exodus event providing the source for the imaginative interpretation of divine causality. The transition from historical summary to prayer and again to historical summary points to the close relationship between prayer and what I have termed negative historical retrospect ("A Liturgy of Wasted Opportunity" [Amos 4:6-12; Isa 9:7–10:4; 5:25-29]). The function of these prayers in cultic contexts is beyond question; what is still unclear is their role in didactic settings, although it is likely that prayers were an occasion for viewing the history of Israel from the perspective of the moral lessons to be gained therefrom.

This survey of eight types of wisdom literature is suggestive rather than exhaustive; other examples for some of the genres could be given, particularly prayer (in Job), allegory (within the description of Dame Wisdom and Madam

Folly), and narrative (cf. Hermisson, *Studien zur israelitischen Spruchweisheit*, 183-86). In time it is hoped that further precision can be given each form, but before such clarity will be possible, a number of unresolved issues must be faced squarely.

III. Unresolved Issues

A desideratum of form critical study of wisdom literature is a standardization of vocabulary, which hopefully will be addressed in the Interpreter's Handbook of Old Testament Form Criticism (see Murphy, "Form Criticism and Wisdom Literature"). The problem is complicated by the difficulty of finding precise English equivalents for German genre terminology and by the variety of terms in use among German scholars. To give a single example, there are at least six words for admonition in use currently (*Mahnwort, Mahnspruch, Mahnrede, Mahnung, Warnung, Rat*).

Far more formidable is the problem of definition: What is meant by wisdom (חָכְמָה)? The scope of wisdom literature, tradition, and thinking is not merely an Israelite phenomenon, for nonbiblical ancient Near Eastern literature must also be taken into consideration, particularly since wisdom literature has been reckoned an "alien body" within the Israelite canon (cf. the highly questionable position of Horst Dietrich Preuss, "Erwägungen zum theologischen Ort alttestamentlicher Weisheitsliteratur," 393-417, particularly 412-17). But how does one discern influence, either of one wisdom tradition upon another or of prophetic and priestly traditions upon the sage? Some progress has been made in this regard, but much more needs to be done (cf. my "Method in Determining Wisdom Influence upon 'Historical' Literature").

Arriving at an operable definition of wisdom is difficult because of the diversity of witness within the wisdom tradition. In view of this remarkable variety of forms and of sociological-theological settings, the composition of a literary history of the genres is virtually impossible. So long as the date of the literary complexes eludes scholarly pursuit, and the precise form of each genre cannot be discerned, real confidence in the results of form critical analysis will be wanting. To illustrate, how does one distinguish the original form of the "better sayings"? Is it מִי . . . טוֹב / מַ, מַ . . . כִּי טוֹב, or (in the negative) טוֹב . . . ב (Qoh 2:24; 3:12; contrast 3:22)? Does not this variety reflect the author's desire to express himself by means of the total linguistic stock available to him (cf. the suggestive remarks of Hermisson in *Studien zur israelitischen Spruchweisheit*, 137-86)? Any attempt, therefore, to date these passages in terms of the form, given our limited knowledge, would be to miss the mark. Nor is the issue any less complicated when one does research in sociological and theological development, for differences of viewpoint and of sophistication may have existed alongside one another in every generation. Certainly a rigid evolutionary scheme of progress must be rejected, even in regard to the religionization of wisdom.

So far very little attention has been devoted to the discovery of the larger structure of wisdom literature, that is, to the intention of the final editor. Of course the recognition of stylistic features that led to larger complexes is a step in this direction, for example, the initial בּ in Prov 11:9-12; לֵב and טוֹב in 15:13-17, the acrostic in Prov 31:10-31, and numerical sayings. But what of architectonic expression now in veiled form? Despite some reserve as to the methodology employed by P. Skehan, I am inclined to applaud his asking of a significiant question. The same may be said about the so-called "new criticism" or structural analysis, which carries its own set of presuppositions, sometimes unawares. Furthermore, what of the relation of wisdom literature and the cult, a crucial issue when one considers Job 31, as well as the תוֹעֵבָה and אַשְׁרֵי sayings (cf. W. Jansen, "'AŠRÊ in the Old Testament," HTR 58 [1965]: 215-26, and Walther Zimmerli, "The Place and Limit of the Wisdom," 153-54)?

Finally, who will take up Muilenburg's challenge to move beyond form criticism to rhetorical criticism? What is the function of refrain (cf. Song of Songs), rhetorical question (Roger N. Whybray, *The Heavenly Counselor in Isaiah xl 13-14*, SOTSMS 1 [London: Cambridge University Press, 1971] 19-26), quotation, imagined speech, and so forth in wisdom literature? These and other questions like them will be given appropriate answers only by scholars who know the tradition but refuse to be enslaved by it.

4 (1993)

Wisdom Literature: Retrospect and Prospect

The publication of the volume entitled *The Sage in Israel and the Ancient Near East*[1] and the updated reprint of *La Sagesse de l'ancien Testament*[2] offer an occasion to reflect on the status of research in wisdom literature.[3] Anyone remotely familiar with the subject must surely be amazed at the sheer quantity of publica-

---

[1]John G. Gammie and Leo G. Perdue, eds. (Winona Lake: Eisenbrauns, 1990). The imprecise notion of wisdom characterizing many essays in this massive work detracts from its value and threatens to retard the progress of research in this area. Part of the problem derives from the impossible design: the underlying assumption that sapiential influence has permeated the entire Hebrew Bible. A few scholars struggled valiantly to carry out their assigned task, esp. in sec. 4; others approach the ludicrous, e.g., Loren R. Mack-Fisher's concluding remarks about what constitutes a sage; and still others put forth highly dubious interpretations of the facts, e.g., Walter Brueggemann's hypothetical construct drawn from sociology, Leo Perdue's identification of Ezra as a sage(!), and John Gammie's wide-ranging inclusivism.

[2]Maurice Gilbert, ed., BETL 51 (Leuven: University Press, 1990). In addition to the authors' updating of their articles and bibliography, the editor has written a brief survey of wisdom research during the decade from 1979 to 1989. He treats (1) introductions and collected works, (2) texts, (3) ancient commentaries, (4) modern commentaries, (5) studies on intertextual relations, and (6) studies devoted to the individual wisdom books.

[3]My own assessment of the past and future of sapiential studies was completed before I read Claus Westermann's *Forschungsgeschichte zur Weisheitsliteratur 1950–1990*, AzTh 71 (Stuttgart: Calwer Verlag, 1991). His focus on the social locus of wisdom and its literary form corresponds to my own isolation of social world and language of discourse as the central issues under discussion in recent publications, although we articulate the matter somewhat differently. For him, the fundamental questions are: "Did Israelite sages function within the family or in a professional setting such as school or court?" "Were the earliest proverbial sayings oral or written?" I share his conviction that the oldest biblical aphorisms derive from the family and were transmitted orally, and I also have serious doubts about the prominent role attributed to wisdom of the clan by Hans Walther Wolff and others. Incidentally, Westermann is mistaken that his essay "Weisheit im Sprichwort," was ignored for many years. I certainly cited it soon after its publication. Holger Delkurt's analysis of the fundamental issues underlying sapiential scholarship ("Grundprobleme alttestamentlicher Weisheit," *Verkündigung und Forschung* 36 [1991]: 38–71) is devoted to the following topics: (1) the definition of wisdom; (2) the place of wisdom; (3) prophecy and wisdom; (4) wisdom as a theology of creation; (5) speech about God in Proverbs; (6) specific themes such as "the appropriate moment for speech and silence," "the poor," and "fate"; and (7) Qoheleth.

tions, all the more surprising because of earlier neglect.[4] Maurice Gilbert's introduction to *La Sagesse de l'ancien Testament*[5] catalogues this vigorous activity over the past decade, so I shall restrict my remarks to analyzing fundamental issues underlying much of the published research. Mirroring the interpretation of the Hebrew Bible in general, a spate of publications about ancient wisdom addresses two questions: (1) Did Israel's sages constitute a professional class,[6] and (2) What characterizes their language of discourse?[7] In other words, what was the social world of the sages and how did they express themselves? Although *sociological* and *literary* interests have prevailed, occasional voices have echoed earlier *conceptual* analyses, particularly about the sages' idea of God.[8]

I. The Social World of the Sages

As R. Norman Whybray's recent essay on this topic shows,[9] no one has succeeded in positioning the sages in any distinct social group. To be sure, scholars use phrases like "elite class," "intellectuals," "urban owners of landed estates," "courtiers," and "professional counselors or teachers."[10] In addition, interpreters usu-

---

[4]One could hardly find a better example of interpretive bias, the point made so often today by practitioners of literary interpretation. The imperialism of a particular view of theology excluded wisdom literature from consideration. Dissatisfaction with salvation history coincided with revived interest in Israel's wisdom, which had earlier captured the imagination after its intimate connection with Egyptian wisdom literature was recognized.

[5]He builds on the survey of S. Pié i Ninot, "La Literatura Sapiencial Biblica: Una actualidad bibliográfica creciente," *Actualidad Bibliográfica* 44 (1985): 202-11, and 46 (1986): 163-74. To this may be added the long section by J. Vilchez Lindez in *Sapienciales I Proverbios* (Madrid: Ediciones Christiandad, 1984) 39-92, preceded by L. Alonso-Schökel's analysis (17-37).

[6]R. N. Whybray, *The Intellectual Tradition in the Old Testament*, BZAW 135 (Berlin: Walter de Gruyter, 1974) has posed the most vigorous challenge to the dominant view, although he appears to moderate his opinion in "The Sage in the Israelite Royal Court," in *The Sage in Israel and the Ancient Near East*, 139: "It is probable, on the other hand, that some parts of Proverbs, especially parts of chaps. 1–9 and 22:17–24:22, were composed as 'text books' for young pupils—though not necessarily at a royal scribal school."

[7]Walter Bühlmann, *Vom Rechten Reden und Schweigen*, OBO 12 (Göttingen: Vandenhoeck & Ruprecht, 1976) shows how self-consciously the ancient sages reflected on speech and its absence.

[8]Johannes Fichtner's synthesis of ancient wisdom literature, *Das Altorientalische Weisheit in ihrer israelitisch-jüdischen Ausprägung*, BZAW 62 (Giessen: A. Töpelmann, 1933) includes a lengthy section on the sages' understanding of God (97-123).

[9]"The Social World of the Wisdom Writers," in *The World of Ancient Israel*, ed. R. E. Clements, 227-50 (Cambridge: Cambridge University Press, 1989). Whybray characterizes the dilemma facing contemporary scholars in this way: (1) Why would royal scribes, even under foreign influence, have ignored the folk wisdom in Israel covering the same topics? (2) Yet the literary quality and clear dependence on foreign models of most of the aphorisms in Proverbs cannot be denied. (3) If education was actually widespread, why limit the authorship of wisdom literature to professional sages? (234-35).

[10]The book of Job is particularly problematic as a source for discerning the status of sages, as Whybray recognizes. Why are Job's three friends not identified as members of a professional class of the wise ("The Social World of the Wisdom Writers," 240)? Moreover, why do the proverbial collections

ally acknowledge an early period when wisdom's origin and transmission occurred within family units[11] and a late epoch during which teachers administered their own private schools,[12] with a possible intermediate stage associated with the royal court.[13] A noticeable lack of continuity stands out above all else, and the imprecise dating of the wisdom corpus complicates matters even more.[14] Indeed, disagreement over the limits of wisdom literature,[15] reflected in the tendency in some quarters to extend sapiential activity from Genesis to Esther,[16] bears witness to the mingling of various groups in Israelite society.

Ancient Near Eastern parallels throw light on the phenomenon of professional sages,[17] while at the same time highlighting distinct differences between Israelite

---

primarily address adults instead of school boys?

[11]Westermann, *Wurzeln der Weisheit* (Göttingen: Vandenhoeck & Ruprecht, 1990) argues forcefully for the prominence of the family in early wisdom instruction. He notes the concentration on topics of central interest to rural populations of simple people (75) and their focus on the "private" life (43). Nevertheless, he rejects the hypothesis of clan wisdom (35) and downplays the cult, asserting that address to God and by God belongs to a wholly different realm of language (142).

[12]Ben Sira's allusion to a building devoted to instruction (51:23) is ordinarily taken literally in contrast to the rhetoric attributed to and descriptive of personified wisdom (Prov 1:20-33; 8:1-36; 9:1-12; Sir 24; Wis 6:12-16; cf. Isa 55:1-3).

[13]The strongest evidence for professional sages at the royal court, the superscription in Prov 25:1, seems to refer to transcriptional activity (הֶעְתִּיקוּ) rather than to literary composition.

[14]The persistence of views that society in general has discarded only exacerbates the difficulty of postulating even relative chronologies for the several wisdom texts. The task becomes impossible when one takes into account the present state of knowledge about Israel's religious pilgrimage, e.g., the beginnings of personal piety, which Franz Josef Steiert, *Die Weisheit Israels—ein Fremdkörper im Alten Testament?* FTS (Freiburg: Herder, 1990) following Jan Assmann, *Weisheit, Loyalismus, und Frömmigkeit* (Freiburg: Herder, 1979), takes as a decisive clue for understanding the wisdom corpus. Michael V. Fox astutely comments: "But he never comes to grips with the fact that whatever their beliefs and assumptions, the Israelite sages never invoke God's law, never reinforce their teachings by appealing to the promises or demands of the covenant, and never draw upon the lessons of Israelite history. . . . Wisdom's avoidance of the particularities of Israelite law and history is a noteworthy and apparently deliberate practice" (review of Steiert, *Die Weisheit Israels* . . . in *JBL* 111 [1992]: 135).

[15]I am firmly convinced that the caveat offered in my article on "Method in Determining Wisdom Influence upon 'Historical' Literature," *JBL* 88 (1969): 129-42, was well placed and that many who cite it approvingly have not really heeded its warning.

[16]Donn Morgan, *Wisdom in the Old Testament Traditions* (Atlanta: John Knox Press, 1981) tries unsuccessfully to legitimate this hermeneutical enterprise.

[17]Two articles by Ronald J. Williams, "The Sage in Egyptian Literature" and "The Function of the Sage in the Egyptian Royal Court," in *The Sage in Israel and the Ancient Near East*, 19-30 and 95-98, update his earlier article "The Sages of Ancient Egypt in the Light of Recent Scholarship," *JAOS* 101 (1981): 1-19 (cf. also Helmut Brunner, *Altägyptische Weisheit* [Zurich, 1988] and Miriam Lichtheim, *Late Egyptian Wisdom Literature in the International Context* [Göttingen: Vandenhoeck & Ruprecht, 1983]). The Mesopotamian scene is treated by Rivkah Harris, "The Female 'Sage' in Mesopotamian Literature (with an Appendix on Egypt)," Samuel Noah Kramer, "The Sage in Sumerian Literature: A Composite Portrait," Ronald F. G. Sweet, "The Sage in Akkadian Literature: A Philological Study," and "The Sage in Mesopotamian Palaces and Royal Courts," in *The Sage in Israel and the Ancient Near East*, 3-18, 31-44, 45-66, and 99-108.

wisdom and Egyptian or Mesopotamian wisdom.[18] From the period of the Old Kingdom learned counselors advised the Pharaoh and his court, the New Kingdom witnessed a growing pietism among the sages responsible for royal instruction and temple ritual,[19] together with a democratizing of the teaching, and the Demotic period saw a ruralization of sages and a growth in skepticism,[20] approaching fatalism. Over the years Mesopotamian wisdom underwent comparable shifts, wisdom's primary locus changing from the tablet house (*edubba*) to the exorcist's place of activity,[21] although some evidence also points to other loci, for example, Sumerian folk proverbs and Babylonian counsels to a prince.[22]

As is well known, wisdom in Egypt and in Mesopotamia was essentially bureaucratic.[23] Instruction, primarily pragmatic, sought to ensure success in the exercise of governmental responsibilities. In the land along the Tigris and Euphrates rivers, professional scribes zealously guarded their unique skills with respect to the complex writing system and secret magical lore, at the same time eroding interest in literature by their very esotericism.[24] Available evidence does not support Gerhard von Rad's claim,[25] reiterated by Walter Brueggemann,[26] that intellectual bureaucratism took hold during the Solomonic era. Only the eighth century comes close to

---

[18]At least two things about Mesopotamian wisdom point to its similarity with and difference from biblical wisdom respectively: (1) the vigorous skeptical tradition in Ludlul, *The Babylonian Theodicy*, and *The Dialogue between a Master and His Slave*; (2) the centrality of magic. In Egypt scribalism and royal courtiers achieved prominence never enjoyed in Israel.

[19]Lichtheim, *Late Egyptian Wisdom Literature in the International Context*, rejects the claim that late Demotic works such as 'Onkhsheshonqy and Papyrus Insinger represent a failure of intellectual nerve that takes refuge in piety, but the conclusions of Hans Heinrich Schmid, *Wesen und Geschichte der Weisheit*, BZAW 101 (Berlin: A. Töpelmann, 1966) cannot easily be set aside.

[20]The first claim stands even if Lichtheim is correct that the sayings in 'Onkhsheshonqy are not overwhelmingly concerned about rural existence (4), for they certainly differ dramatically from earlier royal authorship or court instructions. The second claim hardly excludes belief in a deity's benevolence, for this absent verity fuels the skeptic's comments about fate.

[21]Kramer, "The Sage in Sumerian Literature," 38, brings together the two competing emphases, for he thinks exorcists studied in the tablet house and learned from an *ummia* (cf. Sweet, "The Sage in Akkadian Literature," 60-61).

[22]Were folk proverbs held in less esteem than literary products of professional sages, as Lichtheim thinks was true in Egypt (25)? Perhaps the answer depends on the audience, whether an ordinary citizen or a trained scribe.

[23]In this respect it contrasts sharply with biblical wisdom, which gives almost no evidence of serving bureaucratic ends—unless its conservative and antirevolutionary ethic aimed at preserving the status quo.

[24]A. Livingstone, *Mystical and Mythological Explanatory Works of Assyrian and Babylonian Scholars* (Oxford: Oxford University Press, 1986).

[25]*Wisdom in Israel* (Nashville: Abingdon Press, 1971). His hypothesis about the sweeping away of pan sacralism in a virtual Enlightenment during Solomon's regime has nothing to recommend it and is increasingly rejected.

[26]"The Social Significance of Solomon as a Patron of Wisdom," in *The Sage in Israel and the Ancient Near East*, 117-32. Brueggemann's neat types have rhetorical appeal, but they run roughshod over historical probabilities.

such complex organizational securing of royal interests.[27] As for esoteric knowledge, the simple Hebrew alphabet discouraged any move to withhold literature from the people at large, and magic played a less sanctioned role in Israelite religion than in Egypt or Mesopotamia.[28]

The debate over literacy in ancient Israel has introduced exciting new data into the discussion of the sages' social world.[29] André Lemaire waxes eloquent about a complex system of education during the monarchy embracing most cities in Israel and extending to many remote villages. Drawing on inscriptional data, he imagines the existence of schools as the precondition for the biblical canon, for students needed texts. Others have interpreted the data differently, seeing in them decisive proof of illiteracy throughout the land (misspellings, crude drawings, transpositions of letters). William V. Harris's recent study of *Ancient Literacy* puts Lemaire's optimism under a dark cloud,[30] for if literacy in classical Greece never exceeded ten percent one is entitled to ask how Israel ever reached the high level of literacy that many, if not most, interpreters assume. J. Baines's estimate that literacy in Egypt rarely exceeded one percent is even more sobering.[31]

Stated simply, mass literacy, a recent phenomenon, is a product of the invention of the printing press, Protestantism's emphasis on private reading of the Bible, state and religious funding of education, and the industrial revolution, which made available tangible rewards for educated workers.[32] Ancient Israel lacked these inducements to literacy, at the same time possessing several hindrances to the mastering of reading and writing. First, writing materials were either cumbersome or prohibitively expensive. Second, acquiring an education was not cost effective, especially in an agricultural economy where seasonal work determined one's daily calendar. Third, nothing in the economy demanded a literate populace, and participation in society at large depended on one's oral skills. Fourth, no patron of education assumed the cost of private instruction, and one searches in vain for any mention of philanthropic gifts to education comparable to those in third century Greece.

---

[27]David W. Jamieson-Drake, *Scribes and Schools in Monarchic Judah. A Socio-Archaeological Approach*, JSOTSup 109 (Sheffield: Almond Press, 1991) has demonstrated the improbability that Solomon had the sort of bureaucracy assumed by Brueggemann.

[28]Various biblical allusions to magical practices among the populace indicate that the official position regarding magic and divination did not necessarily commend itself to ordinary citizens.

[29]André Lemaire, "The Sage in School and Temple, " *The Sage in Israel and the Ancient Near East*, 165-81, argues for widespread schools in Israel from early times, but my "Education in Ancient Israel," *JBL* 104 (1985): 601-15, and Menahem Haran, "On the Diffusion of Literacy and Schools in Ancient Israel," VTSup 40 Congress Volume (Jerusalem, 1988) 81-95, take a much more conservative view.

[30](Cambridge & London: Harvard University Press, 1989).

[31]"Literacy and Ancient Egyptian Society," *Man* n.s. (London: Royal Anthropological Institute of Great Britain and Ireland, 1983) 572-99. I am indebted to Rivkah Harris, "The Female 'Sage' in Mesopotamian Literature," 15, for this reference.

[32]Harris, *Ancient Literacy*, 12.

Fifth, members of crafts and guilds requiring literacy of some sort undoubtedly kept membership to a minimum, thus protecting their earning power.

In short, neither a strong desire for literacy nor an opportunity to become literate existed in ancient Israel, with the possible exception of a few guilds.[33] In all likelihood, some moral instruction took place in the family, probably in the form of oral teaching.[34] The overwhelming sense of oral instruction persists into the third century, if by אזן Qoheleth's epilogist alludes to the teacher's manner of listening for insights worthy of dissemination.[35] The legend about the seven *apkallus* in Sumer and the claim that Marduk had four ears at birth emphasize the importance of hearing, as does the phrase designating professional sages as "wide of ear."[36]

The situation in Alexandria, the probable setting of wisdom of Solomon, is unique, as Alan Mendelson's *Secular Education in Philo of Alexandria*[37] effectively demonstrates. There mastering the encyclicals was a means of upward mobility, but knowledge of creation enabled students to move beyond sensory data to what Philo called knowledge of God. Small wonder Wisdom of Solomon actually rattles off the subjects in the school curriculum and dramatically emphasizes the importance of correctly interpreting the "Book of Nature."

The Hebrew Bible does not even provide sufficient data to enable critics to ascertain the identity of those to whom teaching was addressed. Curiously, the proverbial collection that seems to comprise instruction for students, Prov 1–9, actually employs language of family discourse,[38] whereas the oldest collections lack such vocabulary and give the impression of application to adult members of society. In ancient Egyptian and Mesopotamian wisdom, the clientele of proverbs is exclusively masculine. Rivkah Harris has exhaustively documented the exceptions to this masculine hegemony in the ancient Near East.[39] She refers to educated daughters of

---

[33]Economic interests would have led to protectionism with respect to the special knowledge by which guild members earned their wages. Professional pride also encouraged exclusivism, sometimes reinforced by magical rites as in metallurgy. Rivalry resulted from exclusivity, e.g., the struggle for power within priestly circles.

[34]The language of Deut 6:4-9 mentions written signs within an overwhelmingly oral instructional context, and even Prov 1–9, presumably a product of a literary composition as opposed to folk origin, describes the process of learning as oral instruction. The dominance of the verb "hear" (e.g., in 4:1,10; 5:13) stands out, along with the paucity of references to writing (cf. 3:3).

[35]C. F. Whitley, *Koheleth*, BZAW 148 (Berlin & New York: Walter de Gruyter, 1979).

[36]"Four were his eyes, four were his ears. When he moved his lips, fire blazed forth. Each of his four ears grew large and (his) eyes likewise, to see everything" (Sara Denning Bolle, "Wisdom in Akkadian Literature: Expression, Instruction, Dialogue," Ph.D. diss., University of California, Los Angeles, 1982) 58. Erica Reiner, "The Etiological Myth of the 'Seven Sages'," *Orientalia* 30 (1961): 1-11, treats the *apkallus*.

[37]HUCM 7 (Cincinnati: Hebrew Union College Press, 1982).

[38]An exclusive metaphorical understanding of vocabulary such as "my son" and "father" in the sense of student and teacher requires one to ignore clear indications that some of these instructions took place within a family setting (cf. 1:8; 6:20; 4:3-9).

[39]"The Female 'Sage' in Mesopotamian Literature (with an Appendix on Egypt)," 3-18.

royalty and to female scribes who ministered solely to women of the harem, serving as a buffer between the wives of rulers and nonkin males. Although goddesses were patrons of the scribal art in both these lands, Nisaba in Mesopotamia, Seshat in Egypt, this fact did not translate into widespread literacy for women any more than a comparable phenomenon did in the Middle Ages in Europe. On rare occasions women actually composed literature, for example, Sargon's daughter Enheduanna, who described her literary activity as "giving birth" and Ninshatapada, the daughter of Sin-Kashib, the founder of the Old Babylonian dynasty of Uruk.[40] Graphic imagery depicting women as literate, such as scenes showing females with writing implements or written texts, may reflect an *ideal* rather than the *actual* state of things. At least one Egyptian text mentions a wise woman, but this expression suffers from the same ambiguity that חָכָם does in the Hebrew Bible.[41] Does the word in its various forms ever bear a technical sense, "the wise?" Most critics think it does, but few agree on which uses belong to this category. Recent research has cast doubt on the supposed technical use of "counselor" in Mesopotamia,[42] undercutting the claim already on shaky ground textually that the biblical expression "wise woman" refers to a professional sage.[43] Now and again certain remarks reveal the extent to which women suffered from low self-esteem ("Disregard that it is a mere woman who has written and submitted [this] to you") or from calumny (Egyptian graffiti that compares earlier graffiti to the "work of a woman who has no mind").[44]

A different way of discovering the social world of the sages has been applied to Job and Qoheleth, with interesting results. In the book of Job Rainer Albertz discerns infighting between rival groups of upper class citizens, which he characterizes as an unscrupulous enclave bent on amassing wealth at the expense of less fortunate individuals and a pious group who cannot condone such harsh treatment of helpless citizens.[45] How this latter attitude squares with the fact that the

---

[40]Not one female name appears in Dandameyev's study of more than three thousand scribes from the Neo-Babylonia period. In Egypt the New Kingdom witnessed the rise to prominence of several remarkable women, among whom were Hatshepsut, Tiy, and Nefertiti.

[41]Hans-Peter Müller and M. Krause, "חָכַם *chākham*; חָכָם *chākhām*; חָכְמָה *chokhmāh*; חָכְמוֹת *chokhmôth*," *TDOT* (1980) 4:364-85.

[42]Sweet, "The Sage in Akkadian Literature," 64.

[43]P. Kyle McCarter, Jr., "The Sage in the Deuteronomistic History," *The Sage in Israel and the Ancient Near East*, 291, characterizes the woman of Tekoa as an actress "since Joab tells her what to say and do." Does the adjective "wise" in this story simply mean "clever" or "calculating" (cf. also the adjective describing Jonadab)?

[44]The Egyptian *Satire of the Trades* contains an incidental observation more telling than most direct remarks about the status of women ("The weaver in the workshop, he is worse off than a woman. . . . " See Lichtheim, *Ancient Egyptian Literature*, vol. 1 [Berkeley: University of California Press, 1973] 188). The washerman also suffers the indignity of having to clean women's clothes (189).

[45]"Der sozialgeshichtliche Hintergrund des Hiobbuches und der 'Babylonischen Theodizee'," in *Die Botschaft und die Boten. F. S. Wolff* (Neukirchen: Neukirchener-Vluyn, 1981) 349-72.

book is written from the standpoint of a wealthy suffering innocent who expresses contempt for the scum of the earth in chapter 30 needs to be explained, for only with great reservation can it be said this book champions the cause of the poor, a point overlooked by J. David Pleins and Gustavo Gutiérrez in their otherwise perceptive studies.[46] With respect to Qoheleth, Franz Crüsemann has rendered a verdict of "guilty" on charges of heartless surrender to the profit motive regardless of the consequences.[47] Other readers may concur with Elias Bickerman that Qoheleth lived in an acquisitive society, an age characterized by economic ventures aimed at making a fortune,[48] but they recognize that Qoheleth criticized all such mercenary endeavors as futile or absurd. In my view, Qoheleth's remarks about victims of oppression with none to deliver them carry pathos rather than contempt.

Udo Skladny's pioneering efforts to apply a sociological approach to Proverbs did not persuade many critics,[49] but more recent applications of this perspective appear promising. Joe Blenkinsopp understands the preoccupation in Prov 1–9 with foreign women in light of the struggle under Ezra and Nehemiah to rid the community of a perceived threat posed by non-Jewish wives.[50] Pleins and others have analyzed the vocabulary of poverty in Proverbs, with some surprising results.[51] All these efforts to clarify the social world of the sages underline the necessity of postulating different centers of sapiential teaching from time to time. Such diversity gives rise to still another question: did the sages in their several locations use rhetoric that set them apart from the rest of society?

II. The Sages' Language of Discourse

Carol A. Newsom's penetrating analysis of the discourse in Prov 1–9 illustrates the power inherent in a literary study of sapiential texts.[52] Using categories drawn from Mikail Baktin, Emile Benveniste, Jacques Derrida, Mieke Bal, Toril Moi and others, she focuses on the speaking self and the silent addressee, as well as the feminine subject of that talk. In doing so, Newsom highlights the hidden struggle

---

[46]Pleins, "Poverty in the Social World of the Wise," *JSOT* 37 (1987): 61-78, and "Rhetorics of Opposition: Exploring the Diverging Social Visions of the Hebrew Bible, with Special Reference to the Wisdom Tradition," unpub. paper presented in Vienna at the SBL International Meeting; and Gutiérrez, *On Job* (Maryknoll NY: Orbis Books, 1987).

[47]"Die unveränderbare Welt. Überlegungen zur 'Krisis der Weisheit' beim Prediger (Kohelet)," *Der Gott der kleinen Leute*, ed. Willi Schottroff and Wolfgang Stegemann (Munich: Gelnhausen, 1979) 80-104; ET: *The God of the Lowly* (Maryknoll NY: Orbis Books, 1984).

[48]*Four Strange Books of the Bible* (New York: Schocken, 1967) 139-67.

[49]*Die ältesten Spruchsammlungen in Israel* (Göttingen: Vandenhoeck & Ruprecht, 1962).

[50]"The Social Context of the 'Outsider Woman' in Proverbs 1–9," *Bib* 72 (1991): 457-73.

[51]"Poverty in the Social World of the Wise"; R. N. Whybray, *Wealth and Poverty in the Book of Proverbs*, JSOTSup 99 (Sheffield: JSOT Press, 1990); James L. Crenshaw, "Poverty and Punishment in the Book of Proverbs," *Quarterly Review* 9 (1989): 30-43.

[52]"Woman and the Discourse of Patriarchal Wisdom: A Study of Proverbs 1–9," *Gender and Difference in Ancient Israel*, ed. Peggy L. Day (Minneapolis: Fortress, 1989) 142-60.

for power in shaping a world view and the subtle appeal to transcendental authority. Under her critical eye these moral teachings take on their character as life and death decisions by competing generations. Aware of the social consequences of actions, the teachers use every means at their disposal to place the enemy on the margin of existence. In my view, no other interpreter has succeeded to this degree in clarifying the discourse as it unfolds in Prov 1–9.

I have discussed the compositional nature of the sayings of Agur in Prov 30:1–14 under the title "Clanging Symbols."[53] It seems that this entire unit builds on a principle of frustrated expectation, as again and again the anticipated conclusion to a familiar expression does not appear and in its place something wholly unexpected completes the thought. Here both form and content mesh, for the shocking skepticism corresponds to the stylistic iconoclasm.

David Penchansky's *The Betrayal of God* interprets the perceived dissonance in the Book of Job by using categories from Frederic Jameson, Michel Foucault, and Pierre Macherey.[54] For Penchansky, dissonance functions to emphasize the real gaps in divine activity and character, hence should not be explained away as editorial tampering with a seamless text. Such an approach implies that a cloud of darkness hovers over the book from start to finish, and this cloud heightens the mystery and terror associated with the deity depicted in Job. Robert Alter has traced an intricate connection between Job's initial lament and the subsequent theophany; in exquisite detail the divine speech mirrors the earlier human complaint.[55] Alter's sensitivity to the imagery of the text approximates the powerful thrust of Othmar Keel's discussion of Egyptian symbolism for chaos, the hippopotamus and the crocodile.[56] I have noted an additional feature of the theophany, the clash between form and content.[57] The anticipated comforting presence generated by the theophany in context is mitigated by words that ridicule Job and describe a universe virtually devoid of human beings, yet one in which Yahweh takes great pride.

Michael V. Fox has given a new interpretation of multiple voices in Qoheleth, which he understands as various personae of the author.[58] Appealing to a common stylistic device in the ancient world, as well as in more modern works like Joel Chandler Harris's *The Tales of Uncle Remus*, Fox thinks of a single narrator who assumes different personae. The speaker who frames the story then shifts from third person to first person and addresses others as Qoheleth. This approach enables Fox

---

[53]In *Justice and the Holy, Essays in Honor of Walter Harrelson*, ed. Douglas A. Knight and Peter J. Paris (Atlanta: Scholars Press, 1989) 51-64.

[54]Louisville: Westminster/John Knox Press, 1990.

[55]*The Art of Biblical Poetry* (New York: Basic Books, 1985) 85-110.

[56]*Jahwes Entgegnung an Ijob: Eine Deutung von Ijob 38–41 vor dem Hintergrund der Zeitgenössischen Bildkunst* (Göttingen: Vandenhoeck & Ruprecht, 1978).

[57]"When Form and Content Clash: The Theology of Job 38:1–40:5," *Creation in the Biblical Tradition*, ed. John J. Collins and Richard J. Clifford, CBQMS (1992) 70-84.

[58]*Qohelet and His Contradictions* (Sheffield: Almond Press, 1989) and "Frame-Narrative and Composition in the Book of Qohelet," *HUCA* 49 (1977): 83-106.

to argue for unity throughout the book, despite contradictions and apparent epilogues.

Two recent dissertations have examined ancient Near Eastern rhetoric in Sumerian and Akkadian wisdom literature. Robert S. Falkowitz claims in *The Sumerian Rhetoric Collections* that so-called proverb collections are misnamed, for they contain many genres besides proverbial sayings—specifically maxims, riddles, enthymemes, fables, tables, and incantations—and insists that the rhetoric collections were used as texts in schools.[59] Their purpose, in his opinion, was to train scribes in the art of persuasion. Falkowitz thinks many of these genres fluctuated, for example, a proverb became familiar, lost its metaphoric essence, and became a maxim. He also insists that the difference between one genre and another was often hardly noticeable, for metaphors meant to be enigmatic identify riddles and metaphors meant to be understood indicate proverbs. Falkowitz denies that these rhetoric collections ever existed outside the school, despite the traditional appearance akin to folk wisdom, and supposes that rhetoric collections were learned after basic sign lists, lexical lists, and grammatical texts. If he is correct, two observations will impinge heavily on wisdom research: consistency was not of great importance, and one cannot deduce a society's values from its proverbs alone, for they do not necessarily express commonly held truths.[60]

The other analysis of discourse in Akkadian wisdom, Sara Denning Bolle's "Wisdom in Akkadian Literature: Expression, Instruction, Dialogue" interprets the texts from the standpoint of dialogue as understood by Plato and Baktin.[61] Bolle first looks at dialogue in Akkadian narratives such as the *Gilgamesh Epic*, then turns to cult texts (incantations), instructions, contest literature, and dialogical texts, for example, *Theodicy*, *A Dialogue of Pessimism*, and *A Dialogue between a Man and God*. Bolle isolates three features of Platonic dialogue: (1) Socratic *elenchus*, or questioning to expose ignorance, (2) *epagoge*, or arriving at a universal from a particular, and (3) Socratic definition, or searching for the essence. Using Baktin's emphasis on polyphonic dialogue, one that never ends, Bolle analyzes ancient dialogues, including inner dialogues and dialogues within dialogues. She recognizes the rich potential of rhetorical questions, which effect transitions, communicate philosophical, timeless truth, enhance drama, draw readers into the narrative, emphasize, and startle. Noting that instructions address a fictitious audience, Bolle perceives that at a deeper level than the monologue, they address the inner words of mind and heart. Taking issue with her teacher Giorgio Buccellati, she understands the *Theodicy* to be internal dialogue carried on within the heart of a single person (like Qoheleth and *The Dialogue of a Man with His Soul*). She sums up the impor-

---

[59] "The Sumerian Rhetoric Collections," Ph.D. diss., University of Pennsylvania, 1980.

[60] If wisdom and law are integrally related, one would expect proverbial prohibitions to express ancient values. I have explored this putative relationship in an essay entitled "Prohibitions in Proverbs and Qoheleth," forthcoming in the Festschrift for Joseph Blenkinsopp.

[61] Ph.D. diss., University of California, Los Angeles, 1982.

tance of dialogue as follows: "Wisdom is a matter of communication, enlightening, and instructing: dialogue is its vehicle."[62]

Returning to the question with which we began this discussion of literary analysis, did the sages use distinctive rhetoric? As the preceding comments on dialogue indicate, we cannot claim exclusive use of these literary features by ancient sages, but we can affirm special rhetoric in some instances.[63] Still, we lack conclusive criteria for distinguishing in every case exactly which text derives from a sapiential milieu and which one does not. The continuing debate over the provenance of the Book of Job illustrates the slippage in this regard.[64]

III. The Concept of God in Wisdom Literature

Traditional approaches to wisdom literature have by no means vanished from the contemporary scene. Lennart Boström's *The God of the Sages* looks at the view of God in the Book of Proverbs, concentrating on the notion of creation and the belief in a personal relationship between believer and High God.[65] Boström replaces the descriptive term act/consequence with character/consequence, which he thinks more accurately reflects the ancient teaching about order as subject to Yahweh's activity.[66] Boström also discerns a higher degree of readiness in Israel to speak of an intimate relationship with the creator than in Egypt, even during the period of deep piety there.[67] In some respects Boström joins hands with Jon Levenson, whose *Creation and the Persistence of Evil* highlights the resistant force of chaos alluded to in many biblical texts.[68]

In a paper in memory of John Gammie,[69] I looked once more at Johannes Fichtner's conclusions concerning Israelites sages' reluctance to attribute grace to the deity, in contrast with Egyptian and Mesopotamian wisdom literature. On the basis

---

[62]*Wisdom in Akkadian Literature*, 280.

[63]I have attempted to provide some observations on the sages' rhetoric in "Wisdom and Authority: Sapiential Rhetoric and its Warrants," VTSup 32, Congress Volume, Vienna 1981 (Leiden: E. J. Brill, 1982) 10-29.

[64]Katharine J. Dell, *The Book of Job as Sceptical Literature*, BZAW 197 (Berlin & New York: Walter de Gruyter, 1991) 57-107; Bruce Zuckerman, *Job the Silent* (New York: Oxford University Press, 1991); Edwin M. Good, *In Turns of Tempest* (Stanford: Stanford University Press, 1990).

[65]ConBOT 29 (Stockholm: Almquist & Wiksell International, 1990). Tryggve N. D. Mettinger, *In Search of God* (Philadelphia: Fortress Press, 1988) 175-200, emphasizes the transition in the book of Job from a hidden to a revealed God.

[66]On the place of "order" in current research, see my essay, "Murphy's Axiom: Every Gnomic Saying Needs a Balancing Corrective," 1-17 in *The Listening Heart*, ed. Kenneth G. Hoglund et. al., JSOTSup 58 (Sheffield: JSOT Press, 1987). One can posit the importance of order in the ancient sapiential worldview without deifying the concept. In Israel Yahweh had the final word, and the same can probably be said of Egypt's High God.

[67]Ronald J. Williams, "The Sage in Egyptian Literature," 22.

[68](San Francisco: Harper & Row, 1988).

[69]"The Concept of God in Old Testament Wisdom," *In Search of Wisdom: Essays in Memory of John G. Gammie*, ed. Leo G. Perdue and Brandon Scott (Westminster/John Knox, forthcoming).

of a fresh analysis of key texts, it is possible to nuance Fichtner's hypothesis somewhat differently without denying its essential validity.

Conclusion

In this brief survey of recent research, I do not claim to do justice to the many fine articles on wisdom literature falling outside the rubrics selected for discussion. Perhaps I shall be forgiven if I mention one further area of research: the endeavor to locate larger units within collections of proverbs.[70] Of course, these explorations illustrate the much-cited "reader response" theory of literary critics,[71] but the supposed connections between quite diverse sayings also raise the issue that H.J. Hermisson tried to lay to rest,[72] namely the differences between folk and literary proverbs, on which some light has now come from Africa.[73] Michael Fishbane's perceptive studies on inner biblical midrash relate to this problem,[74] for his approach assumes wide familiarity with a written text by many readers. If my conclusions about literacy in Israel are reasonably accurate, scholars will need to exercise considerably more restraint in this regard.[75] In any event, scholarly interest in sociological and literary interpretations of wisdom promises to enrich more conventional approaches. Perhaps all of these endeavors will clarify the manner in which ancient peoples achieved knowledge and explain the esteem in which learning was held.

---

[70]Ted Hildebrandt, "Proverbial Pairs: Compositional Units in Proverbs 10–29," *JBL* 107 (1988): 207-24; Raymond C. van Leeuwen, *Context and Meaning in Proverbs 25–27*, SBLDS 96 (Atlanta: Scholars Press, 1988).

[71]David W. Cotter, *A Study of Job 4–5 in the Light of Contemporary Literary Theory*, SBLDS 124 (Atlanta: Scholars Press, 1992) 97-105.

[72]*Studien zur israelitischen Spruchweisheit* (Neukirchen-Vluyn: Neukirchener, 1968).

[73]Claus Westermann, "Weisheit im Sprichwort," in *Schalom. Studien zu Glaube und Geschichte Israels. Alfred Jepsen um 70. Geburtstag*, ed. K. H. Bernhardt, *ATh* 46 (1971): 73-85; F. W. Golka, "Die israelitische Weisheitsschule oder 'des Kaisers neue Kleider'," *VT* 33 (1983): 257-70; "Die Königs-und Hofsprüche und der Ursprung der israelitischen Weisheit," *VT* 36 (1986): 13-36; "Die Flecken des Leoparden. Biblische und afrikanische Weisheit im Sprichwort," in *Schöpfung und Befreiung: für Claus Westermann zum 80. Geburtstag*, ed. R. Albertz (Stuttgart, 1989) 149-65; and Laurent Naré, *Proverbes Salomoniens et proverbes mossi*, Publications Universitaires Européens (Frankfurt am Main: Peter Lang, 1986).

[74]*Biblical Interpretation in Ancient Israel* (Oxford: Clarendon Press, 1985).

[75]Contrast the monograph on the book of Joel by Siegfried Bergler, *Joel als Schriftinterpret*, BzEATuAJ 16 (Frankfurt am Main: Peter Lang, 1988).

5 (1976)

Studies in Ancient Israelite Wisdom: Prolegomenon

In a sense, wisdom literature can be labeled an orphan in the biblical household. Virtually ignored as an entity until the beginning of this century, "wisdom" suffered the indignity of judgment by alien standards and the embarrassment of physical similarities to non-Israelite parents. In addition, she had a twin (Sirach and Wisdom of Solomon) who was in some circles even excluded from the privileged status of canonical authority, although none could deny her likeness to the more favored sister. Orphans, however, have a champion whose intentions none can frustrate. Perhaps it was inevitable, then, that this special orphan would become queen for a day, and possibly even Queen Mother.

The negative assessment of wisdom arose because it was difficult if not impossible to fit her thought into the reigning theological system. The verdict of G. Ernest Wright represents the dominant position for several decades: "The difficulty of the wisdom movement was that its theological base and interest were too narrowly fixed; and in this respect Proverbs remains near the pagan source of wisdom in which society and the Divine work in history played no real role."[1] In short, wisdom does not accord with the preconceived notion of theology as a recital of God's action in history. As a consequence of the inability to integrate wisdom into salvation history, Gerhard von Rad places wisdom at the end of the first volume of his *Old Testament Theology*[2] and gives it the title "Israel's Response." The inappropriateness of such a procedure has often been noted,[3] for wisdom cannot

---

[1]G. Ernest Wright, *God Who Acts* (1952) 104.

[2]The German edition appeared in 1957. The section has the title "Israel vor Jahwe," with "Die Antwort Israels" in parentheses.

[3]R. E. Murphy, "The Interpretation of Old Testament Wisdom Literature," *Int* 23 (1969): 290; R. B. Y. Scott, "The Study of the Wisdom Literature," *Int* 24 (1970): 41; A. M. Dubarle, "Où en est l'étude de la litterature sapientielle?," *ETL* 44 (1968): 417: "Hardly an apt title, for the wisdom writings, which have no reference to a covenant between Yahweh and his people, can scarcely be considered the response to a summons."

be viewed as an answer to the dominant theme of saving history. Walther Eichrodt's treatment of wisdom,[4] although less bound to a Procrustean bed constructed out of salvation history, offers little improvement, for there is little if any attempt to accept wisdom on her own ground. Rather, later developments in the realm of speculation about Dame Wisdom and the identification of wisdom and spirit are given the lion's share of attention. In one area, however, Eichrodt makes significant strides forward. I refer to his recognition of the importance of creation to the thought of the sages. Still, he views creation largely in terms of divine activity in history.

Even when conscious attention is diverted from the exclusively historical concern of so much Old Testament scholarship, wisdom still gives the impression of a foreign body. Thus Hartmut Gese writes: "It is well known that the wisdom literature constitutes an alien body in the world of the Old Testament."[5] This verdict is substantiated by reference to an absence of (1) a covenant relationship with God, (2) any account of the revelation at Sinai, and (3) a concept of Israel's special election and consequently of Yahweh's saving deeds for his people. Instead, wisdom is said to be directed toward the individual, and consequently to break down all national limits. Gese concludes that "from the point of view of Yahwism wisdom can only appear as wholly secular."[6] Horst D. Preuss moves a step farther afield.[7] The similarities between Israelite wisdom and that of her pagan environment lead him to view wisdom literature as devoid of revelatory content. For him wisdom is Israel's attempt to shape herself in the image of her neighbors, and the resulting creature is paganism pure and simple. The international character of wisdom, its universalistic appeal, is here understood as an inherent deficiency. Wisdom thus suffers the fate of one who is insufficiently Hebraic at a time when a premium is placed on Hebrew thought.

Still another factor contributed to wisdom's minor role in the drama of biblical interpretation. Fully half of her representatives (Sirach and Wisdom of Solomon) enjoy only deuterocanonical status. Inevitably Protestant and Jewish scholars were affected by the fact that there were substantial areas in which canonical and deuterocanonical texts agreed in form, vocabulary, and subject matter. Difficulty in making sharp distinctions between the two bodies of literature resulted in a leveling of the authority granted canonical wisdom.

Theological trends are born, and sooner or later are borne away. Today all three factors that deprived wisdom of her rightful dignity appear to be suffering an

---

[4]*Theology of the Old Testament,* vol. 2 (1967) 80-117.

[5]*Lehre und Wirklichkeit in der alten Weisheit* (1958) 2. Gese refers to the observation of Walter Baumgartner, *Israelitische und altorientalische Weisheit* (1933) 4, 10, 24, and "The Wisdom Literature," in *The Old Testament and Modern Study* (1951) 211.

[6]*Lehre und Wirklichkeit in der alten Weisheit,* 2.

[7]"Erwägungen zum theologischen Ort alttestamentlicher Weisheitsliteratur," *EvT* 30 (1970): 393-417, esp. 416.

eclipse.[8] History as the key to an understanding of the theological distinctiveness of ancient Israel has been found lacking,[9] and with this recognition comes renewed appreciation for those texts which offer a universalistic alternative.[10] The crisis brought on by an exclusive emphasis upon mighty acts of God in history has sent many scholars in search of another refuge. Wisdom's shade tree has suddenly become a haven for many, and the excitement of new discovery fills the air. So, too, do the excesses of exuberant converts. Roland Murphy sums up the situation well: "However, the trend to disregard the wisdom literature has reversed itself. Now the question would rather be, where has Old Testament wisdom failed to appear?"[11] The shrinking planet has renewed our appreciation for the understanding of reality expressed in traditions other than our own, so that wisdom's affinities with Egyptian and Mesopotamian texts has now become an asset rather than a liability. Furthermore, the ecumenical spirit and the sudden explosion of Roman Catholic scholarship in the wake of Vatican II have done much to offset the stigma of deuterocanonicity from which wisdom suffered.

But wisdom remembers yet another day when the discovery of an Egyptian text[12] and the proclamation of its originality at the expense of its Israelite manifestation led to a dozen years when all eyes were focused on her, without any substantial improvement of her status. The orphan, it follows, wears the royal crown, newly bestowed upon her, with supreme modesty. She knows the fickleness of scholarship.

Defining the Term Wisdom

Thus far I have spoken of wisdom as if her identity, if not her status, were a matter of common knowledge. But that is far from the case. Since the year 1908 when Hans Meinhold first recognized her separate existence,[13] she has stood largely

---

[8]See Brevard Childs, *Biblical Theology in Crisis* (1972).

[9]Bertil Albrektson, *History and the Gods* (1967) demonstrated the prevalence of this idea of divine action in history throughout the ancient Near East, thus undercutting the claim of uniqueness.

[10]Walter Brueggemann, *In Man We Trust* (1972) indicates the theological timeliness of wisdom for the contemporary believer, although his account is admittedly onesided.

[11]"The Interpretation of O.T. Wisdom Literature," 290.

[12]*The Instruction of Amenemopet*. Of the thirty sections in this Egyptian text, ten or eleven have more or less exact parallels in Prov 22:17–24:22.

[13]*Die Weisheit Israels in Spruch, Sage und Dichtung*. Meinhold's discussion of wisdom is remarkably modern in some ways. His formal analysis of the literary types (fable, parable, allegory, proverb, or sentence) and the development of the literature from original two-lined sayings to series and larger units differs little from the latest studies in this area (von Rad, for example). Likewise his understanding of the date of the collections in Proverbs, Qoheleth, and Job is remarkably similar to most of the works since that time. Even the numerical values of the names Solomon and Hezekiah as 375 and 136 (or 137) were thought to rest behind the number of proverbs in the two major collections ascribed to Solomon and the

as a mirror image of the scholar painting her portrait. At first almost ubiquitous in the Old Testament, she later settled down in five literary complexes (Proverbs, Job, Qoheleth, Sirach, Wisdom of Solomon), only in recent years taking up residence once again throughout the canonical literature.

The many attempts to define wisdom in ancient Israel have not been altogether successful. Von Rad, for instance, defines wisdom as broadly as possible. For him wisdom is "practical knowledge of the laws of life and of the world, based on experience."[14] At the other extreme is my own definition in terms of four kinds of wisdom: juridical, nature, practical, and theological. "Accordingly, one must distinguish between family/clan wisdom, the goal of which is the mastering of life, the stance hortatory and style proverbial; court wisdom, with the goal of education for a select group, the stance secular, and method didactic; and scribal wisdom, the goal being education for all, the stance dogmatico-religious, and the method dialogico-admonitory." Or again, wisdom is "the quest for self-understanding in terms of relationships with things people and the Creator . . . on three levels: (1) nature wisdom which is an attempt to master things for human survival and well-being, and which includes the drawing up of onomastica and study of natural phenomena as they relate to man and the universe; (2) juridical and *Erfahrungsweisheit* (practical wisdom) with the focus upon human relationships in an ordered society or state; and (3) theological wisdom, which moves in the realm of theodicy, and in so doing affirms God as ultimate meaning" even when denying a purpose to life.[15]

Men of Hezekiah. But the modernity of Meinhold's book is not limited to literary analysis. On the contrary, Meinhold believed that wisdom extended beyond the four major wisdom writings to include Gen 18 and related texts. Indeed, he defined wisdom so broadly that much of the book is devoted to a study of Israelite popular (folk) religion. Wisdom, he thought, takes for granted the prophetic adaptation of folk religion and divination. Meinhold also recognized the importance of Nature. He writes: "Yes, indeed, nature is a book that is rich in wisdom and instruction" (45). The international character of wisdom, too, was clear to Meinhold even at this time. He writes: "The walls of the Jewish church were not sufficiently high or strong to keep out the invasion of oriental and Greek wisdom." There is, however, one jarring note. Throughout the book Meinhold carries on a sharp polemic against Jewish egoism or self love, which he regarded as a theology that arose in the head rather than in the heart, and the individualism that rules out sonship in favor of servanthood.

[14]*Old Testament Theology*, 1:418, 428.

[15]"Method in Determining Wisdom Influence upon 'Historical' Literature," *JBL* 88 (1969): 130, 132. Ernst Würthwein, "Die Weisheit Ägyptens und das Alte Testament," in *Mitteilungen des Universitätsbundes Marburg* (1959), 69, describes wisdom literature similarly. He writes that these books are not only witnesses to an interesting cultural history, but constitute a theological debate over the deepest question of human existence, that of the understanding of God and man, the world and life. Von Rad's observation that "There is no knowledge which does not, before long, throw the one who seeks the knowledge back upon the question of his self-knowledge and his self-understanding" (*Wisdom in Israel*, 67) suggests that we are not as far apart as it appears at first glance. Compare also his additional

Other definitions fall somewhere between these two in their degree of specificity. Henri Cazelles focuses upon the anthropocentricity of wisdom. He writes: "Wisdom is the art of succeeding in human life, both private and collective. It is grounded in humanism, in reflexion on and observation of the course of things and the conduct of man."[16] Guy P. Couturier emphasizes the origins of wisdom as the significant factor, for in this initial stage of development wisdom is "the totality of life experiences transmitted by a father to his son, as a spiritual testament."[17] By far the briefest definition with which I am acquainted is that of Alexander W. Kenworthy, for whom wisdom is "the ability to cope."[18] Recognizing on the one hand the danger of being so general that the result is a tautology, and on the other so specific that the definition is useless or inaccurate, some authorities refuse to offer a definition. But a definite preunderstanding is operative, whether verbalized or not. The boldest step thus far has recently been taken by R. N. Whybray, who avoids the term "wisdom" in favor of "the intellectual tradition."[19] Whybray has discerned better than most the fact that all of these definitions founder at one point or another, for wisdom is an attitude, a body of literature, and a living tradition.

Even when it was deemed impossible to define wisdom, certain pejorative adjectives were used all too frequently. It is little credit to biblical scholars that the corrective came from Egyptologists, who readily discerned the inadequacy of such descriptions as eudaemonistic and humanistic.[20] Still it was left to an Old Testament interpreter, Hans Heinrich Schmid, to break through the additional fallacy of the adjective "nonhistorical."[21] With the discovery that every aphorism or didactic poem has its own history and participates in the historical features of the period in which it arose, the concept of internationalistic wisdom lost something of its cogency. The

---

comment, "In wisdom, however, man was *in search of himself* and took things into his own hands without being able to appeal to a specific, divine commission" (309, italics added).

[16]"Bible, sagesse, science," *RSR* 48 (1960): 42-43.

[17]"Sagesse babylonienne et sagesse israélite," *ScEccl* 14 (1962): 309.

[18]"The Nature and Authority of Old Testament Wisdom Family Ethics, with Special Reference to Proverbs and Sirach," diss., University of Melbourne, 1974.

[19]*The Intellectual Tradition in the Old Testament*, BZAW 135 (1974). He thus takes seriously the objections of W. L. Lambert, *Babylonian Wisdom Literature* (1960), 1, and H. Brunner, "Die Weisheitsliteratur," HO 1 (1952), 90-110. Lambert calls the term a misnomer in Babylonian literature, while Brunner attempts to avoid the word "Weisheit" altogether.

[20]Notably Henri Frankfort, *Ancient Egyptian Religion* (1948) and Hellmut Brunner, "Die Weisheitsliteratur," 90-110, for Egypt; and W. L. Lambert, *Babylonian Wisdom Literature*, vol. 1, for Mesopotamia.

[21]*Wesen und Geschichte der Weisheit*, BZAW 101 (1966). Schmid demonstrated that there was a three-act drama in the wisdom of Egypt, Mesopotamia, and Israel: (1) the formulation of a composition, clothed in a historical garment of a specific time and place, (2) the dogmatic, static solidification, and (3) the testing of maxims and the selection of the ones that accord with personal experience.

consequent search for the distinctive characteristics of wisdom literature that reflect particular histories is still in its infancy, but contains much promise. In any event, it is no longer possible to describe wisdom as eudaemonistic, nonhistorical, humanistic or international.

But the rejection of these terms must not conceal the fact that they have functioned usefully in the past. In truth, wisdom does ask what is good for man, and envisions the good as health, honor, wealth, and length of days. But this pragmatism which sought to secure the good life must be understood in terms of the concept of order ordained by God and entrusted to man's discovery and safekeeping. Thus one may rightfully claim that the emphasis upon man as the center of all values constitutes humanism. But the peculiar religious context within which such humanism flourished demands that one use some qualifying phrase like theological humanism.[22] Similarly, none can deny the universality of wisdom's language and concerns, the timeless problems of human existence and general observations about life. But one must go further to acknowledge the fact that these maxims and reflections are inevitably expressed in the nuances of the particular culture giving birth to the comprehensions of reality falling under the rubric "wisdom."

Both the correction of previous misunderstandings and the working definitions above suggest that significant progress has been made. The matter is further complicated, however, by the *sui generis* character of the book of Job, which has, prompted some scholars to exclude it from the category "wisdom literature."[23] One can appreciate the objections to this masterful enigma, for it does have elements of the lament.[24] Furthermore, it has imbibed the revelatory spirit to a far greater degree than any of the other literary complexes representative of wisdom thought. On the other hand, the book so closely resembles wisdom texts in Mesopotamian literature that one hesitates to exclude it from a discussion of Israelite wisdom. In addition, the subject matter is largely that which claimed the attention of the sages, so one cannot go astray, it seems, by including Job in wisdom literature. Hence I shall work from the assumption that wisdom literature consists of Proverbs, Job, Qoheleth, Sirach, Wisdom of Solomon, and a few Psalms. I am fully aware of the subjective nature of my decision; but this limited view of wisdom literature is more defensible than the equally subjective umbrella approach. The consequence of this minimal stance on my part is obvious: I shall not base any conclusions on such texts as Gen 1–3, the Joseph narrative, the succession narrative, Amos, Isaiah, Habakkuk,

---

[22]Roland Murphy, "The Interpretation of Old Testament Wisdom Literature," 292, opts for theological anthropology, while John F. Priest, "Humanism, Skepticism, and Pessimism in Israel," *JAAR* 36 (1968): 311-26, prefers "sociology" (315).

[23]The list of names is impressive, among whom are Paul Volz, Artur Weiser, Claus Westermann, Paul Humbert, and Heinz Richter.

[24]As seen most clearly by C. Westermann, *Der Aufbau des Buches Hiob*, BHT 23 (1956) and H. Gese, *Lehre und Wirklichkeit in der alten Weisheit*, 63-78.

Jeremiah, Esther, or the like, whatever the merit of the claim that these reflect wisdom thinking.

Queen for a Day: Posing the Problems

Earlier I alluded to the brief period when wisdom had maximum exposure, namely, the years between 1924 and 1936.[25] This unprecedented burst of activity, generated by the discovery of a definite literary relationship between the Egyptian *Instruction of Amenemopet* and Prov 22:17–24:22, set the stage for most subsequent research. The crucial issue, of course, was the question of affinities between a biblical text and an Egyptian Instruction. But still another issue came to the fore during this flurry of scholarship, namely, the structure of wisdom thought.[26] Now and then, too, some acknowledgment of a third set of problems surfaced. I have in mind the question of forms, which means not only the actual delineation of types of literature but also the setting in which they arose, took shape, and acted out their unique histories.[27] This period, then, set the questions occupying the minds of most scholars who labor in the area of wisdom today. The snail's pace we have followed can be discerned by working through Hugo Gressmann's pioneer study of 1925, Walter Baumgartner's two survey articles of 1933 and 1951, and R. B. Y. Scott's assessment of the current state of research in 1970.[28] Significant strides have been taken, nonetheless, and much recent work promises to open new paths leading to fruitful results. In discussing this fifty years of research I shall focus upon the three vital issues already mentioned: (1) affinities, (2) forms, and (3) structure.

---

[25]For bibliography, see Scott, "The Study of Wisdom Literature," *Int* 24 (1970): 23n.3, and Baumgartner, "Die israelitische Weisheitsliteratur," *TRu* 5 (1933): 259-61.

[26]Walther Zimmerli, "Zur Struktur der alttestamentlichen Weisheit," *ZAW* 51 (1933): 177-204.

[27]See Baumgartner, "Die israelitische Weisheitsliteratur," 270-79.

[28]Gressmann, *Israels Spruchweisheit im Zusammenhang der Weltliteratur*; Baumgartner, "Die israelitische Weisheitsliteratur," 259-88, and "The Wisdom Literature," 210-37; Scott, "The Study of the Wisdom Literature," 20-45. See also the surveys of H. H. Schmid, "Hauptprobleme der altorientalischen und alttestamentlichen Weisheitsliteratur," *STU* 35 (1965): 68-74; Dubarle, "Où en est l'étude de la littérature sapientielle?" *ETL* 44 (1968): 407-19; R. E. Murphy, "Assumptions and Problems in Old Testament Wisdom Research," *CBQ* 29 (1967): 101-12; James L. Crenshaw, "Wisdom," in *Old Testament Form Criticism*, ed. John H. Hayes, *TUMSR* 2 (1974), 225-64. R. B. Y. Scott gives another barometer by which to test the progress of scholarship in the area of wisdom, namely, the prominence of the term in periodic assessments of the state of O.T. studies ("The Study of the Wisdom Literature," 24-25). The fact that H. J. Hermisson has been asked to write a new history of research in wisdom literature for *Theologische Rundschau* bears testimony to the progress that has occurred in this area.

I. Affinities

The Bible itself recognizes Israel's kinship with her neighbors in the area of wisdom. Solomon's wisdom, it is claimed, surpassed that of all the peoples of the east and of Egypt (I Kgs. 4:30 M.T. 5:10). The study of the relationship between Israelite wisdom and that of other peoples of the ancient Near East is but a continuation of an ancient endeavor. The question of affinities, however, is greater than mere comparison of Israelite literature with similar texts from Egypt, Ugarit, and Mesopotamia. There is a significant amount of canonical literature outside the above-mentioned wisdom corpus that resembles certain elements of wisdom thought. This literature, too, raises the question of affinity. In short, the problem is both external to the canon and internal.

External Similarities

Israelite wisdom compares herself to that of Edom and Egypt. In the case of Edom little if anything has survived. Robert H. Pfeiffer has attempted to recover Edomitic wisdom in the Bible (Gen 1–11, Job, Qoheleth, Pss 88–89, Prov 30:1–31:9),[29] but the argument cannot compel assent inasmuch as it is purely hypothetical. Even if Job and his friends were non-Israelites, which in itself is debatable, that remarkable fact would not constitute proof that the author of the Book of Job was an Edomite. The patriarchal setting of the story may explain the choice of names and locality. It seems preferable, therefore, to maintain scepticism about the extent of Edomite wisdom within the Bible. Egyptian influence upon the Bible is yet another matter; the shadow of Egypt extends beyond Proverbs as far as Qoheleth and possibly Sirach.

Egyptian presence in the wisdom literature of Israel was acknowledged as early as 1909 by Hermann Gunkel.[30] The extent of this foreign impact was not perceived,

---

[29]"Edomitic Wisdom," *ZAW* 44 (1926): 13-25; Wisdom and Vision in the Old Testament," *ZAW* 52 (1943): 93-102.

[30]"Ägyptische Parallelen zum AT," *ZDMG* 63 (1909): 531-39. We now know about a dozen Egyptian works belonging to the category of wisdom literature. Among the better known Instructions are those of Ptahhotep, (for) Merikare, Amenemhet, Hordedef, Ani, Amenemopet, and 'Onchsheshonqy. Only a few characteristic emphases of these instructions may be noted here. Ptahhotep has a marvelous description of old age (cf. Qoh 12:1ff.), a warning against women, and an emphasis upon good speech. The Instruction for Merikare praises the upright of character over the sacrifice of an evildoer, and encourages silence as a goal of the wise man. Ani emphasizes silence, and warns against women. Similarly Amenomopet stresses the silent one, enjoins care for the widow, and condemns the carrying off of landmarks. 'Onchsheshonqy indicates how deeply religious this literature becomes toward the end of the empire. Two texts express the despair created by social turmoil: *A Dispute over Suicide* and *The Protests of the Eloquent Peasant*. Still other texts set forth the superiority of the scribal profession to all others (*In Praise of Learned Scribes*; *Satire on the*

however, until the epoch-making analysis of Paul Humbert.[31] There is general agreement that the Israelite author of Prov 22:17–24:22 borrowed from an Egyptian source eleven sayings of the original thirty, although the hypothesis of the opposite dependency has been revived relatively recently.[32] Egyptian influence upon Israelite wisdom extends beyond the actual appropriation of sayings from Amenemopet. It surfaces in such metaphors as that of God weighing the heart, righteousness as the foundation of the throne,[33] and possibly the garland of honor in Proverbs. Perhaps, too, Egyptian influence rests behind the satire on the professions in Sir 38:24–39:11, which echoes remarkably the Instruction of Duauf,[34] and the idea of a royal *Bekenntnis* that inspired the form of the early chapters of Qoheleth. Even more important, however, is the role of *ma'at* (order, justice),[35] which appears to have influenced the total thought of Israel's wisdom as well as the concept of a personified Wisdom. While many scholars argue for an Egyptian origin of the metaphor of the righteous man as a flourishing tree and the concept of תּוֹעֵבָה (abomination) of Yahweh, it is probable that these fall into the category of universal language.

Some would argue that the Israelite practice of addressing the pupil as בְּנִי (my son) derives from Egyptian Instructions, in which the father teaches his son all he

---

Trades) or describe scribal characteristics (*Divine Attributes of the Pharaoh*).

[31] *Recherches sur les sources égyptiennes de la littérature sapientiale d'Israël* (1929). Few today would endorse either the approach or the conclusions that Humbert drew, for they claim far too much and often fall into the area of universal human concerns. Still Humbert's work on the relationship between Amenemopet and the biblical Proverbs is decisive, in my estimation. In a concluding summary, Humbert writes that Egyptian influence can be found in the following: the certain borrowing from Amenemopet; literary forms (the fiction of royal authorship; collections of maxims; a more or less philosophical dialogue with occasional narrative; the satire of trades and a panegyric of the sage; the description of the misery of old age); rhetoric and style (familial language with the address of a father to his son; parallelism in the gnomic genre; frequent use of imperatives; synonymous, antithetic, and synthetic stichs; the role of comparison; etc.); expressions; images and conceptions (e.g., the heart being weighed in scales; the negative confession); pedagogical and moral ideas and principles of conduct (184).

[32] Etienne Drioton, "Sur le sagesse d'Aménémopé," in *Mélanges bibliques rédigés en honneur de André Robert*, ed. Henri Cazelles (1957), 254-80, and "Le livre des Proverbs et la sagesse d'Aménémopé," *Sacra Pagina*, ed J. Coppens et al. (1959) 1:229-41; R. J. Williams, "The Alleged Semitic Original of the Wisdom of Amenemope," *JEA* 47 (1961): 100-106; B. Couroyer, "L'origine égyptienne de la sagesse d'Aménémopé," *RB* 44 (1963): 208-24.

[33] H. Brunner, "Gerechtigkeit als Fundament des Thrones," *VT* 8 (1958): 426-28.

[34] Baumgartner, "Die israelitische Weisheitsliteratur," 266.

[35] In addition to Humbert's epoch-making study, see Christa Bauer-Kayatz, *Einführung in die alttestamentliche Weisheit*, BibS(N) 55 (1969) and *Studien zu Proverbien 1–9*, WMANT 22 (1966); Schmid, *Wesen und Geschichte der Weisheit*.

has learned about life.[36] Recent research into the early period of Israelite wisdom in which the leader of the clan instructed his sons in the means of getting the most out of life offers yet another explanation for this form of address, and renders the hypothesis of Egyptian origin both unnecessary and improbable.[37] Others have called attention to the contrast between wise man and hot tempered fool, which finds its parallel in the Egyptian opposite types of men (the silent one and the passionate man).[38] It is noteworthy, however, that "the silent one" or its equivalent does not become a technical term in Israel as it did in Egypt.

The Mesopotamian relationship with Israelite literature differs in kind if not in degree. The literary prototypes of Proverbs, Job, and Qoheleth point more to a commonality of ideas than to direct literary relationship. The problem of innocent suffering prompted literary treatment in early Sumerian times, and representatives of subsequent cultures tried their hand at it as well. The dialogue form prevails in the so-called "Babylonian Theodicy," while the theophany provides the solution in "I Will Praise the Lord of Wisdom." Furthermore, the scepticism surfacing in Qoheleth is even more extreme in "The Pessimistic Dialogue between a Master and his Slave." The impact of Mesopotamian thought upon Qoheleth may extend beyond this text to the Gilgamesh Epic, if the arguments of Oswald Loretz are trustworthy.[39] The case remains open, however; for the advice of Siduri to Gilgamesh, which reappears as a theme in Qoheleth, is probably a universal response to the reality of finitude. In essence, then; the influence of Mesopotamian wisdom thought upon that of Israel consists of literary form and content; in both, the Israelite authors surpassed the prototypes in excellence.

In what way did Israelites come into contact with Egyptian and Mesopotamian wisdom literature? Scholars have assumed the points of contact were the royal courts of Solomon and Hezekiah, where both foreign scribes and Israelite counselors would have worked, the latter of whom may have received their training in foreign courts. The evidence for an institution of wise men at the court is by no means conclusive, however. Those advocating such a function of the wise men must concede that the literary heritage of the sages is scarcely "courtly in subject matter

---

[36]William McKane, *Proverbs*, OTL (1970) has emphasized the importance of Egyptian Instructions for an understanding of Israelite proverbs. It is noteworthy that the Instruction of Ptah-hotep and the Instructions for King Meri-ka-re were intended for grown men upon whom the burden of counsel or rule had either fallen or was about to do so. This is in sharp contrast to the usual assumption that Israelite wisdom was intended for adolescents facing sexual temptation and needing to learn how to cope with life.

[37]Erhard Gerstenberger, *Wesen und Herkunft des "apodiktischen Rechts,"* WMANT 20 (1965).

[38]For a discussion of this emphasis upon the hot-tempered man and the silent one, see my essay "Method in Determining Wisdom Influence upon 'Historical' Literature," 133-34.

[39]*Qohelet und der alte Orient* (1964).

or viewpoint."[40] Perhaps the Canaanites mediated the wisdom tradition to ancient Israel.[41] Unfortunately literary remains from Ras Shamra have yielded minimal support for this theory,[42] for the epithet about El as wise and the lone wisdom text of Babylonian origin offer little encouragement to the notion that Canaanites mediated wisdom to Israel.

I have neglected to mention Greek influence until now; this fact alone points to progress made in wisdom research. Earlier scholars sought to demonstrate Greek influence upon Qoheleth and even saw Job as a Greek drama. But the much-discussed Graecisms in Qoheleth have dwindled to virtual nonexistence,[43] and the cyclic view of nature is now seen against a Near Eastern mythological background. Consequently, Greek presence in Qoheleth no longer functions as the decisive key to understanding its contents. A similar discrediting of Greek influence upon Job has taken place, for any dramatic theory founders since events in the book do not progress toward a climax. Stated differently, the only drama in Job is psychological. Of course Hellenism made a powerful impact upon Sirach and Wisdom of Solomon, both in literary form and in subject matter; yet even here restraint must be exercised. The Greek ideas are by no means taken over without much ado, as Johann Marböck[44] made abundantly clear for Sirach and Patrick Skehan and James Reese[45] demonstrated for Wisdom of Solomon. Greek impact is definitely discernible in, among other things, hymnic praise of the sun, the section in praise of great men, the epithet "He is the All," and belief in immortality (in Sirach), rhetorical devices such as *sorites*, the description of wisdom (in Wisdom of Solomon). In each case, Israelite authors have chosen what could be integrated into Hebraic thought with minimal distortion of the latter. Scholars are becoming much more appreciative today of the care with which foreign matter has been incorporated into Israel's own traditions.

---

[40]Gerhard von Rad, *Wisdom in Israel* (1972), 17. The role of the wise courtier in ancient Israel has recently been studied by Walter Lee Humphreys ("The Motif of the Wise Courtier in the Old Testament," diss., Union Theological Seminary, New York, 1970). Humphreys bases most of his analysis on analogy with Egyptian courtiers, and to some extent Sumerian and Babylonian. In the end he has to admit that "If material designed solely and exclusively for the courtier existed in Israel, it has not survived" (166).

[41]Henri Cazelles, "Les débuts de la sagesse en Israël," *SPOA* (1963), 27-39.

[42]Jean Nougayrol, "Les sagesses babyloniennes: études récentes et textes inédits," *SPOA*, 47-50.

[43]R. Braun, *Kohelet und die frühhellenistische Popularphilosophie*, BZAW 130 (1973) may reopen the whole question of Greek influence.

[44]*Weisheit im Wandel*, BBB 37 (1971).

[45]Patrick W Skehan, *Studies in Israelite Poetry and Wisdom*, CBQMS 1 (1971), 172-236; James M. Reese, *Hellenistic Influence on the Book of Wisdom and its Consequences*, AnBib 41 (1970).

Internal Influence

Ironically at the very moment that caution is the watchword in the area of extrabiblical influence scholars have thrown caution to the wind in assessing wisdom influence within the Bible itself. Various types of argument have been used to prove that sages left their mark outside the literary corpus usually attributed to them. These arguments consist of vocabulary, subject matter, and worldview. Unfortunately they labor under two distinct disadvantages: (1) they cannot escape circular reasoning, and (2) they neglect to take with sufficient seriousness the existence of a common linguistic stock and the universality of many concerns dealing with the human situation. In light of these two facts, wisdom scholarship is in dire need of methodological precision.

The futility of using vocabulary as the clue to wisdom's presence outside the wisdom corpus has been demonstrated recently by R. N. Whybray.[46] More cautious than most interpreters who adopt this method of discerning wisdom's impact upon the nonsapiential corpus, Whybray finally concedes the circularity of his approach. The problem can be stated quite simply: the wisdom corpus alone (itself the result of a subjective decision on the part of each interpreter) defines what is in the last resort "wisdom." The corollary of this minimal assertion is that nothing outside this corpus can be taken as specifically wisdom unless present also in wisdom texts. In short, a word or theme that occurs outside the wisdom corpus cannot be shown to be "wisdom" thought unless used in a purely technical sense. Rather, similarities may be examples of a common linguistic stock. In effect, the recent spate of books and articles arguing the presence of wisdom throughout the biblical canon fail to make their case precisely because of operative presuppositions as to what constitutes wisdom. If, then, the succession narrative is by definition wisdom, a study of thematic considerations in wisdom literature and in the "historical" account turns up nothing that contradicts the hypothesis and proves nothing unassumed from the outset.

Johannes Fichtner's arguments about Isaiah, lately revived and examined in much greater detail by J. William Whedbee and Joseph Jensen,[47] illustrate well the problem of working with vocabulary in common use throughout Israel. For Fichtner the only legitimate explanation for the shared vocabulary (parables, puns, wisdom terminology) was schooling on Isaiah's part at the feet of sages. Two things immediately come to mind. First, Isaiah may have borrowed the language of the wise men (if such it be) for his own purposes, so the hypothesis that the prophet had once been a sage is superfluous. Second, it is by no means certain that Isaiah used distinctive wisdom language. Mere usage of a few words referring to the

---

[46]*The Intellectual Tradition in the Old Testament* (1974).

[47]"Jesaja unter den Weisen," *TLZ* 74 (1949): 75-80; Whedbee, *Isaiah and Wisdom* (1971) and Jensen, *The Use of tôrâ by Isaiah*, CBQMS 3 (1973).

intellectual life of man or the mockery of Egyptian wise men, together with analogies taken from nature, cannot sustain the weight of the theory. Whedbee alters the situation little. The addition of the *hoi* oracles, the use of עֵצָה, and the highly dubious concept of a divine plan prove next to nothing about Isaiah and wisdom.

A much stronger case has been made by Jensen, whose painstaking analysis of the use of תּוֹרָה in Isaiah is in many ways an admirable exercise in caution. Yet even Jensen frequently falls prey to the circularity of reasoning that haunts wisdom research.

For example, Jensen's thesis is considerably weakened where wisdom influence is supported by an appeal to conjectured wisdom texts (Gen 2–3, Deuteronomy, and the like), dubious wisdom themes (possession of the land, way of the people) or everyday linguistic usage (father/son, שָׁמַר, abomination, listen). The procedure of labeling as wisdom any passage that presents special difficulty to the hypothesis of wisdom influence seems highly questionable (Mic. 3: 1), as does an appeal to such commonly shared virtues as concern for the *déclassé* or the idea of authority figures as teachers. Of course God (El) is wise, and together with the king and father, instructs man; but this didactic role of El, the king, and the father does not make them sages. Nor is it legitimate to claim that Isaiah called the wise men back to their genuine theology (wisdom comes from God rather than human investigation) and taught them that man possesses wisdom only as a charismatic gift. Literary dependency like this is no easy matter to document; one must be considerably more cautious in assessing Isaiah's impact upon the thought of the sages.

The situation differs little in regard to the claim that Amos was a product of the spiritual *Heimat* of the sages. First advanced by Samuel Terrien, this thesis was submitted to closer scrutiny by Hans Walter Wolff, who argued that Amos be understood against the background of ancient clan wisdom.[48] I have pointed out the weaknesses of this hypothesis elsewhere, and have sought to demonstrate yet another tradition, the theophanic, behind Amos' words.[49] Wolff's form critical analysis of certain rhetorical features of Amos requires further clarification of the nature of clan wisdom. To lend cogency to his thesis, Wolff needs to distinguish the wisdom of the clan from that of the Israelite court and to demonstrate Amos' similarities with the former. No such demonstration has yet appeared.

---

[48]Terrien, "Amos and Wisdom," in *Israel's Prophetic Heritage*, ed. B. W. Anderson and Walter Harrelson, 108-15 (1962); Wolff, *Amos' geistige Heimat* (1964) (ET: *Amos the Prophet*, 1973).

[49]Crenshaw, "The Influence of the Wise upon Amos," *ZAW* 79 (1967): 42-52; "Amos and the Theophanic Tradition," *ZAW* 80 (1968): 203-15.

A different kind of argument has been advanced to prove the influence of wisdom upon the Joseph story and the Succession Narrative.[50] This line of reasoning falls into categories of thematic interest or worldview. Gerhard von Rad thinks the view of history underlying the Joseph narrative is distinct from the usual understanding of divine action in history. In Gen 37, 39–50 God is depicted as the one who guides history to its destination by working in and through human beings. Such a sophisticated view of providence belongs, according to von Rad, to the worldview of the sages. Thus Joseph is understood as a model of instruction, and the story is said to function as an example of the wise man who overcomes all obstacles and rises to a position of prestige and power. Much in the story detracts from von Rad's theory, as I have attempted to show.[51]

Another example of thematic considerations as the determining factor in attempting to discern wisdom influence is R. N. Whybray's work on the Succession Narrative. Here, too, the manner of viewing God's control of human affairs is decisive. Whybray thus extends von Rad's own procedure one step farther, for the same concept of providence pervades the Joseph story and the account of the collapse of David's family. This view of direct wisdom influence upon the Succession Narrative suffers grievous difficulty, not the least of which is the role played by representatives of wisdom in the story. Whybray's refutation of my objections to his theory hinges upon what appears as subjective assessment of the climactic point in the story and the hypothesis of irony in key passages.[52] For these and other reasons I remain unconvinced.

Similar objections can be raised against H. J. Hermisson's discussion of wisdom and history.[53] While a plausible case can be made for an interest in history by the sages, one must remain alert to areas in which wise men merely share the perspectives of their day. Hence the parallels between the Succession Narrative and wisdom literature prove nothing more than that sages did not isolate themselves from humanity and create their own distinctive vocabulary in every instance. The interpreter must be careful not to assume that only a wise man could cultivate an interest in affairs of the court, the principle of retribution, human psychology, the

---

[50]Von Rad, "The Joseph Narrative and Ancient Wisdom," in *The Problem of the Hexateuch and Other Essays* (1966), 292-300; originally published in SVT 1 (1953); Whybray, *The Succession Narrative*, SBT 2nd ser. 9 (1968).

[51]Crenshaw, "Method in Determining Wisdom Influence upon 'Historical' Literature," 135-37.

[52]*The Intellectual Tradition in the Old Testament*, 89-91. Whybray suggests that my attack against his views is blunted by the fact that he has never said that wisdom was the exclusive background of the Succession Narrative. I find it difficult to understand in any other way the remark that the Succession Narrative was written by a teacher of the wisdom tradition (*The Succession Narrative*, 95).

[53]"Weisheit und Geschichte," in *Probleme biblischer Theologie*, ed. H. W. Wolff (1971), 136-54.

danger of pride, and the power of the spoken word at the right time. Ample evidence that prophets and priests responsible for instruction were not oblivious to these matters exists.

The attempt to understand Gen 1–11 or portions thereof as a product of wise men labors under the same difficulty.[54] While none can deny the presence of vocabulary describing human intelligence, or even of themes focusing upon the consequences of folly, all must admit that these so-called wisdom influences are not the exclusive domain of sages. The similarities between the view of history represented in Gen 1–11 and that of the Deuteronomistic history are too pronounced to be ignored. One could conceivably take note of this similarity and still maintain a wisdom background. No scholar has argued more persuasively for sapiential influence upon Deuteronomy than Moshe Weinfeld,[55] who maintains that a positive relationship between Deuteronomy and wisdom can be discerned in the type of humanism reflected in both and in the didactic characteristics of each literary complex.

Most extreme in his position regarding wisdom's influence is Shemaryahu Talmon,[56] who views Esther as a literary work of the sages. Talmon's thesis rests upon a perceptive analysis of the text of Esther, together with appeal to the role of Nadin in the Story of Ahiqar. Unfortunately Talmon neglected to take seriously numerous points of dissimilarity between Esther and wisdom literature. The result cannot persuade anyone who does not concede Talmon's assumptions, often unexpressed. Those who would see Daniel as a wisdom book are at one with Talmon in ignoring the weight of evidence tipping the scales precariously in a direction other than wisdom. In my view, Daniel's literary category is undoubtedly apocalyptic.

However, if von Rad were correct in his thesis that apocalyptic is the child of wisdom,[57] even this objection would be muted. Evidence does not appear to support von Rad in his endeavor to relate wisdom and apocalyptic. In my judgment, the emphasis upon the "times and seasons" in Daniel has little in common with the earlier wisdom concept of the appropriate time. The same must be said of Hans Peter Müller's hypothesis that mantic wisdom finds expression in Ugarit and in

---

[54]J. L. McKenzie, "Reflections on Wisdom," *JBL* 86 (1967): 1-9; L. Alonso-Schökel, "Motivos sapienciales y de alianza en Gen 2-3," *Bib* 43 (1962) 295-316 (repr: "Sapiential and Covenant Themes in Genesis 2-3," in *Modern Biblical Studies: An Anthology from Theology Digest*, ed. D. J. McCarthy and W. B. Callen [1967], 49-61).

[55]"The Origin of Humanism in Deuteronomy," *JBL* 80 (1961): 241-47; "Deuteronomy—The Present State of Inquiry," *JBL* 86 (1967): 249-62.

[56]"'Wisdom' in the Book of Esther," *VT* 13 (1963): 419-55.

[57]*Old Testament Theology*, vol. 2 (1965), 301-15; *Wisdom in Israel*, 263-83. See also John G. Gammie, "Spatial and Ethical Dualism in Jewish Wisdom and Apocalyptic Literature," *JBL* 93 (1974): 356-85.

Daniel.[58] Such skill in the magical art of incantation has nothing in common with Israelite literature. While the wise man in Egypt and in Mesopotamia was skilled in magical arts, the Israelite sage is never associated with ritual procedure prior to Sirach, and in fact seems antagonistic to the cult.[59]

I have not mentioned every attempt to discover wisdom influence outside the wisdom corpus. But similar objections could be raised to these forays into Exodus, Deuteronomy, Habakkuk, Jonah, Jeremiah, Ezekiel, and so forth.[60] They have not yet succeeded in breaking out of the circular reasoning or in giving sufficient weight to common linguistic stock. Even in rare instances when an author gave some attention to the methodological problems, little progress has been made in demonstrating direct influence. On the other hand, most of these scholars have taken huge strides toward the elucidation of the biblical text. Insights into the rhetorical devices, thematic considerations, and vocabulary of these so-called wisdom texts has been remarkable. The side effect of these strides is less fortunate; wisdom has ceased to have any distinctive meaning. Like Sheol in proverbial lore, its definition is constantly expanding.

In summation, there is at present both a trend toward caution in claiming extra-canonical dependency or positive relationships, and a readiness to find wisdom influence throughout the Bible. The latter reflects the exuberance of new discovery comparable to the period immediately following the identification of the positive relationship between Amenemopet and Proverbs. The excesses of such excitement must not blind scholars to the fact that many of their arguments presuppose what they attempt to demonstrate.

II. Forms

In contrast to research in the area of prophetic literature, very little work has been done on the literary forms characteristic of wisdom.[61] A problem confronts us at the outset: what is the simplest literary unit? It has generally been assumed that the basic unit is the one-line verse, consisting of two stichs in parallelism. Others, however, have argued for a two-line unit as original, often viewing the shorter unit as an inclusio or an abbreviated saying. Customarily various collections have been

---

[58]"Magisch-Mantische Weisheit und die Gestalt Daniels," *UF* 1 (1969): 79-94.

[59]Von Rad's excursus on "Wisdom and Cult" did little more than whet the appetite of those who are interested in the subject (*Wisdom in Israel*, 186-89). One of my students, Leo G. Perdue, is currently completing a Ph.D. dissertation on the role of the cult in wisdom literature.

[60]For bibliography, see Crenshaw, "Method in Determining Wisdom Influence upon 'Historical' Literature," 129n.1 and Whybray, *The Intellectual Tradition in the Old Testament*, 1-2n.1.

[61]Crenshaw, "Wisdom," 226-64 (esp. 229-62); von Rad, *Wisdom in Israel*, 24-50; Baumgartner, "Die literarischen Gattungen in der Weisheit des Jesus Sirach," *ZAW* 34 (1914): 161-98.

dated on the basis of the simplicity of the form, among other factors. Since Prov 1–9 contains several longer units, this seemed to confirm a later date than was thought to be the case in other collections of Proverbs. This dating procedure could then appeal to Sirach, which makes use of frequent paragraph units. Egyptian evidence seemed to confirm such a reading of the facts, until the discovery of the Instruction of ʿOnchsheshonqy. Unfortunately for the simple evolutionistic theory, the literary form of the very late ʿOnchsheshonqy is that of the simplest unit, presumably quite early.[62] In any event, one can no longer date a text simply on the basis of the complexity or simplicity of literary form.

Earlier critics also assumed the existence of popular proverbs prior to the literary stage of development. Appeal was made to such proverbs outside the wisdom corpus, particularly by Otto Eissfeldt in his fundamental study of the מָשָׁל.[63] Eissfeldt's thesis has been submitted to a devastating critique recently by Hermisson,[64] who denies the virtual existence of folk proverbs. Even the so-called folk proverbs give evidence of stylistic composition that is best explained as literary, Hermisson argues. Therefore, the proverbs are products of the schools and reflect the didactic interests and skills of wise men. R. B. Y. Scott has turned to this question in a recent study.[65] Scott rejects Hermisson's conclusions and argues once again for the existence of folk proverbs. While the final word has not yet been written, it seems Scott has the better argument. Consequently, I think one can move beyond the literary stage of proverbial composition to an oral period when the astute observer of human behavior and natural events coined brief maxims that represented the distillate of his knowledge.

If one assumes that the ground form of the proverb was a sentence composed of two members in parallelism, and that some of these proverbs are popular in origin, can he trace the development from one line to longer series within Proverbs? Johannes Hempel has addressed himself to this problem, with considerable success.[66] He writes of expansions by the use of the particle כִּי, the formulation of series, and of thematic and aesthetic units. Various means of linking several proverbs occur: a common letter (Prov 11:9-12b; 20:7-9, 24-26); the same introductory word (Prov 15:13-14, 16-17); the same idea (Prov 16); the use of an acrostic (Prov 31:10-31); paradoxical unity (Prov 26:4-5); and numbers (Prov 30:24-28). Thematic units characterize later proverbs (Prov 1–9) and Sirach, and poems aimed at aesthetics occur with relative frequency in Job, Qoheleth, and Wisdom of Solomon. While much progress has been made in tracing the emergence of larger units, little is

---

[62]W. McKane, *Proverbs* (1970), 117-50, particularly 122.

[63]*Der Maschal im Alten Testament*, BZAW 24 (1913).

[64]*Studien zur israelitischen Spruchweisheit*, WMANT 28 (1968).

[65]"Wise and Foolish, Righteous and Wicked," VTSup 23 (1972): 146-65.

[66]*Die althebräische Literatur und ihr hellenistisch-jüdisches Nachleben*, HLW (1930), 44-56.

known about the perplexing issue of intentional or accidental arrangement of the total sayings in Proverbs or Qoheleth. Zimmerli has recently taken up this problem, concluding that Qoheleth is neither a tractate with a discernible scope and single theme, nor a loose collection of sentences. In short, a decision cannot be made on the basis of the present state of knowledge, for evidence points in both directions.[67] In any case, the final semblance of unity has come a long way from the initial admonition that stood alone. The first undergirding of the authority of admonition by means of motive clauses, reasons, results, or threats has borne rich fruits.

Any investigation into the nature of the forms of wisdom literature must distinguish between constants and variables, or to use the language of Rudolph Bultmann, the constitutive and ornamental features of various forms.[68] I would designate as ornamental such features as paranomasia, rhetorical devices, antithesis, personification, and the like. Each of these enhances the literary character af the sentence, instruction, disputation, or whatever form is being embellished. These ornamental features have a dual purpose, the one aesthetic, and the other practical. Actually the two goals are intrinsically related: the more pleasing to eye or ear, the more persuasive the content. The constitutive features give to the literary piece its wisdom character, hence they cannot be dispensed with if the saying is to retain its integrity.

The basic constitutive form is the proverb, which finds expression either as a sentence or as an instruction. As William McKane has emphasized so convincingly, these two types of proverbs are characteristic of the wisdom literature of Egypt and Mesopotamia as well as of Israel.[69] While it is common knowledge that the instruction strives to teach a moral, even the former of these two, the sentence, may be didactic. I refer to admonition and prohibition, both of which rest on the cumulative authority of tradition. Furthermore, even when the sentence appears to have no didactic intent, one must recognize the effect of the didactic context into which it has ultimately been placed. Hence the sentence is seldom morally neutral. The instruction is consciously pedagogic, and utilizes both motive clause and warning to enhance its persuasive power.

Other constitutive forms, which I have discussed elsewhere,[70] consist of riddle, fable and allegory, hymn and prayer, disputation, autobiographical narrative, lists, and didactic poetry and narrative. The riddle, now in disintegrated form within wisdom literature, may lurk behind certain numerical proverbs and perhaps some of

---

[67]W. Zimmerli, "Das Buch Kohelet—Traktät oder Sentenzensammlung?," *VT* 24 (1974): 221-30.

[68]*Die Geschichte der Synoptische Tradition*, FRLANT 12 (1957), 73-74. H. H. Schmid takes over this distinction between constitutive and ornamental motifs (*Wesen und Geschichte der Weisheit*, 53-54) while H. J. Hermisson questions its value (*Studien zur israelitischen Spruchweisheit*, 139).

[69]*Proverbs*.

[70]Crenshaw, "Wisdom," 229-62.

the erotic proverbs where a *double entendre* is evident. Strictly speaking, the fable is missing from Israelite wisdom, although it abounds in Mesopotamian texts. But the allegory occurs in two places, the first, in germ only, in the description of a wife as a cistern (Prov 5:15-23); the other, fully developed, links up with the one in Prov 5 by referring to a woman as a well (Qoh 12:1-6). The central theme of this text, however, is the debilitating effect of old age. The wisdom hymn praises Yahweh as creator, and introduces the figure of wisdom personified. This hymn eventually sings the praises of wisdom alone and identifies wisdom and torah. A few Psalms (1; 49; 19; 33; 39; 104; 127) closely parallel such hymnic texts and are, therefore, designated Wisdom Psalms. Prayers within wisdom literature contain a strong didactic element; but this didacticism does not distinguish them as a wisdom form, for the doxology of judgment outside wisdom literature makes frequent use of didactic prayers. The disputation consists of a mythological introduction, a debate between friends, and a divine resolution. This is precisely the form of Job, although other elements are present (legal terminology, cultic laments). A variant of the disputation, specifically the "imagined speech," occurs in a number of wisdom texts. The autobiographical narrative (reflexion? confession?) is found in the early chapters of Qoheleth and in Proverbs (4:3-9; 24:30-34). I would suggest that the autobiographical narrative functioned as a certificate of credentials for the head of a school. The presence of onomastica or lists in Israelite wisdom is not certain. There is some evidence, nevertheless, that certain passages in Job and Sirach rest upon onomastica, and Wis 7:17-20 can be understood as a brief list of curricular subjects in Israelite schools. Finally, didactic narrative (Prov 7:21-23), problem poetry (Ps 49), and historical retrospect (Sir 44–50; Wis 10–19), although resembling literature outside the wisdom corpus, have been used with great power by the sages.

So far it has not been possible to ascertain the sociological setting of different literary types. Much recent discussion has centered on wisdom's existence in the period of the Israelite clan. Erhard Gerstenberger has sought to show a close connection between apodictic law and the wisdom of the clan.[71] He places emphasis upon the admonitory style of the father, which resembles absolute prohibition. Against this explanation for the origin of wisdom, Wolfgang Richter has sought to demonstrate the existence of a group ethic rather than a clan ethic.[72] According to Richter, there is a fundamental difference between negatives with לֹא and those with אַל. Each, therefore, reflects a different ethos. Yet a third emphasis comes from Hermisson, who argues for the existence of a school in ancient Israel.[73] Wisdom literature would then be viewed as compositions by professional sages for use in the instruction of other wise men. The evidence for each of these positions is meager; as a result it seems impossible to speak in more than probabilities. Still the balance

---

[71] *Wesen und Herkunft des 'apodiktischen Rechts'.*
[72] *Recht und Ethos*, SANT 15 (1966).
[73] *Studien zur israelitischen Spruchweisheit*, 113-36.

of probability inclines toward the theory of clan wisdom literature. The argument for a temple school has little to commend it, in my view, and rests upon questionable analogy with Egypt and Mesopotamia. Whybray's recent examination of the evidence places a huge question mark over the theory of an Israelite school during the period of the monarchy, and with it, the idea of court wisdom.[74] If he is correct, it will be necessary to reformulate the customary description of wisdom's development during Solomon's reign.

The Solomonic "Aufklärung"

Gerhard von Rad argued that the era of Solomon was revolutionary in character, representing a sharp break with the past. For him, as for Martin Buber, earlier Yahwism was wholly sacral; the Solomonic period abandons all cultic associations in favor of a radically secular understanding of reality. Previously God's action was thought to take place as a mighty intervention and was restricted to a sacred place, charismatic figure, or covenanted people. Now, however, a breath of fresh air flows through Solomon's court. For the first time man becomes aware of himself as man. The discovery of his rational powers and new dimensions of experience effects "a concentration upon the phenomenon of man in the broadest sense, his potentialities and limitations, his psychological complexity and profundity."[75] Providence is now revealed to the eyes of faith in every sphere of life, private or public, and God is thought to work behind the scenes, guiding the course of human events toward the goal which he alone perceives. The impetus for this revolution, so von Rad thinks, was David.

Walter Brueggemann has attempted to develop more fully this understanding of David as the catalyst of the Solomonic enlightenment.[76] He interprets various incidents in the story of David as indicative of spiritual maturity rather than shrewd conduct. The audacity of eating sacred bread is said to reflect David's new idea of the holy; his strange behavior after the death of his infant son is an act of profound faith; the pouring out of the water acquired at such great peril is a sacral act

---

[74]*The Intellectual Tradition in the Old Testament*, 33-43. Even the evidence for schools in Egypt and in Mesopotamia is far from clear; see the discussion by Jacobsen, Landsberger, Wilson, Albright, Oppenheim, Speiser, Grene, Kramer, Parker, Seele, Hoselitz, Gelb, and Güterbock in *City Invincible: A Symposium on Urbanization and Cultural Development in the Ancient Near East*, ed. Carl H. Kraeling and Robert M. Adams (1960), 94-122. The connection between wisdom and schools has been affirmed by H. J. Hermisson: "Israelite wisdom has its center, its origin, and its places of cultivation in the Israelite school" (*Studien zur israelitischen Spruchweisheit*, 192) and by J. J. Van Dijk: "It is . . . highly likely that the school, if it did not actually create wisdom literature, held it in high esteem" (*La sagesse suméro-accadienne* [1953], 23).

[75]*The Problem of the Hexateuch and Other Essays*, 69-74, 202-204.

[76]*In Man We Trust*, 29-47.

expressing a bond with those who risked their lives to satisfy his thirst; the blank check handed David's family is God's way of assuring him that he is free by virtue of God's trust in him.[77]

Both von Rad and Brueggemann think of the Solomonic era as a literary revolution. Scribes, foreign and domestic, grace the court of Solomon, and literature flourishes. Brueggemann even views the Yahwist as David's theologian,[78] and interprets much of the Yahwistic narrative against the background of the Davidic era. Von Rad, on the other hand, insists that the Succession Document was composed prior to the Yahwistic narrative. The latter, he contends, must be understood in terms of (1) the hidden activity of God and (2) the near-fulfillment in David of the ancient tribal territorial claims about the extent of Israel's dominion in the land of promise. Von Rad also sees the Solomonic era as a blossoming of economic and cultural life, leading to an international culture. As an expression of this openness to the world of the ancient Near East, a strong institution of wise men emerges at Solomon's court. In this environment the king becomes proficient—and even creative—in the art of composing proverbs and songs, according to von Rad. Here he appeals to Albrecht Alt's interpretation of the tradition about Solomon's wisdom as encyclopedic knowledge (onomastica) expressed for the first time in poetic form.[79]

This radically altered way of looking at divine activity was not without its hidden dangers, however. Von Rad hints at the chilling blast of scepticism that brought in its wake, though belatedly, the pessimism of Qoheleth. This crisis in the intellectual spirit, and its relationship to the Solomonic era of enlightenment, received its classic expression in an essay by Kurt Galling.[80] Once the action of God is left to the eyes of faith, it soon becomes easy to deny altogether any divine concern for the welfare of mankind. The result is the discovery of life *in tormentis*.

It stands to reason, von Rad argues, that the wise men at the court of Solomon would need an educational model by which to communicate their ideal to potential courtiers. Such a model exists, von Rad claims, in the Joseph story. Here is mani-

---

[77]Still another reading of the incidents is possible, and in my opinion more likely. Thus I see the first incident as David's cunning to save his skin. The second clearly implies that David cringed in fear for seven days, while the pouring out of the precious water was a shrewd move to bind himself more closely to his comrades. The so-called blank check in 2 Sam 7 expresses the vested interests of a priestly group. Finally, David's freedom derives from the power of chieftainship and royalty, not from a knowledge that he is trusted by God.

[78]"David and His Theologian," *CBQ* 30 (1968): 156-81.

[79]"Die Weisheit Salamos," *TLZ* 76 (1951): 139-44. Much has been made of the lists as an ordering of reality. This function is considered doubtful by A. Leo Oppenheim, *Ancient Mesopotamia* (1964), 248.

[80]*Die Krise der Aufklärung in Israel*, 1952. My colleague Lou H. Silberman has pointed out to me the heavy freight borne by the word "Aufklärung." He questions the wisdom of using such a philosophical term to describe the ancient Israelite scene.

fested the educational ideal of early wisdom (Prov 10:1–22:16; 22:17–24:22; 25–29). Von Rad thinks that a court setting for this wisdom is beyond question: "None would dispute the fact that this early wisdom literature belongs within the context of the royal court, and that its principal aim was to build up a competent body of future administrators."[81] Joseph, then, manifests this wisdom ideal of self-control, modesty, intelligence, restraint, godly fear. He demonstrates, among other things, the ability to speak well at the decisive moment, give sound advice, and function effectively at the king's court. Von Rad finds confirmation of this interpretation in the theological prespective of the Joseph story, which tolerates the cult and is sparing in mentioning God. Twice the narrator brings God into the picture, each time at crucial junctures (Gen 45:8 and 50:20). In each of these, good wisdom-theology surfaces, he claims. In short, man proposes but God disposes[82]; the opposition between divine economy and human intention is a central issue in wisdom theology. The chill factor is present, however, according to von Rad; in this regard he points to the element of resignation that undercuts the importance of human activity. In support of his hypothesis, von Rad also claims certain characteristics of normal Israelite thought are absent (historicopolitical interests, a cultic etiological motive, and salvation history), thus indirectly confirming a wisdom background for the Joseph story. He concludes: the "Joseph story, with its strong didactic motive, belongs to the category of early wisdom writing."[83]

This view of the Joseph narrative overlooks a number of essential facts which I have enumerated in the course of a study on methodology in determining wisdom influence upon "historical" literature.[84] The cogency of the argument prompted George Coats to attempt a compromise between the two positions.[85] He proposes to break down the Joseph story into at least two versions, the earlier kernel consisting of Gen 39–41. This story within a story, Coats thinks, does reflect wisdom concerns: "At each stage the focus is on Joseph's skill as a responsible administrator."[86] The emphasis, according to Coats, is upon proper use of power by an administrator already in office, not the means of rising to it. While Coats hesitates to assert wisdom as the sole background for this kernel, he thinks the hypothesis highly probable. Less certain about the existence of a school, however, Coats prefaces his remarks about the Solomonic enlightenment with the adjective "so-called." In the end he minimizes the importance of wisdom, and describes the purpose of the narrative in much broader terms. This threefold purpose includes the

---

[81]*The Problem of the Hexateuch and Other Essays*, 293-94.

[82]K. Sethe, "'Der Mensch denkt, Gott lenkt' bei den alten Aegyptern," in *Nachrichten der Gesellschaft der Wissenschaft* (Göttingen, 1925), 141ff.

[83]*The Problem of the Hexateuch and Other Essays*, 299.

[84]Crenshaw, "Method in Determining Wisdom Influence upon 'Historical' Literature," 135-37.

[85]"The Joseph Story and Ancient Wisdom: A Reappraisal," *CBQ* 35 (1973): 285-97.

[86]Ibid., 289.

tracing of the life of a family through tragic division to reconciliation, the characterizing of political officials who hold the power of life and death, and the positing of hope for one who was believed to be beyond hope.

The ramifications of this theory about a Solomonic enlightenment are manifold. They affect radically the reconstruction of a history of wisdom literature and tradition. Since first advanced as an hypothesis—and without any compelling proof—this theory has become an operative datum for most discussions of wisdom. The time has come, it seems, to ask what evidence exists for the theory of a Solomonic enlightenment. Anticipating the results of this inquiry, there is scant evidence indeed.

The first thing that must be said is that traditions about Solomon's vast wisdom are legendary in character, as R. B. Y. Scott has made clear.[87] Furthermore, references to Solomon in the headings of various collections in Proverbs do not take us back prior to the time of Hezekiah. In essence, then, the only support for a Solomonic enlightenment is inferential; it is based on an analogy with Egyptian court life. While such a view of the facts may be historically probable, one must recognize that nothing demands the existence of an institution of wise men at Solomon's court. Nor is Alt's interpretation of the Solomonic legend, which Anton Causse has called "le mirage salomonien,"[88] the only possible one. The legend may have preceded the actual selection of proverbial collections to be canonized. We simply do not know whether other collections existed or not; Israel at one time may have had proverbs dealing with birds, trees, snakes, and the like, just as she apparently had riddles, now lost to posterity.

Second, there is serious doubt that Israel's literature prior to Solomon can be characterized as pan-sacral. Von Rad overworks this facet of his theory. It is puzzling that the largely secular Samson narrative is overlooked in his argument.[89] These legends are, of course, difficult to date; but the traditions must surely antedate the period of Solomon. In effect they suggest that alongside sacral narratives like the story of King Saul, of which von Rad makes so much, there were also stories of a different sort that breathed a free, secular spirit. There is absolutely no compelling evidence that the Joseph story, the Succession Narrative, and the Yahwist come from the time of David and Solomon. This, too, is an inference, albeit a plausible one. D. B. Redford's analysis points to some of the difficulties in dating the Joseph story at this time[90]; and if Martin Noth is correct that the

---

[87]"Solomon and the Beginning of Wisdom in Israel," VTSup 3 (1960): 262-79.

[88]"La Sagesse et la propagande juive à l'epoque perse et hellenistique," *Werden und Wesen des Alten Testament*, BZAW 66 (1936): 148-54.

[89]For an analysis of this narrative, see my essay in ZAW 86 (1974): 470-504, entitled "The Samson Saga: Filial Devotion or Erotic Attachment?"

[90]D. B. Redford, *A Study of the Biblical Story of Joseph (Genesis 37-50)*, VTSup 20 (1970).

essentials of the Yahwistic narrative existed much earlier than Solomon, then strong doubt is cast upon von Rad's claim that this narrative demonstrates an enlightenment during Solomon's reign. In short, von Rad's theory about literary development from sacral to secular and the sequence of Joseph story, Succession Document, to Yahwist is a doubtful hypothesis. It deserves to be treated as such.

It is highly interesting that von Rad himself insists on making a sharp distinction between the Yahwistic narrative and wisdom. In essence, his student, H. J. Hermisson, was merely carrying von Rad's line of reasoning to its ultimate conclusion.[91] Still von Rad recoils from such a positive relationship between wisdom and history, and insists that the differences are significant.

Class Ethic

A corollary of belief in the existence of an active wisdom movement under Solomon's sponsorship is the emergence of a class ethic. Whoever opts for the existence of class ethics within wisdom literature must face up to certain difficulties.[92] In the first place, a folk origin of aphorisms would suggest that the proverbs reflect the ethos of the total society rather than that of a distinct group within it. Second, Scott's claim that the maxims do not participate in a single worldview or setting, if true, would mean that the assumption of a class ethic is ill conceived. Again, the experiential base of wisdom sayings argues against a class ethic, for the saying can only be valid if it takes into account the totality of experience insofar as it is possible to do so.

One way to skirt these problems is to define class ethic rather broadly as the ethos of a specific social group. As Brian Kovacs has discerned, the tacit assumption of the form criticism enterprise amounts to precisely this sort of thing.[93] A number of scholars have attempted to view the wise men as landed gentry.[94] This presumption of an upper leisure class is based on analogy with the scribal tradition in later Judaism, which has recently been clarified at many points by Ephraim Urbach.[95] The view is also supported by the fact that the wise men seem not to have possessed either the power or the inclination to correct injustice. Such is surely the case in Qoheleth. While this hypothesis of the gentleman farmer as the author and

---

[91]"Weisheit und Geschichte," 126-27; von Rad, *Wisdom in Israel*, 294-95; see also John L. McKenzie, "Primitive History: Form Criticism," *SBLSP* 1 (1974): 87-99.

[92]On class ethic, see Brian Kovacs, "Is There a Class-Ethic in Proverbs?," in *Essays in Old Testament Ethics*, ed. James L. Crenshaw and John T. Willis (New York, 1974), 171-89, and Hermisson, *Studien zur israelitischen Spruchweisheit*, 94-96.

[93]Kovacs, "Is There a Class-Ethic in Proverbs?," 176. I am indebted to my student Brian Kovacs for the following discussion.

[94]Robert Gordis, "The Social Background of Wisdom Literature," *HUCA* 18 (1943/1944): 77-118.

[95]Ephriam E. Urbach, "Class-Status and Leadership in the World of the Palestinian Sages," in *Proceedings of the Israel Academy of Sciences and Humanities* (1966) 2:1-37.

transmittor of wisdom literature is plausible, there is no great emphasis in "the intellectual tradition" on the special concerns of the wealthy farmer.

This leads to a second possible definition of class ethic, that of a restricted in-group morality. The wise men make a sharp distinction between the sage and the fool; the latter has rejected wisdom and is consequently wicked, an agent of chaos. Two different standards apply, then, to the in-group and to outsiders. But this does not necessarily imply closure; Kovacs points out that there are demonstrations of openness in the concern for the déclassé (the widow, the fatherless, the poor, the oppressed, the powerless).[96] Furthermore, the inner disposition was deemed most significant. This concern for intentionality gave the sage a stance from which to attack popular religion in which the deed alone was thought important. Herein lies an element of protest against the status quo. But the wise man was not revolutionary; indeed, there are indications of discrete silence in the face of wrong. I refer to the ambivalent attitude of the sage toward bribery.

What, then, of the professional code of the wise? This brings us to a restrictive definition of class ethic. Clearly there evolves from the literature of the wise a pattern of behavior that is calculated to assure the good life. But can one argue that this code of conduct is intended solely for members of a wisdom establishment? In favor of this narrow view of the code of conduct is the internationalism of wisdom, the high level of continuity among Egyptian, Israelite, and Mesopotamian wisdom texts. Such a shared worldview would seem to argue for a special class with undeniable self-consciousness. On the other hand, there is nothing that demands such an exclusive view of the ethical code in wisdom literature, while much points to a concern for the instruction of young people in general. In this regard it is worth noting that Job uses a cultic text as the standard by which his life is measured (Job 31).[97] Can one really imagine a sage doing that if he thought his own group possessed an exclusive code of ethics?

In short, there is evidence of class ethic in wisdom literature, but not in the narrow sense of the term. Consequently, Kovacs' conclusion merits close attention: "Court and king sayings, instruction and discipline, an ethic of restraint, observance of proprieties, and a system of authority suggest a professional ethic of administrators or officials."[98] My own inclination is to play down the administrative role of wise men, and in its place to put major emphasis upon family ethics. But even the latter type of wisdom had its own view of order, its authoritative spokesman, and its sense of propriety. Perhaps it is even possible to discern three different "class ethics," those of the family, the court, and the "teacher." But, of course, the broader definitions are operative here.

---

[96]Kovacs, "Is There a Class-Ethic in Proverbs?," 178.

[97]Georg Fohrer, "The Righteous Man in Job 31," *Essays in Old Testament Ethics*, 1-22.

[98]"Is There a Class-Ethic in Proverbs?," 186.

Who, then, were the transmittors of the wisdom tradition? If there may not have been an established court wisdom, and if even the existence of an institution "the wise men" is dubious, who is responsible for the compilation and preservation of wisdom literature? Must we resort to the scepticism of R. N. Whybray for whom there is only an intellectual tradition? Perhaps, but Whybray's answer takes us no further than previous theories: it merely recognizes our inability to say precisely who the wise men were.

Can we even speak of a wisdom *movement*, as if there were representatives with common goals and aspirations? Does wisdom represent a fundamentally different phenomenon from prophecy, for example? Such questions indicate how little we really know about wisdom. Much literature has been written about the alleged upper class bias of the wise men, but the evidence for this interpretation of the sages was largely inferential. Robert Gordis' fundamental study of this problem, now supplemented by Urbach's research into the social status of the wise men during the Pharisaic period, is suggestive, but our knowledge of sociological conditions in ancient Israel is still in its infancy.

In short, it is at present neither possible to write a chronological history of the development of wisdom literature nor to place each of the forms within its proper setting. Besides this inability to discern absolute dates and functions of the literature, it is impossible to write a history of the institution or persons responsible for compiling and transmitting the literature. Their origins are obscure, as is the overall development of the tradition. We do not even know whether wise men functioned in each generation as royal advisors, or if they ran a school for the elite members of Israelite society. In actual fact, we do not know who either could have or would have read the literature of the sages, or for what purposes.

III. Structure

The fundamental exploration of the structure of Israelite wisdom took place more than forty years ago. In it Walther Zimmerli[99] underlined the anthropocentric character of wisdom thought, together with its nonauthoritative tone. The wise man, he argued, began with the question: "What is good for man?" In contrast to the powerful prophetic word, which carries the authority of its divine source, the advice (עֵצָה) of the wise man aimed at compelling assent rather than obedience. Zimmerli noted that the wise man refused to appeal to the decrees of creation, but depended solely on the power of persuasion.

---

[99]"Zur Struktur der alttestamentlichen Weisheit." Zimmerli's understanding of wisdom as anthropocentric has been challenged by Hermisson and Schmid. The former writes that man is not the measure of all things, but is measured against the world in which he is placed (*Studien zur israelitischen Spruchweisheit*, 150-51). Schmid, on the other hand, claims that the center is not man but cosmic order, not anthropology but cosmology (*Wesen und Geschichte der Weisheit*, 197).

Subsequent research has called the nonauthoritative nature of the wisdom saying into question.[100] Instrumental in this eroding of the ground upon which Zimmerli stood has been the examination of the spiritual structure of biblical aphoristic literature, the study of the meaning of the root עֵצָה, and the sociological setting within which the wise man uttered his word. Perhaps a useful distinction can be made between the saying addressed to a potential member of the wise men and a word spoken to an outsider. The former saying would, of course, carry the heavy weight of tradition and personal authority. On the other hand, when a wise man confronted those who did not subscribe to the worldview of the sages he had to depend upon his intellectual powers of rational argumentation. One could almost say that clan wisdom would be highly authoritative in that the patriarch speaks to the members of his family, whereas court wisdom depends completely upon the power of logical and psychological persuasion.

In Zimmerli's pioneer study of the structure of wisdom the concept of order does not assume the significance it has in later works. Many scholars today have taken over the Egyptian concept of *ma'at*[101] and define Israelite wisdom in terms of an attempt to discover and maintain order in the personal and social arenas of life. The wise man, according to this understanding, is one who both *creates* order and brings his life into harmony with the *established* order of the universe.

Now the belief in order implies design or purpose, from which man can profit. Much has recently been made of the concept of timeliness or propriety as the goal of all wisdom. The wise man is one who knows the right time and place, the person who exercises propriety. Thus one finds outright contradictions in proverbial sayings, once even juxtaposed (Prov 26:4-5). They are preserved because of a desire to consider all variables in a given situation. Both statements are true, and one must choose which of the two is called for by the situation itself.

The willingness to face up to contradictions arises out of the fact that wisdom is an open system, although a tendency toward frozen dogma in the area of retribution certainly developed. But the sage knew that there were limitations to the comprehension of reality, both in terms of intellectual capacity and divine inscrutability. Ultimately the wise man or woman had to concede the poverty of intellect, for "man proposes but God disposes" (Prov 16:9; 19:21; 21:30-31). The ever present incalculable ingredient to every experience promoted an openness to various possibilities and a recognition of one's limits.

Undergirding the wise person's view of reality was a profound theological conviction. Because reality was created to reward virtue and punish vice, the sage was remarkably at home in the world—so long as the conviction of justice

---

[100]Crenshaw, *Prophetic Conflict*, BZAW 125 (1971): 116-23, esp. excursus B: "'*ēṣâ and dābār*: The Problem of Authority/Certitude in Wisdom and Prophetic Literature."

[101]Most notably Schmid, *Wesen und Geschichte der Weisheit*, and *Gerechtigkeit als Weltordnung*; C. Bauer-Kayatz, *Einführung in die alttestamentliche Weisheit*.

prevailed. In Israel this religious orientation found expression in the recurring theme, "The fear of the Lord is the essence of wisdom." Even outside Israel, both in Egypt and in Mesopotamia, there was a tendency toward monotheism within wisdom thought. Furthermore, this religious sentiment extended beyond the external cultic ritual, reaching as far as the inner motivation. The absence in Israelite wisdom of a concept of divine grace was felt most keenly by Qoheleth, whose religious perspective is devoid of any positive relationship. The cleft between practical maxims based on experience and knowledge acquired through revelation was eased gradually in a process of theologization that is described by J. Coert Rylaarsdam in a profound little book.[102]

This process of theologization is by no means a simple one. In all likelihood it came about in three stages. The first of these is the introduction of the notion of the fear of the Lord as the first principle of wisdom. Much early wisdom appears to have been remarkably "secular" in mood and content; its fundamental purpose was to encapsulate precious observations about reality for the benefit of posterity. The subject matter is largely domestic; agrarian interests and natural phenomena abound. Still those who accumulated this valuable insight into the way things hold together belonged to the people of the Lord, and thus saw themselves as a covenanted people. Small wonder that they came to express their faith in God and in the course of daily happenings in one and the same breath. Indeed the admonitions, motivations, and threats were soon strengthened by appeal to a common faith. Such appeal is no radically new departure, for it links up with the ancient concept of order bestowed upon the universe by a deity who rewards virtue and punishes vice.

The second stage of religionization is the attempt to deal with the difficult problem of divine presence in the world of human discourse. How can it be that truth emerges from an observation of nature and culture? Is it possible that revelation occurs within ordinary human decisions apart from the prophetic oracle, priestly ritual, or poetic vision? The representatives of the wisdom tradition were convinced their observations about reality touched base with the ultimate truth possessed only by God. They expressed this conviction in terms of divine presence, hypostasis. This heavenly figure, Wisdom, enlightens the sages by dwelling in their midst. By this means the sages of Israel managed to salvage something of the ancient Near Eastern fertility concept, namely the highly desirable bride who is more at home in the divine than in the human sphere.

A third kind of theologization came to be employed by Jesus ben Sira. I have in mind the identification of torah with wisdom. Once this equation has been made, it is possible to incorporate the sacred history of Israel into the wisdom tradition. Accordingly, ben Sira goes one step beyond identifying torah and wisdom; he sings

---

[102]*Revelation in Jewish Wisdom Literature*, 1946.

a hymn in praise of the great men in Israel's sacred past. Furthermore, in him one sees the sage at worship: prayers and psalms abound in his collected sayings.[103]

The speculation about Dame Wisdom in Prov 8, Job 28, Sir 24, and Wis 7 may possibly be integrally related to the struggle over divine injustice. In my opinion, however, hypostasis responds to *two* factors: the problem of theodicy and the need to relate wisdom thought to Yahwistic faith. Whybray puts the matter this way: hypostasis was not intended to bridge a gulf between God and man, but between wisdom and Yahwism.[104] Into this void came Dame Wisdom, who seems to be modeled upon the figure of *Ma'at* in Egyptian speculation. The personification of wisdom functions to bestow authority upon wisdom, and to demonstrate divine concern for mankind. The latter was a particularly vexing problem throughout much of the period during which wisdom literature flourished. This claim of a personification of God in wisdom, although not fully developed until Wisdom of Solomon, affirms that God has placed in the human mind a point of contact between heaven and earth, and that this rational principle dwells among the people of Israel in a special manner.

Such a process of religionization exacerbated old problems while softening still others. The assumption of divine control over human affairs to assure the triumph of virtue became more and more difficult to maintain. While some sages closed their eyes to the grim reality of innocent suffering, others wrestled with the problem mightily. Indeed "the Lord of the Old Testament was not one to be painted into a corner by the persistent formulations of the sages."[105] Thus the authors of Job and Qoheleth champion the freedom of God to act contrary to human definitions of justice. The crisis that emerged was the threat of a return to the chaos prior to the creative word; in other words, the mythical *regressus ad initium* takes up residence in the thought of the sages. The close association of creation and retribution has not as yet been formulated satisfactorily, in my opinion. In what follows I shall attempt to break new ground in this difficult area of research.

The Function of Creation Theology

The function of creation theology within the thought of the sages remains something of a mystery to this day. To be sure, scholars have not been completely silent about this fundamental problem. Perhaps the most comprehensive statement is that of Walther Zimmerli: "Wisdom thinks resolutely within a framework of a theology

---

[103]Murphy has observed that, if Gerstenberger and Audet are right about the intimate original connection between law and wisdom, Sirach's insight in associating the two was more brilliant than he realized ("The Hebrew Sage and Openness to the World," in *Christian Action and Openness to the World* [1970] 227).

[104]*Wisdom in Proverbs*, SBT 45 (1965), 104.

[105]Murphy, "The Hebrew Sage and Openness to the World," 231.

of creation. Its theology is creation theology."[106] While making less claim as to the place of creation theology in wisdom, Johannes Fichtner goes farther in describing the nature of the belief in creation. He writes: "Belief in the creator God is connected with faith in the God of retribution in a twofold manner."[107] Fichtner goes on to demonstrate these points of contact between creation and retribution in the areas of divine sovereignty and order, both cosmic and social. Yet neither Zimmerli nor Fichtner gave sufficient attention to the role of creation in wisdom thought to justify their remarks about the centrality of creation theology to the wise men. Astonishingly, to this day no one has devoted a full scale essay to this problem despite the constant refrain in scholarly works that wisdom thought and creation theology are inseparably bound together. Any attempt to provide such an analysis of creation theology within the framework of wisdom needs to clarify the role of creation in the total thought of Israel before going on to demonstrate the distinctiveness of the function of creation theology in wisdom literature. Two points merit consideration.

The first observation takes up the valuable insight associated with Hermann Gunkel.[108] Creation cannot be divorced from the concept of chaos. The implications of this recognition of the absolute necessity for maintaining tension between creation and chaos have not always been felt; the result has been a terminological confusion that distorts most discussions of creation. This semantic lack of clarity has prompted Dennis J. McCarthy to suggest that we should speak in terms of "ordering" rather than "creating".[109] By this means the tension between chaos and creation is given

---

[106]"Ort und Grenze der Weisheit im Rahmen der alttestamentlichen Theologie," *SPOA* (1963), 123: "Die Weisheit des Alten Testaments halt sich ganz entschlossen im Horizonte der Schöpfung. Ihre Theologie ist Schöpfungstheologie." See "The Place and Limit of the Wisdom in the Framework of the Old Testament Theology," 148.

[107]*Die altorientalische Weisheit in ihrer israelitisch-jüdischer Ausprägung*, BZAW 62 (1933), 111. The two links mentioned are the absolute power of God and the idea of order. Fichtner discusses these under the rubrics of creation and retribution. Hans Heinrich Schmid, "Schöpfung, Gerechtigkeit und Heil: Schöpfungstheologie als Gesamthorizont biblischer Theologie," *ZTK* 70 (1973): 16 writes: "The fundamental theme of ancient Near Eastern views of creation was the question of a saving world, that is, of the existing understanding of a comprehensive righteousness." Schmid states further that "Views of order and of creation are two aspects of one and the same complex problem" (18). On this subject see H. P. Müller, "Wie Sprach Qohälät von Gott?," *VT* 18 (1968): 512-16.

[108]*Schöpfung und Chaos in Urzeit und Endzeit*, 1895; see now B. W. Anderson, *Creation Versus Chaos*, 1967.

[109]"'Creation' Motifs in Ancient Hebrew Poetry," *CBQ* 29 (1967): 88-91. See also Claus Westermann, "Neuere Arbeiten zur Schöpfung," *VF* 14 (1969): 11-28, esp. 13. Westermann also notes that high cultures have three basic forms of traditions dealing with creation: "the narrative (myth), the praise of the gods (hymn), and wisdom" (17). He delineates four types: creation through the birth of gods, through battle, through a shaping or forming, and through the word (17).

prominence, although without the unnecessary and unproven assumption of *annual* threats of chaos that Israel had to guard against by correct ritual.

A second observation has to do with the role of creation thought in ancient Israel as currently understood. This consensus of scholarship can be described as follows. Creation is not a primary datum of Israel's faith, but plays a subservient role to redemption. The placing of creation narratives at the beginning of the Hebrew Bible notwithstanding, creation functions to support saving history. Furthermore, the antiquity of a belief in creation is conceded; but its centrality to Canaanite thought posed a threat to Yahwism until Deutero-Isaiah conceived of a brilliant response to that problem. It follows that creation occupies a place on the periphery of Israelite thought, rather than at the center. Hence an Old Testament theology that does justice to the thought of Israel must relegate creation to the sidelines. While this interpretation of the theological importance of belief in creation is associated with Gerhard von Rad,[110] it has been widely accepted.

This widespread understanding of creation's minimal place in the theological enterprise has recently been contested by a specialist in wisdom literature. Hans Heinrich Schmid's[111] investigations in the area of order in the ancient Near East led him to conclude that creation is the framework within which historical views move, that the dominant background of all Old Testament thinking and faith is the idea of the comprehensive world order and with it creation faith in the wider sense of the word and that creation faith is not a peripheral idea in biblical theology but its essence. From yet another perspective, Theodore M. Ludwig[112] joins forces with Schmid in contesting the secondary role of creation. Ludwig examines the traditions of establishing the earth in Deutero-Isaiah; his results suggest to him "that creation faith in Deutero-Isaiah is not merely subsumed under election or redemption faith." My own challenge to the prevailing view of creation was formulated independently of Schmid or Ludwig, and seeks to move a step further by recognizing the tension within the biblical texts themselves. I shall argue that in one sense both von Rad and Schmid are right. The clue to my understanding is the attempt to take seriously the concept of chaos within a discussion of creation. Three points stand out: (1) the threat of chaos in the cosmic, political, and social realms evokes a response in terms of creation theology; (2) in wisdom thought, creation functions primarily as defense of divine justice; and (3) the centrality of the question of God's integrity in Israelite literature places creation theology at the center of the theological enterprise.

---

[110]"The Theological Problem of the Old Testament Doctrine of Creation," in *The Problem of the Hexateuch and Other Essays*, 131-43.

[111]"Schöpfung, Gerechtigkeit und Heil: Schöpfungstheologie als Gesamthorizont biblischer Theologie," 1-19.

[112]"The Traditions of the Establishing of the Earth in Deutero-Isaiah," *JBL* 92 (1973): 345-57.

The Threat of Chaos

It is no longer necessary to justify the claim that the concept of order lies at the heart of wisdom thinking. This conclusion rests on an exhaustive analysis of Israel's wisdom within the context of ancient Near Eastern sapiential literature. Now the order established in the beginning by the creator is ever subject to the threatening forces of chaos, both human and divine. The eruption of disorder came at the very point where the retribution scheme gave way; this crisis of confidence in divine power or goodness surfaced early in Mesopotamia, Egypt, and Israel. The literary deposit of this heroic struggle is living testimony to the awesome power of the forces of chaos that placed a question mark over the belief in a correspondence between virtue and reward. We can recognize the threat of chaos in three fundamental areas. The first realm in which the forces of disorder spill over into the marketplace is that of human perversion.

This intrusion of chaos can be illustrated with reference to Qoheleth, about whom Hans Wilhelm Hertzberg has written: "There is no doubt: the book of Qoheleth was composed with Genesis 1–4 before the eyes of the author; the life view of Qoheleth is formed out of the creation stories."[113] In light of this assessment of the significance for Qoheleth of creation narratives, I turn to Qoh 7:29 ("Lo, only this have I found: God has made man upright [יָשָׁר], but they have sought out many contrivances"). I need not tarry to consider the vast implication of the rare word חִשְּׁבֹנוֹת or the feminine subject of the perversion. It suffices to observe that the former derives largely from a desire to link this verse to 7:25 and 7:27 where a similar word occurs (חֶשְׁבּוֹן), while the latter may be understood generically. In any case, man is only one/one thousandths better than woman. The meaning of the verse is clear in spite of these difficulties. It asserts that mankind alone is responsible for the corruption of the order of the created world.

A similar point pervades Sir 15:14, where Ben Sira responds to a vocal group bent on indicting God for causing human iniquity. Rejecting the assertion that God led man astray, Sirach contends that "It was he who created man in the beginning, and he left him in the power of his own inclination" (cf. 10:18). It has hitherto gone unnoticed that the brief formula of debate, לֹא תֹאמַר, occurs in contexts the overwhelming majority of which wrestle with the problem of divine justice. This propensity of formula and theme is not limited to biblical sources, but also occurs in the Instructions of Ani, Amenemopet, and 'Onchsheshonqy."[114]

Another manifestation of chaos appears in the area of human ignorance. A prominent answer to the problem of evil in Mesopotamia, this stress upon the limits of human comprehension is set within the discussion of creation in Qoheleth as

---

[113]*Der Prediger*, KAT 17 (1963), 229.
[114]Crenshaw, "The Problem of Theodicy in Sirach," *JBL* 94 (1975): 47-64.

well. This is true both of 3:11[115] and of 7:13-14. In the former, Qoheleth writes: "He has made *everything* beautiful in its own time; he has also placed a sense of the remote past and future in their minds, but without man being able to discover the work God does from beginning to end." The avoidance of the Priestly and Yahwistic terminology of creation renders somewhat tenuous Hertzberg's claim that Qoheleth wrote with Genesis 1–4 before him. Still one could claim that the alteration is intentional. More importantly, Qoh 3:11 asserts the orderliness of creation (this must be the meaning of יָפֶה בְעִתּוֹ). At the same time, however, the broken sentence introduces grave qualification to such beauty.[116] God has created man so that he simply cannot know the proper time for anything despite his boasts to the contrary (cf. 8:17). Qoheleth offers further clarification of this ambiguous gift of הָעֹלָם in 3:14 ("I know that whatever God does will remain into the ages; there is no adding to or subtracting from it, for God has made it so that men would fear him"). Here the יִרְאַת יהוה approaches numinous dread rather than the fear of God that is the essence of all knowledge. Coupled with the הָעֹלָם of 3:11, יִרְאַת יהוה gives voice to Qoheleth's existence *in tormentis*. The reason for this torment lies in Qoheleth's recognition that the fundamental premise of wisdom, namely that there is a positive correlation between one's being and one's outward condition, has collapsed under the forces of chaos.

A similar agony rests behind Qoh 7:13-14. Here Qoheleth takes up a proverb that otherwise appears in 1:15 ("The crooked cannot be straightened, nor the missing tallied"), but varies the form considerably ("Consider the work of God; for who can straighten that which he has bent?"). While the use of the rare word תָּקֵן, which elsewhere means to bring disparate voices into harmony (Sir 47:9) or to arrange proverbs (Qoh 12:9), is interesting, it does not seem nearly as significant as עִוְּתוֹ. Used of scales עִוָּה alludes to their falsification (Am. 8:5), but the term can also refer to misleading someone (Ps 119:78; Job 19:6). Especially informative is Lam. 3:34-36, in which it is claimed that the Lord does not delight in (look upon!) the misleading of a man during litigation. It is this sense of perversion that stands out in Job 8;3; 34:12 and Ps 146:9. The twofold question in Job 8:3 is poignant indeed: "Will God pervert (יְעַוֵּת) justice, or Shaddai pervert right?" Here one notes the repetition of the יְעַוֵּת, together with the parallelism of מִשְׁפָּט and צֶדֶק. Similarly, Elihu contends that "Surely God will not act wickedly, nor will Shaddai pervert justice" (34:12). On the other hand, the champion of the prisoner, the righteous, the orphan, and the stranger also perverts the way of the wicked (Ps 146:9).

---

[115]Crenshaw, "The Eternal Gospel (Eccl. 3:11)," *Essays in Old Testament Ethics*, 23-55.

[116]On Qoheleth's use of the broken sentence, see H. P. Müller, "Wie Sprach Qohälat von Gott?," 507-21.

The claim that Zeus can "easily make the crooked straight" which Harry Ranston[117] cites from Hesiod, *Works*, 7 is entirely beside the point, since Qoheleth complains about *man's* inability to correct what is bent. The practical conclusion to this incapacity to alter the divine decrees is provided in Qoh 7:14 ("On the good day be happy and on the evil day consider; this as well as that, God has made so that man is unable to find out anything that will follow him"). Robert Gordis aptly sums up the sense of these two verses: "(they) are an admirable epitome of Koheleth's thought—God is all-powerful, man must resign himself to ignorance regarding the meaning and purpose of life."[118] Of course the verse recalls Job 2:10, with its recognition that both good and evil derive from God and must be accepted as a gift in each instance, that is, with gratitude.

The human inability to penetrate the shield erected by God to prevent the creature from discovering the divine mystery leads on to thought about the work of God in yet another verse (Qoh 11:5). In this instance presumably Qoheleth has reference to the divine creative deed rather than to subsequent redemptive acts, or even to *whatever* God does. The verse argues from the lesser to the greater: "Just as you do not know what the direction of the wind is, or how bones (come) in the womb of a pregnant woman, so you do not know the work of God who does every-thing." In short, human beings know less about God's work and the future than about the mysterious origin of the wind or of a foetus. However, this ignorance of the ultimate mystery of life does not lead to an ignoring of the divine command to replenish the earth. Nor does the recognition that God has placed a limit upon humanity while reserving the truth for himself impel Qoheleth into suicide, in spite of his spiritual kinship with the Babylonian Qoheleth in the matter of limits imposed upon man from without.

Qoheleth is not the only sage who struggled with a conviction about the bankruptcy of human wisdom, whether owing to divine caprice or human fallibility. The skeptical author of Prov 30:1-4 parodies traditional assertions by turning them into rhetorical questions.[119] It occasions little surprise that someone rebukes this sceptic for adding to the words of God (30:5-6), for there is here certainly a new dimension to the affirmation that God has gathered the wind in his fists and wrapped up the waters in a garment. How vastly different is the agonized query: "Who has established (הֵקִים) all the ends of the earth? What is his name, and what is his son's name? Surely you know!" Here one confronts the outer limits of such emphasis on divine inscrutability as is found in Sir 11:4 and 16:21, which describe God's work as wonderful and hidden like a tempest which no one can see.

---

[117]See Hertzberg, *Die Prediger*, 152, for this reference, which I have not been able to verify on p. 74 of Ranston's book.

[118]*Koheleth—The Man and His World* (1951), 274-75.

[119]On these verses see Georg Sauer, *Die Sprüche Agurs* (1963).

While elements of divine caprice have surfaced to some degree in the discussions of responsibility for evil and of human limitations, the arbitrary actions of the creator come to prominence when sin and punishment are addressed. The connection of sickness and guilt survives even the challenge presented by Job, and tempers Sirach's remarks about the place of physicians and medicines (Sir 38:1-15). The evidence of tension within Sirach's mind provides testimony to the force of the argument that sickness is punishment for sin. While he can speak in the spirit of the old view ("He who sins before his Maker, may he fall into the care of a physician," 38:15), Sirach is also convinced that the divine physician created medicines and doctors. Precisely in this area of disparity between inner state and external condition the forces of chaos made their strongest impact.

A third domain in which chaos erupted for the sage concerns the consciousness of divine presence. From the beginning the sage held in creative tension the idea of the presence of the creator who sustains his universe and the recognition of the hiddenness of the distant ruler. Conscious of the ethical dimensions stemming from the fact that rich and poor alike owe their origin to one maker (Prov 14:31; 17:5; cf. 20:12 and 29:13), the sage also knew the silence of eternity that gave rise to despair and ethical nihilism. The result was the inevitable fear of godforsakenness to the destructive forces. In response to this terror over divine abandonment of the order established at the beginning and now threatened, the sages introduced the idea of Dame Wisdom (Prov 3:19-20; 8:22-31; Sir 1:4, 9, 14; 23:20; 24:3, 8-9) within the context of creation thought. There is some evidence, it seems, in support of the position advocated by Burton Mack,[120] namely that hypostasis responds in part to the question of theodicy. The traditions about Wisdom (חָכְמָה) fulfill a desire to make God both accessible and active at a time when serious doubt is cast on his justice.

Creation as Defense of Divine Justice

The question of theodicy lies at the heart of the book of Job; so does creation theology. The juxtaposition of these two themes is even verbalized in several places. When Eliphaz draws to a close the marvelous description of the numinous moment of revelation, he preserves the divine word vouchsafed to him ("Can man be more just than God [אֱלוֹהַ], or a mortal purer than his maker [מֵעֹשֵׂהוּ]?", Job 4: 17). This, indeed, comes to be the crucial issue in Job's confrontation with God, and for his Titanism Job is soundly rebuked by the creator ("Will you even frustrate my own justice; will you condemn me as guilty in order that you may be innocent?", 40:8).

The converse of Job's behavior is voiced by Elihu in 36:3, where we read "I will carry [אֶשָּׂא] my knowledge from afar, and ascribe justice to my maker

---

[120]"Wisdom Myth and Mythology, an Essay in Understanding a Theological Tradition," *Int* 24 (1970): 49-60.

[לְפֹעֲלִי]. In 32:22 Elihu assures us that his word can be trusted, for he does not know how to flatter since "my maker will quickly bear me away" (יִשָּׂאֵנִי). Still another sharp attack upon divine justice occurs in Job's speech recorded in 10:4. Here the victim of divine abuse cries out: "Do you have eyes of flesh, or do you see as man sees?" Job then argues at length that God's hands fashioned and made him like clay, that he poured him out like milk and curdled him like cheese, clothing him with skin and flesh and knitting him together with bones and sinews. Indeed, God granted Job life, covenant love, and happiness of spirit. Why then, Job asks, do you destroy the works that your hands so lovingly fashioned? (10:8-12). In response to Job's query, Elihu avers that God is untouched by human conduct since his greatness does not depend upon man's behavior. Nevertheless, this defendant of God agrees with Job that his creator (עֹשָׂי) [!] gives songs in the night (זְמִרוֹת) and teaches man more than birds and beasts, that is, more than the experiential knowledge of the sages (35:10). Elihu moves on to emphasize the absurdity of Job's Titanism: "Can you, like him, spread out the skies, hard as molten metal?" (37:18).

The divine speeches force Job to recognize his absence when the creative deed was conceived and brought to fruition. By excluding Job from the original creation God impresses upon him the sheer absurdity of Job's attempt to be an equal of God.[121] The puny creature who has boldly faced God and demanded justice now discovers the folly of struggling with one stronger than he. Even the mighty Behemoth, before whom all other creatures cringe in terror, found his strength no match for the creator, but submitted to him docilely. This conqueror of the powers of chaos is equally adept in areas requiring finesse rather than sheer power. His majestic touch scatters snow, hoar frost, or dew upon the whole earth. In short, the divine speeches divest Job of his Titantic defiance by calling attention to the grandeur of creation. The remaining allusions to creation (9:9; 26:1-14; 31:15) are intended to strengthen the case for divine justice, or to highlight the agony of Job deriving from God's failure to use his obvious power in a way that assures universal justice. In a word, creation theology functions in Job to undergird the cogency of the argument for divine justice despite strong and convincing evidence to the contrary.

This same use of creation theology to answer the attacks upon divine justice pervades the thought of Sirach, who moves considerably beyond Job in providing answers for the apparent prosperity of the wicked.[122] Besides the customary responses known to us from Job and Wisdom Psalms, Sirach ventures in virgin territory on two fronts. The first is in the metaphysical realm, the second in the psy-

---

[121]M. Sekine, "Schöpfung und Erlösung im Buche Hiob," BZAW 77 (1958): 220. According to Sekine, the second divine speech brings Job back into the realm of creation along with the original animals and accomplishes his new creation (221-22). Sekine thinks the central place of creation in Job is new to the Old Testament (222). For a similar understanding of Job, see Norman C. Habel, "Appeal to Ancient Tradition as Form," SBLSP 1 (1973): 46.

[122]For a detailed discussion, see my article entitled "The Problem of Theodicy in Sirach."

chological. Sirach contends that creation itself rewards virtue and punishes vice, since God made the universe to consist of complementary pairs of good and evil. In addition, Sirach intimates that God punishes the guilty with excessive *Angst*, specifically in nightmares. But Sirach seems not to have been completely satisfied with such responses to the problem of evil; ultimately he abandons these arguments in favor of a mighty crescendo of praise for the creator of the universe (16:24–17:14; 42:15–43:33; 39:15-35). In each of these hymns creation and theodicy march hand in hand. In the same breath Sirach asserts that "The works of the Lord are all good, and he will supply every need in its hour" (39:33), and "No one can say, 'This is worse than that,' for all things will prove good in their season" (39:34; cf. 39:16-17). Such texts indicate that Sir 18:1 accurately reflects the function of creation in the thought of Ben Sira ("He who lives forever created the whole universe; the Lord alone will be declared just"). One cannot miss the echo in the final clause of the oft-proclaimed "Just art thou, O Lord" within Israel's discussion literature. Here one moves barefoot and with bowed head, for we are privileged to witness the mighty struggle between God and a devotee who discovers the Lord as his enemy, and is nearly driven out of his mind. The combatant finds it difficult beyond imagination to give assent to the maxim that "God has made everything for its purpose (לַמַּעֲנֵהוּ), even the wicked for a day of trouble (he has made)," Prov 16:4. Likewise, he even calls into question the notion of divine prescience actualized in the creative deed (Sir 23:20). In short, creation theology functions as a defense of the justice of God; such a defense is necessitated by the threat of chaos in every dimension of life.

Creation and the Theological Task

If these conclusions are essentially correct about the function of creation theology within the argument over divine justice, I am now in a position to address the broader issue of authority in wisdom thought. Contrary to what would be expected, the wise men do not appeal to creation as direct authority for their counsel. On the other hand, the fundamental premise of their labor to understand the nature of reality is the orderliness of creation. This dependability is grounded in the creative act, at which time an order was established for all time. Creation, then, assures the wise person that the universe is comprehensible, and thus encourages a search for its secrets. Furthermore, creation supplies the principle of order that holds together the cosmic, political, and social fabric of the universe. When this assumed order gives way, appeal to creation surfaces explicitly in wisdom literature, for by this means the sage hopes to persuade himself and others that wholeness is available even when chaos reigns. But the difficulty of attaining the wholeness that has been postulated converts creation faith, once a comforting affirmation, into cause for anxiety and dismay. The final breakthrough comes when Sirach moves away from a rational defense of divine justice to a mighty crescendo of praise of the creator who has made all things in pairs, that is, good and evil. By this tour de force even the forces of chaos are *enlisted in the divine service*, so that both the original creative act and *creatio continua* bear witness to the justice of God.

Such an understanding of the function of creation theology in wisdom literature tends to confirm von Rad's thesis that creation plays a secondary role, although not in the sense in which he saw things. Whereas he thinks of creation as subservient to saving history, I believe creation belongs under the rubric of justice. The function of creation theology, in my view, is to undergird the belief in divine justice. Consequently, I agree with Schmid that creation belongs to the fundamental question of human existence, namely, the integrity of God.[123] It would follow that traditions about creation are at the heart of the theological enterprise, and not on the outer fringes. In a word, the question of divine justice cannot be separated from that of creation, both in the sense of an initial ordering and continual creation in the face of defiant chaos within man and external to him.

So far these remarks have been restricted to the function of creation theology in sapiential thought. The evidence seems to demand a reexamination of the question of creation's role in nonwisdom texts. In studying the use of בָּרָא in the doxologies of Amos and in hymnic texts in Deutero-Isaiah, I came to the conclusion some time ago that this root occurs predominantly within contexts of judgment.[124] I wish to take up that observation once again and to repeat the identification of doxology of judgment in a context of creation thought. In light of the above findings in wisdom literature, my earlier insight into the nature of the doxology of judgment would seem to be confirmed. In those texts, at least, creation and theodicy are interwoven from start to finish. Perhaps there is reason, therefore, to reassess Johannes Hempel's observation that Eve's response to the serpent is a theodicy of universal proportions,[125] coming as it does on the heels of the Priestly and Yahwistic creation narratives. It may turn out that Schmid is, indeed, correct in his judgment that Israel's "views of order and creation are two aspects of one and the same complex problem."[126] If so, we have returned to the state of research when Johannes Fichtner wrote his epochmaking study of Israelite wisdom,[127] even if by way of a long detour along paths carved out for us by von Rad. It remains now for us to

---

[123]Schmid, "Schöpfung, Gerechtigkeit und Heil: Schöpfungstheologie als Gesamthorizont biblischer Theologie," writes that creation is the framework within which historical views move (8), that the dominant background of all Old Testament thinking and faith is the idea of the comprehensive world order and with it creation faith in the wider sense of the word (11), and that creation faith is not a peripheral one in biblical theology, but in essence is its theme (15).

[124]Crenshaw, "*YHWH Ṣebā'ôt Šemô*: A Form-Critical Analysis," *ZAW* 81 (1969): 169-70. See my *Hymnic Affirmation of Divine Justice* (1975).

[125]Cited in von Rad, *Genesis*, OTL (1961), 97.

[126]"Schöpfung, Gerechtigkeit und Heil: Schöpfungstheologie als Gesamthorizont biblischer Theologie," 18.

[127]*Die altorientalische Weisheit in ihrer israelitischjüdischen Ausprägung.*

investigate the theological significance of the interrelatedness of creation and retribution to which Fichtner called our attention four decades ago.[128]

Retrospect and Prospect

This analysis of the present state of research in the area of wisdom literature calls attention to the successes and failures of scholars in the twentieth century. I have the impression that a history of the interpretation of various wisdom books prior to 1900 C.E. would reveal two basic trends: (1) the attempt to bring wisdom thought into line with the more traditional biblical texts, and (2) the viewing of each literary complex in terms of what was desirable in any given era. The former tendency has recently been discussed by S. Holm-Nielsen,[129] who demonstrates the taming process to which Qoheleth was submitted in various early translations (LXX, Syriac, Vulgate) and in the writings of early Christian interpreters. The second trend, that of viewing a text through the mirror of one's own age, is beautifully documented by Nahum Glatzer in regard to the biblical Job.[130] The neglect of wisdom during the heyday of "salvation history" is still another manifestation of this tendency to read the text in light of one's special interests.

As I bring this survey to a close I am conscious of the poverty of our knowledge in so many areas of wisdom research. I have hardly touched upon five topics that will occupy the attention of scholars in the area of wisdom for years to come: (1) wisdom and myth/cult, (2) wisdom and apocalyptic, (3) the role of nature in wisdom thought, (4) intentional arrangement of larger collections of proverbs, and (5) other forms (omens,[131] school questions). As in the study of creation, so also in wisdom research, we stand at the beginning. Hopefully we do not stand before the door of biblical writ without a key.

---

[128]In this endeavor to comprehend the function of creation in wisdom literature one quickly sees the truth of Westermann's observation that "In the investigation of speech about the creator and creation we still stand entirely at the beginning" ("Neuere Arbeiten zur Schöpfung," 13). Similarly, Martin Buber has written: "The biblical story of creation is a legitimate stammering account. . . . But this stammering of his was the only means of doing justice to the task of stating the mystery of how time springs from eternity, and world comes from that which is not world" (*On the Bible* [1968], 11).

[129]"On the Interpretation of Qoheleth in early Christianity," *VT* 24 (1974): 168-77.

[130]"The Book of Job and Its Interpreters," in *Biblical Motifs*, ed. A. Altmann (1966), 197-220.

[131]G. E. Bryce, "Omen-wisdom in Ancient Israel" *JBL* 94 (1975): 19-37, has taken an initial step toward understanding omen-wisdom in Israel.

Selected Bibliography

Albright, W. F. "Some Canaanite-Phoenecian Sources of Hebrew Wisdom." *VTS* 3 (1960): 1-15.

Alonso-Schökel, L. "Sapiential and Covenant Themes in Genesis 2–3." In *Modern Biblical Studies: An Anthology from Theology Digest*, ed. D. J. McCarthy and W. B. Callen, 49-61. Milwaukee, 1967. Orig. in in *Bib* 43 (1962): 295-316.

Alt, A. "Die Weisheit Salomos." *ThLZ* 76 (1951): 139-44.

_____. "Zur literarischen Analyse der Weisheit des Amenemope." *VTS* 3 (1960): 16-25.

Anthes, R. *Lebensregeln und Lebensweisheit der alten Ägypter*. AO 32/2. Leipzig, 1933.

Audet, J. P. "Origines comparées de la double tradition de la loi et de la sagesse dans le Proche-Orient ancien." In *Acten Internationalen Orientalistenkongresses* 1:352-57. Moscow, 1962.

Barton, G. A. *The Book of Ecclesiastes*. ICC. Edinburgh, 1908.

Barucq, A. *Le livre des Proverbes*. SB. Paris, 1964.

_____. *Ecclésiaste*. VS 3. Paris, 1968.

Bauckmann, E. G. "Die Proverbien und die Sprüche des Jesus Sirach." *ZAW* 72 (1960): 33-63.

Bauer-Kayatz, C. *Einführung in die alttestamentliche Weisheit*. BibS(N) 55. Neukirchen, 1969.

_____. *Studien zu Proverbien 1–9*. WMANT 22. 1966.

Baumgartner, W. "Die israelitische Weisheitsliteratur." *TRu* 5 (1933): 259-88.

_____. "Die literarischen Gattungen in der Weisheit des Jesus Sirach." *ZAW* 34 (1914): 161-98.

_____. *Israelitische und altorientalische Weisheit*. SGV 166. 1933.

_____. "The Wisdom Literature." In *The Old Testament and Modern Study*, ed. H. H. Rowley, 210-37. Oxford, 1951.

Beauchamp, E. *Les sages d'Israël, ou le fruit d'une fidelité*. Quebec, 1968.

Bič, M. "Le juste et l'impié dans le livre de Job." VTSup 15 (1965): 33-43.

Bissing, F. W. *Altägyptische Lebensweisheit*, Zurich, 1955.

Blank, S. H. "Wisdom." *IDB* R-Z:852-61.

Blieffert, H. J. *Weltanschauung und Gottesglaube im Buch Kohelet*. Darstellung und Kritik. Rostock, 1938.

Boer, P. A. H. de. "The Counsellor." VTSup 3 (1960): 42-71.

Boström, G. *Proverbiastudien. Die Weisheit und das fremde Weib in Spr. 1–9*. LUÅ 30/3. Lund, 1935.

Braun, R. *Kohelet und die frühhellenistiche Popularphilosophie*. BZAW 130. 1973.

Brueggemann, W. *In Man We Trust*. Richmond, 1972.

_____. "Scripture and an Ecumenical Lifestyle." *Int* 24 (1970): 3-19.

Brunner, H. *Altägyptische Erziehung*. Wiesbaden, 1957.

_____. "Der frei Wille Gottes in der ägyptischen Weisheit." In *SPOA*, 103-20. 1963.

_____. "Die Lehre des Cheti, Sohnes des Duauf." *Äg-Forschungen* H 13. Gluckstadt und Hamburg,]944.

_____. "Die Weisheitsliteratur." *HO* 1/2:90-110. Leiden, 1952.

Bryce, G. E. "'Better' Proverbs: A Historical and Structural Study." In *SBLSP* 1972, 343-54.

_____. "Omen-Wisdom in Ancient Israel." Paper read at the annual meeting of the SBL,

25 Oct 1974, and in *JBL* 94 (1975): 19-37.

Buck, A. De. "Het religieus Karakter der oudste egyptische Wysheid" *NorTT* 31 (1932): 322-49.

Buckers, H. *Die unsterblichkeitslehre des Weisheitsbuches: Ihr Ursprung und ihre Bedeutung. ÄA* 13. Münster, 1938.

Carmichael, C. M. "Deuteronomic Laws, Wisdom, and Historical Traditions." *JSS* 12 (1967): 198-206.

Carstensen, R. N. *Job, Defense of Honor.* Nashville, 1963.

Causse, A. "La sagesse et la propagande juive à l'époque perse et hellénistique." In *Werden und Wesen des Alten Testament*, 148-54. BZAW 66. 1936.

———. "Sagesse égyptienne et sagesse juive." *RHPR* 9 (1929): 149-69.

Cazelles, H. "A propos d'une phrase de H. H. Rowley." VTSup 3 (1960): 26-32.

———. "Les débuts de la sagesse en Israël." In *SPOA*, 27-39. 1963.

Clarke, E. G. *The Wisdom of Solomon.* Cambridge, 1973.

Coats, G. W. "The Joseph Story and Ancient Wisdom: A Reappraisal." *CBQ* 35 (1973): 285-97.

Conrad, J. "Die innere Gliederung der Proverbien." *ZAW* 79 (1967): 67-76.

Cook, A. *The Root of the Thing. A Study of Job and the Song of Songs.* Bloomington, 1968.

Coppens, J. "Le messianisme sapiential et les origines litteraires du fils de l'homme danielique." VTSup 3 (1960): 33-41.

Coughenour, R. A. "Enoch and Wisdom." Dissertation. Case Western Reserve, 1972.

Couturier, G. P. "Sagesse babylonienne et sagesse israélite." *ScEccl* 14 (1962): 293-309.

Crenshaw, James L. "The Eternal Gospel (Eccles. 3:11)." In *Essays in Old Testament Ethics*, ed. James L. Crenshaw and J. T. Willis, 23-55. New York, 1974.

———. "'ēsâ and dābār: The Problem of Authority/Certitude in Wisdom and Prophetic Literature." In *Prophetic Conflict*, 116-23. BZAW 124. Berlin, 1971.

———. "The Influence of the Wise upon Amos." *ZAW* 79 (1967): 42-52.

———. "Method in Determining Wisdom Influence upon 'Historical' Literature." *JBL* 88 (1969): 129-42.

———. "Popular Questioning of the Justice of God in Ancient Israel." *ZAW* 82 (1970): 380-95.

———. "Wisdom." In *Old Testament Form Criticism*, ed. J. H. Hayes, 225-64. *TUMSR* 2. San Antonio, 1974.

Dahood, M. *Proverbs and Northwest Semitic Philology.* Rome, 1963.

———. "Canaanite-Phoenician Influence in Qoheleth." *Bib* 33 (1952): 30-52, 191-221.

———. "Some Northwest-Semitic Words in Job." *Bib* 38 (1957): 306-20.

Damon, S. F. *Blake's Job.* New York, 1969.

Daumas, J. "La naissance de l'humanisme dans la littérature de l'Égypte ancienne." *OrAnt* 1 (1962): 155-84.

Davidson, A. B. *The Book of Job.* CBSC. Cambridge, 1951.

Delitzsch, F. *Proverbs of Solomon.* Edinburgh, 1875.

Dhorme, E. *Job.* London, 1967.

Dijk, J. J. A. van. *La sagesse suméro-accadienne. Recherches sur les genres littéraires des textes sapientiaux.* Leiden, 1953.

Di Lella, A. *The Hebrew Text of Sirach.* London, 1966.

Dillmann, A. *Hiob. KHAT.* Leipzig, ²1891.

Donald, T. "The Semantic Field of 'Folly' in Proverbs, Job, Psalms, and Ecclesiastes." *VT*

13 (1963): 285-92.

_____. "The Semantic Field of Rich and Poor in the Wisdom Literature of Hebrew and Accadian." *OrAnt* 3 (1964): 27-41.

Donner, H. "Die religionsgeschichtlichen Ursprunge von Prov. Sal. 82." *ZÄS* 82 (1957): 8-18.

Driver, G. R. "Problems and Solutions," *VT* 4 (1954): 225-45.

_____, and G. B. Gray. *The Book of Job*. ICC. Edinburgh, 1921.

Drubbel, A. "Le conflit entre la sagesse profane et la sagesse religieuse. Contribution à l'étude des origines de la littérature sapientiale en Israël." *Bib* 17 (1936): 45-70, 407-26.

Dubarle, A. M. "Où en est l'étude de la littérature sapientielle?" *ETL* 44 (1968): 407-19.

_____. *Les sages d'Israël*. LD. Paris, 1946.

Duesberg, H., and I. Fransen. *Les scribes inspirés*. Belgium, 1966.

Dürr, L. *Das Erziehungswesen im Alten Testament und in antiken Orient*. MVAG 36/2. Leipzig, 1932.

Eissfeldt, Otto. *Der Maschal im Alten Testament*. BZAW 24. Giessen, 1913.

Ellermeier, F. *Qohelet*. Herzberg am Harz, 1967.

Engnell, I. "'Knowledge' and 'Life' in the Creation Story." VTSup 3 (1960): 103-19.

Erman, A. *Die Literatur der alten Ägypter*. Leipzig, 1923. ET: *The Ancient Egyptians*, New York, 1966.

_____. "Das Weisheitsbuch des Amenemope." *OLZ* 27 (1924): 241-52.

Feinberg, C. L. "The Poetic Structure of the Book of Job and the Ugaritic Literature." *BSac* 103 (1946): 283-93.

Fensham, F. C. "Widow, Orphan, and the Poor in Ancient Near Eastern Legal and Wisdom Literature." *JNES* 21 (1962): 129-39.

Fichtner, J. *Die altorientalische Weisheit in ihrer israelitisch-jüdischen Ausprägung*. BZAW 62. 1933.

_____. *Gottes Weisheit*. Stuttgart, 1965.

_____. "Jesaja unter den Weisen." *TLZ* 74 (1949): 75-80.

_____. "Die Stellung der Sapientia Salomonis in der Literatur und Geistesgeschichte ihrer Zeit." *ZNW* 36 (1937): 113-32.

_____. *Weisheit Salomos*. HAT 6. Tübingen, 1938.

Fohrer, G. *Das Buch Hiob*. KAT 16. Gütersloh, 1963.

_____. "The Righteous Man in Job 31." In *Essays in Old Testament Ethics*, 1-21. New York, 1974.

_____. *Studien zum Buche Hiob*. Gütersloh, 1963.

_____. "σοφία κτλ. B. Altes Testament." *TWNT* 7:476-96. ET: "σοφία κτλ. B. The Old Testament." *TDNT* 7:476-96.

Frankenberg, W. *Die Sprüche*. HKAT 2.3.1. Göttingen, 1898.

Galling, K. *Die Krise der Aufklärung in Israel*. Mainz, 1952.

_____. "Kohelet-Studien." *ZAW* 50 (1932): 276-99.

_____. *Der Prediger*. HAT 18. Tübingen, 1969.

_____. "Stand und Aufgabe der Kohelet-Forschung." *TRu* 6 (1934): 355-73.

Gammie, John G. "Spatial and Ethical Dualism in Jewish Wisdom and Apocalyptic Literature." *JBL* 93 (1974): 356-85.

Gaspar, J. W. *Social Ideas in the Wisdom Literature of the Old Testament*. Washington, 1947.

Gemser, B. "The Instructions of 'Onchsheshonqy and Biblical Wisdom Literature." VTSup 7 (1960): 102-28.

_____. "The Spiritual Structure of Biblical Aphoristic Wisdom." In *Adhuc Loquitur. Collected Essays of Dr. B. Gemser*, ed. A. Van Selms and A. S. van der Woude, 138-49. Leiden, 1968.

_____. *Sprüche Salomos*. HAT 16. 1963.

Gerleman, G. *Studies in the Septuagint*. 3. *Proverbs*. Gleerup, 1956.

Gerstenberger, E. *Wesen und Herkunft des "apodiktischen Rechts."* WMANT 20. Neukirchen, 1965.

_____. "Zur alttestamentlichen Weisheit." *VF* 14 (1969): 28-43.

Gese, H. "Die Krisis der Weisheit bei Kohelet." *SPOA*, 139-51. 1963.

_____. *Lehre und Wirklichkeit in der alten Weisheit*. Tübingen, 1958.

_____. "Weisheit." *RGG³* 6:1574-77.

_____. "Weisheitsdichtung." *RGG³* 6:1577-81.

Ginsberg, H. Louis. "Job the Patient and Job the Impatient." *Conservative Judaism* 21 (1966–1967): 12-28.

_____. *Studies in Koheleth*, New York, 1950.

_____. "Supplementary Studies in Koheleth." *PAAJR* 21 (1952): 35-62.

Glasser, E. *Le proces du bonheur par Qohelet*. Paris, 1970.

Glatzer, N. N. "The Book of Job and Its Interpreters." In *Biblical Motifs*, ed. A. Altmann, 197-220. Cambridge MA, 1966.

_____, ed. *The Dimension of Job*. New York, 1969.

Godbey, A. H. "The Hebrew Māšāl." *AJSL* 39 (1922–1923): 89-108.

Good, E. M. *Irony in the Old Testament*. Philadelphia, 1965.

Goodman, W. R. "A Study of 1 Esdras 3:1–5:6." Dissertation, Duke University, 1972.

Gordis, R. *The Book of God and Man*. Chicago, 1965.

_____. *Koheleth—The Man and His World*. New York, 1951.

_____. "The Lord out of the Whirlwind." *Jud* 13 (1964): 48-63.

_____. *Poets, Prophets, and Sages: Essays in Biblical Interpretation*. Bloomington, 1971.

_____. "Quotations in Wisdom Literature." *JQR* 30 (1939–1940): 123-247.

_____. "The Social Background of Wisdom Literature." *HUCA* 18 (1943/1944): 77-118.

Gordon, E. I. "Sumerian Proverbs: 'Collection Four'." *JAOS* 77 (1957): 67-79.

_____. "A New Look at the Wisdom of Sumer and Akkad." *BO* 17 (1960): 122-52.

_____. *Sumerian Proverbs. Glimpses of Everyday Life in Ancient Mesopotamia*. Philadelphia, 1959.

_____. "Sumerian Proverbs and Fables." *JCS* 12 (1958): 1-21, 43-75.

Gowan, D. "Habakkuk and Wisdom." *Perspective* 9 (1968): 157-66.

Greenstone, J. H. *Proverbs*. Philadelphia, 1950.

Grelot, P. "Les proverbes Araméens d'Ahiqar." *RB* 68 (1961): 178-94.

Gressmann, H. *Israels Spruchweisheit im Zusammenhang der Weltliteratur*. Berlin, 1925.

_____. "Die neugefundene Lehre des Amenemope und die vorexilische Spruchdichtung Israels." *ZAW* 42 (1924): 272-96.

Gunkel, H. *Die israelitische Literatur* (*Die Kultur der Gegenwart* 1/7). Leipzig, 1925.

_____. "Ägyptische Parallelen zum AT." *ZDMG* 63 (1909): 531-39.

Habel, N. "Appeal to Ancient Tradition as a Literary Form." In *SBLSP* 1973, 34-54.

_____. "The Symbolism of Wisdom in Proverbs 1–9." *Int* 26 (1972): 131-56.

Hain, M. *Rätsel*. Stuttgart, 1966.

_____. *Sprichwort und Volkssprache. Eine volkskündlich-soziologische Dorfuntersuchung*. Giessener Beiträge z. dt. *Philologie* 95. Giessen, 1951.

Hamp, V. "Zukunft und Jenseits in Buche Sirach." In *Alttestamentliche Studien*, ed. I. Nötscher, 86-97. BBB 1. Bonn, 1950.

Harrelson, Walter. "Wisdom and Pastoral Theology." *ANQ* (1966): 3-11.

Harrington, W. "The Wisdom of Israel." *ITQ* 30 (1963): 311-25.

Haspecker, J. *Gottesfurcht bei Jesus Sirach.* AnBib 30. Rome, 1967.

Harvey, J. "Wisdom Literature and Biblical Theology (Part One)." *BTB* 1 (1971): 308-19.

Hausen, A. *Hiob in der französischen Literatur.* Bern und Frankfurt, 1972.

Hempel, J. *Die althebräische Literatur und ihr hellenistisch-jüdisches Nachleben.* Handbuch d. Lit. Wiss. Potsdam, 1930.

_____. "Pathos und Humor in der israelitischen Erziehung." In *Von Ugarit nach Qumran (Festschrift O. Eissfeldt)*, 63-81. BZAW 77. Berlin, 1958.

_____. *Das Ethos des Alten Testament.* BZAW 67. Rev. ed. 1964.

_____. "Das theologische Problem des Hiob." *ZST* 7 (1930): 621-89. Repr: *Apoxysmata*, 114-73. Berlin, 1961.

Herbert, A. S. "The 'Parable' (*Māšāl*) in the Old Testament." *SJT* 7 (1954): 180-96.

Herder, J. G. *Spruch und Bild, insonderheit bei den Morgenlandern, Werke.* Ed. B. Suphan. Bd. 16, 9-27. Berlin, 1887.

Hermisson, H. J. *Studien zur israelitischen Spruchweisheit.* WMANT 28. Neukirchen-Vluyn, 1968.

_____. "Weisheit und Geschichte." In *Probleme biblischer Theologie (Festschrift G. von Rad)*, ed. H. W. Wolff, 136-54. Munchen, 1971.

Hertzberg, H. W. *Der Prediger.* KAT. 1963.

Hölscher, G. *Das Buch Hiob.* HAT 17. Tübingen, 1952.

Holm-Nielsen, S. "On the Interpretation of Qoheleth in Early Christianity." *VT* 24 (1974): 168-77.

Horst, F. *Hiob.* BKAT 16. Neukirchen-Vluyn, 1960–1968.

Horton, E., Jr. "Koheleth's Concept of Opposites." *Numen* 19 (1972): 1-21.

Hudal, A. *Die religiösen und sittlichen Ideen des Spruchbuches. Kritischexegetische Studie.* 1914.

Humbert, P. *Recherches sur les sources égyptiennes de la littérature sapientiale d'Israël.* Neuchatel, 1929.

_____. "Le modernisme de Job." VTSup 3 (1960): 150-61.

Humphreys, W. L. "The Motif of the Wise Courtier in the Old Testament." Dissertation, Union Theological Seminary, 1970.

Imnschoot, P. van. "Sagesse et esprit dans l'ancien Testament." *RB* 47 (1938): 23-49.

Irwin, W. A. "The Wisdom Literature." *IB* 1:212-19. 1952.

Jacob, E. "L'histoire d'Israel vue par Ben Sira." In *Mélanges Bibliques. Rédigés en l'honneur de André Robert*, 288-94. Paris, 1956.

Jansen, H. L. *Die spätjudische Psalmendichtung, ihr Entstehungskreis und ihr Sitz im Leben.* SNVAO 3. 1937.

Jensen, J. *The Use of tôrâ by Isaiah. His Debate with the Wisdom Tradition.* CBQMS 3. 1973.

Johnson, A. R. "*Mashal.*" VTSup 3 (1960): 162-69.

Jolles, A. *Einfache Formen.* Halle, 1956.

Junker, H. *Das Buch Hiob.* EB. Wurzburg, 1962.

Jung, C. G. *Answer to Job.* New York, 1960.

Keimer, L. "The Wisdom of Amenemope and the Proverbs of Solomon." *AJSL* 43

(1926–1927): 8-21.

Kenworthy, A. W. "The Nature and Authority of Old Testament Wisdom Family Ethics: with Special Reference to Proverbs and Sirach." Dissertation, University of Melbourne, 1974.

Kevin, R. O. "The Wisdom of Amenemope and Its Possible Dependence upon the Hebrew Book of Proverbs." *JSOR* 14 (1930): 115-57.

Klostermann, A. "Schulwesen im alten Israel." In *Festschrift für Th. Zahn*, 193-232. Leipzig, 1908.

Koch, K. "Gibt es ein Vergeltungsdogma im Alten Testament." *ZTK* 52 (1955): 1-42.

_____, ed. *Um das Prinzip der Vergeltung in Religion und Recht des Alten Testament*. WF 125. 1972.

Kovacs, B. W. "Is There a Class-Ethic in Proverbs?" In *Essays in Old Testament Ethics*, 171-89. New York, 1974.

Kraeling, C. H., and R. M. Adams, eds. *City Invincible. A Symposium on Urbanization and Cultural Development in the Ancient Near East*. Chicago, 1960. Esp. "Scribal Concepts of Education," 94-123.

Kramer, S. N. "'Man and his God.' A Sumerian Variation on the 'Job' Motif." VTSup 3 (1960): 170-82.

_____. "Schooldays: A Sumerian Composition Relating to the Education of a Scribe." *JAOS* 69 (1949): 199-215.

_____. "Die sumerische Schule." *WZ* 5/4 (1956): 695-704.

Kraus, H.-J. *Die Verkündigung der Weisheit*. BSac 2. Giessen, 1951.

Kroeber, R. *Der Prediger*. SQAW 13. Berlin, 1963.

Kuhn, G. *Beiträge zur Erklärung des Salomonischen Spruchbuches*. BWANT 16. 1931.

_____. *Erklärung des Buches Koheleth*. BZAW 43. Giessen, 1926.

Kuschke, A. "Altbabylonische Texte zum Thema 'Der leidende Gerechte.'" *TLZ* 81 (1956): 69-76.

Kuyper, L. "The Repentance of Job." *VT* 9 (1959): 90-94.

Lagrange, M. J. "Le livre de la Sagesse. Sa doctrine des fins dernieres." *RB* 16 (1907): 85-104.

Lambert, W. G. *Babylonian Wisdom Literature*. Oxford, 1960.

Lamparter, H. *Das Buch der Weisheit, Prediger und Sprüche*. BAT 16. 1959.

Lang, B. *Die weisheitliche Lehrrede. Eine Untersuchung von Sprüche 1–7*. Stuttgart, 1972.

Lange, H. O. *Das Weisheitsbuch des Amenemope, Kgl*. Danske Vid. Selsk., Hist. fil. Med 11/2. Kopenhagen, 1925.

Lapointe, R. "Foi et vérifiabilité dans le langage sapiential de retribution." *Bib* 51 (1970): 349-68.

Larcher, C. *Études sur le livre de la Sagesse*. Paris, 1969.

Lebram, J. Chr. "Nachbiblische Weisheitstraditionen." *VT* 15 (1965): 167-237.

_____. "Die Theologie der späteren Chokma und häretisches Judentum." *ZAW* 77 (1965): 202-11.

Leclant, J. "Documents nouvaux et points de vue recents sur les sagesses de l'Ägypte ancienne." *SPOA*, 5-26. 1963.

Lindblom, J. *La composition du livre de Job*. Lund, 1945.

_____. "Wisdom in the Old Testament Prophets." VTSup 3 (1960): 192-204.

Loretz, O. *Qohelet und der alte Orient*. Freiburg, 1964.

MacDonald, D. B. *The Hebrew Philosophical Genius*. Repr: New York, 1965.

Mack, B. L. "Wisdom Myth and Mythology." *Int* 24 (1970): 46-60.

Malchow, B. V. "The Roots of Israel's Wisdom in Sacral Kingship." Dissertation, Marquette University, 1972.

Malfroy, J. "Sagesse et loi dans le Deutéronome. Études." *VT* 15 (1965): 49-65.

Marböck, J. *Weisheit im Wandel. Untersuchungen zur Weisheitstheologie bei Ben Sira.* BBB 37. Bonn, 1971.

Marcus, R. "On Biblical Hypostases of Wisdom." *HUCA* 23 (1950/1951): 157-71.

Martin, G. W. "Elihu and the Third Cycle in the Book of Job." Dissertation, Princeton University, 1972.

Martin-Achard, R. "Sagesse de Dieu et sagesse humaine chez Esaïe." In *Maqqel Shaqedh (Festschift W. Vischer).* Castelnau, 1960.

Matenko, P. *Two Studies in Yiddish Culture.* Leiden, 1968. Esp. "Job and Faust," 75-162.

McGlinchey, J. M. *The Teaching of Amenemope and the Book of Proverbs.* Washington, 1939.

McKane, W. *Prophets and Wise Men.* SBT 44. London, 1965.

_____. *Proverbs.* OTL. Philadelphia, 1970.

McKenzie, J. L. "Reflections on Wisdom." *JBL* 86 (1967): 1-9.

Meinhold, H. *Die Weisheit Israels in Spruch, Sage und Dichtung.* Leipzig, 1908.

Michel, D. *Israels Glaube im Wandel.* Berlin, 1968.

Montgomery, J. W. "Wisdom as Gift. The Wisdom Concept in Relation to Biblical Messianism." *Int* 16 (1962): 43-57.

Morenz, S. "Ägyptologische Beiträge zur Erforschung der Weisheitsliteratur Israels." *SPOA*, 63-71. 1963.

Mowinckel, S. "Psalms and Wisdom." VTSup 3 (1960): 205-24.

Müller, H. P. *Hiob und seine Freunde.* ThStud 103. 1970.

_____. "Magisch-Mantische Weisheit und die Gestalt Daniels." *UF* 1 (1969): 79-94.

_____. "Wie Sprach Qohälät von Gott?" *VT* 18 (1968): 507-21.

Munch, P. A. "Die jüdischen 'Weisheitspsalmen' und ihr Platz im Leben." *AcOr* 15 (1936): 112-40.

Murphy, R. E. "Assumptions and Problems in Old Testament Wisdom Research." *CBQ* 29 (1967): 102-12.

_____. "The Concept of Wisdom Literature." In *The Bible in Current Catholic Thought,* 46-54. New York, 1962.

_____. "A Consideration of the Classification 'Wisdom Psalms'." VTSup 9 (1963): 156-67.

_____. "Form Criticism and Wisdom Literature." *CBQ* 31 (1969): 475-83.

_____. "The Hebrew Sage and Openness to the World." In *Christian Action and Openness to the World,* 219-44. Villanova University Symposium II, III. 1970.

_____. "The Interpretation of Old Testament Wisdom Literature." *Int* 23 (1969): 289-301.

_____. *Introduction to the Wisdom Literature of the Old Testament.* Colledgeville, 1965.

_____. "The Kerygma of the Book of Proverbs." *Int* 20 (1966): 3-14.

_____. *Seven Books of Wisdom.* Milwaukee, 1960.

_____. "The Wisdom Literature of the Old Testament." In *The Human Reality of Sacred Scripture,* 126-40. 1965.

Nötscher, F. "Biblische und babylonische Weisheit." *BZ* 6 (1962): 120-26.

Noth, M. "Die Bewährung von Salomos 'Gottlicher Weisheit'." VTSup 3 (1960): 225-37.

Nougayrol, J. "Le version ancienne de 'juste souffrant'." *RB* 59 (1952): 239-50.

_____. "Les sagesses babloniennes: études récentes et textes inédits." *SPOA*, 41-50. 1963.

Nowack, W. *Die Sprüche, Prediger, und Hoheslied übersetzt und erklärt.* HAT 2/3. Göttingen, 1898.

Oesterley, W. O. E. *The Book of Proverbs.* London, 1929.

————. *Ecclesiasticus.* Cambridge, 1912.

————. "The 'Teaching of Amenemope' and the Old Testament." *ZAW* 45 (1927): 9-24.

————. *The Wisdom of Egypt and the Old Testament.* London, 1927.

Orelli, C. von. *Die alttestamentliche Weissagung von der Vollendung des Gottesreiches in ihrer geschichtlichen Entwicklung dargestellt.* Vienna, 1882.

Otto, E. "Der Vorwurf an Gott." In *Vorträge der orientalistische Tagung in Marburg,* 1-15. 1950 (1951).

Paterson. J. *The Wisdom of Israel.* Nashville, 1961.

Paulus, J. "Le thème du Juste Souffrant dans la pensée grecque et hebraique." *RHR* 121/122 (1940): 18-66.

Peake, A. S. *Job.* Century Bible. London, 1904.

Pedersen, J. "Scepticisme israelite." *RHPR* 10 (1930): 317-70.

————. "Wisdom and Immortality." VTSup 3 (1960): 238-46.

Peters, N. *Die Weisheitsbücher des Alten Testaments.* Münster i.W., 1914.

Pfeiffer, E. "Die Gottesfurcht im Buche Kohelet." In *Gottes Wort und Gottes Land, Festschrift W. Hertzberg,* 133-58. Göttingen, 1965.

Pfeiffer, R. *Die religiös-sittliche Weltanschauung des Buches der Sprüche.* München, 1897.

Pfeiffer, R. H. "Edomitic Wisdom." *ZAW* 24 (1926): 13-25.

————. "Wisdom and Vision in the Old Testament." *ZAW* 52 (1934): 93-101.

Plöger, O. "Besprechung von U. Skladny, *Die ältesten Spruchsammlungen. . . .* " *Gnomon* 36 (1964): 297-300.

————. "Wahre die richtige Mitte: solch Mass ist in allen das Beste!" In *Gottes Wort und Gottes Land,* 159-73. 1965.

————. "Zur Auslegung der Sentenzensammlungen des Proverbienbuches." In *Probleme biblischer Theologie,* 402-16. München, 1971.

Pope, M. H. *Job.* AB. Garden City NY, 1965.

Porteous, N. W. "Royal Wisdom." VTSup 3 (1960): 247-61.

Preuss, H. D. "Erwägungen zum theologischen Ort alttestamentlicher Weisheitsliteratur." *EvT* 30 (1970): 393-417.

————. "Das Gottesbild der alteren Weisheit Israels." VTSup 23 (1972): 117-45.

Priest, J. F. "Humanism, Skepticism, and Pessimism in Israel." *JAAR* 36 (1968): 311-26.

————. "Where Is Wisdom to be Placed?" *JBR* 31 (1963): 275-82.

Pritchard, J. B., ed. *Ancient Near Eastern Texts Relating to the Old Testament.* Third edition. Princeton NJ, 1969.

Rad, G. von. "Job XXXVIII and Ancient Egyptian Wisdom." In *The Problem of the Hexateuch and Other Essays,* 281-91. Edinburgh and London, 1966.

————. "The Joseph Narrative and Ancient Wisdom." In *The Problem of the Hexateuch and Other Essays,* 292-300.

————. *Old Testament Theology.* Volume 1. Edinburgh and London; New York, 1962. (German edition, 1957.)

————. "Some Aspects of the Old Testament Worldview." In *The Problem of the Hexateuch and Other Essays,* 144-65.

————. "Sprüchebuch." *RGG³* 6:285-88.

————. *Wisdom in Israel.* Nashville, 1972.

Rainey, A. F. "The Scribe at Ugarit. His Position and Influence. *Proceedings of the Israel Academy of Sciences and Humanities* 3-4 (1968): 126-46.

Rankin, O. S. *Israel's Wisdom Literature.* Repr: Edinburgh, 1954.

Ranston, H. *The Old Testament Wisdom Books and Their Teaching.* London, 1930.

Reese, J. M. *Hellenistic Influence on the Book of Wisdom and Its Consequences.* AnBib 41. Rome, 1970.

_____. "Plan and Structure in the Book of Wisdom." *CBQ* 27 (1965): 391-99.

Richter, H. "Die Naturweisheit des Alten Testaments im Buche Hiob." *ZAW* 70-71 (1958–1959): 1-19.

_____. *Studien zu Hiob.* ThArb 11. 1959.

Ringgren, H. *Word and Wisdom. Studies in the Hypostatization of Divine Qualities and Functions in the Ancient Near East.* Lund, 1947.

Röhrrich, L. "Sprichwort," *RGG³* 6:282-84.

Roth, W. M. W. *Numerical Sayings in the Old Testament.* VTSup 13. 1965.

Rowley, H. H. *Job.* New Century Bible. Great Britain, 1970.

Rudolph, W. *Vom Buch Kohelet.* Münster Westf., 1959.

Rüger, H. P. *Text und Textform in hebräischen Sirach.* BZAW 112. Berlin, 1970.

Rylaarsdam, J. C. "Hebrew Wisdom." In *Peake's Commentary on the Bible*, 386-90. London and Edinburgh, 1962.

_____. *Revelation in Jewish Wisdom Literature.* Chicago, 1946.

Sanders, J. A. *Suffering as Divine Discipline in the Old Testament and Postbiblical Judaism.* New York, 1955.

Sanders, P. S. *Twentieth Century Interpretations of the Book of Job.* Englewood Cliffs NJ, 1968.

Sarna, N. "Epic Substratum in the Prose of Job." *JBL* 76 (1957): 13-25.

Sauer, G. *Die Sprüche Agurs.* BWANT 84. 1963.

Schechter, S. "A Glimpse of the Social Life of the Jews in the Age of Jesus the Son of Sirach." In *Studies in Judaism* (2nd ser.), 55-101. Philadelphia, 1908.

Schencke, W. *Die Chokma (Sophia) in der jüdischen Hypostatenspekulation: ein Beitrag zur Geschichte der religiösen Ideen im Zeitalter des Hellenismus*, 1913.

Schmid, H. H. *Gerechtigkeit als Weltordnung.* BHT 40. Tübingen, 1968.

_____. "Hauptprobleme der altorientalischen und alttestamentlichen Weisheitsliteratur." *STU* 35 (1965): 68-74.

_____. *Wesen und Geschichte der Weisheit.* BZAW 101. Berlin, 1966.

Schmidt, J. *Der Ewigkeitsbegriff im Alten Testament.* ÄA 13/5. Münster, 1940.

_____. *Studien zur Stilistik der alttestamentlichen Spruchliteratur.* ÄA 13/1. Münster, 1936.

Schreiner, J. "Die altorientalische Weisheit als Lebenskunde. Israels neues Verständnis und Kritik der Weisheit." In *Wort und Botschaft*, 258-71. Würzburg, 1967.

Scott, R. B. Y. "Folk Proverbs of the Ancient Near East." *Transactions of the Royal Society of Canada* 15 (1961): 47-56.

_____. "Priesthood, Prophecy, Wisdom, and the Knowledge of God." *JBL* 80 (1961): 1-15.

_____. *Proverbs, Ecclesiastes.* AB. New York, 1965.

_____. "Solomon and the Beginnings of Wisdom in Israel." VTSup 3 (1960): 262-79.

_____. "The Study of the Wisdom Literature." *Int* 24 (1970): 20-45.

_____. *The Way of Wisdom in the Old Testament.* New York, 1971.

_____. "Wise and Foolish, Righteous and Wicked." VTSup 23 (1972): 146-65.

Sekine, M. "Schöpfung und Erlösung im Buche Hiob." BZAW 77 (1958): 213-23.

Simpson, D. C. "The Hebrew Book of Proverbs and the Teaching of Amenophis." *JEA* 12 (1926): 232-39.

Skladny, U. *Die ältesten Spruchsammlungen in Israel.* Berlin, 1961.

Smend, R. *Die Weisheit des Jesus Sirach, erklärt von R.S.* Berlin, 1906.

_____. *Die Weisheit des Jesus Sirach, hebräisch und deutsch.* Berlin, 1906.

Snaith, N. H. *The Book of Job.* SBT 11. London, 1968.

Spiegel, J. *Die Präambel des Amenemope und die Zielsetzung der ägyptischen Weisheitsliteratur.* Glückstadt, 1935.

Sprondel, G. *Untersuchungen zum Selbstverständnis und zur Frömmigkeit der alten Weisheit Israels.* Göttingen, 1962.

Stamm, J. J. "Die Theodizee im Babylon und Israel." *JEOL* 9 (1944): 99-107.

Steuernägel, C. *Die Sprüche.* HSAT 2. Tübingen, 1922.

Story, C. I. K. "The Book of Proverbs and Northwest Semitic Literature." *JBL* 64 (1945): 319-37.

Strack, H. L. *Die Sprüche Salomos.* KKANT 6/2. München, 1899.

Suys, E. *La sagesse d'Ani.* AnOr 11. Rome, 1935.

Talmon, S. "'Wisdom' in the Book of Esther." *VT* 13 (1963): 419-55.

Taylor, A. *The Proverb.* Cambridge MA, 1931.

Terrien, S. "Amos and Wisdom." In *Israel's Prophetic Heritage, Festschrift J. Muilenburg,* ed. B. W. Anderson and Walter Harrelson, 108-15. New York, 1962.

_____. "Quelques remarques sur les affinities de Job avec le Deutéro-Esaïe." VTSup 15 (1965): 295-310.

_____. *Job: Poet of Existence.* New York, 1957.

Thomas, D. W. "Textual and Philological Notes on Some Passages in the Book of Proverbs." VTSup 3 (1960): 280-92.

Thompson, J. M. *The Form and Function of Proverbs in Ancient Israel.* Leiden, 1971.

Thompson, K. "Out of the Whirlwind." *Int* 14 (1960): 51-63.

Toombs, L. E. "O.T. Theology and the Wisdom Literature." *JBR* 23 (1955): 193-96.

Torczyner, H. = Tur-Sinai, N. H. "Nachträge und Berichtigungen zu meinen Proverbiastudien." ZDMG 72 (1918): 154-56. (See next.)

_____. "Proverbiastudien." ZDMG 71 (1917): 99-118.

_____. *The Book of Job.* Jerusalem, 1967.

Tournay, R. "Proverbs 1–9: A First Theological Synthesis of the Tradition of the Sages." In *The Dynamism of the Biblical Tradition,* 51-61. New York, 1967.

Toy, C. H. *The Book of Proverbs.* ICC. Edinburgh and New York, 1899.

Tsevat, M. "The Meaning of the Book of Job." *HUCA* 37 (1966): 73-106.

Urbach, E. E. "Class-Status and Leadership in the World of the Palestinian Sages." *Proceedings of the Israel Academy of Sciences and Humanities* 2 (1966): 1-37.

Vergote, J. "La notion de Dieu dans les livres de sagesse égyptiens." *SPOA,* 159-90. 1963.

Vischer, W. "God's Truth and Man's Lie. A Study of the Message of the Book of Job." *Int* 15 (1961): 131-46.

_____. *Der Prediger Salomo.* München, 1926.

Volten, A. "Der Begriff der Ma'at in den Ägyptischen Weisheitstexten." *SPOA,* 73-102. 1963.

_____. *Studien zum Weisheitsbuch des Anii, Kgl. Danske Vid. Selsk.* Hist. fil. Med., 23/3.

Copenhagen, 1937/1938.

_____. *Zwei altägyptische politische Schriften. Die Lehre für König Merikare . . . und die Lehre des Königs Amenemhet, An Aeg* 4. Copenhagen, 1945.

Volz, P. *Hiob und Weisheit. SAT* 3/2. Göttingen, 1921.

Walcot, P. "Hesiod and the Instructions of 'Onchsheshonqy." *JNES* 21 (1962): 215-19.

Walle, B. van de. "Problemes relatifs aux methodes d'enseignement dans l'Égypte ancienne." *SPOA*, 191-207. 1963.

Wallis, G. "Zu den Spruchsammlungen Prov. 10:1–22:16 und 25–29." *TLZ* 85 (1960): 147-48.

Weiden, W. A. van der. *Le livre des Proverbes. Notes philologiques.* BibOr 23. Rome, 1970.

Weinfeld, M. "The Dependence of Deuteronomy upon the Wisdom Literature." In *Yehezkel Kaufmann Jubilee Volume*, 89-108. Jerusalem, 1960.

_____. "Deuteronomy. The Present State of Inquiry." *JBL* 86 (1967): 249-62.

Weiser, A. "Das Problem der sittlichen Weltordnung im Buche Hiob." In *Glaube und Geschichte im Alten Testament*, 9-19. Göttingen, 1961.

Werner, J. *Lateinische Sprichwörter und Sinnsprüche des Mittelalters aus Handschriften gesammelt.* Second edition, ed. P. Flury. Darmstadt, 1966.

Westermann, C. *Der Aufbau des Buches Hiob.* BHT 23. 1956.

_____. "Weisheit im Sprichwort." In *Schalom (Festscrift A. Jepsen)*, 73-85. Stuttgart, 1971.

Whybray, R. N. *The Heavenly Counsellor in Isaiah xl 13-14.* SOTSMS. Cambridge, 1971.

_____. *The Intellectual Tradition in the Old Testament.* BZAW 135. Berlin and New York, 1974.

_____. "Proverbs VIII 22-31 and its Supposed Prototypes." *VT* 15 (1965): 504-14.

_____. *The Succession Narrative.* SBT 2nd ser. 9. 1968.

_____. *Wisdom in Proverbs.* SBT 45. 1965.

Wied, G. "Der Auferstehungsglaube des späten Israels in seiner Bedeutung für das Verhältnis von Apokalyptik und Weisheit." Dissertation, Friedrich-Wilhelms University, Bonn, 1967.

Wildeboer, G. *Die Sprüche.* KHC. Freiburg, 1897.

Williams, J. G. "What Does It Profit a Man?: The Wisdom of Koheleth." *Judaism* 20 (1971): 179-93.

Williams, R. J. "Scribal Training in Ancient Egypt." *JAOS* 92 (1972): 214-21.

_____. "Theodicy in the Ancient Near East." *CJT* 2 (1956): 14-26.

Wolff, H. W. *Amos geistige Heimat.* WMANT 18. 1964. ET: *Amos the Prophet.* Philadelphia, 1973.

Wood, J. *Wisdom Literature.* London, 1967.

Wright, A. G. "Numerical Patterns in the Book of Wisdom." *CBQ* 29 (1967): 524-38.

_____. "The Riddle of the Sphinx: The Structure of the Book of Qoheleth." *CBQ* 30 (1968): 313-34.

_____. "The Structure of the Book of Wisdom." *Bib* 48 (1967): 165-84.

Würthwein, E. "Gott und Mensch in Dialog und Gottesreden des Buches Hiob." In *Wort und Existenz*, 217-95.

_____. "Die Weisheit Ägyptens und das Alte Testament." *Mitt. d. Univ.-bundes Marburg* 1958/1959, H.3/4, 55-69. = *Wort und Existenz*, 197-216.

Zaba, Z. *Les maximes de Ptahhotep.* Ed. de l'Acad. Tchech des Sciences. Prag, 1956.

Ziener, G. *Die theologische Begriffssprache im Buche der Weisheit.* BBB 11. Bonn, 1956.

Zimmerli, W. "Das Buch Kohelet—Traktät oder Sentenzensammlung?" *VT* 24 (1974): 221-30.

_____. *Das Buch des Predigers Salomo*. ATD 16. Göttingen, 1962.

_____. "Ort und Grenze der Weisheit im Rahmen der alttestamentlichen Theologie." *SPOA*. 1963. ET: "The Place and Limit of the Wisdom in the Framework of the Old Testament Theology." *SJT* 17 (1964): 146-58.

_____. "Zur Struktur der alttestamentlichen Weisheit." *ZAW* 51 (1933): 177-204.

_____. "Die Weisheit Israels. Zu einem Buch von Gerhard von Rad." *EvT* 31 (1971): 680-95.

_____. *Die Weisheit des Predigers Salomo*. Berlin, 1936.

Zimmerman, F. "Altägyptische Spruchweisheit in der Bibel." *TGl* 17 (1925): 204-17.

_____. *The Inner World of Koheleth*. New York, 1973.

6 (1983)

Introduction:
The Shift from Theodicy
to Anthropodicy

The human compulsion to deny death[1] is exceeded only by a desire to absolve the deity of responsiblity for injustice.[2] In truth, the two motivating forces are integrally related to one another, for death stands as the ultimate question mark attached to any defense of God.[3] Why, one asks, were we fashioned from such stuff that we shall eventually become food for worms (Sir 10:11)? If, however, death does not constitute the last word, the dark shadow cast over the deity becomes somewhat less ominous. Only gradually did ancient Israel choose to walk along this path as a means towards resolving the enigmas of human existence,[4] and even when she did haltingly profess belief in life after death (Dan 12:2; Isa 26:19) that newfound conviction did not altogether alleviate the misery brought on by the phenomena of evil, suffering, and death. It follows that a study of Israel's attempts to come to terms with death and its minions will introduce us to the pathos of her faith, for both agony and ecstasy characterize that struggle to understand the universal decree, "You must die."[5]

While the problem of theodicy achieves focus in death, especially premature wasting away, the issue is much broader than that. Indeed, every phenomenon that brings into question an assumption of harmony undergirding human existence

---

[1]Ernest Becker, *The Denial of Death* (New York: Free Press, 1973), has demonstrated our obsession with death and has examined in great detail heroic attempts to deny death's reality.

[2]James L. Crenshaw, s.v. "Theodicy," IDBSup.

[3]"Every human order is a community in the face of death. Theodicy represents the attempt to make a pact with death." (P. L. Berger, *The Sacred Canopy* [Garden City NY: Doubleday, 1969] 80).

[4]Hartmut Gese, *Zur biblischen Theologie: Alttestamentliche Vorträge*, BEvT 78 (Munich: Chr. Kaiser, 1977) 31-54; = ET 34-59.

[5]See Sir 14:11; 41:3. See James L. Crenshaw, "The Shadow of Death in Ecclesiastes," in *Israelite Wisdom: Theological and Literary Essays in Honor of Samuel Terrien*, ed. J. G. Gammie et al. (Missoula MT: Scholars Press, 1978) 205-16.

presents additional evidence for the case against God. We may thus define theodic
loosely as the attempt to pronounce a verdict of "Not Guilty" over God for whateve
seems to destroy the order of society and the universe. That wish to protect th
deity's honor surfaced in the very first recorded utterance by a woman in th
Hebrew Bible (Gen 3:2-3). Here the serpent's accusing question cast suspicion upo:
divine goodness; such doubt on the serpent's part evoked a response that furthe
restricted human freedom. A subtle shift occurs in the prohibition, one from *eatin*
to *touching* the forbidden fruit. We shall see that theodicy invariably gnawed awa
at the integrity[6] and dignity of those who felt constrained to come to the defense c
the creator. In short, God's reputation was salvaged at immense cost.[7]

The Search for Meaning

In order to render life bearable the ancients posited a belief in order, both in th
macrocosm and the microcosm.[8] The universe was predictable, within limits, for
was subject to the wishes of the creator. When this assumption threatened to disinte
grate from the impact of the flood waters, the Yahwist took special care to restor
faith in nature's rhythm. The so-called Noachic covenant constitutes the divin
assurance to all peoples that life could go on under changed circumstances brougl
about by the Deluge (Gen 9:8-17). Such an assault from the forces of chaos woul
never again threaten the world; the rainbow exists as a reminder of this promise,
sign that is visible both to the one freely giving it and to those joyfully receivin
its benefits. To be sure, individuals were thereafter subject to attack from evil in it
various manifestations. Therefore, it follows that meaning and not happiness wa
basic to survival. Isolated individuals could endure sporadic irruptions of undeserve
distress in the knowledge that the belief system was not threatened. So long as tha
conviction of order held firm in the universe, essential meaning remained inta«
despite occasional disturbances that made happiness an elusive goal.

What was the precise nature of these disturbances? We may speak of thre
basic phenomena: evil, suffering and death. The first of these unwelcome visito:
consists of moral evil, natural evil, and religious evil. Since nature's destructiv
forces were unleashed by the creator, the distinction between moral and natural ev
becomes somewhat vague in ethical monotheism. Naturally, the situation is differe»

---

[6]Note the manner in which the first man isolates himself, accusing his newly acquir«
wife and God, the generous fashioner of the woman who earlier elicited an ecstatic shout «
satisfaction.

[7]That fact has not escaped C. G. Jung, who suspects that God needed consta:
reassurance that he was just, even at the expense of the truth (*Answer to Job* [Cleveland ar
New York: World, 1960] 32). One may also consult Ernst Bloch (*Atheism in Christiani*
[New York: Herder, 1972]).

[8]Hans Heinrich Schmid, *Wesen und Geschichte der Weisheit*, BZAW 101 (Berli»
Töpelmann, 1966).

where a pantheon of gods exists, for certain deities are responsible for life's disturbing aspects, while others share no responsibility for these vexing phenomena.[9] In Israelite thought one God "kills and brings to life, he brings down to Sheol and raises up" (1 Sam. 2:6), to quote a significant declaration in the Song of Hannah. Similarly, Deutero-Isaiah announces the divine word that "I form light and create darkness, I make weal and create woe, I am the Lord, who do all these things" (Isa 45:7). The consequence of emphasis upon God's incomparability,[10] nay sole existence, was intensified distress about undeserved suffering. Famine, pestilence, and earthquake struck human society without discriminating between the innocent and the guilty.

One way to defuse the situation was to assert that natural forces merely functioned as instruments of divine punishment for sin. While such a claim came to God's defense by reasserting the familiar theme that even Behemoth and Leviathan have been subdued by their creator,[11] this explanation failed to take into account the terrible misery inflicted upon innocent persons who happened to be caught up in the suffering occasioned by nature's fury. A case can even be made for the essential connection between belief in creation and divine justice. Although the rise of creation theology is often associated with saving history, the allusions to God as creator in wisdom literature reinforce belief in divine justice. In short, the one who brought the world into being possesses sufficient power to ensure a balance of order and equity. That is why again and again sages brought together the concepts of creation and justice.[12]

Moral evil is a relational category, but is not necessarily limited to the human sphere. On the vertical dimension issues of morality surface, for individuals seem always eager to subject the deity to norms of justice and virtue that operate among

---

[9]Giorgio Buccellati, "Wisdom and Not: The Case of Mesopotamia," *JAOS* 101 (1981): 36, writes that the texts dealing with theodicy "present a descriptive reflection about the pervasiveness of laws which in their absolute value transcend both the individual gods and the unresolved questions of human life. Thus the Theodicy is not a vindication of a given god or of the open polytheistic system, but rather a statement about the ultimate value of the absolute, both in the divine (or supernatural) and in the human (or political) sphere."

[10]C. J. Labuschagne, *The Incomparability of Yahweh in the Old Testament* (Leiden: Brill, 1966). James L. Crenshaw, *Prophetic Conflict*, BZAW 124 (Berlin and New York: Walter de Gruyter, 1971), emphasizes the consequences for prophecy of belief in one God as giver of good and evil.

[11]John G. Gammie, "Behemoth and Leviathan: On the Didactic and Theological Significance of Job 40:15—41:26," in *Israelite Wisdom*, 217-31.

[12]James L. Crenshaw, *Studies in Ancient Israelite Wisdom* (New York: Ktav, 1976) 26-35, esp. 31-33. For a different view, see Hans-Jürgen Hermisson, "Observations on the Creation Theology in Wisdom," in *Israelite Wisdom*, 43-57. The association of creation and redemption is usually based on a conviction that as creator God possesses sufficient power to save.

human beings. Base and inhumane treatment of others, as well as manipulation for personal ends, comprises moral evil, regardless of its source. The assumption of order on the societal level may permit moral evil to flourish unrecognized and unchallenged, for it enables rulers to justify their position and policies just as it secures a place in the overall scheme of things for those who are governed. This strange circumstance encourages two vastly different kinds of theodicies, one for the oppressor and another for the oppressed. The ensuing situation may explain the emphasis upon God as sustainer of kings and champion of widows and orphans. Each group, the powerful and the powerless, rushed to God's defense where its interests were concerned.

What, then, does the third category of evil entail? Religious evil signifies an inner disposition that perverts authentic response to the holy. That perversion may assume the form of idolatry,[13] where worship is directed away from God to a pale reflection of the ultimate. This type of evil operates wholly on the vertical plane; it concerns human relationship with God and thus extends to the innermost recesses of the imagination.[14] In this respect, religious evil is by its very nature more hidden than the other two, moral and natural evil. It is therefore all the more pernicious since its presence can be easily concealed from human eyes. In fact, some individuals dared to stretch the cloak of secrecy into the heavens, denying God's clarity of vision on grounds of remoteness or indifference.[15] "How can God see through the dark clouds?" they reasoned, whenever they did not actually suggest that the creator lacked interest in terrestrial happenings.

Does not the assumption of order carry in its train a conviction that life has some discernible purpose? Teleology, it would seem, accompanies belief in the harmony of existence. Order implies a goal whereas chaos lacks movement towards some final meaningful destination. Incursions of anomy[16] can at best momentarily divert the march towards a distant goal, but in the last resort such disturbances only hasten progress in the direction of the desired end. They do so by sharpening one's resolve and by shaping character, for adversity does not necessarily weaken individuals.

That brings us to the problem of undeserved suffering, a subject that frequently occupied the thoughts of the ancients as it continues to do in the modern world which has seen the issue present itself definitively and paradigmatically in the great Lisbon earthquake of 1755 and more recently in the nightmares of Auschwitz and

---

[13]Maurice Gilbert, *La critique des dieux dans le Livre de la Sagesse* (*Sg.* 13-15), AnBib 53 (Rome: Biblical Institute Press, 1973).

[14]Although religious evil functions on the vertical plane, it has significant consequences for moral action.

[15]James L. Crenshaw, "Popular Questioning of the Justice of God in Ancient Israel," *ZAW* 82 (1970): 380-95 = *Studies in Ancient Israelite Wisdom*, 289-304.

[16]The term, as used by Peter Berger and others, refers to absence of *nomos*, that which holds society or an individual together.

Hiroshima.[17] What possible response to such puzzling nightmares exists? Space permits us to do no more than name the several approaches to this problem in ancient Israel. These consist of at least seven means of reconciling undeserved suffering with belief in order and purpose. They understand suffering as retributive, disciplinary, revelational, probative, illusory, transitory, or mysterious.[18] Admittedly, an eighth response to this problem achieves prominence in Qoheleth, who denies the possibility of discovering any meaning behind innocent suffering. In this respect such denial resembles the previous response that appeals to the unknown and unknowable (and thus constitutes something approaching an antitheodicy), but it goes one step further and asserts that life under such conditions has no meaning, for no comforter can be found (Eccl 4:1).

In many cases such suffering results in death; we have thus arrived at the third manifestation of anomy mentioned earlier. Now the occurrence of death does not always introduce an element of disturbance requiring explanation. In proper time and manner death resembled the gathering of golden shocks of grain at the season of harvest.[19] Lacking a view of life beyond the grave, save in some ghost-like semblance of existence, Israelites accepted death as inevitable, sometimes, to be sure, with slight tinges of resignation.[20] Entirely different, however, were those instances when death came out of season and violently. How could one believe in God's justice when the ugly dimension of death gained ascendancy?

The issue becomes more perplexing when one pauses to reflect upon the character of the Israelite Lord. Lying at the very heart of her faith is the conviction that Yahweh chose the Israelites and set them apart for special promise and mission. Her sacred narrative and poetry extol God as redeemer of an oppressed people, one who subsequently experienced remarkable demonstrations of divine presence and power. Before this sovereign all earthly rulers must acquiesce, for not even Egypt's might could withstand Yahweh's initiative. Israel's sacred story abounds in divine promises to accompany the chosen ones and assurances that she need not fear enemies from without. Still, circumstances managed to transform such positive words

---

[17]The impact of the Lisbon earthquake upon religious claims is well known, particularly as that conflict emerges in Leibniz and Voltaire. The term theodicy arose with Leibniz.

[18]See, among others, James A. Sanders, *Suffering as Divine Discipline in the Old Testament and Postbiblical Judaism* (Rochester: Colgate Rochester Divinity School, 1955); Erhard Gerstenberger and Wolfgang Schrage, *Leiden* (Stuttgart: Kohlhammer, 1977); and Roland E. Murphy, "Biblical Insights into Suffering: Pathos and Compassion," in *Whither Creativity, Freedom, Suffering?: Humanity, Cosmos, God*, ed. F. A. Eigo, Proceedings of the Theology Institute of Villanova University 13 (Villanova PA: Villanova University Press, 1981) 53-75.

[19]Lloyd R. Bailey, Sr., *Biblical Perspectives on Death*, OBT (Philadelphia: Fortress Press, 1979), emphasizes the Israelite acceptance of death.

[20]2 Sam 12:15-23, especially v. 23: "But now he is dead; why should I fast? Can I bring him back again? I shall go to him, but he will not return to me." Cf. 2 Sam 14:14, "We must all die, we are like water spilt on the ground, which cannot be gathered up again."

into hollow promises devoid of substance. In a word, the covenant relationship exacerbated the problem of theodicy,[21] for the Lord confessed a personal interest in Israel's destiny. In the absence of visible proof that God continues to direct the history of Israel towards a distant goal, what was she supposed to think? Surely that question pressed itself upon the religious leaders in 722 and 587 B.C.E., for the collapse of the northern kingdom and the destruction of Jerusalem were events of no small consequence. The latter calamity was particularly troubling, for Zion had come to represent God's very presence and power, and in fact Josiah's religious reform stood under divine promise articulated in Deuteronomy.[22] The violence which stilled Josiah forever made mockery of God's assurances that success would attend faithful conduct.[23]

The notion of reward and punishment which permeates the Deuteronomistic history and most of the Hebrew Bible presented a ready defense of God: the people are merely reaping what they sowed. In some cases the claim may actually have accorded with reality, especially where "doxologies of judgement" rang forth. In such texts a guilty person or persons confessed God's goodness in pronouncing a sentence of death (see Josh 7:19; Amos 4:13; 5:8-9; 9:5-6, and related passages). But who would contend that all instances of suffering were occasioned by the victims' wickedness? The resulting tension between divine and human culpability was nearly always eased by stressing the latter's sinfulness. In short, defense of God occurred at human expense. As a consequence theodicy was given up, and anthropodicy became the fundamental problem claiming the attention of religious thinkers.[24]

Theodicy in the Old Testament

"It is arrogant to attempt to defend God's justice; it is still more arrogant to assail the deity."[25] Whoever makes such a claim participates minimally in the spirit of the Hebrew Bible, where complaint rises to the God who has revealed the divine

---

[21]Gideon's sharp retort to the divine messenger's assurance of God's presence speaks volumes: "Pray, sir, if the Lord is with us, why then has all this befallen us? And where are all his wonderful deeds which our fathers recounted to us . . . ?" (Judg 6:13).

[22]Stanley Frost, "The Death of Josiah: A Conspiracy of Silence," *JBL* 87 (1968): 369-82.

[23]Religious pragmatism occurs with vengeance in the thought of Jeremiah's opponents in Egypt who argue that it does not pay to serve Yahweh (Jer 44:16-19).

[24]In Job "the problem of theodicy is solved by an *argumentum ad hominem* in the most drastic sense—more accurately, an *argumentum contra hominen*. . . . The question of human sin replaces the question of divine justice" (Berger, *Sacred Canopy*, 74). See A. Jäger, "Theodizee und Anthropodizee bei Karl Marx," *STU* 37 (1967): 14-23, for discussion of the general problem in Marxist thought.

[25]The quotation is attributed to Immanuel Kant by E. G. Kraeling, "A Theodicy—and More," in *The Dimensions of Job*, ed. Nahum N. Glatzer (New York: Schocken Books, 1969) 212. See Immanuel Kant, "Über das Misslingen aller philosophischen Versuche in der Theodizee," in *Werke*, ed. W. Weischedel (Darmstadt, 1964) 6:103-24.

nature as merciful.[26] Nevertheless, even in the Old Testament all rational efforts at theodicy abort, for humans cannot possess firm knowledge of Transcendence.[27] That is why such "rational" theodicies as Job eventually cross over into the realm of feeling and will. Human beings are more than rational creatures; they also possess deep feelings and wishes, which any authentic theodicy must address.

Even those theodicies which sufficiently take feelings and desires into account fail in one important respect: they sacrifice human integrity. In a real sense, Job's silent submission before an awesome display of power amounts to loss of integrity, hence may rightly be termed an argument against humanity.[28]

It may actually be the case that self-abnegation lies at the heart of all theodicy. Only as the individual fades into nothingness can the deity achieve absolute pardon. That loss of individuality may occur in some mystical union wherein one's true selfhood is thought to come to full expression, or it may take place in abject groveling upon the ground before the mighty God. In either case the really human is denigrated, and therein lurks a fatal flaw. Such a condition gives rise to utterances like the following:

> The Lord saw that the wickedness of man was great in the earth, and that every imagination of the thoughts of his heart was only evil continually.
>
> (Gen 6:5 RSV)

In this thinker's view, the flood was wholly justified because humans constituted a *massa perditiones*. The same sort of reasoning occurs to justify the later calamity that befell the southern kingdom in 587.

> Run to and fro through the streets of Jerusalem,
>   look and take note!
> Search her squares to see if you can find a man,
>   one who does justice and seeks truth;
> that I may pardon her.
>
> (Jer 5:1 RSV)

The prophet goes first to the poor people and finds no virtue. Such results are expected, since the poorer classes are ill informed about divine law. So he turns to the upper classes, from whom he expects greater obedience to torah, and makes an astonishing discovery. The elite citizens have also rebelled against decency and have

---

[26]James L. Crenshaw, "The Human Dilemma and Literature of Dissent," in *Tradition and Theology in the Old Testament*, ed. D. A. Knight (Philadelphia: Fortress, 1977) 235-58.

[27]Gerhard von Rad, *Wisdom in Israel* (Nashville: Abingdon Press; London: SCM Press, 1972) 97-110.

[28]For a recent attempt to grapple with the meaning of the divine speeches and Job's response, see J. G. Williams, "Deciphering the Unspoken: The Theophany of Job," *HUCA* 49 (1978): 59-72.

become wholly wanton. In effect, knowledge is not tantamount to obedience, and humans require a new heart (Jer 31:31-34).

In one respect, this text contrasts with another which endeavours to justify wholesale slaughter of the inhabitants of Sodom and Gomorrah. The presence of a single righteous person suffices to spare the holy city, whereas Abraham stopped at ten when bargaining with God over the fate of the doomed cities. To be sure, the narrative in Gen 18:16-33 depicts a responsive deity, and one could argue that the failure was Abraham's, not God's inasmuch as the absence of a single virtuous person in Sodom and Gomorrah is demonstrated by the unfolding story. Since the cities lacked a saving individual, the Judge of the whole earth acted properly, and the patriarch's stunning question, "Shall not the Judge of all the earth do right?" (18:25), loses something of its force.[29]

Such salvaging of God's honor at the expense of human integrity eventuated in a grandiose interpretation of history that amounts to a monumental theodicy. This Deuteronomistic theology justifies national setbacks and political oppression as divine punishment for sin. The portrayal of Israel and Judah as corrupt to the core suffices to justify divine abandonment of the chosen people, but such rescuing of God's sovereignty and freedom was purchased at a high price, the self-esteem of humans.

This tendency to save God's honor by sacrificing human integrity seems to have caught on in ancient Israel, for every effort at theodicy represents a substantial loss of human dignity. The various attempts at theodicy constitute immense sacrifice: of the present, of reality itself, of personal honor, and of the will.

Perhaps the most natural response to the incursion of evil into unexpected circumstances is the surrender of the present moment in favor of future rectification. Without a tiny ray of hope life would become intolerable. The eschatological dimension speaks to this fundamental need by promising that the present calamity will soon pass away, and in its place will come clear signs of God's favor. The further into the future, or indeed into a hidden realm, this expected deliverance is projected, the safer the theodicy, since it becomes less vulnerable to empirical disconfirmation.[30] On the other hand, because the anticipated event is relegated to the remote future, its credibility is likely to fade as generation after generation long for the saving event and experience no fulfilment of that wish. Habakkuk's agonizing cry, "O Lord, how long shall I cry for help, and thou wilt not hear? Or cry to thee,

---

[29]In light of Abraham's question, the sharp accusation directed at Lot by citizens of the doomed cities assumes added significance ("This fellow came to sojourn, and he would play the judge!" Gen. 19:9). For concern over God's compassion resembling Abraham's, see the story about Moses' intercession for a wayward people (Exod 32).

[30]Naturally, Deutero-Isaiah made grand promises that far exceeded the realities of a later generation, even one of fulfilled promises.

'Violence!' and thou wilt not save?" (1:2), cannot be sustained indefinitely unless some indication of divine action presents itself.[31]

One means of dealing with delay in deliverance is to remove the hoped-for event from the realm of experience altogether. That can be achieved in two quite different ways. One can deny the reality of the evil, relegating it to illusion, as the author of Psalm 73 does, or one can shift the arena of God's action to the inner spirit or onto a hidden dimension of reality.[32] This hidden realm may be simultaneous in time, or it may be projected into the next world. Either way, the present experience fades into the shadow cast by anticipated bliss.

Sometimes theodicy seeks to excuse this delay in restoration by interpreting adversity as discipline.[33] Such an explanation for suffering takes many forms, but invariably it assumes that true character cannot emerge apart from testing. This argument pervades the Book of Job, finding frequent expression in the speeches of the three friends as well as in Elihu's angry remarks. As everyone knows, loving parents discipline wayward children, so it should occasion no surprise that God chastens sinful Israel and Judah. From this experience of suffering emerge new insights into selfhood, just as the initial act of disobedience in the garden bestowed valuable knowledge upon the first couple.[34] Often this kind of reasoning is reinforced by the assertion that beauty needs ugliness in order to come to full fruition.

A serious flaw is present in such thinking, specifically the assumption that the universe had to be constituted in such a way that evil is indispensable to goodness. One can readily imagine that a good creator could have made the world differently. What conceivable argument exists for God to enter into a bargain with the Satan to test the faithful servant Job? Or how can one even imagine God demanding that Abraham sacrifice his own son as a test of obedience?[35] No acquisition of fresh insight seems sufficiently precious to justify the private hell initiated by the words:

---

[31]On Habakkuk and theodicy, see D. E. Gowan, *The Triumph of Faith in Habakkuk* (Atlanta: John Knox, 1976) 20-50.

[32]Such a shift occurs in Ben Sira (Sirach) and Wisdom of Solomon, for whom the psychological and metaphysical realms achieve prominence in discussions of theodicy.

[33]Buccellati, "Wisdom and Not: The Case of Mesopotamia," 42-44, discusses the rise of introspection and thus lyric poetry against the backdrop of adversity. He quotes a passage in Aeschylus' *Agamemnon*: He has pointed man on his way to wisdom by having consciousness emerge through suffering: memory of pain, instead of sleep, he will distill into the heart, until it yields the gift of wisdom, even unwanted" (1:43).

[34]Phyllis Trible, *God and the Rhetoric of Sexuality*, OBT (Philadelphia: Fortress Press, 1978) 72-143.

[35]James L. Crenshaw, "Journey into Oblivion: A Structural Analysis of Gen 22:1-19," *Soundings* 58 (1975): 243-56. Søren Kierkegaard's difficulty in "imagining" such a monstrous test prompts him to describe the griefstruck father as eager to protect God's honor, even at his own expense. Abraham reasons that it is better for Isaac to think him a beast than to think God one (*Fear and Trembling* [Garden City NY: Doubleday, 1941] 27).

"Take your son, your only son Isaac, whom you love, and go to the land of Moriah, and offer him there as a burnt offering upon one of the mountains of which I shall tell you" (Gen 22:2). Even less persuasive is Ezekiel's unthinkable declaration to the effect that God gave laws demanding human sacrifice in order to horrify the people (Ezek 20:25-26).[36]

Another sacrifice of human integrity occurs when individuals give up every right to question God's ways. Jeremiah admits at the outset that he must be in the wrong and God in the right, for that is the nature of things.[37]

> Righteous art thou, O LORD,
> when I complain to thee;
>> yet I would plead my case before thee.
> Why does the way of the wicked prosper?
> Why do all who are treacherous thrive? (Jer 12:1 RSV)

An innocent Job smarts from God's challenge, "Will you even put me in the wrong? Will you condemn me that you may be justified?" (Job 40:8), and proceeds to reverse the offense by putting himself in the wrong. Standing before this blustering deity, such a one can only repent in dust and ashes. Where then is his integrity? Has not peace been purchased at too great a cost?

Later attempts to come to grips with human suffering at the hands of cruel oppressors seized this clue and salvaged belief in divine goodness. But that traditional conviction survived at the expense of human dignity, so that it becomes customary to describe society as a *massa damnationis*. The extent to which such thinking can go is manifest in 2 Esdras, where the hero alone is assured divine forgiveness. For the remainder of the people an awful punishment awaited. The seeds sown by Job have found fertile soil in the mind of this tormented individual.[38] Where now is the Lord of covenant love?

Earlier thinkers experienced less consternation over such negative understandings of human virtue, for they believed in something approximating an ontological

---

[36]The poverty of rational defense of God surfaces in Ezekiel's feeble efforts to persuade his opponents that God's ways were just and the people's not just (18:19-29). Here assertion alone is deemed adequate, when claim and counterclaim exist. What makes the prophet's word more credible than theirs?

[37]S. H. Blank, "The Confessions of Jeremiah and the Meaning of Prayer," *HUCA* 21 (1949): 331-54.

[38]Walter Harrelson, "Ezra Among the Wicked in 2 Esdras 3—10," in *The Divine Helmsman: Studies on God's Control of Human Events, Presented to Lou H. Silberman*, ed. James L. Crenshaw and Samuel Sandmel (New York: Ktav, 1980) 21-40. See also A. L. Thompson, *Responsibility for Evil in the Theodicy of IV Ezra*, SBLDS 29 (Missoula MT: Scholars Press, 1977) esp. 330-42. This new response to the problem of theodicy in 4 Ezra (=2 Esdras) is the explanation in terms of an evil *yetzer*. Such a belief in a malevolent principle within the heart came to prominence in later rabbinic speculation.

link which connected an individual genealogically with others in the social group. Here the loss of the self occurs on the level of clan relations, and actual suffering poses no lasting argument against divine goodness, inasmuch as the individual survives in the life of the group. This sacrificing of the self for the welfare of the larger entity has its correlate in subsequent self-denial for the sake of the community or for God.[39]

The powerful idea of a suffering servant who voluntarily endures the afflictions of the larger society and becomes a means of redemption has been called the most profound solution offered by religion to the problem of evil.[40] This chosen one in Deutero-Isaiah takes upon himself the punishment that should have befallen the guilty, and thus spares both God and humans. The picture is not quite so clear, however, for the voluntary nature of his suffering remains uncertain. Both human acquiescence and divine intention combine in the description of the faithful servant.

> Yet it was the will of the Lord to bruise him;
>   he has put him to grief;
> when he makes himself an offering for sin,
>   he shall see his offspring, he shall prolong his days;
> the will of the Lord shall prosper in his hand.   (Isa 53:10 RSV)

One almost gains the impression that the servant had little choice, like the lamb to which he is compared. Beyond that, the vicarious nature of suffering poses an additional problem if it is understood in a manner other than exemplary. How can someone else's suffering remove my guilt?

The preceding discussion has concentrated on the loss of human dignity that accompanies theodicy as it manifests itself in the Hebrew Bible. There is yet another dimension which calls for discussion, namely the loss of essential divine characteristics. These defenses of God's justice strike a compromise in several important respects: they place in jeopardy God's sovereign freedom and self-disclosure, and they imply that another deity exists in opposition to the Lord. One way to justify the presence of human suffering is to associate God directly with that

---

[39]As is well known, both Jeremiah and Ezekiel wrestle with an emerging sense of individuality which complained of suffering for others' crimes (Jer 31:27-30; Ezek 18). The Book of Chronicles applies the concept of reward and retribution on an individual basis, and the Prayer of Manasseh arises as a means of justifying God's patience in sparing this wicked king.

[40]D. D. Raphael, "Tragedy and Religion," in *Twentieth Century Interpretations of the Book of Job*, ed. P. S. Sanders (Englewood Cliffs NJ: Prentice Hall, 1968) 51.

agony. This emphasis upon the divine pathos,[41] which certain prophets stress to the limit, insists that God suffers from the effects of human rebellion.

> How can I give you up, O Ephraim!
>> How can I hand you over, O Israel!
> How can I make you like Admah!
>> How can I treat you like Zeboim!
> My heart recoils within me,
>> my compassion grows warm and tender.
> I will not execute my fierce anger,
>> I will not again destroy Ephraim;
> for I am God and not man,
>> the Holy One in your midst,
>> and I will not come to destroy.[42]   (Hos 11:8-9 RSV)

While some would argue that this loss of perfection in the deity is grievous, others celebrate the limitless potential of a God in process of becoming. This way of speaking about God accords well with the Hebrew Bible's tendency to highlight God's changeability. To be sure, the divine inconstancy arises from human response to prior divine action, but the Bible seems content to describe God as learning through experience.

Without question the greatest threat to the idea of God concerns freedom. The central theological question posed by the suffering Job is whether God is free or not.[43] Are human notions of justice the ultimate arbiter of God's actions? Must God succumb to the magical assumption that lies at the heart of religion as it expresses itself? Or is disinterested righteousness more than an illusion? An affirmative answer to the latter question signifies victory over bondage to magic. Now and then a rare human being will be good for the sake of the good act, not for reward or from fear of punishment.

Insistence upon God's bondage to justice takes a peculiar shape in Jonah's mind, for he objected to merciful actions when they were directed towards foreigners who had occasioned untold suffering in Israel. The ancient creed associated

---

[41]A. J. Heschel, *The Prophets* (New York: Harper & Row, 1962). In his popular treatment *When Bad Things Happen to Good People* (New York: Schocken, 1981), Harold Kushner is attracted to the idea that human anguish over the suffering of innocent people reflects God's anguish and compassion (85). Kushner opts for a limited deity: "He is limited in what he can do by laws of nature and by the evolution of human nature and human moral freedom" (134).

[42]The final decision on God's part remains uncertain, inasmuch as the Hebrew text reads "I will not come into the city," which would probably imply divine withdrawal. A worse punishment is scarcely conceivable.

[43]James L. Crenshaw, *Old Testament Wisdom: An Introduction* (Atlanta: John Knox, 1981) 100-25, 251-54.

with God's self-revelation to a persistent Moses (Exod 34:6-7) proclaimed the compassionate nature of the Lord in unforgettable fashion, while at the same time cautioning against presuming that sin would go unnoticed. Other texts, particularly Deuteronomy and Hosea, carried the emphasis upon Yahweh's graciousness to considerable extreme, arguing that God had chosen Israel through no worth of her own and that wanton conduct could not nullify a profound bond uniting the two. Jonah's anger towards God arose from a conviction that inhumane treatment of others should not be forgiven so readily, particularly when the prophet's reputation for truthfulness was also at stake. A peculiar irony lurks within Jonah's protest[44] since he was himself a recipient of divine compassion for a wayward sinner. How ludicrous, therefore, is the stated basis for Jonah's fury: "For I knew that thou art a gracious God and Merciful, slow to anger, and abounding in steadfast love, and repentest of evil" (4:2b).

The authors of numerous proverbs[45] and Psalm 37 come perilously close to enslaving God, who according to their view *must* reward the good deed and punish the bad one. Indeed, a break with reality has already occurred in Ps 37:25: "I have been young, and now am old; yet I have not seen the righteous forsaken or his children begging bread." That attitude in Job's friends and in Elihu impels them to heap untold misery upon the victim of God's withdrawal.

In Job's case the divine retreat into silence was temporary, and consequently gave way to torrential rebuke. Other theodicies resort to the idea of a chasm separating humans from the divine realm. In this case appeal is made to the *deus absconditus*, the God who hides.[46] Since God is by nature unknowable, this argument is particularly persuasive—except that it is combined with belief in revelation. The self-disclosing one is also the hidden one, and therein lies the problem. Admittedly, withholding of essential nature protects the deity's sovereignty, but why must the mystery begin when injustice raises its ugly head?

Another means of protecting God's honor comes from compromising ethical monotheism, as happens in the old folk tale upon which the story of Job depends. Here the Satan confronts the deity and challenges him to a contest to ascertain the disinterested character of Job's goodness. Since the adversary is designated as a child of God in the employ of the divine court, the shift in responsibility for ensuing atrocities is slight. Ultimately, God is still at fault. A much greater step is therefore taken in Chronicles, where objectionable conduct on God's part in 2 Samuel 24 is attributed to Satan. This understanding of divine action is a great distance from later

---

[44]Terence E. Fretheim, "Jonah and Theodicy," *ZAW* 90 (1978): 227-37.

[45]J. A. Gladson, "Retributive Paradoxes in Proverbs 10—29," Ph.D. diss., Vanderbilt University, 1978.

[46]Samuel Terrien, *The Elusive Presence* (New York: Harper & Row, 1978); James L. Crenshaw, "In Search of Divine Presence: Some Remarks Preliminary to a Theology of Wisdom," *RevExp* 74 (1977): 353-69.

developments where Satan functions in a quasi-dualistic manner. In such apocalyptic theodicies reality fades to the extent that history is demeaned and world-denial championed. Perhaps the personification of wisdom deserves mention, inasmuch as this intriguing figure functions in God's stead, thus ensuring divine presence and power to an age that saw no visible evidence of such. Echoes within this hymnic material approach a compromise in the area of a female associate,[47] but she is not seen as the source of evil.

Conclusion

The preceding discussion of theodicy in the Hebrew Bible has endeavored to present the central theological issues and the basic biblical resources relating to defense of God. Care has been taken to avoid duplication, insofar as possible, of treatments selected for inclusion in this volume. The aim has been to be provocative; in ancient Israel defense of God was no idle chatter but was purchased at great cost, as we have seen. Was the gain worth the loss? In their own way, the ensuing essays will address this important question.

The essays chosen for reproduction in this volume introduce the reader to the scope of the dilemma ancient Israelites faced in coming to grips with phenomena that seemed to deny the force of the claim that justice prevailed on high. The first three articles address the general problem of theodicy, the initial one against the backdrop of a theological theme that organizes Israelite religious thought, specifically that of the covenant, and the following essay against the larger geographical setting of ancient Egypt and Mesopotamia. The third isolates a single issue, whether a dogma of retribution existed in biblical religion, and endeavors to clarify the implications of belief in a sphere of act-consequence. These three essays which present the problem in its broader context are then complemented by special examinations of the theological issue of theodicy in representative texts within the Hebrew canon and in one instance, within the Apocrypha. Those biblical texts are the confessions of Jeremiah, Job, Psalm 73, Sirach (Ecclesiasticus) and Qoheleth (Ecclesiastes). The focus of the entire collection, whether specific or comprehensive, serves as a faithful witness to the earnestness that has characterized investigations ancient or modern into the harrowing questions associated with belief in divine justice.

---

[47]On these important texts, see Burton L. Mack, *Logos und Sophia: Untersuchungen zu Weisheitstheologie im hellenistischen Judentum*, SUNT 10 (Göttingen: Vandenhoeck & Ruprecht, 1973); and Bruce Vawter, "Prov 8:22: Wisdom and Creation," *JBL* 99 (1980): 205-16.

7 (1975)

The Problem of Theodicy in Sirach: On Human Bondage

The race of man stoops in bondage to a heavy yoke. As if the universal decree writ large upon the human heart, "You must surely die" (Sir 14:17), were not sufficient burden for man to bear, another sentence claims absolute sovereignty over humanity. It reads: "You will *fear* death." None escapes the crippling effect of this command, as no one successfully flees from death. Sociological distinctions become meaningless in the face of the prospect of dying; slave and king alike suffer *Angst*. Day and night anxiety reigns; even sleep is turned into an occasion for further consternation when imagined harm exceeds the horrors of actual reality. While anxiety is the lot of every man, it is multiplied sevenfold for the wicked, upon whom fall in good measure such calamities as defy description. Death alone releases a good man from this yoke of bondage; the sinner does not find rest on the day he returns to the mother of all. Instead, he inherits a curse (Sir 40:1-11).

Such reflection upon the human situation, which we have paraphrased rather loosely, is no momentary lapse into Qoheleth-like preoccupation with approaching night on the part of a tired teacher. On the contrary, it joins hands with a host of texts in which Sirach wrestles with the problem of divine injustice. In one and all Sirach takes his point of departure from a set of premises pressed upon him by a vocal group bent on attacking divine justice. While we cannot identify these antagonists, we can discern the basic thrust of their attack. In essence they argue that God's boundless mercy bestows upon his devotees license to sin, that his blessings in material wealth give security, that his power robs man of the freedom to act decisively to avoid sinful conduct, and that his blindness makes evil profitable, especially when the perfidious deed can be concealed from human eyes as well.[1]

The impact of such doubting cries can be discerned in 2:7-11. The thrice-used refrain "You who fear the Lord" suggests that Sirach addresses himself in this instance to the faithful who have begun to feel the cogency of the arguments

---

[1] I have attempted to analyze prophetic literature from the standpoint of controversy literature in *Prophetic Conflict: Its Effect upon Israelite Religion*, BZAW 124 (Berlin/New York: de Gruyter, 1971). The present study is an attempt along similar lines to penetrate beneath the surface of the text of Sirach to the religious controversy calling forth Sirach's remarks.

advanced by Sirach's opponents. The ultimate seriousness of the situation is reflected in the refrain, as well as in the urgency of the exhortations to wait, trust, and hope. In addition, Sirach resorts to an appeal to the past,[2] which constitutes an attempt to enlarge the scope of vision beyond the mere present.

> Consider the ancient generations and see:
> who ever trusted in the Lord
>   and was put to shame?
> Or who ever persevered in the fear of the Lord
>   and was forsaken?
> Or who ever called upon him
>   and was overlooked?   (2:10 RSV)

In short, Sirach's agonizing reflection and polemical thrusts ought to alert us to the disputatious nature of his writing. The latter invites us to penetrate beneath the surface to the central issue at stake in the disputes. That issue can be described in a single word, theodicy. We shall attempt, therefore, in this essay to clarify Sirach's response to his antagonists by examining his use of an ancient debate-form and by studying hymnic contexts in the light of the controversy in which Sirach found himself. To anticipate the results of our study: Sirach availed himself of the entire arsenal of debate forged by earlier figures who wrestled with the issue of theodicy, but he also introduced two new weapons that were deemed most useful by the author of the Wisdom of Solomon. We turn first to the debate-form.

1. Theodicy as a Problem in Sirach

In nine instances Sirach's response to his antagonists makes use of an ancient debate-form.[3] The simple prohibition formula אַל־תֹּאמַר ("Do not say . . . ") can be traced back as far as the Egyptian *Instruction of Ani* and continues in use as late as the *Instructions of 'Onkhsheshonqy*. In OT wisdom literature it barely finds expression in Qoheleth and Proverbs. The relative frequency of its appearance in Sirach is therefore noteworthy. So far it has escaped scholarly notice that there is a remarkable similarity of content in the texts where אַל־תֹּאמַר appears. The overwhelming majority of instances in which this debate-form occurs fall within the discussion of divine justice.

---

[2]Norman Habel, "Appeal to Ancient Tradition as a Literary Form," *SBLSP* 1 (1973): 34-54.

[3]Thomas H. Weber, "Sirach," *JBC* §33.38, writes that 15:11, 15 have the "typical form used to answer an objection in the *bēt midrāš* [בֵּית־מִדְרָשׁ], 'school' (51:23)." If this is correct, the form has a long history. For discussion literature in ancient Egypt, see esp. the informative study by E. Otto, "Der Vorwurf an Gott (Zur Entstehung der ägyptischen Auseinandersetzungsliteratur)," *Vorträge der Orientalistischen Tagung in Marburg: Fachgruppe Ägyptologie, 1950* (Marburg: Universitäts-Verlag, 1951) 1-15.

Do not say, "I am (too) young for thee [thy messenger:
Death] to take," for thou knowest not thy death.
When death comes, he steals away the infant
    which is on its mother's lap
    like him who has reached old age.   (Ani, ANET 420; italics added)

God is (always) in his success,
Whereas man is in his failure;
One thing are the words which men say,
Another is that which the god does.
Say not: "I have no wrongdoing,"
Nor (yet) strain to seek quarreling.   (Amenemopet, ANET 423; italics added)

Do not say: "I have ploughed the field
    but it has not paid";
Plough again, it is good to plough.
Do not say: (Now that) I have this wealth
I will serve neither God nor man,"
Wealth is perfected in the service of God,
    the one who causes it to happen.
Do not say, "The sinner against God lives today,"
But look to the end.
Say (rather):
"A fortunate fate is at the end of old age." ('Onchsheshonqy; italics added)[4]

Say not, "Why were the former days better than these?"
For it is not from wisdom that you ask this. . . .
Consider the work of God;
Who can make straight
    what he has made crooked?   (Qoh 7:10, 13; italics added)[5]

---

[4]The passages from Onchsheshonqy are taken from B. Gemser, "The Instructions of Onchsheshonqy and Biblical Wisdom Literature," *Congress Volume, Oxford 1959* (VTSup 7; Leiden: Brill, 1960) 102-28 (esp. pp. 116, 118).

[5]The debate-form occurs twice in Proverbs (20:22; 24:29). In both passages there is a warning against taking vengeance upon an offender. "*Do not say*, 'I will repay evil'; wait for the Lord, and he will help you" gives a theological motive lacking in "*Do not say*, 'I will do to him as he has done to me; I will pay the man back for what he has done'." Both differ from the usual debate-form in that they do not employ the particle כִּי. Perhaps one should also note Prov 20:9; 24:12; 30:9, each of which refers to a hypothetical statement (who can say, if you say, lest I say). The formal differences, however, between these texts and those in which the debate-form appears are great. Consequently, we shall not use these three passages in drawing conclusions about the debate-form.

Resting behind each of these prohibitions is the painful dilemma of premature death, the inscrutability of the gods that permits the idea of divine caprice to surface, the prosperity of the wicked and delayed rewards of the virtuous, or the divine inactivity after having established a pattern of benevolent deeds. In every instance the debate-form warns against a type of free thinking based on actual experience. The prohibition seldom stands alone, but offers the evidence of broader experience.[6]

Sirach's use of this ancient debate-form throbs with the intensity of agonizing soul searching. From the tone of these contexts in which אַל־תֹּאמֶר occurs we can conclude Sirach felt the threat posed by his antagonists most acutely.

> *Do not say*, "Because of the Lord I left the right way";
>   for he will not do what he hates.
> *Do not say*, "It was he who led me astray";
>   for he has no need of a sinful man.   (15:11-12 RSV; italics added)[7]

> *Do not say*, "I shall be hidden from the Lord,
>   and who from on high will remember me?
> Among so many people I shall not be known,
>   for what is my soul in the boundless creation?"   (16:17 RSV; italics added)

> Do not set your heart on your wealth,
>   *nor say*, "I have enough." [cf. Mic 2:1; Gen 31:29]
> Do not follow your inclination and strength,
>   walking according to the desires of your heart.
> *Do not say*, "Who will have power over me?"
>   for the Lord will surely punish you.
> *Do not say*, "I sinned, and what happened to me?"
>   for the Lord is slow to anger.
> Do not be so confident of atonement
>   that you add sin to sin.
> *Do not say*, "His mercy is great,
>   he will forgive the multitude of my sins,"
> for both mercy and wrath are with him,
>   and his anger rests on sinners.   (5:1-6 RSV; italics added)[8]

---

[6]The Egyptian examples make sporadic use of the third component known from Israelite literature, viz., the refutation introduced by כִּי or its equivalent. Actually, the Egyptian form does not deem it necessary to specify the ground upon which the authority of the statement stands.

[7]For the textual tradition of these verses, see H. P. Rüger, *Text und Textform im hebräischen Sirach*, BZAW 112 (Berlin/New York: de Gruyter, 1970) 75-76.

[8]The textual variants are given in Rüger, *Text und Textform*, 13, 35-37. Alexander A. Di

> *Do not say,* "What do I need,
> and what prosperity could be mine in the future?"
> *Do not say* "I have enough,
> and what calamity could happen to me in the future?"
>
> (11:23-24 RSV; italics added)[9]

Seven times in Sirach the prohibition formula אַל־תֹּאמַר stands in the initial position.[10] Twice it occurs in the second half of a verse (5:1) or in a parallel verse connected by means of a copula (5:6). In most instances we have an initial prohibition formula, a direct quotation, and a refutation introduced by כִּי. Once the כִּי appears in the second of two verses functioning as a refutation (11:23-26), and in still another instance the refutation with כִּי follows the prohibition when it is not in an initial position (5:6).

In sum, the ancient debate-form appears to have functioned primarily, but not exclusively, in contexts dealing with theodicy, both in Egypt and Israel. The precise setting of this form is uncertain, but its presence in early pedagogy seems established. Moreover, the form is relatively fixed, consisting of three elements: (1) the prohibition formula אַל־תֹּאמַר, (2) the direct quotation, and (3) the refutation introduced by כִּי. Finally, Sirach enlists the debate-form to refute antagonists who used the delay in retribution as an excuse to multiply transgression.

Thus far we have said nothing about the great didactic poems (hymns?)[11] that bear the major force of Sirach's refutation of his opponents whose faith has been shattered by the vicissitudes of history. It is here that we discover Sirach's unique

---

Lella, *The Hebrew Text of Sirach* (The Hague: Mouton, 1966) 108-15, discusses 5:4-6 as a select example of retroversion (retranslation from Syriac into Hebrew).

[9]The debate-form also occurs in 7:9 and 31:12 in altered form. *"Do not say,* 'He will consider the multitude of my gifts, and when I make an offering to the Most High God he will accept it.'" "Are you seated at the table of a great man? Do not be greedy at it, and *do not say,* 'There is certainly much upon it!'" In 23:18-19 the debate-form appears to have been transformed into an autobiographical narrative. This passage discusses the self-deceit of the adulterer in terms of an imaginary monologue. It may be, however, that this text, like 20:16 and 36:10, has more in common with the imaginary speeches in the psalms and prophetic literature than with the debate-form being discussed. We shall, therefore, leave all of them out of the present analysis. I have discussed the transformation of a proverb into descriptive narration in "Wisdom," *Old Testament Form Criticism,* TUMSR 2, ed. John H. Hayes (San Antonio TX: Trinity University, 1974) 256-58.

[10]In 15:12 the unusual פֶּן־תֹּאמַר occurs at the beginning of the sentence.

[11]Walter Baumgartner, "Die literarischen Gattungen in der Weisheit des Jesus Sirach," *ZAW* 34 (1914): 170-71, discusses 42:15–43:33 under the category of independent hymns. The other two texts, 16:26–17:24 and 39:12-35, are thought by him to contain hymnic motifs (176, 171-72). He writes that "der Inhalt [of 39:12-35] ist in der Hauptsache nicht hymnisch sondern lehrhaft. . . . Es ist ein didaktisches Lied, aber wohl mit Absicht in hymnischer Form gekleidet . . . " (171-72).

contribution to the resolution of the problem before which a groping humanity stands (Kant). There is, furthermore, a definite link between these poems and the polemical texts already cited. This connection is made by the twice-employed refrain, "No one can say, 'What is this?' 'Why is that?'" (39:17, 21; cf. 39:34). It is precisely in these texts that Sirach's distinctive answers to the problem of theodicy lie. While these three great didactic compositions (16:24–17:14; 39:12-35; 42:15–43:33) have recently been the subject of thorough analysis,[12] they were not examined for the light they throw upon the problem of theodicy. Such a probing of the texts is both timely and absolutely essential, now that Burton Mack has taught us to consider the possibility that theodicy was the formative influence upon the "hypostatization" of wisdom.[13]

The didactic poem in 16:24–17:14 belongs to a larger composition that treats the subject of God's punishment of the sinner (15:11–18:14). The unspoken question of the greater unit is, "Does God observe sin?" An affirmative answer is given in no uncertain terms (17:15-20). The poem supplies a basis for this answer. It meditates upon the vast implications of the creation narrative (Gen 1–2), the Noachic covenant (Gen 9:2), and the account of the fall of man (Genesis 3). With almost mathematical precision the poet sings of divine allocation, a setting of limits, an arranging and a dividing of the eternal created order. Appropriately such rational language is introduced by the instructor's appeal for a hearing, together with a promise that he "will impart instruction by *weight*, and declare knowledge *accurately*." The dominant spirit, however, is not abstract philosophy but a testimony to a vital experience with the living God who made his will known in grace and demand.[14] Here is no cold dogma of an indifferent universe, but a "hymn" of gratitude for the covenant, for knowledge, and for the law of life that the creator has bestowed upon his creatures. In this "hymn" we meet for the first time in wisdom

---

[12]Johannes Marböck, *Weisheit im Wandel*, BBB 37 (Bonn: Hanstein, 1971)—see my review in *JBL* 91 (1972): 543-44. Marböck's influence on the following discussion of hymnic materials is readily discernible to the knowledgeable reader.

[13]"Wisdom Myth and Mythology: An Essay in Understanding a Theological Tradition," *Int* 24 (1970): 46-60. I am inclined to agree with Mack's judgment about the importance of theodicy to the postexilic community. However, I do not accept a late dating of every instance in which the theme of refusing to heed God's warning appears. On one such text, see my essay "A Liturgy of Wasted Opportunity (Am 4:6-12; Isa 9:7–10:4; 5:25-29," *Semitics* 1 (1970): 27-37. The mild tone of many passages used by Mack to support his thesis does not seem sufficiently serious to bear the burden of such a burning issue as theodicy. For that reason I hesitate to endorse Mack's thesis wholeheartedly.

[14]Marböck writes: "Diese Ordnung ist für Ben Sira allerdings nie bloss abstraktes Prinzip, sondern Ausdruck und Offenbarung des lebendigen Gottes. Darum kann und soll sie auch hinfuhren zu Gottesfurcht und zum lebendigen Ausdruck im Gotteslob (17, 8; vgl. 39, 14cd. 15.35)" (*Weisheit im Wandel*, 138).

literature the old idea that man was created in the image of God,[15] interpreted in this setting as a token of sovereignty over all creatures. The purpose of this concept, as of all other ideas in the "hymn," is to emphasize the harmony of the created order. In short, the passage argues that nothing is out of place in all of creation.

But the emphasis upon the fitness of everything raises a question as to natural catastrophes and the like. That is, it leaves unresolved, and indeed intensifies, the issue of natural evil. The second didactic poem alluded to above (39:12-35), wrestles mightily with this difficult problem. The "hymn" opens with an eloquent appeal for a hearing and for others to participate in the singing of praise (39:12-15), and it concludes with a school teacher's personal testimony to the truth of the hymnic declaration that the works of the Lord are all good . . . for all things will prove good in their season" (39:32-34). Thereupon Sirach urges everyone to take up the song of praise (39:35). The "hymn" proper affirms the divine assessment of the finished creative work, viz., that every single thing is very good, and suggests that the secret to such a positive appraisal lies in recognizing the proper time for everything. In decidedly polemical tones the poet affirms God's power and visibility: God sees everything, and his power is unlimited. In infinite wisdom he created good things for the virtuous and evil things for sinners. But even good things are perverted by wicked men and become occasions of stumbling. Thus Sirach claims that evil is attitudinal; faith and obedience are presuppositions for understanding God's ways,[16] and much that goes under the name of evil only appears that way. *In its time* everything will be revealed for what it is, and evil will function punitively in behalf of its creator. Consequently, no man can say one thing is absolutely superior to another.

With this startling conclusion we have stumbled upon a key concept for understanding much of Sirach's thought. This basic idea occurs most clearly, however, in 33:7-15 (Greek, 36:7-15). Here one encounters a concept of opposites or complementary pairs. When God created all things he made them in pairs: "Good is the opposite of evil, and life the opposite of death; so the sinner is the opposite of the godly. Look upon all the works of the Most High; they likewise are in pairs, one the opposite of the other" (33:14-15). In short, the structure of the universe itself is complementary.[17] This does not rule out a decision as to what is better; on the contrary, the wise man can discern what stands under the divine sign of blessing, which is the result of an arbitrary decision on God's part (some he blessed,

---

[15]For a recent discussion of the meaning of this idea, see J. Maxwell Miller, "In the 'Image' and 'Likeness' of God," *JBL* 91 (1972): 289-304.

[16]Gerhard von Rad, *Wisdom in Israel* (London: SCM, 1972) 253. This essay on Sirach first appeared in *EvT* 29 (1969): 113-33. This same ambivalence characterizes Sirach's discussion of the educational tactics of Dame Wisdom. At first she comes with heavy tests, and her yoke appears to be chains and fetters. But he who penetrates *beyond appearance to reality* soon discovers that wisdom's yoke is a golden ornament (4:17-19; 6:18-31; 21:19-21).

[17]Marböck, *Weisheit im Wandel*, 152-54, makes much of this idea of opposites.

others he cursed). Nevertheless, the decision as to what is better is really a discerning of the appropriate time, which Sirach, in contrast to Qoheleth, thinks is open to man.

Both this great hymn in 39:12-35 and the text we have used to illuminate it may imply that even God's actions fall under the rubric of ambivalence.[18] This much Sirach appears to concede to his opponents. The terrible effects of such ambivalence are spelled out in the brief passage with which we began this study (40:1-11). Inasmuch as even the direct intervention of God in the world of men is characterized by ambivalence, a heavy cloud of uneasiness hovers over the human race. At the same time Sirach is convinced that God has really created all things good and that everything has a purpose. Therefore, behind the dark cloud one can discern a smile inclined toward those who please God and a threatening frown turned toward those whose conduct earns his disapproval.

The final didactic hymn that we shall take up (42:15–43:33)[19] shows a decided advance in the direction of praise over polemic. It appears that Sirach himself has begun to sense the utter futility of his earlier rational arguments and has turned more and more to the celebration of God's majesty as manifest in the grandeur of the created order. We do not imply that this hymn completely loses sight of the antagonists; on the contrary, their objections are very much in the poet's mind (42:18, 20, 23-25). But the mood is decidedly different; Sirach is painfully conscious of his inability to proclaim God's praises in an appropriate manner (42:17; 43:27-33). Moving indeed is the religious fervor of Sirach in this hymnic attempt to praise him who is greater than all his works. While one can agree with Norbert Peters that understanding plays for Sirach a greater role than feeling and fantasy,[20] on the basis of this hymn we must credit the author with exceptional powers of poetic description. We refer to such images as that of snow freezing into pointed thorns and of water putting on ice like a breastplate (43:19-20). Rarely does Sirach achieve such exquisite poetry,[21] and his achievement is not entirely unrelated to the grandeur of the subject matter. It is no accident that the words כָּבוֹד, נִפְלָאֹות, and נוֹרָא stand out in this hymn (42:16-17, 25; 43:2, 8, 29). The depth of Sirach's piety and the crisis of faith in his day pervade even his prayers, in one of which Sirach utters the poignant plea: "Show signs anew, and work further wonders; make thy

---

[18]Von Rad, *Wisdom in Israel*, 254, draws this conclusion about the hymn in 39:12-35.

[19]On this hymn, see the translation and notes in Yigael Yadin, *The Ben Sira Scroll from Masada* (Jerusalem: Israel Exploration Society and Shrine of the Book, 1965) 27-34, 45-48.

[20]*Das Buch Jesus Sirach oder Ecclesiasticus*, EHAT 25 (Münster: Aschendorff, 1913) xlviii. Peters writes: "Das Buch ist eben in der Hauptsache die Frucht des diskursiven Denkens des inspirierten Schriftgelehrten, nicht der genialen Intuition des Dichters von Gottes Gnaden. Der Verstand ist mehr an der Arbeit, als das Gefühl und die Phantasie."

[21]To these metaphors one could add the description of the frustration of affliction in terms of a eunuch who embraces a maiden and groans (30:20) and the simile about an arrow stuck in the thigh, which is compared to a word inside a fool (19:12).

hand and thy right arm glorious" (36:6). This text alone is sufficient testimony that the author realized the inadequacy of his arguments for divine justice. The tension between a confession of divine benevolence in the past and a recognition of his inactivity at the moment was felt by Sirach most keenly; but he chose to silence those doubting voices in a mighty crescendo of praise.

The universal decree "You must die" stands in considerable tension with Sirach's understanding of death as punitive. Thus we come to still another attempt on his part to grapple with his opponents' attack on divine justice. In these texts we move beyond hymnic materials in demonstrating that Sirach never entirely freed himself from the necessity of responding to his antagonists. We refer to his argument that the true character of a man cannot be determined until the moment of his death.

> Call no one happy before his death;
> a man will be known through his children.   (11:28 RSV)

Again and again Sirach lays stress upon a divine visitation *at the end*, presumably at the moment of death.

> With him who fears the Lord it will go well *at the end*
> [ἐπ᾽ ἐσχάτων = אַחֲרִית];
> on the day of his death he will be blessed.   (1:13 RSV; italics added)

> A stubborn mind will be afflicted *at the end* [אַחֲרִית],
> and whoever loves danger will perish by it.   (3:26 RSV; italics added)

> Do not envy the honors of a sinner,
> for you do not know what *his end* [יוֹמוֹ] will be.
>   (9:11 RSV; italics added)

The same sense is communicated without the use of a word for "end," by reference either to a sudden shift in the situation or to God's time.

> Do not wonder at the works of a sinner . . . ,
> for it is easy in the sight of the Lord to enrich a poor man
> *quickly* [בְּפֶתַא] and suddenly [פִּתְאֹם].
>   (11:21 RSV; italics added; cf. 11:26)

> Do your work before the appointed time,
> and *in God's time* [בְּעִתּוֹ] he will give you your reward.
>   (51:30 RSV; italics added)

Such passages could easily be multiplied; these suffice, however, to suggest another direction in which Sirach moved in his futile search for a convincing answer to the issue of theodicy. This argument conceals an admission that things are not what they should be *at the moment*, since external circumstances do not always correctly mirror the inner character of a man. A theological motive for this delay in reward and punishment was easy to come by: God's mercy is equal to his wrath (16:12;

17:15-32). Nevertheless, Sirach's passion for justice expresses itself in the not very convincing affirmation that wrath does not delay (7:16; cf. 33:1). Unfortunately, such a claim ignores the presupposition of the assertions that retribution will eventually come, which implies a painful delay of punishment or reward. In truth, it is difficult to avoid the suspicion that Sirach realized in one way or another the utter futility of his efforts at theodicy. If this is correct, perhaps he took renewed strength in his conviction that one must "strive even to death for the truth, and the Lord God will fight for you" (4:28).

2. The Rich Tradition to Which Sirach Was Heir

Sirach was by no means the first Israelite to wrestle with the problem of evil; the fruits of this intellectual and religious pilgrimage were a part of the rich religious traditions to which he was heir. One is not limited to the translator's statement that his grandfather had immersed himself in the study of the Scriptures, for there is proof on almost every page that Sirach was conscious of the prophetic theology of history, the priestly presupposition of reward for obedience, and the dogma of retribution which the sages shared with prophet and priest. The failure of historical events to accord with theological expectation, particularly that of Zion theology, and the shock occasioned by the death of Josiah[22] were familiar experiences of the past. Despite his fundamentally conservative, even proto-Sadducean, bias,[23] the failure of nerve rationally in Job and theologically in Qoheleth had not eluded his grasp, for many of the claims of the wise men had been subjected to empirical disconfirmation. Even the probationary and pedagogical theories of suffering bore within them an inherent denial that physical evil was always a retribution for sin.[24] Moreover, the decisive shift in attitude toward piety and wealth within some psalms indicates a certain hesitancy to view wealth as conclusive proof of God's favor.[25] Even the attempt of the Chronicler, under the sway of extreme individualism, to resolve the question of divine justice was history when Sirach wrestled anew with a vocal group bent on challenging God's power or his goodness.

For Sirach the times were out of joint, since both the Davidic and the Aaronic covenants were jeopardized in his day, and Sirach even imagined himself to be the

---

[22]Stanley Frost, "The Death of Josiah: A Conspiracy of Silence," *JBL* 87 (1968): 369-82.

[23]Alexander A. Di Lella, "Conservative and Progressive Theology: Sirach and Wisdom," *CBQ* 38 (1966): 139-46. Von Rad, *Wisdom in Israel*, 258n.24, has rightly called attention to the fact that *conservative* in Jerusalem does not mean the same as *conservative* in Alexandria, but this fact detracts little from Di Lella's insight.

[24]O. S. Rankin, *Israel's Wisdom Literature* (Edinburgh: T.&T. Clark, 1936) 20.

[25]Arvid S. Kapelrud, "New Ideas in Amos," VTSup 15 (1966): 193-206, argues for an eighth-century dating of this decisive shift in viewpoint. He sees the change in perspective toward the rich and poor as a distinctive contribution of the prophet Amos.

last of a long line of scribes. Such perilous times spawned pessimism and apocalypticism,[26] from the first of which Sirach was not entirely free. As a matter of fact, his emphasis upon final judgment in light of the fact that God sees everything and his divine epithets expressive of transcendentalism, particularly "the Most High,"[27] contributed to the spirit of scepticism that pervades the literature of the last two centuries before the Christian era.[28] Long before Nietzsche had noted that man can live with almost any "how" if he has a "why," the ancient Israelites were struggling to discover a reason for living in the midst of tyranny.

In such a situation the presence of theodicies both conservative and revolutionary, i.e., discrete theodicies of the oppressor and the oppressed, the privileged and the powerless, which we have discussed elsewhere,[29] only complicated matters further. The earlier tendency to unite the ethical and eudaemonistic was giving way, and with this came an energetic reaction from those inclined to view religion pragmatically. Sirach apparently perceived that ethical monotheism stands or falls on its ability to deal with the question of the justice of God, and, like Qoheleth before him, he saw death as the decisive issue in this dilemma.[30] For him theodicy was "the attempt to make a pact with death," since he knew that "the power of religion depends, in the last resort, upon the credibility of the banners it puts in the hands of men as they stand before death, or more accurately, as they walk inevitably toward it."[31] But Sirach can be accused of neither the masochistic response of Job, so prevalent in the Judeo-Christian world, nor the mystical giving up of the problem of theodicy; on the contrary, he attempts a marriage between Hellenism and Hebraism, between Athens and Jerusalem,[32] although he saw to it that Zion wore a chastity belt, the keys of which had been entrusted to the Most High himself.

Now it is possible that we have still not discovered all the answers that Sirach threw into the laps of his critics. Let us return, for a moment, to the text with which

---

[26]For a suggestive treatment of the context and mood of apocalypticism, see Lou H. Silberman, "The Human Deed in a Time of Despair: The Ethics of Apocalyptic," *Essays in Old Testament Ethics: J. Philip Hyatt, in Memoriam*, ed. James L. Crenshaw and John T. Willis (New York: Ktav, 1974) 191-202.

[27]According to Elias Bickerman, *From Ezra to the Last of the Maccabees* (New York: Schocken, 1962) 67, the epithet occurs forty-eight times.

[28]Johannes Pedersen, "Scepticisme israelite," *RHPR* 10 (1930): 317-70.

[29]"Popular Questioning of the Justice of God in Ancient Israel," *ZAW* 82 (1970): 380-95.

[30]For my understanding of Qoheleth's view of God, see "The Eternal Gospel (Eccl 3:11)," in *Essays in Old Testament Ethics*, 23-55.

[31]P. Berger, *The Sacred Canopy* (Garden City NY: Doubleday, 1967) 51. Berger's discussion of theodicy has been particularly helpful in our attempt to come to grips with the difficult issue on a broader scale than that represented by ancient Near Eastern literature.

[32]See esp. Marböck, *Weisheit im Wandel*; Martin Hengel, *Judentum und Hellenismus*, WUNT 10 (Tübingen: Mohr, 1969) 241-75; and T. Middendorp, *Die Stellung Jesu ben Siras zwischen Judentum und Hellenismus* (Leiden: Brill, 1973).

we began this discussion. The phrase "upon sinners seven times more" (40:8) suggests that Sirach may also have ventured into the area of the psychic life as a possible response to the problem of divine injustice.[33] While one could argue conceivably that the reference is only to external calamities such as death, bloodshed, and sword, still the presence of such words as "strife" and "affliction" suggests that Sirach actually thought of *Angst* as punishment for sin. The mention of nightmares in addition to the conscious anxiety over death is especially revealing, for no one has control over the spectres of the night.[34] A limited measure of anxiety is man's common lot, Sirach contends, but the sinner has a lion's share of consternation (cf. 31:1-4). The total context (40:1-11) reinforces such an understanding of the phrase "upon sinners seven times more"; hence we conclude that Sirach viewed a disturbed mental state as punishment for sin.[35]

In sum, the problem of the justice of God was a burning issue in Sirach's day. In no sense of the word can we assume that Job and Qoheleth settled that issue once

---

[33]Such an understanding of dreams is not entirely new to wisdom literature. In Job 7:14 nightmares are said to be a terrible weapon in God's arsenal, while 33:14-18 speaks of them as God's means of bringing a wicked man to his senses. Elihu's discussion of nightmares in the context of revelation has a parallel in Sir 34:1-8. Here Sirach strikes out against those who make free use of dreams in order to predict the future. The cogency of his claim that dreams give wings to fools (34:1) is greatly weakened by the further admission that dreams may be "sent from the Most High as a visitation" (34:6). Of course, there was no way of discerning whether a dream was caused by God, by gluttony (31:19-20), or by any number of factors.

[34]A. Leo Oppenheim, *The Interpretation of Dreams in the Ancient Near East* (Philadelphia: American Philosophical Society, 1956) 197, writes that nightmares were "symptoms of a specific state of mind due to mental stress, disease or malevolent magical activities." Of all the dreams discussed by Oppenheim the most pertinent to this theme are those of Enkidu and Tammuz. Enkidu's well-known dream and awakening scream (which Oppenheim compares to *Richard III*, where the Duke of Clarence dreams he is in hell and foul fiends howled in his ears, "Such hideous cries, that with the very noise / I trembling wak'd, and for a season after / Could not believe but that I was in hell," 1.4.60-62) portend ill for him, although nightmares do not always foretell tragedy. Oppenheim notes that good dreams sometimes announce terrible happenings, whereas bad dreams on occasion proclaim fortune (229). The dream of Tammuz, like that of Enkidu, spells disaster for him. The literary device of a dream with evil content by means of which the author emphasizes the courage of the hero or the inevitability of fate is amply illustrated in the Bible; I refer to Judg 7:13 (the dream of the frightened Midianites who face Gideon in battle) and the dream of Pilate's wife.

[35]Precursors to Sirach's view that mental anxiety was a sign of divine displeasure are certainly present in the OT. I refer to the Saul narrative, which depicts the tragedy of one whom God has driven to madness (cf. also Job 3:25-26 and Prov 10:24). I have discussed the idea of the divine hardening of human hearts in *Prophetic Conflict* (77-90), while the "tragic" dimension is treated in "The Samson Saga: Filial Devotion or Erotic Attachment?" *ZAW* 86 (1974): 470-504.

and for all. In this regard Gerhard von Rad is probably correct in his assessment of the impact of these two documents,[36] although we think that he underestimates their influence. In any event, Sirach struggles to provide a rational basis upon which to view the problem of divine justice. His answers are remarkable ones in many ways:

1. God knows everything even before it comes into being and also sees it at the moment of fruition;
2. past experience proves that God is just;
3. at the appropriate time everything will be rectified;
4. the ultimate response to the grandeur of creation is to surrender before the divine imperative of wonder;
5. from the perspective of the purpose for which all was created, the universe is a marvelous, harmonious order of complementary pairs;
6. God punishes sin by sending great anxiety upon the guilty person.

3. Sirach's Bold Venture

Only the last two of these solutions break new ground in the long-standing debate in ancient Israel. The argument for some sort of divine prescience is a well-known theme of Deutero-Isaiah, who never tires of emphasizing God's prior knowledge and control of all happenings. But Qoheleth, too, knew of God's unique present knowledge; this, at least, seems to be the meaning of the obscure statement that "God seeks what has been driven away" (3:15).[37] The time-worn appeal to tradition appears in both Job and Qoheleth; in each instance little if any credence is given the argument. As is well known, Qoheleth takes up the ancient Egyptian emphasis upon the appropriate time and applies it to the belief in creation (3:1-11),[38] though without reaching the conclusion that Sirach does, viz., that in *its* time all will be rectified (but see the gloss in 2:17). As for the drowning of doubting questions in the rushing crescendo of praise, Job's ultimate surrender amounts to just that.

About Sirach's fifth solution O. S. Rankin has written: "The thought which he develops upon the perfect harmony and adjustment of creation would seem to be his own contribution to theodicy."[39] Gerhard von Rad goes one step further: "Even the

---

[36] *Wisdom in Israel*, 237-39.

[37] That is, God looks again for what he has already seen once. See the discussion of this verse in Robert Gordis, *Koheleth—The Man and His World* (New York: Schocken, 1968) 233-34; and Oswald Loretz, *Qohelet und der Alte Orient* (Freiburg: Herder, 1964) 200n.288. Both Job (10:6) and the author of Ps 39 interpret God's constant vigilance as cause for *dismay*; the latter urges God to look away from him so that he can know gladness (39:13).

[38] "In essence the goal of wisdom instruction was the recognition of the right time, the right place and the right degree of human conduct" (Hans Heinrich Schmid, *Wesen und Geschichte der Weisheit*, BZAW 101 [Berlin/New York: de Gruyter, 1966] 190).

[39] *Israel's Wisdom Literature*, 35. W. O. E. Oesterley, in *APOT* 1:310, thinks Sirach's unique contribution is the idea that God can cause a man's last hours to be so terrible that all former enjoyment of life is obliterated entirely.

wholly direct intervention of God in the world of men is regarded by men as marked by that ambivalence. This attempt to tackle the problem of theodicy is new."[40] With one stroke Sirach has freed man from the odious task of interpreting God's power in comprehensive terms on the basis of a fixed norm. It is precisely at this point, von Rad thinks, that Sirach makes his mark in the theodicy debate. If this is where Sirach takes his stand, however, it is a slippery one. In reality, the emphasis of the text lies elsewhere than on the problem of divine intervention as such, although von Rad is probably correct in drawing the conclusion that the passage also implies the further understanding of God's intervention in human affairs as ambivalent. Nevertheless, the essential point Sirach wishes to make is that *in the creative act* God brought into being a universe that encourages virtue and punishes vice.

To recapitulate, Sirach was faced with a painful dilemma: on the one hand, he courageously refused to accept Hellenism's "easy" solution to the problem of evil,[41] viz., a final resolution in the afterlife; on the other hand, he tenaciously held onto the traditional dogma of retribution in spite of Job and Qoheleth. The challenge presented by these two books prompted Sirach to search for other options. His discoveries represent a flight from reality into the realms of metaphysics and psychology. His own twofold solution was the affirmation that the universe is wondrously made so as to encourage virtue and punish wickedness, and the claim that the wicked are victims of great *Angst*, of nightmares, and of conscious worry and grief.

This flight into psychology and metaphysics was an effective answer to the vexing problem of empirical disconfirmation, for it was akin to the earlier retreat of eschatologists and messianists (as well as the later escape of millenarists) into realms not subject to objective verification. Neither the hellenistic answer nor the dualistic alternative, nor anything akin to the doctrine of karma,[42] is thought worthy of Sirach's allegiance. On the contrary, "again and again Sirach returns to (the idea of) divine retribution, which unfailingly punishes the evil deed and rewards the good

---

[40]*Wisdom in Israel*, 254.

[41]The author of 2 Esdras introduces us to the agony caused by Hellenism's answer to the problem of theodicy. Again and again this sensitive soul chafes at the thought of the eternal damnation awaiting the masses of humanity. Ezra can derive little comfort from reflection upon his own elect state; instead the powerful negative role of the belief in life after death enables him to discern the dark, shadowy side of God that dominates his relationships with mankind. To this ominous character of God Ezra objects most vigorously. For him a congruence between this world and the next was absolutely essential. Therefore, Ezra could not countenance the discernible deep gulf between the present and future ages. For this anxiety on Ezra's part, see 2 Esd 3:1–9:25.

[42]Rankin, *Israel's Wisdom Literature*, 121-23, notes that Judaism eventually found room for such concepts. Evidence for this claim is based on the ideas of *Darkê Tᵉšûbāh* and *Gilgûl*.

deed."[43] In truth "the idea of retribution stands entirely in the center of Sirach's belief about God."[44] What is unique, however, is his belief that retribution manifests itself in the inner life and in the metaphysical realm.

In his flight to areas free from empirical verification, Sirach has ceased to walk in the steps of former sages for whom experience was the ground of all knowledge. Instead, he has allied himself with the dogmatic tradition of prophet, priest, and historian (both deuteronomistic and chronistic). Small wonder that we confront in Sirach for the first time a sage who has made peace with the sacral traditions of a revealed religion.[45] Perhaps we should speak of more than "making peace," for cultic interests dominate the "hymn" in praise of great men (44–50). How revealing in this regard such a text as 33:3 comes to be:

> A man of understanding will trust in the law;
> for him the law is as dependable
> as an inquiry by means of Urim.   (RSV)

What a worldview rests behind this innocent-sounding statement! At the very least we are permitted to see the sacred lot as a symbol for the ultimate in dependability. If we are correct in this interpretation of the texts, it follows that we must part company with von Rad, who would minimize cultic interests in Sirach.[46]

In short, refusing to posit a universe in disharmony and groping desperately for a *nomos*, a "bright 'dayside' of life tenuously held onto against the sinister shadows of the 'night,'"[47] Sirach contends that the marginal situations of life, particularly sleep, fantasy, and death, become occasions of divine vengeance. In his unwillingness to subject his theory to empirical verification, Sirach approaches bad faith, for the inner dialogue between conviction and reality is silenced once and for all.

4. The Impact of Sirach's Answers

We do not possess the necessary data to evaluate the impact of Sirach's answers upon the doubters who stimulated the discussion in the first place. Perhaps we can assume that the multitude of attempts to solve the nagging problem of the delay in retribution indicates that Sirach was never quite happy with any of his

---

[43]Rudolf Smend, *Die Weisheit des Jesus Sirach erklärt* (Berlin: G. Reimer, 1906) xxv.

[44]Alfred Bertholet, *Die jüdische Religion von der Zeit Esras bis zum Zeitalter Christi* (1911) 189.

[45]J. Fichtner, "Zum Problem Glaube und Geschichte in der israelitisch-jüdischen Weisheitsliteratur," *TLZ* 76 (1951): 145-50 (also in *Gottes Weisheit* [Stuttgart: Calwer, 1965] 9-17). For a discussion of the difficult task of recognizing wisdom influence upon nonwisdom texts, see my article "Method in Determining Wisdom Influence upon 'Historical' Literature," *JBL* 88 (1969): 129-42.

[46]*Wisdom in Israel*, 260n.28.

[47]Berger, *The Sacred Canopy*, 23, uses this language in discussing marginal situations and the need for *nomos*.

solutions. On the other hand, we can discern the impact of Sirach's views upon subsequent Jewish literature of the pre-Christian period. We shall limit ourselves to the Wisdom of Solomon.

The author of the Wisdom of Solomon both picks up distinctive views of Sirach and develops them significantly. Here for the first time we have a detailed midrash[48] on the Exodus event understood in terms of Sirach's theory of nightmares for the wicked. The Egyptians are said to have been "prisoners of long night . . . terribly alarmed, and appalled by specters," although thinking themselves hidden from divine scrutiny (17:2-3). In their inner chamber they were not protected from that enemy who can scale any wall, fear.

> Nothing was shining through to them
> except a dreadful, self-kindled fire,
> and in terror they deemed the things which they saw
> to be worse than that unseen appearance. (Wis 17:6 RSV)

Even magical resources were powerless to overcome this terrible state.

> But throughout the night . . .
> they all slept the same sleep,
> and now were driven by monstrous specters,
> and now were paralyzed by their souls' surrender,
> for sudden and unexpected fear overwhelmed them.
> And whoever was there fell down,
> and thus was kept shut up in a prison not made of iron. (Wis 17:14-16 RSV)

In such a chain of darkness even melodious tunes struck terror into the hearts of the Egyptians, for over them spread primordial darkness (17:21). On the other hand, God's holy ones walked under a great light, either in the shape of a pillar of fire that functioned as a compass to guide Israel to the promised inheritance or in the form of a harmless sun.

This author moves even a step beyond Sirach, for he views the nightmarish dreams as God's forewarning "that they might not perish without knowing why they suffered" (18:19). The reason behind this observation is, of course, the desire to exalt God even more by emphasizing not only his justice but also his willingness

---

[48]For a discussion of this terminology and the context within which the Wisdom of Solomon was written, see J. M. Reese, *Hellenistic Influence on the Book of Wisdom and its Consequences*, AnBib 41 (Rome: Biblical Institute, 1970); on midrash, see esp. 91-98. James A. Sanders, "The Ethic of Election in Luke's Great Banquet Parable," in *Essays in Old Testament Ethics*, 247-71, has some pertinent remarks about midrash with particular reference to Merrill P. Miller, "Targum, Midrash and the Use of the Old Testament in the New Testament," *JSJ* 2 (1971): 29-81.

to communicate a knowledge of that justice to the sinner upon whom his oppressive hand falls in wrath.

Sirach's theory about the harmony of the created order likewise receives enthusiastic endorsement in the Wisdom of Solomon.

> For the creation, serving thee who hast made it,
> exerts itself to punish [ἐπιτείνεται εἰς κόλασιν]
>   the unrighteous,
> and in kindness relaxes [ἀνίεται εἰς εὐεργεσίαν]
>   on behalf of those who trust in thee.   (Wis 16:24 RSV)

Here, too, this author moves far beyond Sirach's theory. The Wisdom of Solomon speaks of miraculous transformations or happenings.

> For—most incredible of all—in the water, which quenches all things,
> the fire had still greater effect,
> for the universe defends the righteous.   (Wis 16:17 RSV)

> Snow and ice withstood fire without melting, . . .
> whereas the fire, in order that the righteous might be fed,
> even forgot its native power.   (Wis 16:22a, 23 RSV)

In short, creation punishes the sinner in a way that is appropriate to the sin and rewards the good man in wondrous fashion.

Sirach's appeal to a decisive act of retribution at the end of one's life is also taken over by the Wisdom of Solomon.

> Let us see if his words are true,
> and let us test what will happen at the end of his life
> [ἐν ἐκβάσει αὐτοῦ]; . . .   (Wis 2:17 RSV)

> In the time of their visitation [ἐν καιρῷ ἐπισκοπῆς]
>   they will shine forth,
> and will run like sparks through the stubble.   (Wis 3:7 RSV)

> . . . therefore no one who utters
> unrighteous things will escape notice,
> and justice, when it punishes [ἐλέγχουσα], will not pass him by.
> (Wis 1:8; cf. 4:6, 20 RSV)

Inasmuch as the author of the Wisdom of Solomon believes in the immortality of the soul[49] and retribution in the future life, it is difficult to ascertain whether or not

---

[49]Von Rad, *Wisdom in Israel*, 262, even thinks that some passages in Sirach are amenable to a belief in retribution after death (1:13; 2:3; 7:36; 9:11; 11:26-28; 16:12; 17:23; 18:24). However, he recognizes the question posed to such a view by V. Hamp's study, *Zukunft und Jenseits im Buche Sirach*, BBB 1 (Bonn: P. Hanstein, 1950).

any of these texts refers to a divine visitation in this life. It may be that the two notions of retribution stand in tension, having been incompletely reconciled in the mind of the author.[50]

5. Conclusion

In struggling with the problem of theodicy, Sirach came up with a number of answers, two of which were new at the time. Both were taken up by the author of the Wisdom of Solomon and developed far beyond Sirach's fondest dreams. Neither solution was open to empirical verification, representing as they did an escape into psychology or metaphysics. In light of comparable Greek discussions of Sirach's day,[51] it may be concluded that these answers spoke to the times remarkably well. But, one might ask, how permanently valid are Sirach's solutions to the problem of evil?

David Bakan's recent study of telic decentralization,[52] if accurate, suggests that there may be some truth in Sirach's conviction that wicked men experience excessive nightmares. Of course, it has long been thought that "your cheating heart will tell on you." However, this maxim presupposes an established *nomos* that imposes upon the violator of this norm an intense sense of guilt. Given such a context, the disruptive power of duplicity is astonishing. Sirach's contemporaries may have felt the yoke of conformity more keenly than most earlier Israelites precisely because of the strong temptation to ape Greek ways. In any case, Hellenism had made decisive inroads upon Judaism at the time.[53] The danger implicit in such an argument, however, is the hidden assumption that Jews in Sirach's day were enslaved by a doctrine of righteousness on the basis of works and guilt-ridden because of their inability to achieve perfection. Otto Kaiser[54] has

---

[50]The same tension is observable in Sirach's understanding of the physician whose profession is put under a cloud of suspicion by the belief in sickness as punishment for sin. On this, see Marböck, *Weisheit im Wandel*, 154-60.

[51]Hengel, *Judentum und Hellenismus*, 241-75.

[52]*Disease, Pain, and Sacrifice* (Chicago: University of Chicago Press, 1968).

[53]Bickerman, *From Ezra to the Last of the Maccabees*, 53. R. T. Siebeneck, "May Their Bones Return to Life—Sirach's Praise of the Fathers," *CBQ* 21 (1959): 411-28, emphasizes the hellenistic threat as the primary concern of Sirach. The pedagogy of examples (44:1–50:24) is interpreted against the backdrop of a militant hellenizing movement. Opinions vary as to the role of 44:1-50:24. Ceslas Spicq, *L'Ecclésiastique*, La Sainte Bible, ed. L. Pirot and A. Clamer, 2d ed. (Paris: Letouzey et Ané, 1946), calls the passage a type of concluding doxology, while Bruce Vawter, *The Book of Sirach with a Commentary* (Glen Rock NJ: Paulist, 1962, calls it the heart of the book.

[54]"Die Begründung der Sittlichkeit im Buche Jesus Sirach," *ZTK* 55 (1958) 51-63. The phrase "tote Werkheiligkeit" that Kaiser challenges is taken from L. Couard, *Die religiösen und sittlichen Ausschauungen der alttestamentlichen Apokryphen und Pseudepigraphen* (Gütersloh: Bertelsmann, 1907) 139-42.

certainly provided a much-needed corrective to Dieter Michaelis's treatment of this subject.[55] Kaiser is absolutely right in his positive assessment of Sirach's idea of the fear of God, which rules out any talk about a righteousness that is intrinsic to works.[56] Furthermore, even Bakan's theory of telic decentralization leaves room for the recognition that mental and physical wholeness affect one's sleep or lack of it more powerfully than does one's spiritual condition.

Sirach's flight into metaphysics fares even less well. Leibniz's response to Voltaire suffices to indicate the tenuous nature of any appeal to the harmony of nature in responding favorably to the righteous person and reacting oppressively against the sinner. In our day when nature is itself the tragic victim of human rape in every conceivable way and place, there can be no talk about nature exerting itself in wrath against the sinner and relaxing in compassion toward the good man.[57] Even the effect of the dominical saying that the sun shines upon the just and the unjust has been terribly blunted for a world that can hardly see the sun for pollution. Sirach's further assumption that divine intervention falls into the category of ambivalence thus strikes a responsive chord in hearts devoid of a *nomos* and bereft of hope. The believer today, who has no "bright dayside" and is without hope, can therefore grasp something of the pathos of Sirach's necrophilia. Perhaps his sole recourse is to a kind of gallows humor,[58] an honest self-assessment that may render

---

[55]"Das Buch Jesus Sirach als typischer Ausdruck für das Gottesverhältnis des nachalttestamentlichen Menschen," *TLZ* 83 (1958): 601-608. Michaelis accuses Sirach of humanism and a type of religiosity that is apostasy ("Das Buch Jesus Sirach ist eins der ersten grossen literarischen Zeugnisse jenes Abfalls," col. 608). This theme has recently been taken up again by Horst Dietrich Preuss, "Erwägungen zum theologischen Ort alttestamentlicher Weisheitsliteratur," *EvT* 30 (1970): 393-417. Preuss applies Michaelis's judgment to the entire corpus of wisdom literature, which is understood as Israel's attempt to be like her neighbors; hence it is called paganism. From the other direction Walter Brueggemann, *In Man We Trust* (Richmond: John Knox, 1972), adds a much-needed corrective to an understanding of man that robs him of the dignity bestowed upon him at creation. Brueggemann celebrates the "humanism" in wisdom literature. While we readily agree with him that wisdom literature includes such optimism, we prefer to focus upon the sage's mighty cry *in tormentis*, which has seldom been heard in all its pathos.

[56]Kaiser writes: "Das Gesetz ist der Kompass, der dem Menschen den Weg durch die Sturme des Lebens zeigt, der ihm in aller augenscheinlichen Sinnlosigkeit des Weltgeschehens zu der im Verborgenen waltenden richtenden und segnenden Ordnung Gottes führt" ("Die Begründung," 57). On the fear of God in Sirach, see J. Haspecker, *Gottesfurcht bei Jesus Sirach*, AnBib 30 (Rome: Biblical Institute, 1967).

[57]Unless, of course, we surrender to the overwhelming apocalyptic voices that proclaim a holocaust or a privation. But only the punitive side of Sirach's voice is heard in such a message of doom for the good and the bad.

[58]The term is taken from Hesse, who likewise manifests a fascination with the idea of death (see esp. *Narcissus und Goldmund*, but also *Demian*, *Steppenwolf*, and *Siddhartha*).

him a lonely man of faith[59] in the modern religious marketplace. Perhaps some day he can again join Sirach in the mighty crescendo of praise, and by harnessing his pessimism "to the triumphal chariot of religious faith"[60] he can *live* again.[61] Until that day, the ache within his soul, which unites him with Sirach at the deepest level of human existence, bears living testimony to his ultimate concern and cries out that he has not given God up, though he has lost him.

---

[59]This is the language of J. B. Solovietchek in a marvelous essay, "The Lonely Man of Faith," *Tradition* 7 (1965): 5-67.

[60]C. Zhitlowsky, "Job and Faust," *Two Studies in Yiddish Culture*, trans. P. Matenko (Leiden: Brill, 1968) 98, uses this language to describe Job's response to the Divine Presence. Zhitlowsky asks whether Job lost all courage when the gate of mystery burst open. As Job stands face to face with God, he writes, "The clouds of darkness are dispersed; a feeling of infinite confidence in the world and its Divine Leader arises in his soul and he laughs at the thousand questions, the hungry wolves with burning eyes, and they disappear from his soul" (152).

[61]We refer to the biblical exhortation to choose the Lord and live (Deut 30:19-20; cf. Amos 5:6a).

8 (1970)

Popular Questioning of the Justice of God in Ancient Israel[*]

The task of justifying the ways of God to man has become "a universal religious nightmare"[1]; the problem is not so much the justification of God in the face of actual suffering as it is the *reconciling of evil* with the knowledge that God intends *salvation for mankind*.[2] In essence theodicy is the search for a solution to the problem of meaning,[3] an undertaking that did not begin with modern man, the so-called fourth man, creature come of age.[4]

Neither the ancient Israelite nor his Mesopotamian neighbors shied away from the above-mentioned task,[5] even if for the former one admit the correctness of

---

[*]The presidential address delivered to the Southern Section of the Society of Biblical Literature on 28 March 1969 at the University of South Carolina, meeting jointly with the American Academy of Religion, Southern Section, and the Southern Humanities Conference.

[1]This is the task envisioned by John Milton in *Paradise Lost*. The psychologist Carl G. Jung has observed that theodicy "is no longer a problem for experts in theological seminaries, but a universal religious nightmare" (*Answer to Job* [New York, 1968], 174).

[2]A. Jäger, "Theodizee und Anthropodizee bei Karl Marx," *STU* 37 (1967): 14-23 ("Theodizee ist nicht so sehr eine 'Rechtfertigung' Gottes angesichts des faktischen Leides, als vor allem die 'Rechtfertigung' des Übels im Gegenuber zum Wissen um Gottes Heil für den Menschen," 14).

[3]Ibid.

[4]See K. H. Miskotte, *When the Gods Are Silent* (1967), 1-7 and passim, for discussion of this terminology.

[5]The peculiar failure of Egypt to wrestle with the problem of theodicy has been explained by the fact that the idea of justice as *right* rather than as *favor* never seems to have spread to Egypt, and by the centrality of the belief in immortality (R. J. Williams, "Theodicy in the Ancient Near East," *CJT* 2 [1956]: 18-19). It is customary to call attention to "The Complaints of the Eloquent Peasant," "The Prophecy of Nefer-rohu[ti]," and "A Dispute over Suicide," but the difference between these and Israelite and Mesopotamian literature is great.

the charge of a "conspiracy of silence"[6] on the occasion of the death of Josiah. One might with some justification contend that the conspiracy of silence characterizes contemporary biblical scholars, inasmuch as attempts to wrestle with the problem of theodicy are few indeed. Apart from some discussion in exegetical studies of Job and theological examination of the problem of evil, three special treatments of theodicy have broken the silence of ignorance or timidity. The first, W. Eichrodt's "Vorsehungsglaube und Theodizee im Alten Testament,"[7] is a masterful affirmation of God's providence as proclaimed both explicitly and implicitly in the Old Testament, together with a reminder that the Israelite refused to solve the problem of evil by rational theories, choosing rather (1) the prophetic message of the God who comes (2 Isa, 2 Zech, Ps 22:23-32); (2) the escape to the immediate experience of God's nearness (Ps 73, even in the presence of death; Jer 15:15-21, Ps 16 [Ps 17:15 and 63:4 come close; Job 3—21 attempts this unsuccessfully]); and (3) creation faith, an affirmation of a wondrous creation before which creaturely silence is mandatory (Job 38-41).[8] Eichrodt clearly perceives that the *word of God* in this context, an *addressing of man* by God even in wisdom literature, implies that suffering can only be solved from revelation. The import of the divine creative word is also recognized by J. J. Stamm, whose "Die Theodizee in Babylon und Israel"[9] calls attention to the striking similarities between Job and *The Babylonian Theodicy*, neither of which judges God at the bar of reason. Rather Job pays heed to the revelatory word of the Creator, while the Babylonian sufferer trusts in the religious experience of past generations. In a word, the appeal to revelation or tradition falls far short of a theodicy, the resolution of the problem by human reason.[10] The existential character of the problem of evil does not escape Stamm's vision, for he notes that a crisis of faith rather than intellectual curiosity or literary artistry rests behind the ancient Near Eastern attempts to deal with the problem of theodicy.[11] The

---

[6]S. B. Frost, "The Death of Josiah: A Conspiracy of Silence," *JBL* 87 (1968): 369-82 ("the silence following the death of Josiah which is so profound is the silence of the historiographers," 381).

[7]In *Festschrift O. Procksch* (1934), 45-70.

[8]Ibid., 64-70. The emphasis is upon the necessity for wonder, not man's nothingness. Abraham Heschel, *Man Is Not Alone* (1951), 11ff., replaces Kant's moral imperative with one of wonder, arguing that a capacity for radical amazement separates man from beast.

[9]"Die Theodizee in Babylon und Israel," *Jaarbericht Ex Oriente Lux* 9 (1944): 99-107.

[10]Ibid., 101, 107. Norman H. Snaith, *The Book of Job*, SBT 11 (London, 1968), 33, points to the prophetic influence upon Job, and argues that *The Babylonian Theodicy* served as a model for the biblical work (21-27).

[11]Ibid., 99. For a superb discussion of the crisis through which wisdom passed, see Hans Heinrich Schmid, *Wesen und Geschichte der Weisheit* (1966), 74-78, 131-40, 173-95. John Priest, "Humanism, Skepticism, and Pessimism in Israel," *JAAR* 36 (1968): 321, suggests that Ezekiel's stress upon the transcendence of God and Deuteronomy's elevation of a "Book" contributed to the crisis from which skepticism arose.

purely religious nature of these ancient probings is also grasped by R. J. Williams, whose "Theodicy in the Ancient Near East"[12] discusses the basic literary tradition pertinent to his subject and suggests that the intermediary for whom Job longed, the impartial judge who would even call Yahweh to task, was none other than the Canaanite Baal.[13]

If the literature of ancient Israel and Mesopotamia wrestling with the problem of evil cannot be described as theodicy in the sense intended by Leibniz or Kant, perhaps the reorientation suggested by A. Jäger[14] in the direction of anthropodicy has merit. The crucial question for man is not "How can one reconcile the existence of God with the presence of evil?" but "What positive meaning for man can be had in the face of the tentacles of death?" If this be a proper assessment of our situation, one can approve wholeheartedly the desire of J. Priest to elevate anthropology, or as he prefers, sociology, to at least equal position with theology in Old Testament scholarship.[15] The fruits of such a perspective await our plucking, but Priest's interpretation of Job from the standpoint of the nagging question, "Why am I?," and of Qoheleth as a denial of meaningful history, indicates that a refusal to eat from this tree is folly rather than wisdom. In an article in the *Journal of Biblical Literature*, I have described wisdom literature as Israel's quest for self-understanding in terms of things, people and God,[16] and am now prepared to maintain that the question of meaning is more basic than that of God, indeed that biblical man's point of departure was not God but self. In essence, the God question is secondary to self-understanding.[17]

I. Initial Rumblings:
A Famine in the Land of Promise

Whether theodicy or anthropodicy be the term to describe our present task, the intention is the same, namely to examine the evidence for initial rumblings in Israel indicative of difficulty in answering the question of meaning, to look closely at the

---

[12]"Theodicy in the Ancient Near East," *CJT* 2 (1956): 14-26.

[13]Ibid., 24. The argument rests on the parallel with the Baal and Anat epic (*ANET* 140), which Ginzberg translates by "So I know that triumphant Baal lives, That the prince, lord of the earth, exists!"

[14]Jäger, "Theodizee und Anthropodizee bei Karl Marx," 19.

[15]Priest, "Humanism, Skepticism, and Pessimism in Israel," 311-26.

[16]James L. Crenshaw, "Method in Determining Wisdom Influence upon 'Historical' Literature," *JBL* 88 (1969): 129-42.

[17]This suggests that Old Testament theology should begin with man rather than God as is common in the works adopting a systematic principle. Heschel, *Man Is Not Alone*, 129, observes that "The Bible is not man's theology, but God's anthropology, dealing with man and what [God] asks of him rather than with the nature of God." Also pertinent to this discussion is Heschel's reminder that our "self-concern is a cupful drawn from the spirit of divine concern" (145).

literary deposit expressive of a volcanic eruption (Job and Qoheleth) and to consider the alternative methods of dealing with a loss of meaning, specifically the escape to the comforts provided by religion and the flight from God by the stouthearted.

The use of the expression "famine" above implies that there once was plenty, indicates that the initial rumblings are the result of a privation. But privation from what? From a belief in the efficacy of good works! So long as ancient man thought of the gods in terms of impersonal force, caprice was anticipated and tolerated. However, once personal categories were applied to the gods, man came to expect them to behave in a manner that was humanly predictable, even though free to act in a high-handed fashion on occasion.[18] The belief in the efficacy of good works was characteristic of all three segments of Israelite society. In a recent book entitled "Gerechtigkeit als Weltordnung," H. H. Schmid has demonstrated that basic to the wisdom of the ancient world was the conviction that the Creator had established the universe in an orderly fashion, that a principle of the right or appropriate deed held the created order together, and that man's purpose was to act in harmony with this principle at all times. Although going by different names (*Ma'at* in Egypt, *ME* in Mesopotamia, צֶדֶק in Israel), this principle was thought to have been guaranteed by the king and to have encompassed the areas of law, wisdom, nature (vegetation), warfare (victory over enemies), cult (sacrifice), as well as kingship.[19] Any action that was not in accord with the governing principle of the universe was thought to have upset the balance of nature, to have reintroduced an element of chaos into the created order, hence to be deserving of punishment or death. Conversely, the appropriate deed was rewarded, since it sustained the universe, so that religion became highly utilitarian.

The prophetic theology, with strong ties to covenantal and holy war traditions, was equally positive in the view that the good deed was rewarded. In reality, the basis of a covenantal (or treaty) relationship is a promise that accord with the stipulations of the covenant will bring blessings while a breach of the agreement calls upon the heads of the rebellious all the curses spoken or unspoken. When this is kept in mind, the prophetic theology within individual oracles and in the Deuteronomic history is completely understandable. Furthermore, the holy war traditions, particularly the comforting "Fear not, for I am with you," and the memory of theophanies for judgment upon enemies,[20] coupled with the conviction of Israel's chosenness and uniqueness contributed to the belief that obedience would not pass unnoticed by God. Priestly religion, too, supported the view that good men fare well in this life, both in its relationship with magic and with law. The

---

[18]W. G. Lambert, *Babylonian Wisdom Literature* (London: Oxford University Press, 1960), 6ff.

[19]*Gerechtigkeit als Weltordnung* (1968), 15-77 and passim.

[20]Horst Dietrich Preuss, " . . . Ich will mit dir sein!," *ZAW* 80 (1968): 139-73, and James L. Crenshaw, "Amos and the Theophanic Tradition," *ZAW* 80 (1968): 203-15.

presupposition of the cultic act was that the deity could be moved, whether automatically or by proper conduct matters little as far as the principle is concerned, while the codification of law rests on the premise that God has declared his will for man and will, by the use of the stick or the carrot, punishment or reward, see that it is carried out. Even if we refuse to join K. Koch in affirming a "sphere of destiny" in which the deed activated a principle that guaranteed punishment for transgression,[21] and prefer rather H. Graf Reventlow's view that God's freedom transcends any such nexus of guilt and punishment,[22] the point still stands that priest, prophet and wise man labored under the assumption of a correlation between good conduct and earthly reward.

Undergirding this belief in the efficacy of the good deed was ancient man's sense of solidarity, the corporate merging of the one and the many, making possible the conviction of imputed merit and guilt, and providing a convenient explanation for any divergence from the principle of retribution. But in Israel this balloon was punctured as a result of the rise of a wealthy class and urban culture, the valiant effort to patch the holes by the great prophets succeeding only in increasing the sense of guilt felt by those who refused to sacrifice private interests for the welfare of the group. Even the classical prophets contributed to the breakdown of the correlation between good conduct and reward, both in affirming the grace of God despite Israel's rebellious response, and in making grandiose claims not borne out in actual history, then in escaping to the safe position of expectancy. Both the emergence of false prophecy and the never-fulfilled eschatological hopes (or those only partially fulfilled, as in the case of 2 Isaiah) set the stage for complete loss of faith on the occasions of the death of Josiah, the fall of Jerusalem and collapse of the Davidic dynasty despite 2 Sam 7 and numerous psalms expressing the conviction that Yahweh has established David's throne for eternity.

Such a crisis was not, however, unique to Israel, as H. H. Schmid, "Wesen und Geschichte der Weisheit," has discerned so clearly.[23] Rather both in Egypt and in Mesopotamia wisdom's claims were challenged because of a failure to accord with human experience, particularly during subjugation by enemies who either did not know about the principle governing the universe or did not give any credence to it. Nevertheless, the crisis was more acute in Israel because of the deep *personal relationship* between her and Yahweh, a bond best described by marital or familial imagery, and not even approximated by the conviction of non-Israelites as early as

---

[21]"Gibt es ein Vergeltungsdogma im Alten Testament?" *ZTK* 52 (1955): 21.

[22]"Sein Blut komme über sein Haupt," *VT* 10 (1960): 311. Hartmut Gese, *Lehre und Wirklichkeit in der alten Weisheit* (1958), 45-50, emphasizes Yahweh's freedom from any principle of order. Walter Brueggemann, *Tradition for Crisis* (1968), 78-79, calls attention to Hosea's radical departure in asserting that the blessings promised in Lev 26 and Deut 28 for covenant obedience will befall the *disobedient*!

[23]See n. 11, above.

the Sumerians that the people are the apple of the deity's eye.[24] In Israel the loss of the corporate sense does not begin with Jeremiah and Ezekiel, whose intention was to encourage a generation upon whom the crisis had fallen, but at least as early as the Davidic and Solomonic decisions to alter tribal boundaries, maintain a mercenary army, and ape the ways of neighboring powers. We should expect, therefore, to discover within literature as early as the Davidic era echoes of rumblings brought on by a famine in the land of promise, the inevitable disparity between religious claims and actual experience.

The Yahwistic narrative bears witness to such concern over the conduct of God in the face of extreme wickedness. The account of Abraham's intercession for a doomed Sodom and Gomorrah, although no attack against collective guilt, dares to entertain a radically new understanding of God's righteousness (Gen 18:17-33). The Yahwist recognizes that there is more injustice in the death of a few innocent people than in the sparing of a guilty multitude; his question, however, is "To what limits is the application of this principle subject?" Or put another way, "What determines God's judgment on Sodom, the wickedness of the many or the innocence of the few?" The guilt of the city is beyond question, but the narrator pushes Yahweh to the point of admitting that a very small number of innocent people could spare a great host, so willing is He to save. The fact that Sodom and Gomorrah are inhabited by non-Israelites indicates just how far Yahweh will go in overlooking sin for the sake of a few righteous; Sodom becomes a "pattern of a human community toward which Yahweh's eyes turn in judgment" (G. von Rad). The subsequent angelic removal of all "righteous" people from the doomed cities protects Yahweh from the accusation of injustice, even if the Yahwist did not press God to an admission that one innocent person could spare the city (cf. Am 9:10, where a distinction is made between the guilty and innocent and only the former punished).[25]

Similar rumblings may lie behind the Yahwistic portion of the incident of the golden calf in Ex 32 (25-35). Couched within the Deuteronomic concern for Yahweh's reputation, promise to the fathers and repentance (7-14), this narrative lays stress upon the wrath of God despite the intercessory pleadings of the innocent Moses who dares to lay his life on the altar, hence provides a sort of corrective to anyone who might be disposed to press the principle enunciated in the narrative about Sodom and Gomorrah to his own advantage. In this instance Moses is assured that Yahweh will punish the guilty, little comfort before the brandished swords of

---

[24]Samuel N. Kramer, "Sumer," *IDB* R-Z:463; and Stamm, "Die Theodizee in Babylon und Israel," 105-107.

[25]Gerhard von Rad, *Genesis*, OTL (Philadelphia: Westminster, 1961), 204-209, and John Skinner, *Genesis*, ICC (Edinburgh: T&T Clark, 1910; [2]1925), 305. Hermann Gunkel, *The Legends of Genesis*, trans. W. H. Carruth (repr.: 1964; orig.: Chicago: Open Court, 1901), 60, writes that the storyteller hides from us the most important point in this narrative, Abraham's thoughts while viewing the smoke from Sodom.

the levites, who presumably join Aaron in guilt but escape punishment. The God who can order mass homicide is also capable of carrying out the test of Abraham's faith in the Elohistic narrative of Gen 22. But even here there is a growing suspicion that the demand of human sacrifice is unbecoming to God.

Once the justice of God was questioned, even if obliquely, the everpresent lament intensifies in pathos, for the expressions of confidence lose something of their force. Jeremiah's poignant cry for justice may begin with the conventional confession of God's righteousness (12:1), but the prophetic accusation that Yahweh prospers the wicked, and the divine oracle of hatred for a covenanted people (12:2-13) indicate the shallowness of the claim. Jeremiah's contemporary, Habakkuk, affirms God's justice, however, even in the face of all evidence to the contrary; the final hymn is almost unsurpassed in the Old Testament for grandeur of faith despite one's external situation (cf. Dan 3:16-18). Habakkuk vows that even starvation will not prevent him from rejoicing in God (3:17-19); nevertheless, the perversion of justice and failure of God to respond when the cry of oppression storms the gates of heaven are not nullified by promise of action in the future. The deepest cry of anguish comes, however, not from a prophet, but from a cultic liturgy agonizing over the failure of God to keep his promise to David. Composed of an ancient hymn on the mercies of Yahweh as seen in his victory over Chaos and the election of David, a prophetic oracle promising the permanence of the Davidic dynasty, and a lament over the collapse of that line, psalm 89 may be Israel's reaction to the death of Josiah.[26] Regardless of the historical situation calling forth the psalm, the disparity between God's promise and the reality of the situation finds no rational resolution, and must be stated with a bleeding heart.[27] Little wonder, therefore, that a volcanic eruption takes place, that out of this agony come two masterpieces of the human spirit, Job and Qoheleth.

II. Volcanic Eruption:
Job and Qoheleth

Yehezkel Kaufmann has described the concerns of theodicy as threefold: (1) the origin of natural, or primary evil, (2) of religious evil, and (3) of moral evil.[28] While Job focuses upon the problem of moral evil, both in its social and divine manifestation, and Qoheleth draws attention to natural evil, particularly death, it was left for

---

[26]Hans-Joachim Kraus, *Psalmen*, 2 vols. (Neukirchen-Vluyn: Neukirchener Verlag, 1966), 2:615-25; and Artur Weiser, *The Psalms*, trans. Herbert Hartwell, OTL (Philadelphia: Westminster, 1962), 590-94.

[27]Weiser, *The Psalms*, 593, writes: "Man is not able to resolve by his own thinking the contradiction between the promise and the actual state of affairs; he can only state that contradiction with a bleeding heart."

[28]*The Religion of Israel from Its Beginnings to the Babylonian Exile*, trans. Moshe Greenberg (Chicago: University of Chicago Press, 1960), 332.

the apocalyptic author of 2 Esdras to wrestle with the issue of religious evil, the weakness of Israel apropos foreign empires (cf. Gen 11 and origin of *idolatry*).

Although the biblical Job may be *sui generis*, at least as far as literary classification is concerned, it is but one of several attempts to grapple with innocent suffering in the ancient Near East.[29] At least three solutions to the problem are manifest: (1) man is congenitally evil; (2) the gods are unjust; and (3) our knowledge is partial. The fragmentariness of human understanding was a necessary corollary of the belief in the hiddenness of God, the *Deus absconditus* expressive of true mystery (the *numinous*), but also of his refusal to be controlled by anyone who knows הַשֵּׁם, the Name. The partiality of man's knowledge lent credence to the suggestion that innocent suffering was disciplinary, purgative even, and to the much later belief that all would be set right in a future existence.

The declaration of man's congenital sinfulness goes back to Sumerian times; S. N. Kramer renders the pertinent passage

> Never has a sinless child been born to its mother, . . .
> a sinless workman has not existed from of old.[30]

Similarly the *Babylonian Theodicy* affirms that

> Narru, king of the gods, who created mankind,
> And majestic Zulummar, who dug out their clay,
> And mistress Mami, the queen who fashioned them,
> Gave perverse speech to the human race.
> With lies, and not truth, they endowed them forever.[31]

In full agreement with such sentiment was Eliphaz, Job's miserable comforter, for from him we hear

> Behold, God puts no trust in his holy ones,
>   and the heavens are not clean in his sight;
> how much less one who is abominable and corrupt,
>   a man who drinks iniquity like water!   (15:15 RSV; cf. 4:17)

Likewise Bildad wishes to view man in terms of his own stature; he exclaims

> How then can man be righteous before God?
>   How can he who is born of woman be clean?
> Behold, even the moon is not bright
>   and the stars are not clean in his sight;

---

[29]Lambert, *Babylonian Wisdom Literature*, 21-91, 139-49 and *ANET* 434-40.

[30]"Man and His God: A Sumerian Variation of the 'Job' Motif," in *Wisdom in Israel and in the Ancient Near East*, SVT 3 (1960): 170-82, esp. 179.

[31]Lambert, *Babylonian Wisdom Literature*, 89.

how much less man, who is a maggot,
and the son of man, who is a worm!   (25:4-6 RSV)

Similarly the accusation of the gods as unjust occurs in extra biblical literature as well as in Job, indeed is the presupposition of the works. This comes out most strikingly, however, in "The Babylonian *Pilgrim's Progress*," to use W. G. Lambert's title for *Ludlul bel nemeqi*, where the sufferer complains that he is being treated like an impious one who has neglected prayer, sacrifice, holy days, reverence, God even,[32] and in the *Dialogue of Pessimism*, where such a recognition of the injustice of God lies behind the despair.[33] In Job, too, the justice of God comes under attack, indeed gives way before the might of Titanic Job (9:22-24, 24:1-12).

The incompleteness of human understanding, celebrated in the majestic hymn of Job 28, is emphasized in "The Babylonian *Pilgrim's Progress*" and *The Babylonian Theodicy*. The former complains

I wish I knew that these things were pleasing to one's God!
What is proper to oneself is an offense to one's god,
What in one's own heart seems despicable is proper to one's god.
Who knows the will of the gods in heaven?
Who understands the plans of the underworld gods?
Where have mortals learnt the way of a god?[34]

The Babylonian Theodicy expresses the same sentiment, even if admitting that savants attain to wisdom:

O wise one, O savant, who masters knowledge,
In your anguish you blaspheme the god.
The divine mind, like the center of the heavens, is remote;
Knowledge of it is difficult; the masses do not know it.[35]

It is quite clear that Job is at one with the extrabiblical parallels in the solutions provided. This is true even when one appeals to the theophany as the final resolution of Job's situation, for the same answer is found in "The Babylonian *Pilgrim's Progress*," where Marduk comes to the sufferer and removes all adversity. In view of this affinity between Job and similar works, the assumption of the uniqueness of Job as to *Gattung* is open to question. But what are we to call Job? A רִיב, answered lament, *Streitgespräch*, or what? The kinship with the covenant lawsuit, indeed the legal background, of Job has long been recognized. When one admits the

---

[32]Ibid., 39.
[33]Ibid., 145-49.
[34]Ibid., 41.
[35]Ibid., 87.

close relationship between law and wisdom championed by E. Gerstenberger,[36] the thesis that Job is a רִיב becomes quite possible, as Stamm has already perceived.[37] On the other hand, H. Gese's contention that Job is a paradigm of an answered lament[38] presents serious difficulty, inasmuch as the framework of Job differs radically from that of laments, and even the poetic *dialogue* stands out both in mood and complexion. More attractive than either, however, is the view that Job is a *Streitgespräch*, a controversy dialogue. Such disputations are well known to wisdom literature from its earliest manifestation; their form consists of a mythological introduction followed by a debate between two contestants, the resolution of which is determined by divine judgment.[39] However, the prophetic *Streitgespräch*, which differs as to intensity of argumentation and purpose, namely self-vindication of the prophet, has contributed to the genre as found in Job, and explains the kinship with 2 Isaiah. In Job the mood differs from the calm, almost playful, wisdom discussion of the relative value of things, animals or professions; rather Job employs the controversy dialogue as a weapon of warfare, his own vindication being at stake. In reality, then, Job is rooted in wisdom and prophetic theology, both as to literary genre and final resolution of the problem by a theophany. The key to Job, at least from this perspective, is the emotional outburst of 13: 16 ("This will be my salvation, that a godless man shall not come before him"). Since God comes to Job, he has been vindicated, the problem of meaning is no more, for all things fall into place when in the presence of the Creator of the ends of the earth. For the author of Job, meaning is theological—nothing else matters, neither love (for wife, children, friends), nor desire for earthly goods.

Qoheleth can find no such meaning anywhere; this author is convinced that life is empty, vain, profitless. Neither material possessions, human friendship, nor religious devotion alter the fact that nature is oppressive, that death is the negation of all good, that God is therefore untouched by the plight of creatures. What, then, is man to do? Qoheleth advises him to find some pleasure in wife and children, and to work with dignity, in this way postponing death as long as possible. In Qoheleth there is a challenging of the power of human reason, a recognition of the bankruptcy of wisdom. In Job and in Qoheleth we discern a failure of nerve, the one rational, the other theological![40]

---

[36]*Wesen und Herkunft des "apodiktischen Rechts,"* WMANT 20 (Neukirchen, 1965); and "Covenant and Commandment," *JBL* 84 (1965): 38-51.

[37]Stamm, "Die Theodizee in Babylon und Israel," 104 (with a reference to an article in *Der Grundriss* 5 [1943]: 1ff.).

[38]Gese, *Lehre und Wirklichkeit in der alten Weisheit*, 63-78.

[39]Lambert, *Babylonian Wisdom Literature*, 150-211.

[40]For recent discussions of Qoheleth's manner of speaking about God, see H. P. Müller, "Wie sprach Qohälät von Gott?" *VT* 18 (1968): 507-21; and E. Pfeiffer, "Die Gottesfurcht im Buche Kohelet," in *Gottes Wort und Gottes Land (Festschrift für H. W. Hertzberg)* (1965), 133-58.

In the presence of volcanic fire as seen in Job and Qoheleth, and following the leads suggested by each, two responses are possible: (1) repentance, confession of God's justice despite everything, that is, an affirmation of meaning (Job); and (2) despair, criticism of God for not caring, the denial of divine justice, hence of meaningful existence (Qoheleth). Both responses characterize the popular reaction to the disparity between the promises of faith and the realities of experience.

III. Survival of a Faithful Few: The Doxology of Judgment

The confession of God's justice in the presence of a sentence of death appears in various strata of biblical literature, all of which date from the period of crisis surrounding 587 B. C. and its sequel. The vocabulary of this confession and the act itself led F. Horst to the conclusion that there was within sacral law of Israel (and related peoples) a ceremony in which the guilty person was admonished to give glory to Yahweh (Josh 7:19, Job 4–5, Jer 13:15f., 1 Sam 6:5, Ps 118:17-21, 1 Chr 30:8 (LXX), Amos 4:6-13, 9:1-6), that is, to confess that the Lord is just even when demanding the death penalty.[41] To the literature associated with this occasion Horst gave the title "Doxology of Judgment." His suggestion has been endorsed by G. von Rad and R. Knierim, both of whom provide additional passages to be understood from this perspective (1 Kings 8:3, Ezr 10:7ff., Dan 3:31-34, Neh 9, Ezr 6, Dan 9, Isa 12:1f. [von Rad]; Ps 16:56-60, 29:1-9, 89:7-15, 118:17-21, Mic 1:1, Isa 6:3 [Knierim]).[42] In a work in *Zeitschrift für die alttestamentliche Wissenschaft*[43] I have sought to demonstrate that the doxology of judgment and prophetic recitation of disciplinary punishment characteristic of ancient days of penitence gave way in the exilic and postexilic community to hymnic confessions concluded by the refrain יְהוָה צְבָאוֹת שְׁמוֹ (Jer 10:12-16, 31:35, 51:15-19, Isa 51:15), and finally to cultic confessional prayers (Dan 9, Neh 9, Ezr 9, Jer 32). The centrality of creation faith in these passages is occasioned by the knowledge that it is the Creator who calls all men to judgment, and the striking association of בָּרָא and a theophany for judgment indicates that a new look at the role of creation faith in Israelite thought is mandatory. The peripheral place of creation faith in the Old Testament does not grow out of a refusal to take nature seriously. On the contrary, Bertil Albrektson[44] has laid to rest (once for all, it is hoped) the one-sided emphasis upon God's action in history as opposed to nature as the distinctive of Israelite thought. While it is

---

[41]"Die Doxologien im Amosbuch," *ZAW* 47 (1929): 45-54; repr.: *Gottes Recht* (1961), 155-66.

[42]Gerhard von Rad, *Old Testament Theology*, vol. 1, trans. D. M. G. Stalker (New York: Harper, 1962), 357ff.; and Rolf P. Knierim, "The Vocation of Isaiah," *VT* 18 (1968): 56.

[43]"*YHWH Šᵉbā'ôt Šmô*: A Form-Critical Analysis," *ZAW* 81 (1969): 156-75.

[44]*History and the Gods* (1967).

true, as von Rad has advocated so ably,[45] that the Canaanite threat to the moral integrity of Yahwism constituted a barrier to adoption of creation faith, an obstacle overcome only by 2 Isaiah's stroke of genius in utilizing the Canaanite mythologem to interpret the event of the exodus, nevertheless there must be a better reason for the Israelite hesitance to place creation at the center of his faith. I would venture to propose another possibility: the close association of creation faith with a theophany for judgment was out of place in Israel until the crisis of meaning emerged, the awareness that judgment had fallen. Out of reflection upon the implications of a final judgment came the necessity to postulate a doctrine of creation as central to Yahwism. In a word, such judgment of all mankind can only come from the Creator of all.[46] Against this setting the declaration that Yahweh is צַדִּיק must be understood (Jer 12:1, Ps 119:137, Ezr 9:15, Neh 9:8,33, Ex 9:27, Zeph 3:5, Lam 1:18, Dan 9:14, 2 Chr 12:6; cf. 2 Kings 10: 9).

A related literary phenomenon has come to the attention of S. Frost, who refers to "asseveration by thanksgiving" as a special means of magnifying God's justice even in the context of adversity.[47] Such asseverations of thanksgiving Frost identifies in prophetic and psalmodic literature mostly from the *crisis period* of Israelite faith under discussion here (Isa 42:10-13, 44:23, 49:13, 25:1-5, 12:1b-2,4b-6, Hos 13:4, Jer 20:7-13, Ps 118:21, 116:5, 54:8-9 (Heb.), 86:8-13, 57:22). These positive affirmations of God's justice, like the doxology of judgment and confessional prose prayers interspersed throughout Old Testament literature, are but the Joban popular response to the volcanic eruption in Israelite society. Small wonder that a note of expectancy comes to dominate postexilic literature, for this surrender before the God who comes in judgment must be rewarded, since the justice of God is boldly asserted, hence the eschatological expectation of Hag, Zech, and Mal falls upon ears atune to this frequency. However, such escape by means of an anticipated coming of God in judgment and, *through punishment, in love* was not the only one open to Israel; Qoheleth was not entirely devoid of disciples, although few have been aware of it.

IV. Judgment through Fire:
The Popular Denial of Meaning in Life

In the past, far too little attention has been given to the actual religion of the "man in the streets" in ancient Israel, the spotlight of scholarly scrutiny being turned on the officially sanctioned religion of Israel. There is a growing recognition of the necessity for taking a closer look at Israelite religion as it really was rather than as it was hoped it would be. It is interesting that the study of Amos has led G. Farr

---

[45]"The Theological Problem of the Old Testament Doctrine of Creation," in *The Problem of the Hexateuch and Other Essays* (1966), 131-43; orig. in BZAW 66 (1936).

[46]For further discussion, see my article referred to in n. 43, above.

[47]"Asseveration by Thanksgiving," *VT* 8 (1958): 380-90.

and C. J. Labuschagne in this direction, the latter of whom has promised a mono-graph on what he calls para-theology.[48] In an attempt to solve the enigma of false prophecy I have been forced to take seriously the popular beliefs that constituted a live option for the man of faith. In fact, I would even suggest that the study of prophecy in general and of false prophecy in particular has moved in the direction of taking seriously the voice of the people. Prophetic research began with an emphasis upon the great individualist, ethical monotheist, ecstatic, only later to shift away from the man to his message, both as to its character as doom only or weal *and* woe, and the traditions employed by the prophet. The next logical step, it seems to me, is to discuss the hearers, to discern what they contributed to the dialogue. Fortunately, the voice of the people is not altogether hidden from us; we possess a special source for this phenomenon, namely the prophetic quotations of the oral response to their message. H. W. Wolff's masterful "Das Zitat im Propheten-spruch"[49] provides a useful point of departure, but much more needs to be done. On the basis of prophetic quotations, I would venture to describe Israel's popular religion in terms of arrogant confidence, spiritual insensitivity, taunting defiance, remorseless despair, painful query and historical pragmatism. I shall here limit myself to a glance at some of the evidence for the last two characteristics, painful query and historical pragmatism. The claim that Yahweh was merciful, compassion-ate, and slow to anger was questioned in Jeremiah's day by those who feared that God's anger would last forever (3:4-5a). Ezekiel's contemporaries complained that "The days grow long, and every vision comes to nought" (12:22), in fact, questioned the justice of God ("The way of the Lord is not just" 18:25). Likewise Malachi's opponents complained that "Everyone who does evil is good in the sight of the Lord, and he delights in them" (2:17), "It is vain to serve God. What is the good of our keeping his charge" for "evildoers not only prosper but when they put God to the test they escape" (3:12,15). This painful questioning of God's justice was supplemented by historical pragmatism; the people demanded that God repay their goodness, and when he did not, they turned to other gods or to their own desires. This can be seen in the demand that Yahweh "speed his work that we may see it" (Isa 5:19), and the report that the worship of the queen of heaven paid higher dividends, hence the adulation of Yahweh would be sheer folly (Jer 44:16-19). In the light of this evidence, one must object to the usual assumption that belief in the efficacy of good works, what E. M. Good calls the magical assumption in religion,[50]

---

[48]Farr, "The Language of Amos, Popular or Cultic?" *VT* 16 (1966): 312-24; and C. J. Labuschagne, "Amos's Conception of God and the Popular Theology of His Time," in *Studies on the Books of Hosea and Amos* (1964/1965), 122-33. Th. C. Vriezen, *The Religion of Israel* (1967), 20, writes that a hard core were faithful as in Isaiah's day, "while the great mass of the people must undoubtedly have trimmed their sails to the wind."

[49]*Gesammelte Studien zum Alten Testament* (1964), 36-129; orig. in *BEvT* 4 (1937).

[50]*Irony in the Old Testament* (1965), 196-240.

was of popular origin and typifies the faith of the masses as opposed to that of the religious establishment. No longer ought we to say that the dialogue in Job is an attack on popular religion[51]; on the contrary, both this questioning of God's justice and Qoheleth's denial of any meaning in life have more affinity with popular religion than with official Yahwism. This kinship is particularly noticeable in the prophetic *Streitgespräch*.

On the basis of 2 Isaiah, J. Begrich has observed that the *Streitgespräch* emerged from the concrete situation of the prophet and assumed the form of question and answer, claim and counterclaim.[52] E. Pfeiffer's analysis of the discussions in Malachi indicates that three stages are evident: (1) the initial statement; (2) the objection by the partner in the discussion; and (3) the defense of the original statement, together with the conclusion.[53] My own study of the controversy dialogue has convinced me that it is a weapon of warfare, a self-vindication of the prophet. Accordingly, stylistic devices of rhetorical question and citation of popular theology draw attention to the radicality of the prophetic message, which is reinforced by rational argumentation based on human nature and experience, together with invective and threat. The pedagogic value of the disputation is minimal, owing to the great gulf between prophet and people, a chasm enlarged by abusive language. In essence, the defense of God's justice prominent in prophetic disputations is an effort at self-vindication, a burning issue after the emergence of false prophets.

A thoroughgoing analysis of the disputations that pertain to the justice of God cannot be attempted here, but a few observations are in order. In Mi 2:6-11 the popular demand that the prophet preach שָׁלוֹם is based on the belief that God does not punish his covenant people, and the prophet is forced to defend God's justice. Again, the well known parable of the farmer in Isa 28:23-29, where the point is made that the farmer does the proper thing at the right time, must be interpreted against the backdrop of a denial of the justice of God, as W. Whedbee's recent Yale Dissertation on "Isaiah and Wisdom" has recognized.[54] Here Isaiah is assuring the people of God's justice by promising that God acts in a manner appropriate to the occasion. Likewise, the prophet attacks those who ask, "Who sees us? Who knows us?" by employing a *Streitfabel* calling attention to the absurdity of the clay complaining that the potter has no understanding (29:15f.). A similar questioning of the justice of God prompts 2 Isaiah to praise the Creator as one who does not faint or grow weary, who is unsearchable in understanding, hence the claim that "My way is hid from the Lord, and my right is disregarded by my God" is thought to have no real content. Finally, Malachi addresses himself to the popular rejection of

---

[51]Against G. A. Larue, *Old Testament Life and Literature* (1968), 296, and Stamm, "Die Theodizee in Babylon und Israel," 103.

[52]*Studien zu Deuterojesaja* (1963), 48-51; orig. in BWANT 25 (1938).

[53]"Die Disputationsworte im Buche Maleachi," *EvT* 19 (1959): 546-68.

[54]"Isaiah and Wisdom," Ph.D. diss., Yale, 1968, chap. 2.

God's justice, suggesting that those who deny that God is just or ask "Where is the God of justice?" can find comfort in the expected coming of the messenger of the Lord who will refine Israel's priesthood, indeed, that those who advocate that serving God is vain should take note of the fact that God is keeping a book of remembrance so that eventually there will be a distinction between the righteous and the wicked, and the saints will tread down the sinners on the day when Yahweh acts (2:17—3:5, 3:13–4:3). Are Job and Qoheleth to be silenced so easily? Is there not more integrity in the popular questioning of the justice of God than in Malachi's affirmation of it?[55]

Epilogue:
The Responsibility for Honesty

It would be interesting to pursue the variations of the Joban theme in "Paradise Lost," where one finds God's honor saved at man's expense, "J. B.," where human love provides the hope for one who had discovered that God does not love, but *is*, whereas we *do love*, and Jung's *Answer to Job*, where the eternal gospel that one *can* love God but *must fear him* is altered little by the participation of God in the enigma of human suffering.[56] However, I wish to conclude by raising for your further reflection some questions growing out of this discussion. To what extent are religious leaders responsible for what the masses are asked to believe? When grandiose theological claims are made, must their promulgator assume the responsibility for loss of faith that results when the promises do not materialize? Are prophets culpable for having thought more about vindicating themselves before their attackers than about real communication? Does every appeal to a future act of God cast a positive vote for the Marxist claim that religion is an opiate of the people?[57] Which, then, is preferable, the creed of the blind man ("I have been young, and now am old; yet I have not seen the righteous forsaken or his children begging bread," Ps 37:25), or that of the heart of stone ("It is hopeless, for I have loved strangers, and after them I will go," Jer 2:25b)?

A final thought. Is the current emphasis on wisdom literature indicative of our inability to take revelation seriously any more? Now that we can no longer say כֹּה אָמַר אֲדֹנָי ("Thus hath the Lord spoken") are we reduced to שְׁמַע בְּנִי מוּסַר אָבִיךָ ("My son, listen to your father's advice")? Has the crisis that

---

[55]Heschel, *Man Is Not Alone*, 132, reminds us that "even the cry of despair—There is no justice in heaven!—is a cry in the name of justice that cannot have come out of us and still be missing in the source of ourselves."

[56]C. J. Jung, *Answer to Job*, 169: "That is the eternal, as distinct from the temporal gospel: one can love God but one must fear him"; and Archibald MacLeish, *J.B.* (Boston: Houghton Mifflin, 1958), 151-52: Sarah: "You wanted justice and there was none . . . only love." J.B.: "He [God] does not love. He is." Sarah: "But we do. That's the wonder."

[57]Jäger, "Theodizee und Anthropodizee bei Karl Marx," 22.

confronted Job and Qoheleth invaded the ranks of Old Testament scholarship? Shades of Qoheleth! Is there nothing new under the sun?[58]

---

[58]Hans Heinrich Schmid, "Hauptprobleme der neueren Prophetenforschung," *STU* 35 (1965): 142, asks some pertinent questions about what is meant when the sage learns from experience what prophets proclaim as revelation. This line of thinking opens all sorts of possibilities for Old Testament scholarship.

9 (1993)

The Concept of God in Old Testament Wisdom

As a corrective to abstract treatments in biblical theology, Claus Westermann has proposed that ancient Israelites understood God by means of two fundamental categories: saving and blessing.[1] In his view, canonical literature describes a saving God, except for the wisdom corpus and psalms, which characterize the deity as one who blesses all living creatures. I find this distinction both provocative and problematic. As savior, God acts on behalf of a favored people, who gratefully conduct their lives according to the divine will and in each generation actualize the memory of former deliverances. The blessing God makes life possible by creating an orderly universe in which all creatures benefit from divine generosity. Although the saving God actively participates in the ongoing drama of salvation, the blessing God acts primordially to establish conditions essential to life.

In general, the saving God disregards worth when entering into a covenant relationship with a special group, although inconsistently applying this standard in subsequent dealings with the elect. The blessing God lavishly dispenses bounty without regard to merit and does not play favorites with any group. Yet individual worth determines access to life and riches, so that for many the world of blessing presents itself as a curse, a universe foundering on broken promises. Hence the saving God benefits the few and relates to them and to their enemies with violent jealousy, whereas the blessing God smiles only on those persons who act wisely and virtuously, but that smile too, lacks consistency.

Of course, the saving God resembles ancient Near Eastern patron deities and the blessing God is remarkably like High Gods of Egypt and Mesopotamia. The rarity of saving deeds,[2] which made their recitation all the more poignant, and the

---

[1] *What Does the Old Testament Say about God?* (London: SPCK, 1979).

[2] Jon D. Levenson, *Creation and the Persistence of Evil* (San Francisco: Harper & Row, 1988) observes that "most of the time, God in the Hebrew Bible is doing nothing; the *magnalia Dei* are celebrated in part because of their rarity" (163n.7; punctuation altered).

perceived indifference or hostility of the blessing God suggest that ancient Israel's perception of the Holy[3] does not lend itself to easy categorization.

The essential problem isolated by these remarks surfaces grandly in those rare attempts within the Bible to reflect on God's essential nature, specifically Exod 34:6-8; Gen 18:22-33, Job 1-2, and Jonah 4.[4] The interplay of justice and mercy permeates these texts, each of which addresses the issue in a distinct manner. Does the quality of mercy extend itself so far that human conduct, even wilful idolatry, cannot provoke divine wrath? Can the virtuous character of a few people redound to the benefit of unrepentant sinners? Does God ever act with total disregard for human worth? Does not justice require strict retribution, repentance notwithstanding? These probing explorations into God's character do not mute the unresolved tensions throbbing beneath the surface. At the same time, the several texts take definite moral positions. The Lord's extraordinary capacity for compassion offers no basis for presuming that this gracious, longsuffering deity will be indifferent to sin. In truth, the Judge of the whole earth cares more for the well-being of the group than for exacting strict justice, hence God endorses a principle of vicarious merit. Confronted with a prophet who has personally enjoyed divine forgiveness, God defends the higher principle of spontaneous graciousness that cancels punishment for a repentant city's inhabitants, both human and animal. On the other hand, circumstances occasionally arise that prompt the deity to afflict a supremely virtuous man and to destroy his children and numerous slaves for no discernible reason.

It appears that the categories of justice and mercy cancel one another, necessitating that God opt for one or the other. Even the effort to combine the two qualities by virtue of an elect people encounters difficulty here. The texts concur in the insistence that justice be constituted by compassion. Furthermore, only one of the four texts has a restricted understanding of divine solicitude, the other three addressing God's relationship with non-Israelites.

Although the tension between justice and mercy extends beyond Israel's sapiential literature, it has occasioned wider discussion among modern interpreters of ancient wisdom, for whom the operative term in characterizing the deity, retributor, poses the problem with stark directness. In short, the sages viewed God primarily as the guarantor of a strict system of reward and retribution. According to Johannes Fichtner, whose comprehensive analysis of the wise's view of God remains essential reading,[5] early Israelite wisdom literature maintained complete silence about divine mercy, just as this corpus does not mention such dominant

---

[3]John G. Gammie, *Holiness in Israel* (Minneapolis: Fortress Press, 1989) explores anew the appropriateness of the category of holiness in understanding Israel's God.

[4]Ludwig Schmidt, *De Deo*, BZAW 143 (Berlin and New York: Walter de Gruyter, 1976). Schmidt's analysis suffers from rigid application of source criticism.

[5]*Die altorientalische Weisheit in ihrer israelitisch-jüdischen Ausprägung*, BZAW 62 (Giessen: Alfred Töpelmann, 1933).

ideas and persons outside the wisdom texts as Abraham, Moses, David, the exodus, Sinai, the covenant, the holy city. Fichtner attributes the introduction of a concept of mercy to Sirach's nationalization of wisdom, an unfortunate term for a very real process of integrating older Yahwistic traditions into sapiential teachings.

This understanding of religious development convinced J. Coert Rylaarsdam, who tried to refine and strengthen the argument.[6] On the basis of a fresh study of Israel's wisdom literature in its ancient Near Eastern setting, Horst Dietrich Preuss reached the radical conclusion that biblical wisdom is pagan in all essentials.[7] Unlike Fichtner, who thought Israelite wisdom in its early form excluded divine forgiveness from consideration, although that concept was widely attested in Mesopotamian wisdom, Preuss subsumed biblical wisdom under the encompassing umbrella of Egypt and Mesopotamia. I find myself reacting strongly against Preuss' conclusions and wondering about the accuracy of Fichtner's interpretation of the data. I wish therefore on this occasion to reexamine the sages' understanding of justice and mercy.

* * *

On the surface, the data seem absolutely compelling. Within the Book of Proverbs only 28:13 even remotely accommodates itself to the idea of a compassionate deity, and the sense may well be restricted to human forgiveness.

Whoever hides an offense will not thrive,
but whoever admits (fault) and abandons (perfidy)
    will obtain favor.

The rigid insistence on divine justice within the speeches of Job's three friends is nevertheless tempered by an occasional concession that God inclines toward lenience rather than exact quid pro quo (11:6), but the exasperated sufferer, who asks for his right, not for mercy, adamantly denies any compassion toward him, human or divine. On the basis of content alone, the divine speeches apparently confirm Job's suspicion, for God's solicitude is restricted to the natural world and the animal kingdom. In Qoheleth's view, no distinction between animals and humankind relieves the absurdity of all things. Thus it seems that Fichtner rightly identifies retribution as the dominant notion, albeit a concept that brought considerable consternation because of the indifferent way it manifested itself.

The prominence of divine mercy in Sirach contrasts sharply with this virtual silence in earlier wisdom. Ben Sira seems never to tire of exploring the way God

---

[6]*Revelation in Jewish Wisdom Literature* (Chicago: University of Chicago Press, 1946).

[7]See above all "Das Gottesbild der alteren Weisheit Israel," VTSup 23 (1972): 117-45, and *Einführung in die alttestamentliche Weisheitsliteratur* (Stuttgart, Berlin, Kohn, Mainz: W. Kohlhammer, 1987).

holds justice and mercy in delicate balance. Human weakness and life's brevity evoke divine compassion on all living creatures; this universality of God's mercy differs from human sympathy, which is limited to immediate neighbors (18:8-14). Two powerful forces exist within God, wrath and mercy, neither squelching the other but together issuing in exact reward and retribution (16:11-14). Charitable deeds purchase favorable response from God (29:9, 12), and prayer for forgiveness avails nothing apart from a readiness on the part of the supplicant to forgive human offenses (28:2-4). Delayed punishment offers no reason to presume that wrath is inoperative (5:6), even if God resembles a shepherd and teacher (18:13). Sinners who repent of their deeds obtain forgiveness, although God shows no partiality (35:12).

In the midst of such assertions about God's nature, Ben Sira alludes to ancient Yahwistic texts, most notably the divine proclamation of the so-called thirteen attributes in Exod 34:6-8 and the story of David's offense against God in taking a census, for which he is offered various types of punishment and chooses to fall into divine hands rather than human ones (2 Sam 24:14). Believing that present distress is somehow God's loving means of testing an individual, Ben Sira often resorts to prayer and even expresses himself in the form of a national lament in which he pleads for renewed wonders and deliverance for Israel from her enemies (36:1-17). This prayer, which breathes hatred for foreigners, is worlds removed from earlier wisdom, Israelite or otherwise. The concluding hymn recalls God's mercy, and the praise of the High Priest Simon II mentions his prayer to the merciful Most High. In the final resort when Ben Sira invites young people to come to his house of study, he explicitly encourages them to rejoice over divine mercy. Nevertheless, in all this reflection on God's mercy Ben Sira tenaciously holds on to a belief in retribution (51:30).

The special relationship between God and the elect surfaces again in Wis 3:9, but the reverse side of that bond comes to expression as well. The author remarks that if strict justice befalls the nations hostile to Israel, even after a time of divine indulgence to allow for repentance, those who enjoy God's favor will be punished all the more exactly when they sin (12:20-21). This notion of lenience in the interest of generating repentance occurs elsewhere: "But thou art merciful to all, for thou canst do all things, and thou dost overlook man's sins, that they may repent" (11:23). This author argues that divine justice is beyond question, and because the deity has supreme authority God manifests mildness and patience (12:12-18). In this book we find the usual allusion to God as creator, along with a number of interesting epithets: Lord of your elect, savior, and father.

When we ask how Israel's sages sum up their experience of God, at least two texts come to mind. In response to the divine speeches, Job renounces his previous understanding of God, calling it derivative, and contrasts that earlier rumor about deity with immediate sight. Still, the author exercises extraordinary restraint, and readers do not become privy to the nature of such knowledge. At best, we intuit the silencing effect of new insight on a chastened sufferer. More typical is the response of Elihu to a frightening display of divine power. This awesome manifestation of thunder, lighting, and hail was sufficiently ambiguous to evoke different possibilities in explanation: "Whether for correction, or for land, or for love, [God] causes it to happen" (37:13). To this we compare Qoheleth's bewilderment, presumably about God's actions: "Whether it is love or hate one cannot know" (9:1).

Neither Elihu nor Qoheleth ruled out the possibility that God might smile on humankind. In the former instance, the formulation may suggest all three possibilities as real, the only uncertainty being the actual determination about specific natural manifestations. Indeed, Elihu may even imply that he can identify each of these divine disclosures, for he boasts of having perfect knowledge. Such bold claims are the exception; Israel's sages, like their counterparts in Mesopotamia and Egypt, usually possessed a healthy agnosticism.

The reason was divine freedom, of course, and the sages seem always to have recognized that reality. Human beings may propose, but God disposes; they make plans but God's will works itself out; the lot may fall into the human lap but the deity determines its outcome. Gerhard von Rad has brought this idea into the center of discussion,[8] particularly as it relates to the concept of order that has received considerable attention as a result of Klaus Koch's hypothesis about fate producing deeds,[9] a kind of exact reward and retribution that enslaved the deity also, who at best functioned as midwife assisting an action to reach its specific goal for good or ill. Roland E. Murphy's rejection of order as the controlling concept in biblical wisdom[10] reacts against such excess, which Patrick D. Miller assessed negatively in a study of biblical prophecy.[11] In this connection, Hans Heinrich Schmid has demonstrated the widespread emphasis on order in ancient Near Eastern wisdom, particularly the imagery associated with the goddess ma'at in Egypt.[12]

The sages held another idea as unflinchingly as they did divine freedom. They insisted on the intellect's capacity to assure the good life by word and deed. By using their intellectual gifts the sages hoped to steer their lives safely into harbor, avoiding hazards that brought catastrophe to fools. Unfortunately, the two ideas impinged on one another. God was free to ignore human merit, and responsible conduct guaranteed life's bounty, specifically prosperity, honor, health, and progeny. The interplay of these conflicting ideas lends considerable complexity to the concept of God in biblical wisdom. One can venture the hypothesis that ancient wisdom rested on a fundamental delusion which its concept of God exposed, but in doing

---

[8]*Wisdom in Israel* (Nashville and New York: Abingdon Press, 1972).

[9]"Gibt es ein Vergeltungsdogma in Alten Testament?" *ZTK* 52 (1955) 1-42; ET: in *Theodicy in the Old Testament*, ed. James L. Crenshaw, 57-87 (Philadelphia and London: Fortress Press and SPCK, 1983).

[10]Assessed in James L. Crenshaw, "Murphy's Axiom: Every Gnomic Saying Needs a Balancing Corrective," 1-17 in *The Listening Heart*, ed. by Kenneth G. Hoglund et. al., JSOTS 58 (Sheffield: JSOT Press, 1987).

[11]*Sin and Retribution in the Prophets*, SBLMS 27 (Chico CA: Scholars Press, 1981).

[12]*Wesen und Geschichte der Weisheit*, BZAW 101 (Berlin: A. Töpelmann, 1966).

so the sages introduced ideas about deity that evoked sharply opposing reactions. In other words, the conviction that one escapes vulnerability through proper use of the intellect collapsed before the exercise of divine freedom. At the same time, divine arbitrariness generated skepticism in some people and surrender before a merciful deity in others. These two reactions merely develop implications of earlier wisdom. This statement is obvious with respect to divine freedom and its debilitating consequences, but what about the basis for believing in God's compassion? This one is less obvious, but I think ancient biblical wisdom does offer a rationale for such an understanding of God.

* * *

Where shall we begin? With a study of divine names as Fichtner did? The information here certainly seems to substantiate his claim. The absence in early biblical wisdom of allusions to divine compassion contrasts with the many references to God's mercy in Sirach and Wisdom of Solomon. Sometimes texts can be deceiving. Take, for instance, the sayings of Agur in Prov 30:1-14, which, on the surface at least, appears to be the most God-intoxicated textual unit in wisdom literature. Those who study the divine names could have a field day here, for one finds the following names: El (twice), Qedošim, Elohim, YHWH, Elohai. So much God-talk fails to conceal the substantial distance between Agur and traditional belief in God.[13]

The same point applies to the expressions "fear of YHWH" and "abomination of YHWH," for the first can mean as little as the modern word "religion" and the second may suggest no more than "displeasing," having lost its cultic nuance. In any event, the effort to exclude such references from the oldest wisdom does not seem altogether successful, although that literature does exemplify no great proclivity toward use of the divine name. Furthermore, this early wisdom did not understand YHWH as a patron deity who had entered into an intimate relationship with the nation Israel or any of its official representatives. Instead, YHWH functioned as a precise equivalent of El or Elohim, the more general names for God.

The unique feature of Yahwism, the deity's violent jealousy,[14] makes no appearance in wisdom literature. Job does refer to a גּוֹאֵל, a personal vindicator, but the meaning of this allusion is far from clear. If גּוֹאֵל refers to the institution of redeemer, Job is terribly confused, for he is still very much alive, and if his mono-

---

[13]See my essay "Clanging Symbols," 51-64 in *Justice and the Holy: Essays in Honor of Walter Harrelson*, ed. Douglas A. Knight and Peter J. Paris (Atlanta: Scholars Press, 1989). Contrast, however, Delbert Burkett, "The Son of Man in the Gospel of John," *JSNT* 56 (1991): 51-75.

[14]Tryggve Mettinger, *In Search of God* (Philadelphia: Fortress Press, 1988) 74: "YHWH's violent 'jealousy,' which tolerates no rival, is without parallel in the religious literature of the ancient Near East."

theism rules out another deity who could overpower Job's divine oppressor, we are left with an implausible theory about a split within the deity which throws little light on the text.

On the other hand, Job occupies a special place in God's esteem, and this favoritism brings calamity in its wake. The designation of Job as "my servant" implies a close relationship between deity and human worshipper like that underlying Yahwistic literature. According to Prov 23:10-11, widows occupy a special place in the mind of a redeemer, who pleads their cause forcefully. It is not clear whether the author thought of royalty here or of the ultimate sovereign.

This brief reference to a social institution indicates the complexity of all attempts to clarify the social location of wisdom literature itself.[15] The family must surely have been the primary locus for early wisdom, and this setting offers at least one possibility of thinking about God as merciful. The aphorism about the deity chastening loved ones, an instance of argument by analogy with parental discipline, hardly describes a neutral or indifferent sovereign. Another social locus, the royal court, also provides a strong possibility for compassion to enter the picture. Royal ideology throughout the ancient Near Eastern world emphasized care of widows and orphans, persons on the margins of society who were not thought to have deserved their misfortune. A third social locus, the school, seems ill disposed toward cultivating an emphasis on divine mercy, for scribal discipline was particularly harsh. Yet Sirach, a member of this institution, nourished such thoughts in the early second century BCE and permitted them to flourish.

These social locations of wisdom did not give rise to metaphors that convey special understandings of deity. This astonishing fact has occasioned little comment, all the more noteworthy in light of Thorkild Jacobsen's illuminating analysis of Mesopotamian symbolism in terms of three root metaphors: natural, royal, and familial.[16] We search in vain for comparable metaphors in Israel's wisdom literature, where an occasional allusion to creator almost exhausts the possibilities, unless shepherd in Qoh. 12:11 points beyond King Solomon to the divine source of Qoheleth's teaching. The absence of metaphors from the family and school is puzzling, for parental metaphors were certainly familiar in the ancient world, and nothing could be more natural for the wise than to call God the heavenly teacher (cf. Sir 18:13).

---

[15]R. N. Whybray, "The Social World of the Wisdom Writers," 227-50 in *The World of Ancient Israel*, ed. Ronald E. Clements (Cambridge: Cambridge University Press, 1989); *Wealth and Poverty in the Book of Proverbs*, JSOTSup 99 (Sheffield: JSOT Press, 1990); R. Albertz, "Der sozialgeschichtliche Hintergrund des Hiobbuches und der 'Babylonischen Theodizee'," 349-72 in *Die Botschaft und die Boten* (H. W. Wolff *Festschrift*) (Neukirchen: Neukirchener Verlag, 1981); Frank Crüsemann, "Der unveränderbare Welt. Überlegungen zur 'Krisis der Weisheit' beim Prediger (Kohelet)," 80-104 in *Der Gott der kleinen Leute*, ed. Willi Schottroff and W. Stegemann (Gelnhausen) (ET: *The God of the Lowly*).

[16]*The Treasures of Darkness* (New Haven CT: Yale University Press, 1976).

The pervasive influence on biblical wisdom of ideology derived from speculation about *ma'at* introduced solicitous concern as an important aspect of the relationship between this intermediary figure and human beings. In her biblical expression, she woos young men with exquisite rhetoric, offering them life and riches. Her invitation assumes the character of demand, punctuated with prophetic-sounding threats. This aggressive figure boasts of special relationship with God in primordial times, even of participation in the act of creation, at least as appreciative observer. Nevertheless, she restricts her love to those who love her, thus failing to break out of the mold cast by retributive thinking. In fact, even Mesopotamian wisdom maintains the concept of merit in those places where divine compassion abounds. For example, those individuals who, like Job, suffer afflictions for no apparent reason experience the deity's favor in response to appropriate ritual acts. The correct ritual thus earns restoration and assures divine favor. In this view, mercy is actually the underside of justice, making it possible for deserving persons to climb out of a morass.

Is such forgiveness possible in biblical wisdom? As we have seen, only one text in Proverbs mentions forgiveness, and the silence with respect to the agent conceals its meaning from readers. Does the individual acknowledge a mistake, motivated by a desire to acquire human compassion from an offended person? That reading is certainly possible, but so is the alternative understanding, that the confession of guilt addressed a higher court successfully. On this reading, the text corresponds to Mesopotamian confessions, except for the ritual accompaniments, about which the biblical text is silent. The customary context for creation language in Proverbs indicates that it bears a tiny ingredient of compassion, for the association of creator with the poor stands out. The rich are reminded that their maker also fashioned the poor, and anyone who heaps insults on the unfortunate would do well to recall their creator. The royal obligation to rescue the perishing and give them strong drink to dull their awareness of misery also suggests that strict justice was not always the best thing (Prov 31:1-9).

Analogy with Ben Sira's discussion of physicians implies that comparable questions about favoring the poor might logically have arisen. If the physician risks divine anger by interfering with sickness understood as punishment for sin, an assumption Ben Sira endeavors to undermine, do not those who offer assistance to the lowly undertake a comparable risk?[17] That conclusion would follow upon the strict application of a retributive principle, according to which all people received their proper deserts. We hear no argument against helping the poor; in fact, such kindness is encouraged (cf. Zech 7:9-10). In a society governed by an exact retribution there would be no undeserved misery, but the sages were not that divorced from reality.

---

[17]See my essay "Poverty and Punishment in the Book of Proverbs," *Quarterly Review* 9 (1989): 30-43.

Although the conservative ideology of the wise brought distinct rewards, their motive was not entirely selfish. Their understanding of the cosmic order placed a premium on ethical behavior, which constituted society and prevented the incursion of chaos into daily life. Those individuals who behaved like fools allowed their passions to control them, leading to violence and wholesale destruction of law and order. Such conduct threatened the very fabric of society and the universe, creating a topsy-turvy world in which former slaves rode on horses and individuals who once enjoyed high social status were reduced to traveling on foot. Naturally, the losers in this exchange of status directed thoughts to the heavens, accusing the sovereign of lapsing into a state of unconsciousness.

Such a threat of returning to chaos was real in ancient Israel, as Jeremiah's exquisite poem describing this event attests (4:23-26). The sages as a group never quite abandoned a conviction that God had everything firmly under control, but the divine speeches in Job come very close to acknowledging an area beyond the deity's power. When YHWH challenges Job to overcome human pride in others, does the question conceal an admission that God has found that task formidable? Job stands before God as the supreme example of pride that refuses to bend before the majestic creator. To be sure, this deity was more successful in negating the threat from Behemoth and Leviathan, creatures who represent the chaotic forces within the universe itself.[18] The divine victory over these elements is virtually complete, for they are depicted as little more than playthings with seriously restricted movement. To humans they pose terror on every hand, but God has the primordial beasts under complete control.

If societal turmoil could not be explained as the result of a resurgence of power on the part of Behemoth and Leviathan, and if human perfidy failed to explain the destruction of order, the logical explanation pointed to a change in the face of God. Job saw no other reason for the calamity that befell him, and the possibility of inconstancy in God threatened his world view with collapse. The prospect of serving a useless corvee was distressing, for such an admission struck at the foundation of the sages' understanding of reality. An orderly universe depended on a creator who guaranteed the dispensing of reward and punishment, and when the deity became derelict in this important duty the entire system shattered.

The understanding of God in the Book of Job is complex, necessitating separate analyses of the prose, the individual speeches, and the poem about wisdom's hiddenness. The portrayal of deity in the story combines folkloristic simplicity with an astonishing assumption that human beings do actually worship without thought

---

[18]On these two beasts, see Gammie, "Behemoth and Leviathan: On the Didactic and Theological Significance of Job 40:15–41:26," 217-31 in *Israelite Wisdom: Theological and Literary Essays in Honor of Samuel Terrien*, ed. John G. Gammie et. al. (Missoula MT: Scholars Press, 1978) and Othmar Keel, *Jahwes Entgegnung an Iob*, FRLANT 121 (Göttingen: Vandenhoeck & Ruprecht, 1978).

of the carrot or the stick. The author presents Job as a man who will serve God in all circumstances, gladly accepting divine bounty and refusing to complain about inflicted harm. Job's reasoning, foreign to his wife's comprehension, assumes that we ought to be grateful for anything that God sends our way. In Job's view, humans have no claim on God, and the correct response in all circumstances is gratitude. On the other hand, this story describes God as one who stops at almost nothing, even murder, to prove a point. Furthermore, God admits that the adversary moved the deity to afflict Job without justification. Surprisingly, the deity makes no concession about the deaths of Job's children and servants, who are eradicated and then replaced without a word of apology. Such disregard for human worth stands alongside an amazing acknowledgment of exceptional goodness in one person, whom God twice praises for exemplary conduct in all areas of life, and in the end endorses Job's words as well. This deity expects proper ritual, particularly sacrifice, and responds favorably to Job's intercession for friends after having ignored a similar act on behalf of his children. The God of the story also ties up all loose ends where Job is concerned, guaranteeing that he receives an appropriate reward for his trouble. Having suspended the operation of the retributive world view for a season, God reinstates the system for the benefit of his servant. The disturbing feature of this depiction of God is that a heavenly courtier wields sufficient power to manipulate God and thus to inflict grievous suffering on earth—with God's explicit consent.

Job's God, as presented in his speeches within the Dialogue, is paradoxically both present and absent, an oppressive presence and a hiding friend. Job thinks of God as an enemy determined to destroy him, the imagery fluctuating from wild animal to warrior. Like a lion, God tears apart his prey, and like a strong warrior, God hurls arrows at an exposed target. This tyrant has cast off all capacity for justice, treating Job like a sinner. Eventually, Job charges God with injustice on a much wider scale, mentioning the miserable wretches of society who are victims of oppressive rule. Their cries for help fail to move the deity to pity, leading Job to the conclusion that God turns away from them and thus encourages violence. This picture of the Lord of a chaotic world does not altogether conceal Job's secret hope that God will come to his assistance if only Job can make contact. This search does not reveal a compassionate deity anywhere, and Job despairs over finding the former friend. Of one thing Job is convinced: God is making a mistake and will eventually regret Job's departure. In all this bold accusation and appeal for a trial Job never abandons his conviction that God has sufficient power to do anything.

The three friends emphasize divine justice and power. They cannot accept Job's insistence on innocence, for that concession would condemn the deity as unjust. Therefore they press relentlessly the point of Job's guilt, urging humble repentance and assuring him of God's forgiveness. They, too, celebrate the majesty of the creator of the universe; in doing so, they lessen the status of moral deed on the part of humans. In their view human actions do not affect the deity in any way, so majestic and pure is God. Elihu also emphasizes God's sovereignty and justice, although bringing the disciplinary and educative activity of the deity into focus.

Ironically, by depicting God as a "merciless engineer of the mechanization of divine retribution"[19] they imprison the deity in a rigid system that human beings actually control by their conduct.

The hymn on wisdom's inaccessability stresses divine remoteness, like that of wisdom. Human beings perform incredible feats in search of rare gems; before their efforts, the deepest recesses of the earth yield their precious secrets. Nevertheless, the quest for wisdom ends in frustration, for no human being has access to it, and even Sheol and Abaddon can only boast about having heard a rumor of wisdom's whereabouts. God alone has access to wisdom. In context this celebration of divine intelligence and human ignorance pronounces a powerful negative verdict on Job's bold claim to know the failings of divine conduct. The final declaration that religion is the equivalent of wisdom and hence accessible to everyone seriously negates the force of this poem.

The understanding of God in the whirlwind is the subject of considerable discussion in recent literature. The most comforting reading of the divine speeches emphasizes their aptness as response to Job's two accusations: that God is guilty of criminal activity and that the world lacks any discernible plan. God's twofold response points to human insignificance and ignorance that renders meaningless any charge leveled at the ruler of the universe, and the majesty of the created order contains so much splendour that all creatures are assured a chance to attain their true nature. On this reading, human beings also live in a setting that permits them to achieve their potential. A less positive understanding of this divine lecture on natural wisdom recognizes the creator's virtual silence about humankind. To be sure, this line of argument on God's part exposes anthropocentricity, substituting the mystery of creation and indirectly its creator as the center of all legitimate reflection. In doing so, however, it silences the fundamental questions about human suffering, for God completely ignores the issue and offers no explanation for Job's misfortune.

Still, Job ultimately bends the knee before this deity and places a hand over his mouth, leaving unanswered all kinds of questions. Has he been vindicated because God appeared to Job without crushing him? Has Job seen the error of his argument and repented? Has he given up on his hope of obtaining a fair trial before the heavenly tribunal? Does he acquiesce outwardly but harbor inner rebellion that he determines to stifle for his own protection? How ought one to understand the dismissal of his previous relationship with God as derivative, amounting to hear-say? How can we reconcile the presence of theophany in wisdom literature?

The last question raises the issue of genre, which evokes a variety of suggestions: a lament, a dispute, a drama, a paradigm of an answered lament, a lawsuit. Similarities with lament psalms are obvious, although the dominant genre is not lament. Moshe Weinfeld's typological comparisons with laments in Mesopotamian

---

[19]Mettinger, *In Search of God*, 178.

parallels[20] reinforce Claus Westermann's arguments,[21] but not at the expense of dispute. Here, too, close parallels exist with the acrostic poem known as the Babylonian Theodicy. Does Job's literary form influence the treatment of divine justice?

Qoheleth echoes traditional understandings of God as creator, albeit in quite different language. All things were created beautiful in their time, perhaps in the sense of appropriate for the moment, and God placed something quite valuable within the human mind but rendered it inaccessible (3:11). Before the created world humans stand powerless, either to change the nature of God's finished work or to grasp the mystery of life and death. Qoheleth does not deny God's generosity, but he insists that a probing intellect cannot discern any rationale for the distribution of divine favor. Insofar as Qoheleth can determine, chance reigns and makes a mockery of all sapiential efforts to secure life (the same theme occurs in Papyrus Insinger). This state of affairs is possible because God dwells in remote realms and remains indifferent to the human condition. In God's absence, death has stolen the scene, and its arbitrariness strikes despair in human hearts. Some interpreters view Qoheleth's teachings quite differently, claiming that his summons to enjoyment grows out of complete confidence in divine goodness rather than representing the counsel of despair.[22] Although not wholly rejecting a cultic practice such as making vows to God, Qoheleth advises caution rather than outright negligence, and he calls attention to the vast distance separating God from human beings. For him, all things are futile or absurd. This negative assessment of everything on earth offers no support to those critics who understand the Deus absconditus in a comforting manner. Qoheleth's positive evaluation of life, wine, wisdom and so forth makes all the more poignant his protest against a system that fails to promote virtue. In a society where accident or chance have the final word, one can do absolutely nothing to master the circumstances of existence. In this situation, wisdom has lost its power.

Several wisdom psalms explore the problem of the prosperity of the wicked, but these reflect the communal setting and consequently offer consoling words, either divorced from reality or in spite of all appearances. The author of Ps 37 serves notice that nothing under the heavens suffices to call into question divine justice. Here is another example of hardening dogma like that espoused by Job's three friends and Elihu. For this psalmist, no one in immediate purview has ever experienced undeserved want. In short, always and in every circumstance God dispenses good things to deserving persons and misfortune to offenders. Perhaps, like Job's

---

[20]"Job and its Mesopotamian Parallels—A Typological Analysis," 217-26 in *Text and Context*, JSOTSup 48 (Sheffield: Almond Press, 1988).

[21]*The Structure of the Book of Job* (Philadelphia: Fortress Press, 1981).

[22]Contrast R. N. Whybray, *Ecclesiastes* (Grand Rapids MI: Eerdmans; London: Marshall, Morgan & Scott, 1989) and Graham S. Ogden, *Qoheleth* (Sheffield: JSOT Press, 1987) with James L. Crenshaw, *Ecclesiates* (Philadelphia: Westminster Press; London: SCM Press, 1987) and Michael V. Fox, *Qohelet and His Contradictions* (Sheffield: JSOT Press, 1989). On this matter I cannot agree with Gammie (*Holiness in Israel*, 151-55.)

friends, the psalmist rejects the possibility of achieving the status of righteousness, so that divine injustice is excluded on principle. For the author of Ps 49 the enigmas of human existence fade before God's mystery. Momentary prosperity counts for nought, and death speaks the final word, cancelling all supposed gain. Psalm 73 traces the movement from doubt to trust in great detail. At first the psalmist begins to doubt traditional belief in God's goodness toward the upright, for experience presents far too many examples of prosperous villains. Conscious of teetering on the brink of folly, the psalmist makes a concerted effort to purify such thoughts, receiving support in the assembled congregation of the faithful. Here the psalmist recognizes the insubtantiality and ephemerality of the success enjoyed by the wicked, but more importantly, acquires a fresh awareness of divine nearness. Bolstered by a sense of God's touch and leadership, the psalmist realizes that nothing else in all of the universe quite compares with God's presence. That nearness alone confirms the accuracy of the original credo, and it now becomes permissible to entertain the bold thought that even death's power may yield to a greater force, the God of glory.

* * *

What has this survey indicated? That Fichtner overlooked a few sure signs that Israel's sages believed in divine compassion. Still, his essential point stands, requiring explanation. Why did the situation change dramatically with Ben Sira? Does the key reside in the shift from individual concerns to those of a people who thought of themselves as chosen? In Westermann's terms, the saving God has become dominant over the blessing God. That is, the scandal of particularity has triumphed over universalism. If this is indeed the answer, why does Ben Sira make so little of national concerns outside the encomium[23] in 44–51? Except for occasional allusions to canonical traditions, the lament in ch. 36 alone sounds this particularistic theme.

Perhaps we have not really discerned the nature of the problem. Ben Sira offers a clue when observing that nothing we give our parents can repay them for the gift of life. Perhaps that argument is carried to a higher level in Job 41:11, where God seems to ask: "Who has given to me, that I should repay him?" and then declares that everything under heaven belongs to God, a theme also found in Ps 50:10-12. If human existence is a gift entirely outside the domain of calculating morality, we are already recipients of grace exceeding any merit we may possibly acquire through

---

[23]Burton L. Mack, *Wisdom and the Hebrew Epic* (Chicago: University of Chicago Press, 1985) and Thomas R. Lee, *Studies in the Form of Sirach 44–50*, SBLDS 75 (Atlanta: Scholars Press, 1986).

virtuous conduct.[24] Israel's sages may well have understood reward and retribution in light of an encompassing love of God, a compassionate act of self-manifestation that created the conditions essential to life. To accuse God of failing to maintain an exact correlation between human merit and divine reward amounts to colossal ingratitude for prior generosity.[25] If this point has validity, it follows that justice has always been tempered with mercy, whether or not the sages recognized the interrelationship of the divine attributes.

Why did Ben Sira suddenly articulate this unstated presupposition of wisdom? Did the theological impact of Job's hellish nightmare and Qoheleth's indifference to religious commitment weigh so heavily on Ben Sira's mind that they led to an emphasis on God's mercy and a recovery of the national heritage for a group of sages who had tried to make it on their own abilities? One thing is certain: for Ben Sira, justice alone does not adequately describe God, who turns toward all creatures in abundant mercy. In short, the blessing God is also the saving Lord.

Perhaps this decisive transition from universality to particularism coincides with historical developments in ancient Israel. Although wisdom literature obscures its genesis extremely well, Joe Blenkinsopp has recently described a plausible social setting for polemic against the strange women in Prov 1–9, which he relates to the struggle against marriage between Jews and foreign women in the time of Ezra and Nehemiah.[26] A confident community of sages may well have existed during the expansionism of the eighth century, particularly Hezekiah's rule. Believing themselves capable of controlling their future, these optimists relied on their own knowledge and goodness to face all eventualities. Their confidence was shared by the society at large, one that found expression eventually in the Josianic reforms that turned their ideology into national policy. The catastropic events of 609–587 BCE and the loss of self-government amid a humiliating exile, followed by intense rivalry[27] upon returning to Jerusalem and economic hardship for more than a century gave ample inspiration to someone who fictionalized the problem of suffering and a religious response to injustice. The collapse of family relationships and the emergence of commercialization at the cost of societal obligations and kinship ties seem to lie behind Qoheleth's egocentrism and fascination with wealth. The unreliability

---

[24]Saadia Ben Joseph Al-Fayyumi, *The Book of Theodicy*, trans. L. E. Goodman (New Haven CT and London: Yale University Press) emphasizes this point. Goodman's introduction to Saadia's argument is a model of clarity.

[25]Resulting in bitterness, according to John T. Wilcox, *The Bitterness of Job* (Ann Arbor: University of Michigan Press, 1989).

[26]"The Woman Wisdom and Creation in Proverbs 1–9," a paper read at the national SBL meeting in Anaheim on 19 Nov 1989.

[27]Carol A. Newsom, "Woman and the Discourse of Patriarchal Wisdom: A Study of Proverbs 1–9," 142-60 in *Gender and Difference in Ancient Israel*, ed. Peggy L. Day (Minneapolis: Fortress Press, 1989) gives a brilliant analysis of rival discourse among the sages.

of riches, their tendency to vanish overnight as a result of risky ventures, left a society enamored of wealth highly vulnerable.

Furthermore, the political situation under the Persians and Ptolemys offered little basis for confidence, for the ever-watchful officials of government exacted their taxes and kept the population in check. The Seleucid authorities and rising Hellenistic influence created an anxious populace who desperately needed assurance that God would have mercy on those faithfully turning from sin. In this unprecedented historical setting, belief in the moral order became highly problematic and dependence on God's mercy offered hope to those who had lost confidence in the correspondence between worth and well-being.

Epilogue

For many years I have pondered the puzzling endings of Job and Goethe's *Faust*, both of which seem to "cop out" after having pressed intellectual honesty to the breaking point. Is René Girard right that human societies value order so highly they will go to any extreme, even violence, to maintain it?[28] One can think of ample testimony to belief in reward for effort expended, but rare indeed is the voice of the ancient prophetess who walked through a city with a torch in one hand and a bucket of water in another, her cry echoing through the streets: "Would that I could burn heaven with this flame and extinguish hell's fires with this water, that people would love God for God's sake alone." Can we bear the thought of forsaking all without getting much in return? That dilemma has changed little if any in the centuries since ancient sages struggled with it. On the one hand, we desire a Sovereign who rules the universe justly; on the other hand, we earnestly wish for a solicitous champion of our interests who overlooks human frailty. The sages, too, vacillated in this respect, and this fact demonstrates the validity of Schmid's claim that wisdom literature is in a very real sense historical.[29] The changing views reflect historical events, although obliquely and grudgingly. I do not pretend to have resolved the matter of a shift within wisdom thinking to give greater prominence to divine mercy, but I hope I have shown the complexity of the problem and the rewards of pursuing the question Fichtner posed in his groundbreaking monograph on ancient oriental wisdom in its Israelite-Jewish expression.

---

[28]René Girard, *Job: The Victim of his People* (Stanford: Stanford University Press) 1987.
[29]H. H. Schmid, *Wesen und Geschichte der Weisheit*.

10

The Restraint of Reason, the Humility of Prayer

A fundamental assumption of proverbial wisdom was that an individual could act in such manner as to bring about desirable consequences. This effective use of the intellect was facilitated by the nature of the universe itself, ultimately deriving from the generosity of its creator who guaranteed its general dependability. By studying human conduct and the behavior of animals, as well as observing the phenomena of the heavens, one could in large measure discover how to control destiny. Thus the responsibility for the course of one's life fell directly on human shoulders; so did any praise for successfully avoiding pitfalls along the way.[1]

Such a worldview had an intrinsic flaw: radical egocentrism leading to pride based on significant achievement. In addition, this understanding of reality often encouraged intolerance toward persons of less personal ambition and accomplishment, who sport such tags as "fools" and "lazy bums" in proverbial sayings.[2] Furthermore, this emphasis on self-empowerment stood out because an alternative worldview downplayed the importance of human deeds and emphasized divine providence.[3] Proverbial wisdom resisted this religious emphasis and substituted a remarkably "secular" approach to existence, although the adjective "secular" fails

---

[1] Note the qualifying prepositional phrase "in large measure." The sages understood that exceptions to the rule took place, for not everyone enjoyed the fruit of his or her labors. Moreover, divine freedom and inscrutability imposed limits on human knowledge, forcing individuals to take chance into account. Despite all this, the sages' aphorisms sound remarkably life-affirming, and their message confidently urges hearers to walk in the path that leads to life.

[2] At least seven types of "fools" enliven the sapiential literature, ranging from simple naïf to cruel mocker. I have translated עָצֵל by "lazy bum," because "sluggard" does not quite carry the force of the Hebrew noun.

[3] Because the understanding of the world as reflected in wisdom literature differs radically from the dominant view in Torah and Prophecy, some modern scholars have designated wisdom "an alien body" within the bible and have ignored its teachings in theological discussion. Franz-Josef Steiert, *Die Weisheit Israels—ein Fremdkörper im Alten Testament?*, FTS (Freiburg: Herder, 1990) responds to the question with an emphatic "No."

to capture the thoroughly religious basis for such stress on human possibilities.[4] Hence the nonmoralistic maxims that Hermann Gunkel and Otto Eissfeldt laid claim to in discussing secular wisdom[5] must be interpreted in the light of an assumption that the creator instituted order and also set definite limits on the intellect. The same applies to the political sentences that William McKane used in distinguishing between counsellors who could not afford the luxury of theological convictions and prophets for whom such beliefs dictated their counsel to trust in the Lord.[6] None has seen that fact more clearly than Gerhard von Rad, whose discussion of the limits of knowledge highlights the unpredictable factor that most individuals come up against sooner or later.[7]

Such proverbial wisdom therefore cannot be expected to preserve elements of piety, particularly prayers. An elevated view of human potential negates any need for emphasis on divine compassion, for individuals shaped their own future. The situation is analogous with nineteenth and twentieth century liberal theology's agonizing debate over petitionary prayer, which seemed to contradict the nature of God and the scientific understanding of the universe.[8] Like the modern debate, the sapiential struggle against opposing viewpoints encountered immense resistance from champions of popular religion. In both instances, too, historical circumstances placed huge question marks over an optimistic reading of daily existence. We do not know whether or not instructional wisdom represents a response to Judah's changed

---

[4]Modern distinctions such as sacred and secular ultimately distort the picture of ancient Israelite society, for even the principle of cause and effect was subject to a higher authority. Moreover, adherence to the divinely ordained order was both an ethical and a religious act, one in their view that maintained the structure of the universe.

[5]Eissfeldt's conclusions derive from study of isolated proverbial sayings outside the wisdom corpus; these traditional sayings have been examined in a broader paroemiological context by Carole R. Fontaine (*Traditional Sayings in the Old Testament* [Sheffield: The Almond Press], 1982).

[6]Few interpreters have accepted McKane's thesis in *Prophets and Wise Men* (London: SCM, 1965). His book illustrates the difficulty in trying to grasp the essence of contrasting sapiential traditions, for instructional wisdom is thoroughly religious, as opposed to proverbial sayings.

[7]*Wisdom in Israel* (Nashville and New York: Abingdon, 1972). Although widely praised, this book has significant flaws, which I have noted in "Wisdom in Israel by Gerhard von Rad," *RSR* 6/2 (1976): 6-12.

[8]Perry LeFevre, *Understandings of Prayer* (Philadelphia: Westminster, 1981) has examined this intense debate in the thought of Karl Barth, Henry Nelson Wieman, Paul Tillich, Dietrich Bonhoffer, C. S. Lewis, Thomas Merton, Karl Rahner, and Abraham J. Heschel. The stage was set for this controversy much earlier, particularly in the work of Immanuel Kant, Friedrich Schleiermacher, Ludwig Feuerbach, and Albrecht Ritschl.

circumstances after the fall of Jerusalem to the Babylonians, but theological directives unquestionably incorporate a religious piety into the subject matter.[9]

A comparable shift took place in Egyptian wisdom literature, as Miriam Lichtheim has observed: "It is no longer assumed that righteous living guarantees a successful life. Success and happiness are now thought to depend entirely on the grace of the gods. The individual can achieve nothing without their help; but the will of the gods is inscrutable."[10] In Israel both the book of Job and Qoheleth bear witness to a loss of confidence in the power of the intellect to ensure well-being, but this sense of powerlessness does not give way to devout prayer, except in a comparable text preserved in Prov 30:1-14 and attributed to a foreign sage. Here the restraint of reason issues in the humility of prayer. Gone forever is pride of achievement, as this sage focuses only on modest reward and faithful relationship with God.

The origin of prayer in general remains obscure, although individual prayers have survived throughout the ancient Near East.[11] Their close relationship to magical incantations cannot be refuted, but wherever emphasis falls on a deity's freedom a quite different kind of supplication exists, one characterized by pure praise. Friedrich Heiler's thesis that free prayer by individuals represents the original form and that fixed collective prayers indicate a later, less spiritual, manner of addressing the deity[12] corresponded to the nineteenth century emphasis on great individuals. Likewise, the shift to emphasizing collective prayer as original in the studies by

---

[9]Most scholars today distinguish between sentence literature and instructions; the latter contain overt religious teachings, whereas the former rarely enter this realm of discourse. The difference may derive to some extent from the formal characteristics of each, imperatives functioning best in theological settings, but the issue is more complex than this answer suggests.

[10]*Ancient Egyptian Literature*, vol. 3 (Berkeley: University of California, 1980) 5. Lichtheim goes on to say that life was still prized and that piety demanded that life should be enjoyed.

[11]The importance of prayer to Mesopotamian sages can be gathered from texts that complain of its failure in some instances, e.g., "Ludlul" ("I called to my god, but he did not show his face, I prayed to my goddess, but she did not raise her head. . . . For myself, I gave attention to supplication and prayer: To me prayer was discretion, sacrifice my rule. . . . The king's prayer—that was my joy, and the accompanying music became a delight for me. . . . But I know . . . Sun-god will have mercy . . . [After he has] received my prayers." W. G. Lambert, *Babylonian Wisdom Literature* [Oxford: Clarendon, 1960] 39,41,46,51). The "Babylonian Theodicy" complains that "Those who neglect the god go the way of prosperity, while those who pray to the goddess are impoverished and dispossessed." It adds: "In my mouth I sought the will of my god; with prostration and prayer I followed my goddess. But I was bearing a profitless corvée as a yoke. My god decreed instead of wealth destitution" (Lambert, *Babylonian Wisdom Literature*, 75, 77). Nevertheless, "Counsels of Wisdom" dares to commend prayer: "Prayer, supplication, and prostration offer him daily, and you will get your reward . . . and prayer atones for guilt" (Lambert, *Babylonian Wisdom Literature*, 105).

[12]*Das Gebet* (München: Ernst Reinhardt, 1919).

Sigmund Mowinckel, Erhard Gerstenberger, and Menahem Haran coincided with changed attitudes toward the community as formative in shaping tradition.[13] Perhaps Moshe Greenberg's mediating position describes the situation best, spontaneous prayer having existed contemporaneously with fixed prayer for communal use.[14] A similar controversy has surrounded such issues as individual freedom versus traditional constraints in form critical studies, a debate best illustrated by the individual and the community in the Psalms.[15]

The subject of prayer in wisdom literature has not generated a single article thus far, except for specific studies of two prayers in Sirach.[16] Claus Westermann's recent history of research from 1950 to 1990,[17] which updates my own earlier analysis,[18] isolates two fundamental problems: popular versus professional origins of the literature, oral teachings or written texts. His separate treatment of wisdom literature, *Wurzeln der Weisheit*, fails to bring prayer to the fore even when discussing popular piety.[19] In this respect, Johannes Fichtner's synthesis of ancient Near Eastern wisdom remains instructive, although never really attending to prayer as such.[20]

Even Ronald Clements' *Wisdom in Theology* makes no advance here, despite his demonstrated interest in biblical prayer.[21] My efforts to introduce the topic of prayer into the literature about ancient wisdom grow out of suspicion that such a discussion is long overdue. They also belong to a broader theme, that of human

---

[13]Mowinckel, *The Psalms in Israel's Worship*, 2 vols. (Nashville & New York: Abingdon, 1962); Gerstenberger, *Der bittende Mensch*, WMANT 51 (Neukirchen-Vulyn: Neukirchener, 1980); and Haran, "Priest, Temple, and Worship," *Tarbiz* 48 (1978): 184.

[14]*Biblical Prose Prayer* (Berkeley; University of California, 1983), 43. Greenberg argues that biblical prayers are patterned after daily speech and therefore should not be viewed as purely fictional. The most comprehensive analysis of spontaneous prayer remains that of Adolf Wendel, *Das freie Laiengebet im vorexilischen Israel* (Leipzig: Eduard Pfeiffer, 1932).

[15]Hans-Joachim Kraus, *Theology of the Psalms* (Minneapolis: Fortress, 1992).

[16]P. C. Beentjes, "Sirach 22:27–23:6 in zijn Context," *Bijdragen* 39 (1978), 144-51; Heinrich Germann, "Jesus ben Siras Dankgebet und die Hodajoth," *ThZ* 19 (1963), 81-87; and Johannes Marböck, "Das Gebet um die Rettung Zions Sir 36,1-22 (G 33,1-13a; 36,16b-22) im Zusammenhang der Geschichtsschau Ben Siras," 93-116 in *Memoria Jerusalem*, ed. J. B. Bauer (Jerusalem/Graz: Akademische Druck und Verlagsanstalt, 1977).

[17]*Forschungsgeschichte zur Weisheitsliteratur 1950–1990*, AzT 71 (Stuttgart: Calwer, 1991).

[18]*Studies in Ancient Israelite Wisdom* (New York: Ktav, 1976) 1-6, and "The Wisdom Literature," in *The Hebrew Bible and Its Modern Interpreters*, ed. Douglas A. Knight and Gene M. Tucker, 369-407 (Chico CA: Scholars Press, 1985).

[19]Göttingen: Vandenhoeck und Ruprecht, 1990.

[20]*Die altorientalische Weisheit in ihrer israelitisch-jüdischen Ausprägung*, BZAW 62 (Giessen: A. Töpelmann, 1933) 35-59.

[21]Grand Rapids: Eerdmans, 1992; *In Spirit and in Truth* (Atlanta: John Knox, 1985).

achievement and the necessity for divine assistance, which I have treated at length in an essay entitled "The Concept of God in Old Testament Wisdom."[22]

The relative silence of Israel's sages with regard to the cult, if not actual antipathy toward it, has led to varying interpretation among modern scholars. Leo G. Perdue's comprehensive examination, *Wisdom and Cult*,[23] attributes considerable interest in cultic matters to ancient sages, a claim much enhanced by the changes introduced by Ben Sira in the early second century. Like silence about schools in wisdom literature, which also gives way in Ben Sira's day,[24] the reluctance to speak about the cult has been interpreted in two contradictory ways. Some scholars assume that the cult was simply presupposed while others insist that the sages' silence amounts to intentional rejection of established religion in favor of inner piety or human works.

One thing appears certain, as Clements has recognized. The exile brought about a thorough reconsideration of the cultic apparatus, inasmuch as new circumstances necessitated a different worldview.[25] The existence of the altar had made sacrifice the sole means of atoning for sin,[26] but now another way of achieving that goal had to be devised. External confirmation of inner conviction was visibly removed, and the people were forced to place more emphasis on the sacrifice of the heart and its external expression in praise. Coinciding with an emphasis on prayer and praise was a chastened conscience arising from subjection to foreigners and the religious consequences of such bondage. Those who once viewed themselves as the norm and resident aliens as foreigners now understood themselves as outsiders in an unfamiliar world. Moreover, the family became a refuge replacing the temple, and "neighbors" took on more importance than an extended family, i.e., "brothers," in a different setting. Such far-reaching alterations in worldview accompanied a growing emphasis on God as universal judge rather than champion of an elect people. What Judah Goldin has called demanding prayer[27] could find little support

---

[22]Forthcoming in a volume entitled *In Search of Wisdom: Essays in Memory of John G. Gammie*, ed. Leo G. Perdue and Bernard Brandon Scott (Louisville: Westminster/John Knox).

[23]Missoula: Scholars Press, 1977.

[24]Evidence for schools in Israel is meager (James L. Crenshaw, "Education in Ancient Israel," *JBL* 104 [1985]: 601-15). Even in classical Greece, literacy was less than ten percent, according to William V. Harris, *Ancient Literacy* (Cambridge: Harvard University, 1989).

[25]*Wisdom in Theology*, esp. 26-31.

[26]Elias J. Bickerman, *The Jews in the Greek Age* (Cambridge: Harvard University, 1988) writes that "In the covenanted system of daily oblations a prayer would have been superfluous; the priests only supplicated the Deity to accept the gifts of the chosen people. So long as the temple stood, the altar atoned for Israel" (136). Bickerman suggested that a sense of unworthiness led Jews in Ben Sira's time "to supplement the daily sacrifice with a special prayer for the protection of the chosen people" (137).

[27]*Studies in Midrash and Related Literature*, Barry L. Eichler and Jeffrey H. Tigay, eds. (Philadelphia: Jewish Publication Society, 1988) 331-35.

in such a rigorous concept of deity, one that eventually led to Qoheleth's view of a distant despot, the heavenly record keeper with pen poised to jot down every mistake one makes.

In such circumstances the sages' earlier optimism inevitably gave way to a sense of inadequacy in the face of overwhelming temptations. Restraints on human knowledge produced more than humility; they brought forth a feeling that life had become too much of a burden. Suddenly, a different kind of deity was urgently needed, one who graciously bestows mercy on sinful subjects. The universal judge is somehow balanced by understanding God as father, and people relate to deity as sovereign and parent, the last two of the three metaphors characterizing ancient Mesopotamian religion according to Thorkild Jacobsen.[28] These two concepts of God coexist in tension, for, in Clements words, "If god is the ultimate Ruler and Master of Life, and has established the principles of wisdom which govern all human actions, then what place is left for prayer and a personal relationship with him?"[29]

One could even argue that the sages' elevation of a principle of retribution tilted the scales in the direction of an exacting judge from the very beginning. Clements is undoubtedly wrong in seeing a change in sapiential thought from paternal imagery to that of harsh schoolmaster, but he recognizes the contradiction between a retributive concept of deity and affectionate language. He writes: "The warm personalism of the descriptions of God as 'Father' to human children—presenting a portrait to one who is 'loving and gracious'—yields place to the image of the heavenly Schoolmaster, whose eye misses nothing and who has made the rules and expects everyone of his creatures to abide by them."[30] Actually, reference to deity as "father" rarely occurs in the Hebrew Bible, except to designate YHWH as creator (cf. Deut. 32:6; Jer 3:4,19; Isa 63:16; 64:8[7]; Mal 1:6; 2:10; Ps 68:5[6]; 2 Sam 7:14; Ps 89:27[26]. The expression occurs twice in a prayer by Ben Sira (23:1,4) and once in Tobit (13:4). The ancient credal statement in Exod 34:6-7 never once finds expression in canonical wisdom literature, despite the appropriateness of describing God as demanding judge.[31] Not until Ben Sira does the other half of the confessional formula appear, the affirmation that the Lord is gracious and merciful. This

---

[28] *The Treasures of Darkness* (New Haven & London: Yale University, 1976). The fourth millennium metaphor, that of gods as providers, emphasized the fertility of dying and rising deities. The emergence of powerful cities in the third millennium shifted the emphasis to gods as rulers, and the rise of personal religion in the second millennium brought about still another shift, this time to lift up the parental relationship with the gods as central.

[29] *Wisdom in Theology*, 167.

[30] Ibid, 160.

[31] R. C. Dentan, "The Literary Affinities of Exod. xxxiv 6f.," *VT* 13 (1963): 34-51 claimed that this text represents sapiential teaching, but the idea that a compassionate deity also punishes the wicked occurs throughout the Old Testament.

part of the creed was frequently quoted in prophetic and liturgical texts.[32] Martin Hengel has argued that the book of Job led to excessive reliance on divine mercy and that Ben Sira resisted this trend.[33] If Hengel is correct, this situation constitutes one more instance of religious polemic in which the viewpoint under attack actually dominates the discussion, for Ben Sira mentions divine mercy again and again.

The distancing of God that characterizes the books of Job and Qoheleth eventually led to the introduction of a mediating figure, חָכְמָה (Wisdom). Affectionate language, indeed open expression of passion for a lover,[34] surrounds this fascinating figure who boasts about heavenly origins and who embodies divine instruction. A comparable distancing of God in apocalyptic literature occurred, with angels receiving prayers uttered by men and women in distress. The intertestamental literature witnesses a proliferation of prayers, and that trend continues in the texts from Qumran as well. Our attention will be restricted to the three prayers within wisdom literature.

The only prayer in the book of Proverbs occurs in an astonishing context—within the sayings of the skeptic Agur preserved in Prov 30:1-14. However one reads this unusual text, whether as a dialogue between a skeptic and a believer,[35] or as the cry of an exhausted pious one,[36] the brief prayer in vv 7-9 comes entirely without warning. Furthermore, the prayer does not specify the addressee and surprisingly refers to God in the third person after having begun with second person pronominal suffixes and an implicit transcendent referent. The translation is reasonably straightforward, and the only significant textual variant is the Greek τίς με ὁρᾷ ("who can see me?")

> Two things I ask of you;
>> do not withhold them from me before I die.
> Empty, lying words keep far from me;
>> give me neither poverty nor riches;
>> tear off for me my allotted bread.

---

[32]I have discussed this formula in "Who Knows What YHWH Will Do? The Character of God in the Book of Joel," forthcoming. See also Michael Fishbane, *Biblical Interpretation in Ancient Israel* (Oxford: Clarendon, 1985) 335-50, and Thomas B. Dozeman, "Inner-Biblical Interpretation of Yahweh's Gracious and Compassionate Character," *JBL* 108 (1989): 207-23.

[33]*Judaism and Hellenism* (Philadelphia: Fortress, 1974) 143.

[34]The erotic features of the description of Wisdom in Prov 8:22-31 and beyond have been explored by Samuel Terrien, *Till the Heart Sings* (Philadelphia: Fortress, 1985) 87-120.

[35]James L. Crenshaw, "Clanging Symbols," 51-64 in *Justice and the Holy*, ed. Douglas A. Knight and Peter J. Paris (Atlanta: Scholars, 1989).

[36]Paul Franklyn, "The Sayings of Agur in Proverbs 30: Piety or Scepticism?" *ZAW* 95 (1983): 238-52; compare Rick D. Moore, "A Home for the Alien: Worldly Wisdom and Covenantal Confession in Proverbs 30:1-9," *ZAW* (forthcoming).

Lest I be full and lie,
  saying "who is the Lord?"
or lest being destitute I steal,
  sullying the name of my God.

Formally, the initial request resembles Job's desperate plea in 13:20-21, where the verb הַרְחֵק (keep far away) is also used with reference to the deity.

Only do not do two things to me;
  then I will not hide from your face.
Keep your anger far away from me,
  and let not dread of you terrify me.

This precedent and the absence of versional support for reading a numerical saying in either instance rules out Georg Sauer's emendation, "Two things I ask of you, indeed three. . . . "[37] The presence of three requests in Prov 30:7-9 invites such speculation, however, for the prayer asks for protection from uttering, or uttered, falsehoods and from a life style at either extreme of riches or poverty, but it also seeks a proper portion of food each day.[38] The third petition actually relates to the second, specifying the bare minimum that would prevent one from resorting to theft. If the author of Prov 30:1-14 found inspiration in Job's death-defying determination to be heard and thereby to obtain vindication from the God he addresses directly, the absence of a vocative in vv 7-9 makes sense.

One need not, therefore, assume that the requests look to parents or teachers rather than to God for fulfilment, although this view has much to commend it. Either group could supply these needs, if the first petition is taken to mean the character of the teachings conveyed to students. The lying or empty words in this instance would be someone else's prattle rather than the petitioner's, although one might expect something like "Do not make me hear lying words" if this were its meaning. The reference to God in the third person fits more naturally in requests directed to parents or teachers. Nevertheless, no precedent exists for a student's response in biblical wisdom, although a unique instance of a dialogue between father and son, teacher and student, occurs in the Egyptian Instruction of Ani.[39] For Israel's students, however, Carol Newsom's perceptive assessment stands that their

---

[37]*Die Sprüche Agurs* (Stuttgart: Kohlhammer, 1963) 101.

[38]Compare this Prayer to Thoth in P. Sallier I.8,2-7, which reads: "Supply my needs of bread and beer, and guard my mouth (in) speaking." Lichtheim, *Ancient Egyptian Literature*, vol. 2 (Berkeley: University of California, 1976) 149.

[39]Khonshotep protests that the life of a sage demands too much rigor, but Ani responds that even animals can be taught to conduct themselves differently. Nowhere does the son object to the character of his father's teachings; his complaint is limited to their difficulty.

voice is not heard.[40] Instead an uninterrupted authoritative voice fills instructional wisdom in the bible.

The larger context of the prayer emphasizes the restraint of reason, the acknowledgment that the human intellect knocks at a closed door where ultimate mystery is concerned. Grasping the meaning of Agur's initial remark resembles such an assault on a closed door, as A. H. J. Gunneweg's recent essay demonstrates.[41] His emendation of the twice-recurring לְאִיתִיאֵל to לָאֵה אֵת אֵל yields "who has concerned himself with God" and וָאֻכָל, which he understands as a verbal form of כְּלָא, כּוּל, or יָכֹל, enables him to translate "that I could grasp it." This rendering has no advantage over my own or those of Paul Franklyn and Rick Moore. Whereas I emphasize Agur's ironical dismissal of some sages' optimistic claims about the deity's existence or activity, Franklyn and Moore think of a humble Agur at the hour of death or simply faced with his own limits. Given such consensus with regard to the confession of human ignorance about divine mystery, one expects any prayer in this context to link up with that theme. This one does not. Instead, it concentrates on more mundane things such as deceit and temptations specific to riches and poverty. That fact strengthens my hypothesis that Agur's skeptical opening assault has provoked a devout response, with considerable give and take. Placing opposing viewpoints in direct juxtaposition is an effective rhetorical strategy. One looks in vain for a clearer example of reason's restraint and the humility of prayer.[42]

Elsewhere in the book of Proverbs the sages seldom mention prayer, and the author of the deeply religious opening collection in chapters 1–9 never does. A single chapter, 15, contains two-thirds of these occurrences—a total of two.

> The sacrifice of the wicked is an abomination to YHWH,
>> but the prayer of the just is his delight. (15:8)
> YHWH is far from the wicked,
>> but he hears the prayer of the righteous. (15:29)
> Whoever turns his ear from receiving instruction,
>> even his prayer is an abomination. (28:9)

The same Hebrew word for prayer, תְּפִלָּה, occurs in all three places. References to sacrifice in the book of Proverbs exceed those to prayer by only two, and one of these, 7:14, attests to the worship of a goddess of fertility. The other four allude to

---

[40]"Woman and the Discourse of Patriarchal Wisdom: A Study of Proverbs 1–9," in *Gender and Difference in Ancient Israel*, ed. Peggy L. Day, 142-60 (Minneapolis: Fortress, 1989).

[41]"Weisheit, Prophetie und Kanonformel: Erwägungen zu Proverbia 30,1-9, in *Alttestamentlicher Glaube und Biblische Theologie*, ed. Jutta Hausmann und Hans-Jürgen Zöbel, 253-60 (Stuttgart: Kohlhammer, 1992).

[42]I borrowed this language from Miriam Lichtheim, *Ancient Egyptian Literature*, I, 131.

contentious offerings (17:1) and those brought by unworthy persons (15:8; 21:27) or exalt ethical deeds over sacrificial ritual (21:3). The denial that sacrifice works automatically is balanced by a similar rejection of prayer issuing from the lips of unrepentant sinners. Both assessments indicate the extent to which Israel's sages internalized religion (cf. Ps 50:14).

Arguably technical terms, תּוֹעֲבַת יְהוָה (abomination of the Lord) and תּוֹרָה (instruction), occur in these negative evaluations of sacrifice (15:8) and prayer (28:9), although the former concept appears in Egyptian wisdom literature and the latter may mean no more here than parental teaching. The verb שָׁמַע (to hear, מְשָׁמַע) may also have a technical sense in Prov 28:9 as its equivalent in the concluding section of the Egyptian Instruction of Ptahhotep undoubtedly does. The hearer is one who accepts instruction and internalizes it so that the teaching produces character and deeds commensurate with the four cardinal virtues of integrity, restraint, eloquence, and timeliness.

The sages who wrote the books of Job and Qoheleth also spoke sparingly of prayer. Within the poetic dialogue between Job and his three friends the subject comes up three times. In 16:16-17 Job describes his miserable state despite an admirable relation toward God.

> My face is red from weeping,
> > and on my eyelids—deep darkness,
> although no violence is in my hands
> > and my prayer [תְפִלָּתִי] is pure.

The essential nuance of this defense accords with the broader forensic context, here reinforced by the intensive form of the verb פָּלַל (to pray) and the root זָךְ (to be pure). Job makes a legitimate claim of innocence that seems to be contradicted by his suffering. In 21:15 he rejects the theological argument of evildoers who question the value of being religious. They ask

> Who is Shaddai that we should serve him,
> > and what do we gain that we pray to him [נִפְגַּע־בּוֹ]?

The verb פָּגַע with reference to deity has the sense of "entreat, intercede" as in Jer 7:16, where a combination of terms for intercession occurs.

> But as for you, do not pray [אַל־תִּתְפַּלֵּל]
> > on behalf of this people,
> and do not lift up [אַל־תִּשָּׂא] a cry [רִנָּה]
> > or prayer [וּתְפִלָּה] for them,
> and do not entreat me [וְאַל־תִּפְגַּע־בִּי],
> > for I will not listen to you.

Job's friend Eliphaz urges him to return to God and make peace so that he may eventually offer up a successful prayer.

> You will entreat [תַּעְתִּיר] him and he will hear you,
> then you will complete your vows. (22:27)

Within the speeches by Elihu a similar sentiment unfolds.

> A person will entreat [יֶעְתַּר] Eloah and he will accept him;
> he will look on his face with joyous shout,
> restoring to man his vindicating deeds. (33:26)

One additional text in the poetic dialogue alludes to meditation (שִׂיחַ).

> But you are making fear ineffectual [תָּפֵר]
> and diminishing [וְתִגְרַע] meditation before El. (15:4)

The framing narrative to the book of Job refers to prayer twice in the epilogue—when YHWH rebukes the three friends and then when he recommends his servant Job as a competent intercessor. Both in the initial divine observation and in the narrative report of Job's intercession, the verb פָּלַל occurs (42:8,10).

> And Job my servant will pray for you [יִתְפַּלֵּל]. . . . Then YHWH turned the captivity of Job when he prayed for his friends [בְּהִתְפַּלְלוֹ].

The unusual expression in the Qere, וַיהוָה שָׁב אֶת־שְׁבוּת, occurs only here with relationship to a single individual. Normally it signifies a reversal of national circumstances, specifically the return of exiled peoples to Judah.

A single reference to discourse with a distant deity occurs in Qoh 5:1 [ET 5:2].

> Do not be quick to speak and do not think hastily to cause a word to go forth before God, for God is in heaven and you are on earth, so let your words be few.

The context suggests that vows rather than prayer occupy Qoheleth's thinking here. Gerhard von Rad correctly perceived that Qoheleth had given up on trying to enter into dialogue with God.[43]

The situation differs notably when one turns from the books of Proverbs, Job, and Qoheleth to consider the teachings of Ben Sira. In the words of H. Ludin Jansen, "Thoughts cross over from prayer to instruction. Prayer and instruction go hand in hand. For Sirach that is entirely natural."[44] Josef Haspecker has observed that prayer is mentioned in Sirach as frequently as law,[45] and although this emphasis on prayer supports Haspecker's thesis that fear of YHWH, not torah, occupies center stage, the point stands that Ben Sira talks freely about the importance of prayer. In

---

[43] *Wisdom in Israel,* 233.

[44] *Die spätjüdische Psalmendichtung. Ihr Entstehungskreis und ihr Sitz im Leben* (Oslo, 1937).

[45] *Gottesfurcht bei Jesus Sirach,* AnBib 30 (Rome: Päpstliches Bibelinstitut, 1967) 339.

addition, he incorporates a personal and a national prayer in his teachings, along with a thanksgiving psalm.

According to Ben Sira the occasion for prayer is not restricted to personal distress, although he recognizes that individuals will turn to God in such times. That includes personal distress brought on as a result of sickness (38:9) as well as economic deprivation (4:6; 21:5; 35:13-18). In Ben Sira's view, the impartial judge will execute justice, listening attentively to deserving persons. Prayers by the traditional representatives of this special divine solicitude—widows, orphans, and the poor—pierce the clouds and mount up to heaven. An earlier correlation in the book of Proverbs between laziness and poverty does not deter Ben Sira from sheltering these unfortunate people under divine wings. His discussion of illness has not freed itself entirely from the concept of act and consequence,[46] and this uneasiness manifests itself when Ben Sira attempts to justify the vocation of physicians. Although he argues that the creator put roots on earth that possess medicinal properties, Ben Sira rests his case on the fact that physicians pray for guidance in diagnosing diseases (38:14). Nevertheless, Ben Sira's surrender to the ancient view evokes an incongruous final remark: "Whoever sins before the maker, may he fall into the power of a doctor" (38:15). Just as physicians seek instruction from the Lord, ordinary citizens are urged to pray for guidance in planning their future (37:15), while at the same time paying strict attention to their inner voice.

Where forgiveness is concerned, Ben Sira has more confidence in prayer than in the sacrificial system.[47] Even a host of gifts in the temple does not receive automatic acceptance unless accompanied by prayer and alms (7:10). Repentance reinforces a sinner's plea for acceptance (17:25-26; 21:1; 39:5), provided that the individual abandons all sinful practices (34:26). Anyone who harbors hatred within but prays for forgiveness has no success; in order to obtain forgiveness from God, one must first extend forgiveness to one's fellows (28:2-4). Because human nature embraces both good and evil, God must listen to curses and prayers, responding in an appropriate manner (34:24-26).

Ben Sira places prayer and praise at the very center of the intellectual endeavor. Students try to gain mastery of the torah, prophecy, and wisdom so that they may make an impact on the ruling hierarchy, but above all they rise early to cultivate a spiritual life. They do not stop with petition but move beyond personal need to hymnic praise of the Most High (39:1-6). Such praise in prayer is the fundamental meaning of existence for all people (17:10) and the special calling of sages (15:9-10; 39:6). Ben Sira the teacher offers a fine example for students in this regard

---

[46]Clements, *Wisdom in Theology*, 65-93, has studied the sapiential notion of sickness and health more thoroughly than anyone else, to my knowledge, with the possible exception of Johann Marböck, *Weisheit im Wandel*, BBB 37 (Bonn: Peter Hanstein, 1971) 154-60.

[47]Nevertheless, Saul M. Olyan, "Ben Sira's Relationship to the Priesthood," *HTR* 80 (1987): 261-86, argues forcefully that Ben Sira belonged to the priestly order.

(42:15–43:33). Within the praise of famous men in 44:1–50:24, Ben Sira specifically mentions prayers by Joshua, Samuel, David, and Israel.[48] It is perfectly natural, therefore, that he includes two prayers in the book, one in each half. To them I now turn.

The Hebrew text of 22:27–23:6 has not survived; scholars therefore rely on Greek manuscripts for its content. The prayer belongs to the larger context beginning at 18:15 and extending through 23:27, which is immediately followed by the well-known praise of wisdom and its identification with the Mosaic legislation. As early as 18:30-31 a topos of the prayer is introduced, namely the restraint of sensual appetites. According to P. C. Beentjes[49] the prayer itself divides naturally into two parts, 22:27–23:1 and 23:2-6. The first half of the prayer is then elaborated upon in 23:7-15 and the second half is elucidated in 23:16-27. The prayer begins with a wish, τίς δώσει that was undoubtedly expressed in Hebrew by מִי יֵחֵן, a rhetorical question. Two formulas, each containing three vocatives, follow this initial petition in each half of the prayer (23:1; 23:4). The first reads κύριε, πάτερ, καὶ δέσποτα ζωῆς μου ("Lord, father, and ruler of my life"), and the second varies it slightly to κύριε, πάτερ, καὶ θεὲ ζωῆς μου ("Lord, father, and God of my life"). Beentjes has discerned remarkable consistency in the structure of the two halves.[50]

	A	B
τίς	22:27a	23:2a
καὶ	22:27b	23:2b
ἵνα μὴ	22:27c-d	23:2c-3
κύριε πάτερ	23:1a	23:4a
μὴ	23:1b-c	23:4b-6

He has also recognized chiasm in subject and verb usage within 23:2c-d and 23:3a-b.[51]

$$\text{ἀγνοήμασίν—φείσωνται}$$
$$\text{παρῇ—ἁμαρτήματα}$$
$$\text{πληθυνθῶσιν—ἄγνοιαί}$$
$$\text{ἁμαρτίαι—πλεονάσωσιν}$$

---

[48]Thomas R. Lee, *Studies in the Form of Sirach 44–50*, SBLDS 75 (Atlanta: Scholars Press, 1986) labels the praise of famous men an encomium. Burton L. Mack, *Wisdom and the Hebrew Epic* (Chicago: University of Chicago, 1985) cautiously accepts Lee's hypothesis, but it is vigorously denied by Chris A. Rollston, "The Non-Encomiastic Features of Ben Sira 44–50" (M.A. thesis, Emmanuel School of Religion, 1992).

[49]"Sirach 22:27–23:6 in zijn Context," 145.

[50]Ibid.

[51]Ibid.

Two topics occupy Ben Sira in this prayer: speech and sexual lust. The image of setting a guard over one's mouth occurs also in Ps 141:3.

> YHWH, set a guard over my mouth,
> a sentry over the door of my lips.

Ben Sira opens with a similar request without identifying at first precisely who is being addressed. He desires a sentry, perhaps even a seal that would prevent his lips from parting unless properly attended. Such a guard would save his life from a dangerous tongue (cf. Ahiqar 14b, 15). Having stated the peril in which he finds himself, Ben Sira then names the one from whom he seeks assistance, "YHWH, father, and ruler of my life." In this context he mentions adversaries for whom nothing thus far has paved the way, leading W. O. E. Oesterley to rearrange the prayer so that the pronominal suffix makes sense.[52] One thing is clear: Ben Sira does not want the Lord to abandon him to his enemies, whether his tendency to speak too hastily or others who slander him mercilessly.

The other topic occupies vv 2-6 and thus moves within the human mind to the source of actions. Those at issue here are arrogance and lust of the flesh. Ben Sira asks for whips that will control his thoughts; he also desires a disciplined and informed mind. Such active chastening, an image that realistically draws on familiarity with conditions in ancient classrooms, will alert him to danger and enable him to escape harsher critics, those unspecified adversaries who delight in his discomfiture. He asks to be delivered from self-serving pride and excessive sexual appetite, the characteristics of someone who has lost the capacity to blush. Together the two halves of the prayer cover sin's source and its external expressions. The prayer's motivation arises from fear of being abandoned to merciless foes or to one's own base inclination.

The section immediately following the prayer calls attention to the dangers of unguarded speech (23:7-15), and this valuable advice then gives way to a discussion of sexually loose behavior, first by men and then by women. A familiar aphorism, "To a fornicator all bread tastes sweet," is supplemented by a traditional description of sinners who deny that anyone can observe their clandestine affairs. Ben Sira uses hyperbole to emphasize YHWH's clear gaze: "he does not realize that the eyes of the Lord are ten thousand times brighter than the sun; they look upon all the ways of men and perceive even the hidden places" (23:19). Women, too, who break their marriage vows will suffer for their actions, which bear powerful negative testimony to the sweetness of religious devotion and adherence to the law of Moses. In this final verse (23:27) Ben Sira sums up the two fundamental themes of the entire book, the fear of YHWH and the torah.

The other prayer in Sirach addresses national interests, in doing so resembling ancient laments. Th. Middendorp has questioned the authenticity of 36:1-22 on two

---

[52]*Ecclesiasticus* (Cambridge: University Press, 1912) 150-51.

grounds,[53] its use of language that does not occur elsewhere in the book and its emphasis on themes that seem out of place, specifically hope in divine intervention, the gathering of Israel, high esteem for the prophetic message, polemic, and focus on the nation's discomfiture. Johann Marböck defends the prayer and negates some of Middendorp's arguments, concluding that its authenticity strengthens Ben Sira's stress on historical continuity and that no conflict exists between wisdom and a priestly theocracy, so that the natural place for divine activity and revelation is Israel, hence Zion and the sanctuary.[54]

This prayer has four stanzas, vv 1-5, 6-12, 13-19, 20-22.[55] The first and last verses have a sort of chiastic structure consisting of אֱלֹהֵי :הַכֹּל :כָּל :אֵל. The initial strophe has an inclusio in vv 1 and 5 where the general name for God, אֱלֹהִים, occurs. The epithets for deity throughout the prayer indicate considerable foreign influence, although the state of the text makes it difficult to determine the exact form of the Hebrew. The first verse addresses the deity as "God of all," presumably הַכֹּל אֲדוֹן or אֱלֹוהַ הַכֹּל, an expression also occurring in Ugaritic literature with respect to Baal the ba'lu 'arṣi and in the Bible as אֲדוֹן כֹּל־הָאָרֶץ. The final verse designates the deity as the eternal God, אֵל עוֹלָם. The first two stanzas conclude with the variants of the familiar statement of recognition that Ezekiel uses so often, "Thus they will know . . . that there is no God but you."

The occasion for the nationalistic sentiment was probably the Seleucid victory over the Ptolemaic army at Panium in 198 BCE, which changed the balance of power in Palestine and subjected Judah to the Seleucids. The arrogance of the new rulers provoked the emphasis on the uniqueness of Ben Sira's deity. Rapid deterioration of the political situation revived ancient messianic hopes and prompted fervent prayer for renewed signs and wonders, indeed for the end-time. The prayer opens with a plea for deliverance and closes with a recapitulation of the essential argument that Judah's God will be known as אֵל עוֹלָם, the eternal God. The precarious political situation requires the author of the prayer to resort to a cipher for the Antiochenes, who are identified in the Hebrew as Moab's chiefs, recalling Baalam's oracle in Num 24:17. Similarly, the Hebrew text of v 8 cites Isa 45:9, "who can say, 'what are you doing?'" Ben Sira asks for fresh indication of divine intervention on behalf of Israel, YHWH's firstborn (vv 6, 17), and he concludes with a confession that the Lord is always gracious to Israel.[56] This last remark focalizes the setting for the prayer, which falls directly after an impassioned declaration that

---

[53]*Die Stellung Jesu Ben Siras zwischen Judentum und Hellenismus* (Leiden: E. J. Brill, 1973) 125-36.

[54]"Das Gebet um die Rettung Zions Sir 36,1-22 (G 33,1-13a; 36,16b-22) im Zusammen-hang der Geschichtsschau Ben Siras."

[55]Patrick W. Skehan and Alexander A. Di Lella, *The Wisdom of Ben Sira*, AB 39 (New York: Doubleday, 1987) 420-23.

[56]For the development and form of prayer in the time of Ben Sira and later, see Heinemann, *Prayer in the Talmud*.

the judge of all nations will punish them and defend the cause of those who keep the law.

Elias Bickerman has perceived the signal importance of prayer to Ben Sira. He observes that "If Ben Sira's sage prays to God in order to obtain sapience, the Stoic does the same: the gift of grace is required before either can attain right knowledge."[57] In a word, for Ben Sira prayer is the means to the acquisition of knowledge. We have thus come a long way from the first prayer in wisdom literature, which follows Agur's confession that he could not attain knowledge. Ben Sira has discovered an effective way of overcoming skepticism; he pours out his heart to a merciful ruler and father.

---

[57]Bickerman, *The Jews in the Greek Age*, 173.

11 (1981)

The Contest
of Darius's Guards
in 1 Esdras 3:1–5:3

From time immemorial men and women have striven to discover the quality that endures the baneful effects of time's passage. A victim of the aging process themselves, they have ever sought that lasting powerful force to which they could link their own fragile lives in some meaningful way. One means of discovering what survives the vanishing aeons, and consequently of distinguishing the ephemeral from the eternal, was the question and answer dialogue. By posing a question and offering several answers with differing degrees of adequacy, it was possible to evaluate the relative merits of proposed solutions. Furthermore, the genre gave full rein to rhetorical skills, so that the seriousness of the quest was not permitted to weigh down the rhetoric. Making creative use of traditional material, rhetors developed dialogue into humorous entertainment worthy of the finest ears. Such a dialogue is that attributed to Darius's guards in 1 Esdras 3:1–5:3[6].[1]

The Framing Story

Like the poetic dialogue in the Book of Job, this one is also encased within a framing story, here a contest over the strongest thing in the world. Such contests are well known in comparative literature; two of them deserve special mention because of their great similarity to the one under consideration The first, a Greek account, reports that three Samian girls told riddles while drinking at an Adonis festival, and someone put the riddle about the strongest. The first girl answered "iron," for men dig and cut everything with it and use it for every purpose. The second said "blacksmith," because he bends iron, no matter how strong, and softens it, doing whatever

---

[1]For further reading see S. A. Cook, "I Esdras," in *The Apocrypha and Pseudepigrapha of the Old Testament*, ed. R. H. Charles (Oxford: Clarendon, 1913); Jacob M. Myers, *I & II Esdras*, AB 42 (Garden City NY: Doubleday, 1974) 44-57; C. C. Torrey, *Ezra Studies*, with introduction by W. F. Stinespring (New York: Ktav, 1970; orig. 1910) 37-61.

he pleases with it. The third proposed "penis" as strongest, since even the groaning smith is controlled by it.[2]

The other related text comes from Ethiopia, and lauds woman as strongest:

Iron is strong, and yet fire conquers that.
Fire is strong, and water conquers that.
Water is strong, and the sun conquers it.
The Sun is strong, and a storm cloud conquers it.
A storm cloud is strong, and the earth conquers it.
The Earth is strong, and man conquers it.
Man is strong, and grief conquers him.
Grief is strong, and wine conquers it.
Wine is strong, and sleep conquers that.
But woman is strongest of all.[3]

Such elevation of woman has produced some marvelous stories. A particularly delightful version is preserved by Adam Korczynski dating from 1698. A peasant bought shoes for his wife, and pretended to be afraid to take them home since they were not flawless. Offering them to any man who did not fear his wife, the peasant turned them over to a villager who stoutly denied that he was afraid of his wife. Having persuaded the villager to buy bread, cheese and beer for him in return for the shoes, the peasant then purchased oil and grease for the new shoes and proceeded to rub the smelly ointment all over the villager's shirt and coat, until the unfortunate villager cried out, "Stop, or my wife won't let me into her bed." Grabbing the new shoes, the peasant said, "Look, neighbors, I am fooled," and ran away, leaving the villager to pay for the food.

A Turkish version is even more humorous. A caliph of Iraq, accompanied by his vizier and jester, comes upon a man fleeing from his angry wife, and watches in utter disbelief as the man runs into a tiger's cage. While neither the caliph nor the vizier could believe that a man would prefer a tiger's roar to a wife's rage, the jester uses the occasion to get from the caliph a letter authorizing him to collect one horse from every man in the kingdom who fears his wife. The vizier, the first victim, even gives an extra horse as a bribe to prevent the jester from proclaiming far and near that the king's sage fears his wife. Some time later the jester returns, having traveled from one end of the kingdom to the other, and brings with him numerous horses and a lovely wife for the caliph. The latter is delighted with the

---

[2]I am indebted to William Goodman, Jr., for this interesting parallel ("A Study of 1 Esdras 3:1–5:6" [Ph.D. diss., Duke University, 1971] 210-11). Plays on words dictate the course of this argument: παρὰ ποτόν and παρὰ πόθον (drinking/arousing desire); στένοντα and σθένοντα (groaning/strong).

[3]The text is given in Latin by R. Laqueur, in "Ephoros. Die Proömium," *Hermes* 46 (1911): 172, who found it in Ludolf, *Comentarius ad suam Historiam Aethiopicam* (1681).

gift, but becomes uneasy when the jester praises the young woman loudly enough to be heard by the chief wife in the harem. Once the reason for the caliph's uneasiness is articulated, the jester requests a horse from him also. The old wife, who had overheard the conversation, supports the jester's demand, and he obtains from the exalted caliph a token that a woman rules the "sovereign" of the land.[4]

The facts of the framing story of I Esdras are simple, although fraught with difficulty from the viewpoint of the entire book. After hosting a sumptuous banquet, King Darius found sleep impossible. His three guards passed the night by dreaming up a contest about what is strongest, and let their imaginations run wild in anticipation of great reward for the winner. Placing their answers under the king's pillow, they awaited his summons to defend the individual responses. One wrote "wine," another, "king," and yet another identified "woman" and "truth" as strongest. Upon waking, Darius read the answers and called his lords, together with his guards whom he charged with explaining the meaning behind the enigmatic responses. The dialogue then unfolds, and the third speaker, identified as Zerubbabel, is proclaimed winner. Rather than requesting monetary reward, he reminds Darius of an earlier royal vow to return the vessels stolen from Jerusalem in 587 BCE. The king grants Zerubbabel's request and the story closes as it opened, with feasting and rejoicing.

Tension exists between this story and the dialogue, creating considerable irony. The framework pictures the king acting in his role as strongest; the envisioned rewards throw royal prerogative and favor into special prominence by their language and content. At the same time, the story portrays a king who falls victim to sleep, and the people themselves proclaim the winner of the contest. Within the dialogue, the king's might falters before appetite and sleep, and ultimately death conquers all over whom the verdict ἄδικον (unrighteous) has been pronounced. Still, truth is hailed in regal terminology.

Implausibilities abound within the story, suggesting that it did not always belong to the larger narrative.[5] For example, the framing narrative ignores everything that has gone before, so that the two accounts cannot be reconciled. In addition, the guards themselves determine the nature of the rewards, which are supposed to be given on the basis of the written statements. Furthermore, the story seems confused about whether or not Darius was asleep.

---

[4]Similar folktales may be found in Haim Schwarzbaum, *Studies in Jewish and World Folklore* (Berlin: de Gruyter, 1968) 319-21.

[5]On the composition of the narrative and its relation to its "framework," see further, Frank Zimmerman, "The Story of the three Guardsmen," *JQR* 54 (1963/1964): 179-200, who emphasizes the many incongruities within the present story and explains them as errors resulting from faulty translation from Aramaic into Greek, as well as from pious redaction; K.-F. Pohlmann, *Studien zum dritten Esra* (Göttingen: Vandenhoeck & Ruprecht, 1970) 38-47, who also suggests a Semitic background for the dialogue; see also William Goodman (n. 2 above).

The conclusion of the framing story has been expanded by the application of the incident to special Jewish interests. Nothing in the original framing narrative pointed to Jewish history, except for the intrusive reference to the third speaker as Zerubbabel. In this second conclusion, the sole concern is restoration of the Jerusalem temple, return of its sacred vessels, and general welfare of Jews who journey to Zion surrounded by hostile neighbors.

The absence of special Jewish interests within the original story and dialogue does not demand Greek authorship. Some evidence for translation into Greek from Aramaic does exist, particularly the use of the word τότε (then, thereupon) for continuous narration. Praise of abstract truth stands alongside a doxology lauding the God of Truth, recalling Sirach (Ecclesiasticus) 43:1-5. Here one finds a majestic hymn about the sun that closes on a note of praise for the Lord who made it and sends the obedient sun upon its daily course. In addition, Sir 17:31-32 asks "What is brighter than the sun?" and notes that its light fails nonetheless.

The latter text lends credence to suspicion that a speech in praise of human beings as strongest has fallen out of I Esdras (echoes persist in 1 Esd 4:2,14,37). Sirach 17 praises humans for sovereignty over beasts and birds, and warns about unrighteousness. As tokens of divine favor, and to facilitate mastery of earth, men and women are given strength, logic, knowledge, and favor. Here we recognize a prototype of the dialogue under discussion, one that already combines the themes of endurance and ephemerality, unrighteousness, the sun's splendor, and praise of God who created one and all.

One further word seems appropriate with regard to the dialogue's provenance. Speculation about Dame Wisdom (חָכְמָה: cf. Proverbs 1–9) paved the way for praise of abstract truth, inasmuch as psalmic texts already pictured righteousness and truth as kissing one another. It follows that no reason exists for assuming Greek authorship for the dialogue in its entirety, even if it shows evidence of editorial revision.

Sapiential Traditions concerning Wine, King, and Woman

A brief look at wisdom traditions bearing upon our dialogue shows how copious were the materials from which later scribes could work. The strange workings of wine are described with pathos and humor: on the one hand, it is noted that life without wine is intolerable, while, on the other hand, it is admitted that wine can be destructive, an occasion of stumbling (Sir 31:25-31). In season wine gladdens the soul, but tests the true character of individuals. Those who fail the test posed by this gift of the vine find their strength diminished and become victims of harsh blows. Drunken fools have woe; redness of eyes are but the outer manifestations of a pathetic state in which they see strange things and utter perverse words. Neither the sting of the vine nor the resulting squalor creates in drunkards a resolve to abstinence; combined, they exert precisely the opposite effect, and victims of the cup return to the poison oblivious to blows that invariably follow (Prov 23:29-35). In truth wine is a mocker and strong drink is a brawler, leading fools astray (Prov

20:1) and bringing poverty as its hangover (Prov 21:17). Nevertheless, since wine possesses the power to make people forget their sorry lot (Prov 31:4-7), it should be given to those who are poor and dying, and should be consumed with a happy heart, inasmuch as God has already approved it (Qoh [Ecclesiastes] 9:7). There are those, however, whose responsibility for maintaining a just society demands clarity of thought at all times. Hence wine is not for kings lest they pervert justice (Prov 31:4-7; contrast Qoh 10:17). When wine is coupled with the other great temptress, woman, even intelligent persons go astray (Sir 19:2).

Equally ambiguous are traditions dealing with the king. On the one hand, kingship is accepted as a reality with which one must reckon. Unlike prophetic and historical literature, which has an incisive critique of the concept of monarchy based on the belief that God ruled his people, wisdom literature has no clear attack on kingship as such. The wise did not, however, close their eyes to harsh reality; their proverbs recognize that old kings may become rigid and refuse to take advice (Qoh 4:13-14) and that rationality often gives way to arrogance of position when the king surrounds himself with fools (Qoh 9:17). Indeed, the proud demeanor of kings becomes the subject of mild ridicule (Prov 30:31); and sages concede that undisciplined rulers bring ruin upon their people (Sir 10:3). But the king is supreme, enjoying absolute freedom to do as he chooses (Qoh 8:2-4); consequently it is better to avoid him and his court since his displeasure signals instant execution (Sir 7:4-5). Inasmuch as God dispenses his favors through the king (Prov 21:11) and justice belongs to the royal domain (Prov 20:8), having a monarch is preferable to not having one (Qoh 5:8[9]). This ruler who searches out the unknown (Prov 25:1-7) and whose favor resembles the falling dew (Prov 19:12) is subject to the vicissitudes of history; his power may be stripped from him in a flash (Sir 11:5), and he can be corrupted (Prov 29:26). Since money speaks loudly in his ears, absolute justice comes from the Lord alone. Moreover, wisdom is stronger than ten kings (Qoh 7:19), and today's king is tomorrow's corpse (Sir 10:10). Thus kings take an inferior position to both wisdom and God.

Just as wine perverts the capacity of a king to execute justice, so too woman possesses power to destroy kings (Prov 31:3). The traditions relating to women are likewise ambiguous, as in the case of wine and the king. Many are the texts praising the wife as man's most precious "possession," worth far more than gold (Prov 31:10-31; Sir 7:19; 26:1-4, 16-18; 36:22-25). Such a treasure, the gift of God, is to be appreciated both for her ravishing beauty and sound intelligence. She is indeed the sole source of pleasure and meaning in a silent universe (Qoh 9:9), when death is preferable to life. Nevertheless, more bitter than death is the woman who cannot be trusted (Qoh 7:26), and unfortunately a man cannot entrust his soul to one woman in a thousand (Qoh 7:28). Since the wanton actively engages in bringing about man's downfall (Prov 5:3-14 and passim), and a man's wickedness is better than a woman's goodness (Sir 42:12-14), the person of discretion avoids the strange woman like a plague. Her gifts are, in fact, equally destructive; she leads her victims to the slaughter like dumb animals. Consequently one should not give himself to a woman so that she masters him (Sir 9:2); special care must be taken to shun the female entertainer whose beauty leads the best and wisest man to his doom, and to avoid dinner companions of the fairer sex who are married (Sir 9:1-9). A lack of discrimination enhances woman's seductive powers: whereas a man will choose among possible options, selecting some and rejecting others, a woman will make her well available to any thirsty traveller and open her quiver for any arrow (Sir 26:12; 36:21). The decree from of old stands over this divine gift and Satanic messenger: "you must die" (Sir 14:17). Subject to this decree, too, is the king, and the fruit of the vine passes away. Only truth is worthy of supreme sacrifice, and those who strive to the death for her soon discover that they have a powerful champion on their side—God (Sir 4:28).

On the basis of this brief resumé of traditions focusing upon wine, the king, and woman, it becomes clear that the step from such material to that characterizing the dialogue under consideration is a tiny one.

Rhetorical Features within the Dialogue

Each of the three speeches makes use of a common introductory formula: "Then the first (second; third), who had spoken of the strength of wine (the king; women and truth) began and said (or began to speak)." Similarly, each is concluded with a simple word to the effect that he stopped speaking or ceased. Each spokesman makes skilful use of rhetorical questions. The first speaker sets the tone of the discussion by means of a question ("Gentlemen, how is wine the strongest?") and another to invoke assent ("Gentlemen, is not wine the strongest, since it forces men to do these things?"). The second speaker opens with a false answer in question form, only to correct it promptly ("Gentlemen, are not men strongest who rule over land and sea and all that is in them?"). Such a rhetorical question leads directly to a discussion of him who rules over them all, the supreme monarch. This speaker also appeals for favorable response ("Gentlemen, why is not the king the strongest, since he is to be obeyed in this fashion?"). But the third speech is not content with an introductory and a final rhetorical question; on the contrary, it is punctuated throughout by copious questions (1 Esd 4:14-35):

> Gentlemen, is not the king great, and are not men many, and is not wine strong? Who then is their master, or who is their lord? Is it not women? . . . Do you not labor and toil, and bring everything and give it to women? . . . And now do you not believe me? Is not the king great in his power? Do not all lands fear to touch him? . . . Gentlemen, why are not women strong, since they do such things? . . . Gentlemen, are not women strong? . . . Is he not great who does these things? (RSV)

The third speaker boldly states his view as if only a fool would dare disagree: "Hence you must realize that women rule over you!" (4:22). Such confidence, together with the abundance of rhetorical questions throughout the speech, lead him to dispense with a final question, "Gentlemen, is not truth strongest of all?" in favor of a doxology, "Blessed be the God of truth!"

The first two guards speak briefly and to the point; the third wanders over the broad range of ideas from earth to heavenly manifestation and further abstraction; his speech is twice as long as the other two combined. Whereas the first two spokesmen have no opportunity to respond to the opponents' arguments, but must content themselves with concise defense of their arguments that wine and the king are strongest, the third has the privilege of tearing down the opposing arguments, on the one hand, and defending his own position, on the other. In this regard, as in length, the third speaker has unfair advantage, for he can respond to both speeches.

Furthermore, the speeches display a broadening of focus at each stage in the dialogue. The first speaker sticks to the subject and shows commendable powers of logical coherence; the second introduces a new idea about man as strong, as if another speech had been devoted to that topic; and the third has two "arrows in his bow" to begin with, and even introduces such ideas as the vastness of the earth, the height of heaven and the swiftness of the sun. By modern standards the first speech is superior to the other ones, the third being more bombastic and less tightly reasoned. By reporting that the king and the nobles looked at one another (4:33), the author makes a transition within the third speech from women to truth with great ease. While concealing the slightest hint that the argument has thus far compelled assent, this observation also permits the hearers an opportunity to shift gears before a wholly different answer is defended.

The final speech sustains conscious humor at three places. The image of a man carrying in his hand his most precious possessions and dropping them to gaze open-mouthed at a beautiful woman, both funny and profound (4:18-19), witness to man's ultimate priorities. Such a discovery must have arisen from countless incidents in which man chose a living reality to lifeless things, however precious and priceless. Similarly, the observation that "many men have lost their minds because of women, and have becomes slaves because of them" (4:26), though grim (we might think of Samson, for example), must have provoked a knowing smile among those who listened with appreciation. Even the bold description of the king's love play with his favorite concubine, the otherwise unknown Apame, is calculated to evoke laughter from the king and is carried out with delicacy and apparent success (4:29-31). The reference to the king's gazing at Apame "with mouth agape" takes up the earlier theme of man's reaction to a beautiful woman, and in so doing brings the ruler down to the level of the common man. Before a woman even the king descends from his throne and becomes an ordinary supplicant, flattering and seeking special favor. Thus appropriately the final verdict comes from the gathered nobles rather than from the king alone.

The strongly humorous element in the dialogue gives way before the powerful didactic note in the final discussion of truth. Here we enter the realm of morality and religion. Inasmuch as wine, the king, and woman are creatures they are subject to decay and corruption; hence the verdict for one and all is ἄδικον, unrighteous.

On the other hand, truth has no share in unrighteousness or wickedness, and in her exists no partiality. Here justice alone triumphs, for she possesses both the power to implement justice and full knowledge of past, present and future to ensure equity. Invoked by the whole earth, and blessed by heaven, that is, God, this strongest of all things commends itself to those who are in danger of perishing. Triumphant, then, is truth. But the religious note rings forth with shattering impact, placing even this victor in proper perspective: "Blessed be the God of truth." This combination of subject matter and piety made the dialogue a favorite of Jews and Christians. The rhetoric and traditional material incorporated into the dialogue with consummate artistry set Judaism in the best light possible for Greek and Roman readers, and hence was a favorite of men like Josephus. And the religious fervor clothing the praise of truth especially appealed to Christians, many of whom, like Augustine, found therein prophecy of the Christ.

The Dialogue

The literary artistry of the dialogue is by no means limited to careful but copious use of rhetorical questions, formulae, and humor, or to didactic intentions. The arguments themselves, little masterpieces, say much in few words. We turn, therefore, to brief explication of the meaning of each component in the dialogue. We shall leave aside the intriguing question about the number of speeches in a hypothetical original, as well as the order of the speeches. Evidence does not justify certainty in these areas. The allusion to the power of wine over the king in the first speaker's argument (3:19) cannot be used as evidence for the sequence king-wine-women-truth, for the idea is central to the argument and does not address an earlier speaker's remarks at all. Nor can one remove the discussion of truth from the final speech on the basis of anything other than pure subjectivity. While such a decision may be correct, much favors retaining the discussion as the original solution to the question, "What is the strongest?" We shall examine the dialogue in its present form, even though tempted by 4:2,14,37 to suggest that a defense of man as strongest in terms of the dignity accorded him in the creation account has dropped out.

A. Wine Is Strongest

The knowledge that men and women are rational creatures was not limited to ancient Greeks. While Plato's students, led by Diogenes, may have made fun of his definition of man as a thinking animal without feathers by attaching to a cock the label "philosophical man," the metaphor of human beings as rational has always seemed appropriate in discussions of their essence. *Cogito ergo sum* (I think, therefore I am) removes men and women from their environment and exalts them over all other creatures. Yet this distinctive mark succumbs to the power of the vine, whose product leads astray the keenest mind.

Besides this rational essence, an artificial distinction according to sociological status emerges early. Hence class differences surface, men and women being fitted into appropriate niches on the basis of things over which they have no control (birth) or which have nothing to do with their real selves (possessions). The latter make it possible for one person to subject others to servile obedience, for the rich can enslave those indebted to them. And, of course, there must be someone at the very top of artificial distinctions among people; this person of power and privilege acclaims himself king. Such differences pass away when wine wields its strange power, and now at long last king and lowliest subject stand equal, as do master and slave, rich and poor.

Inasmuch as women and men are thinking creatures upon whom class distinctions have been imposed, above and beyond the ordinary causes for anxiety and remorse, they are ever and again victimized by fear, pain, and sorrow. The sentence of death hangs over their heads, and fertile imagination conjures up all sorts of dangers both real and supposed. Actual pain, both their own and that of those dear to them, increases anxiety about approaching death and heightens agony caused by disappointment, intensifying to the breaking point all psychically based consternation. When wine enters the bodies of men and women, frequently the worry-prone victim of death's messengers, they forget for the moment the power of pain. In place of sorrow and financial woe come a glad heart and freedom from care, so powerful is the blood of the grape. Those who under ordinary circumstances and beset by problems of daily existence can muster minimal self esteem find limitless resources lurking within the cup, which loosens the tongue so that newfound confidence proclaims itself with complete abandon.

Rich experience has taught the values of friendship and the indispensability of fraternal loyalty; without friends or brother, one is vulnerable from every side. Consequently friendship ties and kinship bonds came to occupy a high position in the order of priorities, for nothing was too great a price to pay to assure the perpetuity of those relationships. Even a grievous offense could be overlooked lest the bond with another be severed, and great care was taken to avoid injury to a friend or brother. But persons who have their fill of wine treat such valuable relationships like ordinary refuse, and with reckless abandon pick a quarrel that leads to blows between friends and brothers.

The seasons come, and the seasons go, and with them birth and death. The strange capacity for remembering, that ability to recall selected events, thoughts, and sensations from the shadowy past, survives the powerful sway of time's monotony. Often cause for wonder and astonishment, this memory enables men and women to relive those cherished moments when time and eternity coalesced and the joyous soul cried out, "Stay, thou art so fair." Furthermore, such remembrance of sacral events opens up new possibilities for those to whom primeval event stands as both summons and demand; from its power they receive renewed redemption and ethical motivation. Still, even this astonishing memory bows in submission to the greater power of wine, and the individuals recall nothing that transpired during the drunken stupor.

Wine, then, functions as the great leveler; its mighty floodwaters sweep in the swirling maelstrom all human rationality, memory, psychic states, distinctions both real and artificial, and bonds of friendship and brotherhood. From the murky waters left by the subsiding flood one can pull their corpses, newly transformed into perverted thought, forgetfulness, joviality, boasting, camraderie, and bellicosity. "Gentlemen, is not wine the strongest, since it forces people to do these things?" Such was the brief, but truly cogent, argument of Darius's first guard.

B. The King Is Strongest

The silence of the second speaker with regard to the persuasive points made by the first in defense of wine as strongest puzzles, particularly since he introduces his remarks about the king with a veiled reference to human dominance of the environment. The latter allusion is surely hyperbolic; as the divine speeches in Job 38–41 make perfectly clear, men and women never succeeded in humbling all creatures on land or sea despite the creator's command to do so (Gen 1:28). Hyperbole or not, this reference to human mastery of lesser creatures provides an excellent backdrop against which to focus the comments about ancient oriental kings. No exaggeration, however, occurs in the description of the king as lord and master. Consequently, repeated use of the word "obey" is in order (4:3,5,10,11,12); even when the word is missing, the idea of total obedience pervades the language of understatement. For example, the innocuous word "tell," which occurs frequently (4:4, 7-9), carries the full weight of royal command. Whereas others must utter fruitless commands, the king need only inform his subjects of his slightest wish, and they accomplish it forthwith.

Seven times the phrase, "if he tells," occurs in the portion of the speech preserved in 4:7-9, and another time in 4:4, where it is in parallelism with "send." The sevenfold usage and the subject matter recall Qoh 3:1-9, which juxtaposes similar human actions according to polarities. While Qoheleth arranges fourteen opposites, reduced to seven doublets, in serial fashion, our dialogue has only four opposites, three ideas being left to stand alone. In both we have the opposites kill/heal (or release), and build/cut down. Common to both, also, are references to making war (although this one falls outside the compact unit in 4:7-9), attacking, laying waste, and planting. Comparison with Qoh 3:1-9 is instructive.

> For everything there is a season,
>   and a time for every matter under heaven;
> a time to be born, and a time to die;
> a time to plant, and a time to pluck up what is planted;
> a time to kill, and a time to heal;
> a time to break down, and a time to build up;
> a time to weep, and a time to laugh;
> a time to mourn, and a time to dance;
> a time to cast away stones, and a time to gather stones together;
> a time to embrace, and a time to refrain from embracing;
> a time to seek, and a time to lose;

a time to keep, and a time to cast away;
a time to rend, and a time to sew;
a time to keep silence, and a time to speak;
a time to love, and a time to hate;
a time for war, and a time for peace.
What gain has a worker from his toil?   (RSV)

Of these fourteen opposites only those appropriate to royal command have found a place in our dialogue. Most, however, concern emotional responses and relationships not subject even to the king's wishes. Weeping and laughter, lovemaking and continence, abstemious saving and reckless squandering, silence and speech, loving and despising cannot easily be brought under royal decree. The amazing similarity between the two texts suggests a common fund of traditional motifs, and perhaps, too, a tendency to place opposites over against one another in an effort to arrive at completeness.

The dialogue brings all citizens under the iron hand of the king. It mentions first those directly associated with their lord, the professional army. Subject to the king's slightest whim, the standing army moves at his command. Tossing personal welfare to the wind, and wishing only to gain favor in the eyes of the king, these courageous soldiers gladly give their lives in battle and do not consider for a moment whether the goal of the campaign justifies supreme sacrifice. With stark realism and utter simplicity the second guard describes the accomplishments of such a loyal army: they conquer mountains, walls and towers. An army spurred by royal command is deterred neither by the rugged terrain that must be traversed to arrive at the enemy's territory nor by the protective mountain upon which the fortress rests. Having been sent, the soldiers dare not return until they have trodden upon mountains, broken into walls, and levelled towers to the ground, or until their ranks are decimated so as to render further fighting utter folly. Nevertheless, even spoils of war do not belong to those who risked their lives, but are laid at the feet of him who sent them to the brink of death. Such loyalty is not limited to the army, for the subjects of the king impose upon themselves a heavy tax burden, both in produce and monies.

Twice the speaker interrupts his narrative of subjection to the king in order to point out the absurdity of such sacrifice. In the first instance he observes: "And yet he is only one man!" Again the speaker notes that the king is subject to the same necessities as his subject, and thus must be vulnerable when his eyes are closed in sleep and when his mind tarries on food or drink. The speaker marvels that even when the king is utterly helpless no one lays a hand upon him or ventures to slip away to attend to personal business matters.

No better description of the king's supreme power could have been given than the following terse comment (4:7-9).

If he tells them to kill, they kill;
if he tells them to release, they release;

if he tells them to attack, they attack;
if he tells them to lay waste, they lay waste;
if he tells them to build, they build;
if he tells them to cut down, they cut down;
if he tells them to plant, they plant.   (RSV)

Absolute obedience despite the king's vulnerability—on this fact the second speaker rests his case.

C. Woman Is Strongest, Truth Stronger Still

In the second speech the two answers, men and the king, are intimately related inasmuch as the former heightens the argument about a king's absolute power. The two answers in the third address are totally unrelated, for no logical progression moves from woman to truth. Those commentators who view the section on truth as a later addition are certainly correct in their refusal to see any necessity for it from the standpoint of logic. Since both answers stand alone, we shall discuss them in isolation. First, we turn to the defense of woman as strongest.

In a rhetorical question the speaker alludes in reverse sequence to the three answers previously put forth (king, men, and wine). Yet another rhetorical question takes up the second guard's key terms and suggests that they have been wrongly located: "Who then is their master, or who is their lord?" Denying that the king is the real lord and master, a third rhetorical question introduces the answer to be defended: "Is it not women?" The crowning argument has to do with origins; from the woman's womb came both the king and man who rules over land and sea. Moreover, those who plant the vine also were nourished by women. This is the last we shall hear of wine, save in the final summing up of the argument for truth. Evidently we must assume that the third speaker did not give much credence to the defense of wine as strongest. Precisely the reverse is the case with arguments put forth in favor of the king as strongest; the speaker takes great care to show that men face death in pursuit of a woman's favor more readily than they sacrifice themselves in obedience to the king, and to depict the power that a lovely woman wields over kings themselves. A decisive difference between the service of the king and a lover's devotion is the fact that the latter acts at his own initiative and does not wait to be commanded. Thus he toils for naught but the joy of laying everything at a woman's feet, and he faces every danger from wild beasts,[6] the darkness of the unknown, and human foes, only to bring what he gains to a woman and bask in the radiance of her smile. Furthermore, the spoil that a king's soldiers bring him ultimately adorns the gracious necks of his concubines, while the crown itself may even rest at times upon the lovely head of a woman. This is the point of the humorous

---

[6]The same root that is used for facing a lion also describes man's gazing upon a beautiful woman (θεωρῇ/θεωροῦσιν).

anecdote—approaching burlesque—about the playful, flirtatious behaviour of the king and his favorite lover, Apame.

Twice the third speaker calls attention to a lover's powerful bond over against primary affection for parents. The strong attachment rooted in family relations counts for nought in the face of erotic allurement. Men readily turn their backs on father and mother. Another significant loyalty gives way to a woman's attraction, too. Even love of country fades when a woman enters a man's life. Forgetting parents and country, he follows a woman to foreign lands and dwells among strange people. Such seductive power inevitably eventuated in death, stumbling, sin. Source of life, woman also became an occasion of madness. Like wine, she held the power to reduce rational thought to incoherent babble.

So far the speakers have concentrated on terrestrial affairs.[7] The third speaker shifts the focus toward the skies in order to introduce one who excels over women, earth's strongest inhabitant. The sun encircles the vast earth and high heaven in a single day. Still, truth is greater than the sun. Invoked by the whole earth, and blessed by God, truth has no flaw. Wine, the king, women, and all men are unrighteous,[8] and will consequently perish. Time's relentless march tramples vineyards, topples thrones, lays women low. Above their dust, truth endures forever. To her belongs sovereignty. Before such an impartial judge and righteous ruler, proper human response is a fervent prayer that the God of truth be blessed. Concealed within the prayer, therefore, one discovers yet another answer to the question, "What is the strongest?" The masterful dialogue comes to rest in God.

---

[7]Robert H. Pfeiffer, *History of New Testament Times with an Introduction to the Apocrypha* (New York: Harper & Row, 1949) 256, notes the progress in the argument from lower to higher. He writes that it begins by celebrating material and morally inferior wine, then proceeds to a higher level, the king. He also perceives humor, pathos, comedy, and tragedy in showing the "weaker" sex to be strongest. "Here he ranges . . . from the noblest (mother love and wifely devotion) to the lowest (selfish whims and silly fancies of coquettes bringing ruin to their lovers): even the king is helpless before a woman's wiles. But mightier than anything else is truth: *magna est veritas, et praevalet*! (4:41)."

[8]Paul Humbert, "*Magna est veritas et praevalet* (3 Esra 4:35)," *OLZ* 31 (1928): 148-50, calls attention to striking affinities with Egyptian wisdom (*Ptah-hotep* ¶15 and *The Tale of the Eloquent Peasant* ¶¶92 and 95) and argues for a common saying throughout the ancient world. See James Pritchard, ed., *Ancient Near Eastern Texts Relating to the Old Testament*, 3rd ed. (Princeton: Princeton University, 1969) 412-14, 407-10.

12 (1985)

Education in Ancient Israel

Present knowledge about education in ancient Israel is astonishingly incomplete. This deficiency of hard evidence exists despite many attempts to recover the actual learning situation prior to the first explicit reference to a school, Ben Sira's invitation to acquire an education at his house of study (בֵּית הַמִּדְרָשׁ, 51:23).[1] The flurry of recent activity in researching the problem has failed to alter the state of knowledge appreciably, although it has introduced fresh evidence from Palestinian inscriptions[2] and from the Hellenistic world.[3] The resulting extravagant claims about an elaborate system of schools throughout Palestine prior to the monarchy and after its disappearance require cautious assessment.[4] That is the modest task envisioned in this brief paper.

---

[1]André Lemaire lists the various studies dealing with schools in ancient Israel: *Les écoles et la formation de la Bible dans l'ancien Israël*, OBO 39 (Fribourg: Editions Universitaires; Göttingen: Vandenhoeck & Ruprecht, 1981) 93n.70. These entries cover the period from 1908 through 1979.

[2]Lemaire gives the most complete analysis of inscriptional evidence to date insofar as their relevance to the existence or nonexistence of schools is concerned (*Les écoles et la formation de la Bible dans l'ancien Israël*, 7-33, 86-92).

[3]Bernhard Lang, *Frau Weisheit* (Düsseldorf: Patmos, 1975).

[4]Lemaire concludes that Canaanite capitals had schools (Aphek, Gezer, Megiddo, Shechem, Lachish, Jerusalem), as did Israelite centers (Shiloh, Shechem, Gilgal, Bethel, Hebron, Beersheba). He believes that local schools (Arad, Kadesh-Barnea, Kuntilat-Ajrud) gave elementary education and that regional schools (Lachish) were more advanced. Royal schools at Jerusalem and Samaria taught international relations. Alongside these schools were priestly and prophetic ones, and learning took place at the gates, in the temple, and at the royal palace. From the age of five, boys (and a few girls from elite families) studied, taking advantage of an elaborate curriculum, which Lemaire describes in considerable detail. Naturally, such schools had to develop adequate textbooks. Lemaire traces the formation of the canon as the composing of appropriate texts for classroom use. He thinks such a hypothesis explains the original setting of the Bible, its transmission, and the formation of a canon. Although more modest, Hans-Jürgen Hermisson's claim that "die israelitische Weisheit hat ihr Zentrum, ihre Ursprungs- und Pflegestätte in der israelitischen Schule" says far more than the data warrant (*Studien zur israelitischen Spruchweisheit*, WMANT 28 [Neukirchen-Vluyn: Neukirchener, 1968] 192).

The disputed issue concerns the context within which education occurred: did parents assume primary responsibility for educating their children, or did they entrust boys (and girls)[5] to professional educators? In short, were there schools during the formative period of the monarchy or more generally, before Ben Sira? Since differences of opinion arise from considering the same evidence, the problem could be partly semantic. After all, the term "school" is used in scholarly discussion with reference to a dominant intellectual perspective, as in the Uppsala school, and to a kind of discipleship, as in the Isaianic school. Neither sense is intended here; rather, by school is meant professional education, which involved both reading and writing, at a specific location to which young people came and for which fees were paid to a teacher. This is the sense in which recent interpreters seem to use the word, although they do not formulate the matter so explicitly. The disagreement, therefore, concerns the interpretation of the three kinds of evidence pertaining to the existence of schools in Israel. It comes as no surprise that these three possible sources of clarification are (1) the Hebrew Bible, (2) Palestinian inscriptions, and (3) ancient Near Eastern parallels. We shall examine the evidence from each of these sources in the light of recent scholarship.

I. Education in the Hebrew Bible

Evidence from the Hebrew Bible is largely circumstantial, and some texts say more about literacy in general than about how that ability to read and write was acquired. In August Klostermann's pioneer study of education in Israel, only three texts are taken as conclusive evidence for schools: Isa 28:9-13; 50:4-9; Prov 22:17-21.[6] The first is complicated by its reference to children who have just been weaned. Is it likely that the teaching of reading and writing began at such a tender age? Friedemann Golka answers this question with an emphatic "No" and understands the text as a mockery of infant's babble.[7] Although he thinks of a family setting, such a reading of the passage is not absolutely required; as a matter of fact, Golka

---

[5]Roland de Vaux (*Ancient Israel: Its Life and Institutions* [New York, Toronto, London: McGraw-Hill, 1961] 48-50) is clearly indebted to Lorenz Durr, *Das Erziehungswesen im Alten Testament und im antiken Orient* (Leipzig: J. C. Hinrichs, 1932). That debt is especially noticeable in de Vaux's remark about education for girls. He writes: "Girls remained under the control of their mothers, who taught them what they needed to know for their duty as wives and housekeepers" (50), but one has the impression that Durr's views are less subject to the charge of patriarchalism (see 113, where he emphasizes the breadth of learning acquired by daughters, particularly in Torah).

[6]"Schulwesen im alten Israel," in *Theologische Studien Th. Zahn* (Leipzig: A. Deichert [Georg Bohme], 1908) 193-232.

[7]"Haben denn gerade Entwöhnte, also höchstens Dreijahrige, einen *Lehrer*? Naturlich nicht! Es sind die *Eltern*, in Israel wie bei uns, die sich bei Kindern dieses Alters der Kindersprache zur Unterweisung bedienen" ("Die israelitische Weisheitsschule oder 'des Kaisers neue Kleider'," *VT* 33 [1983]: 260).

must assume that parents instructed their own children in reading and writing. Now it is certainly clear that fathers and mothers taught their offspring moral precepts and instructed them in the art of coping, but all of this may easily have been achieved through oral instruction. What is not so clear is the context in which children learned to read and write, and that is the matter at issue in Isa 28:9-13.[8]

The second passage from the Isaianic corpus uses an expression for a trained tongue[9] and specifically refers to those who are taught. The decisive issue here is whether the prophet's appeal to an authoritative training is adequately explained by parental instruction or whether a greater source of authority is implied. Still, that enhanced authority could be a reference to prophetic discipleship and to the oral instruction involved in such a relationship with a prophetic master. The third text, Prov 22:17-21, is so closely related to the Egyptian Instruction of Amenemopet that it loses much of its evidentiary value.[10] It is conceivable that this foreign material was assimilated into the Israelite ethos[11] at the popular level, although a more probable explanation for the borrowing is that Israelite teachers needed a text for instructing scribes, and this one was precisely the kind of classic instruction for which they were searching. In light of such ambiguous evidence within the Hebrew Bible, modern critics must decide whether the virtual silence about schools is because none existed[12] or because they were so common that no one ever thought it necessary to mention what was obvious to all.

Evidence of a different sort from the Hebrew Bible has often been mustered in defense of professional schools, although it addresses the broader issue of literacy in Israel.[13] The evidence includes, among other things: (1) the existence of a city

---

[8]A. van Selms understands the text in the light of Akkadian ("Isaiah 28:9-13: An Attempt to Give a New Interpretation," *ZAW* 85 [1973]: 332-39). He translates: "Go out! Let him go out! Go out! Let him go out! Wait! Let him wait! Wait! Let him wait! Servant, listen! Servant, listen!"

[9]The Hebrew word is לִמּוּדִים. The further emphasis on hearing in this verse is appropriate to the educative process in the ancient world. The conclusion to the Instruction of Ptahhotep even has an extended pun on the word for hearing. In Egypt "a hearing heart" was essential to learning (cf. the similar expression in Solomon's request to the Lord, 1 Kgs 3:9).

[10]This is also the case if Irene Grumach's theory of a common source for the biblical text and Amen-em-opet should prove true (*Untersuchungen zur Lebenslehre des Amenope* [Munich: Münchner Ägyptologische Studien 23, 1972]).

[11]Glendon Bryce has discussed the process of adaptation, assimilation, and integration (*A Legacy of Wisdom* [Lewisburg PA: Bucknell University Press, 1979]).

[12]"Dass Keine Schulen erwähnt werden, erklärt sich immer noch am besten daraus, dass es keine gab" (Golka, "Die israelitische Weisheitsschule oder 'des Kaisers neue Kleider'," 265).

[13]Some critics emend the text of 2 Sam 12:25 to read that David committed Solomon to Nathan's care, and they understand the reference in 2 Kgs 10:1, 5 to guardians of Ahab's sons as scribal education (cf. 1 Chr 27:32, which states that Jehiel attended David's sons). Others interpret the phrase in 1 Kgs 12:8 ("who had grown up with him," that is, Rehoboam)

named Qiriath-Sepher (City of the Book, or City of the Scribe);[14] (2) the story in Judg 8:13-17 about Gideon's enlisting the aid of a local youth to write down the names of the city officials;[15] (3) Isaiah's determination to bind up the testimony and seal the teaching among his disciples (8:16);[16] (4) Job's desire to have the charges against him written on a document so that he could display them and demonstrate his innocence (31:35-37);[17] (5) Habakkuk's reference to a vision that could be read while one ran through the streets (2:2);[18] (6) allusions to buying knowledge, which is understood as tuition (Prov 4:5; 17:16);[19] (7) presumed scribes and courtiers in the royal court, particularly in the time of David, Solomon and Hezekiah;[20] (8) references to parental instruction in Proverbs (especially 4:1-9; 8:32-36); (9) scattered references to writing (e.g., Isa 10:19; 29:11-12; Prov 3:3; 7:3 [the tablet of the heart]; Jer 8:8 [the false pen of scribes]; Deut 24:1, 3 [a bill of divorce]; Jer 32:12 [deed of purchase]; Josh 18:9; 2 Sam 18:17); (10) vocabulary for teaching and knowledge in Proverbs (cf. also the Oak of Moreh in Gen 12:6, Deut 11:30).

The evidence clearly points to the existence of literate persons at an early period in Israel. What remains unclear, however, is the place where that literacy was acquired. Was the teaching of reading and writing exclusively a parental responsibility, or did professional teachers supplement the learning that occurred at home? Un-

---

in a pregnant sense of "attended school with him" (Hermisson, *Studien zur israelitischen Spruchweisheit*, 117-18).

[14]The meaning of this expression remains hidden. Even if it alludes to a book, it may identify the city as a depository for a document that required periodic public reading. Alternatively, a reference to scribes may suggest that a guild of scribes existed in the city.

[15]Ephraim A. Speiser's remarks about this story have no basis in the text. He describes the youth as an "urchin on the street" and observes that the text almost suggests "that he was a juvenile delinquent" (*City Invincible: A Symposium on Urbanization and Cultural Development in the Ancient Near East*, ed. Carl H. Kraeling and Robert M. Adams [Chicago: University of Chicago Press, 1960] 119).

[16]Scholars have long recognized the existence of a professional group of prophets who gathered around a prophetic leader such as Elijah or Elisha. The close bond between disciples and teacher seems particularly clear in the Isaianic corpus. This fact has often helped to illuminate the so-called Servant Songs and the additions to First Isaiah in general.

[17]Anthony R. Ceresko stresses an influence on this text other than the usual Egyptian oath of innocence (*Job 29-31 in the Light of Northwest Semitic*, BeO 36 [Rome: Biblical Institute Press, 1980]).

[18]There is some question about who the reader is—the prophet who announces the vision or the people.

[19]The language may be symbolic. In that case it would have nothing to say about tuition but would rather refer to the difficulty one endures in acquiring knowledge.

[20]R. N. Whybray, *The Succession Narrative*, SBT 2nd ser. 9 (London: SCM, 1968). E. W. Heaton writes: "[The book of Proverbs] affords the most direct evidence we possess for the school or schools which Solomon must have established in order to train candidates for his new bureaucracy" (*Solomon's New Men* [New York: Pica, 1974] 123).

fortunately, the evidence presented above does not permit a definitive answer to this question.

II. Palestinian Inscriptions

André Lemaire has recently gathered together the cumulative evidence from Palestinian inscriptions. His analysis of the inscriptional data makes free use of qualifying adverbs such as "perhaps" and "probably," which signals the provisional nature of his conclusions. However, the use to which he puts this understanding of the evidence is considerably less cautious, and the results are necessarily problematic.[21] Lemaire isolates the following kinds of evidence that require, in his judgment, the presence of schools throughout Palestine from premonarchic times: (1) abecedaries (Lachish, Kadesh-Barnea, Kuntilat-Ajrud, perhaps Aroer); (2) isolated letters of the alphabet or groups of letters (perhaps Arad); (3) letters of the alphabet grouped by similarities in appearance (perhaps Lachish); (4) words written several times (Arad, Kadesh-Barnea, perhaps Kuntilat-Ajrud); (5) personal names (perhaps Arad and Aroer); (6) formulary beginnings of letters (Kuntilat-Ajrud); (7) lists of months (Gezer); (8) symbols (Kadesh-Barnea); (9) sequence of signs (Kadesh-Barnea); (10) drawings (Kuntilat-Ajrud, probably Lachish); (11) exercises in reading a foreign language, that is, Phoenician (Kuntilat-Ajrud).

The nature of the evidence encourages considerable speculation, both with regard to actual content and intention. Lemaire thinks that many features arose from students' efforts to master the Hebrew script and alphabet, to memorize correct epistolary form and essential information about the agricultural year, to acquire refined techniques in drawing, and to familiarize themselves with proper names. Poor drawings and very large characters are attributed to learners, as are mistakes such as transposed letters. Similarly, the juxtaposition of characters of the alphabet that resemble one another is taken as proof that students are expressing their powers of discrimination.[22]

The evidence to which Lemaire appeals is in some respects impressive: the existence of a clear Phoenician hand, which may indicate a trained scribe; two abecedaries, one of which is in a superior hand; and the juxtaposition of similar letters of the alphabet. One might add to these data the paleographic consistency throughout ancient Israel, which seems to imply authoritative instruction in the art

---

[21]For specifics, see my review in *JBL* 103 (1984): 630-32. Incidentally, Ahiqar instructs his adopted son in the home, although Nadin is destined for the role of a royal courtier. This is strange if James Lindenberger is right that the Ahiqar tradition was compiled "under royal auspices for the purposes of instructing young people who were to be attached to the court" (*The Aramaic Proverbs of Ahiqar* [Baltimore: Johns Hopkins University Press, 1983] 21).

[22]Lemaire gives a convenient summary of his findings (*Les écoles et la formation de la Bible dans l'ancien Israël*, 32). He discusses the inscriptions on 7-33 and provides fourteen figures for clarification.

of writing. Alternative explanations for some of the evidence to which Lemaire appeals readily come to mind. The size of script may indicate poor eyesight, and the disparity in the quality of drawings may mean nothing more than that some persons draw better than others. Nevertheless, the cumulative inscriptional evidence seems to suggest that some people were practicing writing at a few locations. If that is a proper assessment of the evidence, it still leaves unanswered the issue of where children received their instruction.[23] When one takes into account the possibility that the pithoi were brought to the sites from somewhere else, conclusions about where the writing on them occurred are extremely hazardous.

One other bit of evidence has often been brought forward as proof that a school existed in ancient Shechem. W. F. Albright claimed that an Akkadian letter was written by a school teacher to request payment for services rendered.[24] This interpretation of the letter has been challenged,[25] and alternative explanations carry greater conviction, particularly since they do not require textual emendation of the crucial verb.[26] Nevertheless, the letter seems to mention writing, which is being taught, even if to domestics. Perhaps the so-called Gezer Calendar belongs to the discussion at this point, if it actually represents a school boy's practice lesson.

Bernhard Lang has introduced yet another kind of corroborative evidence, the virtual absence of scribal errors in ostraca from Palestine.[27] Here he relies on Lemaire's observation that only four ostraca in about 250 contain errors. It may be that such expertise says more about the simplicity of the Hebrew language than it does about the locus of education. Albright's oft-quoted remarks about the relative simplicity of Hebrew are very much to the point here,[28] especially in the light of

---

[23]Golka writes: "In keinem Fall kann er jedoch den Beweis erbringen, dass diese Funde einer Schule, und nicht dem Privatunterricht nach dem Famulussystem entstammen" ("Die israelitische Weisheitsschule oder 'des Kaisers neue Kleider'," 263n.19). Golka thinks the situation would be entirely different if all the evidence had been found in a single place, especially in Jerusalem.

[24]"A Teacher to a Man of Shechem about 1400 BC," *BASOR* 86 (1942): 28-31. Albright could not make up his mind whether the author was a woman who taught music and dance or a man who headed a school for future cuneiform scribes.

[25]F. M. T. de Liagre-Böhl, "Der Keilschriftbrief aus Sichem," *Baghdader Mitteilungen* 7 (1974): 21-30. In l. 10 *suhārū* is understood as servants, and *lapātu* in l. 11 is taken in the sense of "to write." The result is a letter requesting immediate economic relief. The setting is a domestic one and has nothing to do with a school ("Zwar bleibt er ein Bittbrief, jedoch in der Sphäre des Handels- und Geschäftslebens, was das Verständnis erleichtert," 28).

[26]*Apalu* ("to pay") for *abalu*.

[27]"Schule und Unterricht im alten Israel," *La Sagesse de l'Ancien Testament*, ed. M. Gilbert, BETL 51 (Gembloux: Duculot, 1979) 191.

[28]"Since the forms of the letters are very simple, the 22-letter alphabet could be learned in a day or two by a bright student and in a week or two by the dullest; hence it could spread with great rapidity" (*City Invincible*, 123). Lang is considerably less optimistic about the learning skills of youngsters; he therefore suggests a year or even two years for mastering

such complex languages as Akkadian, Egyptian, and, to a lesser degree, Ugaritic. It follows that the evidence from Palestinian inscriptions, although impressive, is less persuasive than Lemaire admits, and the elaborate system of schools among the Israelite and major neighboring cities that he envisions may never have existed.

III. Education in Egypt, Mesopotamia, and Ugarit

A third kind of evidence is often cited as decisive proof that schools existed in Israel: the irrefutable fact that schools played a vital role in major cultures of the time, specifically in Egypt, Mesopotamia, and Ugarit. The argument usually assumes two forms: first, that many features from these schools appear in biblical texts; and, second, that administrative necessity would have required a presence of schools in Israel's royal courts. For example, use of "my son" as a technical expression for student and "father" for teacher is often taken as decisive proof of Egyptian influence, particularly when combined with common practices such as a free use of corporal punishment. In addition, it is often said that Israel's kings could not have carried out their official business without the assistance of trained officials who understood foreign languages and had mastered various literary skills. For these accomplishments, so it is argued, schools were indispensable.[29]

Now the importance of schools in the ancient world need not be debated. In Egypt from about 1900 BCE a royal school existed for the express purpose of training courtiers, and a specific body of literature bears the identifying title "instructions" (*seboyet*). In these government schools training was provided for potential courtiers, who learned the art of persuasive speech, proper conduct in public, moral values, human psychology, and much more. Most important, they acquired an ability to read and write hieroglyphics. Given the difficulty of this task, it occasions little surprise that numerous errors in the school copies have survived, which suggests that learning did not always accompany copying, inasmuch as students seem often not to have understood the text. A premium fell on handwriting, not understanding; gaps in texts were left without any attempt to fill them in with familiar material, which implies that students did not exercise much original thinking.

One thing is certain: scribes thought highly of their profession. In one text, *The Satire of the Trades*, the scribal profession is exalted above all other occupations (biblical scholars have long known a similar text in Ben Sira 38:24–39:11). Perhaps the excessive cruelty in Egyptian pedagogy could be endured because of the high status bestowed on graduates. In any event, we possess various scribal controversies that testify to the harsh context within which training took place.

---

the Hebrew alphabet ("Schule und Unterricht im alten Israel," 190-91).

[29]Tryggve N. D. Mettinger, *Solomonic State Officials*, ConBOT 5 (Lund: Gleerup, 1971). Hermisson offers the most complete argument and reviews the copious secondary literature (*Studien zur israelitischen Spruchweisheit*, 113-36; cf. also Heaton, *Solomon's New Men*).

These observations apply to secular schools; the existence of temple schools is generally assumed, but conclusive evidence is lacking until comparatively late,[30] when education became remarkably democratic and concentrated on middle-class values.

Sumerian schools are well documented;[31] the school possessed a name, the *edubba* ("tablet house"), and its occupants spoke a special guild language. Members of the tablet house designated themselves "sons" to outsiders, "brothers" to colleagues. The master teacher was "father," and "older brothers" were the preceptors. According to S. N. Kramer, five texts have survived: (1) a schooldays essay; (2) an account by an unhappy father because his son did not choose to be a scribe; (3) a courteous disputation between a supervisor and a scribe; (4) a vituperative debate between two seniors nearing graduation; and (5) a quarrel between two young schoolboys that was resolved by a supervisor. In time the tablet house disappeared, and scribal education fell under the control of families. In Egypt, on the other hand, it appears that education in the family context gave way to governmental instruction.

Certain types of scribal activity had a purely practical aim, for example, the writing of economic contracts. But what about the nonpractical texts? For whom did Sumerian scribes compose their *literary* works? Surely not for the general populace, since most people were illiterate. This included priests, judges, and kings. Only three Mesopotamian kings boasted literacy (Ashurbanipal, Shulgi, and Lipit Ishtar), and their boasts seem empty. Then did scribes write such texts exclusively for themselves and thereby compile a literary canonical tradition? Thus it would seem, and art for art's sake characterized the scribal profession. In a real sense, scribes were caught in a bind. On the one hand, they wanted to guard the prerogatives of their profession and thus to preserve their ranks as "poor aristocrats," whereas on the other hand, they wished to be more responsive to the people and thus to incorporate folklore into their own esoteric teachings. In addition to the complexity of the language, which certainly safeguarded their profession, there was frequent use of technical jargon and secret language (and outright pedantry on occasion). Nevertheless, these Sumerian scribes found a place for popular songs, riddles, and jokes

---

[30]For an extensive bibliography on Egyptian schools, see Lemaire, *Les écoles et la formation de la Bible dans l'ancien Israël*, 94n.73. The following works are particularly important: Hellmut Brunner, *Altägyptische Erziehung* (Wiesbaden: Harrassowitz, 1957); Eberhard Otto, "Bildung und Ausbildung im Alten Ägypten," *Zeitschrift für ägyptische Sprache und Altertumskunde* 81 (1956) 41-48; R. J. Williams, "Scribal Training in Ancient Egypt," *JAOS* 92 (1972): 214-21; and idem, "'A People Come Out of Egypt': An Egyptologist Looks at the Old Testament," *Congress Volume: Edinburgh*, VTSup 28 (Leiden: E. J. Brill, 1975) 238-52.

[31]Kraeling and Adams, *City Invincible*, 94-123; Lemaire, *Les écoles et la formation de la Bible dans l'ancien Israël*, 94n.74; S. N. Kramer *The Sumerians* (Chicago and London: University of Chicago Press, 1963) 229-48.

that arose outside their ranks. It seems that rhetoric played a minor role in Mesopotamian education, whereas original thinking was not altogether scorned. We do not know the precise nature of exams, but one such text has survived, as has encouragement to a student who was fast becoming too old. Those who persevered most probably found employment within the government, with rare exceptions.

Scant information on the Hittites suggests that scribal schools existed,[32] despite the concentration on the royal family in these sources, according to H. G. Güterbock. Nevertheless, a stone at a gate has been diseovered with hieroglyphs of a personal name together with the logogram for scribe. Güterbock thinks that this discovery indicates that trained scribes sat at the city gate and transacted business there. A similar paucity of information exists where Ugarit is concerned, although Anson Rainey has endeavored to piece together the evidence.[33] He thinks that scribes played an important role in ancient Ugarit, a deduction that seems reasonable in light of the literary remains from Ras Shamra.

In short, there were undoubtedly schools in Egypt and Mesopotamia, and their existence in Ugarit is also probable. The emergence of Israel on the historical scene came centuries later than the heyday of schools in either Egypt or Mesopotamia. Is it conceivable that Israel's kings would have imitated her successful neighbors, particularly during Solomon's era? What then do we make of this evidence from Egypt and Mesopotamia? Once again conclusive proof is lacking that these two regions have shaped the form education took in Israel.

The matter is more complicated than is commonly acknowledged. Israel and Egypt were at quite different stages of development in the tenth century.[34] By that time Egypt was an advanced culture, having achieved political sophistication over the course of two millennia, whereas Israel was just beginning her political existence. If comparison is to be made one must set Israel over against a comparable stage in Egypt's development. This correct intuition led Golka to conclude that since early Egyptian education was in the hands of parents, the same was true during the initial stages of Israel's monarchy. The fallacy of the argument lies in the fact that nations do not develop at the same rate, especially when one country can benefit from another's long experience.[35] Besides, differences in complexity of a government affect the picture. The relatively simple Israelite culture made rapid strides, so it will not do to insist that Egypt and Israel developed at the same rate

[32]Kraeling and Adams, *City Invincible*, 121-22.

[33]"The Scribe at Ugarit, His Position and Influence," *Proceedings of the Israel Academy of Sciences and Humanities* 3/4 (1969): 126-24; Lemaire gives a good bibliography of relevant works (*Les écoles et la formation de la Bible dans l'ancien Israël*, 94-95n.75).

[34]Golka, "Die israelitische Weisheitsschule oder 'des Kaisers neue Kleider'," 264-65.

[35]Gerhard von Rad acknowledged the cultural difference between Israel and Egypt, but this admission did not prevent him from concluding that Israel had a school at the royal court (*Wisdom in Israel* [Nashville and New York: Abingdon, 1972] 17).

of speed. It follows that Golka's dismissal of the Egyptian and Mesopotamian parallels is less conclusive than he thinks.

Those parallels are impressive, but do they require a theory of dependence and an equation of settings? Close examination of the extent of similarities[36] must include, among other things, (1) technical language for students and teachers, (2) the use of harsh punishment to reinforce learning, (3) Egyptian loanwords for scribal kit and ink,[37] (4) instructions within the book of Proverbs that closely resemble their Egyptian counterpart,[38] and (5) formal similarities between Job and Qoheleth, on the one hand, and Mesopotamian texts, on the other hand. Besides the striking affinities between Prov 22:17–24:33 and the *Instruction of Amenemopet*, several images occur in Egyptian wisdom and in Israelite (for example, righteousness as the foundation of the throne,[39] a little child [*Ma'at*] playing before the Lord and a goddess who has life in one hand and wisdom in another,[40] weighing the heart in just scales, the reference to heaping coals of fire on an enemy's head [presumably a rite of expiation], a garland around the neck, and a tree of life). Some of these are easily explained on the premise of polygenesis, that is, on the assumption that certain responses naturally accompany the asking of existential questions. Moreover, even if the items in question were actually borrowed by Israelite sages, that fact alone would not necessarily prove that schools existed there. The family setting is equally appropriate for the use of these images and literary genres.

The case for Israelite schools has been reinforced by appeals to the character of wisdom literature. Both Hans-Jürgen Hermisson and Bernhard Lang have argued that the book of Proverbs is didactic in form and therefore functioned as a textbook for students in school.[41] The claim is that conscious rhetoric renders Proverbs an instructional text rather than the product of popular wisdom. Furthermore, didactic units and the portrait of Dame Wisdom are comprehensible, in Lang's view, only

---

[36]See my *Old Testament Wisdom* (Atlanta: John Knox, 1981) 212-28.

[37]Williams, "'A People Come Out of Egypt': An Egyptologist Looks at the Old Testament," 238-39. He understands Hebrew קֶסֶת (scribal kit) as a borrowing from Egyptian *gsti'*, and he reads the Hebrew term יד in Jer 36:18 as a copyist's error for דיר, which "might also be an Egyptian loanword" (239).

[38]William McKane, *Proverbs*, OTL (Philadelphia: Westminster, 1970) 51-150.

[39]Hellmut Brunner, "Gerechtigkeit als Fundament des Thrones," *VT* 8 (1958): 426-28.

[40]Christa Kayatz, *Studien zu Proverbien 1–9*, WMANT 22 (Neukirchen-Vluyn: Neukirch-ener, 1966).

[41]Hermisson, *Studien zur israelitischen Spruchweisheit*, 122-25; Lang, "Schule und Unter-richt im alten Israel," 192-201; idem, *Die Weisheitliche Lehrrede*, SBS 54 (Stuttgart: Katho-lisches Bibelwerk, 1972). Margaret B. Crook thinks that the description of the virtuous wom-an in Proverbs 31 is a sort of academic catalogue for a school that trained wealthy young women in home economics, which includes household administration and instruction in the arts and crafts ("The Marriageable Maiden of Prov. 31:10-31," *JNES* 13 [1954]: 137-40).

if one acknowledges the central position of a school.[42] Gerhard von Rad stated the matter quite simply—one must say, too simply. For him two kinds of deductive arguments were decisive: (1) one from the circumstances in neighboring cultures, and (2) another from the quality of Israel's literary achievement. He concluded: "In Israel, too, writing was known. But writing has to be taught. Handwriting, however, was never taught without accompanying material. It follows from this that there must have been schools of different types in Israel."[43] Von Rad distinguishes several kinds of schools: priestly, royal, levitical, and scribal training required for Ezra's chancellery.

Some of the specifics of von Rad's argument lack cogency. This judgment applies especially to his supposed examination questions and to so-called noun lists (onomastica). The former are common phenomena in popular wisdom, which seems fascinated with such impossible questions.[44] As for the latter, nothing suggests that the authors of Job and Sirach are actually working with noun lists. Rather, they are merely enumerating natural phenomena in a manner that would readily occur to people anywhere.

Yet another line of reasoning has led Tryggve Mettinger to the belief that Israel had schools during Solomon's era.[45] That evidence consists of the list of state officials, which Mettinger thinks indicates strong Egyptian influence. That claim can scarcely be denied, but it hardly adds up to the existence of schools. As a matter of fact, the silence in these texts about an official in charge of education is hard to imagine if alongside all the other royal officials there actually stood a head of schools.[46]

In sum, schools played a vital role in Egyptian and Mesopotamian life, and their influence has certainly reached Israel's learned centers. But precisely what those centers of education in Israel consisted of remains unclear, so much so that R. N. Whybray has even denied the existence of a professional class of sages.[47] In the long run, however, he simply substituted another concept, intellectual tradition,

---

[42]*Frau Weisheit*, 23-53.

[43]*Wisdom in Israel*, 17. The ideal Israelite education, for von Rad, is reflected in 1 Sam 16:18 and consisted of music, warfare, eloquence (and physical attractiveness); see *Old Testament Theology* (Edinburgh and London: Oliver & Boyd, 1962) 1:430.

[44]See my "Questions, dictons et épreuves impossibles," in *La Sagesse de l'Ancien Testament*, 96-111.

[45]*Solomonic State Officials*, 143-57.

[46]Mettinger describes the following royal titles: secretary, herald, friend of the king, "house minister," chief of district prefects, and superintendent of the forced levy (*Solomonic State Officials*, 25-139). It would simplify matters greatly if we knew exactly what the responsibility of certain Israelite officials was, e.g., מַזְכִּיר and סֹפֵר .

[47]*The Intellectual Tradition in the Old Testament*, BZAW 135 (Berlin and New York: Walter de Gruyter, 1974).

for what others call wisdom and located that mental activity in upper-class landowners.

IV. Conclusions: Assessing the Evidence

What then can one say about education in ancient Israel when the three lines of evidence fail to provide a clear picture? In what follows an attempt will be made to work backwards and to describe the situation as nearly as possible. In doing so, a minimalist perspective seems appropriate. In all probability Israelite education was far richer than the resulting account, but erring on the side of caution is preferable to extravagant claims that exceed the evidence.

According to one tradition the high priest Joshua ben Gamla decreed in 63 CE that every town and village would have a school and that all children would attend from the age of six or seven.[48] Regardless of the credence one gives to this tradition, a school certainly existed some 250 years earlier, although its proprietor, Ben Sira, restricted his teaching to those who could afford to pay for it. His professional pride is well known,[49] even if he did also respect other vocations in a way that is entirely absent from the Egyptian *Satire of the Trades*. We cannot be sure just what made up the curriculum in Ben Sira's school, but a combination of scripture and sapiential tradition seems to have occupied his thought.[50] In this respect the curriculum was quite different from the Alexandrian one reflected in Wisdom of Solomon 7:17-22, which includes, among other things, philosophy, physics, history, astronomy, zoology, religion, botany, and medicine.[51]

In the late third century an unknown admirer of Qoheleth described his mentor as one who taught the people (הָעָם).[52] This looks like a claim that a democratization of knowledge occasioned Qoheleth's appearance on the scene. Perhaps that turning to the people dictated his special interest in aesthetics, integrity, and

---

[48]De Vaux, *Ancient Israel*, 50. Some scholars think such education began during the time of John Hyrcanus about 130 BCE (Durr, *Das Erziehungswesen im alten Testament*, 112n.1). R. A. Culpepper acknowledges competing traditions in the Babylonian and Palestinian Talmuds (*Ketub.* 8.8 and *B. Bat.* 21a) with regard to the beginnings of elementary education ("Education," in *The International Standard Bible Encyclopedia*, 3rd ed. [Grand Rapids: Eerdmans, 1982] 2:25).

[49]See my *Old Testament Wisdom*, 28-65, for discussion of the sages as a professional class. Whybray argues quite differently (*The Intellectual Tradition in the Old Testament*, 15-54).

[50]The scriptures made a strong impression on Ben Sira (discussed in my *Old Testament Wisdom*, 149-73, particularly 149-54).

[51]David Winston describes the global nature of the Greek curriculum alluded to here (*The Wisdom of Solomon*, AB 43 [Garden City NY: Doubleday, 1979] 172-77).

[52]On this text, see G. T. Sheppard, "The Epilogue to Qoheleth as Theological Commentary," *CBQ* 39 (1977): 182-89.

context.[53] Moreover, this description of Qoheleth's activity mentions the proverbial form in which he couched his teaching (מְשָׁלִים).[54] From the rest of the book attributed to Qoheleth we can guess that these proverbs and lessons drawn from them were characterized by utter realism and a healthy skepticism.[55] The contrast with Ben Sira's piety can scarcely be greater and may have arisen in part from the two distinct patrons—the people in Qoheleth's case, and elite young men in the case of Ben Sira. It follows that Qoheleth's educational setting can hardly have developed into that over which Ben Sira presided. James F. Ross has proposed an intermediate stage of learning that could link both types of instruction.[56] In trying to understand the decisive shift in perspective within Psalm 73, he envisions a school adjacent to the divine sanctuary. In his view, scholars discussed the perennial problems that threaten faith, such as theodicy, in the immediate environs of the sanctuary. Unfortunately, such an understanding of Ps 73:17 is entirely conjectural.

Education of a different kind is reported in 2 Chr 17:7-9, where King Jehoshaphat is said to have sent five princes, nine Levites, and two priests throughout Judah to teach the book of the law to the people. Of course, this text reveals more about the special interests of its author than about actual history.[57] Nevertheless, it suggests that in the late fifth century a premium was placed on religious education in certain quarters. The earlier task resting on the shoulders of parents, according to the idealized picture in Deut 6:7, is here entrusted to a small band of teachers who enjoy royal favor. For this concept of royal patronage, we can also appeal to the superscription in Prov 25:1, which refers to scribal activity by certain "men of Hezekiah." This brief allusion to copying earlier manuscripts is tantalizingly obscure, but it opens the door to speculation about scribal training under the king's sponsorship. Since Hezekiah consciously imitated Solomon in many ways, it is at least arguable that he did so in this matter as well. After all, the Hebrew text of the Queen of Sheba's praise of Solomon includes the words, "Happy are your men" (1 Kgs 10:8), even if the Greek and Syriac texts have "Happy are your wives."[58] In

---

[53]Aarrhe Lauhe correctly recognizes an aesthetic dimension alongside the ethical one (*Kohelet*, BKAT 19 [Neukirchen-Vluyn: Neukirchener, 1978] 217-20).

[54]Timothy Polk, "Paradigms, Parables, and *Mešālîm*: On reading the *Māšāl* in Scripture,' *CBQ* 45 (1983): 564-83 is the latest in many important studies of מָשָׁל. Two others deserve special notice: George M. Landes, "Jonah: A *Māšāl*? in *Israelite Wisdom*, ed. J. G. Gammie et al. (Missoula MT: Scholars Press, 1978) 137-58; and William McKane, *Proverbs*, 22-33.

[55]See my essay "The Birth of Skepticism in Ancient Israel," in *The Divine Helmsman*, ed. James L. Crenshaw and Samuel Sandmel (New York: Ktav, 1980) 1-19.

[56]"Psalm 73," in *Israelite Wisdom*, 169. For my understanding of this psalm, see *A Whirlpool of Torment*, OBT 12 (Philadelphia: Fortress, 1984) 93-109.

[57]On this text, see Jacob M. Myers, *II Chronicles*, AB 13 (Garden City NY: Doubleday, 1965).

[58]*BHS* favors the reading in the LXX and Syriac, but leaves the matter open.

other words, there is some textual warrant for the presence of a group called "the men of Solomon," at least in the mind of the author responsible for 1 Kgs 10:8.

However, the Deuteronomistic language in the Solomonic legends suffices to give one pause, and the presence of courtiers under David hardly requires the existence of royal schools at this time.[59] The decisive argument would seem to concern the nature of the proverbial sayings transcribed by the men of Hezekiah, for royal interests are conspicuously missing from the collection, and the few references to the king may reflect no more than the usual fascination with persons in authority.[60] In the case of the proverbs attributed to Solomon, the picture is even more astonishing, for the peculiar concerns of the court have made little impact on the authors.

Now if a royal school cannot be documented, where did education take place? An answer to this question can certainly be given: Parents instructed their children in their own homes. No one contests this fact, for the evidence is compelling indeed. The primary sense of father and son within Proverbs must surely reflect a family setting, and the occasional reference to mother cannot rightly be attributed to the demands of parallelism.[61] As a matter of fact, every single use of father and son within Proverbs can be understood as precisely that, a father instructing his son, rather than technical language for teacher and student. But exclusive residence in Whybray's camp may be costly, for it necessitates giving up the sages as a professional group within ancient Israel. Therefore, it seems unwise to insist that all education occurred in the home, despite the paucity of evidence for royal schools.

It follows that the bulk of education may very well have taken place in the family setting, where practical instruction in daily life was provided for boys and girls according to the opportunities open to them. Guilds of various kinds probably broadened the clientele beyond the immediate family while narrowing the scope of learning.[62] For a chosen few, special scribal training may have been provided in Hezekiah's court, and that elite training continued with Ben Sira and eventually fell into priestly hands. Still another kind of education, represented by Qoheleth, sought

---

[59]W. Lee Humphreys discusses the minor role of the court in the book of Proverbs ("The Motif of the Wise Courtier in the Book of Proverbs," in *Israelite Wisdom*, 177-90).

[60]Udo Skladny described Prov 16:1–22:16 as instruction to officials and diplomats and Proverbs 28-29 as an instruction to a prince (*Die ältesten Spruchsammlungen in Israel* [Göttingen: Vandenhoeck & Ruprecht, 1962] 46, 66).

[61]The appeal to stylistic demands as a poetic allusion to the teacher's function *in loco parentis* occurs in Lang, "Schule und Unterricht im alten Israel," 193-95. The Hebrew poet could have invented appropriate expressions to serve in parallelism with father (e.g., the one who begot you); this possibility reduces the cogency of Lang's argument. If father and mother were a "fixed pair," the introduction of the second word may have been almost automatic. However, the variety in Prov 23:22-25, as well as in 31:2, makes that highly unlikely.

[62]Various guilds come to mind: priests, prophets, pottery makers, metal workers, dancers, musicians, and so forth.

to reach the adult population in general, and this effort had its religious counterpart (2 Chr 17:7-9). In short, considerable diversity characterized education in ancient Israel, and scholarly preoccupation with the existence or nonexistence of a school threatens to obscure this significant fact.[63]

---

[63]The article by André Lemaire ("Sagesse et Écoles," *VT* 34 [1984]: 270-81) appeared too late for me to benefit from its contents. Among other things, Lemaire urges scholars to distinguish between oral and written proverbial material, recognizes the inappropriateness of Golka's sociological argument about Egypt and Israel, interprets archaeology's "silence" about schools, and reemphasizes inscriptional evidence for widespread schools in preexilic Israel.

13 (1995)

The Contemplative Life

Introduction

When the sages of ancient Egypt, Mesopotamia, and Israel contemplated reality, they assessed matters in two distinct ways, the one firmly grounded in experience, the other abstract and philosophical. Central to both modes of understanding reality, the principle of analogy facilitated a moving from the better known to the less well known. From the beginning, philosophical ponderings of life's enigmas took the form of extensive dialogue in which opposing viewpoints found expression and vied for acceptance. In contrast to this dialogic way of addressing the world around them, others observed what was accessible to the naked eye and crystallized insights about human beings or nature in brief aphorisms, riddles, and popular sayings. In time the gnomic apperception of reality receded as teachers expanded earlier insights in an effort to communicate with students. Modern scholars therefore distinguish between sayings and instructions. Stimulated by the natural tendency to view the universe in terms of binary opposition, for example, light and darkness, good and evil, this approach encouraged an exploration of deeper reasons for the presence of troublesome aspects of reality along with the good. The two ways of viewing reality therefore reinforced one another.

The Literature

Instructions

In Egypt a technical term, *seba'it*, designates instructions, although the expression also refers to other forms of literature. Among the earliest instructions are some that purport to offer advice from pharaohs to their young sons, the heir apparents. Hence the subject matter was essentially directed toward preparing princes and their high officials for later responsibilities in government: e.g., appropriate etiquette, table manners, conduct in the presence of officials, eloquence, restraint, behavior with respect to women, control of passions, knowing when to speak and when to be silent. Not all instructions were restricted to royalty, for the majority of texts are attributed to courtiers wishing to prepare their sons to succeed them at the royal court. The late Demotic instructions were probably written by ordinary citizens—though literate!—as a sort of manual for self-improvement.

Over the two millennia from the earliest instructions to these products of popularizing reflection, a decisive change is discernible. At first those who formulated these teachings confidently looked on the order of the universe and took the deity's control for granted. In their view persons deserving favor received it and those whose conduct merited punishment did not prosper. With the coming of the Middle Kingdom optimism such as Ptahhotep's "Baseness may seize riches, yet crime never lands its wares" waned and an altogether different mood apparently set in, with serious consequences. Accompanying the anxiety generated by notable social changes was a piety in which individuals sought to incur divine favor by prayer and virtue. During the Demotic period the power of fate began to dominate the surviving instructions, chiefly 'Onkhsheshonqy and P. Insinger. Both instructions stressed the necessity of pleasing the gods, never reconciling the contradiction between fate and the power of the gods but allowing the two notions to function in a complementary manner.

Another decisive change occurred in these late instructions, the adoption of a form that adhered to a single line for each saying. Earlier teachings had begun with a conditional statement, followed by an observation and an explanation or justification for the comment. Because all instructions seek to shape character and to stimulate action, they regularly employ imperatives, a feature biblical scholars have exaggerated in formal analysis. P. Insinger and 'Onkhsheshonqy link the imperatives together in chain fashion, with verbal links connecting anaphoric chains. Whereas older Egyptian instructions influenced biblical Proverbs, the Demotic ones have left their impact on Qoheleth (Ecclesiastes) and Sirach (also known as Ecclesiasticus or Ben Sira), whose text is replete with paragraph-length instructions.

The oldest Mesopotamian proverbs, the Instructions of Shuruppak, use the technical expression "my son" in the sense of student, a characteristic of Egyptian and biblical instructions also. The latter comprise the initial collection in Proverbs, chapters 1–9, as well as a section betraying the influence of the Egyptian Instruction of Amenemope, 22:17–23:22 and a brief unit attributed to King Lemuel's mother in chapter 31:1-10. The Neo-Assyrian text, Counsels to a Prince, also belongs to this instruction genre, as do Counsels of Wisdom and Counsels of a Pessimist.

Sayings

No Egyptian collection of sayings has survived, but numerous traditional sayings and aphorisms are scattered throughout the instructions and are embedded in other literary forms, especially narrative. Collections of proverbs exist in Sumerian and Old Babylonian, just as they do in the Bible, chiefly in Proverbs but also in Qoheleth and Sirach. An Aramaic collection of riddles and proverbs, The Sayings of Ahiqar, resembles Mesopotamian texts and thus renders plausible its narrative framework about a Mesopotamian setting.

Dialogue

The other way of assessing reality, philosophical reflection, deals with weighty matters, especially the problem of life's inequities. Only one text from Egypt, *The Admonitions of Ipuwer*, addresses the issue of theodicy as such, and this particular section may be a later addition. Other works take up many issues typically found in theodicies, especially *The Harper's Songs*, *The Dialogue of a Man with his Ba*, and to some extent *The Tale of the Eloquent Peasant* and *The Book of the Dead*. Two biblical exemplars of this genre, Job and Qoheleth, have greatly influenced Western thinkers. Both Sirach and Wisdom of Solomon contain minidiscussions of the anxiety generated by evil in a universe supposedly created and ruled by a benevolent deity. A few Psalms also broach the issue, either to deny that any problem exists, as in Ps 37, or to forge new insights, as in Pss 49 and 73.

Several examples of theodicy derive from Mesopotamia. The Sumerian *Man and his God* is the oldest known expression of the Job problem, but the later *I Will Praise the Lord of Wisdom* and *The Babylonian Theodicy* develop the form in the direction that the biblical Job adopts. A *Pessimistic Dialogue between a Master and his Slave* struggled with the problematic nature of reality that caused such consternation in Qoheleth. These Mesopotamian texts set precedent for: blaming the gods; recommending repentance and correct ritual; arguing with a friend about God's justice; introducing and concluding poetry with a mythological framing narrative; and considering both sides of opposing intellectual positions.

Composition

Myths

What prompted the authors of these sapiential insights to adopt forms of expression intended to convey their meaning to a wider public? A didactic impulse seems to have accompanied dialogue and instruction—perhaps even sayings—from their inception. This inherent didacticism does not exclude a conscious attempt at a later time to turn simple statements into *literary* products. The functional aspect of knowledge prevailed, its capacity to enrich life in quite tangible ways. According to a royal myth echoed in Pr 25:2, deity and king enacted a reciprocal drama by hiding and seeking valuable facts about the universe and its inhabitants. Presumably, the creator concealed such data in observable reality and thereby presented a challenge for humankind, especially its representative leader, to search for insights that would facilitate steering life's course into safe harbor. The operative word, "What is good for men and women?" survived the very questioning of the intellectual quest's validity. Qoheleth retained the myth of the deity's concealing essential data (3:11) but pronounced a negative judgment on human ability to profit from this dubious gift. Similarly, the author of Job 28 restricted something called wisdom to the deity, announcing that no one else came any closer to it than secondary reporting. Sirach goes a step farther, attributing secrecy to wisdom itself.

Underlying this myth was a significant theological issue—the freedom of God. That prerogative of deity to act without restraint from external sources seems threatened by the sapiential notion of an order governing the universe. In Egypt the principle of *Ma'at* represented this divine order that assured governmental, societal, and individual well-being. A corresponding principle in Mesopotamia seems to be implied by the Tablets of Destiny, *ME*. The Israelite concepts of justice, מִשְׁפָּט, and right dealing, צְדָקָה, functioned in the way *Ma'at* and *ME* did elsewhere.

At first glance this objective order appears to compromise the deity's freedom, but even this principle remained subject to God's free will. At the same time, sages spoke openly of deeds that carried within them the capacity to set into motion events commensurate with the originating act, whether for punishment or for reward. Occasional canonical sayings within the book of Proverbs accentuate the fundamental limits imposed on the human intellect; these reminders that "humans propose but God disposes" resemble sayings in Egyptian instructions. The latest surviving Egyptian instruction, *P. Insinger*, has developed this notion of fate into a refrain while also acknowledging the deity's active involvement in shaping human destiny. Resolving apparently contradictory statements was not essential in the ancient world; rigorous thinkers have always managed to flourish without pressing for closure on disputed matters.

Forms

This open-ended worldview of sages achieved expression in specific forms, chiefly saying and instruction, but also in related ones. Interpreters generally assume that the elemental form, the saying, existed initially as a product of popular insights. Brief maxims and aphorisms simply registered the way things were without pronouncing judgment or advocating corrective action. Several traditional sayings have survived in the narrative and prophetic literature of the bible; others, in expanded form, may be embedded in the wisdom corpus. Occupying a transitional stage between popular saying and didactic poem, riddles captured the surprise of discovery and directed it toward the teaching task. Only Mesopotamian wisdom has preserved riddles intact, but once again Israelite narrative, more particularly, the story of Samson in Judges 14, fills the gap left tantalizingly open by explicit references to riddles as a sapiential concern (Pr 1:6; Sir 39:1-3). Several proverbs structured by ascending numbers betray affinities with riddles, and in one instance the specific allusion to numbers has vanished but the normal interrogative form of riddles takes its place (Sir 1:2-3).

The popular saying, often only a half line, commanded assent by its content alone. Instructions relied on motivation clauses and warnings to persuade others that their teachings were valid. This extended discourse developed into didactic poems which treated single themes at greater length than occurred in sayings and instructions. At this point erotic overtones color the expression of paternal will, either in the form of positive seduction to the intellectual enterprise or in the guise of negative warnings about strange women who lured young men to the grave. Other didactic poems tackle the vexing problem of aging and its final victory, they acknowledge the tyranny of time over all flesh, or they celebrate the worth of a good woman. An impressive group of poems explores the means through which deity communicates with mortals, at first envisioning nothing more than poetic metaphor but afterwards contemplating an actual expression of the divine will in legal form, and eventually opting for a virtual hypostasis in which the deity becomes manifest on earth. Echoes of a polytheistic environment persist in this mythologos, with features deriving from Egyptian *Ma'at* traditions and Isis aretalogies. Didactic poems delve into the wonder and majesty surrounding the creative process, both the divine act by which everything came into existence and the human intellectual adventure that endeavors to make sense of reality as it presents itself to inquiring minds.

Pedagogic interests generated yet another form of communication, the exemplary tale. The autobiographical character of these stories bestows credibility and authority on them. A concerned teacher reports on the fatal attraction of two people who come together for illicit sexual pleasure, an older person recalls near-disastrous personal decisions during his youth, an astute observer calls attention to the undesirable results of laziness, a fictional monarch sums up his life's work and assesses its worth, a sober social analyst registers dismay over society's lack of appreciation for the contribution of scholars, and so on.

Of course, such communicative devices gave birth to related ones, for example, exemplary tale to parable, parable to allegory, and dialogue to dispute. One parable uses the ant's furious pace in preparing for winter's scarcity as incentive to action. Such appeal to lessons from nonhuman creatures played a significant role in ancient wisdom. Mesopotamian disputes between animals or trees over the merits of different species reflect a similar epistemological assumption that nature itself functions as a bearer of knowledge. That polytheistic environment also encouraged informed evaluation of rival deities through disputes. In Israel the dispute form developed into internal debate, a conversation with the self in which Qoheleth considers what he has seen and draws rational conclusions from the available evidence. The Egyptian *Dispute between a Man and his Ba* differs dramatically in its view of an entity, the *ba*, that survives death. The arrangement of aphorisms into a statement, then a contradiction, an objection, or a confirmation demonstrates the sages' fondness for dialogue.

Not all stylistic devices employed by the sages are unique to their literature. The book of Job makes copious use of the lament form, common to the Psalms and to comparable texts from Mesopotamia. Later wisdom, especially Sirach, introduced prayer and hymn into the sapiential vocabulary. Prior to this embracing of religious language, the only prayer occurs in the late excerpt attributed to Agur and the nearest semblance to a hymn heightens the tension between Job and his friends by pointing to the mystery of the universe and its maker. The hymnic praise of the creator comes into its own in Sirach; in addition, Ben Sira adapts a Hellenistic form, the encomium, to heap accolades on heroes of the past.

Social Settings

Do these rhetorical devices indicate the social setting for their use? Unfortunately, one cannot move from literary genre to precise locations in society. This issue must be addressed from country to country, and even within a given environment distinctions readily surface. Egyptian instructions presuppose a royal context, but this intimate connection with the court is not absolute. Scribal schools existed primarily as a function of area temples, instructing religious personnel in the necessary ritual and in theological texts. The language and themes of individual instructions do not provide easy access to the social location of the authors. Villagers can readily discuss royalty and their doings, just as courtiers can talk about agrarian tasks. The fact that only about one-tenth of *'Onkhsheshonqy's* sayings deal with agricultural topics hardly settles the question of origins. The Sumerian school, *edubba*, may have served as a locus for learned discourse, as well as for education at all levels of instruction. Here, as also in Egypt, noun lists, or onomastica, assisted in the study of language and grammar, perhaps also in providing data for a broader education itself.

Ancient Israelite literature derives from several different social contexts. The authors of Proverbs, Job, Ecclesiastes, and Sirach occupied distinct social worlds, and a single book like Proverbs reflects several settings. To be sure, most of the sayings revolve around life in small villages and restrict themselves to the nuclear family. The latter point detracts from the hypothesis of clan wisdom, for members of an extended family are never mentioned. The instructions are directed to yet another group, young urban men, possibly potential officials at the royal court. Given the court's minor role in these sayings and instructions, perhaps one should assume that both forms eventually played a significant role in the scribal school, for which the earliest firm evidence is the second century BCE remark by Ben Sira. Inscriptional evidence has generated an hypothesis of widespread schools in Palestine from early monarchic times, but these data, particularly abecediaries, exercise tablets, crude drawings, and foreign language texts, can be readily explained without resort to the claim of a vast educational network. Literacy in the ancient world rarely exceeded ten percent, and in most instances it ran considerably lower. The modern advance in literacy is a direct result of several factors: the invention of the printing press; the industrial revolution's need for trained workers; state sponsorship of education, assisted by exceptional philanthropists; Protestantism's emphasis on knowing the Bible; the availability of eye glasses; population density sufficient to support public education, and affordable writing materials. Ancient literacy was ordinarily restricted to males with administrative legal functions; exceptions occurred only with respect to the daughters of a few rulers or high officials.

At least three social groups factor into the discussion of the book of Job, according to a recent plausible theory. Two wealthy groups, one of which objects to taking advantage of the poor, contend for supremacy. The cruel upper class against which Job rails has no compassion for the underprivileged who in their view exist only to be used. Qoheleth belonged to an acquisitive society, one in which financial success counted heavily. He has been accused, with dubious justification, of membership in a cruel, calculating upper crust within society that held the poor in contempt. Such a harsh reading of the book ignores the pathos of Qoheleth's observation about defenseless victims of oppression. Strictly speaking, one can only conclude that Qoheleth's *audience* possessed the means to enjoy life that he enjoins as a way of dealing with absurdity everywhere.

Although Egyptian and Mesopotamian wisdom had a positive relationship with the royal court, Israelite attitudes toward kingship and a discernible enthusiasm for simpler societal structures produced conflicting texts. Despite a royal myth that includes attributing collections of sayings and even two entire books, Ecclesiastes and Wisdom of Solomon, to a king, the nature of the proverbial sayings and the celebration of Edomite sagacity imply that in some circles marginal existence apart from society's corrupting influence was viewed as more pristine. Presumably, in that purer state knowledge came much more naturally.

Themes

Creation

The fundamental themes of wisdom literature are religion and knowledge. Beginning with an assumption that truth applies universally and thus was not confined to private experience or limited to any geographical area, sages concentrated on the initiating event that made life possible in its manifold localities and variants. In Israelite wisdom the creative act was placed under the umbrella of divine justice, for it was believed that appropriate reward or punishment could only be dispensed by one who controlled the universe. Even social distinctions on the basis of access to property failed to efface the unique feature uniting all humanity in a single community—their mortality—or to compromise the fact that rich and poor had the same maker. Radical dissenters like Qoheleth did not challenge the common conception that the created world was a thing of beauty, despite occasional examples of twistedness. According to the wisdom myth, the original act of creation culminated in rejoicing on the part of the morning stars and, in one bold text, the creator's youthful female companion, unless one accepts the alternative reading, master craftsman.

One type of creation myth included a battle between the power representing order and an opposing force characterized by instability. This "struggle against chaos" has left its imprint on numerous hymnic texts within the Bible, especially those incorporated in Deutero-Isaiah and the Psalms. This version of creation in which the Israelite deity prevails over chaos has close parallels in ancient Babylon, best known from the conflict between Marduk and Tiamat recorded in *Enuma elish*. The belief that a violent event fashioned the arena for life's drama evoked similar myths throughout the ancient world, competing with the explanation of origins in natural, or sexual imagery. Some interpreters think the struggle between Baal and

Yamm in Ugaritic myth actually disguises the creative act under the story about constructing a palace for Baal.

Israelite sages transformed the chaos myth into a story about domesticating the forces of evil, or more accurately, restricting their scope. Thus the deity who spoke to Job in the whirlwind boasts about setting limits for the chaos monster, circumscribing its movement and wrapping it in swaddling bands. In this version of the myth the real problem of chaos shifts to the human arena, and the faintest hint of divine weakness over against this evil probably achieves expression. In its social dimension evil poses a constant problem requiring perpetual vigilance on the part of deity and virtuous mortals.

Fear of God

The sages' emphasis on creation acknowledged major indebtedness on the part of human beings toward the deity, for life itself derived from the creator. Occasionally this knowledge led to the rejection of any claim with respect to the deity based on virtuous conduct, for no gift to or from God could ever rival the one already freely bestowed on mortals. Given this situation, it is a little surprising that a concept of reward and retribution became common belief, virtually hardening into dogma. At the same time, the sages also recognized their complete dependence on the creator's good will, hence the necessity for proper fear. This notion of fear before the deity included the sense of dread in the presence of a potential threat as well as genuine submission in obedient love. In its fullest sense the expression "fear of God" is the closest the sages ever came to the modern idea connoted by the word religion.

Although the evidence lacks clarity, some interpreters think the sentiment expressing fear of God was originally missing from the sayings. In modern categories, they would have been thoroughly secular. This understanding of the sayings underscores the fact that several aphorisms whose form bears the marks of great antiquity are remarkably silent about any deity, relying solely on human action without regard to transcendent motivation. Such silence does not necessarily mean that the authors of these texts were irreligious. Egyptian wisdom literature also betrays a growing overt pietism as a direct consequence of the collapse of traditional values during the era immediately preceding the composition of *The Instruction of Ani* (18th Dynasty). In this work and in subsequent ones personal piety replaced a strong sense of self-reliance characterizing earlier wisdom. One seems drawn to the conclusion that the world was viewed as less penetrable than had been the case during the early days of Egyptian and Israelite wisdom.

The failure of traditional belief may have affected only a small segment of the population, whereas secular sayings may derive from well-placed individuals at the palace. Perhaps the authors of these precepts saw no need to articulate self-evident views that temple functionaries explicitly mentioned in their literature. A conviction that a person could cope with every eventuality may easily have existed alongside belief that divine assistance was essential to successful endeavor. Hence modern attempts to discern an increase in piety reflecting a crisis of confidence may be correct for only a select group of ancient thinkers.

Although the formula, "Let the initiate instruct the initiate; the uninitiated may not see," does not always imply esoteric knowledge, certain texts in Egypt and in Mesopotamia, intentionally secret, suggest an elitist—perhaps even a mystical—tradition as early as the second millennium, one that goes far beyond the elitism accompanying literacy and possession of information concerning magical ritual. Egyptian initiation texts, e.g. the *Book of Amduat*, the *Book of Gates*, the *Book of the Heavenly Cow*, and the *Book of the Dead* (ch. 148), restrict gnosis to a select group or claim extraordinary knowledge of ritual for a chosen person such as the vizier User. Mesopotamian mystical and mythological explanatory works employ the numerical device, *gematria*; comment on mystical numbers and names of deities; identify gods with various parts of the world through analogy and/or specification; offer mystical descriptions of gods; explain state rituals in terms of the myths by which people lived; and interpret the god's (Marduk's) ordeal existentially. Some of these texts state that the contents are "a secret of the scholar," adding that "the uninitiated shall not see." Occasionally, a scribe expects readers to know another text by heart, for instance, one scholar cites only the first line of *Enuma elish*. An aim of a few texts was identification with a deity, sharing mythic conflicts and victories.

Within seventh century Israel a quasi-mystical surge in the thinking of two prophets, Jeremiah and Ezekiel, may have taken place. Claiming to have been given access to the divine council, Jeremiah insists that his opponents were not similarly gifted. He even uses language that accords with a mystical understanding of the word, which he characterizes as a fire and a hammer (23:29). His contemporary Ezekiel describes the divine departure from the temple of Jerusalem in mystical categories, leading to later restrictions on just who could read these visions. Prophetic books such as Joel cite earlier prophecies and interpret them in new ways; thus an exegetical tradition emerges to prominence in postexilic and Hellenistic Judaism. Apocalyptists soon boasted of esoteric knowledge, comparable to Jeremiah's claim to special disclosure. An elitist tradition flourishes at Qumran and in Pseudepigraphic literature, partly because some contemporaries believed that revealed writings necessarily derived from ancient worthies.

Personified Wisdom

The tension between self-reliance and resort to the deity in special circumstances, or indeed in all circumstances, was eventually eased through a remarkable myth. Israel's poets frequently spoke of abstract divine qualities in a personified manner, for example when picturing righteousness and truth as kissing one another. The wisdom of God naturally lent itself to such personification, as did divine power and speech, which were personified by the Aramaic terms גְּבוּרָה and מֵמְרָא. Wisdom, חָכְמָה, represented the divine logic by which the universe took shape, the structuring of things into a coherent order.

The erotic dimension inherent to all knowledge found suitable expression in this personification of the thought processes, the inexplicable seduction of the human mind by the unknown. Curiously, Israel's stout resistance in official circles to fertility religion did not prevent enthusiastic development of an erotic relationship between students and wisdom. The sages spoke freely about wisdom as a seductress who lures young men to her banquet, but they also conceded that she had a rival in this game of love, one who capitalized on her exceptional physical attributes inflaming youthful passions by smooth limbs and speech. חָכְמָה thus was forced to adopt extreme measures, hence the emphasis on her turning to human beings in love, a notion that does not appear in Egyptian description of a comparable figure, *Ma'at*, the goddess of "right order." In Israelite wisdom, seekers of knowledge are invited to pitch their tent near wisdom's and to pursue her relentlessly, ignoring her initial rebuff in assurance that perseverance will reap rich reward. A partial defusing of this myth occurs in the hellenistic Wisdom of Solomon, where the intellectual quest has achieved its goal and gained wisdom, now the familiar Sophia from Greek philosophy, as wife. Here love's ardor burns under the protective canopy of piety.

Quite a different redirection of erotic ardor takes place in Sirach, where daughters in particular do not receive adequate appreciation—despite Ben Sira's enthusiasm for some women and an appendix to the book that is arguably rich in eroticisms. The development by certain psalmists of something called torah piety led Ben Sira to a bold move, the identification of torah with God's wisdom. In this way a divine attribute has taken up residence in Jerusalem, assuming visible form in the Mosaic covenant, the law. Furthermore, this wisdom evokes comparison with knowledge in the story of the fall, for the paradisaic myth of the rivers recurs here in Ben Sira's musings about the composition of his book.

Why this striving to mediate Transcendence in a tangible manner? The sages' concept of God is remarkably silent with regard to the saving deeds extolled within official Yahwism. This theological position is a corollary of an ethical view emphasizing self-worth, a coping with life on one's own. As confidence in one's ability dwindled, particularly after the collapse of the concept of the extended family and later the state, sages began to recognize their own reliance on divine compassion. Wisdom mediated God's concern for mortals. The transcendent creator draws near and makes known the secrets to success and happiness. Most revealing of all, for those who think of the divine law as oppressive, the person who equates wisdom and torah also introduces the attribute of divine mercy into the discourse of the sages to a degree unprecedented in his time.

Formation of Character

How did wisdom express itself in the lives of sages? Both in Egypt and in Israel four character traits distinguish wise from foolish, good from evil: silence, eloquence, timeliness, and modesty. The first requires control over passions; the silent person does not permit anger, lust, greed, or envy to dominate thought or action. The opposite, the heated individual, gives passion a free rein. The second quality enables sages to persuade others and to communicate effectively, while the third implies an awareness about the appropriate moment for speaking, valuing nonspeaking as a powerful form of communication. The fourth, modesty, indicates humility arising from knowledge that life's mysteries will never fully divulge themselves to those who search for truth.

The premise underlying the sages' elevation of these characteristics is clearly opportunistic. Some interpreters prefer the term eudaemonistic. The fundamental question, "What is good for men and women?" reveals their anthropocentric orientation. Nevertheless, the sages believed that their virtuous conduct did more than guarantee good rewards in the form of wealth, health, progeny, and honor. They also thought their actions sustained the order of the world, preventing a return to chaos. Hence eudaemonism was rooted in ethical philosophy, transforming an apparent selfish act into a moral and religious deed. In their view, the world was always at risk. This fear explains their incessant struggle against those who posed the most formidable threat, fools, and the fervent pleading with vulnerable students, called sons, that they adopt their teacher's worldview.

Sporadic victories by representatives of evil called into question the comfortable eudaemonism and forced sages to reckon with suffering and mortality. The lyrical "I" soon led to a heightened ego, an almost inevitable consequence of the hurting self, and eventuated in uncommon pride of authorship, at least for Ben Sira. With Qoheleth, egoism affects the form of expression, the teacher daring to assess everything as absurd on the basis of his own personal experience. The union of epistemology and theology persists in Qoheleth, who drew the painful conclusion that human beings cannot discern whether or not the deity turns to them in love or hate, all the while speaking effusively about divine gifts. The problem lay in the changed status from one who earned life's rewards to a person depending on divine handouts over which the recipient had no control. More specifically, the apparent arbitrary conduct of the deity generated increased anxiety.

Function

Education

The literature produced by ancient Near Eastern sages served several purposes, all of which belong to the general category of education. Egyptian and Sumerian school texts assisted in the task of instructing students for the many demands of professional life, potentially at the court, but also as scribes responsible for all sorts of economic transactions. Training in requisite languages, contract forms, epistolary style, and regulations pertaining to international commerce probably occurred in the schools, and such instruction required paradigms and exemplars of diverse kinds. Sample examination questions have been identified among surviving Egyptian scribal texts, particularly in P. Anastasi I, indicating that students learned considerable general knowledge of local geography, perhaps while practicing grammar and calligraphy. The complex hieroglyphs and cuneiform signs necessitated close attention to detail beyond the aesthetics of nicely shaped letters. The abecediaries recovered from Palestine probably indicate scribal practice in forming the vastly simpler Hebrew alphabet, but the silence in Hebrew literature concerning schools has elicited opposite explanations: no schools existed; schools were so prevalent that no one ever thought about mentioning them.

Debate

Possibly the most useful texts in implementing pedagogical strategies for advanced students, the philosophical debates covered a wide range of responses to difficult intellectual problems. Such literature offered alternative solutions to the vexing issues encountering the populace every day, although the stellar example of this genre in Israel, the book of Job, portrays its disputants as pastoralists rather than scribes or sages. This unusual feature highlights the simple fact that ancient learning, however academic, did not occur within the confines of an ivory tower but took place at the center of daily activity and addressed pressing questions that directly affected human lives. The same point underlies the description of woman wisdom in Proverbs as a rhetor practicing her trade in busy streets where she had to compete with vendors of all types. In this respect the similarity with Hellenistic peripatetic philosophers comes to mind.

Entertainment

Debate did not always focus on serious existential issues, for the sages found time to enjoy the art of story telling and the clever defense of an intellectual position. An example of the former is the remarkable contest of Darius' guards recorded in 1 Esd 3:1–4:41, which examines the relative merits of wine, king, woman, and truth under the rubric, "What is greatest?" An intriguing remark by the servant in the Babylonian *Dialogue between a Master and Slave* suggests that intellectual exchange occurred at banquets, hence that symposia played a significant role in early education. That incidental remark has parallels in Egyptian wisdom literature also, and the pseudepigrahic Epistle of Aristeas develops the notion of scintillating conversation during meals in great detail. Mesopotamian fables served a dual purpose of entertainment and practice in defending a particular viewpoint. These fables sometimes required students to make discerning judgments about the relative merits of various aspects of society—e.g., tools, animals, vocations, deities. The combined sayings and instructions reflect societal values about numerous topics, but they do not constitute a complete moral code, for some important dimensions of life are strangely missing.

Taxonomies

A few texts from Egypt and many more from Mesopotamia comprise zoological and botanical taxonomies, an exhaustive list of various species. A curious legend in 1 Kings 4:29–34 (Hebrew, 5:9-14) attributes this sort of learning to Solomon, who is said to have compiled proverbs about trees, beasts, birds, reptiles and fish. Those interpreters who consider this text historically credible understand Solomon's contribution to the genre to be the actual formulation of poetic sayings incorporating such taxonomies. Encyclopedic lists in Egypt and Mesopotamia probably served a dual function, facilitating the practice of language and writing.

Ritual

Mesopotamian scribal texts served an important role in ritual, especially magic. Incantations dealing with all kinds of circumstances enabled society to reckon with multiple threats to existence. Liturgical paradigms such as *I Will Praise the Lord of Wisdom* enjoined proper religious response to calamity. Egyptian ritual incantations also claimed the attention of learned scribes, and the biblical Job's protestations of innocence in chapter 31 resemble oaths of innocence in Egypt and Mesopotamia. Otherwise biblical wisdom practiced restraint with respect to religious ritual prior to Ben Sira, whose priestly leanings led to unchecked exuberance at witnessing the High Priest in procession on a holy day. This late biblical sage also compiled an expansive eulogy honoring great men of the past; in doing so he incorporated Yahwistic tradition into wisdom thought.

Polemic

Some sapiential texts functioned polemically to defend the scribal profession, perhaps necessitated by harsh measures employed in the classroom, for which several scribal texts in Egypt and at least one school text from Sumer provide vivid documentation. Ben Sira's defense of the scribe's vocation has some affinity with the much earlier Egyptian *Instruction of Khety*, although the phenomenon of polygenesis may be at work here rather than direct literary dependence. Naturally, opposing views among the sages resulted in literature rich with polemic. Sometimes polemical attacks on outsiders intrude into sapiential texts, as when Ben Sira explodes against traditional enemies of Israel and Wisdom of Solomon launches a verbal assault against Egyptian idolaters.

Counsel

Just as Egyptians had officials at the royal court who needed instruction, Mesopotamians also employed scribes for whom appropriate guidance was necessary, as the story of Ahiqar implies. Whether or not an actual royal counselor advised biblical kings remains unclear, although the story about David mentions two counselors, Ahithophel and Hushai. The obscure title, "men of Hezekiah," alluded to in Pr 25:1 indirectly links these sayings with royalty.

Conclusion

A significant literature from ancient Egypt, Mesopotamia, and Israel possesses sufficient thematic and formal unity to suggest a "common context of origin" and purpose, allowing for distinctions in the several areas. Those texts comprise the ancient effort to acquire knowledge and to embody wisdom in personal character.

To achieve that worthy goal, the sages collected traditional insights of the populace and added their own learned conclusions about reality. In doing so, they bequeathed an important legacy to posterity.

Selected Bibliography

Jan Assmann and J. Hardmeier, eds. *Schrift und Gedächtnis* (1983).
   Collected essays on ancient thought.
Helmut Brunner, *Altägyptische Weisheit: Lehren für das Leben* (1988).
   A translation of ancient Egyptian Wisdom literature.
James L. Crenshaw, *Old Testament Wisdom* (1981).
   A general introduction to Israelite wisdom in its ancient Near Eastern context.
_____, ed. *Studies in Ancient Israelite Wisdom* (1976).
   Extensive collection of essays by various scholars.
Daedalus (Spring 1975). *Wisdom, Revelation, and Doubt: Perspectives on the First Millennium B.C.*
   Perceptive articles by specialists in different ancient cultures—e.g., Israelite, Mesopotamian, Chinese, Greek.
Johannes Fichtner, *Die altorientalische Weisheit in ihrer israelitisch-jüdischen Ausprägung* (1933).
   A valuable synthesis of scholarly interpretation at the time.
John G. Gammie and Leo G. Perdue, eds., *The Sage in Israel and the Ancient Near East* (1990).
   An important collection of articles covering a wide range of topics.
John Gammie et. al. eds., *Israelite Wisdom: Theological and Literary Essays in Honor of Samuel Terrien* (1978).
   Articles on many facets of biblical wisdom.
Maurice Gilbert, ed. *La Sagesse de l'Ancien Testament* (1979; 1990 2nd ed.).
   Essays delivered at a colloquium on Old Testament Wisdom in 1978 at Louvain, recently updated.
Journal of the American Oriental Society 101/1 (Spring 1981). *Oriental Wisdom.*
   Essays on Egyptian, Israelite, Mesopotamian, Arabic, Asian, and Indian wisdom. Also published as a monograph.
W. L. Lambert, *Babylonian Wisdom Literature* (1960).
   Includes texts and translations of major works.
Miriam Lichtheim, *Ancient Egyptian Literature*, 3 vols. (1973–1980).
   Translations of the relevant texts, with notes.
_____. *Late Egyptian Wisdom Literature in the International Context: A Study of Demotic Instructions* (1983).
   An insightful analysis of Demotic wisdom.
Roland E. Murphy, *The Tree of Life* (1990).
   A nontechnical treatment of biblical wisdom literature intended for educated lay readers.

Horst Dietrich Preuss, *Einführung in die alttestamentliche Weisheitsliteratur* (1987).
A useful introduction, often expressing views at variance with much scholarship.

Gerhard von Rad, *Wisdom in Israel* (1972).
Explores the limits of knowledge and provides good analyses of biblical wisdom books.

Les Sagesses du Proche Orient ancien (1963).
Essays from a colloquium in Strasbourg in 1962.

Claus Westermann, *Wurzeln der Weisheit: Die ältesten Sprüche Israels und anderer Völker* (1990).
Studies the social context within which Israelite wisdom flourished.

R. N. Whybray, *The Intellectual Tradition in the Old Testament* (1974).
Views wisdom as a product of upper class intellectuals rather than a professional class.

14 (1980)

Impossible Questions, Sayings, and Tasks

Abstract. Like the related literary forms of riddle, numerical proverb, and question/answer dialogue, impossible questions appeal to generally accepted truth and evoke a sense of mystery. Although interrogative in form, impossible questions function as a strong statement and are particularly effective in didactic settings. Two noteworthy examples of such questions are those in Prov 6:27-28 ("Can a man carry fire in his bosom and his clothes not be burned? Or can one walk upon hot coals without scorching his feet?"). Their function here is to demonstrate the sheer stupidity of adulterous action. Impossible questions, sayings, and tasks heighten the sense of human frailty, inasmuch as they call attention to limits imposed upon intellectual and physical ventures. For example, "Go, weigh for me the weight of fire, or measure for me a measure of wind, or call back for me a day that is past" (2 Esdr 4:5) paves the way toward skepticism in ancient Israel.

Affinities between riddles, numerical proverbs, question and answer dialogue, and impossible questions extend beyond surface similarities to the essential characteristics of each genre. In every instance, argument proceeds from consensus, that which is universally recognized to be true. In addition, certain features of each genre isolate cause for amazement, evoking a sense of awe in the presence of mystery. While tracing the contours of these literary forms, one has the feeling of traveling the road to skepticism. The ancient Israelite sages who ventured forth on this rugged terrain were few; few in number, too, have been contemporary interpreters who have studied the aforementioned genres (Wünsche; Müller; Perdue; Roth; Tur Sinai), with the exception of proverbs (above all: Thompson; McKane). Elsewhere I have attempted to understand the form and function of riddles (1978), as well as the question and answer dialogue (1979). The focus of this essay will therefore fall upon impossible questions, sayings, and tasks. But first I wish to say a few more words about the kinship between riddles, numerical proverbs, question and answer dialogue, and impossible questions.

The riddle Samson proposed to the thirty Philistines who attended his wedding in Timnah signals the essential characteristics of that genre in ancient Israel.

From the *eater food* goes forth,
and from the *powerful one sweetness* proceeds. (Judg 14:14)

Once we penetrate beneath external trappings such as fondness for initial *mem* and succinct poetic form, we discover the essence of riddles: ciphers that function simultaneously as clue and snare. In this brief riddle four Hebrew words function on two fundamentally different levels, which I shall call appearance and essence. "Eater," "food," "powerful one," and "sweetness" represent equivocation on Samson's part. Each cipher points beyond itself to a deeper meaning, which worthy persons comprehend.

On the one hand, cipher language deceives the hearer, leading to false interpretation of the riddle. The transparent meaning of Samson's חִידָה moves on the level of appearance. From a groom (the eater, the powerful one) goes semen (food, sweetness). The story of Joseph's heroic resistance of Potiphar's wife leaves no doubt that such ciphers enriched Israel's vocabulary. Here the narrator emphasizes the only thing Potiphar denied Joseph—the food which he ate (Gen 39:6)—and has the handsome first example of sexual harassment of a worker explain that Potiphar's wife was that food denied him (39:9). Similarly, Prov 30:20 reads: "This is the *modus operandi* of an adulteress—she eats, wipes her mouth, and says, 'I have done nothing amiss.'" From this imagery, it is a small journey to Sirach's brief maxim: "To a fornicator all bread tastes sweet" (23:17), or to Dame Folly's pungent invitation: "Stolen water is sweet, and bread eaten in secret is pleasant" (Prov 9:17 RSV). To recapitulate, Samson coined his riddle in such fashion as to ensnare the Philistines in an erotic net. Failing this, he offered a trap on another surface level. One can readily explain the riddle as vomit which soldiers at the wedding grudgingly gave up.

On a deeper level Samson's ciphers alluded to a lion and honey retrieved from its carcass. That is, they offered a decisive clue that conceals truth at the same time that it divulges important information. Thus it follows that riddles depend upon language's ambiguity. Like myths, which endeavor to communicate heavenly reality in earthly language, riddles must be interpreted (Müller: 472-77). In yet another way riddles resemble myths: once ciphers become familiar language, they lose their depth dimension—the power to trap or to inform concerning ultimate mystery.

In one sense, as André Jolles (131-33) recognized, riddles constitute a test. Their twofold intention can best be compared to examinations within the court room and schools. In the former, an examiner, the prosecuting attorney, endeavors to discover what the examined already knows. In the class room, the examiner knows the answers and tries to identify others who have access to this information. Especially useful in dealing with demonic powers, cipher imagery also avoids straight talk in the erotic realm. On occasion, riddles dispense with language altogether, and symbolic behavior offers simultaneous clue or trap. Naturally, riddles belong to diverse settings: weddings, the royal court, entrance rituals, and schools.

Excitement of discovery accompanies the opening of a riddle. Mystery yields its closely guarded secret to a worthy seeker, who demonstrates ability to avoid traps in the quest for essence. Returning to Samson's riddle, we note that it captures an essential characteristic of the sexual experience: the groom feeds his bride. An ancient Sumerian sage put it this way: "Has she become pregnant without intercourse? Has she become fat without eating?" (Lambert, 247). One wonders whether the well-known Sumerian riddle of the school did not also function as *double entendre*: "One whose eyes are not open enters it, one whose eyes have been opened comes out from it." In any case, the sexual connotation of the imagery of entering and open eyes is indisputable.

In this instance, as in Samson's riddle, disclosed mystery threatens to become commonplace knowledge and forces alternative solutions to be thrust forward. Thus many riddles yield more than one depth meaning, increasing their power to mislead as well as their capacity to communicate. Those riddles for which no additonal solutions presented themselves eventually lost their power to deceive. This is why, I think, so few genuine riddles occur in the Hebrew Scriptures: most of them disintegrated into harmless metaphors. The interpreter is thus faced with the task of reconstructing ancient riddles. A single example suffices. In my view, Qoheleth cites a riddle in his ironic comments about the supposed advantages of life over death: "A living dog is better than a dead lion" (9:4). Both *dog* and *lion* are ciphers signifying members of the lowest and highest social strata respectively. Would not this riddle serve as defense of a widow's remarriage, this time to one who could hardly compare with her former husband? Who knows what surprises await those who patiently search the Scriptures! For the moment, however, I wish to venture forth in still another direction—charting the affinities between riddles and related forms, especially numerical proverbs, question and answer dialogues, and impossible questions.

Proverbs encapsulate the universally true (Thompson, 23). Herein lies their secret sway over human minds: they compel assent at the deeper level of meaning. When numerical proverbs juxtapose several phenomena and introduce excitement of discovery, they penetrate to the level of intrinsic relationship. If ciphers appear, similarities with riddles mount, as Herder saw with exceptional clarity. For example, the comparison of an eagle, a serpent, a ship, and a man with a woman in Prov 30:18-19 employs the cipher "way" and suggests a harmonious universe behind such diverse activity that leaves no trace of its movement. Still, a decisive difference between this proverb and riddles stands out: it lacks an intention to deceive. Unless I am mistaken, all numerical proverbs in the Bible depart from riddles at precisely this point.

Question and answer dialogue, or contest literature, shares a common atmosphere with riddles—strife. In addition, the former uses deceptive understatement to overcome opposition. Nevertheless, such contests sacrifice excitement of discovery by giving the answer at the outset. The exquisite question and answer dialogue in 1 Esdr 3–4 reverses the procedure from what takes place in riddles. The answers (wine, king, women, and truth) provoke great expectations as king and nobles await explanations for these particular responses to the question: "what is strongest?" In this instance emphasis shifts to rhetoric, and entertainment seems to be the desired end (Goodman).

Impossible questions resemble riddles in their fascination for the inconceivable, which evokes disbelief. Confronted by both, the person addressed expresses surprise or astonishment. Riddles and impossible questions strain one's credulity; they frequently give birth to skepticism. Who would ever think that food goes forth from the eater? Or that a wild ass's colt would be born a man? (Job 11:12). When impossible questions use ciphers, affinities with riddles become impressive indeed. It follows that a closer examination of this genre in the Hebrew Scriptures is long overdue. Before attempting such, I wish to call attention to the moods characterizing the forms I have thus far discussed. In my judgment, riddles emphasize malice, numerical proverbs focus upon eros, question and answer dialogue captures humor, often grim, and impossible questions concentrate on wonder.

In form, if not in substance, the Philistines' answer to Samson's riddle resembles impossible questions: "What is sweeter than honey; what is stronger than a lion?" (Judg 14:18). One answer, of course, is love, under whose powerful wings Samson had come to rest. This juxtaposition of riddles and impossible questions (and tasks) occurs also in Arabic legends which expound upon the story of Solomon and Sheba as recorded in the Targum to Esther. I shall mention two of these riddles and one impossible task. The latter asks what thirst-quenching water comes neither from heaven nor from earth. Solomon answers: "Nothing is easier: let a horse gallop and gather the sweat." The two riddles contain implicit questions. The first reads: "It doesn't fall from heaven or spring up from the earth; it runs sweet and bitter from a glass." The answer, of course, is tears, and the cipher "glass" refers to eyes. The other riddle asks about Jonah "The dead lived, the grave moves, and the dead prays—what is that?" (Schechter). Here "grave" functions as a cipher, and the "dead" constitutes an existential paradox.

We shall begin an investigation of biblical impossible questions at Prov 6:27-28.

Can a man carry fire in his bosom and his clothes not be burned?
Or can one walk upon hot coals without scorching his feet?

Occurring within a larger didactic unit (6:20-35), these questions demand a negative answer and function as the equivalent of a strong statement: no one can carry live coals in his garments without setting them on fire, and nobody can walk on glowing coals without burning his feet. Alongside these impossible questions stands another query which requires a positive response: "Do we not despise a thief who steals to satisfy his hunger?" (30). Each type of question appeals to consensus; only one devoid of sense would dare dispute what everyone knows to be true.

The didactic unit consists of a brief familial instruction (20-23), to which has been joined a warning against the arch villain, the adulteress (24-35). The warning consists of an initial statement of the problem (24-26), an argument from consensus (27-28), specific application (29), supporting argument (30-31), and conclusion (32-35). The unit juxtaposes two kinds of fire burning within the human heart: parental teaching, which shines radiantly like a lamp, and consuming passion for another man's wife. A reference to discipline's guidance appropriately links the two fires, inasmuch as sages must practice self-mastery to kindle the one and to extinguish the other. Language of intimacy punctuates the discussion, thereby guarding against taking the threat posed by the adulteress lightly. So do euphemisms. The description of an adulterer as "one who goes into his neighbor's wife" and "one who touches her" suggests that "coals of fire" and "feet" carry an erotic undertone, just as "thief" and "hunger" point beyond a literal sense to theft of sexual favors. Perhaps, too, the allusion to bread as the bargain price a harlot offers as compared to an adulteress was chosen precisely because of its rich double meaning.

Perhaps this *penchant* for *double entendre* explains the strange use of נֹאֵף אִשָּׁה (32), surely a redundant phrase since everywhere else נֹאֵף alone suffices to connote an adulterous act. Inasmuch as a man cannot commit adultery with another man, the specification of woman here hardly seems necessary. Lacking the collective insights of interpreters, who seem not to have noticed the problem, I offer a tentative solution: the author added אִשָּׁה in his concluding observation because of its similarity with אֵשׁ, thus returning to the motif of fire that pervades the entire unit.

The artistry of this textual unit invites closer examination. Verses 20-23 constitute parental teaching, although the imagery is at home in legal and psalmic contexts as well.

> My son, guard your father's directive
>   and do not let fall your mother's teaching.
> Secure them upon your heart always,
>   tie them around your neck.
> When you walk, she [Dame Wisdom] will lead you,
>   when you lie down, she will watch over you,
>   and upon your awaking, she will talk with you.
> For the directive is a lamp, the teaching, a light,
>   reproof and correction, the way to life.

The familial setting for this subunit is virtually assured. Besides using בְּנִי (my son), the author refers to father and mother as the sources of instruction. To be sure, reference to "my son" eventually functions as guild language to designate a student, but it does not seem to have that sense here. In fact, even the imagery accords well with a family setting: going about daily tasks, sleeping, rising.

The synonymous parallelism in verse 20 is strained by the peculiar juxtaposition of positive and negative verbs, as well as by the direct address which occurs only once. In truth, the parallelism takes place at the level of genus: parents, teaching. The father and mother are no more synonymous than are the specific gifts they hand on to their children: מִצְוָה (commandment, directive) and תּוֹרָה (teaching, instruction). The plural suffix in verse 21 distinguishes the paternal directive from the mother's teaching. The verbs emphasize the priceless quality of such parental legacy, which is to be treasured above all else. According to Prov 22:15, folly can be bound up in the heart of a lad, and chastisement can drive it out. In 6:21, the adverb תָּמִיד addresses the possibility that hearts may vacillate: the son must secure the teachings *always*.

The syntax of the three verbs in verse 22 is striking. The first two are infinitive constructs, while the third is a verb followed by the personal pronoun הִיא (she). Presumably, the feminine subject of these verses is Dame Wisdom. The following verse alters the expected sequence noticeably: "for a lamp is the commandment, the teaching, a light." The final colon returns to the original pattern of introducing the metaphor before referring to the actual object of concern: "the way of life (is) correction (and) discipline." The assonance in Hebrew (אוֹר/תּוֹרָה), difficult in English translation, is reproduced in Latin (*lex/lux*).

The next subunit introduces a problem which will be addressed by the legacy bequeathed from parents to children. The initial statement of the danger facing the son occurs in verses 24-26.

> To keep you from the evil wife,
>> from the enticing speech of a foreign woman.
> Do not desire her beauty in your heart,
>> nor be captured by her eyelids.
> For on account of a woman, a harlot, right to a loaf of bread,
>> but a man's wife hunts precious life.

Transition from the previous verses is achieved by means of the verb שָׁמַר, here used of preserving one from danger. Precisely how such teaching accomplishes this goal is not specified. Although the Septuagintal reading of רֵע (stranger) instead of רַע (evil) necessitates no consonantal change, the Massoretic Text makes perfectly good sense. As in verse 20, an active verb gives way to a passive one in verse 25. Lustful stirrings within the heart make one susceptible to coquettish glances. With remarkable power the attractiveness of adultery is acknowledged, particularly in predominantly physical imagery (smooth tongue, lust in the heart, beauty, eyelids). A sharp contrast between an ordinary harlot and a married woman follows: whereas a harlot can be had for a piece of bread—a particularly apt price because of the erotic meaning of bread familiar to ancient sages—a man's wife hunts for something far more expensive. In verse 26 the strange syntax provides a subtle hint of the rake's singleminded race toward sensual gratification (Kidner, 74).

At this point two impossible questions appear (27-28) and make a cogent argument from universally acknowledged fact. No one carries live coals in his clothes with impunity, and nobody walks barefoot on red hot embers without burning his feet. Of course the fire recalls insatiable lust, and the euphemistic use of feet in many contexts suggests that the imagery could hardly be improved.

Verse 29 applies the impossible questions to the danger under discussion.

So is anyone who goes into his neighbor's wife;
    none who touches her will escape punishment.

Wildeboer (21) has perceived the original sense of the verb in the first half of this verse: it referred to a man's entering the part of a tent where women plied their trade. Restraint characterizes this unit from first to last, despite the volatile subject. Euphemisms literally impregnate the vocabulary of this entire text.

Apparently, the author felt the need to buttress his argument in every way possible. Accordingly, a supporting observation underlines the cost of philandering (30-31).

Do we not despise a thief if he steals
    to satisfy his appetite when hungry?
Caught, he will pay sevenfold;
    yea, he will forfeit the entirety of his household goods.

The Massoretic Text does not have the interrogative ה, although some ancient manuscripts do. Perhaps the ה was lost because of the preceding בָּה (Frankenberg, 49). Otherwise, the verse seems to condone theft under certain circumstances, an altogether unlikely view, in my judgment. In any case, the referent seems to shift in verse 31, where the unfortunate person must be the adulterer, for we have already been informed that the starving thief lacks anything with which to pay.

The conclusion (32-35) focuses upon the severe penalty for invading the privacy of marriage.

The adulterer lacks sense,
    whoever does it injures himself.
A beating and disgrace he will discover,
    and (the husband's) anger will not be dispelled.
For a man's fury is jealous;
    he will not display mercy on the day of reckoning.
He will accept no compensation,
    nor will he be moved even if you increase the payoff.

Just as the thief lacked food, the adulterer was devoid of sense. No stronger word could be spoken within a sapiential setting. Qoheleth proceeds to articulate what this text implies. "The *fool* lacks sense" (10:3). In short, the adulterer is a fool.

We note the self-interest underlying this refutation of adultery. Such behavior is not dismissed because it offends divine laws, or even because it violates the sanctity of another individual or family. Joseph may have spurned forbidden pleasure for theological reasons, particularly when accompanied by anthropological-social ones. But this author goes one step further and appeals to self-interest. Under guise of love, another man's wife stalks life itself; touch her, and pay dearly. In Job 31:9-10 and Ahikar 2:6 still another reason is given for avoiding such contact: your own wife will have to surrender to the same ignominy.

Before taking leave of this remarkable didactic unit within which two impossible question are embedded, I wish to call attention to a brief passage in "The Protests of the Eloquent Peasant." Here we find three impossible questions, their practical application, and argument that a thief who is starving can be excused for his action. The impossible questions concern impartial justice: "Does the hand-scale err? Does the stand-balance incline to the side? Is even Thoth indulgent? Then thou (also) mayest work mischief. When thou makest thyself the second [footnote: in the sense of 'companion'] of these three, then thou (also) mayest be indulgent" (Pritchard, 409).

Like the eloquent peasant, Bildad found it impossible to imagine that God could pervert justice. In support of his defense of Shaddai, Job's friend quoted an impossible question that may come from Egyptian wisdom. In any case, the words for papyrus and rushes apparently derive from Egyptian (Tur-Sinai, 149; Pope, 66; Fohrer, 184).

> Can papyrus grow without marsh?
> Rushes flourish without water?   (Job 8:11 AB)

Just as lack of moisture destroys plants which thrive in a watery medium, so absence of virtue leads to an early death. Bildad's certainty in this matter prompts extreme cruelty—the assertion that Job's children had earned their punishment. Conceding that all knowledge is partial, Bildad urged Job to profit from accumulated tradition. The impossible question constitutes such capsular knowledge which was transmitted from one generation to another.

Although tempted to label Bildad's initial question, "Does God pervert justice? Does Shaddai distort the right?" an impossible question comparable to that about Thoth, and consequently to view it as an assertion, the refutation of the charge that God rejects the upright (8:20) makes this identification improbable. Obviously, Bildad's remarks about divine justice are subject to challenge. In short, consensus is lacking on this issue, even if present with regard to the question about papyrus and rushes used in its support.

The structure of Job 8 is terribly elusive, but does not seem to support the interpretation of 8:13 ("Such is the fate of all who forget God; the hope of the impious will perish") as a summary appraisal form (Childs, 133). In my view the entire speech is a tightly woven unit. The introduction alludes to false speech (8:2), offers a theological motto (8:3), and draws a natural conclusion therefrom (8:4). The main body of the speech urges continued loyalty and attempts to demonstrate the truth of the theological affirmation couched in question form. To do so, it distinguishes between external appearance and reality: apparent prosperity will vanish in a moment (8:5-19). The conclusion reaffirms the theological motto (8:20), and acknowledges reversal of the false speech (8:21) and victims of divine punishment (8:22). Because God does not pervert justice, laughter will replace Job's idle banter and his enemies, not his children, will perish.

Still other impossible questions occur in connection with weighing in balances (Job 6:5-6; cf. 6:2).

> Does the ass bray over his grass?
> The bull bellow over his fodder?
> Can flat food be eaten unsalted?
> Is there flavor in slimy cream cheese?   (AB)

Whereas the previously discussed impossible questions were integral to their contexts, these hardly advance the argument. Presumably, Job justifies his complaints in terms of an absence of a functioning reward system.

The student of Amos will recognize affinities with that prophet's argument from consensus:

> Do horses run upon rocks?
> Does one plow the sea with oxen?   (6:12 RSV)

An important difference occurs both here and in Jeremiah:

> Can a maiden forget her ornaments,
> or a bride her attire?   (2:32 RSV)

In each instance the impossible has occurred: the people have turned justice into poison, and those who have pledged their loyalty to the Lord have forgotten him "days without number." The other example in Amos (3:3-8) also departs from the customary form of the impossible question. Here, ordinary actions exercise such power over humans that they cannot resist certain consequences. When lions roar, or battle trumpets sound, it is impossible to vanquish fear. How different these cause and effect questions are from the true impossible question in Jeremiah:

> Can the Ethiopian change his skin
> or the leopard his spots?   (13:23 RSV)

If such transformation were possible, which it isn't, Jeremiah contended, then Judah, accustomed to doing evil, could also do good.

In Sirach the impossible question resembles the numerical proverb:

> The sand of the sea, the drops of rain,
> and the days of eternity—who can count them?
> The height of heaven, the breadth of the earth,
> the abyss, and wisdom—who can search them out?   (1:2-3 RSV)

Here two questions apply to seven items, and come after them. One could easily rephrase the passage as follows: three things cannot be counted, yea, four cannot be found out. Regardless of the form, this text brings us remarkably close to impossible tasks, which folklorists link with impossible questions.

> Go, weigh for me the weight of fire,
>> or measure for me a measure of wind,
>> or call back for me the day that is past.   (2 Esdr 4:5 RSV)

The angel thus poses no small tasks for Ezra, who had complained of inability to believe in divine justice. Recognizing the impossibility of accomplishing any of these assignments, Ezra objects that none born of woman could achieve such things. Undaunted, the angel reverts to impossible questions:

> How many dwellings are in the heart of the sea,
>> or how many streams are at the source of the deep,
>> or how many streams are above the firmament,
>> or which are the exits of hell,
>> or which are the entrances of paradise?   (2 Esdr 4:7 RSV)

In defense, the angel chides Ezra with stark reality—he had earlier asked about things through which Ezra had passed and without which he could not exist (fire, wind, time). The angel's final display of impossible tasks returns to the realm of ordinary experience:

> Count up for me those who have not yet come,
>> and gather for me the scattered raindrops,
>> and make the withered flowers bloom again for me;
>> open for me the closed chambers,
>> and bring forth for me the winds shut up in them,
>> or show me the picture of a voice; . . .   (2 Esdr 5:36-37 RSV)

These impossible questions and tasks within 2 Esdras stand at the apex of an intellectual movement—the birth of skepticism. Numerous passages in Job, Proverbs, and Qoheleth reveal the agony of this birth.

> Who has ascended to heaven and come down?
>> Who has gathered the wind in his fists?
> Who has wrapped up the waters in a garment?
>> Who has established all the ends of the earth?
> What is his name and what is his son's name?
>> Surely you know!   (Prov 30:4 RSV)

This text constitutes a dialogue between a skeptic and a believer; for that reason, it is difficult to determine whether these questions express a faith affirmation or utter skepticism couched in irony.

Regardless of our resolution of this difficult problem we must admit that impossible questions fanned the flames of pessimism and heightened the theodicy question for ancient Israelites accustomed to solving most questions. Certainly, Job 28:12 ("But where shall wisdom be found? And where is the place of understanding?") was not so easily resolved as the equation of wisdom and fear of the Lord in 28:28 implies. The divine questions addressed to Job from the whirlwind only intensified the feeling of impotency that Agur and others like him confessed to constitute a living nightmare.

We are not surprised, therefore, when Qoheleth expresses himself in a similar manner.

> Consider the work of God;
>> who can make straight what he has made crooked?   (7:13 RSV)
> That which is, is far off, and deep, very deep;
>> who can find it out?   (7:24 RSV)

We are thus reminded of a passage in "A Pessimistic Dialogue between Master and Servant" (Pritchard, 438):

> Who is tall enough to ascend to heaven?
> Who is broad enough to embrace the earth?

We may also compare an Akkadian proverb (Pritchard, 425):

> Will ripe grain grow?
> How do we know?
> Will dried grain grow?
> How do we know?

The author of Deut 30:11-14 sought to counteract the force of such skepticism in Israel at an earlier date.

> For this commandment . . . is not too hard for you, neither is it far off. It is not in heaven, that you should say, "Who will go up for us to heaven, and bring it to us, that we may hear it and do it?" Neither is it beyond the sea, that you should say, "Who will go over the sea for us, and bring it to us, that we may hear it and do it?" But the word is very near you; it is in your mouth and in your heart, so that you can do it.   (RSV)

At times we cannot tell whether we are dealing with an impossible question or saying. For example, Job 11:12 may actually be a question: "Can a stupid man get understanding, or can a wild ass's colt be born a man?" On the other hand, it may be a saying similar to Ovid's, "Then will the stag fly!" Actually, we can cite impossible sayings from a Semitic source. In Ahikar, we find the following comment (Charles, 2:737, 739):

> My son, if the waters should stand up without earth,
>> and the sparrow fly without wings,
>> and the raven become white as snow,
>> and the bitter become sweet as honey,
> then may the fool become wise.   (Syr A 2:62)

The Armenian version differs somewhat:

Son, if the rivers pause in their courses,
  or the sun in its career,
  or if the gall become sweet as honey,
  or the raven turn white as the dove,
even so will the senseless man abandon his want of sense
  and the fool become sensible.   (2:83)

In Ahikar we find impossible tasks as well: Building a castle between earth and heaven, making cables from the sand of the river, sewing up a broken millstone. But in these instances Ahikar's ingenuity succeeds in satisfying the person who commissioned the tasks, even if by clever ploys (Charles 2:762-66).

In these examples the impossible sayings occur within a narrative setting (cf. Qoh 1:15). In short, questions have given way to statement or observation that calls attention to the impossible character of certain things. So far we have not mentioned a related form, the paradoxical proverb that Bent Alster has discovered in Sumerian literature (207-208). I list a few examples.

Do not heap up a mountain in the mountains.
Do not cut off the neck of that which has had its neck cut off.
From 3,600 oxen there is no dung.
The dog has climbed up on the roof.
A scribe without a hand, a singer without a throat.
Make the distant side the nearer side.

But here we move into the broader area of paradox, where juxtaposition of incompatible words, like "exalted fool" or "dying, we live" occurs, an expression that also appears in "The Instruction of the Vizier Ptah-Hotep" as "dying while alive every day" (Pritchard, 414). Discussion of the existential paradox takes us beyond the topic announced for this essay.

Before closing, however, I wish to make one observation about the mood characterizing these examples of the impossible question. I have suggested that "wonder" best describes the feeling evoked by this literary form. Now this concentrated focus upon the impossible task early produced a reaction that struck at the very heart of wisdom. Skeptics seized this literary form to attack the possibility of knowing anything significant (Qoh 3:11), and others used the impossible question to squelch open dissent. In the end, emphasis upon God's superior knowledge brought scant comfort to sensitive persons caught up in the paradox of divine grace and wrath. The authors of Deut 30:11-14 and 2 Esdras stand so far apart that none can bring them together. Between wonder as worship and wonder as human incapacity, a deep abyss stretches. "Who can make the distant side near?" This bringing together of two separate realms, essence and appearance, was the distinctive role of riddles. I find it difficult to stifle the suspicion that in doing so, riddles gave birth to an unwanted child—skepticism. During the pangs of childbirth, impossible questions performed midwife service.

Works Consulted

Alster, B.
1975   "Paradoxical Proverbs and Satire in Sumerian Literature." *JCS* 27:201-30.
Bertheau, E.
1847   *Die Sprüche Salomons. Kritische exegetische Handbuch zum Alten Testament.* Leipzig: Weidemanns'sche Buchhandlung.
Box, G. H.
1913   "IV Ezra," in *The Apocrypha and Pseudepigrapha of the Old Testament*, ed. R. H. Charles. Volume 2. Oxford: Clarendon.
Brueggemann, W.
1973   "Jeremiah's Use Of Rhetorical Questions." *JBL* 92:358-74.
Childs, B. S.
1967   *Isaiah and the Assyrian Crisis.* SBT 2/3. London: SCM.
Charles, R. H.
1913/1963   *The Apocrypha and Pseudepigrapha of the Old Testament.* Two volumes. Oxford: Clarendon.
Cohen, A.
1945   *Proverbs.* Chesham: Soncino.
Crenshaw, James L.
1974   "Wisdom." In *Old Testament Form Criticism*, ed. John H. Hayes, 225-64. San Antonio: Trinity University.
1975   "The Problem of Theodicy in Sirach: On Human Bondage." *JBL* 94:47-64.
1976   "Riddle." In *Interpreter's Dictionary of the Bible*, supplementary volume, 749-50. Nashville and London: Abingdon.
1978   *Samson: A Secret Betrayed, A Vow Ignored.* Atlanta: John Knox.
1979   "The Contest of Darius's Pages," submitted for possible publication in *The Old Testament Short Story*, ed. B. O. Long. Missoula MT: Scholars Press.
Dhorme, E.
1967   *A Commentary on the Book of Job.* London: Nelson.
Fohrer, G.
1963   *Das Buch Hiob.* KAT. Gütersloh: Mohn.
Frankenberg, W.
1898   *Die Sprüche, Prediger und Hoheslied.* HKAT. Göttingen: Vandenhoeck & Ruprecht.
Gemser, B.
1963   *Sprüche Salomos.* HAT. Tübingen: Mohr (Siebeck).
Goodman, W. R., Jr.
1971   "A Study of 1 Esdras 3:1–5:6." Ph.D. dissertation, Duke University.
Herder, J. G.
1833   *The Spirit of Hebrew Poetry.* Burlington: Edward Smith.
Jolles, André
1968   *Einfache Formen.* Darmstadt: Wissenschaftliche Buchgesellschaft. (Orig. Tübingen: Niemeyer, 1930).
Kidner, D.
1964   *Proverbs.* TynOTC. Downers Grove IL. InterVarsity.

Lambert, W. G.
1960   *Babylonian Wisdom Literature*. Oxford: Clarendon.
McKane, W.
1970   *Proverbs*. OTL. Philadelphia: Westminster.
Müller, H. P.
1970   "Der Begriff 'Rätsel' im Alten Testament." *VT* 20:465-89.
Perdue, L. G.
1973   "The Riddles of Psalm 49." *JBL* 93:533-42.
Pohlmann, K.-F.
1970   *Studien zum dritten Esra*. Göttingen: Vandenhoeck & Ruprecht.
Pope, M. H.
1973   *Job*. AB 15. Garden City NY: Doubleday.
Pritchard, James B.
1955   *Ancient Near Eastern Texts Relating to the Old Testament*. Second edition. Princeton NJ: Princeton University Press.
Rad, Gerhard von
1972   *Wisdom in Israel*. New York and Nashville: Abingdon.
Roth, W. M. W.
1965   *Numerical Sayings in the Old Testament: A Form-Critical Study*. VTSup 13. Leiden: E. J. Brill.
Sauer, G.
1963   *Die Sprüche Agurs*. BWANT 84. Stuttgart: Kohlhammer.
Schechter, S.
1890   "The Riddles of Solomon in Rabbinic Literature." *Folklore* 1:349-58.
Thompson, John Mark
1974   *The Form and Function of Proverbs in Ancient Israel*. The Hague: Mouton.
Toy, C. H.
1899   *The Book of Proverbs*. ICC. Edinburgh: Clark.
Tur-Sinai, N. H. (Torczyner, H.)
1924   "The Riddle in the Bible." *HUCA* 1:125-49.
1967   *The Book of Job*. Jerusalem: Kiryath Sepher.
Wildeboer, G.
1897   *Die Sprüche*. KHC. Tübingen: Mohr (Siebeck).
Wolff, H. W.
1964   *Amos geistige Heimat*. WMANT 18. Neukirchen-Vluyn: Neukirchener Verlag.
Wünsche, A.
1883   *Die Räthselweisheit bei den Hebräern mit hinblick auf andere alte Völker*. Leipzig: Schulze.

15 (1986)

The Expression
מִי יוֹדֵעַ
in the Hebrew Bible

The expression מִי יוֹדֵעַ occurs ten times in the Hebrew Bible, and most if not all instances are in postexilic texts (2 Sam 12:22; Joel 2:14; Jonah 3:9; Ps 90:11; Esth 4:14; Prov 24:22; Qoh 2:19; 3:21; 6:12; 8:1; the possible exception is 2 Sam 12:22). The subjects of anticipated action vary from God, who is mentioned twice and implied once, to a human being, who happens to be female. Where no action is contemplated, the object of the rhetorical question covers a broad spectrum (an unknown heir, calamity, divine wrath, what is good, the animating life principle, and the interpretation of a word).

In four instances the expression מִי יוֹדֵעַ stands at the beginning of a sentence (2 Sam 12:22; Joel 2:14; Jonah 3:9; Ps 90:11), and once it dangles at the end (Prov 24:22). Three times, possibly four, the rhetorical question follows a conjunction (waw);[1] once מִי יוֹדֵעַ appears after the particle כִּי (Qoh 6:12). Only twice do particles occur to indicate an either/or situation (Esth 4:14, אִם, and Qoh 2:19, אוֹ). Within three texts the expression attracts a specific cluster of words (be gracious; turn and repent; 2 Sam 12:22; Joel 2:14; Jonah 3:9).[2] The semantic field in Qoheleth is broader; the following clauses occur in connection with the rhetorical question, מִי יוֹדֵעַ: who can tell him? who can say? one does not know; the wise know; the dead know nothing (see 8:4, 7; 9:1, 5; 10:14; 11:5-6).

The occurrences of מִי יוֹדֵעַ fall into two distinct groups when viewed from the standpoint of the alternatives presented by the rhetorical question. Five of them leave a door open to possible response that will change the situation for human good, and the other five seem to assume a closed door to any redeeming action. It comes as no surprise that the latter texts occur in Qoheleth, with one exception (Prov 24:22).

---

[1]Esth 4:14; Qoh 2:19; 8:1; and perhaps 3:21 (LXX and Syriac).

[2]The three verbs play a significant role in Moses' intercession for wayward people (Exod 32:12, שׁוּב מֵחֲרוֹן אַפֶּךָ and the disclosure of the deity's nature (Exod 34:6-7 יְהוָה יְהוָה אֵל רַחוּם וְחַנּוּן).

A. An Open Door

1. 2 Sam 12:22: "Who knows whether the Lord will be merciful to me so that the child may live?"[3] Here we have a self-citation attributed to King David; the occasion was the death of Bathsheba's child, the consequence of royal lust. The story of David's desperate attempt to influence God's decision throbs with wonder and astonishment, for the king made a sharp break with traditional behavior under the circumstances. In the face of a prophetic announcement that sealed the infant's fate, David dared to hope that his fasting and weeping might bring about a change in the divine heart. Failing in that endeavor, he promptly proceeded to eat and to get on with the business of living. When questioned about his unusual behavior, David reminded his interrogators that hope remained as long as there was breath,[4] but when that precious commodity was snuffed out not even fasting could reverse the situation. To be sure, David's hope in this instance was ill-founded, but his use of מִי יוֹדֵעַ functions in the same way the prophetic אוּלַי ("perhaps") does in Amos v 15 and comparable passages. The emphasis falls on the sovereignty of God, but human beings still dare to hope that compassion will gain the upper hand.

2. Joel 2:14: "Who knows whether [the Lord] will turn and repent, leaving behind a blessing . . . ?" In vv 1-11 it appears that a prophetic oracle of judgement has shut the door against any future possibility, but a call to repentance is nonetheless introduced in vv 12-14 (But even now). This tiny ray of hope arises from two realities: the divine nature and the power of repentance. The former echoes a revered priestly torah, the credal affirmation from the divine disclosure to Moses (Exod 34:6-8), and the latter pushes beyond ritual practice to genuine moral renewal. Here, too, fasting and weeping find a place, along with hearts, rather than garments, that are torn. We cannot be sure what the impact of this appeal was, though it serves to justify the divine decision to allow the day of the Lord to dawn with terrible consequences for one and all. Nevertheless, the מִי יוֹדֵעַ serves as the prophetic "perhaps," thereby leaving open a remote possibility of reprieve.[5]

3. Jonah 3:9: "Who knows whether God will turn and repent, turning from intense anger so that we do not perish?" The affinities with Joel 2:14 are easily perceived, and if one considers the larger context, they extend to a citation of Exod

---

[3]The translations are mine.

[4]Walter Brueggemann, *In Man We Trust* (Richmond, 1972) 36, sees David's conduct as "an act of profound faith in the face of the most precious tabus of his people." Brueggemann goes further to assert that "it is not freedom from the moment of death, but from the power of death as it has often been described in myth (e.g., Hos 13–14)."

[5]"That the faithful and merciful God is also free in relation to his own anger ('slow to anger' אֶרֶךְ אַפַּיִם) is the foundation of the hope expressed in the 'perhaps'" (Hans Walter Wolff, *Joel and Amos* [Philadelphia, 1977] 50 = *Joel und Amos* [Neukirchen-Vluyn, 1969] 59). Wolff calls attention to Zeph 2:3; Lam 3:29b; and Exod 32:30 for use of אוּלַי in the same sense as מִי יוֹדֵעַ in Joel 2:14.

24:6-8. The king of Nineveh and his nobles proclaimed a fast that embraced all human beings and animals, and that demonstrated true conversion. Although there is no mention of weeping, the text does refer to crying mightily to God, which probably means fervent prayer. Both here and in Joel 2:14 the reference to God's potential turning and repentance may represent a short form of the oft-heard refrain in Deuteronomy and in passages of Jeremiah that reflect Deuteronomistic influence.[6] In any event, Jonah 3:9 uses מִי יוֹדֵעַ in the same way the previous passages from 2 Samuel and Joel do, with one significant difference. In Jonah the human endeavor to change destiny works: God is portrayed as repenting. Whereas the beloved David (and possibly the chosen people) had failed to evoke a favorable response, these despised inhabitants of Nineveh succeeded, much to the chagrin of the prophet Jonah.[7]

4. Esth 4:14: "But if you are indeed silent at this time, help and deliverance will arise for the Jews from another source, and you will die, along with your father's house; and who knows whether you have arrived at the kingdom for a time like this?" It is not necessary in this context to attempt an explanation for the much-discussed phrase מִמָּקוֹם אַחֵר (from another place), although I do not think it conceals an allusion to God, since such an interpretation would suggest that rescue might come at the hands of a deity other than Yahweh.[8] It suffices to note the reference to fasting in the story, and that this act of repentance is clearly intended to influence that heavenly one who is never mentioned in the book of Esther. In this instance Esther was fully prepared to perish if that was her lot, and she did not venture to use מִי יוֹדֵעַ. Instead, she bravely announced: "If I perish, I perish."[9] Here it was Mordecai who took up the expression, who knows?, and urged his niece to seize the opportunity afforded her by providence itself. Perhaps, the story intimates, her very presence in the royal harem was occasioned by the crisis that Haman and his cohorts had brought about.

Once again, מִי יוֹדֵעַ implies that decisive action may alter the present circumstances in ways that are eminently desirable. In this instance, however, the text does not suggest that a change in the deity represents the unknown reality addressed by the מִי יוֹדֵעַ. Whereas the deity in the three previous texts which use the rhetorical question had determined to punish innocent and guilty victims, in

---

[6]For recent study on the book of Jeremiah, see my essay entitled "A Living Tradition: The Book of Jeremiah in Current Research," *Int* 37 (1983): 117-29.

[7]Bruce Vawter, *Job and Jonah* (New York, 1983) 87-117, perceives the critique of prophetic language in Jonah and compares the two radical criticisms of wisdom and prophecy.

[8]To be sure, מָקוֹם came to be used as a surrogate for deity, but the adjective אַחֵר seems to rule that out here, since it would imply a deity other than Yahweh.

[9]The same resolve characterizes the three Hebrews faced with the threat of being thrown into a fiery furnace (Dan 3:17), although the story suggests that their troubles arose from religious conviction rather than from ethnic background.

Esth. iv 14 human beings openly conceived and implemented the threat. Indeed, it seems that such open hostility toward the Jews may be thwarted precisely because God has been at work behind the scenes putting a deliverer in place.[10]

5. Ps 90:11: "Who knows the intensity of your anger, and your wrath according to the fear of you?" The final text in this list of five begins a decisive transition toward the second group still to be examined. Nevertheless, it retains several features of the earlier ones (with the exception of Esth 4:14). Noteworthy is the association of turning and repenting in direct appeal to deity (v 13); naturally, such language grows out of an awareness of divine wrath, which threatens daily existence.

The new departure occurs in the area of meditation: "so teach us to number our days that we may acquire a wise mind" (v 12). Such insight uncovers the fact that God turns human beings to dust and that they vanish like images in a dream;[11] this knowledge also penetrates to the very nature of existence, one punctuated by sighs and toil. Here it is significant that divine reckoning and human time have little in common,[12] but such explanations for the longevity of the deity's wrath threaten to stifle all effort to secure relief. The sorry human predicament almost has a sense of inevitability—although not entirely, for appeal does eventually form on the lips of the poet.

To summarize the results of this investigation: in the first three texts מִי יוֹדֵעַ was used with reference to God's potential change of heart, in the fourth the rhetorical question inquired about the workings of providence and sought to enlist human assistance; and in the fifth text the expression came close to reflecting on the way things were, specifically human existence under divine wrath. In two cases מִי יוֹדֵעַ eventuated in the hoped-for change, and in the other three instances there were implicit grounds for believing that prompt action might affect one's destiny.

---

[10]Sandra Beth Berg, *The Book of Esther: Motifs, Themes, and Structure*, SBLDS 44 (Missoula MT, 1979) 177-79, recognizes a dual causality in the central passage, 4:13-14, and in the structure of the book. She writes: "They indicate that the narrator believed in a hidden causality behind the surface of human history, both concealing and governing the order and significance of events" (178).

[11]Perhaps the boldest expression of this idea occurs in Ps 73:19-20 which may imply that the deity awakes from a dream and obliterates the phantom figures (Martin Buber, "The Heart Determines," in *Theodicy in the Old Testament*, ed. James L. Crenshaw [Philadelphia and London, 1983] 204). On this psalm, see my recent book, *A Whirlpool of Torment* (Philadelphia, 1984) 93-109.

[12]Qoheleth comes close to a Greek conception of cyclical time, not only in the poem about the ceaseless movement of nature (1:3-11) but also in the astonishing assertion that whatever is, already existed, and future events have already occurred, and God seeks that which is driven away (3:15).

B. A Closed Door

The second group of texts in which מִי יוֹדֵעַ occurs differs enormously from those I have just discussed. The essential difference lies in the closed nature of the occurrences in Prov 24:22 and Qoh 2:19; 3:21; 6:12; 8:1. Here the rhetorical question functions overwhelmingly as an expression of skepticism. The emphasis falls on an absence of knowledge, and "who knows?" is a denial that anyone can achieve information in the area under consideration. The mood accompanying the rhetorical question is one of resigned inevitability.

1. Prov 24:22: "For calamity will suddenly arise, and destruction from both of them, who knows?" The two powers against whom a warning is tendered are God and king (v 21), and the person addressed is the son or pupil of a teacher. (Hos 3:5 brings together the Lord and the Davidic king in a similar fashion.) Another interpretation of v 22 is possible, and boasts versional support (Peshitta and Targum). Instead of reading שְׁנֵיהֶם one can point the word to refer to "their years," yielding "and the destruction of their years, who knows?" Alternatively, the ה can be dropped and the word pointed שָׁנִים (those given to change). This would repeat the idea in the preceding verse, which may be emended with the LXX to read "and do not disobey either of them." If, as seems likely, there is a Hebrew root שָׂנָה ("to be, or become, high, or exalted in rank," and also "to shine"), the verse could be translated as follows: "For their calamity will suddenly rise, and destruction from those of high rank, who knows?"[13]

A striking feature of this text is the use of מִי יוֹדֵעַ in the final position. This is the only time that phenomenon occurs. It is interesting that Prov 30:1-14 follows 24:22 in the LXX, and 30:4 has a final כִּי תֵדָע (surely you know). Since Vaticanus and Sinaiticus omit this ironic clause,[14] perhaps it is wise not to speculate about

---

[13]For a discussion of the opinions, see Otto Plöger, *Sprüche Salomos* (*Proverbia*) (Neukirchen/Vluyn, 1983) 264, 284; and William McKane, *Proverbs*, OTL (London and Philadelphia, 1970) 405-406. On the Hebrew root שָׂנָה ("to be, or become, high, or exalted") in Prov 24:21-22, see D. Winton Thomas, "Mitteilungen," *ZAW* 52 (1934): 236-38; L. Kopf, "Arabische Etymologien und Parallelen zum Bibelwörterbuch," *VT* 9 (1959): 280-83; and J. A. Emerton, "The meaning of שֵׂנָא in Psalm 127:2," *VT* 24 (1974): 15-31 (for a discussion of this root in several passages). Emerton accepted it in Prov 5:9; 14:17; 24:21-22, B. Sabb. 10b, and probably Sir 33:7; judged it possible but unlikely in Esth 2:9; considered it unnecessary in Isa 11:11; and thought it more questionable in Hab 3:2; Ps 68:18; Sir 8:1; Dan 7:23. Although Kopf understood Prov 24:22 in the same way as Thomas ("Denn plötzlich kommt ihr Verderben, und wer kennt den Untergang ihres höhen Ranges"), he differed greatly on the meaning of Prov 24:21a, which Kopf repointed to read: "Fürchte Gott, mein Sohn, und erwerbe Besitz" (מֶלַח for מֶלֶךְ).

[14]A similar use of כִּי תֵדָע occurs in Job 38:5, also within a context where questions about the original act of creation emphasize human ignorance and insignificance. The כִּי תֵדָע is reinforced by הַגֵּד אִם־יָדַעְתָּ בִינָה ("declare if you have understanding").

possible relationships between final מִי יוֹדֵעַ and כִּי חַרְעַ. In any event, the rhetorical question in Prov 24:22 serves to deny any useful knowledge about an impending stroke of misfortune.

2. Qoh 2:19: "And who knows whether he will be wise or a fool, but he will have control over all my reward for which I worked wisely under the sun, this also is absurd."[15] Here Qoheleth reflects on the unpleasant prospect of leaving his hard-earned fortune to someone else, who may or may not appreciate the sweat and hard work that went into acquiring it. The larger unit (2:18-23) explores in greater depth this fact that human beings have no permanent grasp on wealth, a point that elicits hatred of the temporary reward for one's labor. Faced with this surrender of life's fleeting gains, Qoheleth concludes that trouble and unrest prevail by day and night. Some critics[16] think this section incorporates a traditional saying as its closing observation: "For all his days are trouble and his striving a pain; even at night his mind does not rest" (v 23), but the evidence is problematic.[17]

3. Qoh 3:21: "Who knows whether the spirit of human beings ascends and the spirit of animals descends?"[18] The מִי יוֹדֵעַ sentence comprises part of Qoheleth's

---

[15]On translating הֶבֶל as "absurd," see the essay by M. V. Fox, "The Meaning of הֶבֶל for Qohelet," forthcoming in *JBL*. See also André Barucq, *Ecclésiaste* (Paris, 1967) passim (*absurdité*) and "Qoheleth (libre de l'Ecclésiaste ou de)," in *Supplément au Dictionnaire de la Bible*, ed. Henri Cazelles and André Feuillet, fasc 50B (Paris, 1977) 609-74, esp. 621 and 635. Even in those instances where הֶבֶל means fleeting, the primary sense of absurdity may also persist (3:19; 11:10; 6:12; 7:15; 9:9). Qoheleth's use of rhetorical questions has been discussed by Daniel Lys, *L'Ecclésiaste ou que vaut la vie?* (Paris, 1977) 263. For this literary device in Second Isaiah, see R. N. Whybray, *The Heavenly Counsellor in Isaiah XL 13-14* (Cambridge, 1971) 21-26 (questions beginning with or containing מִי). He writes that "it is hardly too much to say that the rhetorical question is the principal device of Hebrew rhetoric and oratory" (20). On the expression מִי יוֹדֵעַ, Whybray remarks that it may indicate a hopeful possibility (2 Sam 12:22; Joel 2:14; Jonah 3:9; Esth 4:14), human ignorance (Ps 90:11; Qoh 6:12), or doubt (Qoh 2:19; 3:21; so p. 23).

[16]Kurt Galling, *Der Prediger* (Tübingen, 1969) 91; A. Lauha, *Kohelet* (Neukirchen-Vluyn, 1978) 57.

[17]Adequate criteria for recognizing traditional sayings elude us, although considerable progress has been made. Three studies demonstrate the difficult task confronting interpreters: Robert Gordis, "Virtual Quotations in Job, Sumer, and Qumran," *VT* 31 (1981) 410-27; R. N. Whybray, "The Identification and Use of Quotations in Qoheleth," *Congress Volume: Vienna 1980*, SVT 32 (1981) 435-51; and C. R. Fontaine, *Traditional Sayings in the Old Testament* (Sheffield, 1982). On the prominence of this issue in Qoheleth studies, see my essay in the Gordis *Festschrift* ("Qoheleth in Current Research," *HAR* 7 [1983]: 41-56).

[18]Despite the vocalization of the interrogative ה as if it were an article the copula הִיא requires the translation given above. Although many critics interpret this anomaly as evidence that the Massoretes refused to allow such heterodox views to remain unchanged, Gordis thinks the pointing can be explained as resulting from initial א and ‏ ‎ (*Koheleth—The Man and His World*, 3rd ed. [New York, 1968] 238).

reflection about a common end for all creatures (3:16-22). The section begins with a statement about the universality of wickedness; this strong claim uses two notions that lay at the heart of a just society: justice and righteousness. In Qoheleth's opinion, both qualities had been banished from the human realm. The next verse subscribes to traditional views about divine justice and contradicts Qoheleth's teaching elsewhere (9:10); scholars therefore usually attribute the verse to a later glossator.[19] The following verse (18) introduces the conclusion which Qoheleth has drawn from evil's pervasive character: "I reasoned concerning human beings that God is surely testing them[20] so as to show them that they in themselves are but beasts."[21] Qoheleth then proceeds to offer the reason for this unusual observation and to articulate a practical implication from it. Essentially, Qoheleth argues that all creatures, human and animal, share a common fate, namely death.[22] Since there is no convincing proof that the human life principle goes up toward the heavens and that the animating principle of beasts goes down to the earth, it seems wise to reach out for happiness now. That conclusion is reinforced by the general consensus with regard to the subject of origin and destiny; Qoheleth quotes the popular maxim that "everything originated in dust, and everything will return to dust" (v 20b).[23] Even Qoheleth's practical advice to seize the moment stands under the further reminder that no one can see beyond death: "for who can bring one to see what will take place afterwards?" (v 22b).[24]

4. Qoh 6:12: "For who knows what is good for one in life the number of empty days of life that he spends like a shadow;[25] because who can tell anyone what will occur afterwards under the sun?" According to the Massorah, 6:9/10 marks the mid-

---

[19]Lauha, *Kohelet*, 75; Galling, *Der Prediger*, 96; and many others.

[20]The ל is thus understood as emphatic.

[21]This motif also occurs in Prov 30:2 and Ps 73:22. In each of these texts human ignorance is characterized as brutish conduct. In the former the state seems to be permanent, but in the latter it is transitory.

[22]"The Shadow of Death in Qoheleth," in *Israelite Wisdom: Theological and Literary Essays in Honor of Samuel Terrien*, ed. John G. Gammie et al. (Ann Arbor, 1978) 205-16, gives my views about the importance of this idea to Qoheleth.

[23]Job (1:21) quotes a similar aphorism in his well-known response to the loss of possessions and children (עָרֹם יָצָתִי מִבֶּטֶן אִמִּי וְעָרֹם אָשׁוּב שָׁמָּה); cf. Qoh 5:14. The final word, שָׁמָּה, is a euphemism for Sheol. For a similar idea, see Papyrus Insinger 30:6 ("What comes from the earth returns to it again"; so M. Lichtheim, *Ancient Egyptian Literature III* [Berkeley, Los Angeles, London, 1980] 209). F. Lexa, *Papyrus Insinger* (Paris, 1926) 69, translates as follows: "Celui qui sort de la terre y retourne."

[24]Galling, *Der Prediger*, 97, mentions an inscription on a gravestone from Hellenistic times. It reads θάρσοιοὐδεὶς ἀθάνατος ("Do not worry—no one is immortal").

[25]The Greek rendering, ἐν σχιᾷ, presupposes בְּצֵל. The preposition could be understood as a *beth essentiae*: the translation would be roughly the same ("as a shadow").

point in the versification of the book.[26] It is appropriate, therefore, that vv 10-12 face backwards and forwards, recalling certain themes (determinism, powerlessness, an unknown future) that have already surfaced and pointing forward to further treatment.[27] Although the three verses may have originated independently of one another, they form a semblance of unity in their present position despite their strong difference in formal structure.[28]

Verse 10 is particularly difficult, and slight emendation of the text is required to achieve a meaningful statement. I choose to ignore the position of the 'athnach, and to translate as follows: "Whatever has been, its essence was already named,[29] and it was known what it was; as for man, he cannot really[30] contend with one stronger than he." The next verse understands the contention as verbal, and dismisses verbosity as empty and without profit (cf. 5:1, 6). The argument seems to be that determinism renders human protest null and void, and it is difficult to escape the suspicion that Qoheleth has Job in mind here. If human beings cannot know what is best, what is the purpose of becoming agitated and provoking another's wrath? Here the מִי יוֹדֵעַ denies the possibility of accomplishing the primary goal of wisdom, specifically securing human good,[31] and characterizes existence as nothing more substantial than a fleeting shadow. The effect is particularly touching, for the celebrated life under the sun is relegated to the shadows.[32]

---

[26]A. D. G. Wright has made much of this fact ("The Riddle of the Sphinx: The Structure of the Book of Qoheleth," *CBQ* 30 [1968]: 313-34; "The Riddle of the Sphinx Revisited: Numerical Patterns in the Book of Qoheleth," *CBQ* 42 [1980]: 35-51; and "Additional Numerical Patterns in Qoheleth," *CBQ* 45 [1983]: 32-43).

[27]The close affinities between 6:10 and 3:15 are beyond dispute (cf. also 1:9-10).

[28]Oswald Loretz, *Qohelet und der alte Orient* (Freiburg, Basel, Wien, 1964) 231n.63, emphasizes four independent sayings in 6:10-12. Lauha, *Kohelet*, 118, thinks a thematic and stylistic unity exists in the present form of the verses.

[29]G. Wildeboer understands Qoh 6:10 as deliberately ambiguous about the name אָדָם. Since the name of the original earth creature was related to the word for earth, such a person would be foolish to challenge the creator (*Der Prediger* [Freiburg i. B., Leipzig, and Tübingen, 1898]). Perhaps the passive form is a circumlocution for deity.

[30]The conjunction וְ is taken as asseverative (Charles Francis Whitley, *Koheleth*, BZAW 148 [Berlin and New York, 1979] 61).

[31]Gerhard von Rad, *Weisheit in Israel* (Neukirchen-Vluyn, 1970) ET: *Wisdom in Israel* (London, Nashville, and New York, 1972); and my *Old Testament Wisdom* (Atlanta, 1981).

[32]Perhaps the idea is that a shadow has no independent existence, but owes its very being to something or someone else.

5. Qoh 8:1: "Who is like a sage,[33] and who knows the interpretation[34] of a word?[35] A person's wisdom brightens the face, and the boldness of his countenance is changed." This obscure verse seems unrelated to its context, unless it isolates a specific form of human machinations[36] mentioned in the previous verse. Elsewhere Qoheleth did not flinch from open attack on certain representatives of the school tradition (8:17), and it is possible that 8:1 contains a traditional wisdom boast ("Who is like a sage?"), together with Qoheleth's rebuttal ("Who knows the interpretation of a word?"). Instead of the expected response ("no one is like a sage"), the retort emphasizes the limits of sapiential knowledge. The second half of the verse may preserve an old wisdom saying that calls attention to the positive effect of knowledge on a person's countenance.[37] The final clause seems to refer to a sage's control of emotions regardless of the situation, so that true feelings are concealed when they might be costly if exposed.[38]

Seven variants of the expression מִי יוֹדֵעַ occur within Qoheleth (8:4, 7, 12; 9:1, 5; 11:5, 6). The first two are in a context that discusses the nature of authority (8:2-9). Since a king's power is supreme,[39] his subjects must take special care to observe the changing moods in their ruler and to act in an appropriate manner. After all, no one knows the future, nor can anyone control passion, death, or eventualities such as war. Reflecting on these realities leads Qoheleth to the conviction that human beings rule over others in a manner that produces more evil than good. In 8:4 he acknowledges the power of a king, noting that none can question royal decisions: "Inasmuch as the king's word is supreme, who can say to him, 'what are you doing?'" A similar point is made about God in Job 9:12 and Dan 4:32. Since the verb אָמַר has replaced יָדַע in Qoh 8:4, this verse may have little relevance

---

[33]The LXX has "Who is so wise?"

[34]Qoheleth's affinities with later literature (Daniel and Qumran) are particularly noticeable here (פֵּשֶׁר as a technical term).

[35]According to Hans Wilhelm Hertzberg (*Der Prediger* [Gütersloh, 1963] 140), דְּבָרִים in Qoheleth always means words, whereas דָּבָר connotes either word or thing. The issue is more complex than this suggests, however, and Qoheleth may refer to things here.

[36]The meaning of חִשְּׁבֹנוֹת can be both favorable and unfavorable. In Qoh 7:29 it refers to the use of the imagination for base purposes, hence schemes or devices is an appropriate rendering there.

[37]R. Kroeber, *Der Prediger* (Berlin, 1963) 149.

[38]Norbert Lohfink, *Kohelet* (Wurzburg, 1980) 59, emphasizes the fantasy of the royal court, in this case the Alexandrian. The old proverb refers to the necessity for court officials to conceal their true feelings.

[39]Royal authority was certainly a factor to be reckoned with in daily affairs, but some things were not subject to a king's control. This subtle point is made by the author of 1 Esd 4:1-12, where only those opposites which fall under royal command are taken over from the fourteen pairs in Qoh 3:2-8. On this text see my essay, "The contest of Darius's Guards in 1 Esdras 3:1–5:3," in *Images of Man and God*, ed. Burke O. Long (Sheffield, 1981) 74-88. (This essay is also reprinted above.)

to the present discussion. The participle יוֹדֵעַ does appear in 8:7, but it is preceded by the negative particle. "For no one knows what will take place, because who can tell him precisely what the future holds?"

The larger unit 8:10-15 deals with injustice and its deleterious effects. The delay in punishment for wicked persons actually encourages their conduct, prompting in Qoheleth the advice to eat, drink and enjoy life. Competing viewpoints vie for attention in these verses. The traditional understanding of punishment for the wicked asserts itself in a wholly inappropriate context, where the prosperity of the sinner is openly conceded to be cause for dismay. The traditional attitude uses יוֹדֵעַ as a strong affirmation. "But indeed I know that it will be well for those who fear God because they fear in the divine presence."[40] The following verse proceeds to deny that it will go well for the wicked, who will not be able to prolong their lives like a shadow, because they refused to fear God.

Two texts within 9:1-10 require comment. The larger setting takes up the issue of a single fate for all people, irrespective of their virtue or lack of it, and urges enjoyment during the empty days allotted individuals. The initial verse recognizes divine control over human lives but complains that no one can discern whether the deity's attitude toward humans is characterized by love or hatred. "For I reflected on all this and assessed it, that the righteous and the wise, together with their deeds, are in God's hand; whether love or hate no one knows. Everything before them is fleeting" (if we read הֶבֶל for הַכֹּל and join it to the previous verse).[41] In 10:5 Qoheleth speaks about the advantage that the living possess over the dead, a verse that must surely contain irony: "For the living know that they will die but the dead do not know anything, and they have no more reward, since memory of them is forgotten."

The final unit to be examined is 11:1-6, where practical advice takes into account an element of mystery. Qoheleth counsels diversification of investments and urges action rather than refusal to act because of the uncertainty surrounding daily life. For him ordinary existence has its share of the unknown, for example the miracle of life. "Just as you do not know how breath enters a foetus within its mother's womb, so you do not know the work of God who does everything" (11:5). This verse leads to another that combines the two themes, planting and impregnation. "In the morning sow your seed, and in the evening do not withhold your hand,

---

[40] The grammatical form alone in v 12 (כִּי גַּם־יוֹדֵעַ אָנִי) does not settle the issue of authenticity. Lauha, *Kohelet*, 153, 157, attributes the verse to a redactor (R²), and compares 3:17a; 12:12-14. Gordis, *Koheleth—The Man and his World*, 296-98, thinks Qoheleth quotes earlier wisdom, refuting it in vv 14-15.

[41] E. Podechard, *L'Ecclésiaste* (Paris, 1912) 408.

for you do not know whether the one or the other will prosper, or whether both of them will equally thrive" (11:6).[42]

To recapitulate, the מִי יוֹדֵעַ sayings in Proverbs and Qoheleth serve as strong denials and are thus equivalent to "no one knows." In this respect they can be linked closely with the five rhetorical questions outside Israel's wisdom literature. But a decisive difference exists nonetheless, for מִי יוֹדֵעַ in Qoheleth and Proverbs lacks the potential for surprise that it has elsewhere. In short, a vital ingredient in the nonwisdom texts is missing from Qoheleth and Prov 24:22. The door of hope has been firmly shut. Like Ezekiel before them, the sages in Qoheleth's day made extravagant claims about knowledge that gave birth to an unwanted child whose infant wail was מִי יוֹדֵעַ. In truth, some of life's most profound insights issue from the mouths of babes.[43]

Analysis of the refrain מִי יוֹדֵעַ is more than an aesthetic exercise, which in itself yields significant insights into the thought of one who was himself interested in finding pleasing language to express truth. Qoheleth's use of מִי יוֹדֵעַ functioned to call into question the entire wisdom enterprise. In a sense he was insisting on restraint where claims about knowledge were concerned. From his remarks one can surmise that elaborate boasts were being made by wisdom's champions.[44] It seems

---

[42]In Sir 1:6 the question "who knows them?" occurs in a context of similar questions ("who can count them?" and "who can search them out?" [vv 1, 2, 3]). This list of impossible questions, which may originally have been a numerical proverb, has been extended in some manuscripts by one verse. Two related texts indicate the prevalence of such skepticism in later Judaism. The argument runs from the less to the greater in Judith 8:13-14 (you cannot understand human minds; how do you hope to search out God's thought?). Baruch 3:29-32 asks who has gone up into heaven or crossed the sea, denying that anyone knows the way except the deity who knows all things (cf. Susanna 42, where God is said to be "aware of all things before they come to be").

[43]It is important to note that מִי יוֹדֵעַ has found its way into Jewish liturgy, for it appears in the Passover Seder as an educational device ("One, who knows it? One, I know it . . . "). For the Hebrew text with translation, see *The Passover Haggadah*, ed. Nahum N. Glatzer (New York, 1953) 102-105.

[44]The classic case occurs in 8:17, where Qoheleth boldly rejects every claim made by a sage with respect to *absolute* knowledge. "And I saw every work of God, that one cannot find out the work that is done beneath the sun, however much one labors to search it out he will not find it; even if a wise person claims to know, he is unable to discover it." In this instance Qoheleth dares to assert that his own experience of life's inscrutable aspects carries more force than the claims of traditionists within a school. Elsewhere Qoheleth mentions the profundity of knowledge, its depths that cannot be plumbed by human beings. "All this I tested by means of reason; I said, 'I shall be wise,' but it was remote from me. Distant, whatever occurs, and deep, very deep, who can find it out?" (7:23-24). He makes a similar point in 3:11, regardless of how one translates the enigmatic הָעֹלָם (eternity? darkness or obscurity?). The divine gift does not enable individuals to discover the grand scheme of things, thus acquiring knowledge that would equip them with secrets of success and longev-

that these affirmations about wisdom's potential extended beyond the older assertions about coping with daily experience, perhaps going so far as to insist on knowledge about Transcendence. Qoheleth has been viewed as the peerless defender of divine freedom,[45] although the book was composed in an era characterized by divine hiddenness.[46] One wonders whether there was actually a need for a defender of the deity's sovereignty at this time. Furthermore, Qoheleth certainly pretends to know much about God's will. How can this be if he also is right about the limits of all knowledge? Perhaps an answer emerges when one examines Qoheleth's understanding of divine determination of events. In a word, nothing happens unless the deity wills it; hence whatever occurs has the seal of divine approval. That is why Qoheleth can assert that God has already approved the drinking of wine and enjoyment of life, but that is also the source of Qoheleth's painful laments about oppression of the weak.[47]

Perhaps a comparison with prophetic literature will throw some light on the situation which Qoheleth confronts. Zimmerli's examination of the refrain, "You shall know that I am the Lord," poses the issue in its clearest expression.[48] According to him, the prophet Ezekiel rules out any form of knowledge other than divine confirmation within historical events. In Zimmerli's view, authentic knowledge never moved from below, but invariably came from divine initiative. All human meditation, examination of nature and human nature, and philosophical reflection were destined to abort. However, the price for such exclusive claims about historical revelation was a costly one, for events in history quickly lost their positive revelatory capacity and competing claims soon brought the collapse of the edifice on which prophetic activity occurred.

---

ity. For Qoheleth this does not mean, however, that wisdom has *no* advantage over folly.

[45]Walther Zimmerli, *Das Buch des Predigers Salomo* (Göttingen, 1962) passim.

[46]P. S. Fiddes, "The Hiddenness of Wisdom in the Old Testament and Later Jewish Literature" (D.Phil. diss., Oxford, 1976) 229-76.

[47]L. Gorssen, "La cohérence de la conception de Dieu dans l'Ecclésiaste," *ETL* 46 (1970): 282-324; Hans-Peter Müller, "Neige der althebräischen 'Weisheit'," *ZAW* 90 (1978): 238-64; and Martin Hengel, *Judentum und Hellenismus*, 2nd ed. (Tübingen, 1973) ET: *Judaism and Hellenism* (London and Philadelphia, 1974), emphasize the powerful impact of fatalism on Qoheleth's thought. In my view, the dominant mood in Qoheleth is somber, despite the occasional advice about enjoying life while it is possible to do so. The opposite view has its adherents, the most recent of which is R. N. Whybray, "Qoheleth, Preacher of Joy," *JSOT* 23 (1982): 87-98.

[48]Zimmerli, *Erkenntnis Gottes nach dem Buch Ezechiel* (Zurich, 1954) ET: *I Am Yahweh* (Atlanta, 1982) 29-98. He writes: "Nowhere does the statement of recognition speak of recognition apart from the divine acts which nourish it. There is no room here for knowledge emerging darkly from interior human meditation, from an existential analysis of human beings and the world, or from speculation" (64).

A similar crisis seems to have struck at the very foundation of the wisdom enterprise. Here the issue was roughly the same, although the fundamental problem was imported from revelatory circles. Within sapiential groups a premium was placed on human initiative, as opposed to divine revelation, but that situation changed radically in the book of Job. Here the final resolution to the problem of the dialogue derives from revelation: the deity appears to Job and ties up all loose ends. Qoheleth resists such claims, probably because they could not be tested by reason. Instead of bowing before revealed knowledge, he insisted that no one could gain accurate information about the hidden deity. Furthermore, truth also possessed an unfathomable quality, rendering all claims to possess it ludicrous. In this struggle to demonstrate that the universe was closed, Qoheleth seized upon the useful expression, מִי יוֹדֵעַ, and thereby rendered his opposition speechless, so long as they granted his presuppositions and remained sages.[49]

---

[49]The sages thus fared no better than traditional Yahwism, for whom proof of divine favor was discovered in the historical process. Once her history ceased to give evidence of Israel's special place in the divine plan, doubts inevitably surfaced, shaking the foundations of revelatory faith. Champions of human experience as the realm of demonstrable cosmic intention were equally shaken when they could no longer find proof of a moral universe. The failure of history was devastating to prophecy, and an absence of any discoverable design or purpose dealt a crushing blow to wisdom's proponents. A world characterized by firm convictions had yielded to a skeptical מִי יוֹדֵעַ.

16 (1987)

The Acquisition of Knowledge in Israelite Wisdom Literature

Modern scholars possess a staggering amount of information about ancient Near Eastern sages, thanks to copious texts from Egypt and Mesopotamia. It has become current knowledge that the early sages reflected on the distinct advantages of belonging to an elite class of scholars, described in some detail the rigors associated with study, divided life's span in terms of the years devoted to education as opposed to reaping its benefits, identified the goal of education, characterized wise persons as silent ones and their opposites as hot headed fools of at least six different types, and used in-house language to define the relationships between teachers and students.

But one thing is missing in Israel's wisdom literature and in extrabiblical texts. Where is any reflection on the learning process itself? To be sure, there is talk of pitching camp and peering through Wisdom's windows and speculation about pursuing Dame Wisdom like precious treasure or a bride. But not a whisper about the acquisition of knowledge is heard. How did learning occur, and how was it transmitted? To answer these questions, it may be useful to ponder the underlying presuppositions of perhaps the oldest riddle from the ancient world and to reflect on three fundamentally different kinds of knowledge.

I. A Theory of Knowledge

"Whoever enters it has closed eyes; whoever departs from it has eyes that are wide open. What is it?"[1] Because riddles employ cipher language that offers a clue and conceals a trap at the same time, the secret is to seize the clue without being caught in the hidden trap. It follows that riddles have more than one answer. The first impulse is to answer, "Life," for a child enters the world with closed eyes and at death the eyes must be closed for the individual. Indeed, a son is actually described as the person who closes his father's eyes at the moment of death. Alternatively, one is tempted to respond to the question, "What is it?" along erotic lines, for it is widely acknowledged that love is blind. The mystery of eros certainly

---

[1] The first part of the riddle is obscure; see Samuel Noah Kramer, *The Sumerians* (Chicago and London: University of Chicago Press, 1963) 236-37.

begins in ignorance and ends with eyes that have been opened widely. However, the intended response is, "A school."

What makes the image of open and closed eyes appropriate as a description of the learning process? Because eyes mirror the soul, the symbolism is particularly apt. Just as eyes are paired, so knowledge was of two kinds: systematic and gnomic. The first, systematic knowledge, sought to order reality by means of philosophical reflection, while the second, gnomic apperception, endeavored to capture insights from experience and to clothe them in clever statements that could easily be committed to memory.

The image of closed eyes naturally connotes ignorance; whether the empty head, or the wrongly filled mind, or the one that has an illusion of knowledge. The first, ignorance, is by far the easiest to overcome, and the second, prejudice, is the next easiest, for it merely requires a sweeping away of misinformation and a substituting of accurate facts and perceptions. The illusion of knowledge is highly resistant to education, for a closed mind is subject to stagnation. This situation occurs most often where values are treasured, and that makes religion highly vulnerable.

How did teachers open their students' eyes? First, they beat them vigorously. From ancient Sumer we have a nostalgic speech that might have been given at a class reunion. Here are some of the things this former student recalls: Arriving late, I was caned; my homework was incorrect, my teachers beat me; I whispered in class, and was whipped; I neglected to get permission to stand and was caned; my calligraphy was below standards, and they thrashed me; I loitered on the way to school and my teachers beat me.[2] Second, teachers stimulated lively debate. Perhaps the debate over what is the strongest thing in the world exercised more imaginations than any other topic. One answer to this popular controversy appears in a history of Ethiopia from 1681.[3]

Iron is strong, but fire tempers it.
Fire is awesome, but water extinguishes it.
Water is forceful, but the sun dries it.
The sun is mighty, but a storm cloud conceals it.
A storm cloud is explosive, but the earth subdues it.
The earth is majestic, but humans master it.
Humans are powerful, but grief overtakes them.
Grief is heavy, but wine assuages it.
Wine is powerful, but sleep renders it weak.
Yet woman is strongest of all.

[2]S. Kramer, *The Sumerians*, 238.
[3]The Latin text is printed in R. Laqueur, "Ephoros. Die Proömium," *Hermes* 46 (1911): 172.

The third means of opening eyes was the use of suggestive language. Because students almost without exception were males, wisdom was described as a beautiful bride, and folly was depicted as a harlot enticing young men to destruction. In this way language became highly explosive, and the quest for wisdom suddenly took on erotic dimensions. But teachers often stood in the way of learning, unintentionally encouraging sleep. Two features of the pedagogic method seem counterproductive, for learning was by memorization and by endless copying of texts. The result in Egypt was reproduction with no real grasp of the meaning of the text being copied.

What about those students whose eyes were opened? They encountered three obstacles to moving beyond knowledge to wisdom. Open eyes see many options, recognizing the complexity of knowledge and refusing to give simple answers; they are bombarded with light, producing the insatiable appetite of scholars, a source of permanent discontent; and they also become tired, almost jaded, hence the temptation to skepticism. Another ancient text from Mesopotamia advises a potential philanthropist to go up to the cemetery and look at the numerous skulls there and to ask which one is a malefactor and which is the benefactor.[4]

Such skepticism, nay pessimism, is a daily companion of the knowledgeable student of life. How, then, did teachers overcome these obstacles to higher wisdom? They did so by achieving focus. True wisdom, the Egyptian teachers insisted, is virtue. It consists of knowing the right word for the occasion, arguing persuasively, exercising restraint, and speaking the truth. Thus kaleidoscopic images took on recognizable patterns, and jaded eyes lit up with infinite configurations of insight shaped by dominant images.

Nevertheless, wide open eyes blink and must close in sleep, a poignant acknowledgement that learned men sometimes act like fools. But these teachers never forgot that wisdom (hearing) was a stage beyond knowledge (teaching) and that it meant far more than the accumulation of information. Wisdom, the capacity to use information for human good, includes virtue. By virtue these teachers meant generosity and humility. Perhaps a biblical proverb best sums up what these ancient scholars seem to have meant.

> Three things are too wonderful for me;
>   four I do not understand:
> the way of an eagle in the sky,
>   the way of a serpent on a rock,
> the way of a ship on the high seas,
>   and the way of a man with a maiden. (Prov 30:18-19 RSV)

Life's abundant mysteries evoke gratitude and reverence before the author of wisdom and truth.

---

[4]"The Dialogue of Pessimism," ll. 76-78; see W. G. Lambert, *Babylonian Wisdom Literature* (Oxford: Clarendon, 1960) 149.

II. Three Ways of Acquiring Knowledge

A. Observation of Nature and Human Behavior

After this brief effort to formulate a theory of knowledge for the ancient world and to demonstrate an integral connection between knowledge and virtue, let us turn to an elaboration of knowledge in biblical wisdom. How was knowledge acquired? In a word, knowledge resulted from human inquiry rather than from divine initiative. Actually, this formulation of the situation is not exactly correct, for at creation the deity was said to have taken the initiative, concealing valuable truths within nature itself. From then on, however, it was left to humans to search out these lessons from nature and from human behavior. The means by which they did this was personal observation, and once an insight emerged it had to be transferred from the natural realm to the human by analogy. Some examples should clarify this complex process of reasoning.

God is tested by fire / humans are tried in the furnace of affliction.
Bees produce honey / do not despise little things.
A new friend is like new wine /
    when it has aged you will drink it with pleasure.
A door turns on its hinges / a lazy person turns over and over in bed.
A wooden stake is wedged in a fissure between two stones /
    sin is squeezed in between buying and selling.
Some clouds yield no rain / some people boast of giving and fail to do so.
A continual dripping of rain on a cold day / a nagging wife.
The crackling of thorns in a fire / the laughter of fools.
A bird flitting from nest to nest / an adulterous old man.
Whips to control beasts / discipline for children.
An insatiable appetite like Sheol / a barren womb.
The rich inflict wrong and berate others /
    the poor suffer harm and must apologize.
The rich answer gruffly / the poor are obliged to plead.
A lamb led to the slaughter /
    a young man enticed into the home of an adulteress.

These truth statements are the fruit of personal observation by countless sages, who then endeavored to express their insights in language that was both accurate and memorable. In most instances the poet was content to leave the application of the saying to others, and the teacher's task was therefore to discern the circumstance in which a given saying fit. The lessons had to ring true, else they were quickly extinguished from memory, and they had to apply generally to society regardless of time or place. Often quite different possibilities presented themselves to sages, who reached a decision on the basis of the situation. "Do not answer a fool lest you be like him yourself/answer a fool lest he be wise in his own eyes" (Prov 26:4-5). In such circumstances one can only lose, so a choice must be made either to remain silent and give the impression of defeat before an incompetent, or to speak up and thus bestow dignity on the fool's remarks.

Other observations about human behavior moved beyond simple truth statements to explicit counsel, usually reinforced by elaborate exhortations and warnings. These instructions do not leave interpretation to the student, but freely offer advice that leads to happiness and success. Here the religious dimension comes to prominence, and sexual temptation stands as a major source of human folly. Whereas sages who used truth statements were content to describe reality and therefore to let women and men act on their own reading of the situation, those who preferred instructions imposed parental authority on their hearers. In some instances divine authority was also invoked, especially when parental instruction and the statutes of the Mosaic law seemed to coalesce. A good example of this comingling of the two kinds of authority occurs in Proverbs 6:20-35, which juxtaposes images of two competing flames. The first is the lamp that mothers and fathers light in the hearts of children, while the second is the fire that sexual passion kindles in unbridled thoughts. The former flame, fueled by the divine law, preserves one from the consuming fire.

Do these two distinct types of teaching, truth statements and instructions, go their separate ways, producing two different literary traditions? Not at all. By the second century Ben Sira combines both kinds of teaching, permitting the emphasis to fall on the conscious development of instructions. As a matter of fact, he fashions the teaching into paragraph units which permit him to take up numerous topics and to examine subjects at considerable length. Nevertheless, Ben Sira retains the truth statement as well, and some of his observations demonstrate striking intuition. Take, for example, this maxim: "Dreams give wings to fools" (Sir 34:1). Here in a few words he has captured an important reality, and while it is true that Ben Sira goes on to apply this insight to a specific case of divination, the allusive quality of the truth saying makes it applicable to many circumstances.

If we could only recover the sociological setting for these two kinds of teaching it would enable us to understand them far better.[5] For example, did sages use truth statements when dealing with advanced students and colleagues, while reserving instructions for younger learners? We do not know, but one thing seems clearer today than before. The truth statements were just as authoritative as instructions despite their different literary form. In at least three cases within Proverbs larger instructions quote truth statements as their clinching argument. Dame Folly offers her most persuasive appeal to young men in a truth statement: "Stolen water is sweet, and bread

---

[5]Frank Crüsemann, "The Unchangeable World: The 'Crisis of Wisdom' in Koheleth," *God of the Lowly*, ed. Willi Schottroff and Wolfgang Stegemann (Maryknoll NY: Orbis, 1984) 57-77, is an immensely suggestive attempt to recover the sociological setting for Qoheleth's ideas.

eaten in secret is pleasant" (Prov 9:17). Here is the heart of her seduction, and it rests on an awareness of the incredible power of suggestion. Once the mind has been set on a track, it proceeds to fill in the picture from its store of imagination and desire.

B. Analogy: Creed and Reality

Thus far we have restricted our thoughts to the insights that come through human inquiry. The observation of nature and humans yields dividends precisely because it was believed that laws governed the universe and insured prosperity if one lived in harmony with them. But not all truth was the product of human inquiry. In reality, each passing generation was confronted with the accumulated tradition of truth statements and of instructions, which had lost the freshness of discovery. This treasury from the past came with certain claims of authority and therefore placed new generations in a context of decision. "Do these statements ring true for me?" they had to ask. In a sense, the legacy from the past comprised faith reports, and devotion toward parents complicated matters enormously. The tendency was to accept these faith reports at face value, even when they contradicted the personal experience of later generations. Often this inclination was strengthened by an understanding of the world as becoming progressively worse. Because the golden age lay in the past, they thought, the human intellect may have lost some of its power. It therefore followed that assent could be given to parental convictions even when present reality failed to confirm them. Naturally, dogmas arose as a result of this combination of factors, and nowhere was rigidity of beliefs as destructive as in the area of reward and punishment. The belief that sinners fared badly and virtuous persons prospered was seldom borne out in reality, but this dogma produced crises in Mesopotamia, Egypt, and Israel. When the authority of the past weighed heavily on the present, such a crisis naturally followed.

Canonical wisdom bears impressive witness to the difficulty encountered by those who tested faith reports in the light of their own experience of reality. The unknown author of Job examines this dilemma with immense pathos, finally declaring the bankruptcy of secondhand faith. Such assent to the convictions that once sustained others could not survive divine absence or hostile presence. In the end Job confessed as much, insisting that his spiritual life had always been derivative, despite quite a different assessment of the matter by God and by the narrator in the prologue. For Job the issue was simply hearing as opposed to sight, a strange way of stating things in a community of scholars for whom a sage was best characterized as the hearing, that is, obedient one. Indeed, hearing was equivalent to acting on one's insights, and that was the supreme achievement within wisdom.

Psalm 73 describes a comparable struggle between creed and reality. It opens with a confession of faith that God is truly good to the pure in heart, but the psalmist quickly admits that events render such faith vacuous, for the lion's share of goodies has fallen to wicked persons. Beset by sore temptation, this believer wrestles with doubting thoughts which are recognized as brutish. But a change occurs when the psalmist looks away from prosperous villains and enters the holy place where hearts are purified. There the doubter affirms the faith once more, and soars to hitherto unachieved heights. Suddenly a redefinition of divine goodness overwhelms the psalmist, who realizes for the first time that God's goodness has absolutely nothing to do with things that can be seen and touched, such as material prosperity. Instead, the goodness which comes to decent persons is a feeling of divine presence that bestows confidence regardless of the circumstances. Then at long last the psalmist is able to subscribe to the ancient confession, now that its real meaning has become clear.

The same kind of struggle overtook a traditionalist like Ben Sira, who recounted Israel's sacred story in a time when history gave no evidence that the deity guided the nation Israel toward some unseen destiny. In this instance the scribe complicated matters by taking over traditional faith and linking it with wisdom's universal truths. Whereas he could easily test the latter teachings by his own experience, he could not demonstrate the reliability of claims that God had fought against Pharaoh on behalf of an oppressed people. So what did Ben Sira do in this situation, discard the sacred story? By no means. Instead, he uttered a fervent prayer that God would renew the wondrous signs witnessed by previous generations. Here we see the positive reinforcement of faith that often accompanies experiences which ordinarily render credal affirmations suspect.

C. Encounter with the Transcendent One

So far we have observed two ways through which people arrived at truth. They observed nature, drawing conclusions by means of analogical thinking, and they listened to reports from others who claimed to have discovered valuable insights. There is yet a third way by which knowledge was thought to have reached ancient sages: immediate encounter with the Transcendent One. From one perspective, such claims do not belong in wisdom literature, where a premium is placed on verifiability. How can others test the truth of claims about encountering deity? When the sages resort to this sort of argument they threaten their own fundamental assumption about the capability of the intellect to secure one's existence. The ending to the book of Job, for example, is a response that derives from traditions which are more at home in prophecy and sacred narrative than in wisdom. Here Job claims to have achieved new insight as a direct result of an encounter with deity. The same thing seems to be implied in Psalm 73, where an experience of the deity's hand on the psalmist evokes a splendid acknowledgement that this moment alone is worthy of recollection. The result of the encounter is nothing less than a transvaluation of values, and the psalmist cherishes this sensed presence above all else. A comparable testimony to an encounter with the Holy One occurs in the speech by one of Job's friends, Eliphaz. The account describes an appearance of a numinous figure and the resulting response by a mere earthling. The physical transformation (the hair standing straight up and sense of overwhelming dread) was nothing compared to the knowledge communicated to Eliphaz. In short, the deity is said to have whispered an accusing word: "Shall mortals be more righteous than the creator?" (4:17).

In these appeals to direct encounter with the Most High, a decisive step is taken that opens the door to elaborate theories about communication between creator and creature. The first impressive figure to walk through this door was a woman who identified herself as Wisdom. In many respects, this development is one of the most interesting ones to come out of sapiential thinking. The imagery seems at first to be purely metaphorical, but eventually it signified an actual divine attribute. Egyptian influence is evident at the initial stage, Greek at the very end. Antedating creation, Wisdom assisted the creator and later came to earth in order to communicate the deity's thoughts to all creatures. In Ben Sira's adaptation of the concept, Wisdom established a dwelling in Jerusalem and infused the Mosaic law, with which she became identical. For the author of the Greek Wisdom of Solomon, Wisdom is a pure emanation of the deity. Therefore, whoever acquires wisdom as a bride also possesses the personal attributes of the deity, particularly the four cardinal virtues.

What enabled such ideas to thrive within wisdom literature? An answer appears to lie in the central position that reflections about creation occupied among the sages. A theology of creation is at home in texts which speak of the High God, as opposed to patron deities who guided the affairs of a small clan. The advantage of patron deities was their accessibility in all circumstances, their nearness to devotees. No such assumptions adhere to thoughts about the distant creator, whose task was to govern the universe. Naturally, the need was soon felt to find some means to bridge the great distance separating humans from the High God. One answer came from Hebraic tradition, another from the Hellenic world. The Spirit of God who inspired poets, priests, and prophets was identified with the divine thought, word, and wisdom. Alternatively, the human mind was a microcopy of the divine mind. Hence the human intellect possessed a tiny spark of the divine rationality governing the universe, an idea that linked Israelite sages with Greek philosophers. These two responses to the problem of a transcendent deity implied that the human intellect was in direct touch with ultimate truth.[6]

Belief in direct encounter with transcendence constitutes a link with nonsapiential texts in the biblical canon. However, a decisive difference between the wise and others remained. Perhaps Deuteronomy 30:1-14 comes closest to illustrating this difference. For this author the divine statute is neither too difficult nor too remote, but it is very near and can be kept. The text seems to suggest that detractors were denigrating the divine word because of its accessibility, exalting insights that were acquired at great cost. The author elevates revelation over discoveries resulting from human inquiry. For Israel's sages, revelation occurred at creation, and the goal of men and women was to discover hidden truth.

---

[6]Two skeptical responses to such optimism are Qoheleth and Agur (Prov 30:1-4).

17 (1976)

Wisdom in Israel (Gerhard von Rad): A Review*

"How small a step it was from knowledge to adoration!" (306). In this sentence Gerhard von Rad registers amazement at the way in which Israel's sages easily moved from onomastica, the mere listing of phenomena, to hymnic praise of the creator who fashioned the objects under scrutiny. Von Rad goes on to remark that such a step presented special hazards, particularly the attribution of evil to Yahweh. In spite of the strains placed upon her review of divine integrity, Israel refused to relinquish the belief that Yahweh was Lord of the universe. Wisdom literature bears witness to the heroic struggle to justify the small step from knowledge to adoration.

The key phrase in von Rad's treatment of Israel's wisdom relates to this move from description to praise. That phrase is the title of the second part of the book: "The Liberation of Reason and the Resultant Problems." To what was Israel's wisdom in bondage? Answering this question brings us to the heart of von Rad's understanding of wisdom in Israel.

Patriarchal religion, according to von Rad, was entirely sacral. All of life was brought under the heavy yoke of the holy, and from its power none was free. With Solomon a breath of fresh air swept through the kingdom, dispelling sacral institution and bringing in its trail a secular understanding of reality. The latter was thoroughly religious, but providence governed individual's lives from afar and without resort to the miraculous. In time the secular spirit, threatened by skepticism's veil of resignation, gave way to religious modifications. In short, von Rad postulates an evolution from sacral thinking to secular wisdom and then to religious wisdom. In addition, he distinguishes between old wisdom, the product of the radically secular age, and later wisdom. The latter type of wisdom seldom uses the sentence form, choosing instead the didactic poem, hymn, dispute, and autobiographical narrative, and turns directly to the individual. Old wisdom stressed God's unlimited power and understood the fear of God to mean dependence. Von Rad assumes a school setting for Israel's wisdom, primarily on the basis of analogy with Egyptian

---

*Trans. James D. Martin. Nashville: Abingdon; London: SCM, 1972. Pp. x+330. $12.95.

and Mesopotamian wisdom. He also thinks the quality of Israel's literature and the rhetorical devices employed, such as school questions and catechism, render the hypothesis of school wisdom highly probable. Admitting the possibility of clan wisdom as well, von Rad refrains from discussing its essential character.

Wisdom had a single goal, according to von Rad. It endeavored to "wrest from the chaos of events some semblance of order in which man was not continually at the mercy of the incalculable" (p. 308). In wisdom man was in search of himself, for there is no knowledge that does not sooner of later throw the seeker back upon the question of self-knowledge. The presupposition of all wisdom was trust in Yahweh. With this astounding statement von Rad has baptized Israel's thinking. Thus he can write that wisdom is a form of Yahwism, albeit an unusual one. The presupposition for coping with reality and for "straight talk" in the face of injustice was knowledge and trust in Yahweh and the orders established by him for the human good.

Von Rad's analysis of Israel's wisdom constitutes an inquiry into her search for knowledge, a probing into the way Israel sought to prove herself. His thesis is that trust alone assures reliable knowledge. Faith contributes to knowledge and frees it to ask every conceivable question. It does not hinder knowledge. Such conviction that Israel's wisdom belongs fully within Yahwism rather than on the periphery as an alien body leads von Rad to assert that the fundamental premise of all Israelite wisdom can be summed up in a single sentence: the fear of the Lord is the beginning of wisdom. The diversity within Yahwism thus prompts von Rad to suggest that we consider dropping the singular form "wisdom" and adopt the plural "wisdoms."

In attempting to view reality as Israel saw it, von Rad abandons tradition history in favor of what he calls problem history. By this he means the religious tensions evoking the texts, especially Job and Koheleth. To this concentration on problem history von Rad adds thematic concerns that constitute the principal teachings of sentence literature. Still he reckons with strata within some of the poems, and attributes the various levels to scribal activity. He remarks in passing that the divergent texts dealing with self-manifesting primeval order provide a model of transmitted traditions.

Part one concentrates on the centers and transmitters of didactic traditions, together with the forms employed. Von Rad assumes that wisdom was nurtured in the royal court, but admits that only a small percentage of texts reflects such a setting. He concedes further that the proverbs do not proclaim a code of bureaucratic ethics (for a different view, see Kovacs 1974.) On the contrary, the sociological setting for the majority of proverbs is the landed estate. Those who preserved the traditions were teachers. Ben Sira sees himself as a custodian of valuable traditions; his connection with school is firmly established.

Von Rad's formal analysis of wisdom literature breaks no new ground. He draws heavily upon previous research in treating the literary proverb, numerical sayings, autobiographical stylization, long didactic poems, dialogue, fable and allegory, didactic narrative, and prayers. Certain perceptions of reality could only be expressed in hymnic form, von Rad claims. It follows that the wise were not only faced with the task of artistic formulation of whatever reality they discovered but also with choosing an appropriate literary vehicle. Von Rad observes that we lack a through study of the thought processes characterizing Israel's great dialogues. He writes that the teachers first developed the doxology of judgement into an important literary prayer form. Giving up the usual sharp distinction between poetry and prose, von Rad claims that some of the wisdom literature is written in solemn, poetic prose.

When moving beyond formal analysis to discussion of the liberation of knowledge (part two) and special subjects of instruction (part three), von Rad becomes considerably more polemical. Denying that Israel had a dogma of retribution, he suggests that the rigidity is more typical of modern interpreters than of the ancient wise. Israel's sages, he writes, maintained tension between orders established by the creator and divine freedom. Von Rad asks and leaves unanswered the following question: "Is it faith in Yahweh or in orders?" Rejecting William McKane's theory of secular wisdom (McKane 1965), he appeals to Hesiod for demonstration that a practical, down-to-earth empirical observer can also reflect on fundamental mysteries of the universe. Von Rad refuses to follow his own student, Hans Jürgen Hermisson (1968), in associating wisdom and historical narratives. The Joseph story does not negate this judgment, for it falls into the category of fiction. The succession document and Yahwistic narrative differ from wisdom at two fundamental points: they lack legitimation, and they show no awareness of life's ultimate mysteries. Wisdom, von Rad maintains, always legitimates itself, and never tires of pointing to human limits.

Precisely how does wisdom legitimate herself? Von Rad concludes that Israel's instructions presuppose a theonomous ethos but dialectic ethics. Nowhere do sages appeal to the ethical decalogue or to legal stipulations. On the contrary, they assume the existence of divine orders to which men and women are expected to comply. Von Rad observes that in Israel's culture lessons derived from everyday experience played a much greater role than law codes ever did. The sages therefore appealed to reason, arguing their case by means of motivation clauses and warnings. But the wise also knew their limits. They never compromised the principle of divine freedom.

Considerable attention is given to the relationship between wisdom and apocalyptic. The determination of times in apocalyptic differs sharply from that in prophecy, von Rad argues. Affinities between wisdom and apocalyptic are close, he thinks, so close that apocalyptic must be called a child of wisdom. In apocalyptic the real salvation event moves to the fringes of history, either in the primeval election and determination of decrees or in the anticipation of salvation at the end of time. In prophecy, on the other hand, history is always open to new possibilities, is fraught with potential since it embraces a dialectic of human responses and new decisions by God.

Cultic concerns occupy little of von Rad's time. He thinks the sages had no need of the cult since they listened to a call from creation itself. Even Sirach's celebrated cultic interests are downplayed; von Rad writes that ben Sira's primary concern was with inner motivation and purity of heart, without which cultic acts were useless. The polemic against idols arose from the fact that Israel knew that the created universe points beyond itself to the creator.

The burden of reason's liberation evoked a significant body of protest literature. Von Rad attempts a theological analysis of these texts under the title, "Trust and Attack." Among the psalms are 37, 49, and 73. These remarkable discussions illustrate the potential for good and ill inherent within suffering. Adversity prompts search for meaning, but it also significantly increases the risk of loss of meaning. In this protest literature man goes on the offensive against God for the first time. With Job that attack starts from the position of trust in Yahweh; Koheleth has no such faith relationship to temper his words of dissent. The fundamental issue in Job is: Yahweh *pro me*. Von Rad emphasizes Job's dependence upon the ancient cultic dialogue with God; at this point Job breaks with wisdom. In this regard Job's link with old Yahwistic traditions was stronger than that of his three friends. Von Rad questions whether the sages would have appreciated a religious rebel, although the suggestion that God has become a personal enemy veers sharply from customary belief. The narrative framework of Job does not enter into consideration, since von Rad thinks the poetry and prose cannot be reconciled. God's gamble on Job and its successful outcome stand out in von Rad's discussion of the work. He observes that God could have lost the wager if Job had closed his mind to God's speech.

Koheleth comes off less favorably in von Rad's analysis. Three concerns dominate the book: (1) everything is vanity; (2) God determines every event; and (3) man cannot discern the divine decrees. Death's shadow hovers over everything Koheleth writes. Nevertheless, von Rad asserts, the essential message of Koheleth is quite positive—enjoy life while you can. Von Rad accuses Koheleth of giving up the ancient dialogue of the wise; his words constitute a monologue of an outsider entirely free of tradition. The strong urge to master life has been broken; loss of faith follows. In Koheleth one confronts a man thrown back on his own resources. Von Rad thinks the impact of Job and Koheleth was minimal.

A significant break in Israel's wisdom takes place with Sirach (on this transition in wisdom, see Marböck 1971). The shift is both formal and substantive. Sirach arranges the traditions in large units and shows decided preference for hymnic and didactic material. Von Rad insists that wisdom, not torah, lies behind these teachings. While the theme, "fear of the Lord," pervades Sirach's thought, it is secondary to wisdom. Von Rad perceives the importance of theodicy to Sirach and credits him with a new answer to divine injustice. That response to innocent suffering ventures into the nature of God's intervention in human affairs, which Sirach describes as ambivalent. Von Rad rejects Johannes Fichtner's phrase "nationalization of wisdom" (Fichtner 1933). In its place he speaks of religionization, a term that does not suggest a politicization of wisdom.

In summing up the strengths and weaknesses of Israel's wisdom, von Rad emphasizes the dialectic in her thought. The sages were confident they could recognize God's ways and the limitations imposed upon knowledge. Such confidence in the world and the attacks to which she was subject are said to be unique. Von Rad calls attention to a prominent missing feature: Israel's sages never put together a consistent world view. Instead they speak of an unfinished and unfinishable dialogue about man and the world on the basis of ambivalence. Reliable knowledge, he insists, follows trust. Von Rad marvels at Israel's ability to be at home in the world. Again and again he returns to the theme of creation's summons. The universe itself invites man to knowledge, issues its invitation to love. In short, God lets the created order bear witness to him. Job illustrates the appropriate response: the tiny step from knowledge to adoration.

2

In the preceding observations I have attempted to delineate the essential argument of *Wisdom in Israel*. Much more could profitably be added, for every sentence is pregnant with insight. Rarely can one find such a treasure trove. For me it was a tiny step from knowledge of the book's content to profound appreciation. Original insights into the nature of reality itself crop up again and again. One soon discovers that Israel's quest for self-knowledge illuminates our own search for meaning at decisive points. Modern seekers, too, stand before the mystery of the unknown and unknowable.

Von Rad's masterful style has often been commented upon. I find *Weisheit in Israel* aesthetically less pleasing than most of his works, although numerous exquisite passages fill the pages. The marvel, however, is that the book retains its freshness after repeated readings. I have worked through *Wisdom in Israel* a dozen times, both in German and in translation, and with each reading new insights leap from the pages.

Still I have serious reservations about the book. These objections concern its basic presuppositions and fundamental thesis, as well as many ideas that are less central to von Rad's argument. In what follows I hope to explain why I think the final word has not been said about Israel's wisdom.

Von Rad's fundamental thesis that wisdom is a branch of Yahwism flies in the face of much sapiential scholarship. Hartmut Gese's oft-quoted phrase describing wisdom as an alien body within the Old Testament (Gese 1958, 2) was grounded in firm reality: an absence of the usual Yahwistic concerns until Sirach. Of course much wisdom research drew an extreme conclusion from this undisputed fact—that Israel's early wisdom was purely secular. Von Rad's position offers a necessary corrective, but did he have to baptize wisdom? Sages lived within the covenant community, to be sure, but they chose to ignore virtually every tradition known to prophets and priests. That silence speaks more eloquently than von Rad's immersion of sages into the Yahwistic font suggests.

A collection of proverbs that has traditionally been considered reasonably late, Proverbs 1–9, becomes normative for von Rad's understanding of wisdom. In my opinion, this section of Proverbs cannot bear the weight of von Rad's thesis. The crucial issue does not concern date, which I happen to believe is considerably later that von Rad thinks is the case. I am prepared to admit the possibility of different traditors behind the various collections in Proverbs. However, I think two factors, seldom if ever noticed, warn against a preexilic dating of Proverbs 1–9.

The first concerns the warning against wicked men set on increasing their spoil. If one asks when Israel as we know her would most likely generate such a polemic against doing battle for profit, the answer suggests the period of the struggle between Jews returning from exile and the people who had remained in Judah, or the bitter conflict between Jews and Samaritans during the reforms of Nehemiah and Ezra. Certainly the iron hand of monarchy, whether Israelite or Babylonian, makes an earlier dating of these warnings unlikely.

The other point focuses upon the intensity characterizing a number of proverbs about a foreign adulteress. The reforms of Nehemiah and Ezra leave many husbands without sexual gratification and an equal number of foreign women with little alternative but to fornicate.

Such arguments are, at best, half persuasive. Nevertheless, they are superior to von Rad's unexamined assumption about the early date of Proverbs 1–9. Since all wisdom is a branch of Yahwism, according to von Rad, the explicit theologization in Proverbs 1–9 merely signifies different tradition circles. he may be correct. Still I think a development toward a more explicit religious expression is discernible in the various collections of proverbs (see Scott 1972). Von Rad certainly recognizes such growth in the reflection upon Dame Wisdom, which he rightly characterizes as significantly different from hypostasis.

A phrase that functions programmatically in the first collection of Proverbs (chapters 1–9) becomes normative for the total book in von Rad's eyes. The fear of the Lord is called the essence of all wisdom. Even though the phrase occurs outside the initial collection, its impact differs markedly there. It is inappropriate, therefore, to view the sum total of Israel's wisdom from the standpoint of the distinct piety expressed in Proverbs 1–9.

One of the nicest features of von Rad's discussion of Israel's wisdom is the section on creation's self-revelation. Despite the beauty of this treatment, however, I remain unconvinced by the overkill. The value of this section concerns the elevation of the hymnic material in wisdom, surely a correct move. Nevertheless, von Rad's enthusiasm runs unchecked. It is hardly accurate to claim that *creation* answers Job. On the contrary, *God* speaks to Job and reminds him of his place within creation. Von Rad has pushed a good insight, derived from Egyptian parallels, to the extreme. In the process he has taken metaphorical language too literally and has turned sages into worshippers long before Sirach.

Von Rad's baptism of wisdom responds to a pressing concern on the theological scene today. Does God reveal himself by means other than the prophetic word or priestly תּוֹרוֹת? And if so, what authority does such knowledge have? Von Rad's answer amounts to an equating of "general" and "special" revelation. The former derives from God, although separated from man by a long space of time and mediated by creation. Special revelation, on the other hand, is contemporaneous and mediated by humans (for further discussion, see Zimmerli 1971, 693-94). Such a position raises a serious question about Walther Zimmerli's attempt to describe wisdom's argumentation as advice devoid of authority (Zimmerli 1933). One could conceivably contend that the context makes a significant difference: once proverbs are placed in a sacred collection they take on the authority of tradition. But do they become revelatory? Von Rad's answer rests on an assumption that the creative act bestowed upon God's works an order that possesses potential for revelation, and further, that creation itself eagerly grants its knowledge to the hearing heart. I wonder, however, whether Israel says any more in Psalm 19 than comparable Greek hymns declare about the music of the sphere.

A basic presupposition of the book distorts the picture of wisdom's evolution, in my estimation. Von Rad adopts Martin Buber's concept of pansacrality as an accurate description of early patriarchal religion. This pansacrality vanished with the Davidic-Solomonic monarchy, von Rad asserts, and is replaced by modified secularism, by which he means a secular spirit thoroughly imbued with belief in divine providence. In time Israel's sages are unable to maintain the tension of a distant deity guiding the course of human events, and move to a position of religious affirmation about divine presence in individual lives. In short, von Rad interprets wisdom literature against the evolutionary yardstick of pansacrality, modified secularism, and religious devotion.

The thesis of a Solomonic enlightenment, first proposed in von Rad's epoch-making monograph *The Problem of the Hexateuch*, has governed his thought for decades. No proof has ever been supplied. A thorough examination of the evidence ("The Solomonic Enlightenment: Or the Emperor's New Clothes"), presented by me as a paper to the southern meeting of the Society of Biblical Literature in March 1975, has convinced me that no such enlightenment existed. Instead, sacral and secular strains of thought coexisted throughout Israel's history. Only careful avoidance of certain texts damaging to von Rad's theory, the Samson narrative in particular, permitted him to posit a movement from pansacral ideas to secular to religious thinking. The persistence of sacral ideas in Sirach and Tobit, especially in regard to medical theory and practice, and the secular legends about Samson belie von Rad's hypothesis. Unfortunately von Rad's enthusiasm about the sacral character of holy war prompted him to interpret all of reality in light of this situation.

The attempt to locate Israel's wisdom within the royal court, based primarily on Egyptian parallels, grows out of von Rad's conviction that Solomon either sponsored or promulgated wisdom literature, particularly onomastica. Despite von Rad's damaging admission that virtually none of the proverbs had the royal court as its setting, he interprets the texts from that perspective rather than attempting to come to grips with clan wisdom. Hans Walther Wolff's studies relating Amos and clan wisdom (Wolff 1964, 1969) would seem to call for clarification of that unknown factor. Von Rad ignored the challenge altogether. His defense of school wisdom in Israel demonstrates the paucity of information in this regard (see now H. J. Hermisson 1968, 97-136).

My objection to von Rad's treatment of wisdom extends beyond the basic thesis proposed and the fundamental presupposition about the evolution of wisdom thinking. Despite his perceptive remarks about Koheleth's attack upon God, von Rad fails to do justice to that sage's thought, in my opinion. Is it really correct to describe Koheleth as one devoid of tradition? Surely Koheleth's language makes frequent use of traditional symbolism and imagery, as numerous commentators have noted. While I cannot agree with H.W. Hertzberg that Koheleth wrote with Genesis 1–4 in hand (Hertzberg 1963, 230), I do believe he consciously varies traditional language. A good example is 3:11, where Koheleth alludes to the creation narrative but uses neutral terminology instead of בָּרָא and טֹוב. Well-known traditions rest behind his rejection of them and largely effect what Koheleth says. Furthermore, Koheleth does not claim to have achieved full knowledge. Rather, his allusion to knowledge that sums up reality stands under the qualification "who knows?" In fact, Koheleth complains because God withholds from him certain information necessary for a full life. Unlike von Rad, I do not think Koheleth's positive admonitions have freed themselves from the negative impact of approaching death. Instead, they become all the more pathetic, since everything is profitless.

Von Rad rejects Zimmerli's thesis that Koheleth functions as a guardian of authentic wisdom (Zimmerli 1963, 135-36). The reason is obvious: since, according to von Rad, there was no dogma of retribution, the sages needed no guardian to remind them of their fundamental position about limits to knowledge and concomitant divine freedom. Von Rad's attempt to deny rigidity of thought in Israelite wisdom lacks cogency. The speeches of Job's friends are hardly intelligible when divested of dogmatic assumptions. In this regard it should be noted that the scheme of cause and effect assumed by so many interpreters is no more rigid than von Rad's own analysis in terms of sacral, secular, and devotional.

Von Rad devotes a separate chapter to polemic against idols. This section contributes little to the understanding of wisdom in Israel, particularly since virtually every supporting text stands outside the wisdom corpus. The chapter provides valuable insights into the Israelite world view, but as is so often the case, it tells us little if anything about specific concerns of the wise.

An excursus on the cult is equally disappointing. Sufficient materials exist within wisdom literature to justify fuller treatment and a much greater role of the cult in the sage's life. The importance of the cult for Sirach is underplayed. Both in the selection of members to Israel's hall of fame and in comments about heroes of the past, Sirach reveals his great love for cultic personnel. The final hymn describing the High Priest arises naturally from Sirach's consistently expressed love for the cult. Von Rad's remarks about Sirach's sole interest being the moral presuppositions of the cult fail to do justice to Sirach or the cult. More accurate is his assessment of Job's dependence upon ancient cultic traditions, even if this reliance is described as a departure from wisdom. It is possible that the sages use the cult to embrace communal concerns, inasmuch as they found the exclusively individual focus wanting. In any case, the cultic responses prevail at two points: in matters of theodicy and in learned prayers (see the recent discussion by Leo Perdue 1975).

In one way von Rad's treatment of wisdom is idiosyncratic. He strives to defend a belief that wisdom gave birth to apocalyptic. Crucial to his argument is an analysis of divine determination of times. Von Rad insists that the gulf between the prophetic view of God's control of human destiny and apocalyptic's determinism is unbridgeable. He thinks apocalyptic removes divine action from ordinary events, placing them in the remote past or at the end of history. Von Rad connects this kind of thinking with the sage's belief in the divine fixing of destinies at the beginning of time. But the step from orders of creation to apocalyptic determination of times is a giant one. Much more defensible, in my judgment, is the association of prophecy and apocalyptic (see Peter von der Östen-Sacken 1969).

It is to be expected that many other areas of disagreement between von Rad and the reviewer would exist. Most of them are insignificant. One thing stands out, however, as more than mere difference of opinion. Von Rad consistently resorts to texts outside the wisdom corpus in describing the essential character of wisdom. Baptism of wisdom is evident in more than the analysis of proverbs. Surely it is questionable procedure to draw heavily from such texts as Jeremiah, Isaiah, Habakkuk, and the Joseph narrative in describing the views of sages. Von Rad's admission that the wise never again attempted the sort of literary fiction in the Joseph narrative ("Such a bold mixture of divine activity and guilty human deeds was never attempted again by the teachers," 200), and that Jeremiah developed wisdom thinking about human self-glorification to its zenith ought to warn the reader that something is amiss here. Although I do not want to push the point unnecessarily, I wonder whether von Rad did not prematurely abandon the attempt to date wisdom literature. Such a study might have prevented the abuse of the wisdom corpus that sprang from overlooking its uniqueness among Israel's several traditions.

The prominence of the doxology of judgment in Job receives ample treatment, for the most part (see also von Rad 1971b). Von Rad writes that the sages first developed the judgment doxology in prayer form. This statement needs considerable modification, for its usage in prayer texts of Ezra and Nehemiah certainly antedates the references he has supplied. In need of correction, too, is von Rad's assumption that confession of guilt removed the punishment for sin. Joshua 7:19 and rabbinic instances of execution give no support to von Rad's view. In this regard, a word about von Rad's treatment of theodicy in Sirach is called for. This excellent study of Sirach, first, published separately in *Evangelische Theologie*, places theodicy in the center of Sirach's thinking. Although von Rad stops short, and thus fails to deal with this issue satisfactorily, he does make a good beginning. (For fuller discussion, see Crenshaw 1975a, 47-64).

Seldom does von Rad permit outright contradictions to surface, even in so complicated a book. Perhaps his desire to hold together contrasting viewpoints contributed to the most obvious slipup in the volume. Von Rad writes that it is a mistake to interpret the bitterly serious Dialogue of Pessimism playfully, although in another part of the book he does precisely this ("the question about what is the right thing to do is lost in playful skepticism," 248).

3

Wisdom in Israel is but one of several books on Israelite wisdom. Schmid (1966) devotes full attention to Egyptian and Mesopotamian wisdom, deriving from this discussion the principal rubrics for understanding the development of Israel's wisdom. Von Rad denies any dogma of retribution and crisis in wisdom, central themes in Schmid's book. Hermisson (1968) provides careful stylistic analysis of literary proverbs, rejecting folk proverbs in the process. He also claims that the school nurtured Israel's wisdom and connects historiography and wisdom. Von Rad objects to the latter association. Another of von Rad's students, Bauer-Kayatz (1969) analyzes experiential and theological wisdom, drawing heavily upon Egyptian parallels. Scott (1971) offers a history and typology of Israel's wisdom, along with a discussion of wisdom in revolt that resembles von Rad's section on trust and attack. Brueggemann (1972) seeks to restore Israel's affirmation of human dignity, pointing to the openness of the sage's viewpoint. A Solomonic enlightenment is central to his understanding of Israel's wisdom, although the Davidic era is normative. Whybray (1974) wrestles with the methodological issue I posed in an earlier essay (1969)—an issue von Rad ignores, by the way—and endeavors to develop criteria by which Israel's intellectual tradition may be recognized. My own Prolegomenon to *Studies in Ancient Israelite Wisdom* (1975b) examines affinities between Israel's wisdom and that of Egypt and Mesopotamia, describes the forms of expression employed by Israel's sages, and seeks to clarify the structure of wisdom thinking. It addresses the function of creation in wisdom literature, particularly in contexts of theodicy. Von Rad's *Wisdom in Israel* towers over all these books in its magisterial survey of the phenomenon of Israel's quest for knowledge.

Von rad concluded his study of Israel's wisdom with some observations about what wisdom has and what it does not have. I shall follow suit. *Wisdom in Israel* constitutes von Rad's attempt on a grand scale to span the distance between ancient and modern thinking. The result is a masterpiece in two ways: first, it represents his mature insights into the nature of knowledge, and second, it points to the ultimate mystery that shrouds every attempt to grasp the unknowable. The latter facet of von Rad's own theological struggle surfaces again in his last exquisite little book, *Das Opfer des Abraham* (1971a). Von Rad centers upon *Israelite* wisdom, and in that he is surely right. Only after Israel's wisdom is understood clearly can adequate comparison with other sages be made. Nevertheless, a certain check upon overly Yahwistic readings of wisdom literature was ignored. The book suffers greatly from this failure to look closely at wisdom beyond Israel's boundaries. Lacking, too, are the usual form and traditiohistorical intuitions that have made von Rad's name synonymous with "originality" for a generation. The above criticisms notwithstanding, *Wisdom in Literature* makes a giant stride toward clarifying Israel's quest to know as much about life as can be known.

References

Brueggemann, Walter
1972   *In Man We Trust: The Neglected Side of Biblical Faith.* John Knox Press.
Crenshaw, James L.
1969   "Method in Determining Wisdom Influence Upon 'Historical' Literature." *JBL* 88:129-42.
1975a   "The Problem of Theodicy in Sirach: On Human Bondage." *JBL* 94:47-64.
1975b   *Studies in Ancient Israelite Wisdom.* LBSt. Ktav.
Fichtner, Johannes
1933   *Die altorientalische Weisheit in iher israelitisch- jüdischen Ausprägung: Eine Studie zur Nationalisierung der Weisheit in Israel.* BZAW 62. Giessen: Alfred Töpelmann.
Gese, Hartmut
1958   *Lehre und Wirklichkeit in der alten Weisheit: Studien zu den Sprüchen Salomos und zu dem Buche Hiob.* Tübingen: J. C. B. Mohr (Paul Siebeck).
Hermisson, Hans-Jürgen
1968   *Studien zur israelitischen Spruchweisheit.* WMANT 28. Neukirchen-Vluyn: Neukirchener.
Hertzberg, Hans Wilhelm
1963.   *Der Prediger.* KAT. Gütersloh: Gütersloher Verlaghaus Gerd Mohn.
Kayatz, Christa Bauer
1969   *Einführung in die alttestamentliche Weisheit.* BibS(N) 55. Neukirchen-Vluyn: Neukirchener.
Kovacs, Brian W.
1974   "Is There a Class-Ethic in Proverbs?" In *Essays in Old Testament Ethics: J. Philip Hyatt in Memoriam*, ed. James L. Crenshaw and John T. Willis, 177-89. Ktav.
Marböck, Johann
1971   *Weisheit im Wandel: Untersuchungen zur Weisheitsthologie bei Ben Sira.* BBB 37. Bonn: Peter Hanstein.
McKane, William
1965   *Prophets and Wise Men.* SBT 44. London: SCM.
Östen-Sacken, Peter von der
1969   *Die Apokalyptik in ihrem Verhältnis zu Prophetie und Weisheit.* ThEx 157. Munich: Chr. Kaiser.
Perdue, Leo G.
1975   "Wisdom and Cult." Ph.D. dissertation, Vanderbilt.
Rad, Gerhard von
1971a   *Das Opfer des Abraham.* Munich: Chr. Kaiser.
1971b   "Gerichtsdoxologie." In *Schalom: Studien zu Glaube und Geschichte Israels*, 28-37. AzT 46. Stuttgart: Calwer Verlag.

Schmid, Hans Heinrich
  1966   *Wesen und Geschichte der Weisheit: Eine Untersuchung zur altorientalischen und israelitischen Weisheitsliteratur*. BZAW 101. Berlin: Alfred Töpelmann.
Scott, R. B. Y.
  1971   *The Way of Wisdom in the Old Testament*. Macmillan.
  1972   "Wise and Fool, Righteous and Wicked." VTSup 23:146-65.
Whybray, R. N.
  1974   *The Intellectual Tradition in the Old Testament*. BZAW 135. Berlin and New York: Walter de Gruyter.
Wolff, Hans Walther
  1964   *Amos' geistige Heimat*. WMANT 18. Neukirchen-Vluyn: Neukirchener. ET: 1973. *Amos the Prophet: The Man and His Background*. Fortress.
  1969   *Dodekapropheton: Amos*. BKAT. Neukirchen-Vluyn: Neukirchener.
Zimmerli, Walther
  1933   "Zur Struktur der alttestamentliche Weisheit." *ZAW* 51:177-204.
  1963   "Ort und Grenze der Weisheit im Rahmen der alttestamentlichen Theologie." In *Les sagesses du Proche-Orient ancien: Colloque de Strasbourg 17-19 mai 1962*, 121-37. Paris: Presses Universitarires de France.
  1971   "Die Weisheit Israels: Zu einem Buch von Gerhard von Rad." *EvT* 31:680-95.

18 (1969)

Method
in Determining
Wisdom Influence
upon "Historical" Literature

The influence of wisdom upon nonhagiographic literature is increasingly emphasized. Such kinship is claimed for Gen 1–11, 37, 39–50, Exod 34:6ff., Deut, 2 Sam
9–20, 1 Kings 1–2, Amos, Habakkuk, Isaiah, and Jonah.[1] Impetus for the new tendency was furnished by von Rad's provocative study of the Joseph narrative, an article that has been almost directly responsible for similar claims of wisdom influence
upon Esther and the "succession document."[2] But the publication of new wisdom
texts from Mesopotamia and Ugarit and fresh comparison with Egyptian wisdom

---

[1]For Gen 1–11, R. H. Pfeiffer, "Wisdom and Vision in the Old Testament," *ZAW* 52 (1934): 93-101,
particularly 97ff.; and J. L. McKenzie, "Reflections on Wisdom," *JBL* 86 (1967): 1-9; L. Alonso-Schökel,
"Motivos sapienciales y de alianza en Gen. 2–3," *Bib* 43 (1962): 295-316. For Gen 37, 39–50, Gerhard
von Rad, "The Joseph Narrative and Ancient Wisdom," in *The Problem of the Hexateuch and other
Essays* (1966) 292-300, originally published in SVT 1 (1953). For Exod 34:6ff., R. C. Dentan, "The
Literary Affinities of Exod. XXXIV 6ff.," *VT* 13 (1963): 34-51. For Deut, M. Weinfeld, "The Origin of
Humanism in Deuteronomy," *JBL* 80 (1961): 241-47, and "Deuteronomy—The Present State of Inquiry,"
JBL 86 (1967): 249-62, J. Malfroy, "Sagesse et Loi dans le Deutéronome," *VT* 15 (1965): 49-65; J. R.
Boston, "The Wisdom Influence upon the Song of Moses," *JBL* 88 (1968): 196-202. For 2 Sam 9–20
and 1 Kings 1–2, R. N. Whybray, *The Succession Narrative*, SBT 2nd ser. 9 (1968). For Amos, S.
Terrien, "Amos and Wisdom," *Israel's Prophetic Heritage*, ed. B. W. Anderson and W. Harrelson (1962)
108-15; H. W. Wolff, *Amos' geistige Heimat* (1964) and *Dodekapropheton, Amos* (1967–   ), and for
a critique of the position, J. L. Crenshaw, "The Influence of the Wise upon Amos," *ZAW* 79 (1967): 42-
52. For Hab, D. E. Gowan, "Habakkuk and Wisdom," paper read at the 103rd meeting of SBL (1967).
For Isa, J. Fichtner, "Jesaja unter den Weisen," *ThLZ* 74 (1949): 76-80, and R. J. Anderson, "Was Isaiah
a Scribe?" *JBL* 79 (1960): 57ff. For prophecy in general, J. Lindblom, "Wisdom in the Old Testament
Prophets," SVT 3 (1960): 192-204, and W. McKane, *Prophets and Wise Men*, SBT 44 (1965). For Jonah,
P. L. Trible, *Studies in the Book of Jonah* (diss., Columbia University, 1964) and R. Augé, *Profetes
Menors* (1957).

[2]S. Talmon, " 'Wisdom' in the Book of Esther," *VT* 13 (1963): 419-55, and Whybray, *The Succession Narrative*.

have spurred the trend to unprecedented heights.[3] The excitement of new directions in scholarship has led to exaggerated claims supported by dubious arguments and assumptions, so that a study of methodology in determining wisdom influence is imperative at this juncture. This paper will seek to outline some methodological principles in the study of wisdom influence, and on the basis of these will evaluate the claims about the Joseph narrative, succession document, and Esther.

I. Statement of the Method

Crucial to the study of any movement is its definition, which can be neither too broad nor too narrow, but must be both inclusive and exclusive. A distinction between wisdom literature, wisdom tradition, and wisdom thinking is essential, for these terms refer to the literary deposit of a specifically defined movement characterized by a particular approach to reality.[4] It must be recognized that wisdom speech is not *a se* wisdom,[5] and that several kinds of wisdom are discernible: (1) juridical, (2) nature, (3) practical, and (4) theological—each with a distinct *Sitz im Leben*.[6] Accordingly, one must distinguish between family/clan wisdom, the goal of which is the mastering of life, the stance hortatory and style proverbial;[7] court wisdom, with the goal of education for a select group, the stance secular, and method didactic;[8] and scribal wisdom, the goal being education for all, the stance dogmatico-religious, and the method dialogico-admonitory.[9] Moreover, the wisdom

---

[3]Besides *ANET*, ed. J. B. Pritchard (1955) and *Wisdom in Israel and in the Ancient Near East*, ed. Martin Noth and D. Winton Thomas (1960), the following may be mentioned: J. Van Dijk, *La sagesse suméro accadienne* (1953); W. G. Lambert, *Babylonian Wisdom Literature* (1960); E. I. Gordon, *Sumerian Proverbs* (1959) and "A New Look at the Wisdom of Sumer and Akkad," BibOr 17 (1960): 122-52; *Les sagesses du proche-orient ancien* (1963—which contains excellent articles on wisdom's history and ideology, as well as extensive bibliography, esp. on Egyptian wisdom); H. Gese, *Lehre und Wirklichkeit in der alten Weisheit* (1958); and H. H. Schmid, *Wesen und Geschichte der Weisheit*, BZAW 101 (1966).

[4]Schmid, *Wesen und Geschichte der Weisheit*, 7. It would be less confusing to speak in terms of wisdom literature, παιδεία, and חָכְמָה. The first would refer to Prov, Qoh, Job, Sir, Wisd of Sol, and Wisdom Pss; παιδεία would suggest the wisdom movement itself, its educational curriculum and pedagogy; חָכְמָה would indicate a particular stance, an approach to reality.

[5]Schmid, *Wesen und Geschichte der Weisheit*, 120. Schmid's point is that Sumerian lists (originally an attempt at ordering the world) are taken over by the Babylonians for their philological value.

[6]R. E. Murphy, "Assumptions and Problems in Old Testament Wisdom Research," *CBQ* 29 (1967): 104. It is in this context that Murphy observes that "wisdom language does not constitute wisdom," and rejects both the method of "anthological composition" and "*topoi*" for determining wisdom influence.

[7]E. Gerstenberger, *Wesen und Herkunft des 'Apodiktischen Rechts,'* WMANT 20 (1965) and J. P. Audet, "Origines comparées de la double tradition de la loi et de la sagesse dans la proche-orient ancien," *International Congress of Orientalists* (Moscow, 1960) 1:352-57.

[8]H. Duesberg, *Les scribes inspirés*, has given a helpful analysis of the courtly background of wisdom.

[9]W. Richter, *Recht und Ethos*, SANT 15 (1966) stresses the school as the locus of wisdom. A. Barucq, *Le Livre des Proverbes* (1964) 12-15, thinks the prophets attacked the scribe (court official)

movement is self-critical, Job and Qoheleth emphasizing the disparity between wisdom's claims and reality itself.

The multiplicity of wisdom's representatives and answers[10] must not force one into a definition that is so comprehensive that it becomes unusable. This is the weakness of von Rad's definition of wisdom, taken over by McKenzie. If one views wisdom as "practical knowledge of the laws of life and of the world, based on experience" and thinks that "wisdom had to do with the whole of life, and had to be occupied with all of its departments,"[11] or that wisdom is an "approach to reality," "a firm belief in the validity of experience,"[12] it is little surprise to discover wisdom everywhere, for what literature does not grow out of and reflect experience?

On the other hand, it is likewise true that the understanding of wisdom as eudemonistic, humanistic, international, and nonhistorical is inadequate, for it is both too narrow and false. As Schmid has emphasized, the religious basis of wisdom rests on the assumption that the Creator has established the world so that accord with its governing principle (Ma'at, Me, מִשְׁפָּט) does pay off, but this is not exactly eudemonism.[13] The deep religious cast of wisdom from its earliest stages demands that the claim of humanism be rejected, even though emphasis is placed on man and his behavior. Even the position that wisdom is international is erroneous for Sirach and Wisdom of Solomon, and may be contested at other points. Nevertheless, there is a measure of truth in R. Pautrel's remark that "De toute facon, le genre sapientiel avait été l'une des fenêtres d'Israël sur le monde."[14] Von Rad has discussed the tension between the universal and particular in the ancient Israelite world view of the sage in brilliant fashion, concluding that man "lives within a created order from which ascends an unending hymn of praise, yet he himself hears nothing of it. . . . He must be taught, as if he were blind and deaf, that he lives in a world which could be revealed to him. . . ."[15] As for the view that wisdom is nonhistorical,

---

rather than the sage.

[10]Frankfort, *Ancient Egyptian Religion* (1961; first published in 1948) 4, has characterized ancient thought as a "multiplicity of approaches and answers."

[11]Gerhard von Rad, *Old Testament Theology* 1 (ET 1962) 418, 428. This discussion of wisdom is still perhaps the most provocative available.

[12]McKenzie, "Reflections on Wisdom," 2, 4. Similarly, if one with S. Blank views wisdom as "philosophy rooted in the soil of life: truth springs out of the earth" (*IDB* R-Z:853-61), it follows that a discussion of wisdom in the Old Testament will include Aaron, Moses, Daniel, and others. Again, Lambert (*Babylonian Wisdom Literature*) has even suggested that "a case could be made for including many of the Babylonian epics in the wisdom category, since they deal with cosmological problems" (1).

[13]*Wesen und Geschichte der Weisheit*, 3, 20-22, 115-17, 159-61; see also A. Volten, "Der Begriff der Ma'at in den Ägyptischen Weisheitstexten," in *Les sagesses du proche-orient ancien*, 73-101, and Gese, *Lehre und Wirklichkeit in der alten Weisheit*, 11-21 (and 45-50, where Yahweh's freedom over against this "order" is recognized as an Israelite theme).

[14]*L'Ecclésiaste*, 8.

[15]"Some Aspects of the Old Testament Worldview," *The Problem of the Hexateuch and other Essays*, 164; originally published in *EvTh* 11 (1964).

Schmid has shown convincingly that there is a structural history of wisdom, one that has its changing *Sitzen im Leben*, and that wisdom is itself aware of this history.[16]

It has also been claimed that wisdom is individualistic as opposed to the corporate emphasis of prophecy and priesthood, but even this judgment must be corrected by the recognition that courtly wisdom is social in orientation, especially in its juridical concern.[17] The same may be said of the wisdom of the clan, for there is growing acceptance of the close association of law and wisdom championed by Gerstenberger.[18]

Wisdom, then, may be defined as the quest for self-understanding in terms of relationships with things, people, and the Creator. This search for meaning moves on three levels: (1) nature wisdom which is an attempt to master things for human survival and well-being, and which includes the drawing up of onomastica and study of natural phenomena as they relate to man and the universe;[19] (2) juridical and *Erfahrungsweisheit* (practical wisdom) with the focus upon human relationships in an ordered society or state; and (3) theological wisdom, which moves in the realm of theodicy,[20] and in so doing affirms God as ultimate meaning (even when denying any purpose in life as does Qoheleth, for the pathos of this masterpiece grows out of the fact that the true source of meaning is theological rather than anthropological).[21]

First, then, is the question of definition. A second observation is that wisdom influence can only be proved by a stylistic or ideological peculiarity found primarily in wisdom literature. This implies the exclusion of a common cultural stock, much of which is environmental or derives from the period of the family/clan before the separation into distinct compartments of prophet, priest, and sage. Accordingly, the appeal to Deuteronomy's use of such common words as "hear, know, take, keep,

---

[16]*Wesen und Geschichte der Weisheit*, passim. Furthermore, sacred history plays an important role in Sirach and Wisdom of Solomon. The classic discussion is J. Fichtner, "Zum Problem Glaube und Geschichte in der israelitisch-jüdischen Weisheitsliteratur," *TLZ* 76 (1951): 145-50, repr. in *Gottes Weisheit*, 9-17.

[17]Schmid, *Wesen und Geschichte der Weisheit*, 110-14. Conversely, there is growing recognition that individual responsibility was basic to legal procedure from the earliest times (B. Lindars, "Ezekiel and Individual Responsibility," *VT* 15 [1965]: 452-67, particularly 454).

[18]"Covenant and Commandment," *JBL* 84 (1965): 38-51, particularly 50ff.

[19]See esp. von Rad, "Job XXXVIII and Ancient Egpytian Wisdom," *The Problem of the Hexateuch and other Essays*, 281-91 (orig. SVT 3 [1960]) and W. Zimmerli, "The Place and Limit of the Wisdom in the Framework of the Old Testament Theology," *SJT* 18 (1964): 146-58, originally in *Les sagesses du proche-orient ancien*.

[20]R. J. Williams, "Theodicy in the Ancient Near East," *CJT* 2 (1956): 14-26. A. Bentzen (*Introduction to the Old Testament*, 1:173) quotes an observation by Hylmö that wisdom literature became little by little a literature written by scholars for other scholars. This would be especially pertinent to reflective or theological wisdom.

[21]Gese ("Die Krisis der Weisheit bei Koheleth," *Les sagesses du proche-orient ancien*, 139-51) rightly perceives the deep religious stance of Qoheleth.

law, teach, etc." by Weinfeld and Malfroy carries little cogency.[22] The use of word tabulation is also particularly vulnerable in this regard, unless employed with extreme caution.[23] When one recognizes that wisdom is rooted in experience, it should be no surprise to discover a common vocabulary among sage, prophet, and priest. Moreover, it needs to be pointed out that to call one wise is not to identify him as a sage (cf. Judg 5:29).

This leads to a third observation: differences in nuance must be explained. Whenever a wisdom phrase or motif is found outside wisdom literature the scholar must determine whether or not the meaning has been changed. This can be illustrated by the motif of silence in Egypt and Israel, and by the literary genre of "disputation" in wisdom and prophetic literature.

Egyptian wisdom literature distinguishes between the passionate and the silent man, the latter of whom is like a fertile tree (cf. Ps 1) and is acceptable to the gods who dwell in the land of silence. In the later period the wise man describes himself as the truly silent one (Amenemope; Merikare), and excessive talkativeness (ecstasy and gossip) are viewed as sin. This is in strong contrast to the premium placed on fine speech in the Old Kingdom, at first viewed as a possession of the king or sage, but later recognized even among maid servants at the grindstones (Ptah-hotep—*ANET* 412). But this freedom of speech and high esteem in which it was held posed a political threat, so that both anthropological (contrast between silent man and passionate one) and theological (God of silence favors diplomatic silence) arguments were employed to combat the danger (Ani; Amenemope).[24]

Silence is a prominent theme in Israelite wisdom, but never does it serve as an epithet of the sage. Rather this emphasis is a means of combatting slander and gossip, and depicts the proper reverence before the Holy One (Job 4:12-21, 40:4-5, Hab 2:20, Qoh 5:2; cf. *ANET* 408) and in the presence of death (Amos 6:10, 8:3, 5:13, Judg 3:19, Zeph 1:7, Zech 2:13, Esther 4:14; cf. *ANET* 9, 18, 27, 49, 51, 55, 91, 408, 419n.17). Accordingly it is important to priest and prophet. Not without justification has Y. Kaufmann called the priestly temple the "kingdom of silence."[25] The prophetic emphasis on silence occurs in Amos, where wisdom language may

---

[22]Weinfeld, "The Origin of Humanism in Deuteronomy," and Malfroy, "Sagesse et Loi dans le Deutéronome." Into this category also falls the attempt by B. Couroyer to find literary dependence between Ps 34:13 and Egyptian wisdom ("Idéal sapiential en Egypte et en Israël," *RB* 57 [1950]: 174-79). It may be observed that Weinfeld's thesis that Deuteronomy is the composition of scribes associated with the courts of Hezekiah and Josiah who "achieved a religio-national ideology which was inspired by the sapiential-didactic school" ("Deuteronomy—The Present State of Inquiry," 262) is more ideologically based than philological.

[23]A good example of a judicious use of this method is the recent article by Boston, "The Wisdom Influence upon the Song of Moses."

[24]G. Lanczkowski, "Reden und Schweigen im ägyptischen Verständnis, vornehmlich des Mittleren Reiches," *Ägyptologische Studien* 29 (1955): 186-96. For the importance of silence see *ANET* 414 (silence is better than teftef plants), 418, 420-24, 438.

[25]*The Religion of Israel*, 303.

be used, but with nonwisdom nuance. This is true both of 6:9-10, where a severe epidemic has decimated the city and the prophet urges silence lest the customary benediction remind the destructive deity that survivors have been left, and of 5:13, which suggests that the prudent man will keep silent in such an evil time. If from Amos, this latter statement is full of irony, the wisdom theme being used in a totally new sense, for the last thing Amos would do is keep quiet in the midst of human oppression. In sum, the mere use of wisdom phraseology by a prophet does not make him a sage,[26] for his meaning may be completely alien to wisdom thinking.

A comparison of the "disputation" in wisdom literature and in prophetic traditions (particularly Malachi) indicates that differences in nuance must not be ignored.[27] Whereas the prophetic dispute grows out of and vividly reflects a real confrontation between a prophet and his opponent, and announces the divine decision of judgment and basis for it, the wisdom disputation may be purely literary, often concerns the relative value of things or professions, and resembles the fable in many instances.

Fourth, the negative attitude to wisdom in much of the Old Testament must be kept in mind, especially in looking for changes in nuance. It is certainly striking that wisdom frequently leads to destruction in the historical and prophetic literature. This is true of the wise men of Egypt (Exod 7:8-13), the scheming plan of Jonadab to satisfy Amnon's passion for Tamar (2 Sam 13:3-5), the clever ruse instigated by Joab and articulated by the wise woman of Tekoa (2 Sam 14:1-21), the traitorous behavior of the wise woman of Abel (2 Sam 20), the bloody actions of Solomon upon succeeding David (1 Kings 1-2), the successful deceitful counsel of Hushai (2 Sam 16:23—17:23), the clever serpent (Gen 3), and the foolish advisers of Pharaoh (Isa 19:11ff., 30:1ff., 31:1ff.).[28] Furthermore, the hesitancy to attribute wisdom to Yahweh until quite late indicates an early negative attitude to wisdom,[29] as does the opposition to the building of the Solomonic temple, the achievement of human wisdom (cf. Baal and Anat).

Fifth, wisdom's history must be taken into consideration, insofar as it is possible to determine its structural development, geographic spread, and ideological formulation. The most striking observation here is the change in wisdom reflected in the apocryphal works, specifically the inclusion of priestly and *heilsgeschichtliche*

---

[26]H. Schmid, "Hauptprobleme der neueren Prophetenforschung," *STU* 25 (1965): 142, has asked if a wisdom word in the mouth of a prophet means the same as that word spoken by a teacher. Similarly, in *Wesen und Geschichte der Weisheit*, Schmid recognizes that even etiology can argue from wisdom categories (101), and that wisdom thinking often appears in nonwisdom forms, such as hymns, laws, and omens (110-14, 142).

[27]E. Pfeiffer, "Die Disputationswörte im Buche Maleachi," *EvT* 12 (1959): 546-68.

[28]H. Cazelles, "Les débuts de la Sagesse en Israël," *Les sagesses du proche-orient ancien*, 34-36.

[29]M. Noth, "Die Bewährung von Salomos 'Göttlicher Weisheit,'" *Wisdom in Israel and in the Ancient Near East*, 225-37. McKane, *Prophets and Wise Men*, has dealt with the conflict between prophecy and wisdom, particularly in regard to statecraft.

concerns. Especially important is the recognition of the crisis in wisdom and ensuing dogmatizing and democratizing of wisdom stressed so provocatively by Schmid, a phenomenon common to the wisdom of Egypt, Mesopotamia, and Israel. Moreover, the difference between courtly and clan wisdom, with urban and rural settings respectively, must be recognized, and the literature of each identified. This means that the difficult question of Solomon's role in wisdom must be evaluated, as well as that of Hezekiah.[30] Special attention must be given to the pronounced nationalism of the reforms of Hezekiah and Josiah. Those who claim that these are times of great wisdom influence must show how coexistence with a strongly particularistic governmental policy was possible.

II. Application of the Methodological Observations

A. *The Joseph Narrative.* Von Rad has described the Joseph narrative as an ideal portrait of the courtly wise man, written during the Solomonic enlightenment characterized by anthropological interests. This claim is based on an analysis of the educational ideal and theological ideas permeating Gen 37, 39–50. The fear of the Lord as the point of departure, and the goal of humility, tact, patience, and avoidance of the snares of evil women and hot temperedness are said to be the educational ideals of Egyptian and Israelite wisdom. The absence of cultic etiology, *Heilsgeschichte*, and revelation, together with the presence of a thoroughly religious stance that stresses the hidden providence of God and frustration of man's plans by the Creator (a kind of skepticism that reaches its apex in Qoheleth!) demand for von Rad the conclusion that the *Sitz im Leben* of the narratives is wisdom of the court. Von Rad thinks the parallels with Egyptian wisdom at all these points confirm this hypothesis of a wisdom setting.[31]

Despite the general acceptance of this ingenious hypothesis, a number of questions must be raised, because the case for von Rad's view cannot be said to have been closed. The difficulty in this instance is not so much with definition or failure to consider the history of wisdom, for on both these issues von Rad has much to say in this article, even if the assumption of a Solomonic sponsorship of wisdom is questioned by some. But in view of the other three principles discussed above, von Rad's hypothesis cannot be sustained.

First, wisdom influence can only be proved by stylistic and ideological peculiarities. The argument from psychological interest in the phenomenon of man in its broadest sense overlooks the fact that this is a concern common to much of the ancient literature. Von Rad himself recognizes its presence in the "succession document";[32] one must ask whether there is a qualitative difference between these

---

[30]R. B. Y. Scott, "Solomon and the Beginnings of Wisdom in Israel," *Wisdom in Israel and in the Ancient Near East,* 262-79; and A. Alt, "Die Weisheit Salomos," *ThLZ* 76 (1951): 139-44.

[31]"The Joseph Narrative and Ancient Wisdom," passim.

[32]"The Beginnings of Historical Writing in Ancient Israel," *The Problem of the Hexateuch and other*

two literary complexes and Gen 3, 22, Exod 32, and 1 Kings 13. Moreover, the claim that the Joseph narrative is anthropological in tone overlooks the decisive episode of Joseph's refusing the advances of Potiphar's wife. Here the reason for rejecting her favors is not that Joseph wishes to deal justly with his fellow man, but rather the high point of the reasoning is, "How then can I do this great wickedness, and sin against *God?*" (39:9). Again it must be pointed out that the theme of evil women is a common one, far too ubiquitous to demand wisdom influence.

The third methodological observation that differences in nuance must be explained requires the following correction of von Rad's thesis. In spite of the use of a theme popular in wisdom circles, this story introduces a nuance alien to wisdom. The emphasis on the providence of God, indeed the hidden action of God despite human intentions, is in one particular quite distant from the skepticism of Qoheleth: here the will of God is hidden from evil men, and the wicked schemes are thwarted, while the secrets of God are revealed to Joseph, the favorite of God. There is no place in the Egyptian wisdom literature cited or in Israelite wisdom for this pattern; rather the point of the skeptical emphasis is that there is no one who knows the ways of God, and even the plans of the righteous man may be frustrated by the mysterious God. Still another caveat at this point must be given: the stress on providence is not peculiar to wisdom, but pervades the literature of the Old Testament.[33]

More devastating, however, is the presence in the Joseph narrative of nonwisdom themes. At the outset it may be observed that a man whose story begins and ends in defeat provides a very poor model for the wise men of the court; the story opens with the account of Joseph's frustration in fraternal relations, and ends with the paternal negation of his heart's desire for his sons (48:17-20). Moreover, it is a strange model of education that has as its hero one who has not been trained at a school, and a peculiar propaganda for courtly wisdom that has the ruler choose a man as his counselor on the basis of his "spiritualistic" qualifications. Again, the failure of Joseph to control his emotions must not be overlooked (45:2, 14ff., 50:1, 17), as well as his lack of tact in telling his dreams to his brothers and his harsh treatment of them at a later time (even if the latter is mitigated somewhat by understanding it as a sort of test to ascertain whether the brothers had truly changed).

The nonwisdom themes are numerous, in part growing out of the material itself. These include: (1) the appeal to special revelation and theophanic visions; (2) the emphasis on dreams and divining cup as mediating divine intentions; (3) sacrifice; (4) genealogy (46:8ff.); (5) kosher food (43:31-34); (6) etiology for taxes (47:20ff.); and (7) *Heilsgeschichte* (place names, including Hebron, Shechem, Dothan, Luz, Bethlehem, Beer-sheba; patriarchs and their deities, such as "the God of Isaac," El

---

Essays, 175-204; orig. *AfK* 22 (1944).

[33]Von Rad has taught us, more provocatively than any other, of the significance of this theme in the Hexateuch.

Shaddai, Yahweh,[34] the God of the fathers; the holy war formula, "The Lord was with Joseph" and "I fear God";[35] and the narrative as a prologue to the exodus).

In view of the preceding analysis, von Rad's thesis that the Joseph narrative is a manifestation of the wisdom ideal of education and theology cannot be accepted. What, then, of the other two works stimulated by this article?

B. *The Succession Document.* R. N. Whybray has recently submitted the "succession document" to detailed analysis, reaching the conclusion that it is neither history, (in intention or fact), a novel, a national epic, or a moral-religious tale; rather "it is a work of political propaganda intended to support the regime (of Solomon) by demonstrating its legitimacy and justifying its policies."[36] A comparison of the narrative with Proverbs in regard to the importance of counsel, the ideas of retribution and the hidden control of human destiny by the Creator, and the attitude toward the cult, together with a study of didactic literature in general (use of simile, comparison and narration, dramatization of proverbial wisdom, the irresistible power of a multitude, wisdom and folly, control of sexual passion, humility, learning from experience, danger of treacherous companions, proper speech, education of children, ideal king, ambition, frustration and fulfillment, friendship, loyalty and treachery, and revenge) prompts Whybray to write that the author of the succession narrative "set out deliberately to illustrate specific proverbial teaching for the benefit of the pupils and ex-pupils of the schools."[37] An examination of comparable political novels in Egypt, namely, the Prophecy of Neferty, Kemit, Satire on the Trades, Instruction of Amenemhet, and Story of Sinuhe, all of which were written during the period of Amenemhet and Sesostris, suggests to Whybray that the political novel, sophisticated psychological novel, and narrative based on wisdom themes were known in Egypt long before Solomon, and that the author of the succession narrative probably had such literature among his models.[38]

First, a few words about the general thesis of the book. The conclusion that the succession document is not historical in intention or fact, nor that it is a novel or national epic carries conviction, and is argued with keen insight. However, the rejection of the narrative as a religiomoral tale seems premature, for this view is not negated by the psychological complexity concealing the simple moral. It is difficult to envision a reading of the story without grasping the moral implied about family relations (adultery, sibling rivalry, and sex) and obligations of office and friendship, in spite of (or *because of*) the psychological concerns of the narrative. The hypothesis that the story was written to demonstrate the legitimacy of the Solomonic regime

---

[34]J. L. Crenshaw, "*YHWH Ṣᵉbā'ôt Šmô*: A Form-critical Analysis," forthcoming in *ZAW*.

[35]J. L. Crenshaw, "Amos and the Theophanic Tradition," *ZAW* 80 (1968): 203-15; and K. W. Neubauer, "Erwägungen zu Amos 5:4-15," *ZAW* 78 (1966): 294-302.

[36]*The Succession Narrative*, 55.

[37]Ibid., 95.

[38]Ibid., 116.

and to justify its policies suffers from the well-known fact that neither David nor Solomon is displayed in a favorable light. Quite the contrary, for David's weaknesses and their effect are elaborated in all their poignancy, whereas Solomon is represented as ascending the throne through the scheming plans of the court prophet and the aged Bathsheba, and his first action is almost unsurpassed in the Old Testament for cruelty. In view of this Achilles' heel to Whybray's thesis, a study of his arguments in terms of the five methodological principles enumerated above will be particularly instructive.

The fundamental error of this work of Whybray is the failure to search for stylistic and ideological peculiarities found primarily in wisdom literature. The book suffers grossly from this standpoint. The various themes from Proverbs said to be consciously illustrated by the story are common ones in legal and prophetic literature. It is difficult to see how any story could fail to "illustrate" themes in Proverbs, for this book covers the whole gamut of human existence.[39] The examples below are but a few of the many falling under this category.

The idea of retribution is not only a wisdom theme, but occurs frequently in legal material, where the punishment is made to suit the offense. The hidden control of God over human affairs despite man's intentions is a basic assumption of the Yahwist, Elohist, deuteronomist, and prophecy; furthermore, the tenuous nature of human plans is made all the more finite by the stress upon the demonic in Yahweh and freedom of God to override human intentions.[40] The attitude to the cult in Proverbs has parallels in prophetic literature, and the case is not so clear with the succession document, for sacrifice is practiced, and the absence of the oracle grows out of the fact that David does not go to battle against non-Israelites in the succession document, the oracle in the earlier stories of David being the means of determining whether to wage war or not.[41] The concern for ethical conduct,

---

[39]The prophetic legend in 1 Kings 13 will illustrate the point rather graphically. Nearly every category listed by Whybray in the discussion of parallels between Proverbs and the succession narrative is appropriate here, too. The polarities of wisdom and folly are illustrated by Jeroboam's refusal to listen to the man of God and by the desire of the aged nabi to provide for his existence in Sheol by requesting burial beside the man of God. The danger of pride can be seen in the arrogant boast of the nabi that he was also a prophet, despite the falsity of the statement. The value of experience is recognized both by Jeroboam and the nabi, and the disaster caused by treacherous companions could not be more dramatically depicted. Of course both prophets recognized the necessity of good speech, and the old nabi had taught his children proper respect and obedience, as can be seen from their actions. The value of an ideal king can be recognized by noting its opposite in Jeroboam, while the ambition of the nabi is seen in his desire to associate with the powerful man of God. The frustration of human plans by the hidden God is poignantly depicted, for the fate of the man of God is outside his own hands. The joys of friendship and loyalty, as well as the woes of treachery and revenge, are also illustrated by the relationship between the man of God and the old nabi. Indeed, the man of God would have fared better had he taken seriously the advice about not eating where love is absent, or heeded Prov 22:13 and 26:13.

[40]P. Volz, *Das Dämonische im Jahwe.*

[41]This also explains the attitude to the ark, which was associated with battle. There is one "great exception" to Whybray's thesis about special revelation, as he himself admits (*The Succession Narrative,*

humility, and private prayer is not unique to wisdom, for both prophets and priests shared this interest. Likewise, the רָאִיתִי and וָאֵרֶא formulas[42] are reminiscent of prophetic visions, and use language that every human being employed. Again, it is impossible to converse without using simile and comparison, for the sages did not monopolize metaphorical language. The belief that a multitude is irresistible does not demand wisdom provenance, for Gen 11 uses this idea with special force. Furthermore, the desire to avoid evil women and treacherous companions is a common one (cf. Amos), and the emphasis upon humility and learning from experience is equally as pronounced in Isaiah as in Proverbs.[43] In the same category are the appeal to the use of fine speech and the concern for education. The sages are not sole guardians of either.

Whybray's argument also suffers from a failure to explain nonwisdom emphases in the succession document. Especially damaging to his thesis is the minor role played by wisdom's representatives, indeed the questionable function of each. The total effect of counselors, both private and courtly, is ruinous. This is true of the women of Tekoa and Abel, as well as of Ahithophel, while Hushai's advice is pure treachery. It seems likely that, if Whybray's view were true, the scribes would have presented the wisdom representatives in a far more favorable light. It is difficult to conceive of scribes calling attention to the frustration of Ahithophel's counsel by Yahweh, for this would undermine their position immeasurably.

A third methodological weakness can be observed in the work under investigation. The history of wisdom does not appear to have been considered carefully enough. The hypothesis of the book assumes a fully developed wisdom tradition in the early days of Solomon's reign (indeed, during David's rule!),[44] one that taught proverbial lore now found in Proverbs, and that Egyptian literature had already been mastered this early. This assumption is, at the very least, debatable; to build a whole superstructure on such a flimsy foundation is hazardous indeed.

Finally, differences in nuance between the succession document and wisdom are ignored. Much closer to the truth is von Rad's argument that there is a sharp distinction between the theological standpoints of the Joseph narrative and the succession document, the latter of which does not reflect skepticism as to the hidden control of God over human affairs.[45]

If the preceding arguments have any cogency, the hypothesis of Whybray that the succession narrative is a conscious attempt to illustrate Proverbs by scribes who

---

69), namely, the oracle of Nathan in 2 Sam 12.

[42]Whybray, *The Succession Narrative*, 75.

[43]For the view that wisdom literature made use of the prophetic tradition, see A. Robert's series of articles on Prov 1–9 in *RB* 43-44 (1934–1935) under the title, "Les attaches litteraires bibliques de Proverbs I–IX."

[44]In agreement with McKenzie, "Reflections on Wisdom."

[45]"The Beginnings of Historical Writing in Ancient Israel," 198ff. But the skepticism of the Joseph narrative is much farther from Qoheleth than von Rad admits.

desired to justify Solomon's regime and policies fares no better than von Rad's thesis about the Joseph narrative, and suggests that an examination of Talmon's comparatively recent article on Esther and wisdom is in place.

C. *The Book of Esther.* Taking his cue from von Rad's study of the Joseph narrative and L. A. Rosenthal's demonstration of Esther's dependence on that account,[46] S. Talmon concludes that the Esther narrative is "a historicized wisdom tale," an "enactment of standard wisdom motifs," "having typical wisdom themes and precepts."[47] He thinks that the "outline of the plot and the presentation of the central characters show the wise men in action,"[48] and that the book is made up of an ancient Near Eastern wisdom nucleus in specific biblical variation together with Persian literary motifs.[49] Talmon rests his case on similarities in situations and general trends and ideas in Esther and wisdom, rather than on literary parallels. Accordingly appeal is made to the absence of specifically Jewish religiosity and history, the "concept of an unspecified and remote deity devoid of any individual character," the presence of an individualistic slant and anthropocentric stance, a fondness for court life, and typological concepts (the powerful but witless dupe, the righteous wise, and the conniving schemer).

Talmon has succeeded in forcing biblical scholars to ask a question that would almost never have occurred to them, for it is difficult to conceive of a book more alien to wisdom literature than Esther. A number of his arguments must be challenged, however, as misstatements of fact or erroneous conclusions. First, it is quite a leap from the idea that help may come to the Jews from another source (מִמָּקוֹם אַחֵר) to the wisdom notion of a remote deity, for there is no assurance that the reference is to divine assistance.[50] Again, the argument about typology is singularly unconvincing, for it must resort to an hypothesis about the splitting up of the Ahiqar-Nadin typology, and rests on an analogy between a wise man's adoption of students and the Ugaritic and biblical tales of the loss of progeny by Keret, Danel, and Job. Furthermore, the emphasis upon retribution of the measure-for-measure variety overlooks the natural legal offense, where punishment by human beings is to be expected. As for the claim that Ahasuerus is a type of witless dupe in power, one must note that the impression is certainly a subtle one if that is intended. A more cogent case could be made for the description of Saul in such terms. Particularly weak is Talmon's reference to wise women in Israel, use of sex for desired ends, and erotic interest, all of which prove nothing about the book of

---

[46]"Die Josephgeschichte mit den Büchern Ester und Daniel verglichen," *ZAW* 15 (1895): 278-84, and "Nochmals der Vergleich Ester-Joseph-Daniel," *ZAW* 17 (1897): 126-28.

[47]"'Wisdom' in the Book of Esther," 426.

[48]Ibid., 427.

[49]Ibid., 453.

[50]For opposing views, see A. Spanier, "Die Gottesbezeichnungen המקום und הוא ברוך הקדוש in der frühtalmudischen Literatur," *MGWJ* (1922): 309-14; and H. Bardtke, *Das Buch Esther*, KAT 17/5 (1963) 333.

Esther and wisdom. In this regard, the claim that the inclusion of women courtiers is a novel feature in the ancient Near East overlooks their presence in Canaan (cf. Judg 5), if such they be! Finally, Talmon himself admits that Mordecai is a very poor type of wise man, possessing neither the necessary linguistic ability nor proper tact, the latter illustrated by his refusal to bow before Haman.[51] These observations are reinforced by a study of Talmon's hypothesis from the point of view of the five methodological principles discussed above.

Perhaps the most striking violation of these principles is the failure to reckon with nonwisdom elements. The most glaring of these is the pronounced nationalistic fervor permeating the book of Esther, a spirit that has been an offense to Christian and Jew alike.[52] Any hypothesis that Esther derives from wisdom must explain the presence of narrow nationalism. To ignore this factor is to leave the case hanging in midair.

The history of wisdom is not given proper treatment in this study either, for a kinship between the supposed wisdom of Esther and that of Sirach and Wisdom of Solomon would be expected, since the date of Esther is nearer these works than to older traditions of Proverbs. Therefore, *Heilsgeschichte* and the identification of Torah and wisdom should be present in Esther, while just the reverse is the case (the only link with Israel's sacred history being the Amalekite and Davidic ancestries given Haman and Mordecai, and the mention of the exile of Jeconiah in 2:6).

Lastly, the author consciously limited his study to broad themes and ideas, falling prey to the appeal to ideas common to literature other than wisdom. Despite the mention of individualism as proof of wisdom influence, Talmon admits that both Mordecai and Esther sacrifice private interests for communal weal, and writes that the "glossing over of strictly individual traits enhances the general applicability of the moral illustrated and is perfectly in tune with wisdom literature."[53] To this category of common themes also belong the argument that a description of court life

---

[51]"'Wisdom' in the Book of Esther," 448, 440ff.

[52]Ibid., 428. G. Fohrer (*Introduction to the Old Testament*, 177) writes that Deuteronomy parts company with the sages at precisely this point. The failure of McKenzie ("Reflections on Wisdom") to consider whether sages asked the question of national identity is particularly damaging to an otherwise helpful article. R. B. Y. Scott (*Proverbs and Ecclesiastes*, AB 18 [1965] xvi) sums up the view of most scholars that the sages spoke to individuals, whereas prophets and priests thought of Israel as chosen for a unique mission. There is, it may be admitted, a famous saying that ridicules three peoples, the Edomites, Philistines, and Samaritans in Sir 50:25ff., but this, like so much else in Sirach, is not the normal path of wisdom, and is mild in comparison with Esther. Appeal may also be made to von Rad's contention that wisdom works outwards from the covenant ("The Joseph Narrative and Ancient Wisdom," 295), Murphy's observation that wisdom has its concrete setting in the daily life of a people who believed in God as Savior and Creator ("Assumptions and Problems in Old Testament Wisdom Research," 108ff.), and Zimmerli's discussion of the place of creation theology in Israelite faith ("The Place and Limit of the Wisdom in the Framework of the Old Testament Theology'), all necessary correctives. But this in no way negates the argument that intense nationalism is alien to wisdom.

[53]"'Wisdom' in the Book of Esther," 437, 447.

proves wisdom influence, and the contention that Nehemiah's knowledge of linguistics proves something about courtiers and wisdom.

In conclusion, a study of the arguments for wisdom influence as the exclusive background for the Joseph narrative, succession document, and book of Esther suggests that a negative answer must be given in every case, and demands that modern enthusiasts who rush to find conscious and direct wisdom influence hither and yon would do well to think twice before venturing in that direction.[54]

---

[54]The positive contribution of these works under consideration is the reminder that we have compartmentalized Israelite society far too rigidly, seen already by O. S. Rankin, *Israel's Wisdom Literature*, 14.

19 (1982)

Wisdom and Authority: Sapiential Rhetoric and Its Warrants

In a recent analysis of classical rhetoric George A. Kennedy writes that "the rhetoric of the Old Testament is preconceptual. . . . Indeed, rhetorical consciousness is entirely foreign to the nature of biblical Judaism."[1] Kennedy isolates the essential rhetorical feature in the Hebrew Bible as the "assertion of authority," which leads him to conclude that Old Testament rhetoric "is the simple enunciation of God's truth, uncontaminated by adornment, flattery, or sophistic argumentation" (121). Since divine message-bearers function only as vehicles for God's work, in Kennedy's view, they need no practice in the art of persuasion, for when the time is right, the spirit will move to action those whom God chooses to persuade (122).

One can readily dismiss this misunderstanding of the nature of biblical literature as the inevitable distortion which occurs when specialists attempt to describe the situation outside their respective disciplines.[2] Kennedy's fundamental mistake arises from an assumption that the claim to speak with authority excludes rhetoric. In actual fact, the Hebrew Bible places the two, authority and rhetoric, in uneasy tension in all three canonical divisions, Kennedy's examples notwithstanding.[3] The task of this essay is to throw some light on this strange situation in which persons speak

---

[1]*Classical Rhetoric and Its Christian and Secular Tradition from Ancient to Modern Times* (Chapel Hill, 1980) 120.

[2]R. Alter, "A Literary Approach to the Bible," *Commentary* 60 (December 1975): 71-72, has rightly faulted the profound analysis of Gen 22 by E. Auerbach, *Mimesis* (Princeton, 1953) 3-23, for its sweeping character, since many Hebrew narratives are fraught with foreground (e.g., the David story or Esther).

[3]His choice of covenant speeches by Moses and Joshua, adaptation of the form in prophetic literature, and Dame Wisdom's address as representative of the rhetoric in torah, prophecy, and wisdom inevitably led to superficial treatment.

with authority but self-consciously endeavor to master the art of suasion at the same time. For obvious reasons, I shall limit my remarks to the wisdom literature.[4]

It has long been recognized that authority and rhetoric join hands when personified wisdom emerges to take her place upon the Israelite stage.[5] On the one hand, she speaks with an authority approaching the divine, whether inviting persons to life through her or threatening them with abandonment. On the other, she demonstrates rare skill at persuasion, weaving together an argument that is only slightly less appealing, even on the sensual level, than Dame Folly's invitation. The authority which Dame Wisdom assumes flows from at least three different streams: the divine prototypes for personified wisdom,[6] particularly the Egyptian ma'at,[7] the role of teacher which she adopts,[8] and the reliance upon prophetic language.[9] Similarly, her rhetoric combines appeals to ethos, pathos, and logos; stated differently, persuasive

---

[4]For earlier observations on prophetic authority, see *Prophetic Conflict: Its Effect upon Israelite Religion*, BZAW 124 (Berlin and New York, 1971) 116-23. J. Hempel, "Pathos und Humor in der israelitischen Erziehung," *Von Ugarit nach Qumran*, BZAW 77 (Berlin, 1958) 78, observes that the prophetic claim to divine inspiration resulted in an intimate association between accuracy of prediction and honor; "die Ehre des Weisen aber ist nicht in dem gleichen Ausmass an den pädagogischen Erfolg seines Unterrichtes gebunden." Similarly J. Schmidt singles out wisdom as wholly different from prophecy, poetry, and historical narrative (*Studien zur Stilistik der alttestamentlichen Spruchliteratur* [Munster i. W., 1936] 67).

[5]This union of rhetoric and authority is recognized best in two recent works: Phyllis Trible, "Wisdom Builds a Poem: The Architecture of Proverbs 1:20-33," *JBL* 94 (1975): 509-18 [a chiasmus of four concentric circles converging on the center of the poem], and Maurice Gilbert, "Le discours de la Sagesse en Proverbs, 8. Structure et cohérence," *La Sagesse de l'Ancien Testament* (Gembloux and Leuven, 1979) 202-18.

[6]On the phenomenon of personification of wisdom and its impact upon the New Testament, see P. E. Bonnard, "De la Sagesse personifiée dans l'Ancien Testament à la Sagesse en personne dans le Nouveau," *La Sagesse de l'A.T.*, 117-49.

[7]C. Kayatz, *Studien zu Proverbien 1–9* (Neukirchen, 1966) and H. H. Schmid, *Wesen und Geschichte der Weisheit* (*BZAW* 101; Berlin, 1966) 17-22 and passim.

[8]B. Lang, *Frau Weisheit: Deutung einer biblischen Gestalt* (Düsseldorf, 1975) discovers the key to understanding personified wisdom in the Israelite scribal school. The teacher serves as a model for Dame Wisdom's activity.

[9]"Wisdom is not such an empirical teacher, resting her case on her personal authority; she promulgates wisdom, advice and admonishment with the authority of Yahweh, and the fear of Yahweh is a new מוּסָר. This is the discipline to which she would have her audience submit, and in introducing this direct claim to divine authority for what she teaches she emerges almost as a prophet, except that she still tends to speak the language of a wisdom teacher" (W. McKane, *Proverbs: A New Approach* [London and Philadelphia, 1970] 275). Whether she continues to speak the language of a wisdom teacher is debatable; I would argue that prophetic modes of expression set the distinctive tone here.

technique oscillates among three different poles: the speaker, the audience, and the speech.[10]

The eventual equation of wisdom and torah in Sirach 24 greatly enhances the presumed authority with which Dame Wisdom addresses her clientele, but this transition is accompanied by no diminution of the necessity for skill at persuasion.[11] Ironically, the subsequent relegation of wisdom to Solomon's bride altogether escapes the notion of bridal subservience, for she is portrayed in regal terminology approaching the divine.[12]

At best, then, we can say that a certain uneasy tension exists in those texts which treat personified wisdom. Does that tension extend beyond this minimal corpus to infuse the entire initial collection of Proverbs? A consensus seems to have formed with regard to this question: Prov 1–9 comprises *instruction* literature, which by its very nature makes authoritative claims. Both the setting for these instructions, the school,[13] and the content, theological wisdom, are said to reinforce the heavy hand of authority present in this collection.[14] Rejection of the school hypothesis[15] in favor of a family context alters the situation little, if any, with respect to authoritative teaching for parents spoke to their children with authority comparable to that of teachers who addressed their students. Both parents and teachers

---

[10]These three categories correspond to the three goals in rhetoric: to charm, to move, and to persuade.

[11]J. Marböck's penetrating analysis of this shifting emphasis, *Weisheit im Wandel: Untersuchungen zur Weisheits-theologie bei Ben Sira* (Bonn, 1971) 34-96, has now been supplemented from the standpoint of canonical criticism, with special attention to anthological composition, by G. T. Sheppard, *Wisdom as a Hermeneutical Construct: A Study in the Sapientializing of the Old Testament*, BZAW 151 (Berlin and New York, 1980) 19-71.

[12]"Our author is saying in effect that Wisdom is essentially synonymous with the Divine Mind, and thus represents the creative agent of the Deity" (D. Winston, *The Wisdom of Solomon* [Garden City NY, 1979] 194).

[13]H.-J. Hermisson, *Studien zur israelitischen Spruchweisheit* (Neukirchen, 1968) 113-36, has endeavored to demonstrate the existence of a temple school in Israel. Further discussion of this vexing problem comes from B. Lang (*Frau Weisheit*, passim, and "Schule und Unterricht im alten Israel," *La Sagesse de l'A.T.*, 186-201).

[14]Gerhard von Rad, *Theologie des Alten Testaments 1* (Munich, 1957) 439-51, ET: *Old Testament Theology* 1 (Edinburgh, London and New York, 1962) 441-53; C. Bauer-Kayatz, *Einführung in die alttestamentlichen Weisheit* (Neukirchen, 1969) 36-92.

[15]R. N. Whybray, *The Intellectual Tradition in the Old Testament*, BZAW 135 (Berlin and New York, 1974) 33-43, and "Yahweh Sayings and their Context in Proverbs 10, 1-22, 15," *La Sagesse de l'A.T.*, 155n.8.

recognized the necessity of presenting their message in an attractive form.[16] That is why these brief instructions are rich in persuasive style and vocabulary.

What happens, however, when we move beyond Prov 1–9 and begin to assess the other collections where *sentences* rather than instructions are involved? Does the formal distinction carry in its train a qualitative difference as well? It would seem that the two literary types represent wholly different approaches to reality. Whereas sentences state what is immediately obvious to one and all, once the insight has dawned and achieved verbal articulation, instructions depend upon certain types of legitimating arguments for their cogency.[17] What could be more natural, therefore, than to conclude that the literary types should be distinguished sharply from one another?[18]

The matter is much more complex than this, for in at least four places within Prov 1–9 the two literary types appear hand-in-glove. In each instance a sentence reinforces the argument within an instruction as if to provide irrefutable proof of the position being defended.

We turn first to Prov 1:6–19, an instruction which warns against highway robbery. The threefold address to the student underlines the heinous nature of the crime as well as its special lure. Although the initial address derives from a family setting,

---

[16]W. Bühlmann, *Vom Rechten Reden und Schweigen: Studien zu Proverbien 10–31* (Freiburg, Schweiz, and Göttingen, 1976) 52, writes: "Die schöne Form verleiht einem gesprochene Wort Authorität und Wacht." On the beauty of speech alluded to in Prov 16:21, he observes that "solche Worte nicht nur erfreuen, sondern auch andere zu überzeugen vermögen" (59). Hempel describes the art of persuasion in Proverbs and Qoheleth as rich in the following features: (1) ironic metaphors; (2) question and answer; (3) animal similes and numerical proverbs; (4) animal and human imagery; (5) mythical language; (6) better sayings; and (7) other media such as alliteration, rhyme, appeal to special authority (e.g., the royal testament), and irony ("Pathos und Humor," 71–78).

[17]"The most important formal distinction between Instruction and the wisdom sentence is that the imperative is proper to the first and the indicative to the second. The Instruction commands and exhorts and gives reasons why its directives should be obeyed . . . its aim is to command and persuade. The wisdom sentence is an observation with an impersonal form which states a truth but neither exhorts nor persuades" (McKane, *Proverbs*, 3). But see his recent perceptive analysis of "Functions of Language and Objectives of Discourse according to Proverbs 10–31," *La Sagesse de l'A.T.*, 166–85. Here WcKane distinguishes between transitive and executive language on the one hand and passive speech on the other. On persuasive discourse in Prov 10–31, see also Hermisson, *Studien zur israelitischen Spruchweisheit*, 137–92, and Schmidt, *Studien zur Stilistik der alttestamentlichen Spruchliteratur*, 37–66 (for the entire wisdom corpus).

[18]McKane, *Proverbs*, passim, and C. Westermann, "Weisheit im Sprichwort," in K. H. Bernhardt (ed.), *Schalom: Studien zu Glaube und Geschichte Israels* (Stuttgart, 1971) 73–85. Note the following claim: "Der Aussagespruch sagt, wie es ist. Zu wissen dass es so ist, ist Weisheit. . . . Die Wurde der Weisheit liegt darin, dass sie *nicht* mahnt, *nicht* anstösst, *nicht* auffordert; sie erwartet das Handeln vielmehr als Folge des Erkennens" (76).

nothing else suggests the context of a home, which seems to have been replaced by a school in this instance. The quotation of the robbers' invitation to villainy contains certain elements that bespeak the attitude of a teacher rather than criminals, suggesting that the speech is an imagined one. To illustrate the folly of such plans, the teacher cites a proverb: "For in vain is a net spread in the sight of any bird." The point seems to be that just as birds watch while a net is being prepared and baited but heedlessly proceed to their capture, so those who scheme violence walk resolutely to their own death.[19] Regardless of the actual sense of this difficult proverb, its presence within an instruction suggests that it functions as a warrant for the teacher's specific message.

The second instruction also begins with an address derived from the family setting, but that context seems to persist throughout (6:20-35).[20] The legal tradition furnishes the symbolism for the initial verses, which apply torah attributes to Dame Wisdom. The entire instruction juxtaposes two different kinds of fire: the light of parental instruction and seething passion for another man's wife. The first lamp stands as a powerful antidote to the second fire, which threatens to consume those lacking sense. Rhetoric abounds in this endeavor to frustrate the seductive power of the adulteress, but the crowning argument consists of two impossible questions.[21]

Can a man carry fire in his bosom and his clothes not be burned?
Or can one walk upon hot coals and his feet not be scorched?

(6:27-28 RSV)[22]

These questions function as strong statements which none would dare challenge; as such they constitute an argument from consensus.

The third passage differs from the first two in that it lacks the so-called teacher's call for a hearing; here we stand at a transition from instruction to imaginative discourse or anecdote (Prov 9:13-18). In one sense this description of Madam Folly is derivative, for it clearly serves as a foil to the earlier allusion to Dame Wisdom (Prov 9:1-6). Both women make elaborate use of erotic language,[23] but only one actually invites her guests to sexual pleasures. In all likelihood, Dame

---

[19]D. Winton Thomas, "Textual and Philological Notes on some Passages in the Book of Proverbs," *Wisdom in Israel and in the Ancient Near East*, SVT 3 (Leiden, 1960) 281-82, and McKane, *Proverbs*, 270-71.

[20]For analysis of the structure of this text, see my essay "Questions, dictons et épreuves impossibles," *La Sagesse de l'A.T.*, 100-105.

[21]On this literary category, see my "Impossible Questions, Sayings, and Tasks in Israelite Wisdom," in *Gnomic Wisdom*, ed. Dominic Crossan (Missoula, 1980) 19-34.

[22]Scripture translations are taken from the Revised Standard Version.

[23]The Dead Sea Psalms Scroll preserves a portion of the original concluding poem to Sirach in which *double entendre* abounds, suggesting that such thinking was equally at home among earlier sages.

Wisdom's vocabulary echoes her origins as a goddess,[24] but the sensual aspects have been largely transferred to her antagonist who actively solicits at the center of daily activity. Her invitation is remarkably appealing: "Stolen water is sweet, and bread eaten in secret is pleasant" (9:17).[25] Once again we encounter a proverb at the heart of the argument, confirming our suspicion that teachers reinforced their words with acknowledged authoritative maxims. In this instance the aphorism recalls other sayings, especially the allegorical reference to sexual relations in 5:15-20 and the amusing description of an adulteress as one who "eats, and wipes her mouth, and says, 'I have done no wrong'" (30:20).

Another instruction which cites a sentence as the decisive proof is found in 6:6-11, which advises sluggards to learn a lesson from the ant and warns against the dreadful consequences of laziness.

> A little sleep, a little slumber,
>   a little folding of the hands to rest,
> and poverty will come upon you like a vagabond,
>   and want like an armed man.   (6:10-11)

In 24:30-34, this sentence is quoted yet again, this time within an anecdote and prefaced by the self-reflective comment of a teacher who has learned a valuable lesson from experience. The presence of copious imagery precisely when the clinching argument occurs in another anecdote, Prov 12:6-23, should occasion little surprise. Indeed, the metaphors for self-destruction suggest that a lost sentence may lie behind 12:22-23.

> As an ox goes to the slaughter,
>   or as a stag is caught fast
> till an arrow pierces its entrails;
>   as a bird rushes into a snare. . . .

Nevertheless, the absence of such a sentence in canonical proverbs precludes convincing proof on this point.

The phenomenon of reinforcing an instruction or anecdote by means of a sentence partially explains the peculiar situation in sapiential research where instruction literature is ordinarily distinguished from the remaining proverbs, which are thought to lack an authoritative base. Walther Zimmerli's fundamental analysis

---

[24]B. L. Mack, *Logos und Sophia: Untersuchungen zur Weishseitstheologie im hellenistischen Judentum* (Göttingen, 1973), offers a thoroughgoing analysis from the standpoint of the history of religions. For a recent treatment, see M. Kuchler, *Frühjüdische Weisheitstraditionen: Zum Fortgang weisheitlichen Denkens im Bereich des frühjüdischen Jahweglaubens* (Freiburg, Schweiz, and Göttingen, 1979) 33-53.

[25]On this euphemistic language, see my *Samson: A Secret Betrayed, a Vow Ignored* (Atlanta and London, 1978 and 1979) 114-17.

of the structure of Israelite wisdom[26] lost sight of the fact that sentences spoke with amazing force; indeed, much later, to be sure, Gerhard von Rad went so far as to exalt proverbs over torah in respect to the power they exercised in the daily lives of ancient Israelites.[27] Even those critics who see clearly the authority residing within sentences rarely take the further step toward awareness that the appeal to authority in instructions bears witness to a sense that they lack inner cogency. Thus a peculiar irony persists: precisely where authority is most lacking, that is, in instructions, critics assume its pervading presence, and in sentences, which compel assent without the slightest reinforcement, interpreters emphasize their advisory character. It follows that previous discussions of wisdom and authority stand in need of revision. What follows is only a modest effort from a projected volume on the art of persuasion in Israelite wisdom.

II

In characterizing Dame Wisdom's message I used the categories ethos, pathos, and logos with reference to the speaker, audience, and speech respectively. Now the authority inherent within a spoken or written word derives from one of these three, or any combination of them.[28] For the moment, I shall concentrate on these three warrants for authority in the book of Job.

1. ethos[29]

Job's friends are not sufficiently differentiated to permit one to draw a composite sketch of each one's faith claims. Nevertheless, I shall avoid the tendency to treat their arguments as a single attack on Job. In 8:8-10, Bildad appeals to ethos.

> For inquire, I pray you, of bygone ages,
>   and consider what the fathers have found;

---

[26]"Zur Struktur der alttestamentlichen Weisheit," *ZAW* 51 (1933): 177-204 (ET in *Studies in Ancient Israelite Wisdom*, ed. James L. Crenshaw [New York, 1976] 175-207). To be sure, Zimmerli later modified his position, but the difference is hardly discernible in *Grundriss der alttestamentlichen Theologie* (Stuttgart, Berlin, Köln, Mainz, 1972) 92-93, 136-46. For a corrective, see B. Gemser, "The Spiritual Structure of Biblical Aphoristic Wisdom," in *Adhuc Loquitur: Collected Essays of Dr. B. Gemser*, ed. A. van Selms and A. S. van der Woude (Leiden, 1968) 138-49 (also in *Studies in Ancient Israelite Wisdom*, 208-19). On the meaning of the root עֵצָה see now J. A. Emerton, "The root עֵצָה and some uses of עֵצָה and מוֹעֵצָה in Hebrew," in W. C. van Wyk (ed.) *Studies in Wisdom Literature*, ed. W. C. van Wyk, OTWSA 15 and 16, 13-26.

[27]*Wisdom in Israel* (London, 1972) 26 = *Weisheit in Israel* (Neukirchen, 1970) 41.

[28]The sources of authority include birth, accomplishment, character, and sanction.

[29]Here I am using ethos in a broader sense than nobility of character. It thus combines the essential meaning of ἔθος and ἦθος (custom and character).

for we are but of yesterday, and know nothing,
    for our days on earth are a shadow.
Will they not teach you, and tell you,
    and utter words out of their understanding?

Here the speaker lays claim to a valuable legacy, the tradition acquired and passed on again and again by earlier generations. Indeed, he perceives the fleeting character of existence that forces dependence on accumulated knowledge. That complex system of beliefs, values, and customs was as natural as breathing itself. Upon this solid foundation wise persons took a stand and whatever authority they may have possessed derived from this base. Naturally, those who managed to linger long enough to acquire gray hairs could lay claim to a lion's share of accumulated lore. Accordingly, Eliphaz reminds Job of this fact.

Are you the first man that was born?
    Or were you brought forth before the hills?
Both the gray haired and the aged are among us,
    older than your father.   (15:7, 10)

But traditional knowledge was useless unless confirmed in one's personal experience, and so Eliphaz insists that he has seen "what wise men have told, and their fathers have not hidden" (15:18). Both Bildad and Eliphaz counsel personal appropriation of the inherited tradition, a theme that surfaces in the latter's speeches more than once.

As I have seen, those who plow iniquity
    and sow trouble reap the same.   (4:8; cf. 5:3)
Lo, this we have searched out; it is true.
    Hear,[30] and know it for your good.   (5:27)

Job's arguments also fall within the category of ethos, although he turns the one about age upon its head.

Wisdom is with the aged,
    and understanding in length of days. . . .

---

[30]The importance of hearing was highlighted in Egyptian instructions (cf. Ptah-hotep) in a manner not found in Israel, but the latter sages recognized the necessity of appropriating inherited traditions. Thus Hempel writes: "Demgemass ist auch das wichtigste Erziehungsmittel kein anderes als in den anderen altorientalischen Pädagogien: das 'Horen'" ("Pathos und Humor in der israelitischen Erziehung," 68). H. Brunner, *Altägyptische Erziehung* (Wiesbaden, 1957) 131-36, and H. H. Schmid, *Wesen and Geschichte der Weisheit*, 31-33, discuss the significance of hearing to Egyptian sages. C. F. Whitley understands the difficult אזן in Qoh 12:9 as a reference to listening ("*and he listened* and considered the arrangement of many proverbs": *Koheleth: His Language and Thought*, BZAW 148 [Berlin and New York, 1979] 102).

> He [God] deprives of speech those who are trusted
> and takes away the discernment of the elders. (12:12, 20)

Job, too has kept his eyes open, ever ready to test cherished beliefs.

> Lo, my eye has seen all this,
> my ear has heard and understood it.
> What you know, I also know;
> I am not inferior to you. (13:1-2)[31]

He has also incorporated lessons from afar into those arising in the home.

> Have you not asked those who travel the roads,
> and do not you accept their testimony
> that the wicked man is spared in the day of calamity,
> that he is rescued in the day of wrath? (12:25)

Here the two essential ingredients of ethos, inherited tradition and individual appropriation, stand out with impressive clarity.

This bipolarity of ethos provides an important corrective to the oft-mentioned individualism which characterizes wisdom thinking. In a sense, personal authority depends upon something which comes as a legacy from the past; this valuable gift must be appropriated in a given situation by those who wish to lay claim upon it. In this way individuals point beyond themselves to a greater authority, the collective experience of the community.

2. pathos

Not every appeal to authority concentrates on ethos; another significant warrant for teaching is pathos. Whereas ethos refers to the person of the speaker, pathos focuses upon the audience. Specifically, it consists of the many ways by which the speaker can sway belief or move an audience to action. Often this type of persuasion implies the heightening of certain emotions, such as fear or awe.

Eliphaz waxes eloquent about an experience of the holy which taught him the folly of presumed righteousness.

> Now a word was brought to me stealthily,
> my ear received the whisper of it. . . .
> A spirit glided past my face;
> the hair of my flesh stood up.

---

[31]Note the fundamental difference between Job's bold claim to knowledge and the rhetorician's self-effacement, which functions ironically. Qoheleth's response to sapiential claims (8:17) suggests that the rhetorical effect of putting oneself down arose to counter adverse results of boasting.

It stood still,
> but I could not discern its appearance.

A form was before my eyes;
> there was silence, then I heard a voice:

Can mortal man be righteous before God?

Can a man be pure before his Maker? (4:12-17)[32]

Similarly, Elihu argues from pathos in this remarkable account of divine action upon passive subjects.

For God speaks in one way,
> and in two, though man does not perceive it.

In a dream, in a vision of the night,
> when deep sleep falls upon men,
> while they slumber on their beds,

then he opens the ears of men,
> and terrifies them with warnings. . . . (33:14-18)

Such observations are calculated to instill dread in the hearts of hearers, thus transferring their thoughts from human to divine authority. Occasionally, it is difficult to ascertain whether the allusion points beyond the individual or not, for the reference contains just enough ambiguity to function as personal reinforcement.

But it is the spirit in a man, the breath of the Almighty,
> that makes him understand. (32:8)

This, not age, assures Elihu that his voice should not be stilled while others spout off nonsense. Sometimes this inner voice approximates the modern concept of conscience, for example, when Zophar remarks:

I hear censure which insults me,
> and out of my understanding a spirit answers me. (20:3)

3. logos

A third level on which appeals to authority function is logos, by which I mean the cogency of the speech itself. Such warrants for one's message rely neither on

---

[32]In the light of 40:2 and 25:4, on the one hand, and 32:2, on the other, a translation such as "Can mortal man be more just than God? Can a man be purer than his Maker?" is attractive. The former two texts use a different construction (עִם־אֵל rather than מֵאֱלוֹהַּ), one that presents no ambiguity. The sense of מֵאֱלֹהִים in 32:2 is clearly that Job considered himself more just than God. The context of 4:17 *encourages* this understanding, in my view, and the argument from greater to lesser in 4:18-19 becomes all the more forceful. Still, this literal sense is not demanded, for Num 32:22 and Jer 51:5 indicate that the expression does not *require* a comparison.

the office of the speaker nor on the emotions of the listeners, but endeavor to persuade through logical force alone.[33] Indeed, the actual source of the message may be unknown, and nothing beyond rational clarity may occur, but the authoritative base is present nonetheless.

Perhaps the most obvious appeal to logos takes place when the speaker quotes a saying that compels universal assent, particularly rhetorical questions. In justifying his intemperate outcry against a god who has become a personal antagonist, Job resorts to just such an argument.

> Does the wild ass bray when he has grass,
> or the ox low over his fodder?
> Can that which is tasteless be eaten without salt,
> or is there any taste in the slime of the purslane?   (6:5-6)[34]

Bildad counters with a comparable appeal to consensus.

> Can papyrus grow where there is no marsh?
> Can reeds flourish where there is no water?   (7:8-10)

Zophar, too, takes up the argument from consensus, and thus emphasizes the unlikelihood of acquiring wisdom.

> But a stupid man will get understanding,
> when a wild ass's colt is born a man.   (11:12)[35]

Yet another appeal to logos is the maxim drawn from nature, the so-called nature wisdom.[36] A remarkably powerful example occurs in one of Job's speeches.

> But ask the beasts, and they will teach you;
> the birds of the air, and they will tell you;

---

[33]To be sure, we must make allowances for Israelite fondness for emotion-laden language, hyperbole, and generally extravagant speech.

[34]The difficulty of translating v 6 is illustrated by recent commentaries: "Can flat food be eaten unsalted? Is there flavor in slimy cream cheese?" (M. H. Pope); "Can tasteless food be eaten without salt, or is there any savor in the juice of mallows?" (R. Gordis); "Can one eat spittle, without salt? or is there any taste in the saliva of the dreams?" (N. H. Tur Sinai).

[35]On the basis of Gen 16:12, E. Dhorme understands this *proverb* to mean that a wild ass's colt becomes a master ass, i.e., it acquires the full nature of its breed (*Le livre de Job* [Paris, 1926] 147-48, ET: *A Commentary on the Book of Job* [London, 1967] 163). M. Pope rejects the rendering "wild ass's colt" in favor of male wild ass, and interprets אָדָם as equivalent to אֲדָמָה. Hence he translates: "The inane man will get sense, when a wild ass is born tame" (*Job*, AB 15 [Garden City NY, 1973] 83, 86).

[36]H. Richter, "Die Naturweisheit des Alten Testaments in Buch Hiob," *ZAW* 70-71 (1958-1959): 1-19.

or the plants of the earth, and they will teach you;
and the fish of the sea will declare to you.
Who among all these does not know
that the hand of the Lord has done this? (12:7-9)

One can even argue that the choice of rhetorical questions as the mode of divine address derives from a knowledge that God needs no warrants for his speech, but poses a kind of teacher's examination for Job.[37] To be sure, this is no ordinary test, for the impossible questions heighten the distance between creature and creator, a chasm fragilely spanned by renewed discourse.[38]

III

The preceding analysis of warrants for authority has concentrated on the Book of Job, but it could easily be extended to the entire wisdom corpus.[39] For the moment, I wish instead to shift the attention to the other issue being considered in this essay, namely persuasion. Rather than discussing the general features of biblical rhetoric, I prefer to illustrate that phenomenon through analysis of the contest of Darius's guards in 1 Esd 3:1–5:3. Since I have studied that text in another setting[40] I shall limit my remarks to rhetorical features: choice of material, arrangement of the discussion, vocabulary, and style.

---

[37]von Rad, "Hiob xxxviii und die altägyptische Weisheit," *Wisdom in Israel and in the Ancient Near East*, 293-301, ET: *Studies in Ancient Israelite Wisdom*, 267-91, and *The Problem of the Hexateuch and Other Essays* (Edinburgh and London, 1966) 281-91.

[38]"Es ist das demutsvolle Schweigen des Menschen, dessen Existenz in der Begegnung mit Gott erschüttert und in Frage gestellt worden ist für den solches Schweigen einen neue Weg eröffnet. . . . Doch es ist nicht das Schweigen des sich seiner Nichtigkeit bewussten Menschen, sondern das Schweigen des zu Gott hingekehrten Menschen, der in der Gemeinschaft mit ihm zur Ruhe findet" (G. Fohrer, "Dialog und Kommunikation im Buch Hiob," *La Sagesse de l'A.T.*, 229-30).

[39]Fohrer, *Einleitung in das Alte Testament*, rev. ed. (Heidelberg, 1969) 368-69, ET: *Introduction to the Old Testament* (Nashville and New York, 1968) 339-40, perceives a significant transformation of a simple aphorism into a progressive structure in Qoheleth. E.g., he notes three steps in Qoh 1:16-18, specifically observation, conclusion, and proof in a proverb. Similarly, 3:1-15 yields theme, conclusion, and proverb cited as motivation. "We see here a structural change in wisdom instruction, brought about by a change in the psychological milieu. The individual, the ego, takes on a certain distance from the events or circumstances with which it appears to be linked. The observing subject confronts his observations as an independent personality. In addition, in order to reinforce or justify his views, Qoheleth goes back to earlier proverbs." (340)

[40]The publication of my extensive analysis of this text ("The Contest of Darius's Guards") has appeared in *Images of Man and God: Old Testament Short Stories in Literary Focus*, ed. B. O. Long (Sheffield, 1981) 74-88.

We begin with a look at the conventional material which provided the source for the argument about the strongest thing in the world. I shall isolate two features for discussion: the missing fourth answer and the polarities from Qoheleth concerning a time for everything. As everyone knows, four answers appear in the speeches despite the stipulation that each of the three guards is to give a single response to the question, "What is strongest?" To the answers wine, the king, and woman has been added the victorious response, truth. But certain bits of evidence within the contest point to a further attempt to answer the question in terms of the human capacity for responding to the divine command to subdue the earth.

Echoes of this missing answer persist in 4:2, 14, and 37, where it inserts itself repeatedly. To be sure, the first instance can be explained as a transitional device, but the other two seem to imply that one guard had defended the answer "men." For example, the third speaker begins by referring to the answer defended by the second speaker, then moves to two previous answers: men and wine. In like manner, the summary statement alludes to these three answers but this time in a different order (wine, king, women, men), the latter of which has been expanded to include "all their works." Perhaps this vying for attention on the part of an answer that underwent harsh handling can alert readers to the possibility that the author has adapted conventional material to a new purpose.

This suspicion that older material underlies the contest gains support from another puzzling aspect of the text, this time in the final speech on truth. The crowning argument against wine, king, woman, and men is their unrighteousness, which signals eventual perishing. Now what prompted the reference to the sun in this context? I suggest that two brief hymn-like passages in Sirach provide that fountain from which this stream flows.

In Sir 17:1-3 one reads that God endowed his human creatures with strength like his own, whereas 17:19 likens all their works to the sun, and 17:14 introduces the concept of unrighteousness. Furthermore, Sir 43:1-4 praises the sun but moves beyond the marvelous work to its creator: "Great is the Lord who made it." It would therefore seem probable that a standard literary convention lies behind the text in 1 Esd 4:34-41.[41]

A similar adaptation of traditional material takes place within the praise of king as strongest. In 4:7-9, the phrase "if he tells" ($\dot{\epsilon}\grave{\alpha}\nu$ $\epsilon\dot{\iota}\pi\epsilon\nu$ or $\epsilon\hat{\iota}\pi\epsilon$) occurs seven times; both the sevenfold usage and content recall Qoh 3:1-9. To be sure, formal differences exist, most notably the parallelism in Qoheleth, but striking resemblances

---

[41]Certain themes would naturally appear in any hymn about the sun, but the stress upon its unrighteousness ($\check{\alpha}\delta\iota\kappa o\nu$) must surely exceed normal expectancy. The attempt to discover Semitic parallels to this entire narrative strikes me as essentially on target (K. F. Pohlmann, *Studien zum Dritten Esra: Ein Beitrag zur Frage nach dem ursprünglichen Schluss des Chronistischen Geschichtswerkes* [Göttingen, 1970] 42-46). It follows that I do not think the praise of truth is of Greek origin.

suggest a close relationship (the opposites kill and heal, build and cut down, references to making war, attacking, laying waste, and planting). Of Qoheleth's fourteen opposites,[42] only those appropriate to royal command have commended themselves to the author. The others concern emotional responses and relationships not subject even to a king's wishes. Weeping and laughter, love making and continence, abstemious saving and reckless squandering, silence and speech, loving and despising cannot easily be brought under royal supervision.

Now if adaptation of conventional material[43] best describes the author's choice of subject matter, what characterizes the way he or she endeavors to present the data? A distinct broadening of focus is discernible in the arrangement of the discussion. The initial speaker sticks to the subject and shows considerable powers of logical coherence; the second introduces a new idea about human beings as strong, thus providing a decisive clue about a further speech, now missing; and the third has "two arrows in his bow" to begin with, and proceeds to reminisce about the earth's vastness, the height of heaven, and the swiftness of the sun. Furthermore, the dialogue begins by celebrating material and morally inferior wine and proceeds to a higher level, the king, and finally comes to rest in God.[44] Within the argument about woman, the sequence shifts noticeably. "Here he ranges . . . from the noblest (mother love and wifely devotion) to the lowest (selfish whims and silly fancies of coquettes bringing ruin to their lovers)."[45]

The contest achieves a broadening of focus without resort to extravagant language. Indeed, the vocabulary is particularly suited to logical persuasion. Two features stand out as noteworthy in this regard: the use of ironic understatement and exercise in juxtaposition. A single instance of understatement proclaims the authority of a king more eloquently than hyperbole could ever have done. I refer to the choice of the word "tell" (εἶπεν) in describing royal commands (4:4, 7-9); others may have to raise their voices to attract attention and to insist that certain actions be undertaken, but a king merely tells his subjects the slightest whim and they hasten to turn royal desire into tangible reality.

The second example of restraint in vocabulary appropriate to logical suasion concerns the use of the phrase "look upon with open mouth." It first occurs with reference to a man who holds his most precious possessions in his hands, only to let them go when a beautiful woman passes by, and to stare at her with mouth agape (χάσκοντες τὸ στόμα θεωροῦσιν αὐτήν, 4:18-19). The other exam-

---

[42]J. A. Loader, *Polar Structures in the Book of Qohelet*, BZAW 152 (Berlin and New York, 1979), exaggerates the significance of opposites in Qoheleth, although he correctly perceives evidence of conscious design in the book.

[43]On literary conventions, see Alter, "Biblical Type-Scenes and the Uses of Convention," *Critical Inquiry* (Winter 1978): 355-68.

[44]R. H. Pfeiffer, *History of New Testament Times with an Introduction to the Apocrypha* (New York, 1949) 256.

[45]Ibid.

ple of this phrase brings the king down to the level of ordinary subjects, for it pictures him as a supplicant pleading with a favorite mistress. This beautiful Apame placed the king's crown upon her own head and slapped the king, who gazed at her with mouth agape (χάσκων τὸ στόμα ἐθεώρει αὐτήν, 4:31). No wonder the final decision about the winner in the contest is made by public acclamation, since the democratization of kingship has resulted.

So far I have discussed noteworthy aspects of theme, arrangement, and vocabulary. But what about style? I shall limit myself to observations about introductory and concluding formulae, rhetorical questions, transition, and irony, since these stylistic features seem to be highly significant in this text. Each speech opens and closes with common formulae. The opening formula states: "Then the first (or the second/third) who had spoken of . . . began and said." Likewise each concludes with a statement that the speaker stopped speaking.

By far the most characteristic feature of the speeches is the free use of rhetorical questions. The first speaker sets the tone of the discussion by means of a question ("Gentlemen, how is wine the strongest?") and uses yet another to invoke assent ("Gentlemen, is not wine the strongest, since it forces men to do these things?"). The second speaker opens with a false answer in question form, only to correct it immediately ("Gentlemen, are not men strongest who rule over land and sea and all that is in them?"). A more appropriate introduction to a discussion of the supreme monarch is difficult to imagine. This speaker also appeals for favorable response ("Gentlemen, why is not the king strongest, since he is to be obeyed in this fashion?"). The third speaker is not content with an introductory and final rhetorical question, but punctuates the speech throughout with such questions.

> Gentlemen, is not the king great, and are not men many, and is not wine strong? Who then is their master, or who is their lord? Is it not women? . . . Do you not labor and toil, and bring everything and give it to women? . . . And now do you not believe me? Is not the king great in his power? Do not all lands fear to touch him? . . . Gentlemen, why are not women strong, since they do such things? . . . Gentlemen, are not women strong? . . . Is he not great who does these things?   (1 Esd 4:14, 22b, 28, 32, 34a, 35a)

The impact of these questions is signaled by the bold declaration "Hence you must realize that women rule over you" (4:22a), together with the substitution of a doxology for the concluding rhetorical question—"Blessed be the God of truth!" (4:40c).

Transition from one speech to another is wholly natural so long as the answers correspond to the number of speakers. What happens, however, when an additional answer intrudes? Here transition is achieved in outstanding fashion, for it hints that victory has already come for the third speaker. The brief anecdote about the king's love play and the persuasive defense of woman as strongest allow the speaker to shift attention momentarily to the audience. At that decisive point the transition takes place: "Then the king and the nobles looked at one another; and he began to speak about truth" (4:38). From here on the speaker's thoughts escalate, beginning with the strongest among human beings and soaring from earth to heaven and finally pausing to rest before the God of truth.

Like the Book of Job, this contest consists of a framing narrative and a dialogue. Considerable tension results from this uneasy combination, for the framework pictures the king acting in his capacity as supreme dispenser of favors whereas the speeches challenge that authority with devastating force. On the one hand, the king grants privileges of friendship and fortune, and regal language is applied to truth. On the other, the story portrays a king who falls asleep, and the people themselves usurp royal prerogative in declaring the winner. Furthermore, the dialogue exposes a king's true vulnerability: his might falters before appetite and sleep, when a lone individual could easily be disposed of by others less privileged but at the moment more alert.

These features of theme, arrangement, vocabulary, and style combine to make these speeches truly persuasive.[46] I wish to illustrate the unusual power of the text by reflecting for a moment on the argument concerning wine. The knowledge that men and women are rational creatures was not limited to ancient Greeks. While Plato's students may have made fun of his definition of man as a thinking animal without feathers by attaching to a cock the label "philosophical man," the metaphor of human beings as rational has always seemed appropriate in discussions of their essence. *Cogito ergo sum* removes men and women from their environment and exalts them over all other creatures. Yet this distinctive mark succumbs to the power of the vine, whose product leads astray the keenest mind.

Besides this rational essence, an artificial distinction according to sociological status emerges early. Hence class differences surface, men and women being fitted into appropriate niches on the basis of things over which they have no control (birth) or which have nothing to do with their real selves (possessions). The latter make it possible for one person to subject others to servile obedience, for the rich can enslave those indebted to them. And, of course, there must be someone at the very top of artificial distinctions among people; this person of power and privilege acclaims himself king. Such differences pass away when wine wields its strange power, and now at long last king and lowliest subject stand equal, as do master and slave, rich and poor.

Inasmuch as women and men are thinking creatures upon whom class distinctions have been imposed, above and beyond the ordinary causes for anxiety and remorse, they are ever and again victimized by fear, pain, and sorrow. The sentence of death hangs over their heads, and fertile imagination conjures up all sorts of dangers both real and supposed. Actual pain, both their own and that of those dear to them, increases anxiety about approaching death and heightens agony caused by disappointment, intensifying to the breaking point all psychically based

---

[46]For textual analysis of this story, see the Ph.D. diss. by William Goodman, Jr. ("A Study of 1 Esdras 3:1–5:6," Duke University, 1971).

consternation. When wine enters the bodies of men and women, frequently the worry-prone victims of death's messengers, they forget for the moment the power of pain. In place of sorrow and financial woe come a glad heart and freedom from care, so powerful is the blood of the grape. Those who under ordinary circumstances and beset by problems of daily existence can muster minimal self-esteem find limitless resources lurking within the cup, which loosen the tongue so that newfound confidence proclaims itself with complete abandon.

Rich experience has taught the value of friendship and the indispensability of fraternal loyalty; without friends or brother, one is vulnerable from every side. Consequently, friendship ties and kinship bonds came to occupy a high position in the order of priorities, for nothing was too great a price to pay to assure the perpetuity of those relationships. Even a grievous offence could be overlooked lest the bond with another be severed, and great care was taken to avoid injury to a friend or brother. But persons who have their fill of wine treat such valuable relationships like ordinary refuse, and with reckless abandon pick a quarrel that leads to blows between friends and brothers.

The seasons come, and the seasons go, and with them birth and death. The strange capacity for remembering, that ability to recall selected events, thoughts, and sensations from the shadowy past, survives the powerful sway of time's monotony. Often cause for wonder and astonishment, this memory enables men and women to relive those cherished moments when time and eternity coalesced and the joyous soul cried out, "Stay, thou art so fair." Furthermore, such remembrance of sacral events opens up new possibilities for those to whom primeval event stands as both summons and demand; from its power they receive renewed redemption and ethical motivation. Still, even this astonishing memory bows in submission to the greater power of wine, and individuals recall nothing that transpired during the drunken stupor. Wine, then, functions as the great leveler: its mighty floodwaters sweep in the swirling maelstrom all human rationality, memory, psychic states, distinctions both real and artificial, and bonds of friendship and brotherhood. From the murky waters left by the subsiding flood one can pull their corpses, newly transformed into perverted thought, forgetfulness, joviality, boasting, comradery and bellicosity. "Gentlemen, is not wine the strongest, since it forces people to do these things?" Such was the brief, but truly cogent, argument of Darius's first guard.

IV

What has this brief consideration of authority and persuasion yielded that will enable us to understand the wisdom literature more fully? Minimally, we can say that formal literary distinctions often ignore other factors like subject and function which link together such unlikely candidates as sentence and instruction. The latter, by virtue of the necessity for authoritative claims, possesses less inherent power of persuasion than do sentences. It follows that interpreters need to distinguish between the authority that a teacher endeavors to impose upon students and that bestowed upon texts by their form or intrinsic nature. Still, we must beware of going too far in the opposite direction and asserting that all sentences possessed full authority, for the presence of motivations in a few sentences[47] warns against this extreme position. Furthermore, the multiplication of vivid imagery in sentences easily lends itself to the desire to achieve additional authority.

The sanctions for authority which I have applied to the Book of Job are sufficiently broad, it seems to me, to permit application throughout the sapiential corpus, as are the remarks concerning rhetoric in the contest of Darius's guards. At the same time, the concepts of ethos, pathos, and logos are sufficiently specific to illuminate almost any warrant for one's teaching, just as choice of subject, treatment of the material, vocabulary, and style permit entry into the thought of individual sages. Similar forays into other wisdom texts,[48] which I hope to make in the near future, should reveal extensive mastery of rhetorical technique even where the hand of authority weighs heavily upon the material. In a word, Israel's teachers spoke with authority, but they also developed and refined persuasion to an art.

---

[47]Prov 16:12, 26; 19:19; 21:7, 25; 22:9; 29:19 (cf. 23:16b).

[48]Qoheleth is characterized by the same ambiguity between claim to authority (the royal fiction) and striving for persuasive power (12:9-10). As is well known, the literary fiction of royal authorship fades away after the second chapter, to return again in the epilogue (one Shepherd). The first colophon stresses the sage's great desire to share insights with the populace; to achieve this goal he gave considerable attention to the external form of his words. The emphasis is clearly aesthetic, as well as ethical (Aarre Lauha, *Kohelet* [Neukirchen, 1978] 218).

20 (1987)

Murphy's Axiom:
Every Gnomic Saying
Needs a Balancing Corrective

In 1965 Roland E. Murphy wrote the following:

> Rather, like their Egyptian counterparts, they [Israelite sages] attempted to find the divine order (Egyptian *ma'at*) established in the world. This order must be recognized; man must integrate himself into the divinely established harmony. As Gerhard von Rad has put it, the wisdom movement is an attempt to master reality, to perceive the (divine) laws operating in nature and human society and man himself.
>
> (1965b, 131)

Twenty years later Murphy expressed serious reservations about this widespread interpretation of Israelite wisdom based on Egyptian concepts. He noted that von Rad had not been satisfied with the emphasis on order, for he had posed a revealing question: "Is it faith in the orders or faith in Yahweh?" (1958b, 9). Murphy went on to argue against the interpretation of biblical wisdom as a search for order. In his view an important implication of refusing to endorse the prevailing interpretation was that Israel did not distinguish faith from reason. Murphy therefore insisted that rational knowledge of God, or natural theology, should not be separated from revealed knowledge.[1]

What led to the shift in his thinking about the appropriateness of using an Egyptian concept to clarify Israelite wisdom? Answering this question offers a rare opportunity to catch a glimpse of the things Murphy considers worthy of pursuing

---

[1] A similar point is made in Murphy 1981d.

in the scholarly presentation of Israelite wisdom. This quest will therefore reveal some of the values he has upheld by word and action during the last two decades.[2]

In historical context, Murphy's early acceptance of the characterization of wisdom as a search for order is understandable. For many years scholars assumed that the wisdom literature in the Bible was pragmatic and eudaemonistic.[3] That situation changed when Henri Frankfort recognized the religious presuppositions of Egyptian sages (1961, 62-65). What appeared to be purely utilitarian conduct was actually far more complex. The universe was believed to have been created in a way that would reward actions that sustained the order of things and punish those acts that undermined the cosmic order. Human behavior was thus deeply religious in its motivation. It naturally followed that eudaemonism was grounded in religious conviction, and ordinary conduct had cosmological implications. *Ma'at*, the goddess of truth and justice, was thought to operate as the principle governing the universe. Living in harmony with *Ma'at* brought longevity, wealth, and fortune.[4]

Small wonder biblical interpreters welcomed this means of rescuing proverbial wisdom from the neglect afforded it by a scholarly community whose presuppositions, largely unexamined, placed a premium on saving history. It now appeared that Israel's sages were engaged in a profoundly religious search for the divine order imposed on the universe. Consequently, the pragmatic character of various proverbs ceased to present an embarrassment to interpreters. The so-called secular proverbs were thus provided with religious underpinnings, and the supposed gulf between Yahwism and wisdom narrowed.

The excitement surrounding this new understanding of wisdom can almost be felt as one reads Murphy's guide to wisdom literature that appeared in 1965 (Murphy 1965a). His comments about Egyptian wisdom manifest the enthusiasm of new insight. *Ma'at*, the divine order, must be observed by human beings. Those who integrate their lives into this order by appropriate conduct will enjoy success, whereas individuals who neglect to do so will experience ruin. In such a system sin lacks a personal dimension; instead, it is an aberration, a disturbing of the harmonious integration between creature and cosmos. In this sense sin can be called an abomination of God. The central polarity is order and chaos, and the ethical duty of individuals is to prevent the incursion of disorder into society. That moral

---

[2]That is how long he has been a valued conversational partner in my effort to understand ancient Near Eastern wisdom. His contributions in other areas, e.g., serving as an editor on the boards of *Vetus Testamentum* and *Hermeneia*, and the general coeditorship of the *Jerome Biblical Commentary* will not be discussed here. Nor will the many and varied ways Roland has proclaimed the Christian faith in language that laity could understand and appreciate. In that endeavor he has made countless friends, and one may hazard the guess that his impact will be felt there when his scholarly peers have moved to other interests.

[3]For a discussion of the change in perspective about ancient wisdom, see my prolegomenon to *SAIW*, 1-45.

[4]On *Ma'at*, see Volten 1963.

imperative extends to the simplest of tasks; even proper table manners affect the divinely established harmony. The obligation of teachers ("fathers") toward students ("sons") was to transmit the means whereby the youth could succeed in justice, that is, by observing the rules of the universe, observations based on experience and in harmony with *Ma'at*.

Murphy's early reading of canonical wisdom literature owes much to this interpretation of Egyptian wisdom. He described Proverbs as an attempt to impose control upon the varied experiences of reality. He wrote:

> Hence one must try to bring order into the chaos of the activity of man especially, and of nature. Man's portion before the uncertain and the unknown is solidified when he can point to the usual or to the universal.
>
> (Murphy 1965a, 30)

At this point Murphy used a concept that later came to expression in the thought of von Rad (1972) when he described the sapiential perspective. Murphy noted that nature sometimes yields analogies: Sheol's relentless appetite resembles greedy eyes; remove wood and the fire dies, take away gossip and strife ceases. The animal world also provides clues to solving certain puzzles: a dog returns to his vomit; fools repeat folly. Nevertheless, Murphy called attention to the presence of paradox: one person is generous, yet becomes richer; another is stingy, but gets poorer (Prov 11:24).

Two years later Murphy began to question the appropriateness of transferring *Ma'at* mentality to biblical thinking (1967, 414). He still affirmed the general truth that in a certain sense an *order* underlies the attitude of the sages and their observations. Moreover, he described the sages' task as that of assessing common experiences and putting "order" into these by arriving at correct conclusions: diligence brings prosperity and sloth results in poverty. Murphy based his own objections to the transfer of *Ma'at* thinking to Israelite wisdom on a distinction between what von Rad wrote and what his words had generated in the thought of others. To be sure, von Rad described the process as a rational clarification and ordering, a will to recognize and pin down the orders in human events and natural phenomena. This effort assumes that at the bottom of things an order is at work, silently and often in a scarcely noticeable way, ensuring a balance of events. However, Murphy wrote, von Rad's words do not necessarily mean that Israel's sages thought in terms of a rigid world order comparable to the Egyptian *Ma'at*. After all, von Rad did acknowledge that for Israel the world was more a process than a thing.

Murphy charges Hans Heinrich Schmid (Schmid 1966) with failing to nuance the notion of order in this way. In Murphy's opinion, Schmid had completely transferred an Egyptian world view to Israel, resulting in a polarity between the ethical and the cosmological. As Murphy saw it, a radical shift in perspective occurred here. Whereas Proverbs 10-15 once asked, "How can I contribute to keeping the world in its right course?" now the question was, "How shall I act so that I may stay in the right order, that is, among the just, pious and wise?"[5]

In 1969 Murphy returned to examine this change from action to attitude in the context of reflection on order (Murphy 1969). He emphasized the openness of the sages' observations about reality, their essential character as עֵצָה. Such counsel was subject to further testing in the light of later and different experience. Therefore, Murphy insisted, the sayings are not "rules"; instead, they are observations that must be applied to one's own circumstances. Sometimes silence is a sign of intelligence, and at other times failure to speak indicates ignorance. Inasmuch as answering a fool cuts both ways, it seems inappropriate to say that sages are seeking order. Murphy concluded: "It is correct to say that they are putting some order in the welter of experience, but they do not go beyond this, if they remain faithful to their sources" (1969, 294).

The key to Murphy's argument is divine freedom, which seems threatened by a mechanistic system. He observed that Israel's sages recognized their limitations better than modern thinkers do (he cites Prov 21:30; 16:1-2, 9). Because of this incalculable factor, divine freedom, the Israelite sages could never really secure existence (Prov 16:25). Nevertheless, Murphy conceded that Israelite sages absolutized certain sayings and externalized individual experiences. The result was the dogma of reward and retribution, which came to be understood as automatic.

A year later Murphy again returned to this subject and repeated his objection to an exaggerated emphasis on order (Murphy 1970a). This time he wrote as follows: "The Lord of the Old Testament was not one to be painted into a corner by the persistent formulations of the sages" (1970a, 231). Murphy admitted that many sages froze the teaching, blindly restricting divine freedom. Thus a psalmist implied that God had to punish the wicked and reward the devout (Ps 37:18-20). But other sages, specifically Job and Qoheleth, objected by issuing a warning against presuming on the nature of God. This recognition that some sages challenged the conclusions of others prompted Murphy to posit an axiom: "Any gnomic conclusion relative to God, world, and man needs a balancing corrective" (1970a, 229).

In this connection Murphy rejected the notion of a fate-producing context that von Rad and Klaus Koch (Koch 1955; English translation in Crenshaw 1983, 57-87) had proposed. In their view an act contains within itself, as a seed does its fruit, a good or evil effect. God's role in this process was that of a midwife who watches over the event and assures its coming into existence. Murphy argued that the biblical understanding of God left no room for this hypothetical construct. Although finding this idea of divine freedom in a few proverbs (Prov 3:11-12), Murphy also

---

[5]It could be asked whether a comparable shift occurred in Egyptian wisdom about the time of the *Instruction of Amenemope* (see Lichtheim 1976, 7, 146-47).

referred to the story about the testing of Abraham (Gen 22) as a parade example of God's freedom.

In rejecting an exaggerated emphasis on order Murphy did not abandon his previous acceptance of the general usefulness of the heuristic principle borrowed from specialists in the wisdom literature of ancient Egypt. In fact, he repeated much of his argument from earlier essays. Although a collection of sayings had a didactic function, the primary aim of a saying was "an effort to impose a certain basic order in the chaos of experience" (1970a, 227). Here he accepted von Rad's presupposition that a hidden order underlay all things and events. Therefore, Murphy observed, a wisdom saying is "an insight into a range of experience, from which it draws a steady generalization" (1970a, 228). For example, proud individuals are often discomfited, as pride goes before a fall (Prov 16:18; 18:12). The Israelite sage would have felt the excitement of fresh discovery concerning a regularity in events, but that aspect of the learning process has become lost to modern readers.

At the same time that he endorsed the understanding of Israelite wisdom as a searching for order, Murphy warned against making too much of this idea. Not all proverbs can be explained in this fashion. "There is nothing rigid about empirical observations," he wrote (1970a, 228), for individuals had to be open to every eventuality. The Egyptian view of *Ma'at* is not the same thing as the Israelite view. Furthermore, even if the idea of *Ma'at* has influenced the author of certain biblical proverbs (Murphy mentions the association of wisdom with life),[6] this fact does not justify the transfer of the Egyptian experience of reality to Israel.

Five years later Murphy returned to the same issue (Murphy 1975, 117-26), but this time he was able to appeal to von Rad's own caveat about positing a world order and to offer additional theological reasons for his own position. Here one sees a consequence of emphasizing order: it drives a wedge between Yahwism and wisdom. Murphy's intention was to remove that wedge, for he believed that Israel's sages accepted the fundamental world view of the Yahwists.[7]

According to him, the separation of Yahwism and wisdom resulted from the characterization of wisdom as a search for order, a concept that was grounded in the notion of an act-consequence relationship. Murphy acknowledged the accuracy of Christa Bauer-Kayatz's analysis of the Egyptian influence on the description of wisdom in Proverbs 8 (Bauer-Kayatz 1966). However, he wrote that "it is another thing to say that wisdom is the order of creation . . . and the object of man's inquiry. I would prefer to say that wisdom attempts to establish or impose a kind of order upon the myriad human experiences that form the raw material of wisdom sayings and upon nature itself" (1975, 120). The difference is that sayings arise from

---

[6]See Murphy 1981e, 51-52, for a more comprehensive list of *Ma'at*'s influence on biblical wisdom.

[7]In this regard Murphy and von Rad were quite similar. On the latter, see my review essay (Crenshaw 1976).

experience and impose order on the chaotic events in which people find themselves. Comparisons with nature occur, and analogies are formed, but this activity has nothing to do with discovering an order inherent in the world of human conduct and nature: "There is a coordination of experience and the created world; they illustrate each other" (1975, 121). By capturing and illumining human conduct, the sages shaped ideals.[8] Murphy granted that some proverbs contemplate nature for itself, but he insisted that "one can hardly speak of discovering order. Where order does not clearly appear, as in the stability of events in nature, it is a term of comparison rather than an object of discovery" (1975, 121). He added: "Nature provides for man a language of, and about, God; it is an area in which God is at work, but it does not become a field for the investigation of order" (1975, 121).

The stress falls on divine activity. Murphy admitted that some texts lend themselves to interpretation along lines of act-consequence (Prov 25:26-27), but he claimed that other texts assert that God intervenes directly in rewarding good conduct and punishing evil. Rejecting Koch's compromise—the view that God guarantees the connection between act and consequence—Murphy pointed out that Israel's sages did not attempt to reconcile these opposing views. That would extinguish the flame[9] arising from the profound insight contained within the notion of act and consequence. Then Murphy advanced beyond his earlier argument: this concept or order is overwhelmed by the Israelite notion of a repentant Lord (Jer 18:1-11).[10] Job and Qoheleth do not wrestle with this *concept*, but with *God*.[11] Qoheleth cannot understand God's actions, and Job knows *who* is at fault.[12] This

---

[8]On this process see Murphy 1978a. He writes that the world view and values of the faith community were transmitted within the family, sustained by participation in the liturgy of the community, and challenged by prophetic leadership (1978a, 36).

[9]Murphy thinks a similar extinguishing of the flame occurred in the Hebrew text of Canticles, for he suggests that שַׁלְהֶבֶתְיָה in 8:6 refers to the "flame of Yah" (Murphy 1985a, 3). In "Form-Critical Studies in the Song of Songs," (1973, 422) Murphy claims that the sages understood the songs in terms of wisdom literature. In this connection, he refers to the sayings about human sexuality in Prov 30:19 and 5:18-19.

[10]This theme comes to prominence in "Biblical Insights into Suffering: Pathos and Compassion" (Murphy 1981a). Murphy observes that in Wisdom of Solomon the idea of life after death is not arrived at on the basis of human nature (an immortal soul) but in virtue of justice, one's relationship to God (1981a, 62). He makes the same point in "The Understanding of Revelation in Prophecy and Wisdom," (1978b, 52). Human intimacy is also grounded in divine love, according to Murphy (1979a, 66).

[11]Murphy (1979b) implies that Qoheleth also struggled with human adversaries. In an earlier essay, Murphy suggests that Qoheleth's extreme views are partly attributable to the literary style he adopted (Murphy 1955).

[12]Job took his case directly to God, complaining to God rather than about the deity. Thus Job differs from many modern believers who, according to Murphy, "have lost the art of complaining *in faith* to God in favor of a stoic concept of what obedience or resignation to the divine will really means" (1980, 236).

devout sufferer wants an encounter, and that is another thing than demanding an explanation for the breakdown of an order. At the heart of this struggle is the relationship between God and Job,[13] not some impersonal order. Only by recapturing this truth, Murphy implied, will wisdom retain its rightful place in the canon when subjected to charges of paganism.[14]

A year later Murphy introduced another factor into the discussion of wisdom as a search for order. He labeled this idea of order a modern construct (1976, 187-200; see also Murphy 1983, 28-29).

> The concept of world order, *as opposed to chaos*, is surely present in the OT. Did the sages correlate human conduct with this order, as though it established or diminished the order? I find this [a] very theoretical construct that does not flow from the biblical text itself. (1976, 197)

Murphy went on to say:

> Man remains at the center of the sayings, which are highly anthropocentric. If this is true, the concept of order becomes *our* theological construct. One would do better to speak of man's imposing an order (however provisory) upon the chaotic experiences of life, by analysis and classification. (1976, 197)

In other words, Murphy boldly declared the search for order to be a projection of modern theological concerns on biblical literature. Furthermore, he dared to stand alone against a list of biblical interpreters,[15] referring to his longterm dissatisfaction with the emphasis on order and partially justifying it by noting that von Rad had carefully nuanced a dialectic between the order of human activities and the free ad hoc work of God.

Murphy did not totally reject the concept of order as a correct understanding of some biblical texts, although he qualified his remarks about a possible exception: the notion of retribution for the just. Nevertheless, he labeled this teaching a part of the heritage of Yahwism in general, and therefore implied that it should not be

---

[13]In Murphy's view, the perspective of wisdom is salutary in that it took humans where they were (1979c, 182). Modern preaching should also take the human situation seriously, beginning with the experience of the congregation and moving to the Bible, according to Murphy (1970c, 1, 10, 12). Such an approach would emphasize the *Deus praesens* and *Deus adveniens* (1970b, 590).

[14]This is Murphy's answer to H. D. Preuss, who views wisdom literature as pagan because of its widespread borrowing and, of course, because it lacks the traditional themes in Yahwism (see Preuss 1970; 1972; 1974).

[15]Murphy 1976, 196-97. He mentioned von Rad, Udo Skladny, H. J. Hermission, Hartmut Gese, Walther Zimmerli, Christa Bauer-Kayatz, and H. H. Schmid. In "Hebrew Wisdom," he added James L. Crenshaw and Leo G. Perdue to those scholars who accept the hypothesis of order (1981c, 26).

understood as a distinctive aspect of wisdom. He related the origin of this idea of retribution to divine justice rather than to reflection about order and reality.

In 1978 Murphy implied that he was fighting a losing battle (1978c, 35-42), for he labeled the hypothesis of order an "assured result" of the critics that was badly in need of examination. In this essay he summed up the three objections he had previously raised: (1) the idea of a search for order is a modern reconstruction; (2) it relies too much on the parallel between *Ma'at* and חָכְמָה; and (3) the idea of order describes a presupposition, an aspect of the Israelite understanding of reality that does not bear upon the didactic emphasis of wisdom teaching.[16] Murphy admitted that the idea was logical and probably correct, but he denied that Israel was ever asked such a question as this: "On what conviction is your wisdom based?" He also faulted modern critics for moving from a legitimate insight about wisdom as the art of steering to the notion of mastering life (1978c, 35).

The fundamental weakness of the notion of a fate-producing deed is that it over-looks the idea that the Lord is the primary cause of everything, Murphy declared.[17] This concept, too, may be a valid logical construction; but did it ever exist in reality? Would it have prevailed against the Israelite understanding of God who responds favorably to goodness and unfavorably to sin? Murphy reiterated his earlier argument that when the alleged order broke down in Job and Qoheleth, the Lord, not order, bore the brunt of the attack.[18] The shadow of von Rad made its presence felt, for Murphy acknowledged the magnitude of his contribution to the under-standing of wisdom, while calling for more study.

Murphy's presidential address to the Society of Biblical Literature focused on stylistic features that render suspect the hypothesis of an established order (1985b, 9). In his judgment the lyrical description of wisdom in Proverbs 8 and the accom-panying metaphors are far too personal to be directed toward an order of the uni-verse. The language indicates an amorous relationship, a wooing and eventual marriage. He asked: "who has ever sued for, or been pursued by, order, even in the surrogate form of a woman? The very symbol of Lady Wisdom suggests that order is not the correct correlation. Rather, she is to be somehow identified with the Lord, as indicated by her very origins and her authority. The call of Lady Wisdom is the

---

[16]Murphy 1978c, 41n.4. The first two arguments are much clearer than the third, which Murphy has not yet explained, insofar as I am aware.

[17]Murphy 1978c, 36. In 1981c, 26 he repeated this point: "Yet no one has explained how this view harmonizes with the fundamental Israelite attitude that the Lord is the primary cause of everything, both good and evil." That assumption about divine causality has recently been challenged by Lindstrom 1983.

[18]The force of this argument is weakened by the fact that the author of the addition to the *Admonition of Ipuwer* directs the critique to the deity rather than to an abstract order (Barta 1974).

voice of the Lord. She is, then, the revelation of God, not merely the self-revelation of creation" (1985b, 9).[19]

This new argument appears alongside a reminder that von Rad was not satisfied with the hypothesis of a mysterious but rather abstract order. Murphy also mentioned Schmid's program in biblical theology that posits an order, or justice, as its cornerstone (Schmid 1966, 25; 1973). Although the context does not make it clear, it seems that Murphy rejected the claim that "Creation-faith, that is, the belief that God has created and maintained the world with its manifest orders, is not a marginal theme of biblical theology, it is basically the theme" (1985b, 9n.19). Murphy made the usual concession about a presumption of regularity underlying the sages' observations, but he staunchly denied that they were searching for order.

This analysis of Murphy's attempt to provide a balancing corrective to the dominant approach to biblical wisdom has come to an end. Happily, we can expect further contributions from the one who has forced us all to think more self-consciously about the implications of using Egyptian presuppositions to clarify Israelite wisdom. None can fault Murphy for trying to safeguard divine freedom; there is surely biblical warrant for that endeavor. But this recognition that ancient sages felt compelled to resist frozen dogma may explain why contemporary interpreters have tended to emphasize order. On that score Murphy has consistently adopted a compromise position. That insistence on "both/and" offers the balancing corrective, and that is no small contribution.[20]

---

[19]In 1981b, Murphy described Lady Wisdom as God's intense desire to be more intimately present in the realm of creation, in truth, "God's communication of himself to human beings."

[20]Perhaps proponents of the reigning perspective will need to be more alert to the language they use in discussing order. My own view does not endorse Koch's "mechanistic system" but allows for divine freedom in dealing with individuals. It seems to me that one can speak usefully about the creator hiding the secrets of the universe (i.e., divine revelation) in the natural and animal world, and about the human task of searching for these insights so that by analogy they will be profitable in enabling individuals to cope. We cannot be sure whether ancient sages asked about order or not, but the heuristic value of such thinking seems to justify its use. For me, the crucial issue concerns whether or not ancient sages accepted the world view of Yahwism. Murphy thinks they did; I am not able to accept that position.

Bibliography and Reference List

Barta, W.
1974   Das Gespräch des Ipuwer mit dem Schöpfergott. *SAK* 1:19-33.
Bauer-Kayatz, C.
1966   *Studien zu Proverbien 1-9.* WMANT 22. Neukirchen: Neukirchener.
Crenshaw, James
1976   Review of von Rad, *Wisdom in Israel.* RSR 2/2:6-12.
Crenshaw, James, ed.
1983   *Theodicy in the Old Testament.* Philadelphia: Fortress.
Frankfort, H.
1961   *Ancient Egyptian Religion.* New York: Harper & Row. (Orig. 1948.)
Koch, K.
1955   Gibt es ein Vergeltungsdogma in Alten Testament? ZTK 52:1-42.
Lichtheim, M.
1976   *Ancient Egyptian Literature.* Volume 2. Berkeley: University of California Press.
Lindström, F.
1983   *God and the Origin of Evil.* ConBOT 21. Lund: C. W. K. Gleerup.
Murphy, R.
1955   The Pensées of Coheleth. *CBQ* 17:304-14.
1965a   *Introduction to the Wisdom Literature of the Old Testament.* OTRG 22. Collegeville MN: Liturgical Press.
1965b   The Wisdom Literature of the Old Testament. In *The Human Reality of Sacred Scripture*, ed. P. Benoit, R. E. Murphy and B. van Iersel, 126-40. Concilium 10. New York: Paulist.
1967   Assumptions and Problems in Old Testament Wisdom Research. *CBQ* 29:407-18.
1969   The Interpretation of Old Testament Wisdom Literature, *Int* 23:289-301.
1970a   The Hebrew Sage and Openness to the World. In *Christian Action and Openness to the World*, ed. J. Papin, 219-44. The Villanova University Symposia. Villanova PA: Villanova University Press.
1970b   History, Eschatology and the Old Testament. *Continuum* 7:583-93.
1970c   The Relevance of the Old Testament for Preaching in the 1970s. *Preach* 5:1-12.
1973   Form-Critical Studies in the Song of Songs. *Int* 27:413-22.
1975   Wisdom and Yahwism. In *No Famine in the Land* (J. L. McKenzie Festschrift), ed. J. Flanagan and A. Robinson, 117-26. Missoula MT: Scholars Press.
1976   "Wisdom Theses." In *Wisdom and Knowledge* (J. Papin Festschrift), ed. J. Armenti, 2:187-200. Villanova PA: Villanova University Press.
1978a   Moral Formation. In *Moral Formation and Christianity*, ed. F. Böckle and J. Pohier, 29-36. Concilium 110. New York: Seabury.
1979a   "A Biblical Model of Human Intimacy: The Song of Songs." In *The Family in Crisis or in Transition: A Sociological and Theological Perspective*, ed. A. Greeley, 61-66. Concilium 121. New York: Seabury.

1979b   "Qoheleth's 'Quarrel' with the Fathers." In *From Faith to Faith* (D. G. Miller Festschrift), ed. D. Y. Hadidian, 235-45. PTMS 31. Pittsburg: Pickwick Press.

1979c   "Wisdom and Salvation." In *Sin, Salvation, and the Spirit*, ed. D. Durken, 177-83. Collegeville MN: Liturgical Press.

1980   "The Faith of the Psalmist." *Int* 34:229-39.

1981a   "Biblical Insights into Suffering: Pathos and Compassion." In *Whither Creativity, Freedom, Suffering?: Humanity, Cosmos, God*, ed. F. A. Eigo, 53-75. Proceedings of the Theology Institute of Villanova University 13. Villanova PA: Villanova University Press.

1981b   "The Faces of Wisdom in the Book of Proverbs." In *Mélanges bibliques et orientaux en l'honneur de M. Henri Cazelles*, ed. A. Caquot and M. Delcor, 337-45. AOAT 212. Neukirchen-Vluyn: Neukirchener Verlag.

1981c   "Hebrew Wisdom." JAOS 101:21-34.

1981d   "Israel's Wisdom: A Biblical Model of Salvation." *StMiss* 30:1-43.

1981e   *Wisdom Literature: Job, Proverbs, Ruth Canticles, Ecclesiastes, and Esther.* FOTL 13. Grand Rapids MI: Eerdmans.

1983   *Wisdom Literature and Psalms.* IBT. Nashville: Abingdon.

1985a   "Two Dangerous Books?" *Duke University Letters* 69:3.

1985b   "Wisdom and Creation." *JBL* 104:3-11.

Preuss, H.

1970   "Erwägungen zum theologischen Ort alttestamentlicher Weisheitsliteratur." *EvT* 30:393-417.

1972   "Das Gottesbild der älteren Weisheit Israels." *VTS* 23:117-45.

1974   "Alttestamentliche Weisheit in Christlicher Theologie." In *Questions disputées de l'Ancien Testament*, ed. C. Brekelmans, 165-81. BETL 33. Leuven: Leuven University.

von Rad, Gerhard

1972   *Wisdom in Israel.* Nashville: Abingdon.

Schmid, H.

1966   *Wesen und Geschichte der Weisheit.* BZAW 101. Berlin: Alfred Töpelmann.

1973   "Schöpfung, Gerechtigkeit, und Heil: 'Schöpfungstheologie' als Gesamthoriz-ont biblischer Theologie." *ZTK* 70:1-19.

Volten, A.

1963   "Der Begriff der *Ma'at* in den ägyptischen Weisheitstexten." In *Les Sagesses du Proche-Orient ancien*, 73-99. Paris: Presses Universitaires de France.

21 (1992)

Proverbs

Proverbs, Book of. The twentieth book of the Old Testament in most English versions. The book is an anthology of admonitions and isolated sayings concerning wisdom and wise conduct.

A. Title of the Book
B. Authorship
C. Date
D. Content
E. Function
F. Affinities with Other Biblical Literature
G. Canonization

A. Title of the Book

The Hebrew title for the book of Proverbs, מִשְׁלֵי שְׁלֹמֹה, derives from the superscription in 10:1 (cf. also the longer form in 1:1 and 25:1). Variants to this title are סֵפֶר חָכְמָה and מְשָׁלוֹת (the latter derives from Eusebius and uses a plural form of מָשָׁל otherwise unknown, the usual plural being מְשָׁלִים). The Septuagint (LXX) title is ΠΑΡΟΙΜΙΑΙ; and the Vulgate has *Proverbia*, from which comes the English title "Proverbs." In the Hebrew Bible מָשָׁל designates a wide range of literary types—taunt, allegory, lament, simile, and so on—but its etymology implies likeness, and, in the view of some interpreters, authoritative word (from מָשַׁל, "to rule"). The fundamental feature of the sayings within the book therefore seems to be "comparison." Brief proverbial sayings set one image over against another, making an explicit or implicit comparison. Not every isolated saying compares two things, however, and some sayings extend considerably beyond a single distich, in the process multiplying the number of likenesses under consideration.

B. Authorship

Although certain features of the book associate the name "Solomon" with discrete units, other names also occur in connection with specific sections of the book. Some textual units lack any name whatever. Furthermore, the superscriptions may derive from a time later than the actual composition of the sayings within a given collection. The book therefore takes the shape of an anthology, its individual components coming from various periods of Israel's history. At least two, and probably three, short sections (numbers 3, 6, and 7 below) stem from non-Israelite sources, making the anthology truly international.

Superscriptions set off seven distinct collections from their present context.

1. 1:1–9:18   The Proverbs of Solomon, David's son, king of Israel
2. 10:1–22:16   The Proverbs of Solomon
3. 22:17–24:22 The Words of the Wise
4. 24:23-34   These also belong to the Wise
5. 25:1–29:27   These also are Proverbs of Solomon
                that the Men of Hezekiah, king of Judah, transcribed
6. 30:1-14   The Words of Agur, son of Jakeh, the Massaite
7. 31:1-9   The Words of Lemuel, king of Massa,
                with which his mother instructed him.

The last two brief collections have attracted miscellaneous sayings in the first instance and an alphabetic poem in the second.

8. 30:15-33   Numerical Sayings (except vv 20, 32-33)
9. 31:10-31   An Acrostic poem on a virtuous Woman.

Various signs of disunity within collections one and five, particularly arguments of style, content, and grammar, suggest that even further discrete units once existed (10:1–14:35; 15:1–22:16 and 25:1-27; 28:1–29:27).

In the Septuagint the different location of material and additional sayings indicate conscious acknowledgment of foreign material and a desire to promote specific concepts. The Greek text gathers together the collections of foreign extraction, yielding the following sequence: 22:17–24:22; 30:1-14; 24:23-34; 30:15-33; 31:1-9; 25:1–29:27; 31:10-31. Much additional material in the Septuagint appears toward the end of various collections (e.g., 9:12, 18; 15:27, 29, 33; 16:1-9; 24:22; 27:24-27).

The occurrence of the same proverb in more than one larger entity gives further indication of multiple collections. For example, the same conclusion reinforces instruction about industry akin to the ant's and an object lesson concerning the effects of neglect on a vineyard (6:6-11, 24:30-34). Brief sayings occur more than once in identical form and in slightly altered language, and specific expressions appear in more than one literary context.

A satisfactory explanation has not surfaced for the prominence of Solomon's name in the book of Proverbs on for the implicit attribution of Ecclesiastes to him and explicit mention of him as author in Song of Songs and Wisdom of Solomon. Ordinary citizens venerated kings of the ancient Near East as patrons of wisdom if not actual possessors of extraordinary insight. The praise of Solomon for wisdom surpassing that of all other kings acknowledges this fact and is perhaps a product of subjects' strong wish to be ruled by astute monarchs.

The tradition in 1 Kings 5:8-14 (EVV 4:29-34) that Solomon composed three thousand proverbs and one thousand and five songs actually summarizes their subject matter. One searches almost in vain within the book of Proverbs for sayings and songs about trees, beasts, birds, reptiles, and fish. Such encyclopedic lists have survived in Egypt and Mesopotamia, but biblical onomasticons have vanished if they ever existed. Given the tradition that Solomon's wisdom excelled that of everyone else in the Near East, it seems reasonable to assume that Israelite sages would have vigilantly preserved his noun lists.

Even those interpreters who think the tradition about Solomon's wisdom stems from his patronage of sages rather than from his actual authorship have difficulty explaining the divergence between the descriptions in 1 Kings 5 and the book of Proverbs. Some critics understand the reference in Kings as legend designed to legitimate a harsh regime that operated on the principle of might rather than justice. The apologia certainly depicts the young king as recipient of divine wisdom, which he promptly exemplifies in the judgment concerning the actual mother of a surviving infant, a story found in numerous cultures, and in his riddle contest with the Queen of Sheba. Whether such stories succeeded in counteracting the baneful effects of living memory remains unanswered, for this oppressive side of Solomon's reign was not totally suppressed in the biblical record. In this ancient apologia the climactic place of the references to Solomon's vast wealth may be instructive, for the belief that wise persons prospered became axiomatic at one time. As the wealthiest king in Israel's memory, Solomon must naturally have invited thoughts associating him with extraordinary wisdom. In all likelihood, the allusion to Hezekiah's men represents accurate recollection of a powerful and prosperous king of Judah whose patronage of sages allowed them to collect and transcribe earlier proverbial sayings. The ambiguous expression, men of Hezekiah, recalls the Masoretic text of 1 Kgs 10:8, in which the Queen of Sheba expresses admiration for Solomon: "Happy are your men, happy these your servants who stand before you continually, hearing your wisdom."

The initial collection is preceded by an introductory paragraph similar to the one in the Instruction of Amenemopet. The biblical preface (1:2-6) concludes with a thematic statement (1:7); together they serve as an introduction to the first collection and possibly to the whole book. Technical vocabulary of the wise abounds here: wisdom, discipline, discerning words; perceptive discipline, i.e. correct, fair, and upright; prudence, knowledge, and perspicacity; teaching and steering; simile, enigma, words of the wise, and riddles. In addition, verbs emphasize the learning and teaching process: to know, to perceive, to receive, to give; to hear, to add, to obtain; to understand. Distinct groups of people are also mentioned: the simple, youth, the wise (singular and plural). The thematic statement, "The fear of the Lord is the beginning (רֵאשִׁית) of knowledge; fools despise wisdom and instruction," grounds intellectual pursuits in religion. The word רֵאשִׁית may extend beyond the temporal to the substantive, making piety the fundamental ingredient of all knowledge. The use of the Tetragrammaton, rare in Wisdom Literature such as Job and Ecclesiastes, is very much at home in Proverbs 1–9.

C. Date

Biblical wisdom is notoriously difficult to date, largely because of the timeless quality of its teachings. Sages endeavored to communicate insights that transcend space and time. Their teachings aimed at universal assent by any intelligent individual, Israelite or non-Israelite. Accordingly, the wise remained silent about the specifics of national history, choosing rather to dwell on things accessible to every human being. With Ben Sira a decisive shift took place, and Israel's sacred traditions entered the repertoire of professional teachers. In contrast to earlier Wisdom Literature, Sirach (Ecclesiasticus) can be dated with confidence to the decade between 190 and 180 BCE.

Assigning relative chronology to the various collections in the book of Proverbs must therefore be done with considerable reservation. The previous tendency to date segments of the book on the basis of a form-critical judgment that brief sayings in distich or tristich form (sentences) antedate longer imperatives accompanied by warnings or exhortations (instructions) has collapsed because of Egyptian evidence. The discovery of Papyrus Insinger and the Demotic writings of 'Onkhsheshonky demonstrated the existence in very late times of sentences, whereas instructions from the third millennium have survived. It appears that genre was more a matter of social setting than chronological period; in general, rural folk had a natural affinity for sentences, and members of the court preferred instructions.

Although the form-critical argument for the lateness of Prov 1–9 does not require an early date for this collection, other features do come into play, especially the role of חָכְמָה, whether merely an elaborate metaphor or an actual personification, and the heightened emphasis on piety, possibly even influenced by the Torah in its Deuteronomic form. In addition, the earlier literal use of בְּנִי, "my son," and אָבִיךָ, "your father," appears to have given way to technical nuances for student and teacher, just as חָכָם "intelligent one," has taken on the sense of "professional sage." It follows that the present order of collections in the book of Proverbs does not reflect the chronology of the separate entities, and the clue from the Septuagint that other factors shaped the sequence seems valid for the Hebrew as well. Although conjectural at best, a plausible reconstruction of the various stages of development reads as follows. An ancient collection of family teaching (10:1–22:16) was enlarged by a body of knowledge with conceivably broader application (25:1–29:27), then supplemented by professional instruction, first in a collection that duplicates several instructions preserved elsewhere in an earlier Egyptian text (22:17–24:22) and later by a body of instructions in which Egyptian imagery is completely integrated (1:1–9:18). The miscellaneous collections in 24:23-34 and 30:15-33 may very well have preceded the last mentioned unit, possibly even 22:17–24:22. The sayings of Agur (30:1-14) and instruction of Lemuel's mother (31:1-9) probably followed the larger collections temporally, despite stylistic features in Agur's remarks that echo Canaanite literature. Actually, numerical sayings were widespread in the ancient world; and Agur seems to cite Job and certainly quotes from Psalms and Deuteronomy. His sentiments resemble the words of Qoheleth (Ecclesiastes), who probably was active about the middle of the third century. The latest section in the book of Proverbs, 31:10-31, appears to draw its power from the personification of Wisdom but extols wives of flesh and blood.

An interesting case has been made for the present arrangement of the book as a creative reinterpretation of old wisdom for theological purposes. The essence of the argument is this. Chapters 1–24 have a framing device and cyclic composition, whereas 25–31 use an additive technique. Chapters 1–9 combine two elemental or core blocks (2–4, the personal acquisition of wisdom, and 5–7, ethical advice, mostly about sex). A speech in first person (1:20-33 and 8:1-36) and a framing ring (the prologue, 1:2-7, and the final contrasting "allegory" about wisdom and folly, 9:1-18), enclose the two kernel blocks. Chapter 10 serves as an entrance way into the following collection, and chapter 15 functions as a second theological focus. Verses 4-5 in chapter 10 offer the kernel saying on poverty and riches, and verses 1-8 constitute a minicomposition around older wisdom, infusing new meaning into earlier teaching. Within chapters 10–15 only 14:7 uses the style of instruction, but in 16:1–22:16 it occurs frequently (16:3; 18:22; 19:18, 20, 27; 20:16; 22:6, 10). Instruction style therefore wraps itself around the central unit of proverbial wisdom, providing an effective transition to 22:17–24:22, where imperatives increase noticeably. Chapters 25–27 appear to be more empirical and general, whereas 28–29 contain a pronounced theological bent. A plait pattern is discernible in chapter 29, a linking of a verse with the one after its immediate sequel (1&3, 2&4; 7&9; 12&14; 15&17; 19&21; 20&22).

D. Content

1:1–9:18. This section purports to give parental advice to children. The chief literary device is that of a father (the "I") speaking to a son (the "you"), for the most part warning against rival discourse and thus reinforcing an ideology, the ethos of the family. Readers assume the role of sons who must choose between those values which preserve society and alternative actions that undercut family stability. Various dangers threaten young men, but two stand out here: the encouragement from young companions to unite in an endeavor to get rich quickly through criminal activity and the seductive invitation to sensual pleasure from illicit sources. In both instances the father manipulates the rival discourse, underscoring the dangers accompanying such misconduct. He even reinforces his own authority by appealing metaphorically to a higher level, the transcendental, on which God disciplines wayward children. Furthermore, the father confesses that he was once a child, in this way drawing adults into the discourse and uniting the generations. Occasionally, the father appeals to the authority of torah, a body of teaching that protects those who walk in its paths.

A mother's voice, although never audible, gives additional weight to the warnings against dangerous conduct. Because the principal threat to young men involves a specific kind of woman, the father's discourse receives an ally in feminine form. The voice of Wisdom comes to the assistance of the father, openly inviting young boys to share her feast and, like a prophet, sternly warning those who resist her advances. Together, the two encourage youth to direct their erotic impulses toward their own wives and to pursue knowledge with the same passion. In this context, metaphorical language functions to explore the mystery of eros, which has a dark side in addition to its luminous one. Woman represents access to ecstasy and agony; hence she offers pleasures that seem to justify any risk. That situation enables females whose ways are foreign to wreak havoc as harlots; and adulterous women disseminate their poison, prepared in attractive vials. The discourse acknowledges the power inherent in seductive speech, for it corresponds to secret desire in the hearts of those being addressed. Nevertheless, clear warnings accompany the verbal allure: follow her and die; she speaks folly, behaving unacceptably all the time.

The son's silence contrasts markedly with vocal appeals from various quarters. He faces a choice of allegiance, whether to contribute to consensus or to join the ranks of society's dissidents. He can resist his father's voice, learning how to do so from the very one who urges him to obey parental instruction. An Egyptian instruction, Anii, has a rare instance in which a son actually responds to his dad's teachings, insisting that the vigorous moral demands are beyond his capability although appropriate for the father, who counters such claims with weighty arguments. The son's silence in the book of Proverbs may have contributed to the climate in which the books of Job and Ecclesiastes give voice to rival discourse of a different kind. The call for all readers to adopt the subject position of a son to an authoritative father yields to outright challenge of traditional authority. On his part, the father adheres to belief that allegiance precedes knowledge, so that habitual conduct eventually creates its own ethos in which such behavior becomes natural, like breathing.

Modern interpreters have divided 1:1–9:18 into ten speeches, but they differ on the precise delineation of each unit and the criteria for identifying distinct sections. Introductory formulas consisting of direct address ("my son") and of an appeal to hear or receive instruction suggest the following divisions: (1) 1:8-19; (2) 2:1-22; (3) 3:1-12; (4) 3:21-35; (5) 4:1-9; (6) 4:10-19; (7) 4:20-27; (8) 5:1-23; (9) 6:20-35; (10) 7:1-27. These units assert the personal authority of the teacher and understand wisdom as ordinary human capacity, in contrast to the two places in this larger collection where a personified Wisdom claims to possess godlike power to bestow life and riches.

10:1–22:16. The second collection in the book of Proverbs consists of brief observations about life that make their point in distich form. These two halves of a line balance one another synonymously, antithetically, or synthetically.

1. Condemnation is ready for scoffers,
   and floggings for the backs of fools (19:29).
2. The poor use entreaties, but the rich answer roughly (18:23).

3. The eyes of the Lord are in every place,
      keeping watch on the evil and the good (15:3).

Some observations begin with a particle of existence that functions merely to introduce an anomaly.

There is a way which seems right to a man,
      but its end is the way to death.   (14:12)

Others judge one thing to be preferable to another.

Better is a dry morsel with quiet
      than a house full of feasting with strife.   (17:1)

Still other observations make simple comparisons.

Like vinegar to the teeth, and smoke to the eyes,
      so is the sluggard to those who send him.   (11:26)

Occasionally, a question expresses utter astonishment at incongruities.

Why should a fool have a price in his hand to buy wisdom,
      when he has no mind?   (17:16)

Because these sayings are complete in a single stich, the relationship to the larger context is uncertain. A few modern critics have posited thematic units, particularly in chapters 10–15. For example, 11:3-8 introduces a topic (the just and the wicked), 11:9-14 [17] specifies the effects of conduct on neighbors and society in general, and 11:18-20 repeats the two themes. In verses 9-12, 14 the Hebrew letter כ occupies the initial position, although this phenomenon may be accidental. Similar repetition occurs in 15:13-14 (לֵב, "heart") and in 16:27-29 (אִישׁ, "person"). If the principle linking the individual sayings expresses intentional design, no one has discovered a clue to the structure, which gives the appearance of randomness.

The sayings in this collection lack the distinctive features of the instructions in 1:1–9:18, specifically imperatives and the direct address, "my son" (but see 19:27). The "sentences" capture a single facet of reality, stating the truth in a "matter of fact" way. Readers are expected to give their assent, for the observations derive from collective experience. Hence the sayings dispense with reinforcements of any kind; they thus resemble traditional sayings embedded within biblical narrative and oracular literature, e.g., "The fathers have eaten sour grapes, and the children's teeth are set on edge" (Jer. 31:29; Ezek. 18:2).

The observations constitute astute insights about human behavior, both the good and the bad; and they probe the inner spirit as well: the significance of a wink (16:30), the effectiveness of a bribe (17:8), the unpredictable manner in which generous persons acquire more wealth and stingy ones become poorer (11:24), the posturing of a buyer before and after a purchase (20:14), the necessity of looking beneath the surface of things (13:7), the power of speech to beget good or ill (15:1), the allure of gossip (18:8), the loneliness of the heart in its moments of grief or joy (14:10), the underlying sadness that laughter obscures (14:13). A few proverbial sayings explore the limits imposed by the deity on human beings (16:9,33; 19:21), even on kings (21:1). For the most part these sayings exude optimism (12:21; 13:9; 15:3), a confidence that the Lord holds the reins of the universe securely in hand.

22:17–24:22. The unusual feature of these instructions is their affinity with the earlier Egyptian Instruction of Amenemopet. That relationship has been shown as follows.

Proverbs	Amenemopet	Subject
22:17-18	3:9-11,16	appeal to hear
22:19	1:7	purpose of instruction
22:20	27:7-8	thirty sayings
22:21	1:5-6	learning a worthy response
22:22	4:4-5	do not rob a wretch
22:24	11:13-14	avoid friendship with violent people
22:25	13:8-9	lest a trap ruin you
22:28	7:12-13	do not remove landmarks
22:29	27:16-17	skilful scribes will be courtiers
23:1-3	23:13-18	eat cautiously before an official
23:4-5	9:14–10:5	wealth flies away like an eagle/geese
23:6-7	14:5-10	do not eat a stingy person's food
23:8	14:17-18	vomiting results
23:9	22:11-12	do not speak before just anyone
23:10-11	7:12-15; 8:9-10	do not remove landmarks of widows
24:11	11:6-7	rescue the condemned

The principle of polygenesis may explain some similarities, for identical proverbial sayings occasionally emerge in cultures where no direct contact with one another has taken place. Nevertheless, the astonishing affinities in this instance indicate that the biblical author drew upon the earlier literary tradition or both authors used a common source. The reference to thirty (sayings) becomes understandable in light of the thirty chapters in Amenemopet.

The long rhetorical unit about the dangers associated with excessive drinking (23:29-35) also has a close parallel in Egypt, but nothing here seems to require a theory of dependence. The idea of the deity weighing the heart (24:12) has its closest analogue in Egyptian symbolism about a final judgment of human deeds. Furthermore, the frequent mention of kings and service at the court stands out in this larger unit, 22:17–24:22. Presumably, such notions corresponded to reality in Israel only briefly, although literary conventions persist long after the social conditions giving birth to them have vanished.

24:23-34. A miscellaneous collection, overlapping with 6:6-11, this brief section witnesses to the value of justice in society, offers helpful advice on priorities when embarking on a major undertaking like building a house, and encourages nonretaliation for offenses. The overlap with 6:6-11 has a different introductory scenario, but both discuss the folly of laziness.

25:1–29:27. The essential meaning of מָשָׁל as similitude comes to expression in this early collection, for an impressive number of sayings begin with the preposition of comparison, "like," whereas others achieve the same thing by juxtaposing competing images. The social setting of this collection has generated considerable speculation, one scholar proposing two distinct settings, the court for 25–27 and rural society for 28–29. Evidence hardly supports the thesis that the former unit served as a mirror for princes and the latter unit as advice to peasants. The opening section, 25:2-10, does reflect on the different functions of God and king, pausing to offer sound counsel about the means of securing royal authority and of finding one's appropriate niche in the councils of power. The remaining sayings apply broadly to Israelite society, without dwelling on peculiar concerns of the royal court. To be sure, eloquence and accuracy in reporting facts apply to persons in the king's service, and courtiers profit from keeping a civil tongue. So do other people, who must learn self-discipline, the right time to act, the advantages of breaking free from the rule of lex talionis (an eye for an eye), the necessity of speaking at crucial times and the folly of doing so in some circumstances, the dangers of initiating violence, the advantage of intellectual discussion, and so on. The concluding section in 27:23-27 reverts to royal imagery, specifically wealth and a crown, but makes a sharp transition to the concerns of everyday sustenance.

The contrast between poor and rich surfaces again and again in chapters 28–29, and the responsibility of a ruler to assure justice constitutes a society's deepest hope and harbors its greatest fear at the same time. Experience finds expression in the concession that a king's favor can be bought, so that pure justice rests with Yahweh alone. Nevertheless, the divine empowerment of poor people and their oppressors (29:13) has not escaped this astute observer of human experience.

30:1-14. Extraordinary disagreement characterizes scholars over the scope of this unit and its essential character, whether skeptical or pious. Some interpreters follow the Septuagint's lead in viewing the teaching as humble piety, while others think Agur takes conventional wisdom to task. A strong argument can be made for understanding verses 1-14 as a coherent unit, either as a dialogue between two people or as a teacher citing popular views in order to refute them. More probably, a skeptic challenges traditional wisdom, questioning God's existence and feigning ignorance, although insisting that those who profess orthodox views should demonstrate their knowledge of the Creator. An interlocutor rebukes Agur for heterodoxy, quoting Scripture, and is in turn warned against adding to the teacher's words. A sublime prayer follows, one that by distinguishing social status may mount further attack on the privileged teacher who has forgotten God while basking in the lap of luxury. The concluding section has a transitional statement about servants and masters, one that functions with reference both to humans and to God, together with four incisive observations about types of people who are worse than honest skeptics like Agur: children who dishonor their parents, hypocrites, proud persons, and rapacious cutthroats.

This section demonstrates remarkable skill at rhetoric, utilizing double meanings and clanging symbols, the dashing of expectations. Promising prophetic revelation, it offers human words that are either Delphic gibberish or astonishing confession of practical, at least, atheism. Theophanic language evokes derision in a citation from God's speech in Job ("Surely you know"). The request to be spared poverty and riches demonstrates unusual perception about the role of sociological status in shaping one's religious views. This negative attitude toward wealth accords ill with the prevailing understanding of virtue and its rewards, but Israel's teachers seem to have had difficulty adopting a consistent attitude toward the poor.

30:15-33. Graded numerical sayings alternate with three observations that allude to the four types of persons in 30:11-14. Those who show disrespect for parents will suffer hideously (30:17); adulteresses eat and wipe their mouths without any awareness of offense, consequently remaining pure in their own eyes (30:20); proud individuals ought to refrain from boasting (30:32); and violent people should control their tempers (30:33). The numerical sayings isolate for scrutiny various categories that resemble one another: things that are never satisfied (Sheol, the barren womb, a thirsty ground, fire), movement that leaves no trace (an eagle in the sky, a serpent on a rock, a ship at sea, a young man and a maiden), intolerable circumstances (a king who once was a slave, a fool with a full stomach, a previously spurned woman who weds, a maid who succeeds her mistress), four small creatures able to adapt to circumstances (ants, badgers, locusts, and lizards), and four "prancing" (self-important?) creatures (a lion, a cock, a billy goat, and a king).

31:1-9. This instruction consists of a superscription (31:1), a queen mother's direct appeal to her son (31:2), and four "words" of advice. These admonitions concern relationships with women and excessive drinking. Lemuel's mother tells her royal son to provide strong drink for oppressed victims of society who need something to forget their misery. She also urges him to pay special attention to the matter of justice, becoming a powerful advocate for vulnerable members of society whose voice would otherwise go unheeded. The entire instruction makes effective use of rhetoric, combining terms of endearment, repetition, inclusion, suspension of subject matter, and double entendre.

31:10-31. The personification of Wisdom as a woman served to correct many sayings that emphasize women as temptresses and disrupters of harmony within households. Nevertheless, personified Folly neutralized this embodiment of discernment. Therefore, another means of salvaging women's reputation was needed; the final poem endeavors to do just that. Its effectiveness suffers because of its orientation toward the good wife's contribution to her husband and children. Her worth seems to depend on how successfully she enhances his standing in the community. The description of her entrepreneurship suggests that Israelite women took an active role in business. The religious criterion for evaluating women (31:30) comes as something of an afterthought.

E. Function

During the earliest phases of Israelite society, power rested in elders, who perpetuated their singular authority through legal statute and traditional saying. Apodictic law compelled assent insofar as it voiced the will of respected figures whose wide experience, fairness, and good judgment set them apart from ordinary citizens as custodians of valuable lore. Similarly, proverbial sayings carried the weight of cumulative experience, hence embodied a way of life that was binding on everyone but persons who questioned the fundamental basis of society. These two, law and traditional saying, constitute ancient Israel's attempt to establish and maintain order in complex human relationships.

Although the locus of both law and aphorism reached beyond the privacy of a family's tent to the centers of daily deliberation, particularly the gates where important judicial decisions were rendered, the lofty position of parents in the early system of clans reinforced the authority of these literary forms. This domestic setting left its mark on proverbial teaching, which strengthened its own appeal to hearers by adopting the emotion-laden language of father to son. Older proverbial collections in the book of Proverbs dispensed with such specific designations of speaker and addressee, but ancient Near Eastern parallels from Egypt and Mesopotamia demonstrate the antiquity of this language, which eventually took on the technical sense of teacher (אָב, "father") and student (בְּנִי, "my son") so prevalent in Prov 1–9.

These parental teachings emerged from persistent efforts to penetrate reality so as to order life for maximum success in achieving honor, wealth, health, and offspring. The notion of steering lay at the heart of such instruction, and an appreciable amount of self-discipline too. Optimism prevailed about the extent to which individuals controlled their own destiny. Virtue received its reward and vice, its punishment, with rare exceptions, which emphasized divine freedom. In due time, skepticism made its presence felt, particularly with regard to the impenetrability of the universe. In Egypt a noticeable increase in piety accompanied such pessimism, and the same may actually have occurred in Israel as well. Although an attitude of confident reverence pervades much of the proverbial literature, growing insecurity seems to have evoked opposite responses, skepticism and dogmatic assertions.

The introduction of monarchy in Israel brought about a definite shift in the power base, the center of authority moving from heads of families to a chief of state. This change came slowly and after much resistance on the part of those who watched their status in the community dwindle year by year. Concentration of power in Jerusalem and international commerce hastened the emergence of a professional class of courtiers equipped to handle the complex affairs of state on behalf of royalty. Such learned figures graced the courts of Egypt and Mesopotamia from early times. Precisely when they first appeared in Israel remains a mystery; but they were firmly planted in the eighth century BCE, producing a tradition associating them with the court of King Hezekiah. Even David enjoyed the benefits of two counselors, Ahithopel and Hushai, whether in fact or as a piece of literary fiction.

One can easily imagine the reponsibilities of such courtiers, despite the silence about their duties in Wisdom Literature. International diplomacy must have stood high on their agenda, and thus the mastery of various foreign languages. The educating of young princes may also have fallen to these courtiers, and perhaps, too, the entertaining of nobility with feats of eloquence like those in 1 Esd. 3:1–4:41. The courtiers probably kept records, both political and economic, and prepared propaganda for aspiring and fading regimes. Considerable attention would have gone to the training of young potential courtiers, hence to perpetuating their profession. In all likelihood instructional literature in the book of Proverbs belongs to such "in-house" pedagogy. This scholarship for internal consumption may have encouraged the kinds of philosophical reflection that eventuated in the books of Job and Ecclesiastes.

The disappearance of monarchy in 587 BCE and the drastic alteration of life style, whether in Exile or in the Judean countryside, brought about a radically different job description for professional sages. The accompanying loss in perceived status further fueled fires of discontent, already exacerbated by historical circumstances involving the populace at large. Adversity propelled these learned teachers into strange alliances with the ruling priestly class, or alternatively with persons located on the fringes of society, at least in their conviction that justice had departed once and for all. This retreat in opposite directions suggests that wisdom may always have possessed distinct perspectives corresponding roughly to the differences in literary genre that have complicated all attempts to comprehend the phenomenon. However, the two different orientations, the experiential aphorism and the reflective probing, functioned in a complementary way, possibly to the very end. Their union in Sirach merely continues a trend set in motion by the authors of Job and Ecclesiastes.

The preceding account of professional sages in ancient Israel suggests that they possessed remarkable adaptability, a willingness to change with the times. A Hellenistic text, Wisdom of Solomon, shows how far the sages proceeded in their accomodation to new modes of thought. Such radical departures inevitably threatened to introduce a new entity altogether, making it difficult to determine the actual successors of the wise in later Judaism. Furthermore, this partial rendering of the development of the sapiential enterprise, like the biblical literature itself, maintains silence about onomasticons. One wonders why Israel's teachers did not compile comprehensive taxonomies of flora and fauna, among other things. Perhaps they did, and this particular feature of their intellectual achievement has vanished.

Changes in the meaning of חָכְמָה over the years suggest yet another means of tracing the development of the sapiential enterprise. Just as the adjective חָכָם and its plural assumed a technical sense in some instances (the sage or the wise), the noun חָכְמָה also acquired a rich nuance of astonishing magnitude. Foreign influence definitely played a part in this fascinating speculation about a personified figure who embodied the highest and noblest aspirations of the sages, but Israelite ideas laid the foundation itself. As a matter of fact, prophetic language dominates the initial appearance of חָכְמוֹת (Prov 1:20-33), specifically the image of pouring out the spirit, the description of stubborn refusal to hear, and the references to undesirable consequences of such action. The people refused to listen to the proclamation; they spurned the outstretched hand; Wisdom will mock them in their distress; when they call, she will not answer; unable to find her, they will eat the fruit of their way and gorge themselves on their own misconduct. This threatening posture approximates that of a prophet who speaks in God's name, the prophetic ego merging with the divine. These foolish individuals have not just ignored a human teacher; they have also treated God with contempt.

The plural חָכְמוֹת has caused considerable speculation, none of which satisfactorily explains the form: a plural of abstraction, an ancient Canaanite goddess, an orthographic mistake. Curiously, the next section to introduce this figure, Prov 8:1-36, uses two expressions in parallelism (חָכְמָה and תְּבוּנָה, although referring to a single individual (cf. 7:4). Several links with the earlier text stand out—the place of instruction, the objects of the teaching, the allusions to "seeking and finding" and to fruit, both positive here. New ideas also surface: the extraordinary worth of Wisdom, surpassing the value of jewels; Wisdom's role in the manifest rule of the earth; the integral relationship between Wisdom and morality; and her presence with God at creation.

The latter complex of ideas concerning creation, echoing sentiments from Egypt, particularly the emphasis on her presence before the various creative deeds and the picture of Wisdom as a source of God's pleasure, describes a transcendent figure loftier by far than the earlier prophetic one. The result of God's first creative deed, she therefore preceded earth itself. Either as artisan or darling child, she witnessed the firmament taking shape and rejoiced constantly as Yahweh established order despite chaotic forces of the deep. A merging of egos occurs here too, as Wisdom assures those who find her that they will discover Yahweh's favor and therefore life itself.

The third passage about an extraordinary figure known as חָכְמָה, Prov 9:1-6, describes a building project on a smaller scale. She constructs a house, fashions its seven columns, and prepares a lavish banquet, enlisting the aid of servants to issue an invitation to townspeople. Just as Yahweh had to contend with the waters of the deep, Wisdom must reckon with a rival force who promises sensual pleasure. Given the powerful role of erotic imagination, sweet water and pleasant bread transform a simple meal into a sumptuous feast (Prov 9:13-18).

F. Affinities with Other Biblical Literature

Proverbial sayings occur in various contexts other than the book of Proverbs. Besides traditional sayings preserved in narratives and prophetic literature, one finds similes and aphorisms in Psalms that closely resemble those in Proverbs. For example, Ps. 37:16 expresses the judgment that the meager possessions of virtuous people are better than the abundance of many wicked persons. Similarly, 37:21 states that a wicked individual borrows and cannot repay, but the righteous is generous and gives away. Verse 23 insists that God directs a person's steps, establishing the one who finds divine approval. Psalm 94:8-11 uses rhetorical questions in composing a didactic essay on divine sovereignty that hears, sees, and chastens. The motto in Prov 1:7a occurs in Ps. 111:10a ("The fear of the Lord is the beginning of wisdom"); and the comparison of parental teaching with a lamp and light appears in Ps. 119:105, here with reference to God's word. The sons of youth are likened to arrows in the hands of a warrior in Ps. 127:4.

The use of מִצְוָה and תּוֹרָה in Proverbs raises the possibility that the Mosaic law lies behind the vocabulary about parental instruction. The use of these words with reference to paternal and maternal teaching in 6:20 suggests that they have the same referent in 6:23 ("For the commandment is a lamp and the teaching is a light, instruction and discipline are the way of life"). Nevertheless, an association with Deut. 6:4-9; 11:18-20 seems likely, if unconscious. The Mosaic law may rest behind the language of Prov 28:4, 7, 9; and 29:18, particularly if this last verse also refers to prophecy, but all of these references may have in mind laws of the state.

Although Job and Ecclesiastes represent different genres within Wisdom Literature, they contain many proverbial sayings like those in the book of Proverbs. Perhaps Prov 30:4 alludes to God's mocking remark in Job 38:5 ("surely you know"). Sirach also has numerous proverbial sayings and didactic essays on individual themes, in both instances following in the footsteps of the unknown authors who composed the book of Proverbs. The popularity of such aphorisms is evidenced by their being embedded within devotional narratives such as Tobit (12:7-10).

G. Canonization

The sacred character of Proverbs seems never to have been in doubt, although remarks about its vivid description of a harlot in the act of seduction and about direct contradiction in 26:4-5 have survived in Jewish sources. Christian acceptance of the book seems not to have been contested, and its secular character did not pose any obstacle to considering the book canonical. In some circles, modern scholars have declared its contents pagan, but the criterion they use (proclamation of saving history) leaves much to be desired.

The Greek text has about 130 stichs more than the Hebrew, many of them highly Hellenized. Some haggadic tendencies intermingle with apparent mistakes. Other renderings may harmonize related texts in several different books, especially Psalms, Sirach, and Wisdom of Solomon.

Selected Bibliography

Aletti, J. N.
1977   "Seduction et parole en Proverbs 1–9." *VT* 27:129-44.

Alonso Schökel, L. and Vilchez, J.
1984   *Proverbios*. Nueva Biblia Espanola. Madrid: Ediciones Christiandad.

Barucq, A.
1964   *Le Livre des Proverbes*. SB. Paris: J. Gabalda et Cie, Editeurs.

Bryce, G.
1979   *A Legacy of Wisdom*. Lewisburg PA: Bucknell University Press.

Bühlmann, Walter
1976   *Von Rechten Reden und Schweigen*. OBO 12. Göttingen: Vandenhoeck & Ruprecht.

Camp, C. V.
1985   *Wisdom and the Feminine in the Book of Proverbs*. BLS 11. Sheffield: Almond Press.

Crenshaw, J. L.
1988   "A Mother's Instruction to her Son (Prov 31:1-9)." In *Perspectives on the Hebrew Bible*, ed. James L. Crenshaw, 9-22. Macon GA: Mercer University Press.

1989a   "Clanging Symbols." In *Justice and the Holy*, ed. D. A. Knight and P. Paris, 51-64. Philadelphia: Fortress Press.

1989b   "The Sage in Proverbs." In *The Sage in Israel and the Ancient Near East*, ed. L. G. Perdue and J. Gammie, 205-16. Winona Lake IN: Eisenbrauns.

1989c   "Proverbs." In *The Books of the Bible*, ed B. W. Anderson, 223-30. New York: Scribners.

Crossan, J. D., ed.
1980   *Gnomic Wisdom*. Semeia 17. Chico CA: Scholars Press.

Fontaine, C. R.
1982   *Traditional Sayings in the Old Testament*. BLS 5. Sheffield: Almond Press.

Gese, H.
1984   "Wisdom Literature in the Persian Period." In *Cambridge History of Judaism*, 1:189-218. Cambridge: Cambridge University Press.

Hermisson, H.-J.
1968   *Studien zur israelitischen Spruchweisheit*. WMANT 28. Neukirchen: Neukirchener Verlag des Erziehungsvereins.

Kayatz, Christa
1966   *Studien zu Proverbien 1–9*. WMANT 22. Neukirchen: Neukirchener Verlag des Erziehungsvereins.

Lang. B.
1972   *Die weisheitlichen Lehrrede*. SBS 54. Stuttgart: KBW Verlag.

1986   *Wisdom and the Book of Proverbs*. New York: Pilgrim Press.

Lemaire, A.
1981   *Les écoles et la formation de la Bible dans l'ancien Israël*. OBO 39. Göttingen: Vandenhoeck & Ruprecht.

Lindenberger, J. M.
    1983   *The Aramaic Proverbs of Ahiqar*. Baltimore and London: Johns Hopkins University Press.

Naré, L.
    1986   *Proverbes salomoniens et proverbes Mossi*. Publications Universitaires Européennes. Frankfurt am Main, Bern, New York: Peter Lang.

Nel, P. J.
    1982   *The Structure and Ethos of the Wisdom Admonitions in Proverbs*. BZAW 158. Berlin & New York: Gruyter.

Shupak, N.
    1987   "The 'Sitz im Leben' of the Book of Proverbs in the Light of a Comparison of Biblical and Egyptian Wisdom Literature." *RB* 94:98-119.

Skehan, P.
    1971   *Studies in Ancient Israelite Poetry and Wisdom*. CBQMS 1. Washington: Catholic Biblical Association of America.

Skadny, U.
    1962   *Die ältesten Spruchsammlungen in Israel*. Göttingen: Vandenhoeck & Ruprecht.

Trible, P.
    1975   "Wisdom Builds a Poem: The Architecture of Prov 1:20-33." *JBL* 94:509-18.

Van Leeuwen, R. C.
    1988   *Context and Meaning in Proverbs 25–27*. SBLDS 96. Atlanta: Scholars Press.

Vawter, B.
    1980   "Prov 8:22: Wisdom and Creation." *JBL* 99:205-16.

Whybray, R. N.
    1965   *The Intellectual Tradition in the Old Testament*. BZAW 135. Berlin and New York: W. de Gruyter.

    1972   *Wisdom in Proverbs*. SBT 45. London: SCM Press.

Williams, J. G.
    1981   *Those Who Ponder Proverbs*. Sheffield: JSOT Press.

22 (1989)

Clanging Symbols

Skillful writers weave a pattern of expectation and consequence, introducing just enough ambiguity to alert readers to the possibility of unexpected surprises. Context, shifts in grammar, slight alterations of vocabulary, and so forth attach unaccustomed meaning to familiar phrases. When expressions lead readers along well traveled paths of thought and then veer off in an entirely different direction, they produce a collision of anticipation and result. I call this phenomenon clanging symbols, a formulation that itself illustrates the shift in language from an expected "clanging cymbals."[1]

Edwin M. Good's analysis of the initial poem in Ecclesiastes 1:2-11 closely approximates the approach I have in mind, although Good did not focus on unexpected consequences.[2] Preferring an analogy from music, he replaced the usual mode of viewing a text—which resembles the way one looks at a painting—with a linear view of the process by which the composition came into being. Good noted that a work "sets up in the reader a tendency to respond, arouses the expectation of a consequent, then inhibits the tendency, and finally brings the (or an) expected consequent." An attentive reader distinguishes between the expected consequents and actual ones. In the process, hypothetical meanings yield evident meaning which in turn yields determinate meaning. In Good's view, three stylistic techniques delay the expected consequent: using the interrogative; holding off the key word for some time; and interposing something unexpected.[3] His last point deserves fuller articulation than the study of Eccles. 1:2-11 prompted.

---

[1]The allusion to 1 Cor 13:1 presupposes a familiarity on the part of readers; in the same way, my approach to literary analysis assumes considerable sophistication on the part of authors and interpreters in the ancient world. Literary conventions, formulas, topoi, metaphors, vocabulary, and an intellectual tradition in general weave an intricate tapestry that is capable of multiple designs. The task of modern interpreters is to imagine the several possibilities and to recognize the reasons for the final shape of a given text.

[2]"The Unfilled Sea: Style and Meaning in Ecclesiates 1:2-11," *Israelite Wisdom: Theological and Literary Essays in Honor of Samuel Terrien*, ed. John Gammie et al. (Missoula MT: Scholars Press, 1978) 59-73.

[3]Good, "The Unfilled Sea," 62.

I believe this particular approach illumines many biblical texts in ways not possible when interpreters used more conventional modes of interpretation.[4] I intend, therefore, to apply my version of this manner of reading the Bible to the sayings of Agur in Proverbs 30:1-14.[5] The debate over these aphorisms has so far failed to generate anything resembling consensus.[6] In all probability, that disparity in opinions will continue regardless of the approach taken, but the very inability to clarify its meaning invites a different perspective. I shall concentrate on the surprises that punctuate the text, hoping by that means to understand the present form of the brief section attributed to Agur.

The opening word, דִּבְרֵי, offers an ambiguous clue with regard to the realm of discourse into which readers are drawn. By far the dominant use of this super-scription occurs in prophecy (Jer. 1:1; Amos 1:1; in the singular form, Hos 1:1; Joel 1:1; Mic. 1:1; Zeph. 1:1). Nevertheless, this expression introduces the book of Ecclesiastes (דִּבְרֵי Qoheleth), hence the expectation that a prophetic utterance follows must allow for the remote possibility that sapiential instruction issues forth. If the opening word is prophetic, it will probably be governed by a divine appellation, usually the Tetragrammaton, or by a proper name. Appearance of the divine name would therefore resolve the issue, whereas a proper name would not indicate whether the word is prophetic or sapiential.

In this instance the proper name Agur appears. Elsewhere it does not occur in known Hebrew literature, although the name does show up in northwest Semitic. Precedent from sapiential literature leads one to look for an acronymn, a pen name, or a title.[7] The grammatical form of the name suggests something gathered, unless one drops the initial אָלֶף and derives the word from the verb "to sojourn." The passive participle seems to rule out a title (contrast Qoheleth, the one who assembles). In addition, no clue survives that gives weight to the hypothesis that

---

[4]The recent burst of activity in literary criticism of the Bible continues unabated. Two recent publications bringing that research into focus for the general reader are *The Hebrew Bible in Literary Criticism*, ed. Alex Preminger and Edward L. Greenstein (New York: Ungar, 1986) and *The Literary Guide to the Bible*, ed. Robert Alter and Frank Kermode (Cambridge MA: Harvard University Press, 1987).

[5]In the Septuagint, Prov 30:1-14 was believed to constitute a unity, for it follows the section in Prov 22:17–24:22 in which several sayings from the Egyptian *Instruction of Amen-emopet* appear. The ensuing verses in Hebrew (30:15-33) do not follow immediately in the Septuagint, but are separated from 30:1-14 by 24:23b-33.

[6]For a penetrating study, see the article by my former student Paul Franklyn: "The Say-ings of Agur in Proverbs 30: Piety or Skepticism," *ZAW* 95 (1983): 238-52. Otto Plöger, *Sprüche Salomos (Proverbia)* (Neukirchen Vluyn: Neukirchener Verlag, 1984) 351-62, gives a helpful analysis of the many difficulties in understanding this section.

[7]See my discussion of this issue with regard to the name "Qoheleth" in *Ecclesiastes* (Philadelphia: Westminster Press, 1987) 32-34.

Agur stands for something else. Therefore, we understand it as a name of a foreigner, either prophet or sage.

We expect further identification of Agur, and we are not disappointed. The appositional phrase בִּן־יָקֶה supplies the name of Agur's father, an otherwise unknown Jaqeh. These three consonants have tickled the imagination of one scholar, who thinks they conceal an acronymn, יהוה קָדוֹשׁ הוּא (the Lord is holy).[8] Thus understood, Jaqeh designates Israel's God and Agur stands for the nation as embodied in the sojourner, Jacob. More probably, the reference is to Agur's father.[9] But we still await some information about this unknown Agur, presumably a description of his place of origin or his actual activity. This datum does not follow; instead, we encounter technical vocabulary from prophecy, הַמַּשָּׂא (the oracle, burden). The initial impression that prophetic discourse follows seems to be confirmed at this point, unless we point the word as a gentilic (הַמַּשָּׂאִי, the Massaite) or, less likely, add a prefix in the place of the initial ה, yielding "from Massa." This reading accords with the foreign proper name, Agur, and parallels the geographical designation in Proverbs 31:1.

The words נְאֻם הַגֶּבֶר (whisper or prophetic utterance of the man) return to the realm of prophetic discourse, albeit with an astonishing twist. Technical vocabulary for a divine oracle appears as a human possession. One expects נְאֻם יהוה, נְאֻם יהוה צְבָאוֹת, or something comparable. In no case does one anticipate a human source for an oracle. A more striking juxtaposition of words can scarcely be imagined. They do appear, nevertheless, in two other places (Ps. 36:2 is textually uncertain). The first, Numbers 24:3, resembles Agur's remarks so closely that we suspect conscious interplay (v. 3, בְּעֹר, נְאֻם בְּנוֹ, בְעֹר מְשָׁלוֹ וַיִּשָּׂא;[10] v. 16, נְאֻם שֹׁמֵעַ אִמְרֵי־אֵל וְיֹדֵעַ דַּעַת עֶלְיוֹן). The other place, 2 Sam 23:1, refers to an oracle of David the son of Jesse (נְאֻם דָּוִד בֶּן־יִשַׁי וּנְאֻם הַגֶּבֶר). Both passages supply additional information about the men whose utterance follows, ultimately clarifying the divine origin of the oracles.

The absence of the divine name in connection with a prophetic oracle arouses suspicion of blasphemy, which may find confirmation in the contents itself (לְאִיתִיאֵל לְאִיתִיאֵל וְאֻכָל). "There is no god, there is no god, and I am powerless." Or the message is garbled: "To Ithiel, to Ithiel, and Ukal." The first translation requires the assumption that the foreigner speaks his native tongue, Aramaic. Because Hebrew and Aramaic intermingle elsewhere in the Bible, this possibility gains plausibility here. The second translation takes the initial ל as a sign

---

[8]Patrick W. Skehan, *Studies in Israelite Poetry and Wisdom* (Washington: Catholic Biblical Association, 1971) 42-43.

[9]בֶּן יָקֶה could be translated "son of piety," i.e., the devout one. The pointing of בֶּן is rare regardless of its meaning.

[10]The Septuagint has Agur lift up his מָשָׁל (proverb, analogy). The association of an oracle (מָשָׂא) and the verb וְנָשָׂא occurs in Isa 14:4; Mic 2:4; Hab 2:6, each time with מָשָׁל.

of dedication; in this case the oracle is dedicated to two persons, the first of whom is mentioned twice. The name Ithiel appears in Nehemiah 11:7, and although Ukal does not, the form is appropriate and therefore does not undercut this supposition. On this reading, Agur's utterance resembles a Delphic oracle, a mysterious garbling of sounds that remain meaningless until interpreted by an expert.

Repetition of the first name renders this second option improbable, whereas the reiteration of a solemn declaration heightens the poignancy and reinforces the soundness of this interpretation. The same phenomenon surfaces in Isaiah 24:16 (רָזִי־לִי רָזִי־לִי אוֹי לִי, I languish, I languish! Woe on me!). Similar rhetoric may lie behind Agur's utterance; if one abandons the assumption of blasphemy, an emended text yields the translation: "I am weary, God, I am weary, God, and exhausted."[11] Along similar lines, but in accord with the supposition that Agur's utterance deviates from pious norms, the text has been read, "I am not God, I am not God, and I lack power."[12] Such articulation of the obvious seems highly bland and unlikely as a theological statement.

The second verse offers a rationale for the assertion, thus ruling out the understanding of the utterance as proper names, unless the particle כִּי is emphatic ("Surely").[13] The nature of the rationale, a confession of ignorance, reinforces the emphatic understanding of the particle. Otherwise, one expects Agur to set forth powerful credentials for such expressions of atheism and ennui. That is why many interpreters read Agur's remarks as irony or sarcasm (כִּי בַעַר אָנֹכִי מֵאִישׁ וְלֹא־בִינַת אָדָם לִי, For I am stupid beyond human [norms], and I lack ordinary knowledge). Agur claims that his ignorance removes him from the social realm, linking him with the animal kingdom. Where we expected heavenly wisdom, we must be content with insight from the kingdom of beasts. The sapiential fondness for this image as an indication of ignorance yields another possibility, for at least one psalmist who became aware of brutish reasoning hastened to the holy place and proceeded to purify such thoughts (Ps. 73:22: "As for me, I was stupid and ignorant [וַאֲנִי־בַעַר וְלֹא אֵדָע], I was animalistic toward you [בְּהֵמוֹת הָיִיתִי עִמָּךְ]"). Dare we entertain similar hopes for Agur? No, for he has not finished expressing inadequacy in intellectual circles (וְלֹא־בִינַת אָדָם לִי, nor do I have ordinary human understanding). The genitive relationship, subjective

---

[11] The resemblance to Jer 20:9 has not escaped detection ("Then I said, 'I shall not remember him nor speak any longer in his name,' but it became in my heart like a raging fire shut up in my bones; and I was weary [from] restraining it, and could not [וְנִלְאֵיתִי כַּלְכֵל וְלֹא אוּכָל]." Plöger, Sprüche Salomos (Proverbia), 351, translates Prov 30:1b: "Ich habe mich abgemüht, Gott, auf dass ich es fassen könnte." The previous phrase he understands similarly: "der sich um Gott abmühte."

[12] C. C. Torrey, "Proverbs Chapter 30," JBL 73 (1954): 95-96.

[13] James Muilenburg, "The Linguistic and Rhetorical Usages of the Particle כִּי in the Old Testament," HUCA 32 (1961): 135-60; and Antoon Schoors, "The Particle כִּי," OTS 21(1981): 243-45.

rather than objective, implies that the understanding extends beyond psychology and human nature to embrace knowledge of all kinds, not just information about humankind. The latter point would require an objective genitive (understanding about people).

The sages often join together several intellectual categories in stereometric fashion,[14] each image conveying a different aspect of the scholarly repertoire. The three favorite terms, בִּינָה, חָכְמָה, and דַּעַת occur here in this order. One is tempted to relate the first to anthropology, the second to mythic speculation, and the third to theology. The Septuagint introduces the notion of divine instruction (θεὸς δεδίδαχέν με, God has taught me), in this instance, wisdom. On this reading, the allusion to knowledge of the Holy One (וְדַעַת קְדֹשִׁים אֵדָע)[15] becomes a possession granted Agur, whereas the Hebrew text implies a continuation of the negative, although it is missing (nor do I have knowledge of the Holy One).

An alternative translation of the Hebrew is syntactically possible, inasmuch as the conjunction can be adversative (but I do possess knowledge of the Holy One). Curiously, Agur uses the ambiguous קְדֹשִׁים as an oblique reference to God. The three terms for wisdom, understanding, and knowledge appear together in an instructive proverb (9:10, בִּינָה תְּחִלַּת חָכְמָה יְרְאַת יהוה וְדַעַת קְדֹשִׁים, the fear of the Lord is the beginning of wisdom / and the knowledge of the Holy One is understanding).

The first defense of Agur's radical skepticism restricts itself to the intellectual sphere, even if the words בִּינָה, חָכְמָה, and דַּעַת specify distinct cognitive disciplines. The second rationale for his sharp sarcasm derives from a strong awareness of finitude. The vastness of the universe, like the mysteries of knowledge, lies beyond human access. One can neither comprehend the enigmas of human existence nor control the forces of the universe. In both realms we stand helpless before the unknown and the impossible, wisdom's celebrated claim to enable persons to cope notwithstanding. Four questions using the interrogative particle מִי (who) employ hymnic language in an effort to widen the chasm between creator and creature.[16]

The four questions probe divine sovereignty, specifically the coronation of the universe's ruler, the taming of violent winds, the restricting of the chaotic waters, the establishing of earth's limits. The first hymnic snippet (מִי עָלָה־שָׁמַיִם וַיֵּרַד, who has gone up to heaven and assumed dominion?) requires a slight change in

---

[14]Gerhard von Rad, *Wisdom in Israel* (Nashville: Abingdon Press, 1972) 13, 27, uses this language.

[15]Although increasing evidence points to polytheism in Israel's popular culture, the parallel with Prov 9:10 makes it probable that Agur refers to a single deity. On polytheistic images, see Bernhard Lang, *Wisdom and the Book of Proverbs* (New York: Pilgrim Press, 1986).

[16]For a recent analysis of hymns in Job, see Sharon Waddle, "Dubious Praise: The Form and Context of the Participial Hymns in Job 4-14" (Ph.D. diss., Vanderbilt University, 1987).

vocalization.[17] This format appears vastly superior, inasmuch as the remaining inter-rogatives specify three acts by which the deity exercised sovereignty. Mastery of the powerful winds (מִי אָסַף־רוּחַ בְּחָפְנָיו)[18] for useful purposes facilitated the victory over recalcitrant flood waters (מִי צָרַר־מַיִם בַּשִּׂמְלָה), here imagined as clothing Baby Chaos in a diaper, and eventuated in the delimitation of the earth from heaven (מִי הֵקִים כָּל־אַפְסֵי־אָרֶץ). Mythical images from Enuma elish, mediated through the book of Job, seem to lie behind these questions, however attenuated the symbolism.[19] The divine speeches in the book of Job mock human defiance with such questions designed to crush every delusion of grandeur seething within Job's exalted self-image.

On the basis of similar hymnody in the rest of the Bible one expects a con-cluding refrain that identifies the one who actually achieved these extraordinary feats. No such conclusion occurs, neither יהוה שְׁמוֹ[20] (The Lord is his name) nor the longer variants (יהוה צְבָאוֹת שְׁמוֹ יהוה אֱלֹהֵי צְבָאוֹת שְׁמוֹ). Perhaps in their universalism the sages saw no need for combatting different cultic appearances of idolatry.[21] In Ezekiel's fertile imagination (48:35) the formula יהוה שְׁמוֹ produced the majestic shout יהוה שָׁמָּה (The Lord will be there) as the supreme blessing in the restored eschatological community. The mood in Proverbs 30:4 approaches ridicule, not celebration (מַה־שְּׁמוֹ וּמַה־שֶּׁם בְּנוֹ כִּי תֵדָע). The rhetorical question, "What is his name and what is his son's name? Surely you know!," concludes with a stinging putdown derived from Job 38:5. Rendering the final כִּי תֵדָע differently (if you know) changes its meaning only slightly, if at all. The semantic range of בְּנוֹ may extend beyond the actual family to the relationship between a teacher and student.[22] The implication then is that anyone who achieves such extraordinary accomplishments would obviously attract a student entrusted with transmitting the master's insights to later generations.

The fifth verse serves notice that such nonsense contradicts the community's sacred testimony. Private sentiment must submit to collective judgment

---

[17]וַיֵּרֶד for וַיַּרְד.

[18]The Septuagint implies that God catches the wind in the bosom or fold of a garment, a possible meaning of חֹפֶן (K. J. Cathcart, "Prov 30:4 and Ugaritic HPN, 'Garment'," *CBQ* 32 (1970): 418-20.

[19]Othmar Keel's various publications have greatly clarified our knowledge of ancient symbols.

[20]I have examined this refrain in great detail in *Hymnic Affirmation of Divine Justice* (Missoula MT: Scholars Press, 1975).

[21]How differently the situation became in later Judaism, particularly in Wisdom of Solo-mon. See Maurice Gilbert, *La critique des dieux dans le Livre de la Sagesse* (Rome: Biblical Institute Press, 1973).

[22]The Septuagint took that step, rendering "children" (τοῖς τέκνοις αὐτοῦ) just as it had earlier translated verse 1 by "my son, reverence my words and receive them, and repent."

(כָּל־אִמְרַת אֱלוֹהַּ צְרוּפָה מָגֵן הוּא לַחֹסִים בּוֹ). "Every word of Eloah is reliable; He is a shield for those who trust in him." Scripture bears witness against such blasphemy as Agur expresses it. Here a new speaker takes a sacred scroll and beats Agur over the head with it. Indeed, this advocate of conventional piety may have uttered the כִּי חֶדַע, in effect ridiculing Agur's ignorance. The scriptural allusions echo the language of Psalm 18.31 and 2 Samuel 22:31 (cf. Ps. 119:140). The minimal differences shift the emphasis from an all embracing protectorship to a total reliability of divine words and from exclusive allegiance to Israel's deity to the broader terminology for God employed by foreigners in the book of Job. Expectations explode in this instance, possibly as an accommodation to foreign speech. This explanation will not suffice for the use of an image derived from metallurgy (צְרוּפָה, refined) rather than theological categories like אֱמוּנָה and אֱמֶת (faithfulness, reliable).

Have we taken a false path from the very beginning? Does Agur cite dubious speculation to discredit practical atheism?[23] If this is true, an unknown atheist's confession of ignorance evokes hymnic questions and positive testimony from sacred tradition. Three questions introduced by the interrogatives מִי and מָה combine with an expression of totality, כָּל, to place the unknown thinker in the dunce's chair. In this view, Agur proceeds to warn the uninformed person in the same way ancient teachers harshly rebuked students (אַל־תּוֹסְףְ עַל־דְּבָרָיו פֶּן־יוֹכִיחַ בְּךָ וְנִכְזָבְתָּ, do not add to his words / lest he rebuke you and constitute you a liar). Once again the language echoes similar sentiment in Deuteronomy 4:2 and 13:1 (EV, 12:32), where adding to and taking from the divine decree are mentioned. In many other cases which employ a quotation of questionable ideas to introduce a rejection of such forms of reasoning, the polemicist carefully labels the thinkers fools and charlatans. Lacking some such disclaimer, the actual sayings of Agur probably begin in verse one. They end with the fourth verse, after which confessional theology offers a ringing contrast. Two competing claims collide, the personal testimonies of skeptic and religious devotee. The religious individual appears to assume that putative scripture validates itself, for no rationale reinforces the assertions that divine utterance and deity will stand the test like refined metal.[24]

Agur's feigned humility conceals the dogmatism residing in his denial of Transcendence, whereas his detractor's narrow-mindedness is fully exposed. In this respect, the two thinkers share a fundamental likeness. Absolute statements of both kinds represent a universalization of private experience, which ignores the limitations imposed on human knowledge. Both claims require confirmation from the

---

[23]Franklyn, "The Sayings of Agur in Proverbs 30: Piety or Skepticism," defends this hypothesis.

[24]Literature of dissent in Israel and Mesopotamia cast doubt on assertions of this kind in such a way that traditionalists could no longer assume that divine justice was universally acknowledged.

experiences of others. Agur's faulty logic failed to distinguish between penetrable and impenetrable mystery. Confronting the former, he denied the reality of the latter. His critic also did not take sufficient account of mystery, for this believer presumed too much. This overly optimistic removal of the gulf between the phenomenal and the noumenal realms makes a mockery of realists. The resulting babble estranges as certainly as the confusion of language at the mythical tower of Babel.

What happens then? It appears that the pious critic withdraws from conversation with Agur, despairing of fruitful exchange of ideas. At the very least, we expect some defense of the absolute claims concerning divine revelation, particularly in the light of contradictory experience. This expectation seems imperative after Agur's conscious allusions to Job's struggle to make sense of reality when religious conviction about reward and retribution ebbed away under the impact of harsh circumstances. To one whose integrity hung in the balances, assurances by Job's friends that the old verities retained their power sounded hollow.[25] Perhaps the fragility of their argument did not escape Agur's opponent, who dared to soften the punishment for adding to God's words.[26]

Having given up on Agur, the detractor turns to converse with the one whose existence Agur has denied. The shift from earthly to heavenly audience does not come easily, as we can see from the curious opening words (שְׁתַּיִם שָׁאַלְתִּי מֵאִתָּךְ). Normally, the first word implies a numerical saying,[27] either "two things . . . yea three" or "one thing . . . indeed two." Behind this form of the request may lie Job's plea that the divine enemy do two things so that the afflicted one could present his case before a higher tribunal (13:20). The anticipated number, whether one or two, does not appear in this imitation of Job's speech. Instead, we get a strange intensified petition that seems not to have been thought through carefully, given its cumbersome language (אַל־תִּמְנַע מִמֶּנִּי בְּטֶרֶם אָמוּת, do not withhold them from me before I die). A proper petition would have emphasized the present moment rather than delaying the gifts until some unforeseen hour of death. This anomaly has prompted one interpreter to connect the petition with a dying Agur.[28]

So far nothing in the request requires the hypothesis of a shift into vertical discourse. One human being could ask another to grant a couple of requests, although

---

[25]See the series of articles in the December 1987 issue of *The World and I* (Washington: Washington Times Corporation) 344-97, focusing on the Book of Job: Stephen Mitchell, "The Book of Job," 346-67; Edwin M. Good, "Stephen Mitchell's Job: A Critique," 368-74; James L. Crenshaw, "The High Cost of Preserving God's Honor," 375-82; Lonnie D. Kliever, "The Two Voices of Job," 383-93; and Lionel Abel, "The Book of Job: Its Place in Literature," 394-97; in addition, William Blake's twenty-one illustrations for the Book of Job have been reproduced in their original order.

[26]The earlier promise entailed life and death; here the emphasis falls on rebuke.

[27]Georg Sauer, *Die Sprüche Agurs* (Stuttgart: W. Kohlhammer Verlag, 1963) emphasizes the numerical sayings in Prov 30 and postulates a Canaanite background.

[28]Franklyn, "The Sayings of Agur in Proverbs 30: Piety or Skepticism," 249.

we lack any clue about the sociological context. Indeed, the specific requests, which add up to two only by juggling the figures, do not absolutely demand an interpretation that we have entered the realm of prayer. "Empty, lying words keep far from me" (שָׁוְא וּדְבַר־כָּזָב הַרְחֵק מִמֶּנִּי) is, however, the sort of petition one directs to deity. The same is true of the other request, which has two facets and for which a powerful rationale follows: רֵאשׁ וָעֹשֶׁר אַל־תִּתֶּן־לִי הַטְרִיפֵנִי לֶחֶם חֻקִּי (give me neither poverty nor riches / tear off [for me] my allotted bread). Parents, teachers, even kings could evoke such requests.[29] Do the explanations for the particular petitions settle the matter of addressee?

Not really, although they probably narrow the possibilities to parents or teachers, if this is not a prayer.[30] The first reason for requesting neither extreme, riches or poverty, addresses the dangers accompanying vast wealth: lest I be full and lie and say, "Who is the Lord?" (פֶּן אֶשְׂבַּע וְכִחַשְׁתִּי וְאָמַרְתִּי מִי יהוה).[31] The second rationale for the specific petition recognizes the danger arising from hunger: "lest I be destitute and steal / and I sully the name of my God" (וּפֶן־אִוָּרֵשׁ וְגָנַבְתִּי וְתָפַשְׂתִּי שֵׁם אֱלֹהָי).[32] Surprises abound in this rationale for the two requests. Why does the concept of lying follow the verb for satiety, when one anticipates a reference to godless thought, idolatry, for instance? The Septuagint translator perceived this problem, rendering "who sees me?" for "who is the Lord?" (με ὁρα, which in Hebrew, מִי יֶחֱזֶה, is not orthographically distant from מִי יהוה). In some contexts, the rhetorical question "who sees me?" functioned as an emphatic denial that anyone observed villainy, hence constituted a lie. Another unexpected verb may have the connotation of taking hold of and grasping something precious without recognizing its sanctity.[33] The anticipated allusion to profaning the sacred name does not occur here, despite the surprising personal pronoun (my God).

---

[29]Moshe Greenberg, "On the Refinement of the Conception of Prayer in Hebrew Scriptures," *AJS Review* 1 (1976): 57-92, esp. 59-65.

[30]Defining prayer in the Bible has not been easy, but recent studies have made considerable progress. See esp. Greenberg, "On the Refinement of the Conception of Prayer in Hebrew Scriptures," and *Biblical Prose Prayer as a Window to the Popular Religion of Ancient Israel* (Berkeley, Los Angeles, London: University of California Press, 1983); Jeffrey H. Tigay, "On Some Aspects of Prayer in the Bible," *AJS Review* 1 (1976), 363-79; Ronald E. Clements, *In Spirit and In Truth: Insights from Biblical Prayers* (Atlanta: John Knox Press, 1985); and Samuel E. Balentine, "Prayer in the Wilderness Traditions: In Pursuit of Divine Justice," *HAR* 10 (1986): 53-74.

[31]This negative attitude toward wealth represents a decided shift from the dominant sapiential understandings of rewards that accrued for moral persons.

[32]Prov 6:30 implies that society does not condone theft even if its purpose is to avoid starvation.

[33]William McKane, *Proverbs* (Philadelphia: The Westminster Press, 1970) 650, is drawn to an emendation (תָּפַשְׂתִּי) yielding "I besmirch."

On any understanding of this petition, problems remain. Still, the evidence seems to point toward its interpretation as prayer. Why the coolness? One expects a vocative, "O Lord," and direct address instead of indirect reference to "the name of my God." Although some biblical prayers uttered by persons who believed themselves in disfavor with the deity lack the vocative,[34] the present context may suggest another explanation for its absence in the unit being discussed. Does the prayer for a comfortable existence at neither end of the social scale conceal a stinging attack on Agur, who represents the sapiential privileged class? The request to be spared blasphemous inanities gains poignancy when juxtaposed alongside Agur's opening declaration. If the prayer lingers on the threshold of discourse between humans and communion with the deity,[35] its coolness and distancing from the flame of devotion make sense. Nevertheless, the speaker is drawn closer to the fire, ultimately uttering profound insight: destitute conditions force persons to adopt criminal behavior, and living in luxury's lap tempts individuals to imagine self-sufficiency. The first response sullies the divine name; the second response blinds one to the possibility of Transcendence.[36]

No "Amen" concludes the prayer. An admonition returns to the other side of the threshold: אַל־תַּלְשֵׁן עֶבֶד אֶל־אֲדֹנָו פֶּן־יְקַלֶּלְךָ וְאָשֵׁמְתָּ (do not belittle a servant to his master / lest he curse you and do you harm). If Agur's critic has just slandered him before his heavenly master, one begins to see the utility of this verse as a transition from prayer to human discourse once more. The double meanings of slave and master make the shift possible. This understanding of the verse implies that Agur's integrity has borne fruit, for an unknown individual rushes to his defense and rebukes the defender of traditional spirituality. Astonishingly, Agur's detractor has failed to produce progeny.

The final four verses continue the idea of progeny, each time beginning with the Hebrew word דּוֹר (generation, group, or class).[37] One expects a particle of existence, יֵשׁ, if the series of statements merely observe facts of life without pressing a moral judgment. Because of the earlier negative particles in Agur's opening declaration, contrasting particles at the end would accomplish a fitting closure, especially if doubling also takes place to emphasize a positive viewpoint.

---

[34]Greenberg, *Biblical Prose Prayer as a Window to the Popular Religion of Ancient Israel*, 23.

[35]Ibid. Greenberg insists that prayer followed the patterns of social discourse, hence imaginative or fictive prayers in the Bible actually use authentic language of prayer in Israel's daily life.

[36]"It is rather the deepest form of prayer which instead of seeking 'answers to prayer' in the accustomed way, is concerned to discover 'the Answering One'" (Clements, *In Spirit and in Truth: Insights from Biblical Prayers*, 141).

[37]Peter R. Ackroyd, "The Meaning of Hebrew דּוֹר Considered," *JSS* 13 (1968): 3-10; G. Johannes Botterweck, David Noel Freedman, and J. Lundbom, "דּוֹר *dôr*," *TDOT* 3 (1978) 169-81, esp. 180 (a bad generation).

The conclusion may not be so encouraging; in that case, something like הוֹי (alas, woe to) or תּוֹעֲבַת יְהוָה (an abomination to the Lord) would alert readers to what follows. As the text stands, we have no initial clue about the nature of what follows. דּוֹר אָבִיו יְקַלֵּל וְאֶת־אִמּוֹ לֹא יְבָרֵךְ (a class of people makes light of its father and does not bless its mother). The first two words arouse expectations wholly at odds with what comes next. We await the verb for honoring, obeying, or listening attentively to one's father. Nothing has prepared us for a term of disrespect with reference to the father or for the negative before the verb "bless" associated with mother. Nothing, that is, unless the verse also functions as transition by alluding to the profaning of the heavenly Father's name, a reprehensible act comparable to failure to honor mother and father.

The next verse opens on a promissory note as well (דּוֹר טָהוֹר, a class of people is pure), but it hastens to disabuse anyone of such optimism (בְּעֵינָיו, in its own estimation (literally, eyes) וּמִצֹּאָתוֹ לֹא רֻחָץ, and is not cleansed of its filth). Now that two negative observations have disturbed our thoughts, perhaps we shall encounter offsetting realities. This hope quickly fades (דּוֹר מָה־רָמוּ עֵינָיו וְעַפְעַפָּיו יִנָּשֵׂאוּ, a class, how exalted its eyes [self importance]/ and its eyebrows are raised high). The last verse abandons altogether the initial deception, moving directly into condemnation (דּוֹר חֲרָבוֹת שִׁנָּיו וּמַאֲכָלוֹת מְתַלְּעֹתָיו, a class, sharp its teeth and knives its grinders). Or does it? The answer depends on the sequel, which identifies the victims of such vicious mastication (לֶאֱכֹל עֲנִיִּים מֵאֶרֶץ וְאֶבְיוֹנִים מֵאָדָם, to devour the poor of the earth and the needy of the land). The last word in the Masoretic Text reads מֵאָדָם, which may be a conscious allusion to the earlier ironic comment about ignorance separating one from the human race, although מֵאִשׁ occurs there along with אָדָם. What links this list of inveterate sinners to the foregoing discussion? One conceivable answer is that true brutish conduct extends beyond intellectual poverty to embrace villainy of a far more destructive kind, one that deprives the poor of their humanity.[38]

The sayings of Agur and his detractor seem to end at verse 14. They present readers with an assemblage of clanging symbols. Frustrated expectations and surprises confront us again and again. The different genres—prophetic oracle, hymnic affirmation, debate form, prayer, admonition, and list—join together to form a choir in which singers compete with one another rather than striving for harmony. Nevertheless, nobler instincts strain to introduce a melody that persists ever so faintly despite the cacophony. The words of this melody are barely audible:

> In God's sight persons who claim to possess knowledge of the Holy One but lack respect for parents, behave hypocritically, think too highly of themselves,

---

[38]See the illuminating discussion in Gustavo Gutiérrez, *On Job: God Talk and the Suffering of the Innocent* (Maryknoll NY: Orbis Books, 1987).

and oppress the defenseless are in fact the real atheists of society; for they dissociate justice and the Holy.

If this summary accurately characterizes Agur's tune, I for one shall raise my voice in song along with him. I firmly believe a third voice will reinforce our faint melody; the fervent strains of my former teacher, colleague, and friend, Walter Harrelson, will not be silenced.

23 (1988)

A Mother's Instruction to Her Son (Proverbs 31:1-9)

Two biblical proverbs mention mothers alongside fathers in the context of parental instruction. In each instance a gentle admonition is directed toward pupils, the probable meaning of the technical term בְּנִי (my son).[1] The first example, Prov 1:8, encourages the son to hear the father's corrective teaching (מוּסָר), whereas the second, 6:20, varies the expression appreciably to "My son, guard your dad's command [מִצְוָה]." In this context the Hebrew verb שָׁמַע has the nuance of obedience, an attentiveness resulting in specific action congruent with what the child hears. Both texts emphasize the weight of the father's instruction, which strikes the son as discipline and the interposition of an alien will. Both verses have the same statement about a mother's teaching (תּוֹרָה), specifically "Do not forsake [נָטַשׁ] your mother's teaching." The author of these admonitions could easily have composed anonymously parallel clauses to the one about the father; hence the references to mother throw light on the ancient educational context presupposed by these two sayings. The mention of father and mother implies that both parents taught their sons moral precepts.

The ideal wife and mother in Prov 31:10-31 alludes to this teaching role, although without stating who actually benefitted from her instruction. The observation in 31:26 reads: "She opens her mouth with wisdom, and loyal teaching is on her tongue." That is, she speaks compassionately and wisely. The adjective חֶסֶד connotes steadfastness, an integrity generated by a deep sense of mutual responsibility. All three texts referring to maternal instruction prefer a single expression, תּוֹרָה, and even this word is further qualified in 31:26 to focus on a mother's love. Here

---

[1]Originally, the expression בְּנִי implied an actual father-son relationship. In time, perhaps through the intimacy of guilds, this word בְּנִי received broader usage, coming to denote a student who was not related by blood to the teacher, who concomitantly was addressed as אָבִי, my father. The expression בְּנִי in Prov 1–9 has this technical meaning.

is no hint of harsh discipline, which arguably hovers over the expressions associated with a father's instruction.[2]

An ancient Sumerian text, *The Instructions of Šuruppak*, also refers to instruction from both parents.

> The word of your mother, as if it were the word of your god, do not ignore it. A mother is like the sun, she gives birth to mankind. A father . . . [his?] god shines. A father is [like] a god, his word is just. The instructions of an old man, may you pay attention to them.[3]

Like the Hebrew admonitions, this Sumerian one attaches a negative to the verb associated with maternal teaching (do not forsake, do not ignore) while reserving the unadorned verb for the context of paternal instruction (hear, guard, pay attention to).

Although Egyptian instructions do not attribute teaching to mothers, these texts acknowledge their direct contribution to learning in other ways such as personally accompanying children to the place of instruction and preparing food for them to eat during their stay there.[4] This distancing of mothers from the actual learning process reaches its extreme form in 'Onkhsheshonqy's observation that "Instructing a woman is like having a sack of sand whose side is split open."[5] Such a low opinion of women hardly left room for an astute mother to impart wise counsel. Nevertheless, this same author conceded that "A good woman of noble character is food that comes in time of hunger."[6] So the author did not subscribe to the view that all women were incapable of learning. Furthermore, Papyrus Insinger's perceptive insight that "No instruction can succeed if there is dislike"[7] opens the door for parental teaching, since affection for one's mother predisposed children to receive counsel from her. Thus it comes as no great surprise when The Satire of the Trades concludes the praise of the scribal profession with the following doxology: "Praise god for your father, your mother, who set you on the path of life!"[8]

A biblical text actually preserves a small sample of maternal teaching, but the instruction derives from no ordinary mother. This important remnant of a mother's

---

[2]The use of physical punishment to encourage boys who otherwise neglected their studies is widely documented, both in Egypt and in Mesopotamia.

[3]Bendt Alster, *Studies in Sumerian Proverbs*, Mesopotamia 3 (Copenhagen: Akademisk Forlag, 1975) 137.

[4]Miriam Lichtheim, *Ancient Egyptian Literature*, vol. 2. (Berkeley, Los Angeles, London: University of California Press, 1976) 141 (*The Instruction of Any*).

[5]Lichtheim, *Ancient Egyptian Literature*, vol. 3 (Berkeley, Los Angeles, London; University of California Press, 1980) 170.

[6]Ibid., 178.

[7]Ibid., 192. The expression is sufficiently vague about the object of affection. It could be the subject matter, not the teacher.

[8]Lichtheim, *Ancient Egyptian Literature*, vol. 1 (Berkeley, Los Angeles, London: University of California Press, 1975) 191.

תּוֹרָה comes from a Queen Mother (גְּבִירָה),[9] presumably a non-Israelite from the land of Massa in Transjordan. Her name is missing from Prov 31:1-9, but her son's name has survived in two forms, Lemuel and Lemoel. The probable meaning of the name is "Belonging to God," although "Lim is God" has been proposed on the basis of the Mari texts which refer to a god Lim.[10] A Minaean feminine appellation, Mawil (מוּאֵל) has attracted attention as well.[11] The superscription to this mother's teaching identifies her son and recipient of instruction as a king. The text reads as follows:

> The words of Lemuel, King of Massa,
>   with which his mother instructed him.
> Listen, my son, and listen, son of my womb,
>   and listen, son of my vows.
> Do not give your power to women,
>   nor your sovereignty to women who destroy kings.
> Not to kings, Lemoel, not to kings—drinking wine,
>   nor to rulers—craving strong drink.
> Lest he drink and forget that which has been decreed,
>   and he pervert the justice pertaining to all the afflicted.
> Give strong drink to the perishing
>   and wine to those whose spirit is bitter.
> Let him drink and forget his poverty,
>   and let him not recall again his toil.
> Open your mouth for the speechless,
>   to defend at court all unfortunate ones.
> Open your mouth, judge fairly,
>   and defend the destitute.
>
> (Prov 31:1-9)

The literary genre, royal instruction, has left its mark on ancient wisdom, both in Mesopotamia and in Egypt. A Sumerian text, "The Old Man and the Young Girl,"[12] tells about a miserable old man who sought advice from the king, who first solicited counsel, then transmitted the suggestions to the old man as royal instruction in action. The counsellor's assessment of the situation was that the old man needed a young woman to invigorate him. Accordingly, the king spoke to a maiden and arranged a sexual liaison, probably a marriage. The text breaks off with the girl

---

[9]Israel's historiography credited various queen mothers with considerable influence at the court (2 Kgs 10:13; 1 Kgs 15:13; cf. Jer 13:18 and 29:2).

[10]A. Jirku, "Das n. pr. Lemu'el (Prov 31:1) und der Gott Lim," *ZAW* 66 (1954): 151.

[11]Berend Gemser, *Sprüche Salomos* (Tübingen: J. C. B. Mohr [Paul Siebeck] 1963) 107.

[12]Alster, *Studies in Sumerian Proverbs*, 92-94.

crying jubilantly: "Dance, dance, all young girls, rejoice!"[13] Although this text differs in form and content from actual royal instruction, it shows that Sumerians expected their king to possess unusual insight about human problems. The narrative also demonstrates the ambiguity of the relationship between ruler and sage, for advisors instructed kings, who in turn passed that wisdom along to others.

Egyptian royal instructions determine the actual characteristics of the genre. Only three have survived: *The Instruction of Prince Hardjedef, Merikare*, and *Amenemhet I.*[14] The first, a mere fragment, discusses marriage and death. The second advises Merikare in matters of statecraft, personal character, and religion. Emphasis falls on able officials, wise advisers, compassion, and providence. The third instruction tells the king's son, Sesostris I, how his father died at the hands of treacherous persons within the palace and suggests utmost caution. This advice reeks of cynicism resulting from experience.

A Babylonian text, Advice to a Prince,[15] differs in that it has omen form. The purpose of this text is to protect citizens of Nippur, Sippar, and Babylon from royal abuse of power, especially excessive taxation, corvée, and appropriation of their property. The omen form does not point an accusing finger at the king, but it solemnly announces the dire consequences of accepting bribes and participating in miscarriage of justice.

The close association of viziers and kings which surfaces in the early Sumerian fragment about the old man and the young woman eventually relaxed somewhat; as a result, these wise men transmitted valuable insights to their own sons and to the populace in general. Several Eygptian instructions have survived which envision an audience other than royal sons: Kagemni, Ptahhotep, Any, Amenemope, Ankhsheshonq, and Papyrus Insinger.[16] An Aramaean text, Ahiqar,[17] enjoyed wide dissemination in the ancient world. According to the story, this vizier to King Sennacherib instructed his adopted son, Nadin, who betrayed Ahiqar and caused him much suffering until circumstances required this vizier's service at the royal court and enabled Ahiqar to get revenge as well.

Unlike sentence literature, which expresses an idea in a brief statement, these instructions often have long poems on a single theme. The same subject may extend over several paragraph units. Some topics occur more than once, and that also goes

---

[13]Ibid., 94. E. Lipinski, "Ancient Types of Wisdom Literature in Biblical Narrative," *Isac Leo Seeligmann Volume*, ed. Alexander Rofé and Yair Zakovitch (Jerusalem: E. Rubenstein's Publishing House, 1983) 39-55, writes that the king consulted a cloister woman.

[14]Lichtheim, *Ancient Egyptian Literature*, 1:58-59, 97-109, 135-39.

[15]W. G. Lambert, *Babylonian Wisdom Literature* (Oxford: Clarendon Press, 1960) 110-15.

[16]Lichtheim, *Ancient Egyptian Literature*, 1:59-61 (Kagemni), 1:71-80 (Ptahhotep), 2:135-46 (Any), 2:146-63 (Amenemope), 3:159-84 (Ankhsheshonq), and 1:184-217 (Insinger).

[17]James M. Lindenberger, *The Aramaic Proverbs of Ahiqar* (Baltimore and London: Johns Hopkins University Press) 1983.

for popular proverbs. For example, *The Instruction for Merikare* cites the following proverb twice: "No river lets itself be hidden."[18] For the most part, the instructions take up conventional themes such as the importance of eloquence, good manners, table etiquette, sexual decorum, wise administration, timing, integrity, sobriety, and self control.[19] These traditional subjects sometimes give way to wholly unexpected ones. *The Instruction for Merikare* includes a remarkable confession of wrongdoing.

> Lo, a shameful deed occurred in my time:
> The nome of This was ravaged;
> Though it happened through my doing,
> I learned it after it was done.
> There was retribution for what I had done . . .
> Beware of it! A blow is repaid by its like,
> To every action there is a response.[20]

Perhaps more astonishingly, *The Instruction of King Amenemhet I for his Son Sesostris I* actually describes an uprising within the palace that cost the pharaoh his life.[21] The epilogue to *The Instruction of Ani* stands alone among instructions that have survived. Here Ani's son, Khonshotep, responds to his father's teaching, objecting that the youth cannot possibly observe the moral precepts that come naturally to the father.

> The son, he understands little,
> When he recites the words in the books. . . .
> A boy does not follow the moral instructions,
> Though the writings are on his tongue![22]

The father insists that people can change their dispositions, making the hard teachings easy to keep. As proof of this claim, Ani points to wild animals whose nature has been changed—the fighting bull that becomes like a fattened ox, the savage lion that resembles a timid donkey, the horse, dog, monkey, goose—and to foreigners who learn to speak Egyptian. The example of the beasts fails to convince Khonshotep, who acknowledges that his father's "sayings are excellent, but doing them requires virtues."[23] Ani responds that a crooked stick can be straightened into a noble's staff, or a straight stick can be made into a collar. Knonshotep's final

---

[18]Lichtheim, *Ancient Egyptian Literature*, 1:102 and 106.
[19]Michael V. Fox, "Ancient Egyptian Rhetoric," *Rhetorica* 1 (1983): 9-22, delineates five canons of Egyptian rhetoric: silence, restraint, gentleness, fluency, and truthfulness.
[20]Lichtheim, *Ancient Egyptian Literature*, 1:105.
[21]Ibid., 1:136-37.
[22]Ibid., 2:144.
[23]Ibid., 2:145.

appeal to an infant's nourishment is set aside by Ani, who notes that older children require staple food.[24]

The biblical Instruction for Lemuel lacks any response on his part, but so do all other instructions except Ani. Lemuel's mother opens her teaching with rhetorical flourish,[25] then proceeds to warn her son about women, wine, and dereliction of duty. The instruction consists of a superscription (31:1), a direct appeal to her son (31:2), and four words of counsel (31:3-9). The advice takes various forms: (1) an imperative with a negative (31:3), (2) counsel without a verb, but containing a rationale for the particular course of action (31:4-5); (3) a positively stated imperative with three accompanying jussives (31:6-7); and (4) three imperatives, positively stated (31:8-9).

The Superscription. Like the superscription to the sayings of Agur in Prov 30:1-14,[26] the Instruction for Lemuel has דִּבְרֵי (words) rather than מִשְׁלֵי (proverbial sayings). The expression functions in 30:1 to focus attention on oracular revelation (although tongue-in-cheek), which was reinforced by the pun residing in מָשָׂא, (burdensome oracle; Massa) and by the prophetic formula נְאֻם (whisper, oracle). Ordinarily accompanied by deity, here נְאֻם is governed by the word הַגֶּבֶר (the man). Although the superscriptions to several prophetic books have this word דִּבְרֵי, it accurately describes what follows in Prov 31:2-9. The preferred word in Prov 1-9 is מִשְׁלֵי, perhaps תּוֹרוֹת also. The genitive relationship in Prov 31:1 (words of Lemuel) is an objective one (words directed to Lemuel). As the Massoretes have pointed the Hebrew text, the break comes at מֶלֶךְ (king); one must translate: "The words of King Lemuel, an oracle with which his mother taught him." Because the word for king lacks an article, it is better to associate מָשָׂא, with מֶלֶךְ (king of Massa). According to Gen. 25:14 and 1 Chr. 1:30, the region of Massa was in Transjordan, hence North Arabia. With the shift in the location of the *athnach*, אֲשֶׁר now refers to דִּבְרֵי rather than מָשָׂא, in the sense of oracle. The resulting "with which his mother instructed him" refers back to "words." The use of the verb יִסְּרַתּוּ does not go well with מָשָׂא, in the sense of prophetic oracle, which one "proclaims" rather than "instructs."

The Appeal. The rhetorical flourish by which Lemuel's mother catches her son's attention identifies him as very special. The threefold allusion to the maternal bond moves from the simple Aramaic word[27] for son to the same word qualified by "my womb," and finally to the same word qualified by "my vows." Lemuel was special

---

[24]Ibid.

[25]One recalls the bombastic language of Prov 23:29, which also deals with the problem of excessive drinking. In this instance the question לְמִי occurs six times, whereas מַה appears in Prov 31:2 only three times (assuming that וּמֶה should be read as וּמָה).

[26]See my essay "Clanging Symbols," in *Justice and the Holy*, ed. Douglas A. Knight and Peter Paris (Philadelphia: Fortress Press). (Also repr. above.)

[27]An abundance of Aramaisms mark this instruction: מַה, בְּרִי, לַמְחוֹת, מְלָכִין, and בְּנֵי חֲלוֹף.

in the same way Samuel was, for he had been given to Hannah as a result of divine solicitude, which evoked a promise that the boy would be dedicated to divine service. For obvious reasons, the paternal instructions lack such amplification of the father-son relationship. The bond between mother and child, powerfully different, enabled her to appeal to him in an effective manner. Her nurturing began before his birth, and the care was spiritual as well as physical. That seems to be implied by the reference to vows.

The threefold מָה is variously interpreted. The Septuagint renders it as an interrogative (what), but the Greek translator adds the clause "shall I say to you, Lemuel my first born?" (cf. Isa. 38:15). The Hebrew merely repeats the interrogative "what?" On the basis of 1 Kgs. 12:16 and Cant. 8:4, the מָה has been rendered "Not." The first text uses the interrogative מָה in parallelism with the negative, whereas its parallel in 2 Sam. 20:1 has the negative אֵין instead of מָה. Nevertheless, the meaning is the same whether one translates "What portion do we have in David?" or "We have no portion in David," given the sequel ("for we have no inheritance in the son of Jesse"). The verse in Canticles uses מָה twice as a negative: "Do not awaken and do not arouse love until it pleases." An alternative suggestion derives from Arabic use of מָה as a verb "to listen."[28] The verse thus yields, "Listen, my son; listen, the son of my womb; and listen, the son of my vows." This reading accords with the appeals in other instructions, where hearing is so important that one text, Ptahhotep, concludes with a lengthy discussion of this topic.[29]

The First Admonition. The initial warning takes up a conventional theme in wisdom literature: do not become entangled in sexual relationships that may compromise you or sap your energy. It has been observed that this rather delicate subject is ordinarily the father's responsibility rather than the mother's.[30] The vocabulary of the admonition leaves room for ambiguity about the meaning of the advice. The noun חֵילֶךָ (your might) can also refer to material wealth, and Lemuel's mother may be warning her privileged son not to squander royal resources on women. The second half of the verse seems to advise against sexual liaisons with women of the harem who were favorably placed for plotting intrigue.[31] The unusual word וּדְרָכֶיךָ (and your nobility) need not be changed, inasmuch as the same usage

---

[28]William McKane, *Proverbs* (Philadelphia: Westminster Press, 1970) 408–409, adopts Eliezer ben Jehuda's suggestion in *JPOS* 1 (1920–1921): 114. So does Otto Plöger, *Sprüche Salomos (Proverbia)* (Neukirchen Vluyn: Neukirchener Verlag, 1984) 369.

[29]Lichtheim, *Ancient Egyptian Literature*, 1:73-74.

[30]W. O. E. Oesterley, *The Book of Proverbs* (London: Metheun, 1929) 281. We do not know who assumed responsibility for instructing young boys in matters relating to the opposite sex.

[31]E. Lipinski, "Les 'voyantes des rois' en Prov XXXI, 3," *VT* 23 (1973): 246, thinks of visionaries. He translates: "Do not abandon your vitality to women, nor your ways to kings' visionaries."

occurs in Ugaritic literature. The Hebrew Bible probably has other instances of this meaning for the word דֶּרֶךְ, particularly Amos 8:14 ("Those who swear by Ashimah of Samaria and say, 'As your god lives, Oh Dan, and as the Sovereign lives, Oh Beersheba'.")

On the basis of Sir 47:19, which blames Solomon for laying his loins (יְרֵכֶיךָ) beside women, thereby subjecting himself to them, some interpreters emend the text to יְרֵכֶיךָ (Fichtner in BHS). Others opt for דּוֹדֶיךָ, which they translate in the same way (your loins.)[32] The strange לַמְחוֹת should probably read לְמֹחוֹת (to destroyers), not לְלָהֲנוֹת (to concubines), an emendation that has been suggested because of Dan. 5:2. The final word (מְלָכִין) may be Aramaic מַלְכָּן (counsellors); if so, the half verse refers to women's power to turn the minds of royal advisors from the important tasks of government. The verse appears to restrict itself to one subject, the threat posed by women. Alternatively, the second half verse warns against squandering royal energy on the battlefields, but such an interpretation lacks cogency.

The Second Admonition. Loose sexual conduct was frequently associated with excessive drinking, so the second admonition naturally covers this subject. Surprisingly, the main verb is missing, but the resulting emphasis on the two infinitive constructs achieves stunning rhetorical effect. As in verse 2 where the mother addresses her son, repetition occurs here too. There she repeats the Aramaic word בַּר (son) three times but avoids his actual name. Here in verse 4 she identifies her son, using the variant Lemoel, and repeats the phrase "not for kings," adding a parallel for good measure (rulers). A similar text in 2 Chron. 26:18 throws light on the verbless אַל לַמְלָכִים. It reports that bold individuals opposed King Uzziah, saying to him: "Not for you, Uzziah, to offer incense to the Lord but for consecrated Aaronite priests" to do so. The context implies that the issue is one of appropriateness or propriety. Another text, Mic 3:1, reinforces this understanding of the grammatical form ("Is it not for you to know justice? [הֲלוֹא לָכֶם לָדַעַת אֶת־הַמִּשְׁפָּט]") Micah insists that the people's responsibility is to understand what justice requires of them. Here the sense of duty extends the weaker notion of appropriateness.

The prohibition of drinking, restricted to the ruling class, derives from an elevated view of kingship rather than from nomadic existence. Drinking wine and craving[33] something stronger interferes with the fundamental responsibility of nobility, the promoting of justice. Lemuel's mother may have left the verb unstated, but she clearly offers a rationale for her stringent counsel. The plural gives way to the singular, perhaps to focus the decision on her son alone ("Lest he drink and forget what has been decreed, and he pervert the arbitration of all the needy"). Ancient

---

[32]Plöger, *Sprüche Salomos (Proverbia)*, 371, refers to Dyserinck in this regard. So does D. G. Wildeboer, *Die Sprüche* (Freiburg, B., Leipzig, und Tübingen. J. C. B. Mohr [Paul Siebeck] 1897) 90.

[33]Instead of אֵי, I am reading אַיֵּה.

Near Eastern texts consistently stress the social obligations of kings to champion the cause of widows and orphans.[34] *The Instruction of Šuruppak* even brings together both concerns of Lemuel's mother, advising against judging when drinking. Both Merikare and Amenemhet I emphasize justice and compassion for the widow, the orphan, the poor, and the tearful.

The Third Admonition. With the well being of the destitute still in mind, Lemuel's mother suggests that her son can easily find worthy subjects for liquor and wine. The reversal in the order of these two drinks subtly underscores the harsh realities confronting those who are perishing. Their circumstances require strong medicine. Individuals whose lot, while odious, is nevertheless bearable can soothe their bitter spirit with wine. Again the personalized singular occurs: "Let him drink and forget his poverty, and let him remember his burdensome toil no longer.

In an intriguing section praising the creator, Papyrus Insinger remarks that god created wine to end affliction.[35] In addition, this text notes that wine, women, and food gladden the heart.[36] Within the Hebraic tradition, the exquisite praise of wine as strongest in 1 Esd 3:18-24 acknowledges its power to enable one to forget sorrow and debt. The text also highlights wine's leveling process, the erasing of sociological distinctions. In addition, the author recognizes the effect of wine on cognitive faculties. Kings, like subjects, succumb to its power.[37] It follows that kings who wish to rule wisely and to retain proper distance from their subjects so as to assure respect will avoid enslavement to wine.

The Fourth Admonition. The final admonition isolates instances of special vulnerability under the operative legal system and encourages the king to become a powerful and eloquent advocate for these people. A single verb (פְּתַח) occurs twice in connection with royal advocacy, whereas two different verbs (שְׁפָט and דִּין) clarify the forensic aspect of this speech. Apparently, the word לְאִלֵּם (for the speechless) embraces actual dumbness as well as silence resulting from a disadvantaged social position.

Another reason for this concern on behalf of the speechless derives from the ease with which judges' decisions were influenced by bribes. Lemuel's role as spokesperson for the dumb is set within the larger context of arbitration for all those whom circumstances have overwhelmed (בְּנֵי חֲלוֹף). The exact meaning of this expression remains unclear. The decisive issue, whether or not the two classes of victims are synonymous, can not be ascertained. If the second group represents the

---

[34]C. Fensham, "Widow, Orphan, and the Poor in Ancient Near Eastern Legal and Wisdom Literature," *JNES* 21 (1962): 129-39, repr. in my *Studies in Ancient Israelite Wisdom* (New York: Ktav, 1976) 161-71.

[35]Lichtheim, *Ancient Egyptian Literature*, 3:210.

[36]Ibid., 3:199.

[37]I have discussed this text's rhetorical power in "The Contest of Darius's Guards," *Images of Man and God*, ed. Burke O. Long (Sheffield: Almond Press, 1981) 74-88, 119-20.

same one as the speechless, the Nabataean expression *ḥlp mwt* may offer a clue about the meaning of בְּנֵי חֲלוֹף, perhaps persons overwhelmed by harsh reality.[38] Other possibilities are "children of abandonment" (orphans) or "those who are perishing." Emendations have been proposed, two of which fit the context well (בְּנֵי חֹלִי, weaklings; בְּנֵי עָלוּף, the powerless). The first assumes an error of sight, dittography of the letter ב, and the second presupposes a mistake of sound, the gutteral ע replacing ח. The imperative שְׁפָט governs an accusative צֶדֶק (equitably), while דִּין has a stock phrase as object, עָנִי וְאֶבְיוֹן (the poor and needy), which functions as hendiadys (the poor).

The Egyptian narrative, Protests of an Eloquent Peasant,[39] dramatizes the vulnerability of the lower class when unscrupulous officials forget the obligation to govern justly. In this account the peasant had the requisite persuasive ability to argue his case and to effect the redress of injustice. Not everyone was so fortunate, and those who lacked a voice in the circles of influence lost everything. The person who could effectively guarantee fair treatment of the weak was, of course, the king. Lemuel's mother advises her son to open his mouth to ensure justice for the speechless, not to imbibe intoxicating spirits. The absence of motivation clauses in the mother's instruction is remarkable, for this feature is typical of the genre. The tone of the advice to Lemuel suggests that his mother wished to instill in him a noble concept of kingship so that responsibility rather than privilege would control his daily conduct.

This idealizing of kingship links up with a similar phenomenon throughout the ancient Near East.[40] In Egypt the pharaoh administered *ma'at* (truth, order, justice) by creating cosmos rather than chaos, thereby establishing peace in Upper and Lower Egypt. For this reason, he was looked upon as a shepherd[41] and as a parent[42] who watched over the poor. His largesse extended to care of widows and orphans, feeding the hungry, setting prisoners free, and clothing the naked. Because the pharaoh was god, he possessed understanding (*Sia*) and authority (*Hu*). Nothing escaped his knowledge, not even thoughts, for he tested the hearts of subjects.

---

[38]McKane, *Proverbs*, 411-12.

[39]Lichtheim, *Ancient Egyptian Literature*, 1:169-84. Fox, "Ancient Egyptian Rhetoric," 16-18, contrasts the peasant's verbal virtuosity with the sages' canons of rhetoric ("The most prominent characteristics of the peasant's style are repetiveness, concatenations of extravagant metaphors, and constant wordplay.") Fox thinks this work may be a deliberate polemic against wisdom's emphases on "restraint of anger, brevity of speech, avoidance of sharp answers to superiors, and gentle speech" (17).

[40]Leonidas Kalugila, *The Wise King*, ConBOT 15 (Lund: C. W. K. Gleerup, 1980).

[41]D. Müller, "Der gute Hirte: Ein Beitrag zur Geschichte Ägyptischer Bildrede," *ZÄS* 86 (1961): 126-44.

[42]Thorkild Jacobsen, *The Treasures of Darkness* (New Haven: Yale University Press, 1976) traces the metaphors of deity in Mesopotamia from natural to royal, and ultimately to parental ones.

Normally, this wisdom was thought to have been inherited, but Akhnaton insisted that the god revealed it to him in the same way a teacher instructs a pupil.[43]

Various Mesopotamian kings claimed special favor from the god of wisdom. Hammurabi asserted that his wisdom had no rival; Ashurbanipal credited Nabu, the god of scribal wisdom, with the granting of wisdom; and Nabonidus boasted: "I am wise, I am knowing, I can behold the hidden. . . . The position in heaven of the New Moon, which Adapa composed, this work I surpass, all wisdom is collected with me."[44] Even the king of the underworld was thought to possess the symbol of kingship, namely the tablets of wisdom.

Ugaritic literature celebrates El's wisdom in the well known sentence: "Your decree, O El, is wise; your wisdom is everlasting, a life of good luck is your decree."[45] In another text Asherah observes: "You are great, O El, you are wise; your grey beard certainly instructs you."[46] Although this wisdom is restricted to the god El, human kings probably claimed a share of it. Azitawadda of Adana boasted that he had implemented justice, wisdom, and goodness of heart. Another Phoenician, Bar-Rakib, acknowleged that his father Panammu owned gold and silver because of his wisdom and righteousness. Here as elsewhere, a wise king took care of the poor, especially widows and orphans.[47]

Two Israelite kings, David and Solomon, are credited with wisdom. Neither David nor Solomon is remembered as championing the cause of the poor, although their judicial wisdom probably implies that.[48] The association of wisdom and wealth takes place with Solomon, for his primary interest was self-aggrandizement. This conduct earned him sharp rebuke for amassing horses, slaves, and precious metals, primarily gold and silver (Deut 17:14-17).[49] The king's failure to live up to the ideal eventually stirred disillusioned subjects to envision the birth of a royal child in whom virtue and knowledge would reside. The anticipated ruler in Isa. 9:5 is endowed with the essential elements of royal protocol: wisdom, power, compassion, and well-being. Similarly, the ruler of Isa. 11:2 has wisdom, understanding, counsel,

---

[43]Kalugila, *The Wise King*, 30.

[44]Ibid., 59.

[45]Ibid., 62.

[46]Ibid. In a fascinating twist on this assumption that wisdom accompanies age, Santob de Carrion wrote that he dyed his hair not out of vanity but to keep people from expecting great insight from him. My friend and former colleague Lou Silberman tells me that the same sentiment occurs in rabbinic tradition. On Santob de Carrion, see T. A. Perry, *The Moral Proverbs of Santob de Carrion* (Princeton: Princeton University Press, 1987).

[47]Ibid., 65, 68.

[48]The brutal facts about their rule remained despite such attempts to paint the picture in rosy hues. Perhaps it is noteworthy that Solomon's wisdom is thought to have been a gift in youth rather than something he acquired through long experience.

[49]The repetition of the personal pronoun for himself (לו) stands out here and in the royal fiction of Eccles. 1:4-8 (for myself, לי).

might, and fear of the Lord. These qualities enable him to establish justice and peace.

Unlike the prophets, Israel's sages seem never to have challenged royal action directly, except for imaginary Egyptian rulers. Here the unknown author of Wisd 6:1-11 warns those who exercise power over others that God requires a higher ethical standard from them than from ordinary people.[50] In addition, this author urges kings to receive wisdom from him so that they can stand close examination from the heavenly judge who shows deference to no one.

An astonishing point of view surfaces in Prov 16:10 ("Divination is on the king's lips; in judgment his utterance does not err"). The idea that a king has direct access to the God's will and consequently renders accurate judicial decisions is at home in Egypt. As a matter of fact, this chapter in Proverbs contains several features that find their closest parallels in the land of the Nile. These include the notion of an abomination of the god (16:12), the idea that the royal throne is established on justice (ma'at = צְדָקָה), the image of a messenger of death (16:14), and the belief that life resides in the king's face (16:15).

The other positive remarks in the Book of Proverbs about kings do not come close to these elevated observations. The acknowledgment that kings' special prerogative is to search out what God has hidden and the shrewd comment that no one can comprehend the royal mind stop short of celebrating a king's access to the deity's decrees (Prov 15:2-3). Likewise, the optimal assessment of a king's judicial acumen in 29:14 does not say that the throne was founded on justice, only that a dynasty that promotes justice will endure. This point is reinforced in 29:4, which mentions the stabilizing effect of royal justice on society.[51]

Israel's sages, like their counterparts in Egypt and in Mesopotamia, endeavored to maintain the status quo, for in that way they secured their own privileged position. This conservative stance was rooted in a firm conviction about the universe, which was sustained by an order deriving from its creator.[52] The task of maintaining the divinely ordained order was therefore an ethical and a religious duty, for which appropriate rewards accrued to favored individuals. Curiously, even after Israel's dogma of reward and punishment collapsed, no direct renunciation of kingship per se took place. Indeed, Qoheleth, the most severe critic of traditional wisdom, continued to foster the idealized notion of Solomon as quintessentially wise. At the same time, Qoheleth had some realistic assessments of royal weakness, both in

---

[50]Amos 3:2 makes a similar point.

[51]Of the texts about kings and the court in Proverbs, only 22:21 seems to require a group of courtiers.

[52]Hans Heinrich Schmid, *Gerechtigkeit als Weltordnung*, BHT 40 (Tübingen: J. C. B. Mohr [Paul Siebeck], 1968).

character and in intelligence.[53] Nevertheless, these criticisms did not have royalty as their audience. Only Prov 31:1-9 falls into that category.

To what use were the other sapiential texts put in ancient Israel? Presumably, many early proverbial statements originated among the populace and functioned as a significant force in forming character. The attempt to ascribe greater precision for particular collections has not garnered much support.[54] In any event, collected proverbs probably functioned differently from isolated truth statements. It is tempting to assume a pedagogic setting for collections of proverbs and instructions.[55] If accurate, this educational context even includes one royal instruction in its general teaching for young men who aspired to a scribal profession. Thus one mother's instruction for her royal son became teaching for a wider body of potential scholars. At the same time, Israel's sages receive the teachings of a foreign woman despite their own warnings about embracing the notorious נָכְרִיָּה or אִשָּׁה זָרָה.

---

[53]The pertinent texts are examined in my commentary, *Ecclesiastes* (Philadelphia: Westminster Press, 1987).

[54]Udo Skladny, *Die ältesten Spruchsammlungen in Israel* (Göttingen: Vandenhoeck & Ruprecht, 1962). He thinks of 25-27 as a mirror for peasants and 28-29 as instructions for rulers.

[55]Even R. N. Whybray, "The Sage in the Israelite Royal Court," in *The Sage in Israel and the Ancient Near East*, ed. John G. Gammie and Leo G. Perdue (Winona Lake: Eisenbrauns) writes that "There is little doubt in my mind, on the other hand, that some parts of Proverbs, especially parts of chapters 1–9 and 22:17–24:22, were composed as 'textbooks' for young pupils—though not necessarily at a royal scribal school."

24 (1989)

Poverty and Punishment in the Book of Proverbs

The Book of Proverbs has always stood as a didactic obstacle in the path of biblical salvation faith. Israel's priests and prophets saw Yahweh served when the rich and powerful upheld the rights of the poor. Her sages, however, examined wealth and poverty as if they were separate moral states, in some cases mandated by God. Poverty, like wealth, had a purpose. A look at proverbs concerned with the rich and the poor can provide a counterweight to the claim that there is a single biblical outlook on poverty. In the process, we will also expose the ancient roots of some current economic views.

Retribution and Its Downfall

The poor fit badly in the scheme of things devised by the authors of Proverbs, Job, and Ecclesiastes, who enjoyed the privileges bestowed on society's influential leaders. As advisors to kings, friends of aristocrats, and professional teachers, the wise lived a protected existence. They even convinced themselves, and perhaps others also, that such luxury was their proper reward for the virtuous life style they had adopted. This line of reasoning necessarily implied a less than enviable existence for those unfortunate persons who chose a way of life contrary to that of the teachers. These fools exhibited lack of morality that was matched by a shortage of the things that contributed pleasure and at least a modicum of happiness.

The argument went in the other direction, too. People who found themselves in a miserable situation must surely have possessed some character flaw, sometimes visible but often concealed from public scrutiny. Conversely, individuals who rose high in social standing and acquired the advantages of rank were naturally thought to have superior moral character.

The fundamental premise that produced these conclusions was theological. The creator of the universe took an active interest in its just order, punishing iniquity and rewarding virtue. Ethical decisions affected the essential order of the universe, either threatening its inner harmony or contributing to its stability. Choosing a pattern of life that elicited divine favor transformed the pursuit of pleasure, eudaemonism, into religious performance.

Over the years this conviction became dogma, for sufficient evidence of both aspects of the theory seemed present in society generally. The teachers who promulgated this idea found sufficient data to substantiate their claims, for they were eager to confirm their own favored status, and in doing so they condemned those less fortunate than they. The ambiguous assertion that divine solicitude never fails deserving individuals (Ps. 37:25) cruelly dismisses the poor as morally deficient while at the same time lauding God's providential care for the wealthy.

In the end the teachers actually defended the poor, but not before their own world came crashing down. The story of Job's fall from an exalted position to the ash heap forced the wise to reassess both sides of the equation they earlier championed. It became painfully clear to them that notable exceptions to the theory of reward and retribution occurred at least on the side of virtue. That concession led them to revise their understanding of vice and to admit that not all miserable persons deserved what befell them.

Once the sages acknowledged exceptions, their entire scheme became problematic. Not every deserving person fared well, and not all villains received just punishment. The earlier simplicity and optimism vanished, for now every individual case required careful study to determine whether or not the person's character accorded with external circumstances. The collapse of a cherished conviction precipitated a religious crisis, one which pushed believers over the threshold into the comforting (?) arms of a theophanic creator (Job) and skeptics into the empty abyss of a distant despot (Ecclesiastes).

Thus Israelite sages viewed poverty in the light of a retributive world view, with the emphasis falling on a negative assessment of the poor. The teachers acknowledged an obligation toward the unfortunate, but they harbored suspicion that the poor deserved their misery, which resulted from indolence. Idealizing the poor as special favorites of God, as, for example, in Amos' identification of the righteous with the poor, and Jesus' pronouncement that the poor are blessed (Lk. 6:20), did not find expression in wisdom literature. The wise would hardly have rejoiced to be called Ebionites (the poor ones), as a later sect seems to have done.

The attitude to poverty and its victims remains relatively consistent with the different expressions of wisdom in the Hebrew Bible and the Apocrypha. Furthermore, that understanding of the poor coincided with the sages' teachings in Egypt and Mesopotamia. One exception is an Egyptian text, the Instruction of Ani. Social turmoil in Egypt produced this pious wisdom text, which comes perilously close to claiming a special relationship between the deity and individuals in humble circumstances.

The Poor in Collections of Proverbs

The book of Proverbs gathers together several collections of sayings from various periods and localities. It contains at least three collections of foreign extraction (22:17–24:22; 30:1-14; 31:1-9), each of which has an identifying comment, in one instance mistakenly inserted into the initial saying (22:17). This small unit resembles the Egyptian Instruction of Amenemopet, an earlier text that has thirty chapters. The other two collections derive from Aramaic wisdom, the first from an otherwise unknown Agur and the second from the mother of a king whose name, Lemuel, is given but about whose rule no further evidence has survived.

The remaining collections are associated with the name Solomon, for the most part (1–9; 10:1–22:16; 25–29; exceptions are 24:23-34; 30:15-33; 31:10-31). The tradition in 1 Kings 4:29-34 (EVV) credits this monarch with exceptional literary productivity, but virtually nothing in the collections attributed to Solomon agrees in content with this description of proverbs about trees, beasts, birds, reptiles, and fish. Perhaps Solomon achieved this association with wisdom collections as a reward for sponsoring the wise, although the subject matter rarely relates to special interests of royalty. An alternative explanation for the tradition of Solomonic wisdom relates it to his vast wealth, which must have suggested to many that he was exceptionally wise. Such reasoning was inevitable so long as the theory of reward and retribution flourished. The close juxtaposition of wealth and wisdom in the closing observations of the story about the Queen of Sheba lend credibility to this hypothesis.

The specific origins of the several collections are obscure, although their probable provenance and relative dating seem reasonably clear. The oldest units (10:1-22:16; 25–29) derive from actual family contexts, for the most part imparting parental teachings. Nevertheless, the present form of these proverbs lends itself to wider use, possibly in Israelite schools, for which evidence has vanished, except for a single witness in the second century B.C.E. That sole example was Jesus Eleasar ben Sira, called Sirach for convenience. The latest collections in Proverbs (1–9; 31:10-31) differ immensely from earlier sentences, or aphorisms, employing elaborate paragraphs replete with imperatives, exhortations and threats, or using an alphabetic device that is known as an acrostic. One miscellaneous collection (30:15-33) makes generous use of numerical sayings, both as heightening ("Three things are too wonderful, for me, four I do not understand"), and an absolute number ("Four things on earth are small"). These collections have material that predates Israel's monarchy as well as some from as late as the postexilic period.

Some interpreters have attempted to trace a growing religious influence on the sayings, assuming that the earliest sages were wholly secular. That effort has not been entirely successful, for a religious element probably existed from the very beginning, perhaps becoming more explicit in the latest extensive collection (1–9).

The astonishing thing in Proverbs 1–9 is its virtual silence about the poor. The lone exception, 6:6-11, for which there is a partial parallel in 24:30-34, describes the calamitous results of laziness—poverty will overwhelm the indolent one.

> Go to the ant, O sluggard:
> consider her ways, and be wise.
> Without having any chief, officer, or ruler,
> she prepares her food in summer
> and gathers her sustenance in harvest.
> How long will you lie there, O sluggard?
> When will you arise from your sleep?

A little sleep, a little slumber,
a little folding of the hands to rest,
and poverty will come upon you like a vagabond,
and want like an armed man.   (RSV)

This sharp warning adopts a simplistic approach to the problem posed by needy members of society, a response that many citizens of our own time readily endorse. By this reasoning, the poor only get what they deserve, the just fruits of their own laziness. If 3:27 ("Do not withhold good from those to whom it is due, when it is in your power to do it") actually refers to someone who is destitute, from whom the withholding of promised assistance might have drastic consequences, the collection would escape the charge of unmitigated bias against the poor. Outside 1–9, only two sayings come close to this negative attitude toward the less fortunate. In 10:4 ("A slack hand causes poverty, but the hand of the diligent makes rich") the implicit teaching of 6:6-11 becomes explicit; not only do the indolent suffer need, but the industrious acquire riches. Another explanation for poverty occurs in 21:17 ("He who loves pleasure will be a poor man; he who loves wine and oil will not be rich"), which notes the way individuals squander resources in pursuit of pleasure.

If we are correct in assuming that the students to whom these sayings were ultimately directed came from wealthy families in Judean society, one wonders why the teacher did not try to instill a sense of charity in these young men. (I assume that these students were all males, for they are enjoined to be faithful to the wives of their youth and to spurn the sweet seduction of the foreign woman). On the assumption that the poor were simply malingerers, did teachers think they would incur God's wrath by helping lazy people? This sort of thinking certainly led to ambiguous attitudes toward physicians, at least in the early second century before the Christian era, contrary to the negative view implied in Sirach 38:15 ("He who sins before his Maker, may he fall into the care of a physician"). Ben Sira struggles mightily to defend the medical profession against charges of interfering with divine punishment for evil, namely that by endeavoring to cure the sick, doctors risked shortening the divinely decreed period of affliction that befell sinners.

On Kindness to the Poor

That explanation for the absence in Proverbs 1–9 of any sense of obligation toward alleviating the circumstances of the poor—that they have personally merited their lowly status—depends on an increased emphasis on *individual* retribution, as opposed to a *social* retribution, that is, the poor must be seen as an aggregate of individual sinners, not merely as a more or less suspect segment of Israelite society.

In any event, the earlier "Solomonic" collections openly praise kind actions toward the poor. The profit motive surfaces in 19:17 ("He who is kind lends to the Lord, and he will repay him for his deed"), a saying that presupposes the act/consequence scheme and uses it to good advantage. Those who do a good deed on behalf of the poor, the proverb insists, put the Lord in their debt and eventually receive payment from above. Similarly, 28:27 states that gifts to the poor pay worthy dividends, and 28:8 even asserts that those who lend money on interest will lose it to those who show generosity toward the needy. Such a statement as 21:13 fails to escape charges of self-interest, for it claims that an attentive ear and appropriate action in the cause of the poor ensure the same result if the situation is ever reversed.

The highest stage of blessedness is promised those who show kindness to the poor. Two different verbs indicate the happiness resulting from such considerate action, the first emphasizing the personal disposition and the second stressing others' praise. In 14:21 the charitable person is assured happiness, whereas 22:9 suggests that the needy with whom one has shared bread will sing the praises of their benefactor. The remarkable woman whose praises are heralded in 31:10-31 includes the "poor and needy" in her list of persons who come under her care. For the sum total of her actions, this virtuous wife receives praise from her children and husband. Curiously, the only other use of this combination, "poor and needy," appears in another late collection, the sayings of Agur. Four sayings, each beginning with the word "Generation," describe loathsome individuals who dishonor their parents, practice hypocrisy, think too highly of themselves, and consume the poor and needy. A different word in the initial position does occur in 14:31, which announces that insulting the poor (דָּל) actually demeans the one who made that person, whereas showing compassion for the needy honors "him." Although the pronoun could refer to the needy person, it may also apply to God, for whom the Bible uses masculine pronouns. By deeds of kindness, one honors the Creator.

This tendency to associate God with the poor extends to specific behavior such as ridicule. Whoever mocks the poor insults that person's Maker, according to 17:5, and anyone cruel enough to rejoice when calamity strikes (presumably the same poor person) will pay for such malice. In some instances the wise came very close to urging love for one's enemies; perhaps the motive was conservative self-preservation, but whatever the reason, the teachers decried violence of any kind. The metaphor about heaping coals of fire on an enemy's head by acts of kindness (25:21) remains obscure, although an Egyptian ritual of repentance may throw light on it.

Not every linking of the poor and deity served to protect the lowly against potential oppressors. In 29:13 the neutral statement asserts that a single sovereign empowers both oppressor and victim. No moral judgment appears in the observation, but the larger context probably lends it some small degree of censure. The next verse promises that kings who dispense justice to the poor will reign for a long time. By implication, the heavenly ruler ought to favor the poor over an oppressor.

The wise realized the precarious situation in which poor people existed, particularly in times of unscrupulous or weak rulers. Not all kings subscribed to, or actually implemented, the lofty ideal put forth by Lemuel's Mother (31:9, "Open your mouth, judge righteously, maintain the rights of the poor and needy"). According to 29:7, the poor have certain inalienable rights, which good people recognize but wicked ones fail to grasp. Astonishingly, not all who numbered themselves among the ranks of the poor respected the rights of others in their own social class.

The situation that James abhors, rich Christians (5:1-6) oppressing the poor, is comprehensible if also reprehensible; a rapacious poor person is almost unthinkable. The rich oppressor resembles a torrential rain that destroys vital crops instead of assuring the growth of life-sustaining food. The implication is that a deficient yield would tempt harvesters to neglect the obligation to leave some produce in the fields so that the poor could glean like the ancestress of David in Boaz' grain fields.

The advantageous position of the wealthy was taken for granted, for everyone knew that lenders possessed power over borrowers (Prov 22:7). A curious observation surfaces at the transitional point between the older "Solomonic" collection and the section resembling the Instruction of Amenemopet, where the warning against such conduct appears. The robbing of poor people is at issue here. One would think such action would result in nothing worthwhile, but poverty, like wealth, is relative. Furthermore, the poor offered little resistance, because they lacked access to legal redress. Hence the wise insisted that individuals who take advantage of the poor for personal benefit or who toady to the rich for the same reason will experience need themselves (22:16). The warning against depriving the poor of their meager resources (22:22) actually mentions the place of judicial action, the gate of the city or village. This text also uses the combination "poor and afflicted," the latter term being עָנִי rather than אֶבְיוֹנִים.

Some sayings reflect the adverse social ramifications of poverty. The rich do not lack friends, but the poor cannot even rely on faithfulness from relatives (19:7, "brothers"). On the principle of "How much more!" the teachers assert that if brothers of poor people abandon them, neighbors and friends will avoid the poor even more quickly (19:4; 14:20).

In general, the sayings about the poor acknowledge their desperate plight. Lacking sufficient financial resources to secure their existence, they have no hope (10:15; 13:8), in sharp contrast to the wealthy, who can ransom their lives by prudent use of vast resources. Inherent to their status as wealthy members of society, the rich ignore the pleasantries of polite company, but those who occupy the bottom rungs on the ladder of success are obliged to plead their case (18:23). Even in rare instances when the poor act productively, lawless people seize their profit for themselves (13:23). Such miserable circumstances might have deprived the victims of their integrity, but the teachers saw things otherwise. The lowly people functioned as an example that the proud of spirit would do well to imitate (16:19), and a poor person with integrity was better than a perverse or foolish rich liar (19:1; 28:6). One sentence actually registers approval of a poor individual over an untruthful person (19:22). The wise refused to accept the notion that all poor people were stupid; in fact, one saying asserts that a poor person's grasp of things can be superior to the self-delusion of the rich (28:11).

"Neither Poverty nor Riches"

An intriguing text expresses the view that both wealth and poverty hinder the achievement of a healthy spiritual relationship (Prov 30:7-9). That opinion corresponds to the teachers' general emphasis on moderation in all things, arising from fear that excessive conduct endangers life. A close look at this text seems appropriate at this time.

> Two things I ask of you,
>> do not withhold them from me before I die.
> Emptiness and a deceitful word keep remote from me;
>> give me neither poverty nor riches;
>> tear off for me my portion of bread.
> Lest sated, I lie, saying, "Who is Yahweh?"
> or lest impoverished, I steal,
> besmirching the name of my God.

The external similarity with Job's request that God do two things for him to enable him to appear before the divine tribunal has not escaped notice (Job 13:20), but the contexts differ greatly. In Proverbs, the request seems to be a prayer with no forensic setting intended, whereas Job seeks safe entry into God's courtroom.

The abrupt "two things" engenders expectation that a numerical sequence will follow ("three things"), or that one preceded ("one thing"). What follows as a request takes a peculiar form, for prompt action on God's part is required for the gift to make significant difference. Delaying its receipt until just prior to death makes no sense. The petitionary address implies vertical discourse (prayer, that is) even if this text is the sole example of that genre in Proverbs. Of course, one could direct this request to other human beings such as parents, teachers, or kings, but the probable addressee is the deity.

The first petition actually embraces both ideas that follow, and one has difficulty discovering two requests. Perhaps the person asks to be spared idle thought and destructive conduct. Clearly, the emptiness and deceit relate to denial of Yahweh's claim over one's existence, whereas the full stomach will make it unnecessary for persons to commit desperate acts to stay alive. As illustration of the importance of sociological conditions in shaping human values, the author reflects on the impact of wealth and its absence.

The danger concealed in excessive possessions is that their owner cultivates a false sense of security, thinking nothing can arise for which money does not have an answer (cf. Eccles. 10:19). Like the rich man in Jesus' parable, the hypothetical individual in Proverbs runs the risk of trusting in wealth and forgetting the ultimate owner of everything in the universe. The question, "Who is Yahweh?" amounts to practical atheism, for it implies absolute reliance on one's own resources. The Septuagint, or Greek translation of the Bible, understood the question differently, rendering it "Who sees me?" This reading accords well with the theme of practical atheism in some Psalms and easily derives from a Hebrew text that closely resembles the present one. From the reading in the Greek, one can more readily explain the strange allusion to lying. The question "Who sees me?" functioned as an emphatic denial that anyone observed misconduct, an intellectual position that constituted a spiritual lie.

The problem with poverty was less intellectual, for a hungry stomach forces one to extreme action regardless of its consequences. The ambiguous wording in 6:30 leaves open the possibility that society condones theft resulting from hunger, although the context seems to compensate for the missing sign of the interrogative. I refer to the observation that the thief must pay heavily for lawlessness. The thief's offense may be a grasping after the sacred name without realizing its sanctity, but the nuance of besmirching fits the context better. The choice of the general name for God accords with the foreign nature of the text's origin, a usage softened by the personal pronoun "my."

The coolness of this petition is noteworthy, especially the absence of the vocative "O Lord," and direct address "you" instead of "the name of my God." The lack of a vocative may derive from someone who thought God was unfavorably disposed toward the worshipper, but another explanation seems preferable. The prayer for a comfortable existence on neither end of the social scale contains a stinging attack against Agur, who represents the privileged class of the wise. In light of Agur's blasphemous inanities, as this person saw them, the prayer makes sense. Because it hovers between discourse among humans and communion with God, the cool tone and distancing from the ardor of religious devotion are quite understandable. The speaker did not remain afar off but drew near to the flame and uttered profound truth: destitute conditions force individuals to behave criminally, and living in the lap of luxury tempts persons to imagine self-sufficiency. The first, poverty, forces one to sully the divine name; the second, riches, blinds one to the possibility of transcendence.

The prayer has no concluding "amen." Instead, a transition to human discourse occurs with the ambiguous allusion to servant and master. On one level, the warning against belittling a servant before a master could refer to God, the supreme Lord. On the other level, it connotes human beings.

Whoever wrote this profound prayer could hardly have subscribed to the notable viewpoint expressed in the portrait of personified wisdom, who held vast riches in her hand and invited young men to pursue her like a lover. This remarkable figure, which resembles the Egyptian goddess of truth and justice, Ma'at, claimed to have occupied a favored position with Yahweh before the creation of the world and to have participated actively in that event. She even boasted of being the plaything or artisan of Yahweh, bringing joy to the creator and rejoicing in the finished product. Her largesse also extended to human beings, for she promised to endow her lovers with riches (8:21).

The section of Proverbs that coincides with parts of the Instruction of Amenemopet expresses considerable reservation about the pursuit of wealth, regardless of its source. In that author's opinion, acquired riches quickly vanish, taking wings like an eagle and flying off into the heavens (the Egyptian text has geese).

Conclusion

This examination of attitudes toward poverty and wealth in the book of Proverbs has exposed the ambiguities inherent to both. Those who lacked a fair share of worldly goods often suffered the added indignity of society's scorn, for which religious arguments were advanced. People who held an abundance of possessions also basked in almost universal favor, and this attitude, too, was supported on religious grounds. At least one concerned citizen, the Queen Mother from Massa in Edom, urged her royal son to offer something other than religion as an opiate for the miserable and perishing members of society. That solution was booze (31:6-7), enabling people to forget their poverty by drinking. Such a judgment from one in a position of authority, and therefore having access to better means of reducing want, has been repeated many times over the centuries. Equally dubious was the refusal to take a stand against those in power, shrugging one's shoulders and observing that officials always look out for their own interests (Eccles. 5:8-9).

Rare imaginative individuals, recognizing the inadequacy of such attitudes, saw the plight of the poor among them as an occasion for demonstrating the reality of the faith they professed. If Yahweh championed the cause of widows and orphans, then those who claimed allegiance to this Lord were obliged to extend that compassion to all needy persons. For that grand step to occur, another one was essential: the cessation of placing blame on those who found themselves in lowly circumstances.

Selected Bibliography

Camp, Claudia V. *Wisdom and the Feminine in the Book of Proverbs*. Sheffield: Almond Press, 1985.

Crenshaw, James L. *Old Testament Wisdom*. Atlanta: John Knox, 1981.

_____. *Ecclesiastes*. Philadelphia: Westminster Press, 1987.

_____. "Clanging Symbols." In *Justice and the Holy*, ed. Douglas A. Knight and Peter Paris. Philadelphia: Fortress Press, 1989.

_____. "A Mother's Instruction to her Son (Prov 31:1-9)." In *Perspectives on the Hebrew Bible*, ed. James L. Crenshaw, 9-22. Macon GA: Mercer University Press, 1988.

_____. "The Sage in Proverbs." In *The Sage in Israel and the Ancient Near East*, ed. John G. Gammie and Leo G. Perdue. Winona Lake: Eisenbrauns, 1989.

_____. "Proverbs." Forthcoming in *The Books of the Bible*, ed. Bernhard W. Anderson. New York: Charles Scribner's Sons.

Fontaine, Carole R. "Proverbs." In *Harper Bible Commentary*, ed. James L. Mays, 495-517. San Francisco: Harper & Row, 1988.

Greenberg, Moshe. *Biblical Prose Prayer as a Window to the Popular Religion of Ancient Israel*. Berkeley: University of California Press, 1983.

Gutiérez, Gustavo. *On Job. God Talk and the Suffering of the Innocent*. Maryknoll NY: Orbis, 1987.

Lang, Bernhard. *Wisdom and the Book of Proverbs*. New York: Pilgrim Press, 1988.

McKane, William. *Proverbs*. Philadelphia: Westminster Press, 1970.

Oesterley, W. O. E. *The Book of Proverbs*. London: Methuen & Co. Ltd., 1929.

Rad, Gerhard von. *Wisdom in Israel*. Nashville: Abingdon Press, 1972.

Whybray, R. N. *Wisdom in Proverbs*. London: SCM Press, 1965.

Williams, James G. *Those Who Ponder Proverbs*. Sheffield: Almond Press, 1981.

25 (1990)

The Sage in Proverbs

The Three Main Contexts of Israelite Learning

The Book of Proverbs expresses the views of countless individuals ranging from simple rural folk to a queen mother. These impressions about life's deep secrets and transparent truths have different authors and distinct audiences. Parents tutor their children, often drawing on popular lore from past generations to enable youngsters to succeed. Teachers instruct their students in the ways of the world, particularly in the art of steering the ship of state through treacherous waters. The two fundamental settings, family and school, invite distinct forms of pedagogy.[1] Mothers and fathers appeal to the collective learning of the larger family, and render their fresh discoveries in the form of truth statements, often called *sentences*. By contrast, professional teachers opt for longer *instructions* that have their own rationale built into the imperative—specifically exhortations and warnings—each with supporting arguments.[2] The meaning of sage differed, depending on whether the context of discussion was the family or school.

Despite scant evidence for a third context—the royal court, together with a school that fostered its interest—a case can be made for linking this educational establishment with the subsequent scribal school, for the collapse of the Monarchy in 587 BCE left all surviving teachers and students without a royal patron and notably altered the pattern of their education. No adequate analysis of the sage in Proverbs will ignore these competing groups. Indeed, diversity in viewpoint, style, genre, and intention confirms suspicion that education in ancient Israel occurred in various settings and had multiple goals.

---

[1]William McKane, *Proverbs*, OTL (Philadelphia: Westminster Press, 1970) uses the distinction between instruction and sentence to great advantage. His analysis derives from thorough examination of both forms in Egyptian wisdom, as well as study of Babylonian and Assyrian instructions and sentences.

[2]In some instances sentences are embedded in instructions, thus bringing into question the neat distinction between the two (cf. Prov 1:17; 6:27-28; and 9:17).

The Goals of Learning

The introductions to two collections of instructions (Prov 1–9; 22:17–24:22) offer direct evidence relating to a technical understanding of a sage. The first introduction serves as orientation for the whole book, although specifically focusing on chapters 1–9:

> To know wisdom and discipline,
> to understand perceptive words,
> to receive instruction and astuteness,
> righteousness, justice, and fairness;
> to give prudence to the simple,
> knowledge and discretion to the youth—
> the sage may hear and increase learning,
> and the discerning one may get skill,
> to grasp a proverb and an allusion,
> the words of sages and their riddles. (Prov 1:1-6)

The second introduction has fewer technical terms and concentrates on the practical advantages of an education.

> Orient your ear and listen,
> and put your mind to my knowledge;
> If you retain them [words of the wise][3] in your innermost being,
> they will bring pleasure;
> if they are wholly established on your lips.
> To let your trust be in the Lord,
> I have declared them to you today, yes to you.
> Have I not written for you thirty—[4]
> counsel and knowledge,
> To make known to you correct and reliable observations
> for responding to those who sent you? (Prov 22:17-21)

---

[3]"Mit alten Auslegern wird דִּבְרֵי חֲכָמִים als Überschrift zu verstehen sein"; so Otto Plöger, *Sprüche Salomos (Proverbia)*, BKAT 17 (Neukirchen-Vluyn: Neukirchener, 1983) 262. The Septuagint opens the section with λόγοις σοφῶν παράβαλλε σὸν οὖς (v 17).

[4]*Tanakh* (Philadelphia: New York, Jerusalem: The Jewish Publication Society, 1985) refuses to follow recent scholarship in translating the rare Hebrew word שָׁלִישִׁם (!) on the basis of the thirty chapters in the Egyptian "Instruction of Amenemopet," with which the section introduced by this prologue has much in common.

The religious dimension, which came after the conclusion of Prov 1:1-6 and invites speculation among modern interpreters that it did not belong to the original,[5] appears in the center of the second introduction. Nevertheless, the two assertions of faith differ immensely, for Prov 1:7 emphasizes piety as the first principle or ultimate end of learning ("The fear of the Lord is the beginning [chief ingredient?] of knowledge; ignorant persons despise wisdom and discipline"). The two introductions differ in other significant respects as well; the first one addresses both novices and mature thinkers, seeking to offer appropriate educational material for each group. The second introduction implies that the instruction has a single purpose, to prepare messengers to represent wealthy clients effectively. Whereas the images of the second introduction derive primarily from human anatomy (ears, heart, belly, lips), those of Prov 1:1-6 consist of intellectual abstractions that seem to have special nuances recognizable only to initiates.

A third instruction makes up Prov 31:1-9, but it lacks a specific comment about the goal of learning. The content of the instruction leaves little doubt about the audience and desired result. A mother offers counsel to her son, but she is no ordinary woman and he is no commoner. The queen mother instructs a son who is destined to occupy the throne in Massa, a Transjordanian region.[6] She wishes to help him escape the clutches of wicked women[7] and to avoid the baneful effects of excessive drinking.[8] Curiously, she offers no rationale for the warning about notorious women, a topic so dear to the wise in some circles.[9] Instead, she concentrates solely on the judicial responsibility of kings. In her view, wine enables

---

[5]Theories about a secular wisdom antedating religious sentences and instructions have generally appealed to a number of neutral statements in the Book of Proverbs. Similar traditional sayings exist outside wisdom literature and have been studied recently by Carole Fontaine, *Traditional Sayings in the Old Testament*, BLS 5 (Sheffield: Almond Press, 1982). On secular proverbs, see Frederick M. Wilson, "Sacred and Profane? The Yahwistic Redaction of Proverbs Reconsidered," in *The Listening Heart*, ed. Kenneth G. Hoglund et al., JSOTSup 58 (Sheffield: JSOT Press, 1987) 313-34.

[6]This is the only wisdom instruction that is attributed to a woman, but Claudia V. Camp, in her *Wisdom and the Feminine in the Book of Proverbs*, BLS 11 (Sheffield: Almond Press, 1985) and "Woman Wisdom as Root Metaphor: A Theological Consideration," in *The Listening Heart*, 45-76, has argued for extensive feminine wisdom in ancient Israelite society.

[7]Bernhard Lang, *Wisdom and the Book of Proverbs: An Israelite Goddess Redefined* (New York: Pilgrim Press, 1986) postulates the existence of a goddess in the popular religion of ancient Israelites. If his hypothesis has merit, the struggle against the foreign seductress assumes new dimensions.

[8]Although the text lacks an adjective indicating that excessive drinking is being discussed, scholars note that such an attitude as total abstinence hardly suits a court setting.

[9]As early as the "Instruction of Ani" a warning against the foreign woman appears. It is tempting to wonder whether this fascination with the dangerous woman in Israel helped foster misogyny in later sages such as Ben Sira.

society's castaways (and perhaps condemned criminals) to forget their misery. A king's duty is to speak on behalf of citizens whose lowly estate renders them mute, hence his mind must be clear and his tongue able. Such instruction arises from an exalted concept of the royal office,[10] one easier to achieve in the abstract than in concrete situations of daily existence. The rich rhetoric in this brief unit may derive from an acknowledged discrepancy between the ideal and the actual.

The Formal Setting of Learning— Pragmatic, Secular, and Religious

By nature instructions presuppose a formal educational setting, either a royal or a scribal school. Each one has a distinctive purpose, but the two overlap at important points. The essential task of royal schools coincided with the interests of the state. Diplomacy depended on skilled linguists who could read documents in foreign languages and communicate with official representatives of various heads of state. The domestic economy also relied on trained personnel who recorded revenues and kept accurate accounts of commercial transactions. Besides such utilitarian undertakings, exclusively intellectual enterprises may have existed at the royal court, and perhaps exercises in lighter matters such as rhetorical contests for entertaining royalty.[11] The extent of religious indoctrination varied from time to time, depending on the political and spiritual climate.

Scribal schools maintained the earlier commitment to training an elite group of governmental employees, but these places of instruction also began to function more and more in the religious arena. Fundamental questions of existence attracted the attention of teachers and students. Can virtue exist without positive or negative reinforcement?[12] Does life have any meaning?[13] Where does faith belong in the quest for knowledge?[14] Furthermore, pragmatic interests led to concentration on personal growth. How can one escape the clutches of dangerous seductresses? What types of conduct guarantee success and which ones bring calamity? Above all, do well-intentioned youth have a desirable companion who watches over them and

---

[10]Leonidas Kalugila, *The Wise King*, ConBOT 15 (Lund: Gleerup, 1980).

[11]Scholars have devoted too little attention to the lighter side of ancient wisdom, particularly contests in which the sole or primary purpose was entertainment (cf. "The Protests of the Eloquent Peasant," *ANET* 407-10, which has a serious purpose, and the contest of Darius's guards in 1 Esdras).

[12]Gustavo Gutiérrez, *On Job: God-Talk and the Suffering of the Innocent* (Maryknoll NY: Orbis Books, 1987) offers fresh insight into the biblical masterpiece about the possibility of disinterested righteousness.

[13]I ask this question anew in *Ecclesiastes*, OTL (Philadelphia: Westminster Press, 1987).

[14]Contrasting answers occur in Prov 1–9 and in 30:1-14. On the latter sayings of Agur, see my "Clanging Symbols," in the *Festschrift* for Walter Harrelson (*Justice and the Holy*, ed. Douglas A. Knight and Peter Paris [Philadelphia: Fortress Press, 1989]—repr. above).

bestows insight on them in times of need? These questions seem to have dominated the thoughts of scribal teachers and students.

In due time, religious instruction seized the lion's share of attention, and professional teachers consciously interpreted sacred traditions. Surrendering to this impulse, Ben Sira actually introduced Israel's religious heritage into the body of wisdom literature.[15] Furthermore, he brought about a virtual symbiosis of priestly and sapiential teachings. No wonder Ben Sira called his professional school a house of exegesis (בֵּית־הַמִּדְרָשׁ). The unknown author of Wisdom of Solomon continued this eludication of the biblical text, focusing at length on the story of the exodus.[16]

These two educational settings restricted their enrollment to an elite clientele,[17] whether potential courtiers or religious leaders. Did trained teachers ever address themselves to ordinary citizens, thus instituting a democratization of learning? According to the epilogist responsible for the initial comments about Qoheleth in Eccl 12:9-12, the teacher turned to the populace (הָעָם) with an unusual message of candor. If this language is not a vague substitute for "students," it implies that Qoheleth reached out to the wider citizenry, offering them the benefits of his private investigations.[18] His teaching lacked any connection with the usual aims of royal or scribal training—the preparation of skilled professionals. Instead, he endeavored to inform the public about life's futility. In Qoheleth's view, chance vitiated all attempts to master one's existence for personal gain and decisively undermined the goal of professional wisdom, despite claims to the contrary by representatives of the spiritual hierarchy (Eccl 8:17).

Astonishingly, the instructions and scribal literature rarely touch on topics whose relevance is limited to professional life. The exception occurs in Sir 38:24–39:11, and its connection with the Egyptian "Satire on the Trades" is well

---

[15]Because of their desire to understand Ben Sira in the light of Hellenistic literature, the strong influence of Yahwism does not come to expression in Burton L. Mack, *Wisdom and the Hebrew Epic* (Chicago and London: University of Chicago Press, 1985) and Thomas R. Lee, *Studies in the Form of Sirach 44–50*, SBLDS 75 (Atlanta: Scholars Press, 1986).

[16]The section from Wis 10:15–19:22 excels in psychological insight and striking imagery, indicating the exceptional generative power of the story about deliverance from bondage.

[17]Frank Crüsemann, "Die unveränderbare Welt: Überlegungen zur 'Krisis der Weisheit' beim Prediger (Kohelet)," *Der Gott der kleinen Leute*, ed. Willi Schottroff and Wolfgang Stegemann (Munich: Kaiser, 1979) 1:80-104 (ET in *The God of the Lowly* [Maryknoll NY: Orbis Books, 1984] 57-77), musters arguments in support of an earlier theory that the sages belonged to the privileged class. His case applies more readily to Qoheleth's audience than to their teacher, whose compassionate sentiments are accorded insufficient attention.

[18]Norbert Lohfink, *Kohelet*, NEBib (Stuttgart: Echter Verlag, 1980) also understands הָעָם in this way.

known.[19] Other than Ben Sira, no Israelite scribe mentions a school, although Wis 7:17-22 describes the curriculum in vogue at the time. Particular concerns of the royal court have made no lasting impression on the content of the instructions. The Egyptian instructions likewise seldom call attention to schools,[20] but the existence of these institutions is beyond doubt.[21] Wisdom schools also existed in Mesopotamia, although they served a fundamentally different role in many essentials. Use of analogy from these two countries strengthens the case for schools in Israel, but differences in cultural development and world view suggest caution.[22] This necessity for caution extends to technical vocabulary, whether native to Israel or borrowed from Egypt.[23] Even the Hebrew חָכָם seldom has a technical meaning, a point that has not always been appreciated.[24]

Israelite instructions are profoundly religious. Were they pious from the beginning, or did a later reading of this literature infuse it with religious conviction? In Egypt, a definite development from confident teaching to pious fatalism can be observed, and scholars have argued that Israelite secularism also succumbed to vigorous dogma, conveniently labeled "fear of Yahweh."[25] If this hypothesis prevails, it will undoubtedly influence the understanding of sages. Earlier ones will be characterized as secularists, whereas later sages will be related more closely to religious authorities. Perhaps these professional teachers and students managed to compartmentalize religion and daily existence in the same way folk wisdom did.

---

[19]Miriam Lichtheim, *Ancient Egyptian Literature*, vol. 1 (Berkeley, Los Angeles, London: University of California Press, 1975) 184-92.

[20]E. W. Heaton, *Solomon's New Men* (New York: Pica, 1974) 108.

[21]Lichtheim, *Ancient Egyptian Literature*, vol. 2 (Berkeley, Los Angeles, London: University of California Press, 1976) 167-78.

[22]See my essays "Education in Ancient Israel," *JBL* 104 (1985): 601-15, and "The Acquisition of Knowledge in Israelite Wisdom Literature," *Word and World* 7 (1987): 245-52—both repr. above. See also Friedemann Golka, "Die israelitische Weisheitsschule oder 'des Kaisers neue Kleider'," *VT* 33 (1983): 257-70.

[23]Nili Shupak, "The 'Sitz im Leben' of the Book of Proverbs in the Light of a Comparison of Biblical and Egyptian Wisdom Literature," *RB* 94 (1987): 98-119, assumes that identical vocabulary implies a similar social context and undervalues the possibility of polygenesis (different cultures may have arrived at the same imagery independently). Nevertheless, the striking affinities in language demand an explanation, possibly the one given by Shupak.

[24]R. N. Whybray, *The Intellectual Tradition in the Old Testament*, BZAW 135 (Berlin and New York: Walter de Gruyter, 1974) makes this point with telling force. The word חָכְמָה refers to various kinds of expertise, even to devious and crafty thinking.

[25]McKane, *Proverbs*, endeavors to distinguish different stages in this process of reinterpreting older proverbs, although the criteria for doing so are highly hypothetical.

On the Authors and Audience
of the Sentence Literature

What role did sages play in this sentence literature? Answering that question will require close scrutiny of the remaining collections in the Book of Proverbs. The major portion of these popular aphorisms is associated with Solomon and Hezekiah (Prov 10:1–22:16, chaps. 25–29), although a few lack any identification (Prov 24:23-34; 30:15-33; 31:10-31) and one collection derives from an otherwise unknown Agur (Prov 30:1-14).[26] These secondary superscriptions have less to do with origins than use, except for the last one (Prov 31:1).

Two superscriptions use the technical term for the wise (חֲכָמִים). The first one has been accidentally incorporated into the text of the prologue to the collection that somewhat duplicates eleven instructions in Amenemopet ("Orient your ear and listen to *the words of the wise*"; Prov 22:17). The second superscription using technical vocabulary of the wise boldly asserts that "these also are utterances of the wise" (Prov 24:23). Clearly these texts presuppose professional sages in Israelite society as the authors of the advice that follows.

The content and form of these sayings support the attribution to professional teachers, despite an occasional reference to father and mother. The imperatives with motivations belong to the instruction genre, and the type of counsel seems directed toward future governmental employees: behaving wisely at meals, avoiding drunkenness, recognizing the danger posed by harlots, realizing the power of counsel, refusing to act vindictively, fearing God and the king, judging fairly, and perceiving the perils of laziness. This last topic resembles an instruction in Prov 6:6-11, but the form in Prov 24:30-34 is autobiographical or anecdotal. At one point these sayings actually promise gifted persons that they will come to the attention of kings rather than wasting away in obscurity (Prov 22:29).

Like these minor collections of instructions, which consciously attend to the special interests of professional sages, the initial collection in Proverbs 1–9 discusses items that may have pertained to prospective courtiers: the correct attitude toward power and its revenues, proper respect for truth, the advantage of deference, the dangers of sexual license, the pitfalls of laziness, and the importance of wisdom in establishing and governing the inhabited world. On the other hand, nothing in this collection lies outside the realm of ordinary citizens. That point achieves focus in the references to teaching that derives from parents, an emphasis that becomes particularly personal on occasion (Prov 4:1-6—especially verse 4). This ambivalence about the real context for these instructions, home or school, comes mightily to expression in Prov 5:7-14 where "sons" complain that they disregarded their teachers'

---

[26]Both this text and Prov 31:1-9 have the Hebrew word מַשָּׂא, which probably alludes to the place of origin. The word may also contain a pun on the Hebrew word for oracle or burden, at least in the sayings of Agur.

instructions and almost came to ruin in the assembled congregation. Here one could render "sons" by the word "students," for the expression seems to have taken on a technical meaning.[27] Accordingly, the terms for parents in the other sections of this collection may connote professional teachers who functioned in loco parentis.

In sum, Israel's instructions may very well have been written by professional teachers specifically for potential scribes and courtiers. These elaborate counsels addressed various topics that appealed to young men[28] who aspired to work for kings and nobles. In these collections the wise belong to a privileged class, and the sage stands apart from ordinary citizens regardless of their intellectual achievement. Perhaps the Egyptian influence in these instructions relates in some way to this professionalism. Egyptian sages, too, spoke of a goddess of order (ma'at) who held the symbol of life in one hand and of prosperity in another. They identified the king's throne with righteousness and wrote about God's weighing the heart and rewarding the virtuous with a wreath. They also recognized certain kinds of conduct as an abomination to God, particularly actions that took advantage of the powerless.[29]

On the Interrelationship of Professional Sages, Ascriptions of Royal Authorship, and Popular Wisdom

What place did professional sages occupy in popular wisdom,[30] which expresses itself in the sentence literature in Prov 10:1–22:16 and chaps. 25–29? Use of the term "popular wisdom" already suggests an answer: this body of knowledge derives from the populace at large and identifies concerns of general application. Then what do the ascriptions to Solomon mean, who were Hezekiah's men, and why did someone make this connection between royalty and folk wisdom?

In the Psalter many psalms have the superscription "to David," perhaps in the sense of "pertaining to" rather than "belonging to." Having nothing to do with authorship, the ascription nevertheless identifies the particular psalms as in some way associated with Israel's great king, David. Various traditions linked him with music, making it entirely appropriate to connect his name with the Psalter, whether as patron or as representative of a musical style. A similar phenomenon may have taken

---

[27]The reference to "mother" militates against a technical sense for the word אָב (father), but guilds in which parents taught their own sons and others may eventually have led to a technical meaning of אָב and בְּנִי.

[28]At least two things suggest that Israelite students were exclusively masculine. First, they are consistently addressed as sons, and second, they are admonished to remain faithful to their own wives and to shun foreign women.

[29]Glendon E. Bryce, *A Legacy of Wisdom* (Lewisburg PA: Bucknell University Press, 1979) gives a comprehensive analysis of Israel's transformation of borrowings from Egypt.

[30]Laurent Naré, *Proverbes salomoniens et proverbes mossi* (Frankfurt am Main: Peter Lang, 1986) examines Prov 25–29 in the light of African popular wisdom. His insights often illuminate the biblical text.

place among the sages, who knew the centrality of the pharaohs in Egyptian wisdom and who acknowledged the force of traditions about Solomon's exceptional sagacity.

In their present form, those popular reflections on Solomon's wisdom are wholly immersed in fantasy, although they may rest on authentic memory. The recollections that have the strongest claim to accuracy attribute to him a type of aphorism that rarely appears in the Book of Proverbs. That missing form is nature wisdom, possibly nominal lists (onomastica). The closest thing to such wisdom in the biblical canon occurs in the anonymous supplement to the sayings of Agur. These numerical proverbs draw moral lessons primarily from observing nature (Prov 30:15-33). The literary character of this evidence and its dissimilarity from the actual utterances associated with Solomon in the Book of Proverbs are not easily accommodated to a view of Solomonic authorship or patronage.

Sociological analysis of this king's place in the ancient Near East may lend support to the historicity of the later legends, but the method hardly offers the final answers that some interpreters attribute to it. No amount of special pleading will erase the harsh fact that Solomon's regime was oppressive and bloodletting. Reconciling these practices with "enlightenment" mentality requires considerable mental reservation.[31]

Still, Solomon's diplomacy probably introduced a professional class of the wise into Israelite society. The "men of Hezekiah" may have continued this intellectual tradition, perhaps copying[32] earlier truth statements of popular origin and providing a context for these utterances. In neither case did the wise compose the sayings that appear in the collections attributed to Solomon and associated with Hezekiah's men. Even if a small section of the latter collection actually functions as a mirror for aspiring rulers (Prov 28–29),[33] which is improbable, the vast majority of these truth statements address ordinary citizens. In them the word חָכָם (wise) has a moral connotation and lacks any reference to a profession.

Exceptions to this summary statement do occur. The most notable one concerns the making of war, which ordinarily belonged to kings (Prov 20:18). This observation about the importance of counselors in preparing strategy for a battle may, of course, derive from premonarchic times when family leaders gathered persons of discernment to discuss an approaching skirmish. Nevertheless, the larger context has several statements that exalt kings and allude to righteousness as the foundation of the throne, an idea that also appears in Egyptian wisdom literature.[34] Nowhere in these two collections of truth statements does Egyptian influence shape the ex-

---

[31]Surely it is significant that the consistent teachings in biblical proverbs condemn the abuses of power and privilege for which Solomon was known.

[32]These men of Hezekiah are called copiers (הֶעְתִּיקוּ), not sages (חֲכָמִים).

[33]Udo Skladny, *Die ältesten Spruchsammlungen in Israel* (Göttingen: Vandenhoeck & Ruprecht, 1962), has defended this hypothesis.

[34]Helmut Brunner, "Gerechtigkeit als Fundament des Thrones," *VT* 8 (1958): 426-28.

pression more notably than in chapter 16, which goes so far as to assert that royal judgments cannot err because God directs the king's thinking (Prov 16:10). Here the ruler's goodness is grounded in the fact that his throne is established by righteousness (צְדָקָה = ma'at), and his approval of integrity is assured (Prov 16:12-13). Although a king's anger is a messenger of death, his favor distills life-giving rain (Prov 16:14-15). Such assertions do not appear to communicate folk wisdom.[35]

This intermingling of popular aphorisms and language from Egyptian courtiers illustrates the complexity of Israelite wisdom literature. No single sociological group was responsible for the sapiential corpus, whether family or royal court. Considerable crossover probably occurred, the same persons belonging to different settings over the years. Consequently, neat divisions of the literature may be more heuristically than historically accurate. Folk wisdom, above all, registers the insights of individuals from the total society.

It follows that many viewpoints surface in these truth assertions. Persons of humble circumstances and individuals of substance observe human nature and draw universal insights from frequent repetition. Some sayings reflect pious presuppositions, others do not take the transcendent realm into account at all. Some focus entirely on domestic situations, others think only of commerce. Some recognize psychological dimensions of various experiences, others seem content to describe what is visible to the naked eye. Moreover, common folk may have reflected about kings and the dangers associated with life at the royal court, while courtiers who owned farms may have talked about matters related to successful breeding of herds and growing sufficient food for people and animals. That is why subject matter alone offers a dubious criterion for determining the social setting of a given aphorism.[36]

A preponderance of evidence still points to popular origin for the truth statements associated with Solomon and Hezekiah's men. Many of these utterances may betray literary retouching at the hands of trained sages,[37] but eloquence was not wholly missing from untutored individuals, as an Egyptian sage acknowledged.[38] In all probability, parents devoted considerable energy to instructing their children, and the oft-repeated appeal "my son" points first and foremost to the family context. Numerous sayings are directed to youngsters who faced the perils of growing up, but other utterances presuppose a married clientele with responsibilities in the larger society.

---

[35]Do the errors of Hebrew in chapters 15–16 reinforce suspicion that foreign hands have helped shape this section of the book? Sylistic differences have long been noted as well.

[36]Form critics have always paid attention to social setting, a point that some interpreters seem to overlook in their excitement over a method in vogue at the moment.

[37]H.-J. Hermisson, *Studien zur israelitischen Spruchweisheit* (Neukirchen-Vluyn: Neukirchener, 1968).

[38]"Good speech is more hidden than greenstone,/ Yet may be found among maids at the grindstones" ("Instruction of Ptahhotep"; see Lichtheim, *Ancient Egyptian Literature* 1:63).

Concluding Remarks on the Confidence, Character, and Universalism of the Sages

Regardless of the social context of these utterances, they possessed astonishing confidence in the power of the intellect. By living according to the accumulated insights of past generations, individuals guaranteed prosperity, long life, honor, and well being. For these optimists, the universe seemed to operate in an orderly manner, rewarding virtue and punishing vice. Behind this discernible order[39] stood a benevolent creator whose providential care brought security to those who practiced "fear of the Lord." In their eyes, the wise were righteous and fools were wicked; hence to be a sage meant adopting a way of life characterized by devout conduct. That was by no means all, for these aphorisms also describe sages as diligent, self-controlled, modest, chaste, temperate, and respectful. In other words, the wise enabled society to function successfully. Fools disturbed the calm, necessitating rigorous measures at the hands of gentler people. Sages therefore recognized the reality of evil, but they believed in their own ability to cope in the face of adversity.

Why did the sages compile the several collections of proverbs? Presumably, instructions arose in an educational context and served as texts in classrooms.[40] Did folk wisdom also function in this setting? Although the wise left no clue about the rationale for the compilation of the Book of Proverbs other than the prologues to chaps. 1–9 and 22:17–24:22, they undoubtedly recognized the educational value of popular wisdom. Precisely when this collecting of proverbs took place remains a mystery, but the initial activity may date from the Solomonic era. This quest to preserve insights from the past probably blossomed under Hezekiah, when political circumstances combined to foster respect for the past and to usher in a sense of urgency that surrounds a people who aspires to greatness against impossible odds. In any event, the collectors added nothing that enables modern scholars to date their work. They may actually have brought the collections together in Josiah's reign or during some later period. Strangely, these later sages respected their predecessors' wish to maintain universal appeal, for they introduced no distinctive feature of Yahwism. That departure from wisdom's usual realm of discourse was left to Ben Sira, a sage quite distinct from those who composed and collected the Book of Proverbs.

---

[39]On current debate about the appropriateness of using the concept of order with reference to biblical wisdom, see my essay "Murphy's Axiom: Every Gnomic Saying Needs a Balancing Corrective," in *The Listening Heart*, 1-17—also repr. above.

[40]André Lemaire, *Les écoles et la formation de la Bible dans l'ancien Israël*, OBO 39 (Göttingen: Vandenhoeck & Ruprecht, 1981) makes this point, although with less restraint than the evidence requires.

26 (1993)

Prohibitions
in Proverbs and Qoheleth

In a recent examination of poverty in the laws of the ancient Near East and of the Bible, Norbert Lohfink[1] lends his voice to earlier claims[2] that Israelite law and wisdom are integrally related. With regard to the emphasis on the poor in the Covenant Code, he remarks that these statutes "take up well-known themes of traditional

---

[1] "Poverty in the Laws of the Ancient Near East and of the Bible," *Theological Studies* 52 (1991): 34-50. Lohfink's description of evolving attitudes toward the poor within the several legal codes (Covenant, Deuteronomic, and Holiness) rests on structural and linguistic arguments. That is particularly true of his conclusions about Deuteronomy, which he thinks sought to "create a world in which one can be a stranger, an orphan, or a widow without being poor" (44). Lohfink writes that the authors of the Holiness Code "tried to bring things back to reality" (47), for the existence of the poor was a fact of daily existence. Deuteronomy's dream of eliminating the poor thus lost out to realistic politics. One feature of Lohfink's investigation of Mesopotamian law codes, the absence of laws about the poor or oppressed despite eloquent rhetoric concerning their well-being in the prologues and epilogues, points to the distinctiveness of the biblical legal corpora even though both the Mesopotamian codes and Deuteronomy imagine an ideal society.

[2] Most notably, Erhard Gerstenberger, Wolfgang Richter, and J. P. Audet. Gerstenberger ("Covenant and Commandment," *JBL* 84 (1965): 49-51) claims that both in form and content legal maxims and wisdom are alike, and the guardians of the precepts are not priests or prophets but fathers, tribal heads, wise men. He also makes the point (*Wesen und Herkunft des apodiktischen Rechts*, WMANT 20 [Neukirchen: Neukirchener Verlag, 1965]) that Israel was not conscious of conflict between wisdom's admonition and legal commands, for wisdom warnings are fundamentally identical with law. Wolfgang Richter (*Recht und Ethos: Versuch einer Ortung des weisheitlichen Mahnspruches*, SANT 15 [Munich: Kösel Verlag, 1966]) and J. P. Audet ("Origines comparées de la double tradition de la loi et de la sagesse dans le prôche-orient ancien," *International Congress of Orientalists I* [Moscow, 1960] 1:352-57]) make the same point. In a discussion of ancient Near Eastern royal ideology Leonidas Kalugila (*The Wise King*, ConBOT 15 [Lund: CWK Gleerup, 1980] 37) comments: "The king was a shepherd, a father and mother of his subjects, taking care of the poor, the widows, the orphans, feeding the hungry, releasing the prisoners, clothing the naked etc." Care for widows and orphans is mentioned in the Ugaritic Dan'el text (*ydn dn 'almnt / ytpt tpt ytm*; "He decides the case of the widow, he judges the suit of the orphan").

Ancient Near Eastern education and royal ideology: to be just and good to the poor in daily life, in business and at court."[3] Lohfink goes on to compare the general tone of the whole series of laws to Egyptian wisdom texts and prayers. He concludes that these biblical laws arose in a rural area but that the authors were familiar with ancient Near Eastern schools and may even have borrowed specific teachings from them.

Having dismissed the hypothesis of a "Deuteronomic" reworking of these laws within the Covenant Code,[4] Lohfink is inclined to opt for direct literary borrowing from outside. He insists, however, on the historically embedded nature of the idea of the stranger and the word לָחַץ with reference to the oppression of a stranger.[5] In his view this verb does not derive from law or wisdom admonition but reflects Israel's particular experience, possibly the result of "massive migration from the north to the south after the destruction of Samaria."[6]

R. N. Whybray's analysis in *Wealth and Poverty in the Book of Proverbs*[7] reaches an altogether different conclusion about the social context of the sayings about the poor. After providing a thorough study of the older aphorisms in 10:1–22:16 and 25–29, he writes that "there is nothing in them to suggest that they were composed as tribal law or to form part of a system of education."[8] Whybray rejects the view that the form of these sayings demonstrates a literary culture, for

---

[3]"Poverty in the Laws," 40.

[4]Ibid., 39. He therefore cannot explain wisdom influence as mediated through Deuteronomy, which Moshe Weinfeld in *Deuteronomy and the Deuteronomic School* (Oxford: Oxford University Press, 1972) attributes to ancient sages. If Lohfink's theory is correct that Deuteronomy changes "the structures of society so as to provide support for those groups which, for very different reasons, are not in a position to live off their own land" (44), the attempt to reorganize society fits badly into ancient wisdom, which endeavored to sustain the status quo. Even such radical sages as the authors of Job and Qoheleth did not propose a new social order, despite the injustice they witnessed.

[5]"Poverty in the Laws," 42. Lohfink thinks the Covenant Code marks the origin of the traditional group of *personae miserae*, the stranger, the orphan, the widow (40).

[6]"Poverty in the Laws," 41.

[7]JSOTSup 99 (Sheffield: JSOT Press, 1990).

[8]*Wealth and Poverty*, 74. Whybray concludes that the instructions in 1-9, 22:17–24:22; 30:1-9; 31:10-31 derive from different circles entirely from the working class responsible for the sentences in 10:1–2:16; 25-29; 24:23-24 (*sic*, 34); 30; and miscellaneous sayings in 1-9. The authors of the first two instructions belonged to the upper class and wrote for students, some of whom may have been preparing for responsibilities at the royal court. Two of these instructions, 31:1-9; 31:10-31, reflect the views of those persons who have already reached the top of the social ladder. Whybray (*Wealth and Poverty*, 116) identifies four social strata in Proverbs: officials of the court, members of the educated urban society, prosperous farmers, and small farmers earning a precarious living.

African folk proverbs have many of the same characteristics that in the Bible have led some interpreters to argue for "literary" formation.[9] In the debate over the accuracy of the claim that wisdom and law shared a common origin in the ancient clan, Lohfink clearly belongs to the camp in which Joseph Blenkinsopp has pitched his tent. Blenkinsopp's view finds expression in *Wisdom and Law in the Old Testament*,[10] where he suggests that casuistic law closely resembled aphoristic wisdom, whereas apodictic law bore a striking resemblance to instructions.[11] His understanding of wisdom as an attempt "to bring human conduct into line with a cosmic law of regularity and order observable in the sequence of seasons, the movements of the heavenly bodies and the like"[12] made a comparison between law and wisdom a logical consequence. His definition of wisdom as living in conformity with the law of nature[13] strengthened that logic considerably.

In light of Claus Westermann's observations in *Wurzeln der Weisheit*[14] that the older proverbial sayings never refer to relationships within the larger clan nor do they champion such a family structure,[15] perhaps we should think instead of the

---

[9]Laurent Naré, (*Proverbes salomoniens et proverbes mossi*, Publications Universitaires Européennes [Frankfurt: Peter Lang, 1986]) compares Prov 25–29 and African proverbs. The chief proponent of the literary character of canonical proverbs is Hans-Jürgen Hermisson (*Studien zur israelitischen Spruchweisheit*, WMANT 28 [Neukirchen-Vluyn: Neukirchener Verlag, 1968]).

[10](Oxford: Oxford University Press, 1983).

[11]Blenkinsopp writes: "If, as noted above, case law is in some respects comparable with proverbial wisdom, categoric law exemplified in the decalogue has analogies with the admonitions and instructions of the sages" (*Wisdom and Law*, 81). The distinction made by Claus Westermann between sayings, which originated among ordinary people and were circulated orally, and admonitions, which arose in educational circles, might accommodate this understanding of two types of laws ("Weisheit im Sprichwort," *Schalom. Studien zu Glaube und Geschichte Israel. Alfred Jepsen zum 70. Geburtstag*, ed. K. H. Bernhardt, AzT 46 [1971] 73-85). Westermann thinks of sayings as universal, while the admonitions are specific to a particular people (*Forschungsgeschichte zur Weisheitsliteratur 1950–1990*, AzT 71 [Stuttgart: Calwer Verlag, 1991]) 17.

[12]*Wisdom and Law*, 19.

[13]*Wisdom and Law*, 19. Blenkinsopp (28) notices that the same pattern, imperative or prohibition with motivation, occurs in the *Intruction of Amenemope* and in the Decalogue, as well as in other biblical legislation.

[14](Göttingen: Vandenhoeck & Ruprecht, 1990).

[15]*Wurzeln*, 35-36. He writes: "Eine über die Familie (Vater-Mutter-Kind) hinausreichende grössere familiäre Gemeinschaftsform 'Sippe' kommt in der Proverbien niemals, in keinem Spruch vor; niemals wird das Denken oder das Handeln auf eine grössere Gemeinschaftsform, niemals auf weitere Verwandte bezogen" (35). The second reason to consider *Sippen-ethos* problematic is: "Mit 'Sippe' kann nur eine familiär strukturierte Gemeinschaftsform gemeint sein. Von der Familie aber, von Vorgängen in der Familie, von Verhältnissen

nuclear family unit. Far too much has already been made of the clan ethos as a wisdom locus for the summons to pay attention, with misleading conclusions that link prophets closely with the sapiential tradition.[16] Nevertheless, a family setting for law and wisdom may still be proposed, the authoritative father being the promulgator of both types of command.[17]

Space does not permit me to evaluate the strength or weakness of the argument about law and wisdom. Instead, I shall address a more modest task—to provide some data that ought to precede such discussions. In short, how do the proverbial sayings express prohibitions? The assumption that a common origin issues in similarity of form makes such comparative information desirable, indeed essential. I shall leave to specialists in Israelite law the further task of applying these data to the several legal codes within the Bible.

I. Prohibitions in the Book of Proverbs

As one might expect, most of the prohibitions are found in instructions; in them the huge diversity of form immediately comes to mind. Warnings and negatively stated admonitions using direct address are expressed in many different ways, as the following examples demonstrate.

1. either בְּנִי or בָּנִים accompanied by one or two jussives with אַל, stated either synonymously or antithetically (3:1, 11; 5:7; 6:20; 24:21);

---

zwischen Familiengliedern oder von familiären Problemen handeln die Sprüche nur äusserst wenig, sie spielen eine grössere Rolle fast nur im Bereich der Erziehung" (35-36). Arguments from silence are never entirely satisfactory, a fact that interpreters who study the problem of schools in ancient Israel have come to appreciate. In Westermann's view, the world of the oldest proverbs is the simple village, and their language is that of daily discourse. R. N. Whybray ("The Social World of the Wisdom Writers," in *The World of Ancient Israel*, ed. R. E. Clements, 227-50 [Cambridge: Cambridge University Press, 1989]) writes that "Israelite tribal wisdom is a somewhat shadowy postulate" (233).

[16]Hans Walter Wolff has argued repeatedly that the prophetic appeal for a hearing originated in an educational setting of the wise. In itself a dubious claim, this hypothesis has led Wolff to posit wisdom influence on several minor prophets (Hosea, Amos, Micah, Joel, Jonah). On Joel 1:2-3, e.g., he writes: "The book's opening employs in v 2a the ancient 'call to receive instruction' (*Lehreröffnungsruf*), a form especially popular in wisdom circles, used to arouse attentiveness" (*Joel and Amos* [Philadelphia: Fortress Press, 1977] 20).

[17]Gerstenberger, "Covenant and Commandment," 51. Philip Johannes Nel (*The Structure and Ethos of the Wisdom Admonitions in Proverbs*, BZAW 158 [Berlin and New York: Walter de Gruyter, 1982] 89) concludes that the authority of wisdom is intrinsic (i.e., rests in its truth) and therefore does not depend on an authority figure such as a father or an institution like the family. On this problem, see my "Wisdom and Authority: Sapiential Rhetoric and its Warrants," *Congress Volume Vienna 1980*, VTSup 32 (Leiden: E. J. Brill, 1981) 10-29.

2. a conditional clause introduced by אִם and followed by a single jussive with אַל (1:10);

3. a jussive without any explicit reference to sons, but with implicit address to them (3:7, 25, 27-31; 4:6, 14, 21, 27; 5:8; 6:25; 7:25; 8:33; 9:8; 20:13, 19, 22; 22:22, 24, 26, 28; 23:3, 4, 6, 10, 13, 17, 20, 31; 24:1, 15, 17, 19, 28-29; 25:6; 26:4; 27:1; 30:6-8, 10; 31:3);

4. the mention of objects first, then a jussive with or without a suffix (3:3; 23:23; 27:10);

5. an imperative followed by a single or multiple jussive (3:5; 4:5, 13, 15; 6:3-4; 23:22-23);

6. וְעַתָּה and vocative בָנִים plus imperative and לִי with accompanying jussive (5:7);

7. an imperative and antithetic jussive (23:23);

8. a verbless warning (31:4); and

9. a relative clause as the object followed by a jussive (25:7b-8) or a participle followed by a jussive (26:24-25).

A striking example of indirect address or impersonal speech, Prov 28:17, lacks אִם although its conditional nature appears likely. In one instance, 20:19, לֹא with the imperfect occurs where it cannot be explained as a verb that prefers לֹא to אַל inasmuch as the same form תִּתְעָרֵב is negated by אַל in 24:21. Occasionally, a motive clause has a prohibition (4:2).

The motive clause is equally varied; at least eleven ways of expressing motivation can be detected.

1. כִּי in the same verse or the next one (1:8-9; 3:1-2, 25-26; 4:21-22; 7:25-26; 22:22-23; 23:9, 10-11, 17-18, 20-21; 24:1-2, 15-16, 19-20, 21-22; 25:6-7; 26:25; 27:1);

2. כִּי at the end of a series (3:5, 7, 12; 4:5, 6, 13-16; 23:6-7);

3. כִּי plus כֵּן (1:16-19) or כִּי and antithesis (3:31-32; 6:26);

4. וְ copulative (3:3-4, 21-22, 28, 29; 20:22);

5. בְּ temporalis (3:27) within an infinitive construct;

6. adverbial אִם (3:30) and conditional (22:26-27);

7. פֶּן (9:8; 20:13; 22:24-25; 24:17-18; 25:8-10; 26:4,5; 30:6, 8-10, 31:3-5);

8. פֶּן and פֶּן, followed by וְ and וְ (5:7-10);

9. אַשְׁרֵי with כִּי (8:33-35);

10. כִּי in the sense of when (23:13);

11. a summary statement (23:31)

The motivation is conspicuously absent in 4:27; 6:4-5; 22:28; 23:22-23; 24:28-29. A preference for פֶּן over כִּי is observable in instructions attributed to Agur and to Lemuel's mother, but פֶּן also occurs in sayings where one does not expect to find them (25:9-10; 26:4-5). Verbal forms show decided preference for *qal* and *piel*, although *hiphil* forms occur often, with an occasional *niphal* and *hithpael*.

II. Prohibitions in Qoheleth

Within Qoheleth eight, possibly nine, varieties of prohibition indicate that later wisdom retained stylistic fluidity akin to earlier instructions.

1. אַל with the jussive plus לְ and the infinitive, a dative of administration and a motive clause introduced by כִּי (5:1[2], 3[4]);
2. אַל plus וְאַל and jussives, followed by a question with לָמָה as introductory particle (5:5[6]; 7:16-17);
3. אַל with the jussive plus a motive clause introduced by כִּי (7:9-10);
4. אַל plus וְאַל and jussives followed by a motive clause with כִּי (8:2-3; cf. 10:20);
5. אַל with jussive but without an immediate motive clause (9:8; cf. כִּי in 9:9);
6. a conditional clause introduced by אִם, followed by אַל and a jussive, with a motive clause beginning with כִּי (5:7; 10:4);
7. אַל with a jussive followed by לֹא and the imperfect, coupled with a motive clause and כִּי (7:21-22);
8. an imperative plus אַל with a jussive, followed by a motive clause with כִּי (11:6);
9. טוֹב followed by a relative and לֹא with an imperfect, plus partitive מִן (5:4[5]).

The diversity in Qoheleth extends beyond form to syntax, grammar, topic, and semantic field. No single form appears to be normative, either in quantity or in aesthetic appeal. Warning or admonition, vetitive, and motive clause comprise essential components, although ambiguity persists with regard to the formal or functional nature of these categories.[18]

* * *

Armed with this information about the actual variety of prohibitions in proverbial wisdom, interpreters should be able to assess claims about similarities between law and wisdom. One significant test case exists within Proverbs itself, although its resolution alone will not settle the argument.

Proverbs 22:28 is one of those rare sayings with multiple variants (23:10-11; Deut 19:14; 27:17; cf. Jb 24:2). No motive occurs in Prov 22:28, only a terse warning (אַל־תַּסֵּג גְּבוּל עוֹלָם אֲשֶׁר עָשׂוּ אֲבוֹתֶיךָ) = "Do not remove the age-old

---

[18]The trail was laid out by unknown authors of earlier sayings, but Ben Sira made it familiar territory. I have discussed his use of an ancient debate form in "The Problem of Theodicy in Sirach," *JBL* 94 (1975): 47-64.

boundary that your ancestors set up"). The Egyptian parallel from the *Instruction of Amenemope* adds a religious justification for the prohibition, which *ANET* omits ("Do not carry off the landmark at the boundaries of the arable land . . . nor encroach upon the boundaries of the widow"). Loss of land meant exclusion from the divine promise, and violation of established order was a serious offense. As is well known, respect for boundaries was not unique to the Egyptians and Israelites, for the Greeks praised Zeus as protector of borders and the Romans honored Terminus in an annual festival.[19] Within Proverbs itself, 15:25 asserts that YHWH is committed to maintaining widows' boundary stones, a belief presupposed also by the passage from Amenemopet cited above (but with a different deity, of course; cf. Deut 32:8; Ps 74:17).

In Prov 23:10 the oft-proposed change of עוֹלָם to אַלְמָנָה improves the symmetry;[20] the motive clause in the next verse describes YHWH as the one accepting social responsibility for the nearest of kin and argues a case within the judicial system. In early times the office of גֹּאֵל functioned, among other things, in cases of blood revenge occasioned by murder or serious sexual offenses.[21] The clause, "He will plead their case against you" recalls Prov 22:23, "For YHWH will plead their case" which is further reinforced by assurance that the deity will despoil the despoilers. Here the victims of oppression belong to the ranks of the marginalized (the poor, דָּל, and helpless, עָנִי).[22] In this particular case the injustice occurred precisely in the place where justice was supposed to be carried out (בְּשַׁעַר, "in the gate"). Presumably the agent of this miscarriage of justice was a bribe, for which practice the sayings provide ample evidence. To curb such abuse of power and wealth reflected, for example, in Job 24:2, an epithet describing YHWH as "father of the fatherless, champion of the widow," came into existence (Ps 68:5[6]; cf. Exod 22:21-22; Job 10:13).

Differences between Prov 22:28 and Deut 19:14 discredit the attempt to relate the two texts in any way other than subject matter: לֹא with imperfect, רֵעֶךָ instead of עוֹלָם (or אַלְמָנָה), רֵאשֹׁנִים for אֲבוֹתֶיךָ, נֹבְלוּ for עָשֹׂוּ and typical

---

[19]Crawford H. Toy, *The Book of Proverbs*, ICC (New York: Charles Scribner's Sons, 1902) 427.

[20]The versions offer no evidence that the translators read אַלְמָנָה, but the parallel from *Amenemope* and the frequent biblical association of widows and orphans (Exod 22:21; Deut 10:18; Ps 68:6; 146:9; Isa 1:17; Jer 7:6; 22:3) favor this emendation (Otto Plöger, *Sprüche Salomos (Proverbia)*, BKAT 17 (Neukirchen-Vluyn: Neukirchener Verlag, 1981]) 272.

[21]Helmer Ringgren, "גָּאַל *gā'al*, גֹּאֵל *gō'ēl*, גְּאֻלָּה *ge'ullāh*," *Theological Dictionary of the Old Testament*, vol. 2 (Grand Rapids MI: Eerdmans, 1975) 350-55; and J. J. Stamm, "גאל *g'l erlösen*," *Theologisches Handwörterbuch zum Alten Testament* (München: Chr. Kaiser Verlag, 1978) cols. 383-94.

[22]On the understanding of poverty as a sign of divine displeasure, see my essay entitled "Poverty and Punishment in the Book of Proverbs," *Quarterly Review* 9/3 (1989): 30-43—also repr. above.

Deuteronomic rhetoric ("in the inheritance which you will hold in the land YHWH your god gives you to possess"). The only point of similarity occurs in the two words גְּבוּל תַּסֵּג. The ancient curse in Deut 27:17 (אָרוּר מַסִּיג גְּבוּל רֵעֵהוּ) is closer to the other legal text, Deut 19:14, than to the passages from Proverbs. In the curse against one who removes a neighbor's boundary mark the participle occurs rather than the imperfect, the oath particle functions as negation, and רֵעֵהוּ has third-person singular suffix instead of second person, for indirect address chracterizes the genre of curse (cf. Job 3:4, 6, 7, 9-10). Such differences among these texts exclude direct dependence, and the functional use of the curse as a prohibition implies that maxims may have played a similar role.

Some evidence supports the claim that positively stated maxims occasionally amounted to prohibitions. Proverbs 3:7a has the usual prohibitive form (אַל־תְּהִי חָכָם בְּעֵינֶיךָ), but the folly of this inordinate pride is condemned in proverbial sayings such as דֶּרֶךְ אֱוִיל יָשָׁר בְּעֵינָיו (12:15)[23] and "Do you see a person wise in his own eyes? There is more hope for a fool than for him" (26:12). The emphasis falls on reluctant students who think they already have all the answers and therefore do not need to learn from superiors.[24] All three texts aim at a single goal—to effect an openness to instruction. Functionally, all three are identical, despite their differences in syntax.

Another type of prohibition in Proverbs complicates the attempt to correlate law and wisdom. In three instances אַל־תֹּאמַר occurs; one of these legislates speech, while two of them place constraints on thought itself. The first, 3:28, issues a warning against requiring a debtor to grovel at the creditor's feet; for such delay in advancing a loan only lowers borrowers' self-respect. The second verse, 20:22, cautions against repaying evil deeds in kind and urges patience made possible by a conviction that YHWH will provide the desired retribution. In the third instance, 24:29, a warning against enforcing the principle of lex talionis seems to presuppose divine response for the purpose of punishing offenders in due time.[25] The same

---

[23]Otto Plöger, (*Sprüche Salomos [Proverbia]*, 151) writes that the fool establishes his own standard, refusing to hear advice from wiser individuals. The scandalous stories in Judg 19-21 describe chaotic circumstances resulting from a society ruled by independent judgments at odds with any sense of obligation to the community at large. These stories serve as a powerful apology for kingship ("In those days there was no king in Israel; everyone did what suited him" (אִישׁ הַיָּשָׁר בְּעֵינָיו יַעֲשֶׂה, Jdg 21:25). According to Prov 21:2 the fool has plenty of company, for human beings generally set their own standards, although YHWH weighs hearts (כָּל־דֶּרֶךְ־אִישׁ יָשָׁר בְּעֵינָיו וְתֹכֵן לִבּוֹת יהוה).

[24]I have examined "Resistance to Learning in Ancient Egypt and Israel" in a plenary address presented at the national meeting of the Catholic Biblical Association in Los Angeles, 10-13 August 1991. This paper, part of a larger work to be published later, deals with the conclusion to *Ani*, *Papyrus Insinger*, and Ben Sira, among other texts.

[25]William McKane, (*Proverbs* [Philadelphia: Westminster Press, 1970] 574-75) calls attention to the Babylonian "Precepts and Admonitions": ("Do not return evil to the man who

sentiment underlies *Ahiqar* 79 ("My enemies will die, but not by my sword"), which also leaves the matter of instrumentality open. The belief in the inevitable consequence of an evil deed, the conviction that the deity will punish villainy, and the knowledge that everyone must die make this saying richly ambiguous in one sense but absolutely certain in yet another sense.[26]

* * *

This survey of prohibitions in Proverbs and Qoheleth indicates the rich diversity of ancient sapiential speech. Preliminary examination suggests that similar variety characterizes prohibitions in Job and Sirach, but the data must await future study. In a few instances where identical prohibitions exist in law and wisdom, the differences of expression stand out. At the very least, those interpreters who identify wisdom and law as a common phenomenon will need to explain the sharp divergencies. Why would fathers choose such distinct language if both law and wisdom derive from family paraenesis? And why are most of the prohibitions found in instructions which originated in educational circles? Perhaps an adequate explanation can be found, but the question should not be ignored. As Westermann's history of research in wisdom literature during the years from 1950 to 1990 makes abundantly clear, scholars have yet to resolve the issue of wisdom's origins, whether oral or literary, and locus, whether family or school. Until further clarity is achieved on these crucial matters, claims about a common origin of law and wisdom must remain highly suggestive but at the same time equally problematic.

---

disputes with you. Requite with kindness your evildoer. Maintain justice to your enemy. Smile on your adversary"). McKane resists any theological reading of Prov 24:28.

[26]James M. Lindenberger, *The Aramaic Proverbs of Ahiqar* (Baltimore and London: Johns Hopkins University Press, 1983) 178.

27 (1992)

Job

Job, Book of. A book in the third division of the Hebrew Bible (the "Writings") that recounts the story of Job, a righteous man whose motives for being righteous are tested through a series of personal tragedies and sufferings. When three old friends arrive to console him, they all engage in a dialogue focusing not only on the cause of Job's personal misfortune but also more generally on the problem of evil. Their dialogue (or, more properly, "dispute"), in which Job sharply questions the nature of divine justice, ends without resolution, whereupon yet another character, the young Elihu, appears to offer his own observations on the nature of Job's predicament. Eventually God appears on the scene to upbraid Job for complaining, and to restore Job's family, property, and health.

- A. Contents
- B. Structure
  - 1. On the Basis of Diction
  - 2. On the Basis of Dramatic Movement
  - 3. On the Basis of Individual Components
- C. Scholarly Issues
- D. Competing Arguments
- E. Composition
- F. Date and Language
- G. Related Works in the Ancient World
- H. Canon and Text
- I. History of Interpretation

A. Contents

The book of Job consists of a narrative framework and a poetic core. The prose section is divided into a prologue (1:1–2:13) and an epilogue (42:7-17); the poetry is embedded between these two. Together prose and poetry examine the possibility of being good without thought of either reward or punishment and explore the nature of innocent suffering; whether or not it exists, how one ought to act in the presence of misery, and why such injustice occurs. The prose framework deals with loss and eventual restoration without so much as a raised voice, and in its simplicity embraces and makes possible the eruption of volcanic emotions in the poetry.

Emphasizing the historical gap between the time of the hero and the subsequent narrating of the events, the narrative sets the action in (pre)patriarchal times. Job's possessions, like those of the patriarchs, consist of cattle and servants; not only his three friends but also his enemies (nomadic Sabeans and Chaldeans) come from the greater environment associated with Abraham's wanderings; the monetary unit קְשִׂיטָה (42:11) belongs to that ancient era (cf. Gen 33:19); Job's life span exceeds that of the patriarchs; and his sacrifice of animals corresponds to the practice prior to official priests. The name Job recalls a folk hero associated in Ezek 14:14,20 with Noah and Daniel, probably the Dan'el of Canaanite epic texts. Although the meaning of Job's name is uncertain, similar forms are attested from early times in Egypt and Mesopotamia with the meanings "Where is the divine father?" and "Inveterate Foe/Hated One." In accord with the universality typical of early wisdom, the hero seems to have been an Edomite, famous for the wisdom of its inhabitants, and the setting in the land of Uz echoes the noun עֵצָה (counsel).

The action of the prologue (1:1–2:13) alternates between earth and heaven, the events of the latter hidden from Job. The hero, perfect outwardly and inwardly according to irrefutable testimony (1:3,8), enjoys the fruits of virtue—until God directs the Adversary's attention to him, eliciting suspicion of Job's motive for being good and provoking a test to determine the truth. Calamity befalls Job without warning, intruding on a serene setting of festivity. Marauding Sabeans strike Job's property, then fire continues the destruction; Chaldeans wield the penultimate stroke, and a fierce windstorm levels the house in which Job's children are eating and drinking. Messengers convey the news, their formulaic expressions heightening the pain. This narrative strategy informs readers of these events at the same time it informs Job (Weiss 1983). Having lost his children and possessions, Job blesses the Lord as source of good and ill (1:21). A second heavenly scene ensues, with God's "I told you so" and the Adversary's insistence that a real test must touch the actual person (2:3-5). God accedes once more, insisting that Job's life must not be taken. The final scene depicts a sorely afflicted Job, but one who retains his integrity despite his wife's urging to curse God and die (2:9-10). This time Job's confession takes interrogative form, but he does not curse God. Having heard of Job's misfortune, three of Job's friends, Eliphaz, Bildad, and Zophar, journey from their homes in Teman, Shuah, and Naaman respectively to offer comfort in adversity. Twice the narrator enters the story to pronounce the obvious judgment that in all this Job did not sin, adding "with his lips" the second time. The slight alteration suggests, at least to some people, a gulf between outward expression and inward resentment (*Baba Bathra* 16b). A *Leitwort* (leading, or theme, word) in 1:9 and 2:3 (חִנָּם, for nothing, without cause) links the prologue with the poetry (cf. 9:17; 22:6).

The poetic dialogue consists of three distinct units: Job versus Eliphaz, Bildad, and Zophar (chaps. 3–31), Elihu's attack on Job's friends and Job (chaps. 32–37), and God's lectures to Job (38:1–42:6, with brief responses by Job in 40:3-5 and 42:1-6). Job opens the dispute with a curse, but not against God except indirectly as creator of the birthday Job damns (chap. 3). He invokes uninterrupted darkness on that day, preferring that his mother had remained in a state of perpetual pregnancy or that he had died at birth, finding rest and equality in Sheol. His hidden fear that calamity might befall him had prompted excessive religious scrupulosity in the story (1:5) and erupts again in 3:25. From here on, each friend in turn responds to Job. This alternation of speakers occurs in three cycles, with the order of the friends being Eliphaz (chaps. 4–5, 15, 22), Bildad (chaps. 8, 18, 25), and Zophar (chaps. 11, 20—note that Zophar has no response in the third cycle). Job answers each of them in turn (chaps. 6–7, 9–10, 12–14, 16–17, 19, 21, 23–24, 26–27). Once the friends are reduced to silence, Job contrasts his former happiness (chap. 29) with his present misery (chap. 30) and utters an oath of innocence designed to force God's hand (chap. 31). Unlike most oaths in the Bible, Job's imprecations actually state the penalty that will beset the guilty person. He disavows, among other things, idolatry, lying, adultery, lust, greed, abuse of power, lack of concern for the poor, and misuse of land.

Surprisingly, Job's extreme action yields an unexpected interlocutor (chaps. 32–37), the youthful Elihu, whose name means "He is my God." Having stood by silently while Job's friends tried to answer his arguments, Elihu can contain his words no longer. Lashing out first at the comforters-turned-accusers, he then turns against Job with comparable contempt, claiming that God speaks through nocturnal experiences (33:15-16) and disciplines by means of adversity, both to elicit repentance (33:19-30). Citing Job's own words (e.g., 33:33 and 6:25; 33:24 and 6:23; 33:22 and 6:29), Elihu endeavors to overwhelm him with his own "perfect knowledge," a characteristic of his God as well. Elihu denies that one who hates justice will govern, and notes that God's all-encompassing power rules out any need for partiality (34:17-20). Like Zophar, Elihu exalts God to the point of rendering human deeds worthless insofar as God is concerned: good and evil affect human beings but do not touch God in any way. Such thinking naturally issues in majestic praise of the creator (chaps. 36–37), who now speaks from a storm (38:1). God asks Job question after question, forcing him to recognize that he knows very little about the mysteries of the universe (chaps. 38–39). The heavenly teacher lectures Job on the wonders of nature and calls to mind wild animals who live outside the human domain. God parades these creatures before Job: lion, mountain goat, wild ass, wild ox, ostrich, horse, hawk and eagle (chap. 39).

Not content with Job's initial repentance (40:3-5), God boasts about two special creatures, Behemoth and Leviathan (chaps. 40–41). In introducing them, God seems to concede that human pride and wickedness in general present a challenge even to the creator (40:10-14). Although God transforms the mighty Behemoth and Leviathan into innocuous playthings for the deity's amusement, the puny Job is no match for their strength. Realizing that his earlier Titanism was ludicrous, Job relents (42:1-6). The dispute has not been a total disaster, for Job's secondhand knowledge of God vanishes before the immediacy of sight. Hearing gives way to seeing, which enables Job to gain a proper perspective on his place in the universe. Complaint also acquiesces to profound silence. No longer does Job claim to be the measure of all things.

The epilogue (42:7-17) ties up all loose ends. Having repented, of what is unclear, Job intercedes on behalf of the three friends, at whom God is angry because they did not speak truth about God *as Job did*. A temporal connection between prayer and restoration occurs, and Job returns to his previous state, with one bonus: his three daughters possess unsurpassed beauty, besides an inheritance. Seven times the verb בָּרַךְ occurs in the story (1:5, 10, 11, 21; 2:5, 9; 42:12), alternating between the meanings "curse" and "bless" except the last two, which are reversed.

B. Structure

To some extent the shape of the book depends on one's predisposition, but three different ways of viewing the structure commend themselves. Readers may emphasize (1) the diction, (2) the dramatic movement, and (3) the individual components in outline form. By discounting brief prosaic introductions and observations, the first approach yields two parts, prose and poetry. The second perspective uses narrative introductions—and to some extent conclusions—to distinguish three divisions, specifically 1:1–2:10; 2:11–31:40; 32:1–42:17. The third approach divides the book into five discrete sections: chaps. 1–2; 3–31; 32–37; 38:1–42:6; 42:7-17.

1. On the Basis of Diction

Perhaps the most noticeable feature of the book is its use of a story to enclose a poetic center. This device was widely employed among sages of the ANE to provide a specific historical framework within which to interpret teachings that had broad application, whether philosophical ruminations about innocent suffering and the governance of the universe or collections of aphorisms to enable others to make wise decisions. For example, Ahiqar and 'Onkhsheshanqy have left significant proverbial sayings for posterity, but in each instance an account of the teacher's personal adversity encloses the collection of maxims. Little effort to connect this prose framework with the poetic teachings is evident, so that both story and poetry stand on their own. Nevertheless, the juxtaposition of the two parts of the book offers a way of understanding the teaching that would otherwise not occur. Just as a simple frame enhances a painting, delineating its original features and drawing attention away from itself to the art, so these brief biographies give vital data about the hero's words and character.

In a sense, the Joban poetry interrupts the story, which suspends Job's destiny in midair until the poetry has reached its goal; only then does the tale resume and achieve closure. The narrator of the story, who freely intrudes twice to pass independent judgment on the hero (1:22; 2:10), recedes in the poetry so that other voices may be heard. The lyrical poetry of Job, whose threatened ego fights for survival against overwhelming odds, the confident assurances of Eliphaz and his companions, Elihu's brash rebuttal of all four, and the divine interrogation—all this takes place while the narrator creates a story within an earlier story, the folktale. The narrator's resumption of the tale after Job's claim to have seen the deity gives the impression of returning to reality, at least a realm that ordinary people comprehend. *Do ut des* (I give in order to receive) still functions in this land of Uz, for divine anger departs as a result of Job's obedient deed, and God restores Job at this time. Prologue elicits dialogue, and epilogue terminates it. The epilogue does more than end the dialogue, for the force of "anti-wisdom" within the poetry evaporates under the heavy hand of the narrator. Viewpoints collide everywhere, not just in the dialogue. The prose framework and that in the poetic core speak opposing views: the former ultimately seems to affirm the reward of the innocent (Job is at least compensated for his suffering, if not rewarded for his virtue) while the latter proclaims most persuasively that the innocent are not rewarded. To this day no satisfactory harmonization has been found.

2. On the Basis of Dramatic Movement

Introductions at 1:1-5, 2:11-13, and 32:1-5 suggest another way of dividing the book. The first introduces Job and gives essential insights into his character, which will soon be assailed mightily. The second introduction identifies Job's three friends and sets up expectations about their role as comforters, whereas the third introduction describes Elihu's boldness in venturing to address his elders without their consent and justifies his fury at the level of discourse so far. Thus understood, the book of Job becomes a drama consisting of three episodes: God afflicts Job, Job challenges God, God challenges Job. Another way of stating the drama is the hidden conflict, the conflict explored, and the conflict resolved (Habel 1985). This interpretation depends on an understanding of narration through dialogue, so that the fundamental category of the book is said to be prose with the poetic dialogues retarding the movement of plot and heightening the emotional pitch.

This approach encounters difficulties other than the brevity of the first part, since Job's laconic confessions in this section differ from his outpouring of resentment in the second unit, although his two repentant statements in part three balance the shorter confessions nicely. More to the point, the narrator's commendation of Job's conduct (1:22; 2:10) marks two closures, and although section two ends appropriately (31:40, "The words of Job are ended"), the third section concludes reluctantly. God's first speech evokes Job's final words, or so he says (40:4-5), only to give way to a second divine speech and an additional response from Job (42:2-6). Each indecision necessitates further brief introductions of speakers, but these comments play no role in the suggested structuring of the book. The description of plot development also presents difficulty, for Elihu's speeches hardly contribute to resolving the conflict between Job and God. Actually, the epilogue alone describes the resolution, the divine speeches functioning as disciplinary chastening of the hero.

3. On the Basis of Individual Components

Yet another means of structuring the book derives its clues from the distinctive components in it: (1) a story about Job's affliction, (2) a dispute between him and three friends, (3) the speeches of Elihu, (4) divine speeches punctuated by Job's submission, and (5) a story about Job's restoration. The second division fails to qualify as a consistent dispute, for the third cycle breaks off without Zophar's final speech and thereafter Job appears either to address the divine enemy or to enter into nostalgic monologue. This approach does not disparage the dialogue by labeling it an almost interminable retardation of the plot, since the poetic speeches possess value in their own right apart from any progress they may signal toward some unspoken telos. Because the action moves toward a divine pronunciation of Job's innocence in the debate between Job and his friends, the dialogue gives an impression of progress, particularly the emergence of references to the figure of an "advocate" or "redeemer." Emotional changes and high points mark still another kind of movement in the poetry, indicating that progress does occur even when opposing intellectual positions come no closer together than at the beginning.

C. Scholarly Issues

More critical problems surround the book of Job than perhaps any other book of the Old Testament. Many of these problems relate to the structure of the book itself.

Perhaps the most obvious problem concerns the composition of the book, more specifically the relationship of the prose framework to the poetic core (see E below). Even though prose and poetry can be intermixed with great literary effect (e.g., Jonah), a number of apparent inconsistencies are associated with this prose/poetry distinction. The patient Job of the prose framework contrasts with the defiant Job of the poetic core; and the God who is proud of Job and commends him in the prologue/epilogue rebukes him in the dialogue. However, these contrasts can be an understandable function of the plot development. More seriously, the "happy ending" effected by God (42:10-17) seems to undermine the integrity and force of Job's penetrating argument as presented in the dialogue (i.e., that God does not guarantee "happy endings"). Thus, some questions have been raised about the literary relationship between the prose framework and the poetic dialogue: initially the framework was thought to be secondary, although the dominant hypothesis now is that this framework reflects an original folktale that was subsequently embellished by the poetic dialogue.

Indeed, some tension seems to exist between the prose prologue and epilogue. The Satan—whose penetrating questions about the ultimate motives for human righteousness precipitated the "testing" of Job in the prologue—is never mentioned in the epilogue. Moreover, the epilogue does not even return to the issue of the "test."

In the poetic dialogue itself, the most noticeable structural feature is the predictable "roundtable" cycle of the debate, with each friend speaking in turn. Yet in the third cycle of the debate (esp. chaps. 25–28) this symmetry dissolves: Bildad's third speech is surprisingly brief (chap. 25), Zophar has no third speech, Job paradoxically seems to express sentiments that previously have been found only on the lips of his three friends (26:5-14), and there are literary clues that several

"Job speeches" may have been spliced together (e.g., 27:1; 29:1). Some scholars have attempted to reconstruct a third speech for Zophar out of Job's paradoxical statements, while others hold that the hymnic reflections on wisdom (chap. 28) are secondary.

The nature and function of the Elihu speeches (chaps. 32–37) are problematic. Are these speeches secondary or original? Most scholars opt for the former, pointing out that their appearance breaks an otherwise clear pattern: Job never replies to Elihu, and in the epilogue neither God nor the narrator acknowledges his presence and participation in the dialogue (as they do Eliphaz, Bildad, and Zophar; 42:7-9). Indeed, the speeches seem intrusive—something even Elihu must apologetically admit (32:6-22): they delay the smooth movement from Job's plea that God appear and respond (chap. 31) to God's actual appearance and response (chap. 38). However, Elihu's speeches fail to provide the anticipated "breakthrough solution." Is the resultant sense of disappointment unintended (i.e., does the text of Job preserve the remains of a clumsy author [or secondary redactor?] who, like Elihu, tried unsuccessfully to steer the issue to a clear resolution)? Or does the author have some specific reason for introducing Elihu and having his arguments prove so noticeably inadequate; and if so, what is that reason?

Similarly, the nature and function of the theophany (chaps. 38–40) have presented other problems. Was it original, and why are there *two* divine speeches (38:1ff.; 40:6ff.), each ending with a capitulation by Job? Does Yahweh "contaminate" the test of Job's character by appearing in this manner, or has the test already been decisively resolved? Does Yahweh not attempt to "bully" Job into submission just as Job had cynically predicted (i.e., Yahweh forces the issue back to the question of his power, not his justice)?

Other "historical" questions have centered on the time and circumstance of the writing (see F below) and possible connections with other ANE writings (see G below). The more "philosophical" questions, however, have centered on the various "answers" that are (or are not) given for the "problem of human suffering" (see G below). The quest for such "answers" is an understandable human desire, but it may be unfair to expect the book of Job to answer these questions.

However, if he had wanted to, the author undoubtedly *could* have provided some (perhaps even satisfactory) resolution to the story. If he wished to retain the dialogue, the author could have explicitly addressed its point (or its pointlessness?) and the ambiguity of Job's final reaction, explicitly telling the reader whether or not the test was resolved, and if so, how it was resolved. The author similarly could have had God more explicitly underscore the fact that no human being (neither Job nor the reader) can know or understand why the world operates the way it does (i.e., have God exercise his "power play" more obviously and directly on the reader). Indeed, to some extent the author seems to permit the plot to devolve toward this insight.

If he eliminated (or ignored) the dialogue altogether, the author *literarily* could have resolved some aspects of the narrative. For example, he could have portrayed a resolute Job who never complained and who made a complete *and unselfish* submission to God. He could even have depicted this Job continually suffering and eventually dying in pain. In this scenario, Satan would lose the wager, but the narrative could have still ended on the upbeat note that God still retained pride in (the now-deceased) Job (assuming the author cannot portray Job being resurrected from the dead). The reader would at least still be left with a moral example (Job), and whatever vague hopes might be associated with the notion of retaining divine favor posthumously.

Or the author could have depicted Job finally and decisively cursing God and having Satan thereby win the wager. Such a scenario conceding the truth of the Satan's claim could have itself constituted not only a profound authropological lesson into human motivation (that even the best of human intentions *are* colored by self-interest) but also a touching theological lesson about the predicament of God (who, despite the unconditional love shown for humans, can only be loved conditionally for the benefits rendered, not unconditionally for God's sake).

It is of course unfair to expect an ancient author to write a literary piece to provide satisfying answers to the questions raised by subsequent generations of readers. Nevertheless, many readers have wished that the author could have explicitly cited the "Fall" and "Original Sin" (Genesis 3–4) to explain human suffering, more explicitly drawing the conclusion that (for the time being?) the world does not operate according to God's original intent at Creation. Again, some readers have wished that the author could have developed the figure of a more diabolical "Satan," thereby portraying a sort of cosmic dualism that explains suffering as caused by an evil presence actively working to undo God's otherwise harmonious and just creation.

Regardless of how satisfying or unsatisfying they may be to subsequent readers, all these hypothetical resolutions would at least represent clear and deliberate attempts to resolve the profound problem of human suffering. The fact that the author of the finished book seems not to make such an explicit attempt perhaps reveals an awareness of how intractable the problem is. Perhaps the author was content merely to raise the issues, knowing from experience, reflection, and realization that any answer that human beings can articulate and comprehend is necessarily inadequate.

D. Competing Arguments

In a book that features a deity who asks copious questions, it occasions little surprise that the central theme of the book is stated interrogatively: does anyone serve God for nothing (1:9)? Society seems to take for granted the principle of retribution, the reaping of what one sows, despite occasional exceptions. Job's case stretches the belief to the limit, and in doing so the book probes an even profounder mystery: can religious trust survive every eventuality? The author recognizes that religion cannot endure unless its adherents transcend self-interest and reject all relationships grounded in the hope of reward for service duly rendered or fear of punishment for failing to meet expected standards of belief or practice.

As one might expect, an ambiguous answer rises above the heat of conflict, and the ambiguity penetrates to the very core of the story as well as the poetic dispute. On the surface, it appears that Job utterly rejects every semblance of a magical concept of reality whereby human beings manipulate deity for their benefit. After all, he retains his loyalty to God in the face of extreme adversity, explaining that we ought to accept weal and woe as equally sent by God. Still, the story endorses the principle of reward and retribution in subtle ways (Job is supremely virtuous and rich) as well as not so subtle (Job offers sacrifices to propitiate deity, and God seems to reward Job in the end for faithfulness). Despite its radical challenge to dogma, especially in the undeserved fate of Job's children, the story ultimately bows to tradition.

The center of gravity shifts in the poetic dispute, where the fundamental order of the universe comes under attack. Job questions the moral underpinnings of human existence, for he no longer receives appropriate dividends from above. Ironically, his complaint presupposes the very principle that he denies, else he would have no basis for dispute with God. The question, "Does God rule justly?" alternates with another, "How should a person respond to undeserved suffering?" Like the Mesopotamian *I Will Praise the Lord of Wisdom*, the book of Job functions as a paradigm of an answered lament, a model for those undergoing present suffering. The model consists of four movements: undeserved affliction, complaint, hearkening, restoration (Gese 1958). It gives free rein to the expression of anger, while at the same time urging the individual to submit humbly to the mystery and majesty of creation. The book offers no satisfactory answer to the agonizing query, the shortest question of all, "Why?" Even if the arrangement between God and the Adversary does not really constitute a wager, the idea of testing a faithful servant is only slightly more palpable, at least to modern consciences.

The Book of Job addresses more than one question and proposes several competing answers. Presumably, the author's answer, insofar as one option takes precedence over all opposing views, is hidden within the divine speeches. These lectures on the wonders of nature argue for a morality that transcends human values and contend that God governs the universe wisely. The frightening monsters, described in language that conjures up images of crocodiles and hippopotami, posed a threat to order in Egyptian mythology but yielded to divine domestication according to this astonishing text (Keel 1978). The deity's activity in providing for the needs of wild animals and in causing rain to fall beyond the regions of human habitation implies that caprice does not speak the final word. Saadia Gaon makes the argument more explicit: the gift of life satisfies the issue of divine justice, and anything beyond that falls into the category of mercy. Owing their very existence to the creator, human beings have no claim on God.

This line of reasoning comes closest to Eliphaz' insistence that human deeds have no effect on God, who does not even trust holy ones. For Eliphaz, the basic issue becomes clear in a terrifying revelation: "Can a mortal be more righteous than God? Can a man be purer than his Maker?" (4:17). Not content to rest his case on a word from God, he appeals to proverbial wisdom (reaping and sowing) and to ancestral teaching ("We are older than you"). At first gentle toward Job and holding out hope of eventual restoration as a result of submission, Eliphaz becomes increasingly less patient, accusing Job of heinous crimes. In doing so, Eliphaz fails to see the inconsistency with his earlier insistence that God derives no pleasure from human morality.

Although Eliphaz alludes to human existence as drinking iniquity like water, Bildad extends this point to include the birth process itself. He also expresses an exceedingly low estimate of human worth. Matters lack any ambiguity whatsoever for Bildad; Job's children sinned and paid for it, for God does not pervert justice. It follows that Job's repentance will accomplish restoration. Zophar's contribution to the argument skirts the issue of justice altogether: God takes mercy into account, punishing less than people deserve. Moreover, Zophar bears witness to an inner voice that announces the brevity of ill-gotten wages.

Elihu plows the same furrow Job's three friends have opened, as if youth inevitably do so. Like Eliphaz, he thinks God warns mortals by means of frightening dreams and visions; Elihu also questions the effect of virtue or wickedness on God, concluding that morality concerns human beings only (35:8). Like Bildad, Elihu cannot even imagine the possibility God rules unjustly. Like Zophar, Elihu thinks favored persons escape penalty for their sins. His arguments lay greater stress on educative discipline and the role of a mediator in moving the deity to compassion.

Job also entertains thoughts about an advocate who will plead his case and press for vindication. This daring concept (9:33) disappears almost as abruptly as it occurs, only to return a second (16:19) and third time (19:25) with greater tenacity. Job remains adamant in his protests of innocence, and this unyielding stance obliges him to attribute fault to God. Failing to obtain a hearing in the divine court, Job concludes that God has abandoned justice altogether. Because Job believes in the unlimited power of God, he naturally assumes that the problem belongs to the realm of will. The deity clearly does not want to execute justice throughout the land, Job charges, and with this concession Job broadens his scope to include the miserable wretches of society who know nothing but deprivation from birth to death. Fleeting thoughts about survival beyond the grave only distress Job, who denies the likelihood itself. He soon realizes that his only hope consists in a formal pronouncement of innocence within a court of law. To this end he pleads with God to write out the crimes for which he now suffers, vowing to parade the charges for all to see. In desperation, he enters into an oath of innocence, a self-imprecation designed to force God to answer. Confused to the end, Job forgets that human action has no control over arbitrary deities—or free ones (Hempel 1961). Readers forget this point too, frequently remarking that such action forced God to respond. Even Israel's sages knew better; neither curses nor oaths automatically move from word to deed.

E. Composition

A noticeable lack of coherence within the book implies that more than one author contributed to its final form. Differences between framework and core suggest that the author of the poetry used a popular folktale to pose the religious problem to be examined in the dispute. The depiction of the hero differs sharply in the two parts, a model of patience in the story, a defiant rebel in the poetry. The names for God differ, Yahweh in the prose, El, Eloah, Shaddai in the dispute (with one exception). The story endorses the principle of reward and retribution, despite Job's temporary misfortune, but neither Job nor God subscribes to the theory. Job rejects it outright and God ignores it completely. The epilogue has God condemn the friends for speaking lies about the creator and praise Job for telling the truth, whereas the divine speeches adopt quite a different attitude toward Job's attempt to justify himself at God's expense.

Confusion also exists within the poetic section. The third cycle of speeches breaks off prematurely with no response by Zophar; furthermore, Job's arguments at this point become wholly out of character. He seems to surrender to the friends' understanding of things, which contradicts everything he has said previously and makes nonsense of what follows. Various rearrangements of chapters 24–27 restore Zophar's last speech; perhaps Job's final remarks to the friends were so blasphemous that later readers replaced them with Zophar's sentiments. Chapter 29 presents a problem, for it interprets the argument and offers a feeble rationale for religion. The poem pronounces wisdom off limits for humans (Job seeks God, not wisdom!) but then concedes that God has made it accessible to everyone who is religious and moral, a conclusion Job only reaches after God's speeches. Furthermore, wisdom has two different meanings; practical knowledge in the dialogue, the nature of the universe in the poem. Elihu appears without advance warning and cites previous material with great familiarity. He may represent the later Jewish community's dissatisfaction with the divine speeches. Both God and the narrator in the epilogue ignore Elihu, as does Job. Moreover, the oath in chapter 31 arouses expectation of a divine visitor, which Elihu delays interminably. The divine speeches also seem to suggest supplementation. The primary problem extends beyond particular sections that differ markedly from the rest, especially the descriptions of horse and ostrich, to the simple fact that God speaks twice and elicits two submissions from Job. The second speech has struck many readers as excessive browbeating.

Literary unity within the dialogue has its defenders, who offer various justifications for rejecting a theory of textual accretion. The breakdown of the third cycle is a subtle way of declaring Job the victor (but why does Job endorse their view of retribution?). Job 28 functions as an interlude, retarding the action of the drama and assuaging human emotions. Elihu serves as an ironic foil to the deity, and the citation of earlier speeches constitutes instances of literary anticipation or foreshadowing. Variety in style and vocabulary is a mark of literary craft, and God's two speeches address Job's dual charges. Stylistic affinities between the hymn on wisdom's inaccessability and the Elihu narratives, on the one hand, and the rest of the poetry, on the other hand, have led some interpreters to posit common authorship over a long period of time. The silence about Elihu in the epilogue baffles critics of all persuasions.

The folktale may have developed by stages, with the wife and friends playing somewhat different roles from the ones in the present book (Vermeylen 1986). The three friends may once have functioned in the way the Adversary does now. Inasmuch as these verses featuring "the Satan" can be omitted without serious loss, the story in all essentials probably existed long before the addition of the motif of a heavenly adversary. The story manifests exquisite style, causing one interpreter to question the appropriateness of using the term folktale (Good 1988) and leading another to postulate an epic substratum (Sarna 1957).

F. Date and Language

Although the book is set in pre-Mosaic times, the actual time of composition is much later. Linguistic evidence seems to indicate a date in the sixth century or later (Hurvitz 1974), despite the complete silence about the national calamity in 587 BCE. Specific indicators for dating the book are exceedingly rare. Job's powerful outcry about the desirability of incising his testimony on a rock with lead inlay may allude to the Behistun Rock on which the Persian King Darius proclaimed his accomplishments to all passersby. Mention of caravans from Teman and Sheba (6:19) and the nomenclature of officials (kings, counselors, princes) in 3:14-15 corresponds to Persian hierarchy. The use of the definite article הַ with שָׂטָן suggests a stage in the development of the figure prior to the Chronicler and parallel to Zechariah. The abundance of Aramaisms, while problematic, may indicate a date in the late sixth or fifth century. The relationship between Job and comparable laments or lyrical texts in Jeremiah and Deutero-Isaiah is difficult to assess, but priority may go to the latter books. Similarities between Job and theological probings within the Psalter (37, 49, 73) certainly exist, but the uncertain dates of these psalms render them dubious witnesses about the actual date of the book of Job. The possible allusion to Job in Qoheleth 6:10-11 may echo familiarity with the folktale, and the recently discovered Targum of Job from Qumran, dating from the second or third century BCE, suggests a considerably earlier date for the book of Job.

An attempt to provide a specific historical setting for the book in Teman lacks cogency. According to this hypothesis, the book was written between 552 and 542 BCE, when Nabonidus conquered Tema and marauding soldiers took Job's possessions, forcing him to ransom his life (Guillaume 1968). Likewise, an effort to understand the book as a paracultic tragedy intended for use at the New Year Festival (Terrien) has failed to persuade many readers. Two astonishing features of the book remain unresolved: why did the author choose an Edomite for its hero, and why did the analogy between Job's affliction and Israel's defeat by Babylon and enforced exile not affect the depiction of the hero? Given the hostile sentiments toward Edom in prophetic texts from the exilic and postexilic period, the identification of the perfectly righteous man as an Edomite, made explicit in an appendix to the book in the LXX, seems strange until one recognizes the universalism of wisdom literature. Moreover, having set the story in (pre)patriarchal times, the author could not have introduced an Israelite, for the nation did not appear on the historical scene until centuries later.

Two other factors, sometimes thought to indicate a late date for Job, alter the situation little: the emergence of monotheism and monogamy. The heavenly Adversary can act only insofar as God allows it to do so, and the divine speeches also insist on the creator's authority over the entire cosmos. Such "modified monotheism" still employs mythic language about antagonists over whom the creator exercises control. Moreover, Job imagines the possibility of a mediator's forcing a guilty deity to acknowledge Job's innocence. One hesitates to label such thinking "monotheism," although it resolutely refuses to exonerate God by positing a rival deity. The noteworthy assumption that a wealthy man like Job in patriarchal times had only one wife may suggest that monogamy had become the rule rather than the exception when the author composed the folktale.

The language of the book contains more rare words than any other biblical work, Hosea being its nearest rival. The linguistic forms have caused interpreters to posit theories of composition in another language, primarily Aramaic. Much clarity of language and syntax comes from Northwest Semitic, so that theories of translation into Hebrew from another language seem superfluous. Nevertheless, the rare dialect of the book often defies understanding, and the frequent references to obscure animals and natural objects do not help matters. A single example illustrates the problem. In 4:10-11 five different words for lion stretch modern translators' wits to the breaking point.

G. Related Works in the Ancient World

Belief in the moral governance of the universe was widespread in the ancient world. Gradually this conviction gave rise to confidence that certain actions ensured well-being most of the time. By behaving in specific ways, individuals controlled the gods, who also benefitted from human attention to the cult and to ethics. During periods of social turmoil, doubt about the deity's benevolence became prevalent and produced literary texts resembling the book of Job in some ways. From Egypt come three works of this nature: *The Admonitions of Ipuwer*, *The Dispute Between a Man and his Ba*, and *The Eloquent Peasant* (*ANET* 441-44, 405-10), all dating from the twelfth Dynasty (1990–1785 BCE).

A section of *The Admonitions of Ipuwer* cites conventional belief ("He [God] is the herdsman of all; there is no evil in his heart. His herds are few, but he spends the days herding them") only to lament the wickedness that the deity allowed to stand. Because of social upheaval, the author denies the existence of a providential deity guiding human affairs. He asks: "Where is he today? Is he asleep?" and insists that "his power is not seen." Although the god possesses authority, knowledge, and truth, "turmoil is what you let happen in the land, and the noise of strife." Death naturally follows, and the poet entertains the possibility that the divine herdsman loves death. *The Dispute Between a Man and his Ba* (*ANET* 405-407) describes a miserable person who tries to persuade his soul to join him in a pact to commit suicide, primarily because his name reeks and he lacks companions who act virtuously. The man longs for death, which is "like a sick man's recovery," "like the fragrance of myrrh (and lotus)," "like a well-trodden way," "like the clearing of the sky," "like a man's longing to see his home." *The Eloquent Peasant* (*ANET* 407-10) complains bitterly to a government official, Rensi, son of Meru, about a lesser functionary who robbed him. Because of his rhetoric, the peasant is imprisoned and encouraged to plead his case; unknown to him, scribes record his speeches for the entertainment of the court. The peasant speaks nine petitions, becoming more exasperated over time and threatening to appeal to Anubis. When servants come from Rensi to reward the peasant, he mistakes their purpose and welcomes death with the words: "A thirsty man's approach to water, an infant's mouth reaching for milk, thus is a longed-for death seen coming, thus does his death arrive at last." Like the book of Job, these texts have prose frameworks enclosing poetic complaints.

From Mesopotamia come at least four texts that explore the problem of unjust suffering: *Man and his God, I Will Praise the Lord of Wisdom, The Babylonian Theodicy,* and *A Dialogue Between a Master and his Slave.* In the Sumerian *Man and his God* (second millennium; *ANET* 589-91), a sufferer complains to the gods but confesses guilt and is restored. He accuses the deity, here called a "righteous shepherd," of becoming angry, thereby encouraging human enemies to conspire against the sufferer without fear of divine retaliation. Appealing to the intimate relationship of father and son, the sufferer asks how long the deity will leave him unprotected. Nevertheless, he surrenders all right to protest divine conduct and subscribes to conventional wisdom: "Never has a sinless child been born to its mother; a sinless workman has not existed from of old." *I Will Praise the Lord of Wisdom* (*ANET* 434-37) discovers a solution in the inscrutability of the gods and the necessity for human beings to perform proper cultic acts. The sufferer believes in divine compassion ("I will praise the Lord of wisdom . . . whose heart is merciful . . . whose gentle hand sustains the dying . . . ") despite his own wretched state. Contrasting his earlier prestige with his present dishonor, he complains about inability to discover the face of the one to whom he prays. Circumstances compel him to conclude that the gods may have a different value system from the one constructed by human beings. This concession leads him to ask: "Who can know the will of the gods in heaven? Who can understand the plans of the underworld gods? Where have humans learned the way of a god?"

The Babylonian Theodicy (ca. 1100 BCE; *ANET* 601-604) resembles Job in that a sufferer engages in dispute with a learned friend. An acrostic poem of twenty-seven stanzas with eleven lines each, this dispute entertains the possibility of divine culpability ("Narru king of the gods, who created mankind, and majestic Zulummar, who pinched off the clay for them, and goddess Mami, the queen who fashioned them, gave twisted speech to the human race. With lies, and not truth, they endowed them forever.") The sufferer complains of having been orphaned early, and his friend reminds him that we all die. When told that wild asses trample fields and lions kill, the friend points out that the wild animals pay with their lives and that the plan of the gods is remote. The sufferer insists that his good deeds have not brought favorable response from the gods, and this remark arouses the friend's anger over such blasphemy. The friend does concede that the one who bears the god's yoke may have sparse food, but this situation can change for the better in a moment. The sufferer lingers on the notion that morality yields no profit. In the end, the complainant prays that the shepherd (i.e., god) who abandoned him will yet "pasture his flock as a god should."

The Dialogue between a Master and His Slave (*ANET* 437-38) resembles Ecclesiastes more than the book of Job, but some features of the Dialogue echo the conditions underlying Job's distress. A master determines to pursue a course of action and his servant, the proverbial aye-sayer, encourages him. The master changes his mind and the slave defends this decision. Nothing commends itself to the master—not dining, marrying, hunting, philanthropy, or anything else—except suicide, better still, murdering the slave. This poor wretch, caught in his rhetoric, seems to say that the master would gladly join him in death within three days.

The Canaanite epic of Keret (*ANET* 142-49) bears some resemblance to the book of Job. The hero loses his wife and sons but eventually finds favor with the gods and acquires a new wife and additional children. More remote parallels such as Prometheus Bound have been compared with Job, but differences stand out (Prometheus was a Titan, not a human being, and he suffered the wrath of Zeus through wilful conduct). An Indian tale about a discussion among the gods over the existence of pure goodness among earthly creatures singles out a certain Harischandra, whom the god Shiva submits to a test that demonstrates his incredible virtue.

The author of the book of Job may have known about the Mesopotamian (and Egyptian?) prototypes, but the biblical text cannot be explained solely on the basis of earlier parallels. These explorations of the governance of the universe and unjust suffering may have provided an intellectual stimulus, but the biblical author has produced something that stands alone as *sui generis*. Still, structural similarities (framework enclosing poetic disputes) and common ideas place the biblical work in the wider context of intellectual and religious foment. This observation also extends to specific units within the book of Job, for example, the oath of innocence in chapter 31, for which Egyptian execration oaths offer a close parallel (Fohrer 1963).

The claim that the book of Job is *sui generis* does not imply originality for everything in Job. In fact, striking similarities exist between elements within this book and other biblical material: the laments in Jeremiah (chaps. 3 and 20) and in the Psalms, hymnic passages in Amos (4:13; 5:8-9; 9:5-6) and Deutero-Isaiah, the book of Ruth, prophetic lawsuits, and proverbial wisdom. Sometimes the author seems to offer a parody of biblical texts (e.g., Job 3 and Genesis 1; Job 7:17-21 and

Psalm 8). Occasionally Job shares expressions in common with another textual unit (e.g. 38:5 with Ps 30:4, "Surely you know"; and 13:20 with Prov 30:7, "Two things"—but the connection between these texts is unclear).

The book of Job is usually discussed in connection with Proverbs, Ecclesiastes, Sirach, Wisdom of Solomon, and a few Psalms (e.g., 37, 49, 73). Modern scholars call these works "wisdom literature" and consider their closest parallels to be in Egypt and Mesopotamia rather than in the rest of the biblical canon. In some ways Job resists inclusion in this corpus, primarily because of the dominance of the lament genre and the theophany. Nevertheless, it seems best to designate the book "wisdom" and to recognize that, like Sirach some years later, the author of Job begins to widen the scope of traditions accessible to the sages.

On the basis of the texts to which modern critics have given the title wisdom literature, four quite distinct types are discernible: proverbial sayings, religious or philosophical reflections in discourse form, nature wisdom, and mantic revelation. The book of Job lacks the last of these types. Collections of aphorisms from the third millennium to the third century BCE have survived in Egypt, and Mesopotamian proverbs date from the third and second millennium. The philosophical probings from both areas rival the proverbial sayings in antiquity. The book of Job unites these two types of wisdom—the brief saying and reflective discourse—while restricting nature wisdom to a discrete unit, specifically chaps. 38–40. In general, the aphorisms present a positive view of reality, resting on belief in a reliable order and in the capacity of the human intellect to control one's actions and thus to promote well-being.

On the other hand, the intellectual reflection about the problem of suffering and the meaning of life is markedly less optimistic. The former type of thinking, by means of aphorisms, has a decidedly practical purpose, although its utilitarianism possessed a profound religious grounding: because right conduct sustained the order of the universe, the gods reward appropriate behavior. The reflective discourses question such certainty as found in these brief aphorisms, comprising a sort of "anti-wisdom." The sages therefore demonstrate unusual willingness to examine their presuppositions and to criticize themselves. The author of Psalm 37 affirms traditional belief in the face of all evidence that seems to indicate otherwise, but Psalm 49 takes human frailty much more seriously, and Psalm 73 probes deeply into the nature of the relationships between worshipper and deity. Here the assurance that God is good to the upright appears dubious when taking into account the prosperity of evildoers, until the psalmist goes to the holy place and reflects on the destiny of the evil ones. Then the intimacy with God becomes a source of unsurpassed joy and divine presence more precious than anything else in all creation.

Although the nature wisdom in the book of Job resembles lists of flora and fauna from onomastica in ancient Egypt—where encyclopedic knowledge of different subjects seems to have served to train young courtiers (von Rad 1972)—decisive differences make the identification of Job 38–40 as lists highly doubtful (Fox 1986). Ancient sages study nature as a means of learning more about human beings through analogy, for the wise assume that the same laws govern the universe, animals, and humans.

Because undeserved suffering posed an immense intellectual and religious problem for the sages, they sought arduously for a satisfactory answer. Their most common understanding, the *retributive*, is grounded in the order of the universe and the will of its creator. A second explanation, the *disciplinary*, derives from the context of the family, where well-intentioned parents punish their children as an act of love, hoping thus to shape character and to protect the young ones from harm. In time, the school also endorses this method of controlling the actions of youth. A third approach to suffering, the *probative*, bears impressive witness to the disinterested nature of religion. God tests human hearts to ascertain whether or not religion is pure, and in doing so replaces human self-interest with the centrality of holiness. A fourth interpretation, the *eschatological*, contrasts present discomfort with future restoration, indicating that hope springs eternal in the human breast. A fifth suggestion, the *redemptive*, derives from the sacrificial system and the idea that the spilling of blood alone makes atonement. A sixth response, the *revelatory*, takes suffering as an occasion for divine disclosure of previously hidden truth, both human pride and the mystery of the living God. A seventh understanding of suffering, the *ineffable*, is a humble admission of ignorance before unspeakable mystery, one so profound that a self-revealing deity in the book of Job remains silent about the reason for his suffering and fails to affirm meaning behind such agony. An eighth explanation for suffering, the *incidental*, implies that an indifferent deity stands by and thereby encourages evil, which seems trivial to the High God who fashioned mortals to be subject to suffering as the human condition. All these understandings of suffering in one way or another find expression in the book of Job.

H. Canon and Text

As in the case of Qoheleth (Ecclesiastes), the disturbing thoughts of Job did not prevent its acceptance in the biblical canon. An occasional rabbinic dissent against the historicity of the character Job has survived (*Baba Bathra* 15a), and one Christian thinker, Theodore of Mopsuestia, questioned the book's sacred authority. The sequence of writings varied at first, Job falling between Psalms and Proverbs in the Talmud, and in Codex Alexandrinus, but preceding Psalms and Proverbs in Cyril of Jerusalem, Epiphanius, Jerome, Rufinus, and the Apostolic Canons. Jewish tradition designates the two different sequences by the acrostic abbreviations אֱמֶת ("truth") for Job (אִיֹּוב), Proverbs (מִשְׁלֵי), and Psalms (תְּהִלִּים), and תֹּאַם ("twin") for Psalms, Job, and Proverbs. The Council of Trent fixed the order with Job in the initial position.

Textual problems abound in the book, and the much shorter Greek versions seldom resolve the difficulties. Often merely a paraphrase, the Greek text sometimes elucidates a theological bias in the present Masoretic text, for example the repointing of a negative particle in 13:15 to affirm trust in God even when faced with the prospect of death at the deity's hand (Pope 1973, 95-96). The Syriac

Peshitta assists in clarifying obscure meanings of the Hebrew text. Enough of the Targum from Qumran has survived to confirm the same disorder in chaps. 24–27 as that in the Hebrew. One surprising feature of the Targum is its termination at 42:11 instead of 42:17. Jerome's Latin translation of the Hebrew text of Job was influenced by the Greek translations of Aquila, Theodotion, Symmachus and the Alexandrian version as mediated by Origen's Hexapla.

I. History of Interpretation

The *Testament of Job*, the oldest surviving interpretation of the book of Job, probably comes from Alexandria in the first century BCE. One of many such "last words" of a famous person, it is characterized by zeal against idols, extensive speculation about Satan, cosmological dualism, interest in women, burial customs, magic, merkabah mysticism, angelic glossolalia, and patience. The *Testament of Job* differs considerably from the biblical story. The essential variations are that (1) Job destroys Satan's idol, incurring wrath, but an angel reveals Satan's identity to Job; (2) Job's possessions and good works are magnified in haggadic fashion; (3) Job's devoted wife, Sitis, begs for bread and eventually sells her hair to enable them to survive; (4) Satan concedes defeat in wrestling with Job; (5) Baldad poses "difficult questions" and Zophar offers royal physicians, but Job relies on the one who created physicians; (6) Sitis refuses to die until she knows that her children receive proper burial, and Job assures her that their creator and king has already taken them up; (7) God condemns the friends for not speaking truth *about Job*; (8) Job's daughters inherit magical items, enabling them to speak ecstatically; and (9) chariots take Job into heaven.

Unlike the Epistle of James (5:11), early opinions about Job's character did not always emphasize his patient endurance. The *Abot de Rabbi-Nathan* accuses Job of sinning with his heart and in this way defends divine justice. Rashi faults Job for talking too much. According to Glatzer (1966), later interpreters went beyond calling Job a saint or an imperfectly pious man to quite different categories: a rebel (Ibn Ezra, Nachmanides), a dualist (Sforno), a pious man searching for truth (Saadia Gaon), one who lacked the love of God (Maimonides), an Aristotelian denier of providence (Gersonides), one who confused the work of God and Satan (Simeon ben Semah Duran), a determinist (Jospeh Albo), one who failed to pacify Satan, a scapegoat, and isolationist (the Zohar), one who suffered as a sign of divine love (the Zohar, Moses ben Hayyim). In Jewish legend, God turned Job over to Samael (Satan) to keep him occupied while the Jewish people escaping from Egypt crossed the Red Sea, then God rescued Job from the enemy power at the last moment.

The early church stressed Job's suffering as a lesson in living and had readings from Job in the liturgy of the dead. Gregory the Great wrote thirty-five books of Sermons on Job, and Augustine read the book as an example of divine grace. Thomas Aquinas saw the book of Job as the starting point for discussing the metaphysical problem of divine providence (Damico and Yaffe 1989). Calvin wrote 159 sermons on Job, mostly polemical defenses of providence (Dekker 1952). This early Christian concentration on the suffering hero of faith gave way in the 17th and 18th centuries to an emphasis on Job as a rebel. For instance, Voltaire saw Job as a representative of the universal human condition (Hausen 1972).

Modern critics continue the tendency to understand Job in the light of prevailing intellectual or religious sentiments. For Carl Jung, psychological insights provide the key to understanding Job. Jung emphasizes the importance of a marriage between an unreflective but powerful deity, Job's afflicter, and חָכְמָה (wisdom), who taught God that the Cross, not abusive force, was the answer to Job. Jack Kahn draws on modern psychiatry to understand the grief process through which Job passed. Two literary treatments of Job have greatly influenced Western thinking about the problem of evil, Goethe's *Faust* and Archibald MacLeish's *J.B.* An anthropological approach to the book of Job emphasizes the people's desire to establish order by sacrificing Job as a scapegoat (Girard 1987), and a liberation theologian stresses Job's identification with the causes of the poor (Gutiérrez 1987). A philosopher explains Job's offense as ingratitude, a bitterness of spirit that harbors resentment toward God for allowing affliction to strike a heavy blow against Job's security (Wilcox 1989). Artists depict Job's suffering in the light of Greek mythology (William Blake) and the Holocaust (Hans Fronius). A Yiddish interpreter uses Goethe's *Faust* as a lens through which to view Job positively (Chaim Zhitlowsky 1919); a contemporary novelist likens the Jewish fate under Hitler to Job's affliction (Elie Wiesel) and is opposed by a humanist who contrasts Job's survival with the victims of Auschwitz and Dachau (Rubenstein). Some existentialist writers seem to have used Job as an example of the human situation (Camus, Kafka), and at least one Marxist philosopher thinks of Job as an exemplary rebel against theism and abusive power that religion fosters in the western world (Ernst Bloch).

The current fascination with literary theory has produced several different understandings of the book of Job. In one instance, readings are offered from the perspective of feminism, vegetarianism, materialism, and New Testament ideology (Clines 1989). An older reading of the book as drama has been revitalized (Alonso-Schökel 1977), and a shift from viewing Job as tragedy to comedy has occurred. In this view, Job's final restoration qualifies the book as a comedy in the classical sense of the word (Whedbee 1970). Attention has come to the ways modern interpreters silence the shrill voice of dissent, whether in the revised Roman Catholic liturgy (Rouillard 1983) or in the act of interpretation itself (Tilley 1989). In providing a fresh translation, a contemporary poet (Stephen Mitchell) has taken great license and removed the sting of Job's *cri de coeur* by omitting crucial verses.

Specialists in Hebrew Bible continue to wrestle with the meaning of key texts in the book of Job, particularly 19:23-27 and 42:6. Confronted with several possible translations (and probable textual confusion in 19:23-27), interpreters concede the impossibility of certainty. A parallel in the Canaanite epic of Baal and Anat may explain Job's daring thought that extends the concept of a גּוֹאֵל to the realm of the gods, but the matter is complicated by the two previous allusions to an umpire (מוֹכִיחַ, 9:33) and a witness (עֵדִי || שָׂהֲדִי, 16:19, 21). Such foreshadowing occurs throughout the book of Job: 9:17 and 38:1–42:6; 11:5-6 and 38:1–42:6; 13:7-12 and 42:7-9; 22:30 and 42:10; 9:32-35 and 32-37 (ironically); 8:6-7 and 42:10-17 (Habel 1985). Moreover, the ambiguity of Job's remarks in 19:23-26 leaves unclear Job's personal circumstances at the time of seeing God. Does Job expect vindication before death, or is his expectation considerably more bold? With respect to the missing object in 42:6, the suggestions are varied: Job repents of his finitude, he rejects (drops) his anticipated lawsuit, he falls down to the earth in shame, he only pretends to repent, knowing how to manipulate an unjust ruler, he rejects God, he recants his earlier words. Less likely, the verb מאס is understood reflexively (I loathe myself, I melt away, I abase myself).

One conclusion seems to force itself on readers: the author of the book does not believe that the natural order is moral (Tsevat 1966). The God whom Job worships and accuses of injustice transcends morality. Consequently, this book does not present a comforting deity nor a particularly accommodating universe. Perhaps that attitude is appropriate in an examination of the possibility of disinterested goodness. Nevertheless, the evocative power of this book "crashes into the abyss of radical aloneness" (Susman 1969) and arouses high praise in many readers, for example: "Here, in our view, is the most sublime monument in literature, not only of written language, nor of philosophy and poetry, but the most sublime monument of the human soul. Here is the great eternal drama with three actors who embody everything: but what actors! God, humankind, and Destiny" (Alphonse de Lamartine, cited in Hausen 1972, 145).

Bibliography

Alonso-Schökel, L.
    1977   "Toward a Dramatic Reading of the Book of Job." *Semeia* 7: 45-59.
Aufrecht, W. E., ed.
    1985   *Studies in the Book of Job*. SRSup 16. Waterloo, Ontario.
Barr, J.
    1971–1972   "The Book of Job and Its Modern Interpreters." *BJRL* 54:28-46.
Ceresko, A. R.
    1980   *Job in the Light of Northwest Semitic*. Rome.
Clines, D. J. A.
    1989   "Job." In *The Books of the Bible*, ed. B. W. Anderson, 181-201. New York.
Crenshaw, James L.
    1981   *Old Testament Wisdom*. Atlanta.
    1983   (editor) *Theodicy in the Old Testament*. Philadelphia and London.
    1984   *A Whirlpool of Torment*. Philadelphia.
Crossan, J. D., ed.
    1981   *The Book of Job and Ricoeur's Hermeneutics*. Semeia 19. Chico CA.
Curtis, J. B.
    1983   "On Job's Witness in Heaven." *JBL* 102:549-62.
Damico, A. and Yaffe, M. D. eds.
    1989   *Thomas Aquinas: The Literal Exposition on Job*. Atlanta.

Damon, S. F.
1966   *Blake's Job*. New York.
Dekker, H., ed.
1952   *Sermons from Job: John Calvin*. Grand Rapids.
Dick, M. B.
1979   "The Legal Metaphor in Job 31." *CBQ* 41:37-50.
Duquoc, C., and C. Floristan, eds.
1983   *Job and the Silence of God*. Concilium 169. New York.
Fohrer, G.
1963   *Das Buch Hiob*. KAT 16. Gütersloh: Gütersloher Verlagshaus Gerd Mohn.
1983   *Studien zum Buche Hiob (1956–1979)*. BZAW 159. Berlin and New York.
Fox, M. V.
1986   "Egyptian Onomastica and Biblical Wisdom." *VT* 36:302-10.
Freedman, D. N.
1968   "The Elihu Speeches in the Book of Job." *HTR* 61:51-59.
1968   "The Structure of Job 3." *Bib* 49:503-508.
Gese, H.
1958   *Lehre und Wirklichkeit in der Alten Weisheit*. Tübingen.
Girard, R.
1987   *Job: The Victim of His People*. Stanford.
Glatzer, N. N.
1966   "The Book of Job and Its Interpreters." In *Biblical Motifs*, ed. A. Altmann, 197-220. Cambridge MA.
1969   (editor) *The Dimensions of Job*. New York.
Good, E. M.
1988   "Job." *HBC* 407-32.
Goodman, L. E., trans.
1988   *The Book of Theodicy. Translation and Commentary on the Book of Job by Saadiah Ben Joseph Al-Fayyumi*. New Haven.
Gordis, R.
1978   *The Book of Job*. New York.
Guillaume, A.
1968   *Studies in the Book of Job, with a New Translation*. Leiden.
Gutiérrez, G.
1987   *On Job: God Talk and the Suffering of the Innocent*. Maryknoll NY.
Habel, N. C.
1985   *The Book of Job*. Philadelphia.
Hausen, A.
1972   *Hiob in der französischen Literatur*. Bern and Frankfurt.
Hempel, J.
1961   *Apoxysmata*. BZAW 81. Berlin.
Hurvitz, A.
1974   "The Date of the Prose Tale of Job Linguistically Reconsidered." *HTR* 67:17-34.
Janzen, J. G.
1985   *Job*. Atlanta.

Kahn, J. H.
    1975   *Job's Illness: Loss, Grief, and Integration*. Oxford.
Keel, O.
    1978   *Jahwes Entgegnung an Ijob*. FRLANT 121. Göttingen.
Kegler, J.
    1977   "Hauptlinien der Hiobforschung seit 1956." In C. Westermann, *Der Aufbau des Buches Hiob*, 9-25. Stuttgart.
Kubina, V.
    1979   *Die Gottesreden im Buche Hiob*. FTS 115. Freiburg.
Leveque, J.
    1970   *Job et son Dieu*. Paris.
Matenko, P.
    1968   *Two Studies in Yiddish Culture*. Leiden.
Mettinger, T. N. D.
    1988   *In Search of God*. Philadelphia.
Michel, W. L.
    1987   *Job in the Light of Northwest Semitic*. Volume 1. BeO 42. Rome.
Muenchow, C.
    1989   "Dust and Dirt in Job 42:6." *JBL* 108:597-611.
Müller, H. P.
    1970   *Hiob und seine Freunde*. Zurich.
    1977   "Alt und Nues zum Buch Hiob." *EvT* 37:284-304.
    1978   *Das Hiobproblem*. Darmstadt.
Oorschot, J. V.
    1987   *Gott als Grenze*. BZAW 170. Berlin and New York.
Ploeg, J. P. M. van der, and A. S. van der Woude, eds.
    1972   *Le Targum de Job de la Grotte XI de Qumran*. Leiden.
Pope. M.
    1973   *Job*. AB 15. Garden City NY: Doubleday.
Rad, Gerhard von
    1972   *Wisdom in Israel*. Nashville.
Roberts, J. J. M.
    1977   "Job and the Israelite Tradition." *ZAW* 89:107-14.
Rouillard, P.
    1983   "The Figure of Job in the Liturgy: Indignation, Resignation, or Silence?" In *Job and the Silence of God*, ed. C. Duquoc and C. Floristan, 8-12. Concilium 169. New York.
Sanders, P. S., ed.
    1968   *Twentieth Century Interpretations of the Book of Job*. Englewood Cliffs NJ.
Sarna, N. M.
    1957   "Epic Substratum in the Prose of Job." *JBL* 76:13-25.
Schmid, H. H.
    1966   *Wesen und Geschichte der Weisheit*. BZAW 101. Berlin.
Schmidt, L.
    1976   *De Deo*. BZAW 143. Berlin.
Susman, M.
    1969   "God the Creator." In *The Dimensions of Job*, ed. Glatzer, 86-92. New York.

Terrien, S.
    1957   *Job: Poet of Existence.* Indianapolis.
    1965   "Quelques remarques sur les affinites de Job avec la Deutéro-Esaie." In
            Volume du Congres: Geneve, 1965, 295-310. VTSup 15. Leiden.
Tilley, T. W.
    1989   "God and the Silencing of Job." *Modern Theology* 5:257-70.
Tsevat, M.
    1966   "The Meaning of the Book of Job." *HUCA* 37:73-106.
Van Selms, A.
    1985   *Job.* Grand Rapids.
Vawter, B.
    1983   *Job and Jonah: Questioning the Hidden God.* New York.
Vermeylen, J.
    1986   *Job, ses Amis et son Dieu.* Leiden.
Weiss, M.
    1983   *The Story of Job's Beginning.* Jerusalem.
Westermann, C.
    1981   *The Structure of the Book of Job.* Philadelphia.
Whedbee, W.
    1970   "The Comedy of Job." *Semeia* 7:1-39.
Wilcox, J. T.
    1989   *The Bitterness of Job: A Philosophical Reading.* Ann Arbor.
Wilde, A. de
    1981   *Das Buch Hiob.* OTS 22. Leiden.
Zerafa, P. P.
    1978   *The Wisdom of God in the Book of Job.* Rome.
Zhitlowsky, C.
    1919   "Job and Faust." In *Two Studies in Yiddish Culture,* ed. P. Matenko, 75-162.
            Leiden.

28 (1992)

Job the Silent
or Job the Affirmer?

Job the Silent: A Study in Historical Counterpoint. By Bruce Zuckerman. New York: Oxford University Press, 1991. Pp. vii+294. Cloth, $29.95.

The decade of the 1990s has opened auspiciously for the interpretation of the Book of Job. Edwin Good's stimulating commentary *In Turns of Tempest* (Stanford: Stanford University Press, 1990) and Leo G. Perdue's *Wisdom in Revolt* (Sheffield: JSOT Press, 1991) have been complemented by Bruce Zuckerman's scintillating study of the biblical book in light of Shalom Spiegel's analysis of the Akedah tradition and Y. L. Perets's short story "Bontsye Shvayg."

Zuckerman understands the Book of Job as a parody combatting popular expectation of the resurrection of the righteous. He thinks such false hopes accompanied oral traditions about the hero Job as reflected in the prose framework to the poetry, just as Ugaritic legend undoubtedly, in his opinion, concluded with the resurrection of the murdered Aqhat. The biblical story of the sacrifice of Isaac in Genesis 22:1-19 provides the point of departure for this understanding of the Book of Job, particularly the final verse which implies Isaac was actually slain on the altar. Relying on postbiblical evidence that confirms the reality of speculation about Isaac's death at Abraham's hand, Zuckerman turns to a similar phenomenon in Yiddish literature, the popular story about Bontsye the Silent. Here too a much-loved story gave rise to an attempt to parody its teachings, but Perets's version quickly fell victim to historical circumstances, the pogroms in the 1880s and the Holocaust. As a result of the changed ethos, the strong mocking of popular piety in Perets's account was lost and in its place emerged a reinforcement of this piety. This denial of everything Perets hoped to achieve through well-placed signals in the text found expression in minor revisions of his story in translation.

Returning to the Book of Job, Zuckerman detects the same process at work. A popular legend about a patient Job who lost everything and received it all back again as reward for his patience under suffering so angered a brilliant poet that he wrote a scathing indictment of such wishful thinking. Drawing on traditional genres, particularly Dialogue and Appeal, and using the legal metaphor for a lawsuit, although in this instance astonishingly applied to God, the poet mocks popular beliefs about resurrection from the dead and turns the patient Job into Job the impatient. Here, too, historical events led to the gradual attenuation of the extreme views expressed by the poem.

This tampering with the original message occurred in several stages: first, the addition of the Elihu speeches in 32–37, the addition of the hymn about wisdom's hiddenness in 28, the disarray of the third cycle of speeches and the resulting attribution of traditional piety to Job, the addition of the Satan figure, and the changing of the friends' role; second, the legendary accretions that now appear in The Testament of Job and in the Qumran manuscript of Job, the changes within the LXX, and the Masoretic retouchings in the form of suspended nun, euphemisms, and minor textual alterations; third, the statement in the Epistle of James about the patience of Job, which influenced all later Christian views about the book and virtually erased the memory of the impatient Job of the poetry.

This alternating of theme and countertheme within the book and in later interpretation leads Zuckerman to use musical terminology to describe the situation as he sees it. Thus historical counterpoint and fugue become the categories through which he interprets the Book of Job. Zuckerman listens to the various themes and counterthemes, melodies and opposing melodies, that characterize the prose and poetry. In many ways his work reminds one of David Penchansky's examination of literary dissonance in the Book of Job (*The Betrayal of God* [Louisville: Westminster/John Knox, 1990]), although Penchansky employs literary categories rather than musical ones. One may also compare John T. Wilcox's use of philosophical categories to understand the book of Job (*The Bitterness of Job* [Ann Arbor: University of Michigan Press, 1989]).

The speculative nature of Zuckerman's enterprise is freely embraced, but that does not seem to have tempered his conclusions in many instances where caution would have been wise. His numerous assumptions should be laid out for readers to see. The ones to which I shall call attention below are the most dominant, although by no means do they represent a complete list.

Crucial to everything Zuckerman writes is the assumption that popular expectations of a resurrection characterized ancient religion. Evidence for this hope is meager, one might even say nonexistent. While I agree that the final verse in the story about the sacrifice of Isaac probably points to an earlier stage of the legend in which an actual sacrifice took place—on which I have written essays in *Soundings* and in *A Whirlpool of Torment* (Philadelphia: Fortress Press, 1984)—that Zuckerman overlooks, I think the speculation about the Akedah is considerably later than the account in Genesis and owes much to the burning issue of theodicy during the late Hellenistic period and the Roman era. I do not think the Job legend ever included a story about the resurrection of his children.

The author of this story has little if any interest in protecting God's reputation; the deaths of slaves and children merely serve to advance the plot, and the replacement of these children with others satisfies the author, for whom God does exactly as the deity pleases without thought of the moral implications. One could accuse the author responsible for the gloss about the Satan of a desire to provide a buffer between the cruel God of the story and the usual Yahwistic understanding of the deity as compassionate, but Zuckerman thinks of this effort to salvage God's reputation as late. Zuckerman observes that this belief in a resurrection characterized Canaanite myths as well, but the slight support he offers, a restoration of the agricultural season of fertility, is slender evidence for such an elaborate theory. The logic would compel him to conclude that Aqhat died and rose each year. Moreover, the reasons that produced competing traditions in Judaism, orthodoxy versus heterodoxy, are lacking within Canaanite literature, for there was no canonical version. The very idea of a sacred canon was a novel concept introduced by Judaism.

The assumption does not seem warranted that the reference in the Epistle of James to the patience of Job implies the existence of a variant tradition to the written one. Ancient wisdom literature often uses the verb "to hear" with reference to receiving written tradition, for example, the *Instruction of Ptahhotep*. It has long been recognized that the Epistle of James preserves maxims from the wisdom tradition, and therefore the use of "You have heard" probably recalls the written Book of Job. After all, few people possessed copies of the Bible in the early church. What they knew of the sacred story came from oral preaching and reading in the synagogues. Zuckerman admits that narrative rules the day, for people tend to believe narrators far more than poetic observations, which are by nature polyvalent. The Frame Narrative has the final word, and it extols a hero who affirms trust in the deity in all circumstances. Here I think Zuckerman's description of Job in the story as silent misses the point: Job is not silent like Bontsye but expresses complete trust in God who gives both good and evil.

One further point about the Epistle of James may be relevant here. Zuckerman tries to recreate the ethos within which this book was read, but in doing so he neglects the important interpreters who claim that an old Jewish moral treatise has been reworked into a Christian document by the addition of minor glosses. Even if they are wrong, the reference to the patience of Job in a Christian work strikes one as strange, for the mention of Jesus' patience in suffering would have been much more effective as an example for believers to follow.

Zuckerman's dependence on Hurvitz's relative dating of the prose and poetry of the Book of Job is not above criticism. In fact, Zuckerman acknowledges the difficulty inherent in this assumption, particularly the comparison of two different types of writing, but he relies on the fact that no such dramatic difference between prose and poetry exists elsewhere. Naturally, this opinion is subject to challenge. Hurvitz's conclusions may therefore not support Zuckerman's hypothesis. Given the probability of glosses within a given book, it is virtually impossible to determine the date the original was composed.

The examination of the legal metaphor within the Book of Job, which relies on the research of Sylvia Scholnick, is almost as crucial to the argument as is the assumption about the resurrection. Zuckerman states that the essence of biblical literature elsewhere affirms divine justice, but anyone who studies the problem of theodicy in the Hebrew Bible knows that such a claim cannot stand. One could almost say that the genius of the Bible is precisely the opposite, the freedom with which faithful people challenge God's actions and appeal to a higher justice than that manifest at the moment, which is precisely Job's tactic. Zuckerman's discussion of divine justice teems with difficulties, including among others an ambiguous use of the word "trial"; an assumption that human virtue obligates the deity; a belief that whatever the deity does is "just," for Power determines right; and an attempt to separate legal terminology from appeal, despite Jeremiah's clear combination of the two concepts in 12:1-6.

On at least two occasions Zuckerman writes that the criterion of literary worth governed the inclusion of the Book of Job in the canon, or stated another way, prevented its exclusion. I doubt those who introduced this book into the canon really thought about it as a venerable and consummate work of literature. We do not know what entered the minds of those who chose the contents of the canon, but I suspect that use and popularity were the main criteria. A consummate work of literature such as Second Esdras was excluded from the canon, its literary merit notwithstanding, although its language probably led to the decision to reject the book.

Like many critics, Zuckerman fails to see that the traditional view about a merciful deity does not characterize wisdom literature in the Bible, where a concept of reward and retribution reigns. In a world that rewards piety and punishes wickedness, divine mercy has little place. The pioneering work of Johannes Fichtner, *Die Altorientalische Weisheit in ihrer israelitische-jüdische Ausprägung* (Berlin: Walter de Gruyter, 1933) called attention to this anomaly and contrasted the biblical reticence about speaking of divine mercy in the wisdom literature with the more vocal Mesopotamian and Egyptian wisdom tradition. One can trace a growing willingness to ascribe mercy to the biblical deity in Ben Sira, where the concept becomes important because of rival Hellenistic teachings, adverse historical circumstances, and a theology of divine hiddenness.

The assumption that silence about Elihu within the epilogue indicates censure may not be justified, for the narrator certainly does not hesitate to express twice a narratorial view of Job's sinlessness. One would therefore expect this narrator to state exactly what the reader should think about Elihu too.

I wonder about Zuckerman's observation that a book is more dangerous if left outside the canon. To be sure, the Book of Job is now placed within a context that tempers its heterodoxy, but it seems to me that religious people could simply ignore works that do not comprise part of the canon, just as they ignored some noncanonical works. I doubt, therefore, that the Book of Job was included in the canon as a means of softening its effect on readers. Like Song of Songs, the Book of Job expressed some of the deepest sentiments of the people that could hardly be suppressed by officials without a popular clamor.

From this discussion of assumptions that underlie Zuckerman's interpretations of the Book of Job one can readily see how fragile the hypothesis is and how questionable the evidence in some instances must be. Nevertheless, Zuckerman is aware of most of the assumptions and offers strong reasons for choosing the path he does. The argument is tightly reasoned, the documentation thorough in most cases, and the judgments are balanced and fair. The result is a magnificent counterpoint to the traditional interpretation of the biblical Book of Job. In discussing Mesopotamian dialogues, Zuckerman does precisely what he observed as taking place within the history of the Bontsye Shvayg legend—he omits the punch line of the *Pessimistic Dialogue between a Master and His Slave*, thus distorting the conclusion. In doing so, he is sincerely wrong in the same way interpreters of Job err in assessing him.

Job the Silent offers so much food for thought that one could choose virtually any topic and comment positively and negatively on Zuckerman's treatment. The elaboration of Shalom Spiegel's *The Last Trial* (New York: Schocken, 1967) includes many important insights, and the discussion of Bontsye Shvayg is an exquisite example of attentiveness to the sociology of knowledge. Zuckerman's analysis of the historical events that affected the way Jews read the story must surely offer a model for scholarly study of biblical material. Unfortunately, the historical data are not sufficient for such an analysis of Job or any other book.

At times I think Zuckerman overlooks important alternative readings of the facts. For example, he objects that Bontsye Shvayg did not offer intercessory prayer for the hundred million suffering people on earth, but this censure ignores the fundamental character of suffering, the turning inward resulting from extreme pain and the threat to one's existence. Here a moment's reflection on the psychology of suffering would have provided some insight into the validity of the description of Bontsye the Silent. Zuckerman thinks God cannot be hauled into a court of justice because God is not a human being, which is certainly true, but at least one biblical author did not hesitate to use the metaphor "man of war" with reference to God. Surely the strong tradition of dissent in the Bible laid the foundation for pronouncing judgment on God when the offense justifies such action. Furthermore, the Hebrew text of Job 4:17 can legitimately be rendered, "Can a mortal be more just than God?" (cf. 40:8). Again, the claim that the Book of Job is the most death-oriented one in the Hebrew Bible may not stand, for Qoheleth probably surpasses this book in the stench of the tomb. Zuckerman's rejection of Egyptian imagery for Leviathan in favor of Canaanite ignores the powerful evidence provided by Othmar Keel for the mythological use of crocodile and hippopotamus.

Zuckerman remarks that the true purpose of the Book of Job—to counter the view that good people will be resurrected—has not been recognized in scholarly literature, but there may be a reason for that fact. The Book of Job may not have had such a purpose. A similar skepticism may be appropriate with regard to Zuckerman's thesis that paraody is the essence of the Poem. If the example of parody that he provides, Amos 5:18, is any indication, we should look for clear and obvious signs of this genre rather than the obscure ones Zuckerman detects. The nature of Amos' remarks can hardly be missed; that is not the case with the Poem. Zuckerman's further observation that the Poem examines the nature of God has much to commend it, as Tryggve N. D. Mettinger has discerned (*In Search of God* [Philadelphia: Fortress Press, 1988]).

A final thought. If the Poem is really a parody, Job's response in 42:5-6 requires considerably more analysis than occurs in Zuckerman's account of the matter. Of course, recent literary interpretations of these verses as irony support Zuckerman's thesis, but such an understanding of Job's response to the divine speeches is clearly open to objection.

Having registered these critical observations, I hasten to add that I found Zuckerman's treatment of Job one of the most stimulating books I have read in some time (in this respect, like Good's *In Turns of Tempest*). I recommend it highly as a possible, and in many ways plausible, reading of the book. Given the high quality of the scholarship, it is a pity that so many printing errors (I spotted twenty-four) and even grammatical mistakes managed to get into the final form of the book. In a volume that devotes such careful attention to extensive references, it is also disconcerting to find one of my essays attributed to the editor of the volume in which it appears.

29 (1993)

When Form and Content Clash: The Theology of Job 38:1–40:5

The first speech from the tempest presents Job—and all subsequent readers—with a fine example of the collision between literary form and its religious content.[1] One can hardly say that in this instance the medium is the message, for the singular function of theophany,[2] the bringing near of the one who until now has dwelt in concealment, clashes with the content of the speech, the shattering of every human illusion of occupying a special place in God's sight.[3] In examining this remarkable text, I shall address three issues: (1) the logic of the argument attributed to Yahweh; (2) the appropriateness of the subject matter in context; (3) and the theological significance of the divine speech, together with Job's response to it.

The Logic of the Argument

In his dispute with the three friends Job levels two fundamental charges against the God whom he has faithfully served. First, God fails to govern the universe prop-

---

[1]For a study of this phenomenon in the book of Proverbs, see my essay "Clanging Symbols," in *Justice and the Holy: Essays in Honor of Walter Harrelson*, ed. Douglas A. Knight and Peter J. Paris, 51-64 (Atlanta: Scholars Press, 1989).

[2]Perhaps this clash is built into the very essence of theophany in the ancient world, particularly because of its close association with natural phenomena and warrior ideology. On the one hand, the manifestation of awesome natural forces elicited terror in persons who witnessed a theophany. On the other hand, the martial imagery ordinarily implied that the deity had come to bestow assistance on the one favored by divine unveiling.

[3]Several interpreters have made this point, none quite so emphatically as Robert Gordis in *The Book of God and Man* (Chicago and London: University of Chicago Press, 1965) and, for popular consumption, David Neiman, *The Book of Job* (Jerusalem: Massada, 1972) who frequently writes about the human illusion of the central position.

erly, that is, in such a manner that virtuous people thrive and wicked individuals come to grief. Second, at the very least God is guilty of criminal negligence.[4]

By placing himself under an oath of innocence[5] and daring to state the dreadful content of individual punishments, Job hopes to compel God to appear in court and defend the divine conduct.[6] If Job is guilty, the curses will crush him, but if innocent, he will escape unscathed and the verdict of guilt will point in another direction. The onus will then fall on God's shoulders to prove divine innocence in the face of weighty evidence to the contrary. It thus appears that Job has seized the initiative and gained the upper hand in the debate.

That impression explains the disappointment often acknowledged over the speeches from the tempest. This discomfiture takes various forms. From a pastoral perspective, a verbose lecture on cosmogony, meteorology, and zoology seems strange comfort for one whose soul aches as a result of personal isolation and loss of family, possessions, and honor. From a legal perspective, the threefold interrogation—did you witness? do you know? are you able?—shifts the focus from the accused and transforms Job into the unfortunate object of calumny. From a literary perspective, the nature wisdom skirts the profound questions being explored, specifically "Does disinterested righteousness exist?" and "How can one explain undeserved suffering?"

In truth, the opening and closing references in the zoological section to the violent preying on weaker victims amount to bold admission that in the animal world the strong survive at the expense of the weak. The lioness and raven provide for their own; from aloft the hawk and vulture search for food so that their young may be gorged with blood. In this world "might makes right," if one may justifiably introduce the subject of justice at all. The implication that power alone lights up God's eyes can hardly escape Job's notice, but does that principle operate in the human realm too?

It would seem so, on the basis of the entire divine speech. Dismissing the previous debate (Job's? Elihu's?) with a flick of the hand, God orders Job to prepare for

---

[4]Tryggve N. D. Mettinger, *In Search of God* (Philadelphia: Fortress Press, 1988) 175-200, offers a recent assessment of these accusations and emphasizes the move from a hidden God (*Deus absconditus*) to a present one (*Deus praesens*). Norman Habel, *The Book of Job*, OTL (Philadelphia: Westminster Press, 1985) 528, writes: "Job's heroic faith has provoked the *deus absconditus* into becoming the *deus revelatus*, even before Sinai."

[5]Georg Fohrer, "The Righteous Man in Job 31," in *Essays in Old Testament Ethics*, ed. James L. Crenshaw and John T. Willis, 1-21 (New York: Ktav, 1974) underscores the complex manner in which the poet uses a wisdom form to suggest tension between the claim of inner purity and the presence of hybris as well.

[6]Various critics have stressed the legal metaphor in the book, most notably Heinz Richter, *Studien zu Hiob*, ThArb 11 (Berlin: Evangelische Verlagsanstalt, 1959) and Sylvia Huberman Scholnick, "The Meaning of מִשְׁפָּט in the Book of Job," *JBL* 101 (1982): 521-29, and "Lawsuit Drama in the Book of Job" (Ph.D. diss., Brandeis, 1975).

intellectual combat,[7] at the same time echoing Job's earlier curse on the day an announcement declared the birth of a boy (literally, גֶּבֶר, 3:3). The one who presumed to challenge the creator listens as God asks if he were present at the birth of land and sea, light and darkness (38:4-21). This evocation of certain features of the creation myth leaves virtually no room for chaos to exercise any threat whatever.[8] The emphasis falls on God's design and control over the elements. Job was not present when the creator laid earth's foundations, determined its dimensions, measured it exactly and set its cornerstone in place. Nothing is left to chance here, and festive celebration by a celestial choir accompanied the completion of the building.

Then God supervised the birth of the sea, mentioned here because this turbulent water symbolized chaos in ancient myth. After clothing its unruly waves in dense cloud, Yahweh restricts the sea's domain by a powerladen decree. Having secured the earth on its pillars, God moves on to single out light from darkness (Sheol), asking Job if he has ever commanded dawn to take hold of earth's fringes and to shake out the denizens of wickedness like vermin in a blanket[9] or if he has descended to the Underworld and learned the secrets of death and its realm.[10] The operative word here is certainly "power," but a subtle hint implies that God somehow attends to the problem of controlling wickedness, concentrated in nocturnal activity, and the suggestion of definite order in the universe moves far beyond mere hinting. The question about Job's ability to conquer evil advances by degrees as the speeches progress—from human wickedness to natural evil, symbolized by Behemoth, and supernatural evil, personified in Leviathan.[11]

Yahweh's references to cosmogony conclude with ironic mockery of Job's brief existence, then a shift to discussion of meteorology occurs (38:22-38). Here, too, a

---

[7]Cyrus Gordon understands the imagery differently. For him, Yahweh uses an allusion to belt wrestling (*HUCA* 23 [1950–1951]: 131-36).

[8]Jon D. Levenson, *Creation and the Persistence of Evil* (San Francisco: Harper & Row, 1988) discovers various degrees of opposition to Yahweh in the several accounts of creation within the Hebrew Bible and attempts to place these different traditions on a temporal continuum. All such efforts, however ingenious, are rendered dubious by the likelihood that the views derive from competing guardians of the tradition about creation, some of whom may have lived at the same time.

[9]The NEB (and REB) indicate the difficulty presented by this text, which may actually contain a reference to a constellation rather than to wickedness.

[10]Behind this allusion may rest a rich tradition about descent into the Underworld, one that is illuminated nicely by texts from Mesopotamia. We cannot be sure how much familiarity with this myth the author of Job had.

[11]This distinction between Behemoth and Leviathan may press the symbolism excessively. In any event, the restrained language encourages caution with respect to the necessity for talking about mythic creatures here. In my view, the animals are real, but they conjure up images of beasts from the realm of myth.

curious ambivalence surfaces, for Yahweh claims that hail is reserved for the time of warfare. Neither here nor in the earlier allusion to shaking wicked ones out of the horizon does one find any assurance based on the sort of calculating morality that permeates the arguments in the dispute. Furthermore, God emphasizes the impartiality of life-giving rain, which falls on terrain as yet undisturbed by human feet. Throughout this section, the imagery of generation and parturition seems to echo Job's earlier complaint about his own conception and birth.[12] Job's inability to command the constellations, order lightning to do his bidding, or channel the rain for his own ends merely underscores his utter helplessness in mastering the rules that govern the heavens.

The section on zoology restricts itself to wild animals, with the notable exception of the mighty war horse, which excites the Lord greatly. Besides the aforementioned violent creatures, the following beasts parade before Job in splendid formation: the mountain goat, the wild doe, the wild ass, the wild ox, the ostrich, the horse, the hippopotamus, the crocodile. Yahweh questions Job about the sexual habits of goat and deer, asking if he serves as midwife to them, and about the freedom of ass and ox, inquiring whether he can tame them for domestic service. The description of the ostrich draws on popular lore about its stupidity, curiously referring to God in the third person,[13] and affirming that God denies wisdom to this strange creature who can outrun horse and rider. The second divine speech continues this zoological description, turning first to the hippopotamus and concluding with the crocodile. At the outset, however, God challenges Job to accomplish a feat that even the deity seems to find daunting, namely abasing proud human beings.

The divine argument possesses a certain kind of logic, one suggested by the creation myth and by Job's radical attack on that event concentrated in his own birth. Cosmogony, meteorology, and zoology constitute the mythic liturgical tradition as seen in the Priestly account, while one searches the speeches in vain for the other creation tradition, the fashioning of men and women.[14] This missing datum is surely no accident, for the absence of any human being at creation gives resounding testimony to Job's littleness. In the whole speech God makes only a

---

[12]Robert Alter, *The Art of Biblical Poetry* (New York: Basic Books, 1985) 99. Alter's insights on the relationship between chap. 3 and the divine speeches are fresh and compelling.

[13]The same phenomenon occurs in more than one place where the Hebrew text alludes to the punishment of Sodom and Gomorrah. Although God is represented as the speaker, a shift takes place to refer to Elohim in the third person as instigator of the calamity (cf. Amos 4:11).

[14]Rainer Albertz, *Weltschöpfung und Menschenschöpfung: Untersucht bei Deuterojesaja, Hiob und in der Psalmen*, CalTM 3 (Stuttgart: Calwer, 1974) develops this distinction as it applies to the book of Job, while P. Doll, *Menschenschöpfung und Weltschöpfung in der alttestamentlichen Weisheit*, SBS 117 (Stuttgart: Katholisches Bibelwerk, 1985) extends the discussion to include Proverbs as well.

casual allusion to a rider astride a mighty steed. Still, Job could derive some comfort from the fact that he is being addressed by the creator, even though both the mode of speech and its content betray a spirit of mockery.[15]

Perhaps Job could also find solace in Yahweh's refusal to offer simple solutions to complex questions, for gain in access to life's mystery could only come at the expense of forgoing the condition of human existence. The most one can do is discover an analogous situation, to wit that suffering and evil belong in the category with the unknown and unknowable, like the origins of the universe and the marvelous instincts of creatures over whom human beings exercise no control. Moreover, Job could derive confidence from the assurance that God has created the world in a way that allows every creature to develop according to its nature,[16] although one's place in the pecking order would surely temper that confidence.

The Appropriateness of the Content

One expects that Lord to respond to Job's charges and to demonstrate their falsity, thus exonerating the deity. We remember, however, that the Prologue has Yahweh concede that the adversary has incited the Lord to strike out against a loyal servant without cause. Nevertheless, the divine speech will have none of this willingness to accept responsibility for Job's misery. Instead, Yahweh labels Job a faultfinder and accuses him of obscuring the divine design of things by ignorant talk. It appears that the prologue also prepares us for the possibility of two divine speeches, analogous to the twofold unfolding of calamity and Job's response to each affliction.[17] If this is correct, one may legitimately conclude that the two speeches address the two charges leveled at the deity.

---

[15]Gerhard von Rad, *Wisdom in Israel* (Nashville and New York: Abingdon, 1972) 225, writes: "All commentators find the divine speech highly scandalous, in so far as it bypasses completely Job's particular concerns, and because in it Yahweh in no way condescends to any kind of self-interpretation." Luis Alonso-Schökel, "God's Answer to Job," in *Job and the Silence of God*, ed. Christian Duquoc and Casiano Floristan (New York: Paulist, 1983) 45, cites interesting examples of comments by scandalized interpreters.

[16]According to L. E. Goodman, Saadiah explains the divine speeches in terms of three conceptual themes: (1) the pure grace of creation; (2) the constitution of natures in things; and (3) the provision of each creature with its own niche (*The Book of Theodicy*, YJS 25 [New Haven and London: Yale University, 1988]).

[17]On one reading of the book, Job's initial confession (1:21) gives way to one that contains considerable ambiguity (2:10). Similarly, the first response to the divine speeches expresses ambiguity (40:4-5) and the final one returns to the confessional stance (42:2-6). This neat *a b b' a'* pattern is broken by the presence of great uncertainty as to the meaning in the last words of Job.

Recent interpreters have emphasized the cogency of the two speeches as responses to Job's charges that the universe lacks order and that God is a criminal.[18] In their view, the first speech denies the accusation of criminality and the second speech addresses the matter of divine governance of things. The first argument is a subtle one; the Lord implies that the creator who watches over every creature and provides daily sustenance can scarcely be guilty of cruelty toward any living thing. If anything, this solicitous ruler actually deserves the title of "Bountiful Provider," for God dispenses largesse without regard to need or merit, indeed pours out precious rain on uninhabited soil.

It seems to me that this initial speech also addresses the charge that God presides over a chaotic world, for in describing the creation of the world Yahweh uses language of precise measurement, secure foundations, and cornerstones. The same point is made differently when Yahweh claims to have laid a statute on the sea, commandments on the morning, and ordinances on the heavens. In Yahweh's view, even the rain has channels and lightning has paths, while snow and hail are held in abeyance until their proper time.

Such language about Yahweh's complete control over the created order is every bit as effective in responding to the issue of a chaotic world as the second speech. There Yahweh launches an attack on Job, challenging him to overcome all human pride and to conquer all wickedness.

Are we to deduce from this description of things the slightest concession that Yahweh faces a task that even the sovereign creator finds to be at best difficult? If so, this monumental concession must be viewed in the light of the extraordinary ease with which the Lord overcomes the symbolic forces of evil, Behemoth and Leviathan. The choice of these two beasts can hardly be accidental, for their mythic role in the Egyptian worldview illuminates the description in chapters 40–41 wonderfully.[19] Even the forces of evil are subject to their creator's will, Yahweh insists, and mighty Behemoth enjoys special status because of temporal priority. Leviathan, too, stands as king over all proud creatures. Job's puny darts have bounced off the Lord like human missiles hurled at the powerful crocodile, who must surely symbolize deity in this context.[20]

It thus seems likely that the two divine speeches respond *after a fashion* to the two accusations Job has leveled against God, but the deity's silence with respect to

---

[18]Othmar Keel, *Jahwes Entgegnung an Ijob: Eine Deutung von Ijob 38–41 vor dem Hintergrund der Zeitgenossischen Bildkunst* (Göttingen: Vandenhoeck und Ruprecht, 1978) and Veronika Kubina, *Die Gottesreden im Buche Hiob* (Freiburg: Herder, 1979). The latter author's emphasis on the historical dimension of the divine speeches lacks persuasiveness.

[19]Keel, *Jahwes Entgegnung an Ijob.*

[20]John T. Wilcox, *The Bitterness of Job* (Ann Arbor: University of Michigan Press, 1989) thinks the speeches celebrate certain aspects of fertility religion, evoking in Job a renewed appreciation for the sexual. The evidence Wilcox adduces is not very convincing to me, especially the conclusions based on the names Job gives to his daughters.

the significant issues of the book other than the forensic ones strikes many readers as strange. In one sense the divine speeches utter sublime irrelevance, for they offer no insight into the fundamental existential dilemma confronting Job. What conceivable justification exists for human suffering, particularly undeserved suffering? More to the point, how should one respond to innocent suffering?

The author of the book has certainly shown little reticence about offering various traditional understandings of suffering, merited or otherwise: it comes as punishment for wickedness; as disciplinary warning; as a test intended to expose or to shape true character; as a means of purifying one's innermost being; it will vanish when God acts; it reveals hidden truth, human and divine. The poet's silence about suffering in the divine speeches probably amounts to an admission that none of these explanations satisfactorily unveils the mystery of suffering. If the poet, wisely, we think, refrained from offering a simple answer for ultimate mystery, that is still no reason for failing to offer guidelines on how human beings ought to respond during undeserved suffering.[21]

Perhaps the speeches and Job's reluctant responses do say something important with regard to the proper way to behave during suffering. The difficulty lies in the ambiguity of Job's responses. The first answer, forced on him by a persistent deity, emphasizes Job's insignificance, his lightweight status in competing in a heavy-weight arena. The use of an expression for smallness contrasts with the weightiness of the Lord,[22] but how should one understand the concession? If I am so worthless, what can I answer?[23] Because of my littleness, what shall I say? In other words, is this response tantamount to a refusal to concede the dispute? This reading actually paves the way for a second divine speech, which aims at eliciting a more acceptable response from Job.

Unfortunately, the second response continues the ambiguity of the first.[24] Does Job reject his legal claim, his attack on God, his God, himself, his repentance? Does he melt, abase himself, and derive comfort from his ritual acts? Or does Job maintain his rebellion to the end? What does he mean by dismissing all previous

---

[21]The contrast with the Mesopotamian "I Will Praise the Lord of Wisdom" is noteworthy, for this text emphasizes liturgical remedies for affliction, constituting the whole thing a paradigm of an answered lament.

[22]The Hebrew word קַלֹּתִי implies that Yahweh's speech has certainly impressed Job with his puny stature when compared with the mighty creator whose honor (כָּבוֹד), although challenged, was still heavy indeed.

[23]J. Gerald Janzen, *Job* (Atlanta: John Knox, 1985) 243, understands the opening word הֵן as "if" rather than "behold." Walter L. Michel, *Job in the Light of Northwest Semitic*, vol. 1, BeO 42 (Rome: Biblical Institute, 1987) 95, interprets 4:18 and probably 15:15 and 25:6 the same way (i.e., הֵן as "if").

[24]Charles Muenchow, "Dust and Dirt in Job 42:6," *JBL* 108 (1989): 597-611, endeavors to throw light on the difficult text by appealing to the sociocultural milieu in which the book was written.

experience of God as derivative in favor of immediate sight? We do not know the answers to these important questions. Thus far the text of the theophany has emphasized speech, remaining completely silent about the actual form which the poet imagines God to have assumed. Why, then, does Job give voice to such daring confession? Has his hope of vindication become reality? After all, he claims to have stood before God with impunity (13:16), indeed to have beheld deity and survived. If Job has been vindicated, his speech in 42:6 may properly signal final acquiescence, a willing surrender before divine majesty.

Subtle changes occur even when the two Joban responses and God's immediate challenge to Job that he offer an answer cite earlier language. At first Job is accused of obscuring (literally, "darkening") the design imposed on the universe by its creator (38:2), whereas later in the text God uses the image of concealing the divine plan of things (42:3). Even within the first divine speech, God's language varies when urging Job to respond. In 38:4 Yahweh orders him to declare if he knows "understanding," (בִּינָה), but 38:18 has "Declare if you know all of it" (כֻלָּה).

What about the question attributed to the adversary as the decisive issue under discussion: "Will anyone serve God for nothing in return?" The speeches from the storm ignore this question altogether. Does the poet assume that Job's confessions of trust and submission within the prose settle this matter once and for all time? That can hardly be true, for Job quickly alters that position in the dialogue. One could possibly interpret the divine speeches as indirect response to the question about disinterested righteousness. They imply that the abundance of divine favor, indeed its almost wasteful excess, leaves no room for human claims to serve God without thought of reward. Grace comes to all creatures in such superfluity that the matter of merit can find no place of entry.[25] Accordingly, all creatures owe their very existence to a generous deity. Such an understanding of the text presses it to the limit, particularly in light of what appears to be divine badgering of Job.

This point raises the issue of God's rhetoric. Often characterized as excessive, bombastic, nagging, and the like, this constant belittling of a hurting creature may reflect an educational setting, if the harsh treatment of students by their teachers in Mesopotamia and in Egypt permits one to assume that the author of Job knew this phenomenon and used his knowledge to good effect.[26] Furthermore, the choice of medium for the divine appearance seems especially cruel, given the earlier mention of a tempest in the prose.[27] Curiously, the breakthrough in the story about the theophany to Elijah on Mt. Horeb does not express itself within the sapiential resort

---

[25]This point occurs often in Saadiah's commentary on Job (*The Book of Theodicy*) esp. on 360, but also note Goodman's introductory comment on 37.

[26]On ancient pedagogy, see my essays entitled "Education in Ancient Israel," *JBL* 104 (1985): 601-15, and "The Acquisition of Knowledge in Israelite Wisdom Literature," *Word and World* 7 (1987): 245-52.

[27]The actual words differ, רוּחַ גְּדוֹלָה in 1:19, סְעָרָה in 38:1.

to revelation through a special appearance of the deity.[28] Must the poet convey the impression of power regardless of the consequences?

Although the interrogative form of the divine speeches reduces adult questions to the status of schoolroom exams, this choice of questioning has been called an essential veil for presenting ideas worthy of deity.[29] In prophetic literature the supposed enigmatic character of divine oracles functioned similarly to erect an imaginary wall between ordinary discourse and transcendent speech. This point can be pushed too far, for the hymnic passages in the dialogue and in Elihu's address closely resemble the divine speeches, and prophetic literature teems with oracular speech that makes no apology for attributing the views to God.

Perhaps the questioning form functions in yet another way—to shift the emphasis from Job's goodness to his knowledge. As long as the issue pertained to Job's virtue, no one could fault him, for in the prose even God bore witness to his singular character.[30] Therefore, the questions in Yahweh's speeches draw attention away from Job's exemplary conduct to his partial knowledge. Consequently, some interpreters take note of the fact that Job's flaw existed in the cognitive domain (e.g., Maimonides, Aquinas). In their view, he was a good man with only partial knowledge. After all, he does confess that he was ignorant prior to the divine revelation, which replaced rumor with firsthand experience. Such a way of formulating the discovery of fresh insight strikes one as peculiar in an ethos that normally highlighted hearing as the way new information was acquired.[31]

---

[28]If critics are right in assuming that wisdom literature normally limits itself to observable phenomena, this resort to theophany is astonishing, as is Eliphaz' earlier description. Perhaps it is better to acknowledge different forms of wisdom, in one of which present revelation plays a significant role. In another form, revelation took place at creation when the deity locked secrets of the universal order in the cosmos and left them there for human discovery at some subsequent time. In any event, one would expect sages to stress communication by means of an inner still voice rather than one associated with great commotion.

[29]Matitiahu Tsevat, "The Meaning of the Book of Job," in *Studies in Ancient Israelite Wisdom*, ed. James L. Crenshaw, 341-74 (New York: Ktav, 1976) insists that the solution to the book must have *intellectual* content. For him, the God who turns to Job is neither just nor unjust, but God. Why then does Job say, "My eye sees *you*"?

[30]Some literary critics would assert that an even more unimpeachable source, the omniscient narrator, attests to Job's purity (1:22; 2:10).

[31]The conclusion to Ptahhotep has a fine wordplay that develops this aural aspect of learning at great length, but the same emphasis on hearing occurs widely in wisdom literature where instruction often took the form of oral recitation.

Theological Significance of the Speeches

Interpreters have consistently seen the book of Job as a radical challenge of traditional views about the relationship between act and consequence.[32] They have not been quick to recognize that the divine speeches constitute an equally radical criticism of the anthropocentric presupposition of ancient sages.[33] Human hybris bursts before this rapturous celebration of a universe in which women and men play no role other than that of awestruck witness to grandeur and terror. On the one hand, Job challenges the view of God as benevolent creator, insisting that the deity is both malicious and hidden. On the other hand, the poet has Yahweh express genuine excitement over creatures who strike terror in humans. Job's parody of Psalm 8 pales in comparison with the Lord's virtual silence about humankind.

This revolutionary perspective occurs with amazing poetic restraint. We read simply, "Then Yahweh answered Job from the tempest" (38:1). No elaboration of Yahweh's appearance, no reference to accompanying seraphs or cherubs, no stress on the inadequacy of linguistic representation of deity can be found here. The poet does not even try to defend the use of a genre that belongs to liturgical traditions more readily than to sapiential ones. The language of theophany is reported in a matter of fact way; the extraordinary has become ordinary.[34] Such restraint contrasts sharply with the actual content of the divine speeches, where rhetorical flourish abounds.

Not only do the divine speeches demolish human pride. They also reveal a problem for what it is, a mystery.[35] The intellectual and religious quandary becomes even more perplexing after the divine input, for the partial answers that the poet exposes in the prose and dialogue have not taken into account the complexity of the universe as unveiled by its maker. In a sense, the poet has Yahweh announce the collapse of the sapiential enterprise,[36] for the human intellect cannot guarantee well-

---

[32]Lennart Boström, *The God of the Sages*, CB 29 (Lund: Almqvist and Wiksell, 1990) 90, characterizes the relationship as character-consequence rather than act-consequence.

[33]M. Sekine, "Schöpfung und Erlösung im Buche Hiob," *BZAW* 77 (1958): 213-23, emphasizes the manner in which the divine speeches take Job back to primordial times in order to actualize his redemption in the present.

[34]The effects, however, of this divine manifestation are far from ordinary, even if Job refuses to cower in fear before his accuser.

[35]Georg Fohrer, "Dialog und Kommunikation im Buche Hiob," in *Studien zum Buche Hiob (1956–1979)*, 135-46, BZAW 159 (Berlin and New York: Walter de Gruyter, 1983). Gustavo Gutiérrez, *On Job* (Maryknoll NY: Orbis, 1985) xviii, also thinks silence is central to the mystery of God, but the problem of the book, as he sees it, concerns proper speaking about God in suffering.

[36]Bruce Vawter, *Job and Jonah* (New York: Paulist, 1983) 86: "Wisdom, philosophy, in other words, is pronounced a dead end. . . . The God of the theophany of Job is a *deus absconditus* even more remote than the God on whom Job refused to call."

being in the kind of world that Yahweh parades before a chastened Job. Perhaps the introduction of a theophany into the book of Job functions to convey this awareness of wisdom's ultimate ineffectiveness. When confronted by a problem, the intellect knows almost no limit, but the situation changes drastically once mystery enters the picture. Problems are susceptible to solutions; mysteries can only be illuminated. We exercise control over problems, whereas mystery seizes us and generates in us a sense of wonder.

The claim that Yahweh speaks and resolves the book's intellectual probing poses a special kind of problem. For obvious reasons, religious people tend to grant more authority to the Lord's words than to mere human speech.[37] Naturally, the poet gave a privileged position to Yahweh for precisely this reason. What happens, however, when views attributed to God cause embarrassment of one kind or another? In this instance, Yahweh's description of the ostrich preserves folklore that does not coincide with actual reality. When this strange creature abandons her eggs—or her young—she does so to lure predators away from her brood. This point illustrates a fundamental problem associated with scripture, namely the tendency to confuse human words with divine communication.[38] That mistake worsens as a result of the literary fiction of divine speech.

Another problem about the book has immense theological significance. Job's responses to his calamities and to the speeches from the tempest use terribly ambiguous language. Does that fact suggest that human response to deity inevitably bears a doublesidedness? That, because life unfolds in such obscure fashion, men and women hedge their bets? Faced with one whose power can crush him in a second, does Job resort to verbal ambiguity and hope that Yahweh will fail to recognize the shady nuance?[39] The difficulty with this detection of irony in Job's response is that it ignores the sages' belief that God saw into the depths of human hearts. Such duplicity on Job's part would not have escaped Yahweh's sight, in the sages' view. Therefore, the ambiguity must result from poetic ineptness, which is unlikely, or it must function theologically to acknowledge that all divine-human encounter is cloaked in ambiguity. The very assertion that human beings enjoy such high status as addressees of transcendence is subject to counter claim or outright denial, hence the necessity for language that suggests the tenuousness of the situation.

---

[37]The search for the exact words of God in prophetic criticism of a recent era was undoubtedly fueled by such an assumption, as if removing all glosses placed one in the presence of authentic revelation.

[38]Red letter editions of the Bible foster this illusion that one has access to Jesus' actual speech, glossing over the fact that those words passed through extensive theological shaping at the hands of early Christian theologians.

[39]Some such assumption characterizes those interpreters who view Job's response as ironical, e.g., James G. Williams, "'You Have Not Spoken Truth of Me': Mystery and Irony in Job," *ZAW* 83 (1971): 231-55, and "Deciphering the Unspoken: The Theophany of Job," *HUCA* 49 (1978): 59-72.

This observation leads to a general point about the metaphorical nature of all theological discourse. As is well known, all language about God is necessarily symbolic; we use metaphors because we wish to describe the unknown in terms of the known. In the end, however, we succeed only in fashioning fragile stained-glass windows[40] through which we behold our own images of ultimate reality. No human being will ever know whether or not those images correspond with anything in the transcendent realm, for that certainty would require one to forfeit the condition of finitude.

Having said that, I hasten to add that the text depicts an ambiguous sovereign, one who can best be described by means of two metaphors, creator and warrior.[41] The first is obvious, the second less so. Yet the elusive references to the presence of recalcitrant forces in the world despite Yahweh's immense power justifies the adoption of the image of the Lord as one who continues to engage the forces of evil in combat.[42] Astonishingly, the traditional symbols of chaotic powers, Behemoth and Leviathan, seem to pose less of a threat than does human pride. In this ongoing battle, the Lord enlists Job's assistance,[43] but acknowledges that the task is beyond human achievement. Then does the text imply that eventual victory over evil will come through divine agency? Such an apocalyptic reading of the crucial verse (38:23) offers more hope than the text seems to suggest.

Indeed, the total impression left by reading the book of Job conveys little comfort. The God of the prologue yields to manipulation, and despite confidence in at least one exemplary human being acquiesces in a set of events that leaves havoc in its wake. What is more, this deity expresses no dismay over wanton destruction of life and property, although complaining about being incited to afflict a favorite servant without cause. The deity of the epilogue waxes hot against Job's three friends, who must surely have offered the best answers to Job's suffering that they could muster. Moreover, this God bestows favor on Job once more and replaces his lost children as if this action makes all things right. Even if this restoration of Job

---

[40]"God is above and beyond; the images and symbols should remain what they are: not solid prison walls, but the fragile stained-glass windows of transcendence." (Mettinger, *In Search of God*, 207).

[41]It may be more accurate to conflate these metaphors, for the imagery of battle is inherent to a full expression of the idea of creation.

[42]In the prolegomenon to my *Studies in Ancient Israelite Wisdom*, I call attention to the continuing conflict between God and chaos, a point that Levenson, *Creation and the Persistence of Evil*, skillfully develops.

[43]Perhaps this interpretation of God's challenge to Job bestows far more dignity on the human subject than the text allows, for the point certainly highlights Job's inability to overcome pride in himself or in others.

does not fall into the category of reward for something,[44] whether integrity or intercessory prayer, it has certainly struck many interpreters as odd.

The depiction of God in the poetry is equally troubling. The friend's understanding of God removes the deity from the human scene, save for terrifying moments, and separates mortals from their creator by a chasm so vast that human deeds count for nothing. Elihu's disciplinary God is a little more palatable, although in the end Elihu also envisions a supreme and remote being untouched by human frailty or accomplishments. At the other end of the spectrum, Job's God presents two faces,[45] malevolence and absence. Readers who expect the divine speeches to bring relief from this litany of undesirable divine attributes are disappointed. If anything, the portrayal of deity in the speeches increases the distance between human beings and their maker. This distancing takes place, paradoxically, despite a literary form that emphasizes incredible closeness. Here form and content clash, with the latter gaining supremacy. Must "the greater glory of God" always require a belittling of human beings?[46]

---

[44] Most interpreters have understood the restoration of Job as reward for faithfulness, which contrasts with the lying words of the three friends, according to the perspective articulated in the epilogue. One can conceivably view the restoration as further sign of divine munificence that does not take merit into account.

[45] Claus Westermann, "The Two Faces of Job," in *Job and the Silence of God*, 15-22, discusses the analogous contrasting descriptions of God's servant Job.

[46] For the theological elucidation of this point, see my introduction to *Theodicy in the Old Testament* (Philadelphia and London: Fortress Press and SPCK, 1983) 1-16. By taking the theophany as normative, we conclude with Wilcox that "the book as a whole is profoundly skeptical, agnostic; its message is largely a counsel of silence" (Wilcox, *The Bitterness of Job*, 122).

30 (1987)

The High Cost
of Preserving God's Honor

Mitchell's Job excuses a capricious God too easily and misconstrues the rhetoric of the divine speech.

The denial of death[1] and the impulse to exonerate the deity[2] pose the supreme intellectual challenge to every generation. The Book of Job exposes the integral link between the two facets of this existential dilemma. Its exquisite language has provoked such widely divergent responses as Blaise Pascal's gamble on behalf of a benevolent deity and Ernst Bloch's vehement denial of theism.

In Mitchell's view, however, the voice in the whirlwind ushers Job into a new dimension of reality where his eyes light up with joy inspired by the dance of death and life.[3] Engulfed in primal energy, Job recognizes the triviality of his quest for justice. Despite Mitchell's insights into the language of the biblical masterpiece, he misses its pathos. Divine perfidy and human suffering ought to evoke a loud outcry that can be heard above Job's enforced silence.

The Suffering of the Innocent

For millennia, students of life's mysteries have known that prosperity and adversity introduce tests into human lives that both disclose and shape character.

In the oldest myths of origins, even the gods encountered opposition, both during the initial creation of the universe and subsequently when representatives of chaos, superhuman and human, cavorted within restricted boundaries. Ancient Babylonians adapted a Sumerian myth describing mortal combat between the gods Marduk and Tiamat, which resulted in the creation of heaven and earth from the slain Tiamat and, as an afterthought, humans from the blood of her consort Kingu.

---

[1] Ernest Beeker, *The Denial of Death* (New York: The Free Press, 1973).

[2] James L. Crenshaw, ed., *Theodicy in the Old Testament* (Philadelphia and London: Fortress Press and SPCK, 1983). See also my textual studies on divine testing, *A Whirlpool of Torment* (Philadelphia: Fortress Press, 1984).

[3] *The Book of Job* (San Francisco: North Point Press, 1987).

Ugaritic texts celebrate a struggle between the Canaanite god Baal and his rivals Yam or Mot, and the Egyptian literature records a battle between the sun god Re and the nocturnal demon Apophis. Within the Hebrew Bible, echoes of the Babylonian myth resound in the priestly creation account of Genesis 1:1–2:4a. The continuing fight with agents of chaos forms the subject of poems in Psalms, Second Isaiah, and Job that extol Israel's God for domesticating these mythological creatures, identified as Rahab, Leviathan, Tannin, and Behemoth.

The outcome of this struggle assured law and order, a universe that operated on a principle of reward for virtue and punishment for vice. This conviction that goodness paid worthy dividends and that evil produced an unwelcome harvest became axiomatic throughout the ancient Near East. This step was taken subsequent to the shift in metaphors for the gods from natural images to personal ones, such as king and parent.[4] In Israel the several traditions—priestly, prophetic, sapiential, and apocalyptic—perpetuated the magical assumption that ultimately enthroned human beings and their wishes and needs. Such religion functioned to satisfy the desires of its devotees, as Ludwig Feuerbach perceived with extraordinary clarity. The heavenly adversary in the prologue to the Book of Job voiced the creed that all religious devotion arises from self-interest. The biblical aphorisms in Proverbs weave a fantasy world in which, with rare exceptions, right prevails over wrong, truth over deceit, goodness over evil.

The Deuteronomistic history (Joshua, Judges, Samuel, Kings) stands as a monumental defense of the claim that Israel's God acted justly in sending conquering armies against its citizens, burning the capital cities, and marching their survivors into exile far beyond the Jordan. An occasional psalmist, willfully blind, boasted that he had achieved wisdom with increased age but had never seen good people suffering deprivation of any sort (Psalm 37). Like their heavenly counterparts, rulers were thought to champion the cause of justice. A conservative ethos believed to be ordained by God thus reinforced the status quo. The goddess *Ma'at* guaranteed equity in Upper and Lower Egypt; Israel's personification of Wisdom relies heavily on this popular figure who held symbols of life and prosperity in her hands. These biblical sages also came perilously close to personifying evil as a seductress.

Defense of God's goodness is the subject of Eve's first words, provoked by a stinging accusation in question form, that the creator is really a despot. This same primeval story has a petulant God issue a solemn oath that chaos will never again threaten civilization. In the Middle Ages the rainbow's arc provoked the daring thought that God had aimed an arrow toward heaven.

My bow between you and me
In the firmament shall be.

---

[4]Thorkild Jacobsen, *The Treasures of Darkness* (New Haven and London: Yale University Press, 1976).

> The string is turned toward you
> And toward me is bent the bow,
> That such weather shall never show
> And this beheet I thee.[5]

This repentant deity tarries before Abraham long enough to listen to a stinging reminder that the judge of the whole world should practice justice. But the necessary ten righteous individuals were lacking in Sodom and Gomorrah; and in Jeremiah's day the city of Jerusalem could not even muster one just person. Although regretting the experiment that resulted in human beings whose evil disposition reigned supreme, Israel's God attempted to juggle election and justice, an impossible task even for a deity. The chosen people awaited a new heart and a different covenant, all the while proclaiming God's justice in the face of overwhelming evidence to the contrary. A seduced and raped Jeremiah voices sheer bafflement, but he prefaces his remarks with a lame acknowledgment that by the nature of things the deity is innocent of all charges.

Ethical monotheism only confounded the issue. A single deity kills and makes alive, bestows weal and woe. Implicit in election is teleology, the movement toward a future paradise. Those who were not chosen could anticipate no such golden moment in the sun, a source of anguish to sensitive souls like Ezra who uttered the unthinkable opinion that it would have been better if God had not created anyone rather than sentencing virtually everyone to perdition. The problem of evil gnawed at Ezra's insides and formulated an obsessive torrent of agonizing questions about divine justice.

Israel's effort to analyze the problem of evil encountered three fundamental expressions: moral, natural, and religious. The first, moral evil, points to the relational aspect of betrayal, rebellion, and deceit. Natural evil enforces the universal decree, "You must die," introducing overwhelming powers that wreak havoc in society: the germ, earthquakes, drought, and much more. Religious evil cloaks an inner perversion of the mind and heart, concealing idolatry and a pernicious disposition. The universal human nightmare, Auschwitz and Hiroshima, prefigured by the Lisbon earthquake in 1755 which resulted in a mass exodus of the clergy from the church, endures—the bomb, the hole in the ozone layer, famine, AIDS. Responsibility for evil in its various forms falls on human and divine shoulders, a fact implicit in the presence of the serpent in Eden and explicit in persistent stories about a God who hardened hearts and deceived prophets.

Suffering, a necessary by-product of evil, sometimes strikes the undeserving. Hence the essential problem occasioned by suffering is its unfair distribution, which chips away at the foundation of an orderly universe sustained by a benevolent creator. The special world of suffering causes its victims to imagine that their experience is unique. A heightened ego results, for pain focuses thoughts inward and the

---

[5]A medieval play entitled *Noah's Flood*.

self feels threatened by a formidable enemy. Isolation from the community follows, a sense of alienation in dispersion. A simultaneous drive toward a universal community takes place, for suffering spares no one. Aristocrat and commoner generate sympathy for each other precisely because both have felt pain and isolation.

A concentration of suffering often occurs, personal and social dimensions erupting in wholesale death from famine, disease, and war. Advances in technology revive the ancient threat of total annihilation, producing a society that cannot escape the ultimate Angst. In response to suffering, mental and physical, a special language evolved. Lyrical poetry laden with emotion employs hyperbole to cover the full range of feelings. Throughout Mesopotamia and Palestine, personal pronouns focused agony and ecstasy in laments. By selecting rare words and elemental expressions, these poets concentrated the individual outcry and announced to the heavens that the world had fallen out of kilter. At the same time, the elaborate choice of similes and metaphors underscored the poverty of adequate language to describe the misery wrought by hostile invasion.

How did the ancients cope when confronting suffering? Perhaps the earliest response sprang from a realistic observation that human beings cannot avoid evil conduct despite noble resolve. This concession was later articulated in Paul's powerful language: "For the good that I wish to do, I cannot, but I do the evil that I want to shun" (Rom. 7:14; the same idea occurs in the works of the Greek philosopher Epictetus and the Roman poet Ovid). Suffering therefore functioned as punishment for sin. The inadequacy of this view—forcefully underlined by Jesus' response to the question seeking to place blame on the blind man or his parents and by the aphorism about sun and rain striking good and evil alike—has not hastened its demise.

Parental discipline suggested another response to the presence of pain, inasmuch as God was worshiped as heavenly parent. A curious development of this insight issues from the mouths of Job's friends, who insist that the deity punishes special favorites. The same theme shocks Amos' audience: "You only have I chosen; therefore I will punish you for all your iniquities." The playwright Neil Simon attempted to modernize Job by capitalizing on this notion in God's Favorite.[6] Biblical precedent—the profoundly moving test of Abraham (Gen. 22:1-19), the artful prologue to the Book of Job,[7] and the Passion narrative—achieve heights that dwarf Simon's play.

Because suffering does not always bring death prematurely emphasis fell on its fleeting character. In some circles the hope rose that an era would soon dawn where pain and tears were altogether foreign. Delayed gratification did not destroy this hope, but a change took place. That hope became temporally and spatially separated from existenee on this earth. A distinction between the world to come and the present world pervaded apocalyptic thought, which flourished during times of oppres-

---

[6]Neil Simon, *God's Favorite* (New York: Random House, 1975).
[7]Meir Weiss, *The Story of Job's Beginning* (Jerusalem: The Magnes Press, 1983).

sion. Such extreme adversity provided the intellectual stimulus to think boldly, eventuating in a conviction that death did not utter the last word. In the next life wrongs would be rectified, for every hidden thing would be exposed to the light of day.

Another answer to suffering attacked the essential egocentricity engendered by pain. Enduring undeserved misery on behalf of others gave suffering a redemptive quality. The shocking death of the suffering servant in Isaiah (52:13–53:12) made sense only if understood as vicarious sacrifice. The same reasoning reconciled Jesus' innocence and violent death. Even guilty criminals possessed the possibility of transforming their execution into redemptive suffering that absolved their own guilt, according to Joshua 7:19 and subsequent rabbinic practice, which persists in muted form into modern times.

A single biblical psalm (73) combines two entirely irreconcilable concepts of suffering. For wicked persons both prosperity and adversity resemble images in a divine dream, hence are illusory. Those persons whose only desire finds fulfillment in divine presence discover to their utter surprise that the goodness of God has nothing to do with the proverbial carrot or stick. For these fortunate individuals, the touch of the divine hand endures as their portion, solid as rock.

The Book of Job

The concluding episode in the Book of Job explodes with revelation and mystery. Israel's God invariably concealed more than was disclosed at any one time. Other deities guarded their secret names lest they lose sovereignty to unscrupulous rivals. The Israelite God's self-revelation has this same caution, but the multiple possibilities for translating the Hebrew disclosure to Moses (Exod 3:14) suffice as a communicative act. For Job, the divine harangue exposed the absurdity of facing the sovereign of the universe in a court of justice. This is what Job recants, the persistent demand that the guilty deity stand trial for criminal activity. Nevertheless, the hope that extreme suffering may issue in revelatory insight superior by far to derivative tradition (hearsay) does not change the inevitable fact that mystery cloaks the seeing. After all, the divine speeches skirt the issue of innocent suffering altogether, producing what has been called sublime irrelevance.

A more radical view refuses to acknowledge any purpose to the misery that envelopes earthly existence, one characterized as utter futility and absurdity. The unknown author of Ecclesiastes transcends his own egocentrism momentarily when beholding the tears of hopeless victims for whom no comforter exists. In his view, however, the distant Despot remains indifferent to human misery, shedding no tears for the oppressed and generating no anger toward oppressors. This concept of deity has no place for a patient Lord who delays punishment in the hope that sinners will repent.

Such an extreme view of an indifferent deity contrasts sharply with other parts of the Hebrew Bible. These texts stress God's active involvement in suffering, which is not limited to the human sphere. This acknowledgement of divine pathos gives a whole new dimension to the problem of suffering, in effect rendering Mitchell's reading of Job's final insight trivial. The nature of life, its subjection to genesis and destruction, the harm inflicted by some persons on others, and the placing of the self at the center of the universe inflict pain on the Lord of Life. Just as some suffering ultimately triumphed over its human victims, Christians believe God embodied that agony at Calvary. The symbol of the resurrection moves beyond tragedy, affirming the dominion of God in the face of apparent defeat. An unfortunate by-product of this hope, the failure to face squarely the lack of any means to confirm this faith in the ultimate triumph of virtue, entices Christians to dodge the complexity of the problem symbolized by death.

For ancient Israel, death at the right time and in an appropriate manner evoked little consternation, in sharp contrast to the Gilgamesh Epic, whose hero determined to achieve immortality at any cost, only to fall victim to a serpent's appetite for the branch retrieved from the tree of life. Premature, violent death did disturb biblical women and men, but they drew a modicum of comfort from a concept of corporate solidarity. An ontological link spanned the centuries, assuring that each individual would survive through the social group. Popular thought extolled a miracle-working deity who occasionally restored a corpse to life, whereas more skeptical minds denied the possibility of return from Sheol (2 Sam 12:23). Still, the symbol of national resurrection fanned the flames of devotion as proclaimed by the prophets Hosea and Ezekiel. Dead bones can spring to life, they insisted. Eventually, the expectation of victory over death's sway became more than a symbol for Daniel (12:6) and the unknown author of Isaiah 26:19. An entirely different basis for survival entered the back door when the author of the Wisdom of Solomon endorsed the Greek notion of an immortal soul.

Mitchell's assessment of the Book of Job owes more to Eastern than to ancient Near Eastern religious concepts. His Nietzschean emphasis on a perspective that transcends human morals contrasts with a recent commentary on Job by a leading liberation theologian from Peru, Gustavo Gutiérrez.[8] In his view the book of Job addresses the question: how can we speak of God in the midst of suffering? Like Mitchell, Gutiérrez concedes that "utility is not the primary reason for God's action" since "the creative breath of God is inspired by beauty and joy."[9] But Gutiérrez thinks Job's fortunes began to change when he discovered the needs of his neighbors, a view already attributed to the rabbis on the basis of Job's intercession for his friends. Gutiérrez recognized the heart of the biblical book that "nothing, no human work however valuable, merits grace, for if it did, grace would cease to be grace."[10] But this insight did not impel him to a position that allows one to look on

---

[8]Gustavo Gutiérrez, *On Job* (Maryknoll NY: Orbis Books, 1987).
[9]Gutiérrez, *On Job*, 75.
[10]Gutiérrez, *On Job*, 88-89.

oppression without a sense of moral outrage. For Gutiérrez, "the work is written with a faith that has been drenched in tears and reddened by blood."[11]

Mitchell's anecdote about a Zen teacher who taught him that everything is a matter of perspective finds beautiful expression here.[12] Gutiérrez reads the Book of Job and endeavors to speak meaningfully of God even in the face of cruel poverty. Mitchell's post-Holocaust reading, however, summons victims to faith in a new kind of God, one indifferent to human notions of morality.[13]

I find many insights in Mitchell's introduction, although I am astonished at its dated and limited secondary resources, particularly in light of the explosion of literary activity dealing with wisdom literature during the last two decades.[14] These rich discussions of Job in its ancient setting render Mitchell's introduction uninformed and insular. The recent translation of Job by the Jewish Publication Society will undoubtedly weaken the impact of Mitchell's poetic rendering.[15]

Moreover, Mitchell's translation suffers from an attempt to reproduce an original poem without giving sufficient attention to its numerous stages and additions. Unfortunately, he operates on faulty principles of reconstruction. Anyone familiar with scholarly discussion of the various stages of the Book of Job[16] cannot be satisfied with what Mitchell has done. How can he justify the inclusion of Satan when the oldest form of the story lacked this character and viewed Job's wife as the antagonist? Why did Mitchell omit the narrator's comments about Job's sinfulness after successive temptations? How can he possibly drop the Elihu narratives (32–37) and the poem about wisdom's inaccessibility (28) from the book, granted their secondary nature? In short, what Book of Job is he translating? His rearranging of the text on the basis of modern logical progression reminds one of certain kinds of biblical scholarship done nearly fifty years ago.[17]

Mitchell emphasizes the special favor Job's three daughters enjoyed. It should be noted that the Testament of Job elevates the young women even more.[18]

---

[11]Gutiérrez, *On Job*, 14.

[12]Mitchell asked why fecal matter stank and was told that it tasted like candy to a fly.

[13]Mitchell writes: "It is an experience of the Sabbath vision: looking at reality, the world of starving children and nuclear menace, and recognizing that it is very *good*" (xxi). How differently Dostoevsky saw the problem of a child's suffering (*The Brothers Karamazov*)!

[14]James L. Crenshaw, *Old Testament Wisdom* (Atlanta and London: John Knox Press and SCM, 1981) and Gerhard von Rad, *Wisdom in Israel* (Nashville: Abingdon Press, 1973) provide comprehensive analyses.

[15]*The Book of Job* (Philadelphia: Jewish Publication Society of America 5740/1980).

[16]See J. Vermeylen, *Job, ses amis et son Dieu* (Leiden: E. J. Brill, 1986) and Hans-Peter Müller, *Das Hiobproblem* (Darmstadt: Wissenschaftliche Buchgesellschaft, 1978).

[17]The best example is Julian Morgenstern's "Amos Studies," *Hebrew Union College Annual* 32 (1961): 295-350.

[18]R. P. Spittler, "The Testament of Job," in *The Old Testament Pseudepigrapha*, vol. 1, ed. James Charlesworth, 829-68 (Garden City NY: Doubleday, 1983) 829-68.

Mitchell's failure to examine the Sumerian and Babylonian prototypes for the biblical book, as well as later developments in the Pseudepigrapha, leaves one wondering what he would have said about its literary form. What is the book—dispute, drama, dialogue, lament, lawsuit (see "The Book of Job—Its Place in Literature" in Book World's Commentary)? Is it tragic or comic, an issue that has evoked considerable recent discussion?[19] Do the divine speeches offer a parody on Israel's teachers, and does the book signal the bankruptcy of wisdom just as Jonah describes the demise of prophecy?[20] Is the dissonance resulting from juxtaposed prose and poetry intentional? Like Goethe's *Faust*, does the Book of Job suffer from bad faith at the end, refusing to face a world that does not reward virtue? Why is this hero of the sages a non-Jew, and why is wisdom not one of his four celebrated virtues? How can Job serve as a paradigm for everyone, when his virtue as described by God had no parallel in the ancient world? Surely the theme is more than the Jewish one,[21] for "the victim" is ubiquitous. And Job retains his integrity, so it is inaccurate to call him not upright (יָשָׁר) just because he was "pulled down into the dust by the gravity of his anguish."[22]

Some insights in Mitchell's introduction ring true. The biblical book teaches that virtue is its own reward and that a Shiva aspect of God, which Carl Jung developed extensively in *Answer to Job*,[23] offers "a healthy shock to those who believe in a moral God."[24] But Job's silence says more about his own effort to play God than about endorsing an amoral perspective.

Readers will find much in Mitchell's book to stimulate thought, and they will rejoice in his vibrant images. If he prompts them to think once more about the fundamental issue facing theism, that of disinterested righteousness, his work will not have been in vain. One hopes, however, that readers will not exonerate God so quickly, for that response to the Book of Job misses its agony and ecstasy. Evil's multiple expressions may very well appear differently from God's vantage point, but mere mortals must wrestle with anomie from their limited experience.[25]

For them, pain and evil are more than an optical illusion. If God is unmoved by human misery—as MacLeish implies with the words: "God does not love; he is,"[26] presumably an echo of the divine revelation to Moses in Exodus

---

[19]See Robert Polzin and David Robertson, eds., *Studies in the Book of Job* (Missoula MT: Scholars Press, 1977).

[20]Bruce Vawter, *Job and Jonah* (New York: Paulist Press, 1983)

[21]Mitchell, *The Book of Job*, vii.

[22]Mitchell, *The Book of Job*, xi.

[23]Carl Jung, *Answer to Job* (Cleveland/New York: World Publishing Company), 1954.

[24]Mitchell, *The Book of Job*, xxiv.

[25]Note the recent psychological interpretation of the book of Job by J. H. Kahn (*Job's Illness: Loss, Grief, and Integration* [Oxford: Pergamon Press, 1975]).

[26]Archibald MacLeish, *J.B.* (Boston: Houghton Mifflin Company, 1956). Sarah's response to J.B. recalls the superiority of humans at this point: "But we do (love). That's the wonder."

(3:14)—the pin has pricked a mighty bubble indeed. Then the lights in the heavens have truly gone out, and many voices in the Bible proclaiming divine pathos are silenced like Job.

31 (1977)

Job as Drama

The Twofold Search:
A Response to Luis Alonso Schökel

The attempt to understand the Book of Job in the light of Greek drama lacks persuasiveness. One looks in vain for action, except in the initial scene. For this reason others have emphasized the psychological drama unfolding upon the pages of the book.[1] Luis Alonso Schökel yields to this temptation, stressing an intellectual drama consisting of *passion* and *search*. Action of a different sort fills both the narrative and the dialogue. The intensity of feeling and scope of the quest justify the term drama, even if in a loose usage. I have no quarrel with an heuristic use of the category, insofar as it enriches our knowledge of a profound disputation.[2]

I would describe the "drama" quite differently from Alonso Schökel's suggestive delineation of plot and action. In my view the play consists of two acts running concurrently and performed on different stages. They accomplish the masking and unmasking of God. One act portrays Satan's search for disinterested righteousness. The other dramatizes Job's quest for the real character of God.[3] Both acts stand in tension with one another in literary form and content. This tension persists, whether viewed as drama or otherwise. The book's prose and poetry cannot be harmonized. Suspense fills the universe as the heavenly audience awaits the outcome of the two quests. At long last God, the director of the strange play, abandons the spectator role and assumes that of actor. Ironically, at that moment his mask vanishes, and Job sees God for who he is.

---

[1]Most recently Albert Cook. He characterizes the frame story as God's dramatization for Satan of Job's fidelity, and views the physical situation of the speakers as something approaching a scene. He writes: "The dung heap at Job's feet stages his despair, and the open universe surrounding all the speakers stages the cosmos, which keeps entering the dialogue, finally to dominate it" (9). Cook describes the ritual silence as staged contrast to the dialogues, and interprets God and Elihu as silent spectators who cross the line from audience to stagegroup.

[2]For my understanding of Job as a disputation, see Crenshaw 1970, 1974, and 1975.

[3]Johannes Hempel writes of "a personal struggle for the last truth about God."

The Masking of God

The initial act concerns the character of men and women. Satan, the divine CIA agent, inquires into human motivation: will anyone serve God for nothing? In his view, both God and creature are culpable. Humans serve God because it pays to do so; God, for his part, rewards virtue and punishes vice. Satan's creed, "all that a man has, even his religion, he will give up for his life," moves God to relinquish absolute sovereignty. To satisfy Satan's curiosity god sacrifices Job's well-being, together with the lives of countless others.

Disregarding the poetic dialogue, a cyclic structure emerges: God hedges in his loyal servant; Satan roots up the protective border; and God plants it again. From one perspective, that of the prose narrative, the play confirms Satan in his fundamental attack on God and humans. Obedience to God constitutes self-serving.

In the poetic dialogue Job does not entirely free himself from the charge of acquisitiveness. Even his desperate and defiant final act, courageous as it is, arises from a compulsion to clear his name. Job seeks vindication, his version of the highest good. Self interest gives birth to his titanic challenge of God. Satan's creed stands, despite Job's heroism.

Job's friends fare no better. They, too, live and breathe within a world operating on the principle of self-interest. Religious devotion capitalizes on the positive side of this governing principle. The friends act because they believe God will react. Job's wife, much maligned, gives voice to the same conviction. "Curse God and die." Do something heinous, she urges her husband, so God will punish you by sending relief in the form of death.

Conveniently removed from the scene of suffering, either as inflictor or as victim and commiserator, God wears his mask unperturbed. Others perform deeds, endure agony, cry out against heaven. Unmoved, God sits on his throne while others expose their identity.

The Unmasking of God

On a different stage the second act unmasks God. In it Job searches for God's real character. His quest to remove the divine mask contrasts with God's passive resistance. Narrator and poet contradict one another on the matter of divine character. Ambiguity reigns to the end, where God concedes the veracity of Job's accusations (see Williams) and the error inherent within pious confessions on the lips of Job's friends. Inner tension characterizes Job's thoughts, for his attack upon God presupposes what he denies at the same time. If the principle of retribution has become inoperative, Job's basis for complaint vanishes. God escapes culpability so long as the universe operates from caprice. Such a universe exists, according to Job's words themselves.

Additional tension surfaces within the dialogue. In rare nostalgic moments Job recalls the intimacy of a trusting relationship with God (10:12; 12:4). Astonishment abounds, therefore, when Job acquiesces to the divine charge of speaking without knowledge. Here Job insists that he has been speaking from derivative experience rather than from primary relationships. Where now is Job's integrity?

Job's quest for God's true identity exposes divine freedom as never before. The book's purpose, in my view, revolves around God's freedom. Indirectly it poses a test for the sages who gave birth to the play; does your world view reckon with gaps in the principle of retribution? For this reason I cannot accept Alonso Schökel's interpretation of the lawsuit as a force to which God was subject. Neither legal challenge nor, for that matter, ritual curse (contra Robertson and Good) possessed power over God. The fundamental point of the book leaves no room for divine necessity. Alonso Schökel's language echoes that of Job's friends: God *must* intervene.

In my view God cannot be forced to act, either by a curse or by a lawsuit. Furthermore, God does not *need* words. Instead, this divine eavesdropper performs his own drama of silence. When he ventures onto the main stage his performance constitutes sublime irrelevance. One recalls the profound observations recorded in Prov 26:4-5. Job's dilemma—or was it God's?—gave him no alternative. To answer a fool prevented arrogance on the latter's part, but it increased the number of fools by one. God's bombastic display satisfies no one. Alonso Schökel writes that assurance of retribution would provide no comfort to Job after his experience. True, but even that small comfort beats news that God acts capriciously, approaching the demonic. Such a God, like *J.B.*'s deity, hardly deserves a moment's reflection.

Job is not the only person hoisted on his own petard. The audience, both ancient and modern, fall victim to the view under attack. Reason sits upon the throne, and dogma stands in the shadows. Ancient spectators, at least, bristled at Job's extreme language and blasphemous behavior. To them Job's conduct earned rebuke. We applaud Job's words, for like him we pass judgment upon God. Divine freedom falls before our concept of equity. The play's purpose fails in this way, not in the audience's refusal to climb upon the stage.

The twofold drama accomplishes the unmasking of God. One wonders whether the quest was worth the effort. Job discovers the dreadful truth about God: that he acts with total disregard for human well being. If we limit our attention to Job, forgetting the other innocents sacrificed to prove a point, we cannot rest content with reconstituted dialogue. How can talking past one another qualify as dialogue? In essence divine silence gives way to human silence: Job clams up. Confronted with One whose sole concern is to abase the proud, Job acquiesces. In God's presence he counts for naught.

Job learned his lesson well. Henceforth he will not encroach upon God's territory. From this moment forward Job will never again doubt God's freedom to act as he chooses. What about God? Does he learn anything from the twofold search? We cannot be sure God profited at all, save in the eyes of Satan. In our weaker moments we think, like Job, that God regretted his experiment. Still, we have no evidence that God's eyes ever became moist with tears shed over his servant Job.

Here, too, we creatures discover the chasm between us and god. We read about Job and see ourselves in the hero, or the villain. We lack the power to remain untouched by the profundity of the drama. In this respect, Jung stumbled upon a valid intuition: the one who reads Job does so with passion. Both Alonso Schökel and I confess an inability to remain neutral when confronted with the book that must have shaken the very foundation of knowledge in ancient Israel.

Works Consulted

Cook, A.
    1968   *The Root of the Thing*. Bloomington: Indiana University Press.
Crenshaw, James
    1970   "Popular Questioning of the Justice of God in Ancient Israel." *ZAW* 82:380-95.
    1974   "Wisdom." In *Old Testament Form Criticism*, ed. John Hayes, 225-64. San Antonio: Trinity University Press.
    1975   *Studies in Ancient Israelite Wisdom*. New York: Ktav.
Good, Edwin M.
    1973   "Job and the Literary Task: A Response." *Soundings* 56:470-84.
Hempel, Johannes
    1938   "The Contents of the Literature." In *Record and Revelation*, ed. H. Wheeler Robinson. Oxford: Clarendon Press.
Kallen, H. M.
    1959   *The Book of Job as a Greek Tragedy*. New York: Hill and Wang.
Robertson, David
    1973   "The Book of Job: A Literary Study." *Soundings* 56:446-69.
Williams, James G.
    1971   "'You have not spoken truth of me': Mystery and Irony in Job." *ZAW* 83:231-55.

The editors have received from Professor Alonso Schökel a response to the above response. He writes:

When I say that God must speak, God must intervene, I am not making a theological statement—as the friends do—but a literary one: namely, that the dynamics of the play or work demand that the character God speak. Moreover, I do not equate the character of God in the Book of Job with the metaphysical reality we usually call God. References and referents are mediated by the work, and are not immediately there (cf. Paul Ricoeur, *La métaphore vive*). I hope that this note will clear me of the accusation of taking sides with Job's friends.

32 (1977)

In Search of Divine Presence

(Some Remarks Preliminary to a Theology of Wisdom)

The task envisioned in this essay is a modest one: to provide some preliminary observations about a theology of Israel's wisdom literature.[1] Any attempt to understand the theological perspective of canonical Hebrew wisdom[2] must take into account diverse materials within Proverbs, Job, and Qoheleth.[3] The several collections in

---

[1]Significant Studies in this area include Walter Zimmerli, "Ort und Grenze der Weisheit im Rahmen der alttestamentlichen Theologie," in *Les sagesses du Proche-Orient ancien* (Paris: Presses Universitaires de France, 1963) 121-37, ET: "The Place and Limit of the Wisdom in the Framework of the Old Testament Theology," *SJT* 17 (1964): 146-58, and in *Studies in Ancient Israelite Wisdom*, ed. James L. Crenshaw (New York: KTAV, 1976) 314-26; J. Coert Rylaarsdam, *Revelation in Jewish Wisdom Literature* (Chicago; University of Chicago Press, 1946); Lawrence E. Toombs, "O.T. Theology and the Wisdom Literature," *JBR* 23 (1955): 193-96; John F. Priest, "Where Is Wisdom to Be Placed?," *JAAR* 31 (1963): 275-82, = *Studies in Ancient Israelite Wisdom*, 281-88; Gerhard von Rad, *Old Testament Theology*, vol. 1 (New York: Harper & Row, 1962) 418-59; idem, *Wisdom in Israel* (Nashville: Abingdon, 1972); Horst Dietrich Preuss, "Erwägungen zum theologischen Ort alttestamentlicher Weisheitsliteratur," *EvT* 30 (1970): 393-417; "Alttestamentliche Weisheit in Christlicher Theologie?" in *Questions disputées d'Ancien Testament*, ed. C. Brekelmans, 165-81, BETL 33 (Belgique: J. Ducolot & Leuven University Press, 1974); J. Lévêque, "Le countrepoint théologique apporté par la réflexion sapientielle," in ibid, 183-202; Roland E. Murphy, "Wisdom and Yahwism," in *No Famine in the Land*, ed. James W. Flanagan and Anita Weisbrod Robinson, 117-26 (Missoula MT: Scholars Press, 1975). Unfortunately, Hans-Jürgen Hermisson's essay on wisdom theology, scheduled to appear in the Samuel Terrien *Festschrift*, is not yet available to me.

[2]Space does not permit discussion of Sirach and Wisdom of Solomon, in both of which one encounters wisdom in transition, to use the apt title of Johann Marböck's study of Ben Sira (*Weisheit im Wandel: Untersuchungen zur Weisheitstheologie bei Ben Sira*, BBB 37 [Bonn: Peter Hanstein Verlag, 1971]). On the change that wisdom underwent in these two books, see above all Johannes Fichtner, *Die altorientalische Weisheit in ihrer israelitisch-jüdischen Ausprägung*, BZAW 62 (Giessen: Töpelmann, 1933).

[3]We thus consciously exclude from this treatment the profoundly theological wisdom psalms. In addition, we have had to forego discussion of possible sapiential literature elsewhere within the Hebrew Bible, as well as comparable ancient Near Eastern texts.

Proverbs go their own ways, and individual proverbs within a single collection differ greatly from one another.[4] In addition, both Job[5] and Qoheleth[6] depart radically in form and content from these collected proverbs. On the other hand, all three biblical works share a common way of thinking[7] and belong to a single worldview[8] that we customarily label "wisdom."[9] A direct consequence grows out of this fact: a comprehensive unifying theme permeates all three books. It follows that a theology of wisdom must attend to three fundamental matters: the diverse traditions, the understanding of reality presupposed, and the unifying themes that set wisdom-thinking apart from all other theological reflection in ancient Israel.[10]

The Diverse Traditions

We shall begin the descriptive task with Proverbs. Inasmuch as the sages focused upon ordinary realities of daily existence,[11] such a starting point seems highly appropriate. The largest collection (10:1–22:16)[12] deals with a wide range of everyday situations. It passes judgment on various kinds of behavior, ranging from secret actions like bribery to open vilification of the poor. All conduct falls into one

---

[4]See Udo Skladny, *Die ältesten Spruchsammlungen in Israel* (Göttingen: Vandenhoeck & Ruprecht, 1962) and William McKane, *Proverbs*, OTL (Philadelphia: Westminster, 1970).

[5]Georg Fohrer, *Das Buch Hiob*, KAT 16 (Gütersloh: Gerd Mohn, 1963) and Marvin H. Pope, *Job*, AB 15 (Garden City NY: Doubleday, 1973) contain ample bibliography of pertinent secondary literature.

[6]H. W. Hertzberg, *Der Prediger*, KAT 17 (Gütersloh: Gerd Mohn, 1963); Robert Gordis, *Koheleth—the Man and His World* (New York: Schocken, 1968); Rudi Kroeber, *Der Prediger*, SQAW 13 (Berlin: Akademi Verlag, 1963); and Oswald Loretz, *Qoheleth und der Alte Orient* (Freiburg: Herder, 1964).

[7]Walther Zimmerli, "Zur Struktur der alttestamentlichen Weisheit," *ZAW* 51 (1933): 177-204, ET: in *Studies in Ancient Israelite Wisdom*, 175-209.

[8]For opposing interpretations, consult Hans Heinrich Schmid, *Wesen und Geschichte der Weisheit*, BZAW 101 (Berlin: Töpelmann, 1966) and Gerhard von Rad, "Some Aspects of the Old Testament Worldview," in *The Problem of the Hexateuch and Other Essays*, 144-65 (Edinburgh and London: Oliver & Boyd, 1966) and idem, *Wisdom in Israel*.

[9]R. N. Whybray has recently opted for an entirely different label (*The Intellectual Tradition in the Old Testament*, BZAW 135 [Berlin & New York: Walter de Gruyter, 1974]).

[10]*Studies in Ancient Israelite Wisdom*, 1-45, gives the author's analysis in three areas: relationship with other literature, forms, and structure. One may also wish to consult my "Wisdom in the OT," IDBSup (1976) 952-56.

[11]Perception of the extraordinary depths concealed within everyday occurrence did not preclude occasional flights of fantasy, during which Israel's sages reflected upon primordial creatures and remote regions of the universe.

[12]The heading of this collection reads simply "Solomonic Proverbs." Two additional collections are associated with Solomon (25–29; 1–9) but have fuller inscriptions ("These also are Solomonic Proverbs which the men of Hezekiah, King of Judah, copied" and "Proverbs of Solomon, son of David, King of Israel").

of two categories: wisdom or folly.[13] The stringency of the language describing fools gives the impression that everyone agrees on essential traits of the one who refuses to follow the sages' advice. Nevertheless, ambiguity remains. Riches do not always constitute good, nor does poverty necessarily represent divine disfavor. Scant fare with love is better than abundant food with hatred. Even wisdom does not always avail. Men and women make elaborate plans, but God shapes the courses of their lives.[14] He controls the outcome of less planned endeavors as well; the lot falls in the way God determines. Kings, too, are subject to his will; their lives are like streams in God's hands. His eyes cover the entire universe; how much more human hearts are wide open to God.[15]

Certain things can be depended upon without fail. Laziness and excessive sleep bring poverty, just as gossip and talkativeness lead to disgrace. Diligence lays in store for future times of hardship, and obedience brings honor and riches. God rewards virtue and punishes vice, although sometimes he delays both.[16] Pride eventuates in one's downfall, and deferred hope brings sickness. Anxiety accompanies folly, giving birth to shame and disgrace. Sages exercise control over their passions, restraining themselves in both joy and grief.[17] Passionate persons bring destruction, whereas those who control their temper prosper. Dissimulation may work in many instances, but God distinguishes between sacrifices offered by wicked people and those brought by devout persons.[18] Whoever uses false scales provokes God's anger, as do mockers of the poor. In ridiculing unfortunate victims of society, one curses their maker.

Moral growth does not come easily. Discipline, both human and divine, functions in a thoroughly positive manner. Children upon whom the whip has fallen

---

[13]T. Donald, "The Semantic Field of 'Folly' in Proverbs, Job, Psalms, and Ecclesiastes," *VT* 13 (1963): 285-92; R. B. Y. Scott, "Wise and Foolish, Righteous and Wicked," *VTS* 23 (1972): 146-65.

[14]Von Rad, *Wisdom in Israel*, 97-110 ("Limits of Wisdom").

[15]On this notion of God's watchful eye, see above all J. Fichtner, *Die altorientalische Weisheit in ihrer israelitisch-jüdischen Ausprägung*, 97-123 (esp. 117).

[16]See my essays entitled "Popular Questioning of the Justice of God in Ancient Israel," *ZAW* 82 (1970): 380-95, ET in *Studies in Ancient Israelite Wisdom*, 289-304; "The Problem of Theodicy in Sirach: On Human Bondage," *JBL* 94 (1975): 47-64; and "Theodicy," IDBSup 895-96—the first two of which are reprinted above.

[17]Self-control was so highly treasured in Egyptian wisdom that "the silent one" became a designation for the sage, whereas "passionate one" referred to his opposite. A similar phenomenon occurred in Israel, where we find a sharp contrast between one who has mastered his temper and a person given to uncontrollable anger.

[18]We lack clarity as to the sages' attitude to the cult. On this difficult problem, see Leo G. Perdue's Ph.D. diss. (Vanderbilt, 1975: *Wisdom and Cult*, scheduled to appear shortly in the SBL diss. series); von Rad, *Wisdom in Israel*, 186-89; and J. G. Snaith, "Ben Sira's Supposed Love of Liturgy," *VT* 25 (1975): 167-74.

often will honor their aged parents. Rebuke rather than praise bears fruit, resulting in gratitude and extended friendship. Through discipline one attains an honorable reputation and a lasting name. But propriety dictates that certain people not be whipped. Sages speak appropriate words for every occasion; they learn such an art through arduous self-discipline. Generous in word and deed, they prize integrity and loathe a lie. Particularly abhorrent is the person who practices deceitful body language, winking and bowing outwardly while inwardly planning mischief.

Life, the sage's most precious commodity, is God's gift to those who please him. Longevity, wealth, and honor accompany one who acquires a good wife, her husband's crown. Genuine fear of the Lord brings one to the fountain of life. An adulteress leads him in the opposite direction, as does wine in excess.

Another collection also attributed to Solomon, Proverbs 25–29, differs noticeably in form.[19] Nevertheless, it covers many of the same themes. The initial verse distinguishes between God's glory to conceal and the king's glory to search things out. In a sense this allusion to royalty seems an apt beginning, for the king plays a more prominent role in this collection.[20] In his presence one should practice proper restraint.

Considerable care has gone into the formulation of useful advice in various circumstances. One should not wear out his or her welcome at the home of a friend, nor speak flattering words freely. Wise persons observe the situation and discern the appropriate word for the moment. They do not sing songs to one whose heart is weighed down with sorrow. Knowledge about the power inherent within an apt word does not render one incapable of silence. There is a time for no response. Hidden love avails less, however, than open rebuke. Love directed to one's enemies reaps greater dividends than retaliation for wrongs. Just as one must impose strict controls on a desire for revenge, he or she must curb a ravenous appetite.

Many of the proverbs in this collection echo those in Proverbs 10:1–22:16. These bemoan the power of a contentious woman, warn against gossip, make fun of the sluggard who turns on his bed like a door on its hinges, admonish lustful men to avoid loose women, encourage humility, enjoin strict accuracy in reporting facts, and encourage free use of the rod in disciplining children. In addition, these proverbs recognize the powerful role "chance" plays in human endeavor, and urge reserve in planning for the future. Inasmuch as riches do not last forever, the sage looks to basics like sufficient lambs and goats to provide food and clothing.

Yet another collection appears in Proverbs 22:17–24:22. Connection with the Egyptian Instruction of Amenemope[21] attests to the international character of Israel's

---

[19]Note the antithetic parallelism in 10-15 especially.

[20]Even von Rad concedes that Israel's proverbs seldom reflect a court setting (*Wisdom in Israel*, 17).

[21]D. C. Simpson's convenient comparison of passages in Proverbs and Amenemope can be found in *ANET* 424. According to Walther Eichrodt, "Knowledge of Nature, and the

wisdom. The ethical tone of these sayings is distinctive. They advise against oppression of the poor who have no defense against injury and warn against removing ancient landmarks.[22] Widows, orphans, and the poor have the Lord as their redeemer; he weighs persons' hearts and keeps watch over their deeds.

Prudential morality also dominates these texts. Accordingly, they instruct aspiring courtiers[23] to watch their eating habits carefully in the presence of a ruler, and urge that one refuse to eat the food of a stingy host. These proverbs also encourage strict discipline of children, and warn against drunkenness by means of a singularly apt description of strong drink's power. Equally dangerous, the harlot constitutes a deep pit. Like a robber, she lies in wait and surprises her victim with calamity. Honor for parents, compassion for enemies, the fleeting quality of wealth, and punishment of the wicked widen the circle of these proverbs.

Several smaller collections highlight many of the themes already mentioned. Proverbs 24:23-34 touches upon the necessity of toil and the positive correlation between work and wealth. It also urges love for one's enemies, warns against partiality in judging, and recognizes the power of the right word in every situation. In Proverbs 30:1-9, a foreign skeptic laments his inability and ignorance.[24] He asks weighty questions about the foundation of the universe and travel between heaven and earth, and assumes that such questions defy answer. A believer appends a confession of faith, which is followed by a rebuke for adding to his words. The short collection ends with a profound prayer:[25] remove falsehood and lying from me, and give me neither poverty nor riches lest, having everything, I forget thee, or being in want, I steal.

Different in form from most of the proverbs already described, the brief collection of numerical proverbs in 30:10-33 calls attention to certain similarities in animal and human behavior. These proverbs deal with an insatiable lust, wondrous mystery (particularly eros), haughtiness, tiny creatures that accomplish much, and the striding of a self-important one. Perhaps the allusion to love's ecstasy prompted a picturesque depiction of an adulteress as one who eats, wipes her mouth, and says nonchalantly, "I have not erred."

---

moulding of the individual life, formed a bridge between Israel and the pagan world" (*Theology of the Old Testament*, vol. 2 [London: SCM; Philadelphia: Westminster, 1967]) 87.

[22]Some scholars substitute אַלְמָנָה for עוֹלָם in 23:10, largely on the basis of the parallel in Amenemope, but McKane remains unconvinced (*Proverbs*, 380). The presence of יְתוֹמִים (orphans) in this verse supports the emendation, in my view.

[23]W. L. Humphreys, "The Motif of the Wise Courtier in the Old Testament" (Ph.D. diss., Union Theological Seminary, 1970); George W. Coats, *From Canaan to Egypt*, CBQMS 4 (1976).

[24]Georg Sauer, *Die Sprüche Agurs*, BWANT n.f. 4 (Stuttgart: Kohlhammer, 1963).

[25]Prayer intrudes more and more into the sages' thought in Sirach and Wisdom of Solomon.

Another non-Israelite summarizes his mother's teachings in 31:1-9. The queen mother counseled Lemuel against squandering his strength with women, steered him away from strong drink, which suffices for condemned criminals and the impoverished, and urged him to give careful attention to his judicial function. There follows an acrostic on the ideal wife (31:10-31). A rare find, she basks in her children's and husband's praise for the honor and wealth she brings to her household.

The final collection (1–9) introduces a new tone and develops certain themes in altogether new ways. Here Dame Wisdom[26] and Madam Folly compete with one another for individuals' affections. Like a teacher, Dame Wisdom goes to the market places and proclaims her message. But she threatens those who ignore her in a manner highly reminiscent of prophetic utterances. Her students await a sumptuous banquet in a royal palace, and can rely on her for long life. Her opposite, Madam Folly, plies her trade like a common harlot, and destroys anyone who eats her "stolen bread" or drinks from her cistern.

Wisdom enjoyed preexistence, long before God created the universe. His precious delight, she rejoiced in his presence (and sang with the morning stars!) when God brought the earth into being. Given such a privileged status, Wisdom's summons and threat carry the weight of divine authority. Anyone who rejects her instruction invites death, but those who heed her words discover the tree of life. Upon their heads she places a garland, and pendants on their necks.

This collection reflects consciously on the task of the sage.[27] The goal of learning—wisdom, instruction, understanding, righteousness, justice, equity, prudence, discretion, hearing, learning, skill—has as its first principle the fear of the Lord. In short, wisdom consists of religious devotion.

Many themes in this collection correspond to those discussed in regard to the other entities. Here one finds warnings against laziness, jealousy, violence, going surety, and similar practices. Here, too, one discovers admonitions to honor God with one's substance and to keep the commandments, prizing wisdom above all else. Inasmuch as God beholds everything that transpires, the lamp of his gaze will illuminate all secret sins. Choice between the two ways faces everyone, and a wise person heeds sound advice. In addition, this collection contains a numerical proverb that develops the notion of body language in an unusual direction and advises sluggards to take lessons from ants.

When we move from Proverbs to Job and Qoheleth, we encounter many of these same themes in other forms. But essential differences stand out with considerably more prominence, partly because of the literary forms of each work.[28] These

---

[26]For the latest study, see Bernhard Lang, *Frau Weisheit* (Dusseldorf: Patmos-Verlag, 1975).

[27]Compare Sir 38:24–39:11, and somewhat differently, Wisd 7:17-22.

[28]For discussion of wisdom forms, see my essay "Wisdom" in *Old Testament Form Criticism*, ed. John H. Hayes, TUMSR 2 (San Antonio: Trinity University Press, 1974) 225-64.

singular religious struggles share a common spirit with Agur's scepticism and rare proverbs like 14:13 ("Even in laughter the heart is sad and the end of joy is grief"), but they stand in dialectic with views informed by the rich proverbial tradition we have described above.

The Book of Job consists of a prose framing-story into which a poetic dialogue has been inserted.[29] The old folk tale begins with a heavenly scene, which gives rise to events below. Challenged by the Satan to name one person who qualified for the award, "Disinterested Righteous One," God singled out his faithful servant Job and cast a decisive ballot in his favor. The Adversary's blows failed to deter Job in his integrity, and when his own wife urged a special kind of euthanasia, Job remained firm in his resolve to honor God in weal and woe. The epilogue tells how God rewarded Job for demonstrating disinterested righteousness: he hedged Job in once again with life's good things—children, wealth, honor, and long life.

The poetic dialogue presents a different Job, one who persisted in defending his own integrity even at God's expense.[30] Again and again, Job accused God of betraying him. God, not Job, has broken the bond that his servant cherished beyond description. Faithful in word and thought. Job refused to plead guilty: his integrity was at stake. Convinced that God attacked him as a personal enemy, Job struggled to understand this new face of God. His emotions plumbed the depths as he recalled past memories and contemplated present realities. Longingly, he reached out for hope in any form; in the end he recognized that death would speak the final word.[31] In desperation, Job uttered an oath of innocence[32] and thus hoped to secure God's judgment that he was not guilty.

Job's three friends used every argument available to them in an attempt to demonstrate his culpability. Honorable in their intention, they hoped to lead Job to knowledge and repentance. Unable to entertain such dreadful thoughts that God might confront his favored servant as an antagonist, these critics could not conceive of God as unjust. It follows that they must uncover Job's guilt, regardless of the strains such an effort imposed upon their friendship. In the end they rescued God at man's expense. Using hymnic material about God's grandeur, they emphasized the great gulf between God and humanity. Ultimately, they succeeded in removing man from the domain of divine concern.

Recognizing the inadequacy of such arguments, but fully persuaded that Job stood condemned, Elihu paraded onto the stage and offered his own "perfect knowl-

---

[29]Francis I. Andersen, *Job*, TynOTC (London: Inter-Varsity Press, 1976) 36-37, views the book as a unity and describes it as narrative with poetic dialogue.

[30]Roger N. Carstensen, *Job, Defense of Honor* (Nashville: Abingdon, 1963).

[31]Samuel Terrien, *Job: Poet of Existence* (New York: Bobbs-Merrill, 1957) 40-65; and my forthcoming essay in the Samuel Terrien *Festschrift* ("The Shadow of Death in Qoheleth"—also repr. below).

[32]Georg Fohrer, "The Righteous Man in Job 31," in *Essays in Old Testament Ethics*, ed. J. L. Crenshaw and J. T. Willis, 1-22 (New York: Ktav, 1974).

edge." Once we have removed the verbiage, we find a cogent defense of the educative or disciplinary theory of suffering.[33] In addition, Elihu succeeded in relating man and God much more positively than the three friends had done.

The final participant in the debate had remained silent when under sharp attack by an angry Job, but deigned to set him right on one score: suffering cannot be construed in every instance as punishment for sin. The character of God's speech from the whirlwind, the source of destruction in the prose narrative, approaches confirmation of the friends' view that a human being counts for nothing in God's eyes. The arsenal of rhetorical questions forced Job to concede that he was not the center of things.[34] Indeed, the entire theophanic speech deals with the nonhuman world, as if God wanted to say that the universe can get along without people. Still, that would be a misreading of the facts, for God does condescend to talk with Job. Even the challenge to play God, if they can, places human beings above every single creature that God paraded before Job. In addition, Job's repentance, however interpreted, signifies a possibility of relationship that conceals wonderful promise.

The necessity for awe in divine presence fills the poem on wisdom's whereabouts in chapter 28. The poet expresses sheer wonder that men successfully enter the earth's core in search of precious minerals, but concedes that the quest for wisdom has invariably failed. Although the Underworld has heard a rumor about her, only God knows Wisdom's locality. Humans must content themselves with the fear of the Lord, which amounts to authentic wisdom.

Whereas Job wrestled with God strengthened by a hope that, like Jacob, he would acquire a blessing, Qoheleth possessed no such trust.[35] A single theme runs through his reflections from first to last: vanity of vanities, everything is vanity. All human effort was as counterproductive as chasing the wind. Convinced that nothing new presented itself to a weary generation, Qoheleth made a series of experiments that led him to hatred of life. He sought lasting value in pleasures of all kinds, from wines to women, as well as in work and fame. In each instance he found no profit, and came to view wisdom as only relatively superior to folly.

Unable to free himself from the ever-present stench of the tomb, he noted that human beings and beast meet a single fate. That death angel hardly made moral distinctions either, for justice could not be found. Oppression ran unchecked, and no one comforted the victims of cruelty. Quite the contrary, for upon their death wicked men received eulogies. In the face of such harsh reality, Qoheleth savored

---

[33]Jim Alvin Sanders, *Suffering as Divine Discipline in the Old Testament and Postbiblical Judaism* (Rochester NY: Colgate Rochester Divinity School, 1955).

[34]Robert Gordis, *The Book of God and Man* (Chicago: University of Chicago Press, 1965).

[35]Von Rad, *Wisdom in Israel*, 234 ("If he felt himself unprotected from events and 'vulnerable on every side' [Zimmerli], then this was not due to the greater sharpness of his gifts of observation but to a loss of trust").

light's sweetness[36] and counseled enjoyment of life's fleeting pleasures during the strength of youth. For a brief moment, he grasped the necessity of sociality, although unable to trust any woman and only one man in a thousand. Nevertheless, he accused God of concealing vital knowledge about the appropriate time for any single thing.[37] Still, he wished to avoid God's field of vision, and advised moderate behavior. Qoheleth's final description of death's power[38] stands as a compelling reason for remembering one's wife and grave, each reality tempering one's conduct magnificently.

Several proverbs strengthen Qoheleth's contention that the day of death is better than the hour of birth, and give voice to similar pessimistic thoughts. Others sparkle with humor, and scarcely advance the claim that everything, including wisdom, is vain. An epilogue places some distance between the editor and the traditions under consideration, and justifies Qoheleth's deeply religious gropings by summing up their impact as he sees it: fear God and keep his commandments.

The Sages' Worldview

Once we move beyond the descriptive task, we encounter the problem of interpreting these traditions in their own context. Viewed from one perspective, proverbial wisdom strikes one as very much concerned with "ordinary reality." We must not conclude from this focus upon common, everyday matters that such wisdom lacks a religious base. On the contrary, Johannes Fichtner did not overstate the case at all with his observation that "Religion is for the Israelite sages in no case only a peripheral matter, but the principal feature of wisdom, its heart; indeed more than that: wisdom is religion."[39]

The study of the totality of human experience aimed at a single target: to secure God's gift of life. Experience taught sages that life consisted of more than full bellies and barns, however important these may have been. They learned quickly that certain kinds of behavior hastened the day of death, and such knowledge introduced them to psychic stress. Life characterized by anxiety left something to be desired. Emphasis upon the quality of life led to an early recognition that divine favor made a decisive difference between authentic and inauthentic existence. Trust in human ability left no place for divine mercy in proverbial wisdom:[40] virtue sailed

---

[36]Kornelius H. Miskotte, *When the Gods Are Silent* (New York: Harper & Row, 1967) 450-60.

[37]For discussion of this difficult text, see my essay "The Eternal Gospel (Eccl 3:11)," in *Essays in Old Testament Ethics*, 23-55—also repr. below.

[38]See "The Shadow of Death in Qoheleth"—also repr. below.

[39]*Die altorientalische Weisheit in ihrer israelitisch-jüdischen Ausprägung*, 57.

[40]Rylaarsdam, *Revelation in Jewish Wisdom Literature*, 26, and often thereafter ("Mercy in God indicates a loss of human self-confidence about the capacity to discover and fulfill the demands of God," 65; "The Hebrew wisdom movement's recognition of human creaturehood conditioned it from the beginning to enter either the path of despair or the path of faith

into the harbor unmolested, and vice deserved and experienced inevitable shipwreck. On account of this amazing confidence in the inner harmony between the universe and its creator, these sages never decried a lack of divine compassion. Perhaps one could even say that the sages' scorn for fools arose from the same trust in human potential; since one can do what he or she chooses, the fool must wish to be morally bankrupt.

While proverbialists refused to rely upon divine compassion, they did catch a glimpse of the benefits to be derived from his presence. Although most proverbs subsume divine presence under other categories, the desire to relate God and humanity more directly gave birth to "mythological" reflection about Wisdom. Through her, God made his presence felt in the lives of his creatures, and in this way made known his great desire to communicate with humankind. In the person of Wisdom, the wise eventually forged a valuable link with prophetic revelation.

This acknowledgment of extraordinary concourse between God and humanity necessitated no demeaning of ordinary reality. All of creation was pregnant with meaning. The wise did not need to travel to heaven above or Sheol below to discover wisdom, for fragments of knowledge filled everything. They had only to open their eyes and search for God's mysteries, which willingly presented themselves to all who desired to learn. The whole universe became the scene of a marvelous game: God hid facets of knowledge under every nook and cranny, and human beings hunted excitedly for as many of them as time allowed.

Not all discoveries evoked ecstasy. Interspersed with the wondrous bits of truth were realities that most people prefer to avoid: murder, slander, lying, pride, laziness, and so forth. These, too, taught the sages to search within their own hearts and to ask serious questions about their innermost thoughts. As a consequence, they perceived the ambiguities of life. Riches may capture one's ultimate allegiance, knowledge may instill pride in the knower, and silence may imply consent or inability to think of a proper response. Such valuable insights enabled sages to make necessary distinctions and thus to penetrate beneath surface manifestations. In addition, awareness of limits imposed upon all knowledge equipped the wise for their biggest struggle of all, the fight to understand divine enmity and indifference.

Inasmuch as Israel's wisdom concentrated on the individual, it drew no solace from the age-old belief in corporate solidarity. In time, both the nation and individuals within it nullified the claim that justice inevitably triumphs. Far too often good people watched their hopes vanish in flames, and stood helplessly while cruelty overwhelmed innocent children. Others, however, watched from a safe

---

and disgrace," 75). It should be noted that H. Wheeler Robinson sees a great lacuna in wisdom theology: nowhere does it speak of regeneration of the heart (*Inspiration and Revelation in the Old Testament* [Oxford: Clarendon Press, 1946] 261). Similarly, Lawrence Toombs thinks the recognition of man's dependence on grace in Prov 2 opens a door by which wisdom may be brought into O.T. theology ("O.T. Theology and the Wisdom Literature," 196).

distance while base persons got what was coming to them; such onlookers found no reason to discard their fundamental faith in the order underlying the universe. Thus the stage was set for a battle that threatened to destroy the whole wisdom enterprise.

The Book of Job bears witness to the incredible harshness of this struggle. Fast friends stooped to personal vilification because neither willingly gave up cherished beliefs. Youth threw off restraint, claiming superior insight to gray haired ones. A distraught wife felt constrained to encourage her miserable husband to precipitate the death sentence.[41] More importantly, God deigned to reveal a face that inspired terror in one who had earlier dwelt in the shadow of his solicitous care, and innocent sons and daughters fell victims to fatal blows wielded, with God's express permission, by a member of his heavenly court.

In the book several understandings of God clash. None of them accords with Yahweh as he had come to be known and revered. The framing narrative depicts one who permits wanton destruction and incredible human torture for no apparent reason at all. A faithful servant stands over against a faithless God, and praises him in prosperity and in adversity. This God's unshakable faith in Job's integrity contrasts with the Satan's cynicism, but scarcely atones for the horror story he orchestrates.

Job's three friends cherished fixed faith more than a vital relationship with the living God. Their deity was a rational being, predictable and enslaved by a greater principle: justice. As Johannes Hempel saw with unusual clarity, two principles ruled the world, and the first was not God.[42] In such a system, the deity was reduced to the category of *reaction*. Without fail, suffering pointed to guilt, and extreme suffering, to heinous offense. No personal relationship with God created the illusion of human importance; instead, man's actions made little if any difference to God. Vast reaches of space separated God and humanity, and irreconcilable difference, too, in purity kept the two worlds apart. The creator of the universe had better things to attend to than puny earthlings. His commitment to justice did assure restoration, however, for the properly repentant individual. In the end, that commitment allowed no questioning of God's integrity even if that view were purchased at the expense of a great man's honor.

In his extreme misery, Job pushed beyond the philosophical question, "Why does God permit me to suffer?" to the bold formulation, "Why does he *make* me suffer these things?"[43] God, not suffering, had become problematic. Torn by the disparity between present reality and past memory, Job found it next to impossible to reconcile the two faces of God. Cherished recollection of divine favor in bygone

---

[41]For discussion of various traditions about Job's wife, see Hans-Peter Müller, *Hiob und seine Freunde*, ThStud 103 (Zurich: EZV Verlag, 1970) 17-21.

[42]"Das theologische Problem des Hiob," *ZST* 6 (1929): 621-89 = *Apoxysmata*, BZAW 81 (Berlin: Töpelmann, 1961) 114-73.

[43]Martin Buber, *The Prophetic Faith* (New York: Harper & Row, 1960) 187-97, esp. 189.

days rendered the present fury directed against him unintelligible. A single question burned itself into Job's poisoned mind: Is God for me or against me?[44] Intuition told him that no one had a claim on God, but reason insisted that God ruled the universe according to a principle of strict justice. Job's complaint lacked force unless the latter assumption held sway. Paradoxically, his attack on God destroyed the very ground on which he stood: nothing in Job's present experience confirmed a belief that God acted in a just manner.

Perhaps Job could have endured God's fury if it had not been followed by his withdrawal, which shut off all dialogue. Precisely at the moment of Job's most pressing need for answers, an eclipse of God took place. Faced with silence from his former dialogue partner, and confronted with empty words from human substitutes, Job adopted extreme measures of provocation.[45] The boldness of his charges against God arose from a single impulse: to evoke God's response at any cost. Confident that a sinner could not stand before God, Job believed that success in overcoming divine silence would constitute personal vindication.

God's self-image in the eyes of the poetic author of the book confirms none of the above views. Although he succumbed to Job's persistent attempts to discover the hidden face and provoke a word, any word, this Puppeteer put on quite a show. In essence, he forced Job to take a journey in uncharted terrain.[46] That lonely trip took him to realms devoid of human influence, and ultimately, to the beginning of time when primordial creatures cavorted before their maker. Such a journey exploded for all time Job's "illusion of the central position."[47] Henceforth, he would not judge God from a human standpoint, nor would he pretend superiority to his creator. Admittedly, God's response to Job ignored all his burning questions and offered no compelling answers to life's enigmas. Still, even such a rebuke is preferable to stony silence. Relationship has been restored, although infused now with weighty ambiguity. One marvels at the sheer honesty of the poet, who described life just as he saw it.

Consciousness of divine anger followed by oppressive silence was not the only problem confronting Israel's sages. In some ways another face of God caused considerably more consternation. That face signified indifference to the universe for which he was responsible. Before such a God one neither bowed in fear nor uttered praise; instead, one simply took advantage of every possible pleasure while stamina

---

[44]Von Rad, *Wisdom in Israel*, 221 ("What concerned Job above all else was the credibility of God. For this reason he was passionately concerned with the question, 'Yahweh pro me?'").

[45]David Robertson, "The Book of Job: A Literary Study," *Soundings* 56 (1973): 446-69; Edwin M. Good, "Job and the Literary Task: A Response," ibid., 470-84.

[46]Masao Sekine, "Schöpfung und Erlösung in Buche Hiob," *Von Ugarit nach Qumran*, BZAW 77 (Berlin: Töpelmann, 1958) 213-23.

[47]David Neiman, *The Book of Job* (Jerusalem: Massada, 1972).

persisted. Qoheleth experienced the religious bankruptcy of life emptied of trust in God.

Certain positive features accrue to an understanding of God as wholly indifferent to ordinary human endeavor, particularly when the alternative is the many-faceted God in the Book of Job. In the first place, God does not gird himself for battle against a favored devotee. Neither friend nor foe, God cannot be relied upon in time of distress, and he will not create hideous misery as a sort of test. Second, life coheres under an indifferent deity, especially if one avoids conduct that provokes humans to wrath. Third, God's indifference rested upon certain knowledge that the universe had been created with great care, so that everything was appropriate to its time. Hence, one could depend upon the cosmos; indeed, the universe was so reliable that it generated a sense of monotony in those who observed various phenomena. In addition, God gave prior approval to every human action, either by beholding it in his time before it actually took place, or simply by allowing it to occur at all.

On the other hand, such a view of God lacked essential ingredients that prompted Job to take his life in his hands and press to the very limit for restored discourse with his most treasured friend. Qoheleth's God concealed all important knowledge that would have permitted a sage to say and do the right thing in its time. Stinginess characterized this God in another matter as well: he withheld the "whole" of everything, granting only a tiny portion. Moreover, God held this tidbit in his own hands, condemning humankind to a life of dependency. Still, this dispenser of goodies did not see himself as a good shepherd over human beings. For that matter, human being and beast stood together in God's sight, just as they were felled by the same wielder of the scythe. Since this death angel made no distinction between good people and wicked ones, it followed that humans had no advantage over animals. It further followed that God did not govern the world justly. Small wonder that such a deity consigned humankind to extinction, for death spoke the final word for an indifferent God. Man returned to his eternal home, and God went blithely on his way.

The tortuous journey from full confidence in God and his universe to knowledge of God turned enemy, and ultimately to consciousness of an indifferent deity must have taken a heavy toll in human life. For some, it must surely have led to Agur's isolated tent. Like him, they lost all faith in God and in their own ability. Others divorced faith from reality altogether, and in that way salvaged a cherished creed. In assessing this spiritual trial through which the sages passed, we must guard against a chronological fallacy: the belief that the wise underwent three distinct eras corresponding to the understandings of God. While we can truthfully speak of a certain movement from one view to another, we must also acknowledge the probability that a single generation, indeed a lone individual, may have experienced all three phenomena.

Thematic Coherence

The bankruptcy of the usual approaches to Old Testament theology has long been recognized when applied to wisdom literature. Absence of weighty theological traditions such as the exodus, patriarchs, Mosaic revelation, Davidic covenant, and election of a people renders the customary rubrics pointless. In addition, the character of the wisdom corpus resists all attempts to impose Yahwism as the norm by which to assess its validity. Wisdom's diversity demands that multiple categories be employed; her integrity insists upon appropriate ones derived from wisdom's own world of thought.

Various attempts to discover fundamental unity have borne rich fruit. Four deserve special attention.

1. Wisdom Theology Is Creation Theology.

Walther Zimmerli's well known judgment that "Wisdom thinks resolutely within the framework of a theology of creation"[48] has seemed compelling to many interpreters. Based on wisdom's universalism, this thesis acknowledges the validity of torah's commission entrusted to humanity as articulated in Genesis 1. God sends human beings into the world to master it. The sage's attempt to establish order rests on prior divine command and reflects faith in the efficacy of human deeds. Accordingly, the sage appropriates God's blessings by going out into the world and establishing a society in which human relations reflect order. But this endeavor eventuates in extreme scepticism. Qoheleth considers the effort fruitless, "even a pain under a curse." Encountering the "reality of the creator more clearly than any other Israelite wise man before him," he views death as the force that robs everyone of the power of the whole creation.

Zimmerli's conclusion that creation functions as the pulse of sapiential thought arose from study of Proverbs and Qoheleth. Evidence from Job strengthens the thesis greatly, for the hymnic creation tradition punctuates the dialogue. Both Job and his friends reflect on the power of the Creator, and God directs Job's attention to the wonders of the created order. In this stance, appropriation of the divine blessing has become problematic.

Predictably, such emphasis upon creation and wisdom thinking prompted interpreters to attribute the creation accounts in Genesis to Israel's sages.[49] In this way,

---

[48]"The Place and Limit of the Wisdom in the Framework of the Old Testament Theology," 148; but note the minimal role of this theme in *Grundriss der alttestamentlichen Theologie*, ThW 3 (Stuttgart: Kohlhammer, 1972) 136-46, and "Erwägungen zur Gestalt einer alttestamentlichen Theologie," *Studien zur alttestamentlichen Theologie und Prophetie*, TBü 51 (München: Kaiser, 1974) 27-54, esp. 46-51.

[49]Most importantly, Luis Alonso-Schökel, "Sapiential and Covenant Themes in Genesis 2–3," *TD* 13 (1965): 3-10 = in *Studies in Ancient Israelite Wisdom*, 468-80.

wisdom acquired actual narratives describing the process of creation, which was otherwise only presupposed. Certain linguistic features in the Genesis stories gave plausibility to the claim of sapiential origin, and the universality of the accounts hardly belonged to sacred traditions about an elected people.

Emphasis upon universal features of wisdom tended to minimize the significance of unique features of Yahwism. Reaction arose in defense of special revelation. Horst Dietrich Preuss[50] rejected Israel's wisdom in toto, labeling the whole enterprise paganism. In his view, wisdom represents a human effort to generate its own salvation. Such an endeavor makes mockery of God's revelation in Jesus Christ, he thinks, for it deceives men and women into thinking salvation results from their own deeds. Preuss objects to the emphasis upon creation on the grounds that all peoples have creation stories. Since Israel shares her creation theology with other nations, one searches these narratives in vain for special revelation. It follows, in Preuss's view, that wisdom creation theology is doubly pagan.

2. Wisdom Thinking Is a Search for Order.

Hans Heinrich Schmid[51] proposed an alternative theory without discarding the prominence of creation: wisdom's goal is the establishing of order, both cosmic and social. Deriving his cue from the Egyptian concept of Maat, variously translated as order or justice, Schmid viewed creation as the divine establishing of primeval order, which humans reconstituted through the appropriate deed at the right moment. In such a universe ethical conduct possesses cosmic significance. The goal of wisdom, it followed, was the discovery of the hidden order established in the beginning, and the resultant harmonizing of one's life with that order.

In Schmid's view, this way of thinking gave rise to an intellectual crisis throughout the ancient world. Earlier trust in the order of the cosmos gave way, and solidified into a dogma devoid of reality. Eventually, piety prevailed, and God intervened between the order established originally and human appropriation of reward or punishment. Self-reliance faded away more and more, while dependence upon divine mercy gained ground. Such movement away from trust in the order of things in the direction of distrust characterizes Israel's sages as well, where pathos swells to the bursting point because of the character of Israel's deity.

Schmid went one step further. He linked together creation and order as two aspects of a single problem.[52] Subsuming cosmic, political, and social order as a unity within the notion of creation, he argued that creation provides the framework within which historical events occur. This means that creation is soteriological and,

---

[50]"Erwägungen zum theologischen Ort alttestamentlicher Weisheitsliteratur," and "Alttestamentliche Weisheit in Christlicher Theologie?"

[51]*Wesen und Geschichte der Weisheit.*

[52]"Schöpfung, Gerechtigkeit und Heil: 'Schöpfungstheologie' als Gesamthorizont biblischer Theologie," *ZTK* 70 (1973): 1-19.

further, that it is the essence and theme of biblical theology. Fundamentally, the theme of creation was the holy world, in other words, an all-encompassing justice.

My own research led in a similar direction independent of Schmid's conclusions.[53] Israel's sages do indeed relate creation and justice; the texts bear this claim out with striking force. But the emphasis falls upon divine justice instead of creation. It follows that creation functions in the sages' thoughts to undergird God's justice which came under attack with increasing vigor. Confronted with life's terrors that undercut belief in God's justice, the sages appealed to various features of creation faith in an effort to shelter God from brutal attack. This suggests that order, justice, righteousness rather than creation functions at the heart of wisdom thought. The fact that creation appears now and then in contexts of serenity[54] hardly alters this conclusion, for hymnic affirmation constitutes one major answer to the theodicy question.

3. Wisdom Is Trust in and Openness to the World.

Objecting to Schmid's emphasis on order as the imposition of scholarly dogma upon sapiential thought, Gerhard von Rad[55] sought to grasp Israel's wisdom in terms of remarkable trust in a world that addresses humans with a divine summons. In his opinion, faith freed knowledge to achieve incredible heights, while at the same time allowing for limits to all attempts to comprehend ultimate mystery. Von Rad exalts the concept of the fear of the Lord as fundamental to everything the sage says and does. In the end he understands wisdom as another form of Yahwism.

Others have seized upon individual themes put forth by von Rad, particularly those dealing with the goodness of creation. Walter Brueggemann[56] emphasized again and again human responsibility and God's willingness to trust his creatures. Objecting to theologians' heavy stress upon the grace of God and human inability to do good, Brueggemann sought to restore trust in humanity as a legitimate theological response. In his view, wisdom summons God's creatures to live up to their full potential upon the good earth. Because God trusts men and women, they can live fully, free to secure the cosmos in its political and social manifestations. Similarly, Roland Murphy[57] singled out the idea of openness to the world as a significant contribution of wisdom literature. Israel's sages believed that the world yielded many of its important secrets to those who asked apt questions. According to Murphy, the sages derived their openness from profound trust in Yahweh. In

---

[53] *Studies in Ancient Israelite Wisdom*, 26-35.

[54] Walter Brueggemann, review of *Studies in Ancient Israelite Wisdom*, *JBL* 95 (1976): 691.

[55] *Wisdom in Israel*.

[56] *In Man We Trust* (Richmond: John Knox, 1972).

[57] "The Hebrew Sage and Openness to the World," in *Christian Action and Openness to the World*, Villanova University Symposium II-III (1970) 219-44.

effect, sages were participants in the Yahwistic cult, although they never spoke about what everyone took for granted.

4. Wisdom Concerns the Cosmos and the Mystery of Human Beings.

J. Lévêque[58] has recently renewed the old comprehensive approach to wisdom in terms of two realities: the cosmos and human beings. But he introduces a useful term for relating Yahwism and wisdom, a perennial problem. According to Lévêque, the idea of counterpoint in music theory aids scholars in treating two entirely different phenomena. Just as one melody functions in counterpoint to the dominant one but retains its own integrity and contributes to the final musical composition, so wisdom and Yahwism together make glorious music.

Lévêque's actual discussion of Israel's wisdom relies heavily upon von Rad's *Wisdom in Israel*. Man's astonishing intellectual freedom never threatened the role of faith, for the fear of Yahweh prevented any elevation of human rationality. In addition, the world directed a message to human beings and taught them its limits. Faced with such obstacles to knowledge, men and women doubled their praise and acknowledged that they could only arrive at the fringes of God's wonders. In regard to humankind, the sages came up against an inner scandal: retribution. God held the reins, and phenomena were ambiguous. Revolt against limits imposed upon humans surfaced, particularly in Qoheleth.

Three themes stand out in Lévêque's discussion of humans: the ethical base, humanity's historicity, and the knowledge of God. Submission to reality was surrender to God. In short, God's will was effected in the cosmos. In time wisdom incorporated prophetic revelation into her thinking, and equated torah with wisdom. The sages focused on the individual in the world, that is, on ordinary events in life. In this connection Lévêque insists that the Israelite summoned to the covenant with Yahweh was also "everyday man." Lévêque's comments about the knowledge of God rise to great heights. He emphasizes Job's terrible negation of divine holiness, wisdom, and righteousness, and links this view with comparable texts outside the wisdom corpus. He concludes that every question about humanity is at heart a question about God.

5. Order Derives from Divine Presence.

To these four, I wish to add yet another perspective from which to view Israel's wisdom. Far from constituting the primary fact of life, order depends upon divine presence and favor. Where God and his will become manifest, life coheres. Order reigns in all human relationships that enjoy divine approval. Absence of God results in disorder, producing chaos. Failure to bring life into harmony with his purposes gives birth to alien designs, disharmony, and corruption. By studying all of life, one

---

[58]"Le countrepoint théologique apporté par la réflexion sapientielle," in *Questions disputées d'Ancien Testament*, ed. C. Brekelmans (see n. 1, above).

discovers rules for conduct. Certain actions generally assure God's blessing, while other actions result in frustration, infamy, or death. In time these lessons for living become valuable collections of learned traditions, legacies transmitted from one generation to the next. Only a hearing heart can appropriate such treasures; each lesson must be validated anew. As situations change, and motivations vanish because they were not specified, past legacies pose a very real danger: they tend to harden into dogma that stifles life.[59]

Life's ambiguities make it highly desirable, if not absolutely essential, to secure God's presence. By living in accord with the rules of the universe established at creation, one obtains God's presence. In addition, God comes to meet his creatures in Dame Wisdom. Human discovery and divine disclosure stand in a complementary relationship. But human discovery is grounded in God's prior action, for he wishes to make known the secrets of the universe, which in reality are divine mysteries. Observation of the natural order and human behavior leads to insight into the fundamental nature of reality. At that moment the essential unity of creation comes into view.

God's presence is not automatic, despite a desire to be known. Dame Wisdom calls, invites, celebrates with her guests, but she also threatens those who show no appreciation for her wares. She must compete with Madam Folly, whose power to destroy remains hidden until the last second. Unfortunately, those who treasure God's presence cannot count on continued blessing. Virtue does not always bring divine presence in its wake. Good people sometimes experience divine absence, however much they long for his presence. Such withdrawal may constitute a test, or it may defy explanation.

From this brief discussion of various attempts to unite the diverse streams within Israel's wisdom, one gains insight into the difficulty of the task facing modern interpreters. When one considers that this essay has concentrated on the descriptive task of what Israel's sages thought, that is, on *meaning back then*, it follows that a significant theological task remains: to translate that meaning into language that addresses people today. In my view, the fundamental link between then and now can be found in a search for divine presence. Creation, order, openness, cosmos, and humans—all pale alongside God's presence. Success in that perilous quest brings unspeakable joy and unbelievable agony. Failure brings—nothing.

---

[59]For analysis of this problem, see my "The Human Dilemma and Literature of Dissent," in *Tradition and Theology in the Old Testament*, ed. Douglas Knight (Philadelphia: Fortress Press, 1977).

33 (1992)

Ecclesiastes (Qoheleth)

Ecclesiastes (Qoheleth). One of the Five Megilloth (Scrolls), this biblical book characterizes life as utter futility, like shepherding or chasing the wind.

A. The Meaning of the Name
B. Literary Integrity
C. The Structure of the Book
D. The Historical Setting
E. The Literary Expression
F. Qoheleth's Teachings
G. The Larger Environment
H. Canonization
I. The Text

A. The Meaning of the Name

The Hebrew title of the book is "Qoheleth." "Qoheleth," from which the name "Ecclesiastes" derives, has been variously explained as a personal name, a nom de plume, an acronym, and a function. The difficulty of comprehending the meaning of the word "Qoheleth" is compounded by the fact that it seems to be understood differently within the book itself, where "Qoheleth" has the article at least once (12:8, although the same verse occurs in 1:2 where Qoheleth lacks the article). In all likelihood, the article also appears in 7:27, where "Qoheleth" has a feminine verb form, although the word "Qoheleth" is otherwise always construed as a masculine. The LXX supports a redivision of the consonants in 7:27, yielding אָמַר הַקֹּהֶלֶת ("says the Qoheleth"). The name occurs seven times:

1. The words of *Qoheleth*, son of David, King in Jerusalem. (1:1)
2. The ultimate absurdity, says *Qoheleth*, the ultimate absurdity; everything is absurd. (1:2)
3. I *Qoheleth* have been king over Israel in Jerusalem. (1:12)
4. Look, I have discovered this—says *Qoheleth*— adding one to one in order to find the sum. (7:27)
5. The ultimate absurdity, says the *Qoheleth*, everything is absurd. (12:8)
6. In addition to the fact that *Qoheleth* was a sage, he also taught the people knowledge. (12:9a-b)

7. *Qoheleth* sought to find pleasing words
and accurately wrote down trustworthy sayings. (12:10)

Although the word "Qoheleth" is understood as masculine, its form is qal feminine participle. Elsewhere the root קָהַל is always *Hip'il* or *Nip'al* (causative or reflexive/passive). It thus means "to convoke," "to assemble" (*Hip'il*) or "to be gathered" (*Nip'al*). Precedent exists for a masculine personal name with a feminine ending (Alameth, 1 Chr 7:8). This interpretation as a personal name clearly underlies the identification of Qoheleth as son of David, which occurs in the superscription to the book (1:1), but the idea of royal authorship ultimately derives from the book itself (1:12).

Three things weaken the argument for viewing "Qoheleth" as a personal name, a substitute for "Solomon": (1) the use of the article; (2) the identification of Qoheleth as a wise man (חָכָם), presumably a technical term in this instance (12:9); and (3) the point of view from which the book is written, except for the royal fiction in 1:12–2:26. Elsewhere the author writes from the perspective of a subject powerless to redress the injustices perpetrated by higher officials. Of course, an additional factor renders impossible the identification of Qoheleth with royalty: David did not have a son named Qoheleth who succeeded him, for Solomon occupied the throne after his father's health failed.

Then is "Qoheleth" a nickname for Solomon? The link between this unusual form and Solomon could easily have arisen from the language in 1 Kgs 8:1-12, which reports that the king assembled the representatives of the people to Jerusalem. But the initiative to look for such a suitable text must surely have sprung from the author's self-presentation in 1:12–2:26, for Solomon's vast wealth supplies the imagined context for the royal experiment described in these verses. As we shall see, the Egyptian royal testament offers a prototype for this section of the book, but Qoheleth was not content to restrict his sayings to this literary form. Conceivably, the allusion to one shepherd in 12:11 reverts to the royal fiction earlier abandoned by the author, inasmuch as the image of the pharaohs as shepherds circulated widely in Egypt. Nevertheless, Qoheleth usually speaks as a teacher, not a king; therefore, another explanation for the name must be sought.

Does the strange form conceal an otherwise unknown identity? Is "Qoheleth" an acronym? It has been argued (Skehan 1971, 42-43) that the name for Agur's father in Prov 30:1a, Jakeh, represents the first letters of a sentence (יהוה קָדוֹשׁ יְ = יקה הוּא). Following this analogy, קֹהֶלֶת constitutes the abbeviation of a four-word sentence. But what would those words have been? So far, no satisfactory explanation along these lines has come to light. Some have even thought that Qoheleth stood for personified wisdom, a walking assembly of wise sayings, but elsewhere Dame Wisdom is always called חָכְמָה. The most compelling answer to the enigma of the name points to two instances of a feminine participle functioning as an office (Ezra 2:55,57; Neh 7:59). Two different occupations lie behind the personal names in these verses (a scribe and a binder of gazelles). Accordingly,

Qoheleth refers to an office that was related in some way to assembling people. The LXX renders the word in this way, associating the noun for "assembly" with the word for a public gathering (ἐκκλησία). Jerome continued that line of reasoning in the Vulgate, but stressed the role of speaking in the presence of an assembly. Now if Qoheleth gathered people, did he summon them to a cultic assembly? This understanding led to the Reformers' use of *Prediger* ("Preacher") with reference to this book, but biblical evidence for such a meaning does not exist. Whatever else Qoheleth did, he did not preach, at least not in the modern sense of the word.

Did Qoheleth assemble people to a school? That kind of activity accords with the epilogist's description in 12:9. The difficulty remains that Qoheleth consistently opposes traditional wisdom. To be sure, school wisdom possibly possessed the capacity to criticize itself in the manner demonstrated by the book. One could even say that Qoheleth democratizes wisdom, turning away form professional students to ordinary citizens. The use of הָעָם "the people," in 12:9, where one would naturally expect a reference to students, favors this interpretation of the situation. Furthermore, if the form קְהִלָּה in Neh 5:7 actually means "harangue," then the word "Qoheleth" might refer to an office of "arguer" or "haranguer." However, Qoheleth does not present his observations in a manner that would justify this particular interpretation of the word under consideration.

The verb קָהַל always occurs with reference to an assembly of people. If the sense of the word could extend to the gathering of objects, then "Qoheleth" might refer to "collecting proverbs," the task for which the epilogist remembers the teacher (12:9-11). Qoheleth kept an ear in readiness to hear something worthwhile; he searched high and low for appropriate insights; and he grouped the resulting sayings in an understandable way. This instance would not be the only one in which Qoheleth departed from ordinary usage, for he forged a language and syntax peculiar to this book. Furthermore, he saw no fundamental distinction between humans and animals with respect to death; one could therefore argue that Qoheleth assembled sayings (1:1) and that 7:27 contains a veiled allusion to this understanding of the title ("One to one to discover the sum"). In short, Qoheleth collected sayings and in doing so arrived at the complete picture that life amounts to a huge zero.

B. Literary Integrity

We have already had occasion to mention an epilogist who commented on the achievement of the teacher. Naturally, the presence of an epilogue of this sort introduces the question of literary integrity. Did Qoheleth write the complete book, or have several authors contributed to its present form? Answers to these questions vary, but four different responses have commended themselves to interpreters: (1) the author wrote the bulk of the book, but editorial glosses entered at a later time; (2) the author cites traditional wisdom and refutes it; (3) the author enters into dialogue with an interlocutor, real or imagined; and (4) the book reflects a single author's changing viewpoints over the years, as well as life's ambiguities.

By analogy with superscriptions throughout the canon, it can be safely argued that 1:1 does not derive from Qoheleth's hand. This superscription identifies the author with David's son who held the office of king in Jerusalem. The expression "words of Qoheleth" echoes a similar superscription in Prov 30:1a, but the form also occurs in prophetic collections (e.g., Amos 1:1a; Jer 1:1a). The book of Qoheleth really begins at 1:12 ("I Qoheleth have been king over Israel in Jerusalem"). Furthermore, a thematic statement in 1:2 and 12:8 functions as an inclusio, setting off the beginning and the end of Qoheleth's teaching. Only in these verses does the superlative form הֲבֵל הֲבָלִים occur. The additional verses in 12:9-14 derive from one epilogist, or more probably two. To this point in analysis a virtual consensus exists in scholarly discussion.

Within the body of Qoheleth's teachings as delineated above (1:3-12:7), one searches in vain for a consistent argument. It appears that later editors have toned down the extreme views of the teacher. Theories of multiple redactors (Qoheleth, a Sadducean, a sage, a pious one, and another editor) have lost their attraction in the latest analyses, although most interpreters still reckon with at least one glossator who corrected Qoheleth's views about reward and retribution (2:26a; 3:17a; 8:12-13; 11:9b; perhaps 5:18 and 7:26b). Whether or not these glosses derive from the second epilogist, also responsible for 12:12-14, remains uncertain, but the hypothesis has plausibility.

The effort to attribute the entire book to Qoheleth lacks persuasiveness for at least two reasons. First, it overlooks the probability that the same sort of editorial activity that took place during the preservation of the other books of the Hebrew Bible would also have occurred in this one. Indeed, the radical character of Qoheleth's views invited editorial comments. Second, the claim that Qoheleth could easily have referred to himself in the third person, as he apparently did in 7:27, obscures the appreciable differences in attitude between the rest of the book and the final epilogue (12:12-14). These differences go beyond use of language such as בְּנִי, "my son," to religious views like the admonition to "fear God and keep the commandments" and the warning that the deity will bring every hidden thing into the light of day, presumably at a final judgment. One has the impression that Qoheleth's epitaph appears in 12:9-11, and that a less appreciative assessment of the teacher's unusual views about life follows.

Throughout the book one encounters teachings that stand in considerable tension with each other. A strong case has been made for understanding these contrasting opinions as instances in which Qoheleth cites traditional wisdom. An adversarial stance toward established dogma is beyond dispute, for Qoheleth actually warns against an uncritical acceptance of claims about absolute truth (8:17). In one instance Qoheleth's language almost requires the addition of something like "he asks" ("There is an individual who has no heir, whether son or brother, but there is no end to all his work, and also his eyes are never content with his wealth—'for whom am I toiling and depriving myself of good things?' [he asks]; this also is absurd and grievous bother," 4:8).

Traditional sayings dot the observations of Qoheleth, as has been recognized for some time, for example, "the crooked cannot be straightened and what is missing cannot be counted" (1:15). One investigation (Whybray 1981b) has isolated eight quotations on the basis of affinities in form and content between the oldest collections in Proverbs and aphorisms in Qoheleth (2:14a; 4:5; 4:6; 7:5-6a; 9:17; 10:2; 10:12). Those scholars who believe they have found quotations in Qoheleth's observations emphasize the variety with which these traditional sayings are used. Some he quotes with full approval (7:5-6; 10:2, 12), but he gave them a radically new interpretation. Others serve to confirm the first stage in the characteristic two-part argument, the so-called broken sentence in which Qoheleth stated a truth only to qualify it by appealing to a fact of life that contradicted it. This phenomenon of quotations, widespread in the ancient Near East, has four main categories: (1) the verbalization of a speaker's or writer's unexpressed ideas or sentiments; (2) the sentiment of a subject other than the writer or speaker; (3) use in argument and debate; and (4) indirect quotations without a *verbum dicendi* (Gordis 1976).

Early Christian theologians perceived the apparent contradictions within Qoheleth's thought and attributed the different views to two persons, a speaker and an interlocutor, real or imagined. The dialogical character of the book thus came to expression, despite the strong tendency to neutralize Qoheleth's unorthodox sentiments. Thesis stands over against antithesis in such a way that all teachings are relativized. J. G. Herder endorsed this view of the book, and contemporary interpreters have sought to bolster the argument by appealing to the juxtaposition of a *bonum* and a *malum* and by an intricate analysis of polar structures in the book. Although some of the proposed thirty-eight chiastic structures and sixty polar structures result from much too general criteria, for instance, desirable and undesirable, one can scarcely deny the force of the hypothesis as such. After all, Qoheleth did arrange his argument in a group of fourteen polarities in at least one literary unit (3:1-8).

Of course, the application of modern standards of logical consistency may bestow too much weight on the Greek heritage. Qoheleth may never actually have reconciled the disparities between faith and experience, but such a view elevates the religious dimension to a degree that Qoheleth probably never permitted. Perhaps two additional factors strengthen this particular approach to the contradictions in Qoheleth's thought. The teachings in the book may represent the fruit of a lifetime's research, having been given literary expression over a long period. Furthermore, life's ambiguities themselves may have struck Qoheleth as worthy of noting, particularly as historical situations changed from time to time. There may indeed be some truth in the claim that the confrontation between Hebraism and Hellenism produced a compromise position, best exemplified by Qoheleth. However, the Jewish tradition alone had its share of ambiguities, and these disparities between religious conviction and actual reality found expression in Qoheleth's realism.

Signs of thematic unity and a single tone largely offset these indications of tension within Qoheleth's thought, or between his views and those of later editors.

Nevertheless, some segments of the book have not been successfully integrated into its logical scheme, above all the collection of sayings in 10:1-4, 8-20, which discourages the view that Qoheleth wrote a unified treatise. Although neither characterization of the book, treatise or collection of sentences, explains the situation adequately, it may be instructive to think of a kaleidoscopic image whereby apparently incongruent features of the text come together in many different meaningful configurations. Even if one accepts this reading of the disparate material, the difficult task of ascertaining the powerful force that brings a semblance of order out of apparent disarray remains. In a word, what shape does the book take; what identifies its internal structure?

C. The Structure of the Book

One can easily recognize the outer frame of the book. Leaving aside the superscription in 1:1, there remain a thematic refrain (1:2) and a poem (1:3-11) at the beginning and a poem (11:7–12:7) plus a thematic refrain (12:8) at the end. Together with the superscription, the two epilogues (12:9-11, 12-14) enclose the book in a kind of envelope. The first poem demonstrates the aptness of the thematic statement in the realm of nature, and the final poem shows the accuracy of the theme on the human scene. Nature's ceaseless repetition illustrates the utter futility of things, as does the eventual disintegration of the human body.

Within Qoheleth's teachings bracketed by a thematic statement and a poem, a few distinct units stand out, either because of content or because of introductory and concluding formulas. For example, a single thread holds together the royal experiment in 1:12–2:26, specifically the idea that a powerful monarch indulges himself in a vain search for something that will withstand time's ravages. A second example, this one smaller in scope, 4:9-12, discusses the advantages of teaming up with another person. So far, however, no satisfactory scheme has surfaced to explain all the units of Qoheleth's teachings. Often determining where one unit begins and another ends cannot be done. Therefore scholars vary widely in their calculation of the number of literary units within the book.

If the text lacks clear demarcations of the several units, how can one decide on the extent of each? Perhaps a clue exists in Egyptian Instructions, clearly divided into sections or chapters. Analogy with Papyrus Insinger, roughly contemporary with Qoheleth, may suggest that refrains mark off larger units in the Hebrew text. One refrain seems especially suggestive in this regard, the sevenfold exhortation to eat, drink, and enjoy one's portion of life's good things (2:24-26; 3:12-13; 3:22; 5:17-19; 8:15; 9:7-10; and 11:7-10). But the first and last of these texts illustrate the difficulty of this approach, for the refrain in 3:24-26 certainly concludes a unit, and the formula in 11:7-10 just as certainly begins a new unit.

As a matter of fact, the book has a wealth of formulaic expressions, and these repeated phrases and sentences probably function to delineate units of thought. Wright has seized these data to arrive at an arrangement of the entire book. According to his view, a single refrain sets off the different units in the first half of the book, whereas two formulaic expressions indicate subsections in the second half. The first refrain, "All [this] is absurd and a chasing after wind" occurs six times in 1:12–6:9, yielding the following literary units (2:1-11; 2:12-17; 2:18-26; 3:1-4:6; 4:7-16; 4:17–6:9). In 6:10–11:6 the repeated phrases "not find out" and "who can find out?" indicate four subsections (7:1-14; 7:15-24; 7:25-29; 8:1-17) and "cannot know" also points to four sections (9:1-12; 9:13–10:15; 10:16–11:2; 11:3-6). This theory is then reinforced by an involved numerological analysis that takes its clue from the number of uses of the Hebrew word הֶבֶל, as well as the numerical value of its three consonants.

This elaborate hypothesis appears to press a valid intuition too far. In some instances, the formulaic expression occurs in the midst of a thought unit rather than at the end (for example, 11:2). Moreover, the repeated phrases sometimes do not enter into consideration (4:4, "striving after wind"), and other formulaic expressions are ignored altogether ("this is absurd," "under the sun," "I turned and considered"). In addition, the units perceived in the analysis under discussion vary in length, forcing one to wonder about the utility of such an approach. Despite the claims for objectivity, the decision to ignore some formulaic expressions and to concentrate on just these three ("This is absurd and a chasing after wind," "not find out" / "who can find out," and "cannot know") undercuts that claim, and the many assumptions necessitated by the numerological proof weaken the argument greatly.

Not all attempts to discover the book's structure have taken refrains as the starting point. Of course, many interpreters have searched for logically consistent units. Two recent theories illustrate this approach and demonstrate the sophisticated nature of such analyses of the book. Both interpretations apply the refined methods of literary criticism to the biblical text, although such literary analysis developed as a means of understanding quite different material. Loader's approach (1979) stresses the polar structures in the book and arrives at twelve fundamental units (1:2-11; 1:12–2:26; 3:1–4:16; 4:17–5:8; 6:10–8:1; 8:2-9; 8:10–9:10; 9:11–10:11; 10:12-20; 11:1-6; 11:7–12:8). Lohfink's approach emphasizes the Greek background of the book, which he understands as a philosophical treatise. In his view, Ecclesiastes has the form of a palindrome, a complete balancing of material so that the second half repeats the substance of the first half. Such a reading leads to the following structure:

1:2-3	Frame
1:4-11	Cosmology (poetic)
1:12–3:15	Anthropology
3:16–4:16	Social Criticism I
4:17–5:6	Criticism of Religion I (poetic)
5:7–6:10	Social Criticism II
6:11–9:6	Ideology Critique (*Refutatio*)
9:7–12:7	Ethics (poetic at the end)
12:8	Frame

Even if one conceded the far-from-obvious premise that the book uses Greek rhetoric, several questions remain. Why did the author allow the intruding critique of religion in 4:17–5:6 to mar the perfect palindrome? Has Lohfink chosen adequate rubrics? For example, is anthropology missing from the passage where Qoheleth offers a low opinion of men and an even lower estimate of women (7:25-29)? Can one rightly restrict ethics to 9:7–12:7 in light of persistent efforts to view the entire second half of the book as the practical, or ethical, implications of the worldview advanced in the first half of Ecclesiastes (1:2–6:9)?

Without committing oneself wholly to either clue, refrain or logical coherence, one can certainly discern a semblance of structure in the book. One of the most attractive interpretations (Schoors 1982b) divides the book as follows:

1:1	title
1:2	general theme of the book
1:3–2:26	Solomon's confession
3:1-22	human beings under the law of time
4:1-16	life in society
4:17–5:8	the advantage of silence over unreflected speech
5:9–6:9	on wealth
6:10-12	transitional unit
7:1–9:10	the experience of life and death
9:11–10:20	wisdom and folly
11:1-6	the necessity of taking risks
11:7–12:7	the necessity of enjoying life
12:8	inclusion: the general theme of the book
12:9-14	epilogue

Attractive as this analysis may be, it still does not answer all the questions that result from general rubrics such as "life in society" and "wisdom and folly." Because other sections also deal with social relations and knowledge or its opposite, it appears that every attempt to discover the book's structure serves as little more than a heuristic device.

So far this discussion has said nothing about another unifying principle, the tone of the book. The individual units combine to give a single impression. An honest and forthright teacher observes life's ambiguities and reflects on their meaning for human existence under the sun. Furthermore, a unity of themes and topoi reinforces this tonal unity, as a glance at the vocabulary of the book quickly confirms. Qoheleth uses certain words with such frequency that they almost induce a hypnotic state in the listener or reader. By their frequency of occurrence these words send a distant echo through the corridors of the mind erected by this skillful teacher: do/work, good, wise, time, know, toil, see, under the sun, fool, profit, portion.

D. The Historical Setting

If all attempts to discern the book's structure remain inconclusive, the same verdict characterizes efforts to locate it in a particular place and time. For a brief period, scholars endeavored to demonstrate that the original language was Aramaic, but this trend has virtually disappeared. The discovery at Qumran of Hebrew fragments from the book to which a date in the mid-second century BCE seemed appropriate has hastened the demise of the theory of an Aramaic original. Such an early dating of a Hebrew version of Ecclesiastes left little time between its composition and the Qumran fragments. However, the decisive refutation of the Aramaic origin lay in the inability of its proponents to show how the present form of the book required a theory of translation to explain its peculiar style and syntax.

The fact remains that the book is written in an Aramaizing Hebrew, a language with strong Mishnaic tendencies. The vocabulary contains a high percentage of Aramaisms, and in this regard it belongs alongside certain other late canonical books. Occasional Persian loan words also appear, for example, פַּרְדֵּס "park" and מְדִינָה "province." Greek influence, once believed to lie behind the phrase "under the sun" and "to see the good," no longer seems likely; the ancient Semitic world attests to the former expression and the latter phrase is authentic Hebrew.

On the basis of certain commercial terms and usages, as well as orthography, a setting for the book in Phoenicia has been proposed (Dahood 1952). This theory of the book's origin has made little impact on the scholarly community. The suggestion of Egyptian provenance, based largely on the allusion to natural phenomena in 1:5-7, has been less convincing. The references to reservoirs (2:6), leaky roofs (10:18), wells (12:6), farmers' attention to the wind (11:4), and the Temple (4:17; 8:10) are perfectly appropriate for a literary composition in Palestine (Hertzberg *Prediger* KAT). Nevertheless, the evidence is inconclusive, for ancient authors openly received material from various sources. The so-called historical references in 4:13-16; 8:2-4; 9:13-15; and 10:16-17 function typically. Therefore, they offer no real assistance in dating the book or in locating its cultural setting.

Many factors point to a relatively late date for the composition of Ecclesiastes. The vocabulary itself shows signs of being very late, for example סוֹף, "end"; פֵּשֶׁר, "interpretation"; מָשָׁל, "rule"; שָׁלַט, "rule"; פִּתְגָם, "decision"; זְמָן, "time"; עִנְיָן, "worry"; the relative pronoun שֶׁ, "that, which," attached to another word, and the personal pronoun אֲנִי, "I," used alongside אָנֹכִי, "I," with almost equal frequency. Moreover, the *waw* consecutive occurs only twice, although the literary types in the book do not lend themselves to frequent use of this verbal form. A Hellenistic coloring may rest behind the vocabulary for rulers, perhaps also the observations about individuals whose responsibilities brought them in regular contact with the royal court. At least one of the rhetorical questions, a literary device that the author uses nearly thirty times, occurs only in arguably postexilic texts. This rhetorical question, מִי יוֹדֵעַ "who knows?," functions as a strong assertion equivalent to "no one knows." Another stylistic peculiarity of the book, the use of participles with personal pronouns, forms a late feature of the language.

The meager political data that scholars have detected in the book point to a period prior to the Maccabean revolt in 164 BCE, for the attitude toward foreign rulers fits best in the Ptolemaic period. The Zenon archives reflect a political situation of economic prosperity for the upper echelons of Jewish society about 250 BCE. It has been plausibly argued that Qoheleth belonged to the privileged class (Gordis 1968), although on the basis of highly inferential evidence. More probably his students came from privileged families, hence could act on their teacher's advice about wearing fine clothes and anointing themselves with expensive oils. The severe policies of Antiochus IV restricted such freedom to follow one's inclinations, whether personal or religious. Furthermore, Ben Sira probably knew and used the book about 190 BCE, although Whitley has attempted to show that Qoheleth actually used Ecclesiasticus. The bases for this late dating of Qoheleth lack cogency: that the language of Daniel is earlier, that the mishnaic tongue was widely used, that Qoheleth wrote before 140 but after Jonathan's appointment in 152 BCE and its accompanying political changes. A date for Qoheleth between 225 and 250 therefore still seems the most likely one.

E. The Literary Expression

What literary type best characterizes the book? Although several different types come to expression, the dominant one is reflection arising from personal observation. Qoheleth's language calls attention to both aspects, the observing and subsequent reflection ("I said in my heart" [1:16; 2:1,15; 3:17]; "I gave my heart" [1:13,17; 8:9,16]; "I saw" [1:14; 2:24; 3:10,16; 4:1,4,15; 5:17; 6:1; 7:15; 8:9,10; 9:11,13; 10:5,7]; "I know" [1:17; 2:14; 3:12,14; 8:12]; "there is" [2:21; 6:1,12; 8:14; 10:5]). Naturally, the reflection varies from time to time, prompting some interpreters to distinguish between unifed critical and broken critical reflections or meditative reflection and simple meditation. Not every critic thinks that such language adequately describes Qoheleth's dominant literary type; three alternatives have received some attention: מָשָׁל (a similitude or comparison), diatribe, and royal testament. The latter of these, royal testament, occurs only in the "fiction" in 1:12–2:16 (perhaps also the conclusion resulting from the royal experiment, 2:17-26). From Qoheleth's language, "monologue" more accurately describes the material than "diatribe," for he emphasizes the debate within his own mind. The term מָשָׁל has too broad, or too specific, a scope to be useful in describing the book's literary type.

Qoheleth also uses such literary types as autobiographical narrative, example story, anecdote, parable (often called an allegorical poem), antithesis, and proverb. The last of these occurs in many of its forms: the truth statements (or sentences), "better" sayings, numerical sayings, instructions, traditional sayings, malediction and benediction. Qoheleth had particular fondness for "better" sayings, for they enabled him to pretend to endorse conventional wisdom but actually to challenge its veracity by introducing a wholly different consideration (4:3, 6, 9, 13; 5:4[5]; 6:3, 9; 7:1, 2,

3, 5, 8; 9:4, 16, 18). He also used the emphatic form, "nothing is better" (2:24; 3:12, 22; 8:15).

F. Qoheleth's Teachings

What did Qoheleth communicate by means of these diverse literary types? According to the thematic statement in 1:2 and 12:8, he sought to demonstrate the claim that life lacked profit and therefore was totally absurd. In support of this thesis, Qoheleth argued: (1) that wisdom could not achieve its goal; (2) that a remote God ruled over a crooked world; and (3) that death did not take virtue or vice into consideration. Hence (4), he advocated enjoyment as the wisest course of action during youth before the cares of advancing years made that response impossible.

(1) *Wisdom could not achieve its goal.* The purpose of being wise, according to Qoheleth, was to discover the good for men and women. In other words, sages searched for ways to ensure success, specifically of living long, prosperous lives surrounded by children and admired by friends and neighbors. For many generations this quest for success had occupied the thoughts of Qoheleth's predecessors, whose conclusions the book of Proverbs preserves. In general, they considered it possible to achieve the goal of wisdom, although reckoning with incalculable divine actions now and again. Consequently, these early sages exuded optimism about the chances of living well. They based their hope on the conviction that a moral order existed, having been established by the creator who continued to guarantee it. These sages went about their work with confidence that the wise would prosper and fools would experience ruin.

But something happened that dashed such comforting thoughts, which had hardened into dogma. Mounting evidence that injustice often prevailed produced a religious and intellectual crisis. The books of Job and Ecclesiastes surfaced from this turmoil and offered a different perspective on the universe. The wisest man in the East underwent horrendous suffering that defied explanation, and wisdom possessed only limited value. It appeared that the moral order had collapsed, and this event had serious religious implications, making it no longer clear whether or not the deity turned toward humans benevolently.

Qoheleth recognized the futility of striving for success, because he saw such efforts being frustrated on every hand. The fastest runner did not always win the race, nor did the strong warrior necessarily achieve victory. The intelligent person did not always receive food, and the skillful were sometimes overlooked. Chance became the supreme factor in human experience, and none could exercise control over it. Qoheleth examined all those things thought to offer happiness—sensual pleasure, achievement, fame, fortune—but dismissed them as utterly absurd.

Whereas earlier sages had believed they could achieve wisdom, Qoheleth thought it impenetrable. Human resolve to possess her only enabled them to discover Wisdom's remoteness and profundity. Of course, limited bits of insight were accessible, enabling their possessors to walk in light rather than darkness. Nevertheless, no one could really discover wisdom's hiding place, however much he or she claimed to have done so. Consequently, the future remained hidden and mysterious, even for the wise, who could not discern the right moment for any given action. Although Qoheleth characterized the natural universe and the human scene by monotonous repetition, he noted that none could profit from this element of predictability. In this respect, Qoheleth refused to yield a toe hold to practitioners of the science of predicting the future, a technique of wisdom, popular in Mesopotamia, that used omens to discover what lay in the immediate future.

(2) *God was remote and the world crooked.* A devout Job directed his complaint to God in heated dialogue, but Qoheleth refused to address the deity at all. He warned those who approached the holy place that since God dwelt in heaven and they resided on earth, their words should be few. Qoheleth noticed that religious vows were a source of danger, inasmuch as some people forgot their promises once the occasion for the original vows had passed. He thus advised caution with respect to religious obligation. Qoheleth had the same attitude toward deeds of morality that he did toward acts of piety. He suggested that individuals adopt a moderate lifestyle, being neither excessively devout nor extremely virtuous. The suffering of Job indicated what could happen when a person became too good. Although Qoheleth did not refer to Job by name, he did counsel against striving with a stronger person, which some interpreters have plausibly taken as an allusion to Job's fruitless struggle with God.

Although Qoheleth freely referred to God's activity, he seemed unclear about the nature of the divine work. It appears that he thought the deity tested human beings in order to demonstrate their kinship with animals. Hence God showed individuals that they would die just like animals, with the implication that decomposition awaited as the final event for all creatures. Although Qoheleth mentioned a judgment, it seems nothing more than another way of talking about death. Some references to judgment must imply a forensic setting, presumably after death, but they probably constitute glosses in the spirit of the second epilogue.

In any event, oppression had gained the upper hand on earth, and the hierarchy of authority ultimately reached the sovereign of the universe, also implicated by such tyranny. Utter mystery characterized God's actions, both in the enlivening of a fetus and in the granting of power to enjoy the fruits of one's labor. Although Qoheleth freely talked about divine gifts, he did not know what disposition characterized the deity, whether love or hatred. To be sure, God bestowed generous gifts on human beings, but no apparent rationale for these acts of kindness existed. Instead, God dispensed these gifts with complete disregard for character. Consequently, nobody could ever ensure that the deity would grant only good things as reward for faithfulness.

Earlier sages had also believed that the High God transcended the universe, which owed its origin to the deity. But they proclaimed nearness as well, for they believed that God sustained a moral order. Qoheleth agreed that God created the universe; the language, however, differs sharply from the Priestly account of creation that seems to provide the source for Qoheleth's observations. God made everything appropriate for its time. This declaration substitutes a nontheological expression and an aesthetic category for the language in Genesis 1. Nevertheless, the created universe can not be faulted, for human beings have perverted the beautiful and appropriate creation.

Qoheleth recognized an order inherent to things, but he denied that anyone could discover the right time for action. The creator placed some unknown gift in the human mind but made it impossible to use the divine mystery profitably. A time to laugh and a time to cry existed, but how did one know when those different moments presented themselves? What if a person looked for peace when the occasion called for war? Perhaps this anomaly prompted Qoheleth to spy out and explore all knowledge, for only by embracing the many polarities of existence could one ever hope to know the proper time for anything. Nevertheless, Qoheleth conceded that nobody really knows the meaning of a thing.

It made little difference that the universe had integrity, so long as human beings had an innate disposition to do evil. God's achievements could not be changed; the crooked could not be straightened and the straight could not be made crooked. This popular proverb, which Qoheleth quoted with approval (1:15; 7:13), hardly accords with Qoheleth's statement that men and women have used their ingenuity in the service of evil—unless, that is, God bears indirect responsibility for human contrivance.

In this oppressive world Qoheleth recognized a need for companionship, although he judged others on the basis of the contribution they could make to his comfort. A friend would rescue him from a pit, fight off robbers and brigands, and keep him warm on a cold night. Although Wisdom Literature usually moves within the general area of self-interest, that feature of Qoheleth's thought comes to prominence in the royal fiction, with indulgence the operative word. Only once did a pained conscience speak out in behalf of oppressed citizens, and the repetition of the cry "There was no comforter" reveals the impact of their suffering on Qoheleth.

(3) *Death did not take virtue or vice into consideration.* Qoheleth was not the first person to reflect on the finality of death, but he dwelt on it so much that it became central to his thought. Indeed, he once expressed hatred of life because he lacked the power to control his fate. Nevertheless, he stopped short of encouraging suicide, a natural consequence of his disdain for life. In this regard, Qoheleth differed from the unknown author of the *Dialogue between a Master and His Slave* (*ANET* 437-38).

The thought that death cancels all human achievements prompted Qoheleth to consider life pointless. When one's accumulated wealth fell into the hands of a stranger or a fool, it seemed to mock personal ambition and frugality. Qoheleth imagined that memory of persons disappeared almost as quickly as their bodies decomposed. Furthermore, death's clutches caught some people even before they breathed that last breath, so that they could not gain any pleasure in life. Faced with such grim prospects, these unfortunate individuals would be better off dead, and better still if they had never been born. Qoheleth characterized the stillborn's condition as rest, whereas those who have entered this world undergo buffeting from all directions. Although he quoted a proverb that "a living dog is better than a dead lion," Qoheleth made it clear that the living have a dubious advantage. Knowing that one must die seems hardly worthwhile information; in this instance, as in most, knowledge brings suffering. Critics therefore generally assume that Qoheleth spoke ironically when citing the proverb.

Qoheleth's predecessors had also recognized death's inevitability, but they had assumed that a positive correlation existed between one's virtue and the manner and time of death. In addition, they had managed to deal with exceptions by appealing to the larger entity, the community. Neither source of solace remained for Qoheleth, who recognized death's arbitrary nature and who rarely transcended egocentrism. The same fate befell wise and fool, humankind and animals. Moreover, no one knew what happened after death, but the prospects did not look promising.

The concluding poem (11:7–12:7) depicts this common fate in unforgettable images. The decline of one's powers in old age resembles the collapse of a stately house, and the restrictions on activity contrast with nature's annual rejuvenation. The darkness of approaching death falls on humankind, but nature stands unmoved. Then comes the final silencing of men and women, depicted in two images. The first describes an expensive lamp that falls from the wall and experiences ruin; the second portrays a well at which the pulley breaks and the container for drawing water falls to the bottom and shatters. The language emphasizes the priceless commodities that come to ruin or cease to benefit anyone—silver, gold, light, water. The brief existence under the sun seems to constitute a single act of breathing on the part of the creator, who now takes back the vivifying breath. The death angel takes flight, bearing its reluctant burden into the realms of the night. Qoheleth may have despised life and envied the condition of the aborted birth, but he still did not welcome this destruction of personal identity.

(4) *The wisest course of action was to enjoy life during youth before the cares of advancing years made that response impossible.* Of course not everyone had the capacity to enjoy good food, women, expensive clothing and perfumes. Qoheleth seems to have addressed young men who had adequate resources, enabling them to indulge in pleasure. Unless his advice was entirely divorced from reality, Qoheleth probably taught individuals from the privileged class. In any case, he implies that they had access to persons in important positions of authority and that they possessed sufficient resources for living comfortably.

Qoheleth did not encourage total abandon to sensual desire, for such behavior carried too many risks. Instead, he advised young people to enjoy the simple pleasures avilable to them without resorting to extremes of austerity or debauchery. Although the language about enjoying "the woman you love" is unusual, Qoheleth may not have meant someone other than the young man's wife. However, Qoheleth warns of a future judgment, and a moment's reflection on this sober prospect may explain why he praised those who visited the house of mourning rather than the ones who chose to frequent places of levity.

Such somber warnings detract from Qoheleth's positive counsel, for he seemed unwilling to believe that anything really softened the impact of this conclusion about life's utter futility. Therefore he encouraged enjoyment and reminded those practitioners of pleasure about life's ephemerality and absurdity. Presumably, the little joys available to humans merely made an otherwise intolerable situation bearable. On the other hand, Qoheleth's view that God has already approved one's actions has a remarkably emancipating effect. Life introduces enough risks without the additional factor of a scrupulous conscience. Qoheleth thus left no room for anxiety about religious duty, for life was complex enough without complicating things by becoming a religious zealot. The truth of Qoheleth's observations about human existence speaks for itself. One can hardly escape the wisdom in his advice to enjoy the simple pleasures of daily existence while the strength and financial means to do so endure.

To sum up, Qoheleth taught by means of various literary types that earlier optimistic claims about wisdom's power to secure one's existence have no validity. No discernible principle of order governs the universe, rewarding virtue and punishing evil. The creator, distant and uninvolved, acts as judge only (if at all) in extreme cases of flagrant affront (for example, reneging on religious vows). Death cancels all imagined gains, rendering life under the sun absurd. Therefore the best policy is to enjoy one's wife, together with good food and drink, during youth, for old age and death will soon put an end to this "relative" good. In short, Qoheleth examined all of life and discovered no absolute good that would survive death's effect. He then proceeded to report this discovery and to counsel young people on the best option in the light of stark reality. It follows that Qoheleth bears witness to an intellectual crisis in ancient Israel, at least in the circles among whom he taught.

G. The Larger Environment

An intellectual crisis struck other cultures also, but not at the same time. One expects, therefore, to find some common themes throughout the ancient Near East. This expectation has led to exaggerated claims of literary dependence on Qoheleth's part. Given the probable date of the book, Hellenistic influence has seemed most likely. Qoheleth's concept of chance (מִקְרֶה) has been related to τύχη; absurdity (הֶבֶל) to τῦφος; profit (יִתְרוֹן) to ὠφελος; portion (חֵלֶק) to μηρίς; "under the sun" (תַּחַת הַשָּׁמֶשׁ) to ὑπὸ τὸν ἥλιον. One recent critic (Lohfink 1980) has postulated competing places of learning in Jerusalem, private schools in which the Greek language was spoken and Temple schools using Hebrew. This author argues that Qoheleth struck a compromise with Hebrew wisdom as the background and Greek—especially Homer, Sophocles, Plato, Aristotle, and contemporary philosophers—the inspiration. Other interpreters plausibly suggest that Qoheleth's knowledge of Greek thought amounts to no more than what any Jew would have absorbed simply by living in Jerusalem during the late third century.

What about literary relationships with ancient Egypt? To be sure, Qoheleth issues a *carpe diem* similar to the advice contained in the Harper's Songs, but this determination to enjoy sensual pleasure seems universal. The preoccupation with death in Qoheleth recalls a similar emphasis in the *Dialogue of a Man with His Soul*, (*ANET* 405-407) and the royal testament must surely correspond to this literary type in such instructions as those for Merikare (*ANET* 414-18). Nevertheless, Qoheleth does not offer a legacy for a successor, and the royal fiction disappears after chapter 2. Verbal similarities do occur with late Eygptian texts, particularly *Papyrus Insinger* (*AEL* 3:184-217) and the *Instruction of 'Onkhsheshonqy* (*AEL* 3:159-84). For example, the hiddenness of God and divine determination of fate characterize both Insinger and Qoheleth, whereas 'Onkhsheshonqy and Qoheleth advise casting bread (or a good deed) on the water and promise a profitable return, and both use the phrase "house of eternity." However, the counsel about casting bread on water has a different sense, and the euphemism for the grave occurs widely.

Perhaps the most striking verbal similarity occurs in a Mesopotamian text, the Gilgamesh Epic (*ANET* 72-99, 503-507). The alewife Siduri's advice to Gilgamesh that he enjoy his wife, fine clothes, and tasty food finds an echo in Qoheleth's positive advice. Qoheleth omits one significant thing, the allusion to the pleasure that Gilgamesh would receive from his child. The Gilgamesh Epic also deals with the themes of death, life's ephemerality, the importance of one's name, and memory of a person after death. According to *I Will Praise the Lord of Wisdom* (*ANET* 596-600), divine decrees are hidden from humans, a view that Qoheleth advocates in 3:11, 8:12-14, and 8:17. The *Babylonian Theodicy* (*ANET* 601-604) has a fundamentally pessimistic mood, whereas Qoheleth shrinks from blaming all evil on God (cf. 7:29). The *Dialogue between a Master and His Slave* recognizes the threat posed by women and sets up polarities in a way that commends neither alternative. Qoheleth also voices a low opinion of women (7:26) and juxtaposes positive and negative activities (3:1-8).

H. Canonization

Qoheleth's radical views have branded his teachings an alien body within the Hebrew Bible. How, then, did the book find acceptance in the canon? The usual answer, that the attribution to Solomon paved the way for its approval as Scripture, does not take sufficiently into account the fact that a similar device failed to gain acceptance in the canon for Wisdom of Solomon or for the Odes of Solomon. Their use of Greek may have canceled the effect of the claim to Solomonic authorship. A better answer to the question, that the book received two epilogues, the last of which removed the sting from Qoheleth's skepticism and advocated traditional views concerning observance of Torah, presents itself. Evidence from the second century CE indicates that the book of Ecclesiastes was mentioned, along with Song of Songs, Esther, Ezekiel, and Proverbs, in a discussion about books that "defile the hands" because of their sacred character, but the attitude of Hillel prevailed over the Shammaite contingency. On the Jewish side, Akiba recognized Qoheleth's canonical authority just before the middle of the second century. The book appears in the list drawn up by the Christian Melito of Sardis about 190 CE, but in the fifth century Theodore of Mopsuestia first raised objection to its sacred character.

Precisely how early Qoheleth became canonical cannot be determined. A few verbal similarities between the book and Sirach exist (for example, "everything is beautiful in its time" [3:11; 39:16], "God seeks" [3:15; 5:3], "wise of heart" and "change of face" [8:1; 13:24], "either for good or for evil" [12:14; 13:24]). In addition, verbal echoes also occur in "one in a thousand," and "the end of the matter," but these comprise stock expressions in Wisdom Literature. Although Sirach was probably familiar with the book of Ecclesiastes, the evidence remains inconclusive. A similar situation exists with regard to Wisdom of Solomon, often thought to attack Qoheleth's views about enjoying life's sensual pleasures. If the author of chapter 2 has Qoheleth in mind, it clearly implies a misreading of his teachings, for Qoheleth did not advocate robbery.

I. The Text

The Hebrew text of Qoheleth is in good condition. Fragments dating from the middle of the second century BCE, discovered at Qumran, include part of 5:13-17, substantial portions of 6:3-8, and five words from 7:7-9. The Greek version may be the work of some disciples of Aquila, whereas the Syriac translation in the Peshitta may rest on a Hebrew text very similar to the Masoretic one. The Vulgate strove for faithfulness to the Hebrew, although Jerome hastily completed the translation of Proverbs, Ecclesiastes, and Song of Songs ("in three days").

Selected Bibliography

Barucq, A.
 1968 *Ecclésiaste*. Verbum Salutis, 3. Paris.
Brown, R.
 1973 *Kohelet und die frühhellenistische Popularphilosophie*. BZAW 130. Berlin.
Crenshaw, J. L.
 1974 "The Eternal Gospel (Eccl 3:11)." In in *Essays in Old Testament Ethics*, ed. J. L. Crenshaw and J. T. Willis, 23-55. New York.
 1978 "The Shadow of Death in Qoheleth." In *Israelite Wisdom: Theological and Literary Essays*, ed. Gammie et al. (1978), 205-16.
 1981 *Old Testament Wisdom*. Atlanta.
 1983 "Qoheleth in Current Research." *HAR* 7:41-56.
 1986 "Youth and Old Age in Qoheleth." *HAR* 10:1-13.
 1987 *Ecclesiastes*. OTL. Philadelphia.
Crüseman, F.
 1979a "Die unveränderbare Welt. Überlegungen zur Krisis der Weisheit beim Prediger (Kohelet)." In 80-104 in *Der Gott der kleinen Leute*, ed. W. Schottroff and W. Stegemann, 80-104. Munich. (ET)
 1979b "Hiob und Kohelet. Ein Beitrag zum Verständnis des Hiobbuches." In *Werden und Wirken des Alten Testaments; Festschrift für C. Westermann*, ed. R. Albertz et al., 373-93. Göttingen.
Dahood, M.
 1952 "Canaanite-Phoenician Influence in Qoheleth." *Bib* 33:30-52, 191-221.
Ellermeier, F.
 1967 *Qoheleth I: Untersuchungen zum Buche Qoheleth*. Herzberg am Harz.
 1970 *Qohelet I*. Abschnitt 2/7. Herzberg am Harz.
Fox, M. V.
 1977 "Frame-Narrative and Composition in the Book of Qoheleth. *HUCA* 48:83-106.
Galling, K.
 1932 "Kohelet-Studien." *ZAW* 50:276-99.
 1934 "Stand und Aufgabe der Kohelet-Forschung." *TRu* n.f. 6:355-73.
Gammie, J. G., W. A. Brueggemann, W. L. Humphreys, and J. M. Ward, eds.
 1978 *Israelite Wisdom: Theological and Literary Essays in Honor of Samuel Terrien*. Missoula MT.
Gese, H.
 1958 *Lehre und Wirklichkeit in der alten Weisheit*. Tübingen.
 1963 "Die Krisis der Weisheit bei Koheleth." In *Les Sagesses du Proche-Orient ancien*, ed. F. Wendel, 139-51. Paris. ET: in *Theodicy in the Old Testament*, ed. J. L. Crenshaw, 141-53. Philadelphia, 1983.
Gilbert, M.
 1981 "La description de la viellesse en Qohelet XII.7, est elle allegorique?" In *Congress Volume, Vienna*, 96-109. VTSup 32. Leiden.
Ginsberg, H. L.
 1955 "The Structure and Contents of the Book of Koheleth." VTSup 3:138-49.

Ginsburg, C. D.
1857   *The Song of Songs and Qoheleth*. Repr. New York, 1970.
Goldin, J.
1966   "The End of Ecclesiastes: Literal Exegesis and its Transformation." *Lown Institute for Judaistic Studies* 3:135-58.
Good, E. M.
1978   "The Unfilled Sea: Style and Meaning in Ecclesiastes 1:2-11." In Gammie et al., eds. (1978) 59-73.
Gordis, R.
1968   *Koheleth: The Man and His World*. New York.
1976   *The Word and the Book: Studies in Biblical Language and Literature*. New York.
Gorssen, L.
1970   "La Cohérence de la conception de Dieu dans l'Ecclésiaste." *ETL* 46:282-324.
Hengel, M.
1974   *Judaism and Hellenism*. Trans. J. Bowden. Philadelphia.
Holm-Nielsen, S.
1974   "On the Interpretation of Qoheleth in Early Christianity." *VT* 24:168-77.
1956   "The Book of Ecclesiastes and the Interpretation of It in Jewish and Christian Theology." *ASTI* 10:38-96.
Horton, E.
1972   "Koheleth's Concept of Opposites." *Numen* 19:1-21.
Johnson, R. F.
1973   "A Form Critical Analysis of the Sayings in the Book of Ecclesiastes." Ph.D. diss., Emory.
Klopfenstein, M.A.
1972   "Die Skepsis des Qohelet." *TZ* 28:97-109.
Kroeber, R.
1963   *Der Prediger*. SQAW. Berlin.
Lauha, A.
1955   "Die Krise des religiösen Glaubens bei Kohelet." VTSup 3:183-91.
1981   "Kohelets Verhältnis zur Geschichte."In *Die Botschaft und die Boten: Festschrift für Hans Walter Wolff zum 70. Geburtstag*, ed. J. Jeremias and L. Perlitt, 393-401. Neukirchen-Vluyn.
Loader, J. A.
1979   *Polar Structures in the Book of Qohelet*. BZAW 152. Berlin.
Lohfink, N.
1979   "War Kohelet ein Frauenfeind? Ein Versuch, die Logik und den Gegenstand von Qoh., 7,23-28, 1a herauszufinden." In *La Sagesse de l'Ancien Testament*, ed. M. Gilbert, 259-87. Gembloux.
1980   *Kohelet*. NEBib. Stuttgart.
1981   "*Melek, šallit*, und *môšēl* bei Kohelet und die Abfassungszeit des Buch." *Bib* 62:535-43.
Loretz, O.
1964   *Qohelet und der Alte Orient*. Freiburg.
1980   "Altorientalische und Kananäische Topoi in Buche Kohelet." *UF* 12:267-78.

Lys, D.
1977   *L'ecclésiaste ou que vaut la vie?* Paris.
Muilenburg, J.
1954   "A Qoheleth Scroll from Qumran." *BASOR* 135:20-28.
Müller, H. P.
1968   "Wie sprach Qohälät von Gott?" *VT* 18:507-21.
1978   "Neige der althebräischen 'Weisheit.' Zum Denken Qohäläts." *ZAW* 90:238-64.
Murphy, R. E.
1979   "Qoheleth's 'Quarrel' with the Fathers." In *From Faith to Faith*, ed. G. Y. Hadidian, 235-45. Pittsburgh.
1981   *Wisdom Literature: Job, Proverbs, Ruth, Canticles, Ecclesiastes, Esther.* FOTL 13. Grand Rapids MI.
1982   "Qoheleth Interpreted: The Bearing of the Past on the Present." *VT* 32:331-37.
Ogden, G. S.
1977   "The 'Better'-Proverb (Tob-Spruch), Rhetorical Criticism, and Qoheleth." *JBL* 96:489-505.
1979   "Qoheleth's Use of the 'Nothing Is Better' Form." *JBL* 98:339-50.
1980a   "Historical Allusion in Qoheleth iv 13-16?" *VT* 30:309-15.
1980b   "Qoheleth ix 17 - x 20. Variations on the Theme of Wisdom's Strength and Vulnerability." *VT* 30:27-37.
1982   "Qoheleth ix 1-16." *VT* 32:158-69.
1984   "Qoheleth xi 7 - xii 8: Qoheleth's Summons to Enjoyment and Reflection." *VT* 34:27-38.
1987   *Qoheleth.* Sheffield.
Pfeiffer, E.
1965   "Die Gottesfurcht im Buche Kohelet." In *Gottes Wort und Gottes Land: Festschrift für H. W. Hertzberg*, ed. H. G. Reventlow, 133-58. Göttingen.
Podechard, E.
1912   *L'Eccléesiaste.* Etudes bibliques. Paris.
Rad, Gerhard von
1972   *Wisdom in Israel.* Nashville.
Rousseau, F.
1981   "Structure de Qohelet I 4-11 et plan du livre." *VT* 31:200-17.
Rudolph, W.
1959   *Vom Buch Kohelet.* Münster.
Sawyer, J. F. A.
1975   "The Ruined House in Ecclesiastes 12: A Reconstruction of the Original Parable." *JBL* 94:519-31.
Schmid, H. H.
1966   *Wesen und Geschichte der Weisheit.* BZAW 101. Berlin.
Schoors, A.
1982a   "Kethibh-Qere in Ecclesiastes." In *Studia Paulo Naster Oblata II Orientalia Antiqua*, ed. J. Quaegebeur, 215-22. Leuvain.
1982b   "La structure litteraire de Qoheleth." *OLP* 13:91-116.
Sheppard, G. T.
1977   "The Epilogue to Qoheleth as Theological Commentary." *CBQ* 39:182-89.

Skehan, P. W.
 1971   *Studies in Israelite Poetry and Wisdom.* CBQMS 1. Washington DC.
Stiglmair, A.
 1974   "Weisheit und Jahweglaube im Buche Kohelet." *TTZ* 83:257-83.
Whitley, C. F.
 1979a *Koheleth.* BZAW 148. Berlin.
 1979b "Koheleth and Ugaritic Parallels." *UF* 11:811-24.
Whybray, R. N.
 1978   "Qoheleth the Immoralist (Qoh 7:16-17)." In Gammie et al., eds. (1978) 191-204.
 1979   "Conservatisme et radicalisme dans Qohelet." In *Sagesse et Religion (Colloque de Strasbourg Octobre 1976)*, ed. E. Jacob, 65-81. Paris.
 1980   *Two Jewish Theologies: Job and Ecclesiastes.* Hull.
 1981a "Qoheleth, Preacher of Joy." *JSOT* 23:87-98.
 1981b "The Identification and Use of Quotations in Qoheleth." VTSup 32:435-51.
Williams, J. G.
 1981   *Those Who Ponder Proverbs: Aphoristic Thinking and Biblical Literature.* Sheffield.
Witzenrath, H.
 1979   *Süss ist das Licht . . . Ein literaturwissenschaftliche Untersuchung zu Kohelet 11, 7-12, 7.* St. Ottilien.
Wright, A. D. G.
 1968   "The Riddle of the Sphinx: The Structure of the Book of Qoheleth." *CBQ* 30:313-34.
 1980   "The Riddle of the Sphinx Revisited: Numerical Patterns in the Book of Qoheleth." *CBQ* 42:35-51.
 1983   "Additional Numerical Patterns in Qoheleth." *CBQ* 45:32-43.
Zimmerli, Walther
 1964 "The Place and Limit of the Wisdom in the Framework of the Old Testament Theology." *SJT* 17:145-58.
 1974   "Das Buch Kohelet—Traktat oder Sentenzensammlung?" *VT* 24:221-30.
Zimmermann, F.
 1973   *The Inner World of Qoheleth.* New York.

Qoheleth
in Current Research

Ten years ago a survey of Qoheleth research was published by Breton (1973) in *Biblical Theology Bulletin*. The essay treats commentaries first, then deals with special studies on particular problems of interpretation. Under the first category, Breton described current thinking about the following seven topics: (1) place and date of origin; (2) influences and language; (3) unity; (4) style; (5) Qoheleth and traditional wisdom; (6) pessimism and faith; and (7) הֶבֶל. The section on special studies, somewhat more extensive, discusses recent essays on (1) philology, (2) style, (3) structure, (4) wisdom, (5) God, (6) pessimism, (7) time, (8) the relationship between Qoheleth and other biblical books, (9) historical data in Qoheleth, and (10) death. Breton emphasized the inadequacy of traditional approaches to the book, expressing the opinion that much of modern research merely restates older views. Thus Barucq (1968) quotes Podechard (1912) more than sixty times, Hertzberg (1963) relies heavily upon Delitzsch (1877), while both Loretz (1964) and Ellermeier (1967) underline the significance of older authors again and again. Anyone who has compared commentaries must surely concur in this judgment, and thus stands face to face with a shocking claim of Qoheleth: "There is nothing new under the sun" (1:9b). What follows, therefore, is an attempt to bring up to date the story of research into the book that evokes such contradictory responses in those who wrestle with its presence in the Hebrew Bible. Although I shall emphasize the last ten years, those publications will be set in the larger context of research during the last half century.

Unlike Breton, I envision an interpretive history of research. My mentor in this respect is Galling, whose comprehensive surveys of Qoheleth research appeared in *Zeitschrift für die alttestamentliche Wissenschaft* (1932) and in *Theologische Rundschau* (1934). In the first of them, Galling isolated four main issues for discussion: (1) the theme of the book; (2) the autobiographical form; (3) the relationship between Qoheleth and ancient Near Eastern wisdom; and (4) the influence of Greek philosophy upon the book. Galling concluded that Qoheleth lacks a unified theme and an organic structure. Instead, it consists of thirty-seven separate sentences or aphoristic units. The royal fiction, of Egyptian vintage, is wholly devoid of biographical value, Galling insisted, and therefore provides no historical information about the unknown author. Indeed, that fiction of royal authorship quickly fades, and the rest of the book takes the form of a dispute with "school wisdom." The chief stylistic medium in this debate is the broken sentence, in which the first part presents traditional views only to be corrected by the author's understanding of the real situation. The major part of Galling's survey is actually a thorough presentation of this phenomenon of broken sentences in the book. The third issue, forced upon biblical critics by the remarkable discovery a few years earlier that the Egyptian Instruction of Amenemope influenced Prov 22:17–23:33, did not seem promising to Galling, who does not push beyond Humbert's findings (1929). Even those Egyptian borrowings, such as the literary device of royal authorship, the allusion in 10:16-17 to cultivated fields of the king, and the philosophy encapsulated in the slogan *carpe diem*, bear Qoheleth's individual stamp. The final issue, that of Greek influence upon the book, was set aside, since Galling intended to publish a separate essay on Theognis. So far as I can determine, that essay never materialized.

The second survey essay by Galling spreads its net wider still, focusing on seven topics: (1) the text, language, and date of the book; (2) its unity; (3) its composition; (4) Qoheleth and Greek philosophy; (5) the relationship with Egyptian wisdom; (6) an analysis of the book's structure; and (7) its theological perspective. Galling opted for a third century date in Jerusalem, and conceded that Aramaisms are sprinkled throughout the book. He argued for the presence of editorial additions in 3:17; 8:5, 12, 13; 11:9b; 12:7b; and the epilogues. Two other texts, 2:26 and 7:26, usually thought to be additions, are understood in a nonmoral sense, and are therefore retained as authentic teachings of Qoheleth. Galling rejected an organic unity, insisting on individual sentences. While acknowledging the atmosphere of popular Greek philosophy in Qoheleth, Galling denied a Greek source for such phrases as "the good that is beautiful" (5:17), "chance" (cf. 1 Sam 6:9; Ruth 2:3 for similar use of מִקְרֶה), and "to see (enjoy) good" (cf. 2 Sam 12:18). Furthermore, he noted the absence in Qoheleth of a contrast between aristocracy and plebes, so essential to Theognis. Egyptian influence seemed undeniable to Galling, who mentioned the following verses in this regard: 1:12; 8:2, 10; 10:4; 7:10, 13f; 8:13. He did note, however, that Papyrus Insinger lacks the distinctly personal touch in Qoheleth, who found no place for a hymn to the creator. In this respect, Ben Sira demonstrates clear affinities with Insinger.[1] As far as internal structure is concerned, Galling rejected attempts to see a pervasive influence of the Yahwistic creation narrative upon the book. He went so far as to deny familiarity with Israel's history of creation. That led Galling to discuss the theological perspective of the book. Far from speaking out of the category of revelation, Qoheleth maintained distance

---

[1]The kinship between Ben Sira and Papyrus Insinger has recently been examined by J. Sanders, in *Ben Sira and Demotic Wisdom*, SBLMS 28 (Chico CA: Scholars Press, 1983.

between creature and creator and spoke for the people. In Galling's judgment, Qoheleth dwelt on the periphery of Yahwism.[2]

Explaining Inconsistencies within the Book

Is it possible to ascertain a common theme in Qoheleth research during the period under review? Unless I am mistaken the essential issue for more than fifty years has been the search for an adequate means of explaining inconsistencies within the book. A more pressing concern seems to have motivated this endeavor, even though frequently waiting inconspicuously in the shadows. That desire was to determine authentic teachings of Qoheleth. One suspects that historical interest alone cannot explain this compulsion. That is why theological issues always seem to surface in discussions of Qoheleth.

Qoheleth affirms divine action, both punishment and reward (7:18, 26; 3:11, 14; 11:5), but he also contends that God is so far away that no one can comprehend the divine ways (8:17; 5:1). Life is better than death (9:4-6), but the dead are more fortunate (4:2), and Qoheleth hates life (2:17). Wisdom is unprofitable and empty (1:17-18; 2:13-16), but it is an advantage when accompanied by a heritage (7:11); it is useful (7:19) and preferable to force (9:16-18). Joy is empty (2:2-3, 10-11), but it is good (5:19; 8:15) and comes from God (2:24-26). Work is grievous and unprofitable (1:13-14; 2:11, 18; 3:10; 4:6), but God gives it for human enjoyment (5:18). Woman lacks real worth (not one in a thousand, 7:26-27), but a man ought to enjoy the wife he loves (9:9). Retribution does not operate (8:10-14), and all are equal in the grave (9:2-3), but God keeps a tally of merits (7:18, 26) and will eventually judge everyone (11:9).[3]

Naturally, such inconsistency in the book produces opposing interpretations, even with respect to the overall tone. Was Qoheleth an optimist despite everything, or was he a pessimist? Von Rad (1972, p. 231; cf. Whybray, 1981a) thought Qoheleth's heart beat with gusto when the subject of enjoying life's pleasures presented itself, and Rousseau (1981) has opted for the dominance of that refrain over the more frequent one asserting life's absurdity. Of course, a moderate position commends itself to others, for example Klopfenstein (1972), who conceded that skepticism has invaded Qoheleth's thoughts and taken up residence, but that doubt concerns human ability and never extends to God. I have argued (1981, 126-48, 254-56) for the prominence of pessimism, largely on the basis of the consistent qualification that Qoheleth attaches to each allusion to enjoyment. In another essay

---

[2]One other survey of research on Qoheleth appeared in 1980 (P. C. Beentjes, "Recente visies op Qohelet," *Bijdragen: Tÿdschrift voor Filosofie en Theologie* 41:346-444) but it is largely devoted to a single monograph: C. F. Whitley, *Koheleth*.

[3]On such inconsistencies within Qoheleth, see A. Barucq, "Qoheleth (Livre de l'ecclésiaste ou de)," p. 613 in *Supplément au Dictionnaire de la Bible*, 50B (1977).

(1980) I insisted that skepticism, which perceives the disparity between present reality and a vision of a just society, passes over into pessimism in this book.

A related question has prompted considerable debate: was Qoheleth the guardian of authentic Yahwism or did he circle around biblical faith, remaining on the outermost fringes? Zimmerli (1964) has insisted that Qoheleth preserved the old belief in Yahweh's freedom and grounded human response in proper fear, working his theology out of the revelatory category of creation. On the other hand, von Rad (1972, 232-37) has located Qoheleth's thought on the perimeter of Israelite faith, in this judgment concurring in Gese's declaration that Qoheleth, and wisdom in general, was an alien body in the canon (1958). Hertzberg (1963) and Forman (1960) attempted to demonstrate Qoheleth's indebtedness to the Yahwistic creation narrative, while Sheppard (1977) and Childs (1979, 580-89) discussed the significance of the final epilogue in setting the tone for reading the entire book. Goldin (1966) and Holm-Nielsen (1974; 1975/1976; cf. Murphy 1982) examined varying attitudes in Judaism and Christianity to the epilogue and to the whole book respectively.

Differences persist in other matters as well. Was Qoheleth a misogynist? Did he advocate nothing in excess, not even virtue? Was he a conservative or a radical? Lohfink (1979) has addressed the first question, that of Qoheleth's attitude to women. Largely by appealing to several stages in the development of the ideas found in 7:23-28, Lohfink sought to exonerate Qoheleth of prejudice against women, who on the other reading of the text are only one-thousandth less trustworthy than men. The crucial verse was taken by Lohfink to be a citation from traditional wisdom, which Qoheleth refuted. Whybray (1979) has sought to isolate conservative and radical tendencies in Qoheleth's thought. In his view, Qoheleth draws heavily upon Jewish wisdom, not Egyptian, Greek or Mesopotamian, but he interprets these traditions in a radical manner. In another essay Whybray (1978) has stoutly refused to concede immoral advice to this sage. By means of a syntactical analysis of 7:16-17, he challenged the usual understanding of this passage. It does not, he insisted, commend a middle course between virtue and vice, but attacks self-righteousness.

Perhaps the most frequently used word to characterize Qoheleth is crisis (Crüsemann 1979a; Hengel 1974). Even here opposite viewpoints exist. Gese (1963) has put forth the thesis that in Qoheleth a crisis of wisdom explodes the atmosphere of a doctrinaire school. Schmid (1966, 186-96) has offered a slight revision, but his view virtually amounts to the same thing: Qoheleth has given up all hope of securing existence through wisdom, since its ability to cope has vanished. Schmid noted the remarkable inconsequence that Qoheleth did not give up faith in God. On the other hand, Lauha (1955; cf. Crüsemann 1979b) compared Job and Qoheleth, the former as *homo religiosus* and the latter as a secular individual. For Lauha, the crisis occurs in the realm of faith: God no longer guarantees an order in which goodness receives divine favor and wickedness results in punishment (cf. Müller 1978).

To recapitulate, contradictions within the book of Qoheleth evoke opposing interpretations of the real thought to be attributed to the teacher. Critics cannot agree where the emphasis falls, and the result has been lively debate that so far has generated little consensus. How can the tensions within the book be explained? Four responses to this difficult question govern the course of contemporary discussion. The contradictory views derive from a redactor, they are citations of traditional wisdom, they reflect life's ambiguities and time's passage, or they represent conscious effort to provide thesis and antithesis and thus to capture life's fullness.

Dominant Hypotheses

(1) Contradictory Views Derive from a Redactor

Lauha (1978) has recently reasserted the hypothesis of editorial activity throughout the book. In his view two redactors worked over the book, R^1 adding 1:1, 2; 12:8, 9-11 and rearranging 1:3-11 to its present position, and R^2 correcting Qoheleth's unorthodox theology, particularly on the touchy subject of retribution. This redactor's hand is evident in 2:26a ; 3:17a; 5:18; 7:26b; 8:12-13; 11:9b; 12:12-14. Acknowledgment of redactional activity did not lead Lauha to reject a certain kind of unity, that of style and thought. In this regard he followed Loretz (1964, 196-216) in recognizing a unity of *topoi* with their own inner connections. Lauha insisted that the *topoi* were typical ones drawn from traditional wisdom, but they achieved a distinctive tone in Qoheleth's nimble fingers. Since the first redactor assumed that Qoheleth's membership in the professional guild of the חֲכָמִים was common knowledge, it follows that the teacher had access to the *topoi* promulgated in the schools. Surprisingly, Qoheleth referred to himself as king rather than sage, but he surely meant this bit of royal fiction, quickly abandoned after the second chapter, to be understood as an allusion to sapiential status. The first redactor altered this reference by making it specific; the phrase "son of David" thus historicized what had earlier been a general allusion. Lauha considered it significant that the first colophonist ignores the royal fiction altogether. Naturally, this claim depends upon reading the words "one shepherd" as an allusion to God rather than the teacher.[4]

Zimmerli (1962) had earlier developed Galling's views about an adversarial relationship between Qoheleth and school wisdom into open hostility, a view recently emphasized by Murphy (1979). At one point Qoheleth boldly asserted that the mere claim to possess knowledge was not to be trusted, even if put forth by a sage (8:17). This conviction that wisdom cannot achieve its goal struck at the fundamental premise of the school. For Qoheleth, wisdom has lost its power and chance has ascended the throne (cf. Müller, 1978). Such crushing of the very foundation stone upon which the sages had built their school was a bold enterprise. Was it too daring? Did Qoheleth vacillate from one position to another, at one time endorsing

---

[4]On the imagery of shepherd in Egyptian thought, see D. Müller, "Der gute Hirte: Ein Beitrag zur Geschichte ägyptischer Bildrede," *ZÄS* (1961) 86:126-44.

divine reward and punishment, at another denying them? Thus it would seem—unless Qoheleth cites traditional claims in order to refute them.

(2) The Author Quotes Traditional Wisdom

A decisive step forward was made when Gordis recognized the presence of quotations within the book attributed to Qoheleth (Gordis: 1939/40), a thesis that was subsequently strengthened by analysis of other biblical, rabbinic, and ancient Near Eastern literature (Gordis 1949a). The fruit of this research is conveniently summarized in a recent essay, where Gordis distinguishes eleven different types of citations (Gordis 1981). He proposes four major categories of quotations: (1) the verbalization of a speaker or writer's unexpressed ideas or sentiments; (2) the sentiment of a subject other than the writer or speaker; (3) use in argument and debate; and (4) indirect quotations without a *verbum dicendi*. Under the first category Gordis delineates six subtypes: (a) presentation of a speaker's unspoken thought; (b) citations from current folk or literary wisdom; (c) citation of a proverb with or without comment, or expanded by additional observation by the author supporting or opposing it; (d) citation of prayers; (e) presentation of ideas previously held by the speaker or writer; (f) a hypothetical idea that would or should have occurred to the subject. Two subtypes fall under the second major category: (a) direct quotation of words of foes, friends, God, or people, and (b) development of elaborate dialogue where various speakers must be inferred. Similarly, two subtypes appear under category three: (a) use of contrasting proverbs to negate one view and affirm another, with the second being the author's view; and (b) presentation of the arguments of one's opponents in order to refute them; the citation, which exaggerates and distorts the original, is never literal.

Whybray has recently examined Qoheleth from the perspective of quotations, searching for agreement in form and content between sayings in the oldest collections of the Book of Proverbs and Qoheleth (Whybray 1981b). Eight quotations in Qoheleth meet this criterion, in Whybray's judgment (2:14a; 4:5; 4:6; 7:6a; 9:17; 10:2; 10:12). Like Gordis, Whybray emphasizes the many uses of such quotations. Some are quoted with full approval (7:5-6; 10:2, 12) but Qoheleth gave them a radically new interpretation. Others he employed to confirm the first stage in the characteristic two-part argument, the so-called broken sentence in which he posited a truth and then "gravely qualified it by stating a fact of life which runs counter to it."

(3) Inconsistencies Reflect Life's Ambiguities and Time's Passage

Not all critics attribute diversity of viewpoint within the book to different authors. Delitzsch (1877) had long ago contended that Qoheleth should not be judged by logical standards derived from Greek thought, and Wildeboer (1898) had emphasized the inevitable conflict between faith and experience as the source of inconsistency. When one combines these recognitions with an understanding of the literary form of the book as a teacher's notebook or diary, then time's passage lends credibility to the argument. After all, opinions change with age and shifting political circumstances. In this regard, even wisdom is historical, as Schmid (1966) has perceived with great clarity. Rudolph (1959) went so far as to explain Qoheleth's inconsistency as the fruit of the confrontation between Judaism and Hellenism, coupled with the psychology of the individual. In this judgment Rudolph exercised considerably more restraint than Zimmermann (1973), who thought he found evidence that Qoheleth suffered from the classic symptoms Freud described so graphically: incest, impotency, Oedipal conflicts, and so forth. Maillot (1971) drew the analogy of a kaleidoscope, insisting that like life itself Qoheleth's views create a kaleidoscopic demonstration that eventually forms a fixed image. Barucq (1977) found such an explanation for the shifting positions in Qoheleth attractive, although he did not rule out the possibility of glosses.

(4) Inconsistencies Represent a Desire to Embrace All of Life

Herder's suggestion (See Barucq 1977, 612) that Qoheleth juxtaposes two voices, thesis and antithesis, has been taken up again by Müller (1968) and Loader (1979), the latter in great detail. According to him Qoheleth structured his entire argument around polar viewpoints. Loader claimed to have isolated thirty-eight chiastic structures and sixty polar structures within the book. In all these polarities a negative follows a positive in such a way as to draw attention to the resulting הֶבֶל. In addition, an intricate system of cross reference joins together numerous lesser polarities and connects the separate verses and larger units. In Loader's view the tension within the book and that between the form and subject matter testify to the conflict between Qoheleth and school wisdom. In short, we have here a version of the theory of quotations. One could argue that Qoheleth's desire to cover all of reality dictated the decision to utter opposing sentiments. In this case he would have recognized some truth in each claim and would have expected his hearers to judge which one applied in a given situation.

Another attempt to understand the competing voices has resorted to the explanation that Qoheleth borrowed heavily from Greek thought. Lohfink (1980) claimed that the form of the book is that of a palindrome, while its content constitutes a diatribe. In a palindrome the symmetry is so perfect that a work reads the same forwards and backwards. The following scheme is proposed for outlining the book.

1:2-3	Frame
1:4-11	Cosmology (poetic)
1:12–3:15	Anthropology
3:16–4:16	Social Criticism I
4:17–5:6	Criticism of Religion (poetry; a sort of intrusion)
5:7–6:10	Social Criticism II
6:11–9:6	Ideology Critique (Refutatio, denying retribution)
9:7–12:7	Ethic (poetic at the end)
12:8	Frame

Lohfink granted that the criticism of religion mars an otherwise perfect specimen of the palindrome. Undaunted, he argued that Qoheleth was written as a compromise for the school at Jerusalem, where Alexandrian influence was manifest. Although intended to preserve Hebrew values while endorsing Hellenistic ones, the book owes its inspiration to Greek education. Lohfink asserted that Greek syntax and stereotypical expressions are scattered throughout the book in the same way English appears in German literature today. Qoheleth was a leader of those seeking education and gathered the people just as wandering Greek philosophers did. Since the book was later canonized, Lohfink thought that it must have been used as a text and that its author was probably a member of the wealthy class. The hypothesis of use as a text book has received support from Lemaire's (1981) study of inscriptional and other evidence that schools existed in early Israel.[5]

The designation of the form of the book as a palindrome and the message as a diatribe was only the first step in Lohfink's endeavor to buttress an argument for Greek influence upon Qoheleth. Without trying to be exhaustive, I offer the following bits of evidence drawn from the commentary at large:

1. the myth of eternal return (which Lohfink views as a positive statement)
2. the name Qoheleth, which resembles that of Hegesias the Cyrenian, a wandering teacher who was known as the "commender of suicide"
3. the motto in 1:1 which is developed in 1:2–2:2 after the fashion of Cynic diatribes
4. the Hebrew word תּוּר for spying out or searching, with the audial resemblance to τηρεῖν
5. Menander's observation that king and wise, clever and rich are alike in death
6. the comparison of humans to animals, familiar from Epicureans, popular philosophers and Satirics
7. Euripides' distinction of earthly things from αἰθήρ, which ascends at death
8. the praise of the dead and the unborn in Homer and Hegesias
9. Menander's warning that God will not forget oaths sworn to him
10. the cynic phrases "lover of ease" and "lover of gold" (φιλόπλουλος / φιλάργυρος)
11. the expressions ἀγαθόν ὅτι καλόν and καλόν φίλον
12. Menander's advice not to oppose God
13. Pindar's observation that humans possess no means of finding out what is best for them

---

[5]The inscriptional evidence on which Lemaire draws may be read quite differently. Even if one accepts the claim that reverse writing, poor spelling and drawing, and so forth suggest children's efforts at acquiring scribal skills, it is still another jump from that to the existence of schools. I plan to address this issue in the near future in connection with a presentation at the national meeting of the Society of Biblical Literature in Dallas, 18-20 Dec 1983.

14. Archilochos' counsel to be happy in health and not to fret in misfortune, since people rise and fall
15. Diogenes Laertius's judgment that there is an inner connection between uncertainty and delusion
16. Simonides' comparison of women to a net
17. Theognis's assertion that life is meaningless and the search for knowledge is futile
18. Euripides' claim that whoever is alive has hope
19. Homer's description of death as a net
20. Euripides' saying that it is sweet to behold the light

Such an attempt to locate Qoheleth squarely within the intellectual community of ancient Greece joined hands with that of Braun (1973), who emphasized the influence of popular philosophy upon the book. The hypothesis was advanced long before by Ranston (1930), but it had fallen into disfavor, particularly through Loretz' (1964, 90-134) defense of Babylonian parallels and the ever-increasing recognition of Egyptian affinities, especially with Papyrus Insinger. On another front Horton (1972) has pointed to similarities between Qoheleth and Taoist writings, a powerful argument for the universal character of the themes within the book.

Internal inconsistencies in Qoheleth have rendered all attempts to discover the structure of the book problematic. However, this fact has failed to halt the publication of several essays in recent years (Ginsberg 1955; Wright 1968, 1980, 1983; Rousseau 1981; Schoors 1982b; cf. Fox 1977; Good 1978; Osborn 1970). The problem is complicated by uncertainty with regard to the actual form of the book, whether it consists of individual "sentences" or a sustained treatise on life's vanity. Zimmerli (1974) speaks for many when arguing that the evidence points in both directions. Form critical analyses have failed to throw much light on this vexing problem (Johnson 1973; Loretz 1964; Witzenrath 1979; cf. Ogden 1977, 1979), as have philological studies (Whitley 1979a; Ceresko 1982).

Attempts to determine the linguistic background and sociological setting for Qoheleth have encountered difficulty because of conflicting tendencies (Ellermeier 1967; Fox and Porten 1978; Whitley 1979b; Loretz 1980). Ambiguous conclusions have also surrounded efforts to relate the book to its particular historical setting (Ogden 1980a; Lohfink 1981; cf. Lauha 1981). In one area, at least, a consistent attitude persists. That is the matter of allusions to the shadow of death (Crenshaw 1978; cf. Sawyer 1975; Gilbert, 1981). Nevertheless, Eaton (1983) reads Qoheleth in such a manner as to remove every radical teaching. The relationship between Yahwism and Qoheleth's views is the subject of much speculation, particularly because modern theologians have been unable to reckon with wisdom in a predominantly "historical" scheme (Armstrong 1983). In any event, the significance of creation (Crenshaw 1974) and fear of God (Pfeiffer 1965) to Qoheleth seems beyond doubt.[6]

It would be presumptuous to pronounce judgment upon the sum total of this research. Instead, let me say what will characterize my commentary on Qoheleth for the Old Testament Library. First, the refrains will be taken as a decisive argument for thematic unity as well as for the pessimistic impact of the book. Second, the magic rod, i.e., a theory of broken sentences, will be subjected to critical scrutiny in the light of clear evidence of redactional activity, both in the epilogues and within the book itself. Third, the Jewish background for Qoheleth's thought will be highlighted at the expense of Greek or Egyptian sources for themes that are much more adequately explained by the notion of polygenesis. Fourth, the radical nature of the book will receive notice; this applies particularly to the claim that creation faith somehow redeems Qoheleth's unorthodox views and to the positive understanding of the notion of fear before God. Finally, I shall apply aesthetic criticism to the book, emphasizing literary and theological dimensions. It may be that in the last resort Qoheleth is a mirror which reflects the soul of the interpreter. If so, there is sufficient vanity in scholarship to appreciate reliable mirrors.

---

[6]This survey has not taken into account several important essays on specific topics on which Gordis has written at some length (Qoheleth and Qumran; the language of the original book, whether Aramaic or Hebrew; the text, especially the כְּתִב and קְרֵא readings) and many exegetical studies of individual units. Such an inquiry would far exceed the limits of this publication.

Bibliography

Armstrong, J. F.
1983 "Ecclesiastes in Old Testament Theology." *The Princeton Seminary Bulletin* 94:16-25.
Barucq, A.
1968 *Ecclésiaste*. VS 3. Paris.
1977 "Qoheleth." *Supplément au Dictionaire de la Bible*, ed. H. Cazelles and A. Feuillet, 609-74. Paris.
Beentjes, P. C.
1980 "Recente visies op Qohelet." *Bijdragen: Tijdschrift voor Filosofie en Theologie* 41:436-44.
Braun, R.
1973 *Kohelet und die frühhellenistische Popularphilosophie*. BZAW 130. Berlin and New York.
Breton, S.
1973 "Qoheleth Studies." *BTB* 3:22-50.
Ceresko, A. R.
1982 "The Function of Antanaclasis (*mṣ'* "to find" ‖ *mṣ'* "to reach, overtake, grasp") in Hebrew Poetry, Especially in the Book of Qoheleth." *CBQ* 44:551-69.
Childs, B.
1979 *Introduction to the Old Testament as Scripture*. Philadelphia.
Crenshaw, J. L.
1974 "The Eternal Gospel (Eccl. 3:11)." In *Essays in Old Testament Ethics*, ed. J. L. Crenshaw and J. T. Willis, 23-35. New York.
1978 "The Shadow of Death in Qoheleth." In *Israelite Wisdom*, ed. J. Gammie et al., 205-16. Missoula.
1980 "The Birth of Skepticism in Ancient Israel." In *The Divine Helmsman*, ed. J. L. Crenshaw and S. Sandmel, 1-19. New York.
1981 *Old Testament Wisdom*. Atlanta and London.
Crüsemann, F.
1979a "Die unveränderbare Welt. Überlegungen zur 'Krisis der Weisheit' beim Prediger (Kohelet)." In *Der Gott der kleinen Leute*, ed. W. Schottroff and W. Stegemann, 80-104. München.
1979b "Hiob und Kohelet. Ein Beitrag zum Verständnis des Hiobbuches." In *Werden und Wirken des Alten Testaments*, ed. R. Albertz et al., 373-93. Göttingen.
Delitzsch, F.
1877 *Commentary on the Song of Songs and Ecclesiastes*. Edinburgh.
Eaton, M. A.
1983 *Ecclesiastes: An Introduction and Commentary*. Leicester/Downers Grove IL.
Ellermeier, F.
1967 *Qoheleth, I. Untersuchungen zum Buche Qoheleth*. Herzberg.
Forman, C.
1960 "Koheleth's Use of Genesis." *JSS* 5:256-63.

Fox, M. V.
1977   "Frame-Narrative and Composition in the Book of Qoheleth." *HUCA* 48:83-106.
Fox, M. V., and B. Porten.
1978   "Unsought Discoveries: Qohelet 7:23–8:1a." *Hebrew Studies* 19:26-38.
Galling, K.
1932   "Kohelet-Studien." *ZAW* 50:276-99.
1934   "Stand und Aufgabe der Kohelet-Forschung." *TRu* n.f. 6:355-73.
Gese, H.
1958   *Lehre und Wirklichkeit in der alten Weisheit.* Tübingen.
1963   "Die Krisis der Weisheit bei Koheleth." *Les Sagesses du Proche-Orient Ancien*, ed. F. Wendel, 139-51. Paris. ET in *Theodicy in the Old Testament*, ed. J. L. Crenshaw, 141-53. Philadelphia and London, 1983.
Gilbert, M.
1981   "La description de la viellesse en Qohelet XII-7, est elle allegorique?" *Congress Volume, Vienna*, 96-109. VTSup. Leiden.
Ginsberg, H. L.
1955   "The Structure and Contents of the Book of Koheleth." VTSup 3:138-49.
Goldin,
1966   "The End of Ecclesiastes: Literal Exegesis and Its Transformation." *Lown Institute for Judaistic Studies* 3:135-58.
Golka, F.
1983   "Die israelitische Weisheitsschule oder 'des Kaisers neue Kleider'." *VT* 33:257-70.
Good, E. M.
1978   "The Unfilled Sea: Style and Meaning in Ecclesiastes 1:2-11." In *Israelite Wisdom*, 59-73. Missoula.
Gordis, R.
1939/1940 "Quotations in Wisdom Literature." *JQR* 30:123-47.
1946   "The Original Language of Qohelet." *JQR* 37:76-84. Repr. in *The Word and the Book: Studies in Biblical Language and Literature*, 231-48. New York, 1976.
1949a   "Quotations in Oriental, Biblical, and Rabbinic Literature." *HUCA* 22:157-219. Repr. in Gordis, *Poets, Prophets and Sages: Essays in Biblical Interpretation*. Bloomington IN.
1949b   "The Translation Theory of Qohelet Reexamined." *JQR* 39:103-16 = *The Word and the Book*, 249-62.
1952   "Koheleth—Hebrew or Aramaic?" *JBL* 71:93-109 = *The Word and the Book*, 263-79.
1955   "Was Koheleth a Phoenician?" *JBL* 74:103-14 = *The Word and the Book*, 280-91.
1960   "Qoheleth and Qumran—A Study of Style." *Bib* 41:395-410 = *The Word and the Book*, 292-307.
1968   *Koheleth: the Man and His World.* New York. Orig. 1951.
1981   "Virtual Quotations in Job, Sumer and Qumran." *VT* 31:410-27.
Hengel, M.
1974   *Judaism and Hellenism*, 115-30. Philadelphia.

Hertzberg, W.
1963   *Der Prediger.* KAT 17. Gütersloh.
Holm-Nielson, S.
1974   "On the Interpretation of Qoheleth in Early Christianity." *VT* 24:168-77.
1975–1976 "The Book of Ecclesiastes and the Interpretation of It in Jewish and Christian Theology." *Annual of the Swedish Theological Institute* 10:38-96.
Horton, E.
1972   "Koheleth's Concept of Opposites." *Numen* 19:1-21.
Humbert, P.
1929   *Recherches sur les sources égyptiennes de la litterature sapientiale d'Israël.* Neuchâtel.
Johnson, R. F.
1973   "A Form Critical Analysis of the Sayings in the Book of Ecclesiastes." Ph.D. diss., Emory University.
Klopfenstein, M. A.
1972   "Die Skepsis des Qohelet." *TZ* 28:97-109.
Lauha, A.
1955   "Die krise des religiösen Glaubens bei Kohelet." VTSup 3:183-91.
1978   *Kohelet.* BKAT 19. Neukirchen-Vluyn.
1981   "Kohelets Verhältnis zur Geschichte." *Die Botschaft und die Boten*, ed. J. Jeremias and L. Perlit, 393-401. Neukirchen/Vluyn.
Lemaire, A.
1981   *Les écoles et la formation de la Bible dans l'ancien Israël.* OBO 39. Fribourg and Göttingen.
Loader, J. A.
1979   *Polar Structures in the Book of Qohelet.* BZAW 152. Berlin and New York.
Lohfink, N.
1979   "War Kohelet ein Frauenfeind? Ein Versuch, die Logik und den Gegenstand von Qoh., 7, 23-28, la herauszufinden." In *La Sagesse de l'Ancien Testament*, ed. M. Gilbert, 259-87. Gembloux.
1980   *Kohelet.* NEBib. Stuttgart.
1981   "melek, šallît, und môšēl bei Kohelet und die Abfassungszeit des Buchs." *Bib* 62:535-43.
Loretz, O.
1964   *Qohelet und der Alte Orient.* Freiburg, Basel, Wien.
1980   "Altorientalische und kananäische Topoi in Buche Kohelet." *UF* 12:267-78.
Maillot, A.
1971   *La contestation. Commentaire de l'Ecclésiaste.* Lyon.
Müller, H. P.
1968   "Wie sprach Qohälät von Gott?" *VT* 18:507-21.
1978   "Neige der althebräischen 'Weisheit': Zum Denken Qohäläts." *ZAW* 90:238-64.
Murphy, R. E.
1979   "Qoheleth's 'Quarrel' with the Fathers." In *From Faith to Faith*, ed. G. Y. Hadidian, 235-45. Pittsburgh.
1981   *Wisdom Literature: Job, Proverbs, Ruth, Canticles, Ecclesiastes, Esther.* FOTL 13. Grand Rapids.

1982   "Qohelet Interpreted: The Bearing of the Past on the Present." *VT* 32:331-37.

Ogden, G. S.
1977   "The 'Better'-Proverb (Tôb-Spruch), Rhetorical Criticism, and Qoheleth." *JBL* 96:489-505.
1979   "Qoheleth's Use of the 'Nothing is Better' Form." *JBL* 98:339-50.
1980a   "Historical Allusion in Qoheleth iv 13-16?" *VT* 30:309-15.
1980b   "Qoheleth ix 17-x 20. Variations on the Theme of Wisdom's Strength and Vulnerability." *VT* 30:27-37.
1982   "Qoheleth ix 1-16." *VT* 32:158-69.

Osborn, N. D.
1970   "A Guide for Balanced Living. An Exegetical Study of Ecclesiastes 7:1-14." *Bible Translator* 21:185-96.

Pfeiffer, E.
1965   "Die Gottesfurcht im Buche Kohelet." *Gottes Wort und Gottes Land*, ed. H. G. Reventlow, 133-58. Göttingen.

Podechard, E.
1912   *L'Ecclésiaste*. Études bibliques. Paris.

Ranston, H.
1930   *The Old Testament Wisdom Books and Their Teaching*. London.

Rousseau, F.
1981   "Structure de Qohelet I 4-11 et plan du livre." *VT* 31:200-17.

Rudolph, W.
1959   *Vom Buch Kohelet*. Münster.

Sawyer, J. F. A.
1975   "The Ruined House in Ecclesiastes 12: A Reconstruction of the Original Parable." *JBL* 94:519-31.

Schmid, H. H.
1966   *Wesen und Geschichte der Weisheit*. BZAW 101. Berlin.

Schoors, A.
1982a   "Kethibh-Qere in Ecclesiastes." *Studia Paulo Naster Oblata II Orientalia Antiqua*, ed. J. Quaegebeur, 215-22. Leuven.
1982b   "La Structure littéraire de Qoheleth." *Orientalia Lovaniensia Periodica* 13:91-116.

Sheppard, G. T.
1977   "The Epilogue to Qoheleth as Theological Commentary." *CBQ* 39:182-89.

Stiglmair, A.
1974   "Weisheit und Jahweglaube im Buche Kohelet." *Trierer Theologische Zeitschrift* 83:257-83.

Von Rad, G.
1972   *Wisdom in Israel*. Nashville and London.

Whitley, C. F.
1979a   *Koheleth*. BZAW 148. Berlin and New York.
1979b   "Koheleth and Ugaritic Parallels." *UF* 11:811-24.

Whybray, R. N.
1978   "Qoheleth the Immoralist (Qoh 7:16-17)." *Israelite Wisdom*, 191-204.
1979   "Conservatisme et radicalisme dans Qohelet." In *Sagesse et Religion (Colloque de Strasbourg Octobre 1976)*, ed. E. Jacob, 65-81. Paris.

1980   *Two Jewish Theologies: Job and Ecclesiastes.* Hull.
1981a   "Qoheleth, Preacher of Joy." *JSOT* 23:87-98.
1981b   "The Identification and Use of Quotations in Qoheleth." In *Congress Volume, Vienna,* 435-51. VTSup 32. Leiden.

Wildeboer, G.
1898   *Der Prediger.* KHC 17. Tübingen.

Williams, J. G.
1981   *Those Who Ponder Proverbs: Aphoristic Thinking and Biblical Literature.* Sheffield.

Witzenrath, H.
1979   *Süss ist das Licht . . . : Ein literaturwissentschaftliche Untersuchung zu Kohelet 11, 7-12, 7.* St. Ottilien.

Wright, A. D. G.
1968   "The Riddle of the Sphinx: The Structure of the book of Qoheleth." *CBQ* 30:313-34.
1980   "The Riddle of the Sphinx Revisited: Numerical Patterns in the Book of Qoheleth." *CBQ* 42:35-51.
1983   "Additional Numerical Patterns in Qoheleth." *CBQ* 45:32-43.

Zimmerli, W.
1962   *Das Buch des Predigers Salomo.* ATD 16. Göttingen.
1964   "The Place and Limit of the Wisdom in the Framework of the Old Testament Theology." *SJT* 17:145-58.
1974   "Das Buch Kohelet—Traktat oder Sentenzensammlung." *VT* 24:221-30.

Zimmermann F.
1973   *The Inner World of Qoheleth.* New York.

35 (1986)

Youth and Old Age in Qoheleth*

The association of advanced age with wisdom is made in Ugarit, Mesopotamia, Egypt and Israel. Because this link is generally acknowledged, a few examples suffice. After mentioning El's advanced years, Athirat praises him: "You are wise indeed. . . . The gray of your beard has truly instructed you. . . . You are wise for eternity."[1] The Sumerian Instructions of Suruppak assert that the teachings of an old man are precious (5:13).[2] Egyptian Instructions constitute the insights of aged Pharaohs or viziers,[3] and Job's friends insist that age is on their side, and with it, superior wisdom.[4]

---

*This essay is part of a larger research project on "The Depiction of Old Age in Ancient Near Eastern Wisdom Literature," which was generously funded by the John Simon Guggenheim Memorial Foundation for the academic year 1984–1985.

[1]The translation in *ANET* takes *rbt* to imply greatness instead of age: "Art great indeed, O El, and wise, thy beard's gray hair instructs thee (*šbt dqnk ltsrk*). Anath's praise of El is rendered as follows: "Thy decree, O El, is wise; Wisdom with ever-life thy portion" (138).

[2]Alster (1974, 35) translates: "The Instructions of an old man are precious, may you submit to them!"

[3]*The Instruction of Ptahhotep* is purported to have been written by the aged vizier of King Izezi of the Fifth Dynasty (ca. 2350 BCE). Here one reads: "How good for a son to grasp his father's words, He will reach old age through them" (Lichtheim 1973, 74). Other Instructions include: *The Instruction for Merikare* by the old pharaoh to his son (ca. the end of the 22nd century BCE), *The Instruction of Amenemhet I* for his son Sesostris I (ca. 1960 BCE), *The Instruction of Hordedef* for his (27th century BCE, text from ca. 1250–1150), *The Instruction of Ani* by a middle class father to his son Khonshotep (toward the end of the Egyptian Empire), *The Instruction of Amenemopet* (10th to 6th c. BCE), *The Instruction of 'Onkhsheshonky* (Ptolemaic period), *The Instruction of Papyrus Insinger* (Ptolemaic period).

[4]"Both the gray-haired and the aged are among us, older than your father" (Job 15:10), a view that Elihu challenges: "It is not the old that are wise, nor the aged that understand what is right" (32:9, emended text). Naturally, Job also refuses to concede the claim that advanced years automatically bring superior understanding. An enthusiast for the torah also came to the conclusion that a younger person could surpass elders in knowledge: "I have more understanding than all my teachers, for thy testimonies are my meditation. I understand more than the aged, for I keep thy precepts" (Ps 119:99-100).

Of course, the ancients recognized that the link between old age and wisdom was not inevitable, for exceptions did occur. The author of Psalm 119, which exalts the Torah, claimed to have more knowledge than the aged precisely because of obedience to the divine precepts (v. 100), and Job's unjustified suffering, intensified by the unfair accusations of his friends, prompted him to oppose the learning of his older critics, a rashness that inspired the youthful Ehihu to speak his piece. This recognition that age did not necessarily bring superior wisdom achieves classic expression in 2 Maccabees, which refers to a certain Auranus as a man advanced in years and no less advanced in folly (4:40). One may compare the remark attributed to Joseph ben Tobias: "Pardon him because of his age; for surely you are not unaware that old people and infants are likely to have the same level of intelligence."[5] For this reason Ben Sira pokes fun at adulterous old men who resemble birds flying from one nest to another.

Youth, on the other hand, is viewed as a time of passion, naivete, and folly. Lacking self-control, youngsters speak when they should be silent,[6] they readily succumb to a trap set by an ever-present seductress, and they quickly express anger and resort to violence. Devoid of experience, young men drift into habits that society frowns on as disruptive.

The characteristic manner of viewing youth and old age becomes almost paradigmatic in the account of the transition of power from Solomon to his son, Rehoboam. True to form, the older counsellors advised a course of moderation, whereas the brash youth urged a show of force.[7] The reality of the political situation favored the counsel of the elders, on whose side was a combination of astuteness and compassion. But greed and arrogance prevailed, with unfortunate consequences for the empire.

Those who believed that the elderly embodied the human ideal were not blind to the discomfiture of old age. A Sumerian fragment faces this unpleasant fact without flinching.

---

[5]ὃ δε συγγινώσκε φησὶν αὐτῷ διὰ τὸ γῆρας. Οὐ γαρ λανθάνει σε πάντως ὅτι καὶ τοὺς πρεσβύτας καὶ τὰ νηπία τὴν αὐτὴν διάνοιαν ἔχειν συμβέβηκεν (*Antiquities of the Jews*, 12.172). I thank Ray Newell for this reference.

[6]According to Ben Sira, it is fitting for old persons to speak at a feast, if they have their facts straight and do not interrupt the music, but young men should speak only when asked to do so, and never more than twice (32:3, 7).

[7]The old men who had served Solomon counselled conciliation, but Rehoboam's peer group added insult to injury. Their language is coarse and harsh: "My little finger (*virum membrile*) is thicker than my father's loins. . . . My father chastised you with whips, but I will chastise you with scorpions" (1 Kgs 12:10-11). It required little intelligence on the part of representatives of the northern tribes to discern that they had no portion in David's kingdom.

My grain roasting fails,
Now my youthful vigor, strength and personal god
    have left my loins like an exhausted ass.
My black mountain has produced white gypsum.
My mother has brought in a man from the forest;
    he gave me captivity.
My mongoose which used to eat strong smelling things
    does not stretch its neck towards beer and butter.
My urine used to flow in a strong torrent,
    but now you flee from my wind.
My child whom I used to feed with butter and milk,
    I can no more support it.
And I have had to sell my little slave girl;
    an evil demon makes me sick.   (Alster 1975, 93)

Some of the images are perfectly clear, others less so. The roasting of grain symbolizes digestion; black mountain stands for the head, which is adorned with white hair; the man from the forest that relegated the speaker to captive existence represents a walking stick; the mongoose aptly evokes the thought of a hearty appetite. The straightforward descriptions leave little to the imagination: exhaustion, malfunctioning kidneys and painful flatulation.[8] The allusions to a child and slave girl are less clear, but they seem to specify wife and concubine. If so, the allusions imply that although sexual desire is still present, it no longer achieves satisfaction. The Egyptian Instruction of Ptahhotep sounds the same note.

Oldness has come; old age has descended. Feebleness has arrived; dotage is coming anew. The heart sleeps wearily every day. The eyes are weak, the ears are deaf, the strength is disappearing because of weariness of heart, and the mouth is silent and cannot speak. The mind is forgetful and cannot recall yesterday. The bone suffers old age. Good is become evil. All taste is gone. What old age does to people is evil in every respect. The nose is stopped up and cannot breathe. Simply to stand up or to sit down is difficult.[9]

Roughly two thousand years later the author of Papyrus Insinger expressed a similar sentiment.

He who has passed sixty years,
    everything has passed for him.
If his heart loves wine,
    he cannot drink to drunkenness.

---

[8]Compare the proverb in Lambert (1960, 260), "A thing which has not occurred since time immemorial: a young girl broke wind in her husband's bosom."
[9]The translation is taken from *ANET* (412).

If he desires food,
    he cannot eat as he used to.
If his heart desires a woman,
    her moment does not come.[10]

This unknown author divides the human life span into forty years of preparation, twenty golden years, and forty years of unpleasantness. Before the onset of old age at forty, ten years are devoted to learning about life and death, the next ten years to vocational training, the third decade to acquiring possessions, and the fourth decade to gaining maturity. In this assessment, only twenty years, ages forty to sixty, are pleasant. This golden age is a good time in life because of its gentleness. The astonishing thing is that the author refuses to relinquish the conviction that old age is the human ideal.

A contemporary of this author, Qoheleth, who in all likelihood lived in Jerusalem,[11] clung to the realistic description of the aging process but let go of the conviction that the best years in life accompanied white hair. In an important article on "The Unchangeable World: The 'Crisis of Wisdom' in Koheleth," Crüsemann observes that "the deterioration of old age and the picture of its obnoxiousness that is given in 12:1-8 represent a typical reversal of segmentary thinking, according to which the elderly embody the human ideal."[12] What enabled Qoheleth to take this step into virgin territory? Was it the sight of young athletes, strong of body and alert of mind, the reminder of a Greek culture that had achieved incredible things? Was it something far more radical?

In Crüsemann's analysis, Qoheleth belonged to the wealthy class of landowners who eventually gave up their kinship ties because such obligations were not economically profitable. Building on the initial insight of Gordis (1943/1944, 77-118)[13]

---

[10]Lichtheim (1976, 199). *The Sixteenth Instruction*, ll. 11-14, advises individuals to provide for their old age, arguing that a brief old age is preferable to one in which the unfortunate person is reduced to begging. Nevertheless, the author acknowledges that nothing can alter one's alloted life span.

[11]Neither the Egyptian influence on Qoheleth (the royal fiction in 1:12-2:26, the reference to casting bread on the waters, the concept of chance, the *carpe diem* theme, the image of the grave as an eternal tomb) nor Phoenician vocabulary and orthography requires an origin for the book outside Judah. The content fits Palestine (cisterns, snakes in rock walls, clouds and rain, and grain, wine, and oil as the basic economic products), and many interpreters assume that Qoheleth wrote in Jerusalem.

[12]An English translation appears in Schottroff and Stegemann (1984, 57-77). The quotation is from 69.

[13]He writes: "It is the thesis of this paper that Wisdom Literature, which reached its apogee during the earlier centuries of the Second Temple, roughly between the fifth and the first half of the second centuries BCE, was fundamentally the product of the upper classes in society, who lived principally in the capital, Jerusalem" (81). The existence of wisdom academies, which presupposes a leisure class; the warning against sexual relations outside

and its elaboration by Bickerman (1967, 139-67)[14] in terms of an acquisitive society like that underlying the Zenon correspondence,[15] Crüsemann searches for evidence of class conflict in Qoheleth's teachings. The breakdown of segmentary thinking is particularly evident, Crüsemann believes, in Qoheleth's individualism that cannot even derive satisfaction from knowledge that an heir continues one's name. Like Gese (1963, 139-51)[16] Crüsemann stresses the crisis that resulted from the collapse of the connection between act and consequence.

Belief in an impenetrable deity is a corollary of this intellectual crisis. A benevolent creator and sustainer of order no longer undergirds a world view according to which one's status as good or evil was evidenced by a person's conduct and position in society.[17] Behind this old view of things Crüsemann posits a social class, specifically the landed upper class. Ownership of the land was a family matter that was perpetuated by economic self-sufficiency. In this context, a צַדִּיק was one who met the requirements set by the group and lived in harmony with their norms. For the rich, segmentary ties with the poor were an expensive luxury. Under the Ptolemaic rulers, the urban aristocracy became an instrument of a heavy taxation policy, resulting in its alienation from the rest of society. A developing monetary economy, a decline in rural self-sufficiency, and a heavy burden of taxation hastened the collapse of traditional norms, which were no longer in harmony with social reality. Qoheleth's repudiation of the Yahwistic tradition and surrender to a calculative mentality of materialistic thought on an individualistic level "give death a fascination that eclipses everything else."[18] Personal ethics thus place a premium on

---

marriage; the references to precious stones, expensive clothes, wine to drink and meat to eat; the utilitarian morality, and virtue of charity; the refusal to endorse belief in life after death as the answer to the dilemma of reward and punishment, which was acute for the oppressed but not for the wealthy; the lack of enthusiasm for the Temple cult or religious exercises in general; the attitude toward labor and trade; and the conservative political and social ideas—these are some of the things leading Gordis to the conclusion that the sages belonged to the wealthy classes.

[14]Bickerman conjectures that Qoheleth was possibly tried in the wrong way, with rewards (147). Unlike some Greek philosophers, Qoheleth asks his hearers to share their wealth with their bodies rather than with others (165).

[15]A prominent businessman in the middle of the third century BCE, Zenon has bequeathed his archives to posterity. The refrain of his correspondence, according to Bickerman, is "Hurry up," for his business was his life (159). Hengel (1974, 116) also places the composition of Qoheleth in the period of the Zeno(n) papyri when "considerable political and economic activity was developing in Palestine which could not in the end fail to make its mark in the intellectual sphere."

[16]An English translation appears in Crenshaw (1983, 141-53).

[17]The clearest and most extreme presentation of the act-consequence relationship is by Koch (1955, 1-42). An English translation appears in Crenshaw (1983, 57-87).

[18]Crüsemann (1984, 68). The basis for this assessment of Qoheleth as calculating is the use of the word חֶשְׁבּוֹן (sum), the expression "one to one to discover the total," the word

conduct that avoids risk. Even oppression is explained as an inevitable consequence of the hierarchic organization of the state, and Qoheleth appears to stop short of criticizing the king. In one place Qoheleth uses religious terminology to lend support to the authority of the king (מִצְוָה, שְׁבוּעַת אֱלֹהִים).[19]

It is unfortunate that Crüsemann did not take into consideration several studies of the role of elders in ancient Israel, which offer an alternative explanation for the loss of esteem in which society held its older citizens. The pioneer study by Seesemann, "*Die Ältesten im Alten Testament*"[20] concluded that Israel's monarchs deliberately suppressed the power of family chiefs, breaking up their solidarity as a deliberative body and replacing them with persons who posed no threat to the power of the crown. With the disappearance of the monarchy, the elders emerged once more to a position of authority. Van der Ploeg (1961) refined the latter point, noting that the centrality of the law during the exile turned the council of elders into a governing body that issued decisions on the basis of the written law. In time the influence of the heads of families decreased and that of teachers of the Mosaic law increased. McKenzie (1959)[21] isolates loss of land as an important factor in the decline of elders' authority, although he thinks the policies of various monarchs were decisive in eroding the power of local family chiefs. The complexity of the situation after the exile comes to expression in Conrad's essay on "זָקֵן" in *TDOT* (1980) who distinguishes between elders, whose authority was virtually nonexistent, and heads of distinguished families, who exercised considerable power.

Crüsemann's conclusions are significant nonetheless, for they greatly clarify Qoheleth's readiness to abandon traditional teachings, particularly with respect to youth and old age. But Crüsemann fails to do justice to Qoheleth's profundity in this as in other teachings. The tone of Crüsemann's essay is judgmental, and Qoheleth is summarily dismissed as a callous rich man whose ethical and political views

---

יִתְרוֹן (profit), and the general emphasis on עָמָל, both the toil and its monetary yield. On the prominence of the idea of death in Qoheleth, see Crenshaw (1978, 205-16).

[19]Eccl 8:2, 5. The text of 8:2 is difficult. Interpreters have emended the initial אֲנִי to אֵת or בְּנִי or they have retained אֲנִי and added אָמַרְתִּי on the basis of 2:1; 3:17, 18. A remarkably similar text in Ahiqar (*hzy qdmtk mnd'm qšh ['l'] npy m[lk] 'l tqwm . . . 'nt 'stmr lk*) prompted Whitley (1979, 71-72) to translate Eccl 8:2 by "Take heed in the presence of a king." Lindenberger (1983, 81) renders the Aramaic as follows: "Here is a difficult thing for you: do not stand opposed to the king . . . look out for yourself," thus raising serious objection to Whitley's interpretation of the verse. The sacred oath is either subjective or objective genitive (God's oath concerning kingship or a subject's expression of loyalty taken in God's name). Ambiguity also surrounds the word מִצְוָה in 8:5, which may refer to a royal edict or to a divine statute. The word מִשְׁפָּט may connote procedure as in Judg 13:12.

[20]I have not seen this Leipzig dissertation from 1895. Its contents are summarized in van der Ploeg (1961, 185).

[21]The biblical literature from this period is not entirely consistent in the way it describes the role of the elders.

eventuated in those criminal activities attacked by the author of Wisdom of Solomon.[22] The evidence does not support the claim that Qoheleth was wealthy,[23] and the force of the poignant expression which occurs twice in connection with the discussion of oppressed victims of society—and they had no comforter—is overlooked in Crüsemann's effort to place a wedge between Qoheleth and the poor.[24] Therefore, another look at Qoheleth's attitude to youth and old age seems appropriate.

Qoheleth has little to say about youth, apart from his remarks that are juxtaposed with a depiction of old age and death. The two exceptions are 4:13-16 and 10:16. The former text contrasts a poor and wise youth (יֶלֶד [25] מִסְכֵּן וְחָכָם) and an old and foolish king (מֶלֶךְ זָקֵן וּכְסִיל) who refuses to take advice. From this point on, the text is somewhat obscure, but it seems to say that the poor youth had risen from poverty and imprisonment in the king's territory, eventually to sit on the throne. The allusion to a second youth[26] muddies the waters, but it probably refers to the poor man who became king, unless it means that there was yet another young man who usurped power. Qoheleth's point is that the crowd is fickle, forgetting rulers of accomplishment in record time.

The other text pronounces a malediction on the land that has a child (נַעַר) as king so that the princes feast in the morning, but utters a benediction over the land when the king is born of nobility (בֶּן־חוֹרִים)[27] and princes feast at the right time and

---

[22]Crüsemann (73) distinguishes between Qoheleth's actual teaching and its political and social consequences, which are "closely related" and which make the attack in Wisdom of Solomon appear to be not "so wide of the mark."

[23]I understand the royal experiment in 1:12–2:26 as fiction, hence worthless for determining the author's social status, and I do not distinguish between the author and Qoheleth; for an opposing view, see Fox (1977, 83-106). The references to money, fine clothes, expensive perfumes, drinking wine, and so forth say more about Qoheleth's audience than they do about his standing in society. He may very well have been wealthy, but the evidence is inconclusive.

[24]In my judgment Qoheleth's compassion for the oppressed is genuine and should not be viewed as a wealthy man's light dismissal of well-deserved misery.

[25]The only uses of מִסְכֵּן in the Bible are in Eccl 4:13 and 9:15-16, although Ben Sira also uses it twice (4:3; 30:14). The Mari documents and the laws of Hammurabi have a similar word for the underprivileged (*muskenum*).

[26]The allusion to the second (הַשֵּׁנִי) links this verse with the previous unit (4:7-12) which deals with the advantages of having a companion. In context הַשֵּׁנִי seems to mean "another," or it refers to the second youth who emerged from poverty to riches. The point appears to be that changes in kingship occur repeatedly and the masses quickly forget previous rulers regardless of their achievements.

[27]One expects a contrast with נַעַר such as זָקֵן. Instead Qoheleth uses a rare expression that means free men. Elsewhere nobility is expressed by חוֹרִים (1 Kgs 21:8, 11; Jer 27:20; 39:6; Neh 2:16; 5:7). Parallels to Qoheleth's use appear in Gittin 4:6 (בֶּן חוֹרִין) and Ahiqar 217 (בַּר חרן), and Jewish coins of the First and Second Revolts use the abstract term "freedom" (חרות).

for the correct reason.[28] Two things make this verse problematic in determining Qoheleth's view about youth. The semantic range of נַעַר is vast, from a child to a vigorous warrior, which places age over against social status, posing a special problem. Here, as in the previous text, historical allusions and typical examples merge, making it impossible to determine the precise context. The drone of Ptolemaic politics mutes the echoes of the Joseph narrative.

The other references to youth in Qoheleth occur in the exquisite depiction of old age and death (11:7–12:7).[29] Here the abstract terms בָּחוּר, יַלְדוּת, and שַׁחֲרוּת specify prime years when the hair is black or when one is experiencing the dawn of life.[30] Qoheleth urges young persons to seize this period and make the most of it, daring to do the forbidden,[31] and throwing caution to the wind. In a time of sensual gratification, one obeys the dictates of sight and imagination, leaving no place for responsible thought or physical pain. Such is the conduct that Qoheleth recommends before the deterioration of the body begins. Youth is the bright antechamber in which one resides before entering an increasingly dark tomb.[32]

But what characterizes old age? Qoheleth describes it in unforgettable, if mixed, images and metaphors. The earthly house crumbles and its inhabitants are severed from contact with the essentials of life, ushering them into residence in an eternal house.[33] Guardians of the terrestrial abode lose their strength, men of property stoop with age, slave women stop grinding flour because the inhabitants are so few,[34] and the mistresses of the house are obscured, perhaps because they wear black or because they have lost interest in the world and seldom appear at the windows to see what is happening in the streets below.[35] Although the doors are closed for

---

[28]The advice of Lemuel's mother is that rulers should scorn wine lest they pervert justice, but that strong drink be given to individuals who are in misery (Prov 31:4-7).

[29]Four recent studies of this text reach different conclusions: Sawyer (1975), Gilbert (1980), Ogden (1984), and Witzenrath (1979).

[30]In Job 30:30 the root שחר has the connotation darkness (עוֹרִי שָׁחַר מֵעָלָי), but the root also indicates the dawn (כַּעֲלוֹת הַשַּׁחַר, 1 Sam 9:26). The latter sense also occurs in the Mesha Inscription (1.15, *mbk' hšhrt*).

[31]A warning against following the organs of desire, the heart and eyes, is found in Num 15:39.

[32]Witzenrath (1979) emphasizes the significance of the images of light and darkness in this poem.

[33]The expression "eternal home" refers to the grave in a Palmyrene inscription from the end of the second century BCE (*bt 'lm 'qbr' dnh dy bnh zbd'th*), a Punic inscription (*hdr bt 'lm*), Egyptian usage; the Targum on Isa 14:18; and Sanhedrin 19a; cf. Tobit 3:6, which has τόπος αἰώνιος.

[34]If the subject of the verb were the grinding women, one would expect Qoheleth to say that they work all the more vigorously because of their decrease in numbers. An impersonal subject for inhabitants seems required.

[35]If the description of a funeral procession governs more than 12:5, the allusion may be to the clothing worn by grieving women.

privacy, sexual activity is rare, and the chirping of a bird awakens the man whose sources of sensual gratification have departed.[36] Terror reigns in the form of fear of heights and dread of the unknown on ordinary paths. Digestion ceases to function and physical desire fails to respond to aphrodisiacs.[37] A moving from one house to another takes place, presaged by professional mourners parading the streets. Then all at once death strikes: a shattered lamp spills its precious oil, a broken pulley hurls its pitcher into the well, where its water flows freely,[38] and the body disintegrates into dust, releasing the divine breath.[39]

The essential thought is the same if one interprets the images allegorically.[40] It is then the human body that is being described rather than an estate. Arms and legs tremble, the back stoops, teeth fall out, eyes are darkened, hearing is impaired, the voice becomes shrill, the hair turns white, the joints creak, and sexual desire disappears. Because the images are literal in some instances, it seems wiser to avoid the allegorical interpretation.[41] Even if one accedes to the claim that the second part of the description contrasts nature's rebirth with a collapsing house,[42] the attitude to youth and old age remains unchanged. There is nothing pleasant about old age and death, regardless of how one approaches this text. This point stands in spite of Sawyer's remark (1975, 523) that Qoheleth was not particularly interested in old age, an opinion that Ogden shares (1984, 35).

There are two troublesome comments in Qoheleth's advice to youth: "But know that God will bring you into judgment for all this. . . . For youth and black hair are fleeting." Two attempts have been made to rob the first observation of its sting: (1) viewing the *waw* as conjunctive (and know that God will judge you if you overlook such pleasures; Gordis 1951, 336); and (2) understanding מִשְׁפָּט in a nonforensic sense (Gorssen 1970, esp. 304-305). More probable is the explanation that the warning was added by an editor who adhered to traditional piety and sought to neutralize Qoheleth's heterodoxy (Sheppard 1977). The second observation that youth is short-lived accords with Qoheleth's understanding of reality. The contrast

---

[36]The slightest noise disturbs the elderly, whose sleep is light and who awake before wishing to do so.

[37]The precise meaning of "caperberry" is unclear, although its use as an aphrodisiac makes sense in this context.

[38]The association of water with life is natural; here the flowing of vital fluid from its container signifies death.

[39]The idea is that the creator breathed life into human beings and takes back that life-breath at the moment of death. This understanding of mortality has no positive feature, for the pessimistic refrain dashes all such hopes.

[40]The difficulty of maintaining a consistent interpretation of this kind is increasingly recognized, although a few images do lend themselves to an allegorical reading.

[41]This claim does not deny the existence of powerful imagery and metaphorical profundity within the poem.

[42]That is the understanding of the poem advocated by Sawyer (1975).

between a brief period of pleasure and an extended stay in Sheol does more than justify the description of everything as futile;[43] it also provides an image of death's power to obliterate all memory of pleasure.

These two assessments of youth suggest that Qoheleth has not altogether relinquished the older attitude toward youth. His abandonment of the conviction that old age was the human ideal does not carry with it the belief that youth is the ideal time of life. Youth was fleeting, perhaps futile as well.[44] Because Qoheleth subscribed to the view that the end of a thing was better than the beginning, it was impossible for him to see youth as the optimal age. Furthermore, the role of chance[45] cancelled the advantages of athletic training, for superior athletes did not always win the race. For Qoheleth, youth was preferable to old age because in the early years one had the capacity to enjoy life. But the advantage was a relative one, like that of sages over fools.[46] In terms of absolute profit, which was the measure of all things for Qoheleth, youth and old age alike were futile, absurd, and without substance.

Qoheleth's gloomy picture of old age is set over against a brighter portrayal of nature. Elsewhere the universe itself is subjected to the same dark brush. Deutero-Isaiah envisions the future decay of the universe like a garment (51:6), and Ben Sira observes that everything decays, including leaves and generations (14:17-19).[47] Second Esdras extends the thought further, remarking that the world has lost its youth, times begin to grow old, weakness and increased evil accompany age (14:10-18).[48]

Desperate measures were adopted in a vain attempt to rejuvenate the aged. A Sumerian king was advised to find a beautiful young woman who would restore his vitality (Alster 1975, 92-94) and David followed the same strategem. One Egyptian response to this problem of waning powers approaches voyeurism.[49] The afflicted Pharaoh was told to search for nubile women who would row his barque while he observed the rhythmic movements of their naked bodies. But some people made peace with their dwindling powers; the octogenarian Barzillai declined David's offer of a place at the court, conceding that his ability to discriminate tastes had vanished, along with his appreciation for sensual pleasure with women. Others, like Sinuhe, began the journey into eternity by returning home at any cost (Lichtheim 1973, 222-35).

---

[43]On translating הֶבֶל see Fox (1986). Fox argues for the translation "absurd."

[44]The essential meaning of the root הֶבֶל was ephemerality (breath) and insubstantiality (idols).

[45]The concept of chance (מִקְרֶה) is central to Qoheleth's thinking, but it also looms large in the Insinger Papyrus.

[46]No scholar has emphasized the relative teaching of Qoheleth more than Loader (1979).

[47]In his view, personal circumstances determined whether this gradual decay was greeted with open arms or with dismay.

[48]The idea was not unique to Israel, as the description of human decline in terms of a golden age that gave way to silver, copper, and iron ages demonstrates.

[49]Lichtheim (1973, 216-17) understands the diversion as royal amusement.

However, the epithet for God, the Ancient of Days, in the book of Daniel pre-serves the earlier attitude toward old age. The comforting power of this image be-comes clear by reflecting on two texts, one from the legal codes and the other from exilic prophecy. In Lev 19:32 we read: "You shall rise up before the hoary head and honor the face of an old person, and you shall fear your God; I am the Lord." The point is not merely the obvious one of showing respect for authority,[50] for a much bolder thought struggles to be born in the command. The natural flow of thought from the aged to God implies that our most eloquent witness to the reality of the living God is a hoary head and wrinkled visage. The other word comes from Isa 46:4 ("Even to your old age I am the One, and to gray hairs I will carry you. I have made, and I will bear; I will carry and will save"). Here is the unforgettable image of the Ancient of Days cradling the people of Israel like babes in solicitous but powerful arms. This breathtaking image is the poet's response to a persistent suspi-cion that God might forsake one in old age, a fear that evokes a prayer in Ps 71:9, 18. Like Deutero-Isaiah's proclamation of something extraordinarily new, this one also fell on deaf ears as far as Qoheleth was concerned. How chilling his teachings must have been to those individuals who had already experienced their golden years! And how sobering to those who still possessed youthful vigor![51]

---

[50]Compare the acknowledged superiority of the aged in Job 12:12.

[51]The attitude to youth and old age in the ancient Near East serves as a window through which modern interpreters may be able to view Israel's intellectual development. This essay is but one of several essays that will be necessary before the reliability of such viewing can be assessed.

Bibliography

Alster, B.
1974   *The Instructions of Šuruppak*. Copenhagen.
1975   *Studies in Sumerian Proverbs*. Copenhagen.
Bickerman, E.
1967   *Four Strange Books of the Bible*. New York.
Crenshaw, J. L.
1978   "The Shadow of Death in Qoheleth." In *Israelite Wisdom: Theological and Literary Essays in Honor of Samuel Terrien*, ed. J. G. Gammie et al., 205-16. Missoula MT.
1983   (editor) *Theodicy in the Old Testament*. Philadelphia and London.
Conrad, J.
1980   "זָקֵן *zāqēn*." *TDOT* 4:122-31.
Crüsemann, F.
1984   "The Unchangeable World: The 'Crisis of Wisdom' in Koheleth." In *God of the Lowly*, ed. W. Schottroff and W. Stegemann, 57-77. Maryknoll NY.
Fox, M. V.
1977   "Frame-Narrative and Composition in the Book of Qoheleth." *HUCA* 48:83-106.
1986   "The Meaning of *Hebel* for Qoheleth." *JBL* 105:409-27.
Gese, H.
1963   "Die Krisis der Weisheit bei Kohelet." In *Les sagesse du Proche-Orient ancien. Colloque de Strasbourg 1962*, 139-51. ET in Crenshaw 1983, 141-53.
Gilbert, M.
1980   "La description de la viellesse en Qohelet XII 1-7 est elle allegorique?" *Congress Volume Vienna 1980*, 96-109. VTSup 32.
Gordis, R.
1943/1944 "The Social Background of Wisdom Literature." *HUCA* 18:77-118.
1951   *Koheleth: the Man and His World*. New York.
Gorssen, L.
1970   "La cohérence de la conception de Dieu dans l'Ecclésiaste." *ETL* 46:282-324.
Hengel, M.
1974   *Judaism and Hellenism*. Philadelphia.
Koch, K.
1955   "Gibt es ein Vergeltungsdogma im Alten Testament?" *ZTK* 52:1-42. ET in Crenshaw 1983, 57-87.
Lambert, W. L.
1960   *Babylonian Wisdom Literature*. Oxford.
Lichtheim, M.
1973,1976,1980 *Ancient Egyptian Literature*. Volumes 1–3. Berkeley.
Lindenberger, J. M.
1983   *The Aramaic Proverbs of Ahiqar*. Baltimore.
Loader, J. A.
1979   *Polar Structures in the Book of Qohelet*. BZAW 152. Berlin and New York.

McKenzie, J.
    1959   "The Elders in the Old Testament." *Bib* 40: 522-40.
Ogden, G. S.
    1984   "Qohelet XI 7-XII 8: Qoheleth's Summons to Enjoyment and Reflection." *VT*
            34:27-38.
Sawyer, J. F. A.
    1975   "The Ruined House in Ecclesiastes 12: A Reconstruction of the Original
            Parable." *JBL* 94:519-31.
Schottroff, W. and W. Stegemann, editors
    1984   *God of the Lowly*. Maryknoll NY.
Sheppard, G. T.
    1977   "The Epilogue to Qoheleth as Theological Commentary." *CBQ* 39:182-89.
van der Ploeg, J.
            "Les anciens dans l'Ancien Testament." *Lex Tua Veritas. H. Junker
            Festschrift*, ed. H. Gross and F. Mussner, 175-91. Trier.
Whitley, C. F.
    1979   *Koheleth*. BZAW 148. Berlin and New York.
Witzenrath, H.
    1979   *Süss ist das Licht*. St. Ottilien.

36 (1974)

The Eternal Gospel (Ecclesiastes 3:11)

"That is the eternal, as distinct from the temporal gospel: one can love God but one must fear him."[1] With these words Carl Jung gives voice to a universal human experience in the presence of the holy. Such terror before God is a common element in Israelite religion, of course; but the experienced grace of Yahweh, who stood in a covenant relationship with his chosen people, tempered the fear. There is one book in the Old Testament where the fear of God seems to stand alone without any hint of divine compassion. That book is Ecclesiastes.[2] The focal passage for a study of its thought is 3:1-15, for it is here that the *Angst* awakened in the human breast before the hidden God manifests itself with unforgettable poignancy and raises the burning question: "Is man the object of divine compassion or caprice?"

I.

Both style and content suggest that 3:1-15 is a separate unit. The refrain[3] in 2:26 functions as a concluding summation, after which one expects a new departure. While there is no similar refrain or stylistic device at the end of 3:1-15, the content changes noticeably in 3:16. The argument for the unity of 3:1-15 based on subject matter is twofold. First, there is remarkable coherence (for Qoheleth!)[4] in 3:1-15,

---

[1]C. G. Jung, *Answer to Job* (1969) 169.

[2]E. Pfeiffer, "Die Gottesfurcht im Buche Kohelet," *Gottes Wort und Gottes Land. Festschrift für H. W. Hertzberg* (1965) 133-58, examines the textual basis for J. Fichtner's thesis that Qoheleth uses the fear of God in its original numinous sense; Pfeiffer's essay, replete with extensive quotations of pertinent literature, appears to confirm Fichtner's observations; see *Die altorientalische Weisheit in ihrer israelitisch-jüdischen Ausprägung*, BZAW 62 (1933) 52-53.

[3]"This also is vanity and a striving after wind." The refrain appears in various forms at 1:14; 2:11, 17, 26; 4:4, 16; 6:9; with which may be compared 2:15, 19, 21, 23; 3:19; 4:8; 5:9[10]; 6:2; 8:10, 14; 11:7.

[4]"Das Spruchgefüge ist eine Einheit, wie es auch einem Skopus hat, den von der Zeit als *Kairós* und *aion*": K. Galling, *Der Prediger*, HAT (1940) 59. G. von Rad, *Weisheit in Israel* (1970) 293, thinks there is an inner unity of the entire book, one that is not of linear thought development but the unity of style, topic, and theme.

where the "riddle of time" and its consequences for human conduct are treated. Second, 3:16–4:3 is a thematic unit; it treats the so-called problem of retribution, namely the prosperity of the wicked and oppression of the righteous individual. The pivotal role of 3:1-15 is noteworthy; again and again the author returns to the themes introduced in this section (see esp. 3:17; 8:5-6, 9; 9:11-12).[5]

The relationship between 3:1-15 and the rest of the book is an intimate one, suggesting that the author himself recognized the centrality of the unit. The initial section (3:1-9) recalls 1:3-11, a didactic poem describing the divorce between history and nature. In 3:10 the verbal similarity with 1:13b is striking, while 3:12-13 takes up Qoheleth's advice to enjoy life as expressed in 2:24. The emphasis upon the durability of divine creativity recalls the observation in 1:4, which differs sharply from Deutero-Isaiah's proclamation that the word of God stands forever (Isa 40:8). Again 3:15 returns to and expands the statement found in 1:9, although the meaning of the elaboration is unclear despite the close parallel in Sir 5:3.[6] The affinity between 3:1-15 and the rest of the book is not limited to what precedes the unit; on the contrary, many of its ideas recur at later junctures. The observation that everything has its appropriate time is repeated in 3:17, but here in a judgmental context. The tragic pessimism of 3:11 is permitted to surface again in 7:13-14 and 8:17 (perhaps also in 7:29 and 11:5), just as the conclusion to eat, drink and enjoy life (3:13) crops up at crucial stages of the argument (3:22; 5:17 [EVV 18]; 8:15; cf. 9:7-10).

Both in syntax and vocabulary the peculiar stylistic features of the author are well represented in this small unit. Fourteen antithetic pairs expressive of totality[7] are juxtaposed in serial fashion (cf. 7:1-10), a stylistic trait particularly appropriate for an author who wishes to emphasize the relative value of all things under the sun (that is, on earth). The rhetorical question that functions as a negative assertion, a favorite device of the author,[8] stands in 3:9. The broken sentence,[9] still another special feature of Eccl appears in 3:11, perhaps twice (גַּם and מִבְּלִי). The

---

[5]H. Gese, "Die Krisis der Weisheit bei Koheleth," *SPOA* (1963) 148.

[6]Literally, "God is seeking the circle of things gone by." Does it mean that he has no interest in human affairs, R. Gordis, *Koheleth, the Man and His World* (1951) 234? The verse in Qoheleth may be a gloss from 1:9 or 3:14, meaning "Er verwirklicht, was verwirklicht werden muss": Galling, *Der Prediger*, 63.

[7]J. Pedersen, "Scepticisme israélite," *RHPR* 10 (1930): 352; P. Boccaccio, "I termini contrari come espressioni della totalità in ebraico," *Bib* 33 (1952): 173-90. However, the reduplication of עֵת constitutes a problem for this view, as Galling, "Die Rätsel der Zeit im Urteil Kohelets (Koh. 3:1-15)," *ZTK* 58 (1961): 5-6, has recognized.

[8]R. Kroeber, *Der Prediger* (1963) 37, counts 29 rhetorical questions, not one of which is a real question.

[9]K. Galling, "Stand und Aufgabe der Kohelet-Forschung," *TRu* 6 (1934): 369. Indicators of broken sentences are: וְגַם (2:14; 3:13; 7:6), גַּם זֶה (2:24), וּבְכֵן (8:10), כִּי גַּם־יוֹדֵעַ אָנִי (8:12), and וְ (9:18).

preference for participles also finds expression here (3:9), even with a pronoun, as do words otherwise found only in relatively late Old Testament texts (זְמָן ;סוֹף; שֶׁ). Attention should also be called to the extraordinary calm mood[10] despite the churning beneath the surface; the impersonal style employed in some sections does little to conceal the burning genuineness of Qoheleth's teachings. The favorite expressions of the author make their appearance in this small unit; here one encounters "under heaven," "toil," "gain," "gift of God," "*the* God," "I saw," "I knew," "time," and "end." Noteworthy omissions are "vanity of vanities" and "striving after wind."[11]

Inasmuch as the structure of the book is still a mystery, it is impossible to place 3:1-15 within the total argument. The attempts at structural analysis on the basis of logical coherence and stylistic characteristics have failed to create a consensus,[12] due chiefly to their subjective nature. Perhaps this failure bears witness to the aphoristic quality of the book, and suggests that the author may not have arranged his "collection of sentences" in any logical fashion, but permitted random observations to intrude at will.

Literary analysis of 3:1-15 is relatively certain. It consists of two subsections:[13] (1) Inexorable Law (vv. 1-9) and (2) Human Response (vv. 10-15). The first is composed of an introduction (3:1), fourteen contrasting pairs (3:2-8), and a rhetorical question (3:9), providing the transition to the second subsection. The latter is made up of reflections on the nature of reality (3:10-11), observations about the proper human response to the way things are (3:12-13), and further reflection on the grounds for the conclusions about human conduct (3:14-15). Within the first subsection the author has made use of chiasmus[14] to isolate the antitheses; the fourteen pairs of contrasts are introduced by the chief *Grenzsituationen* over which man has no control (birth and death) and are concluded by the great historical contingencies

---

[10]Pedersen, "Scepticisme israélite," 341. W. Zimmerli, *Der Prediger*, ATD (1962) thinks of incipient rebellion in three places (1:13; 3:10; 6:10). See the commentary on these verses.

[11]Kroeber, *Der Prediger*, 30-42 (esp. 37-42) perceives that the broken sentence is more than a pedagogical method, inasmuch as it denotes the inner breach of wisdom. Therefore he writes: "Die Widersprüche Qoheleths sind nicht Zeichen gedanklicher Unklarheit, sondern als Spiegelbilder der Wirklichkeit das Merkmal seiner realistischen Lebensbeziehung" (37). Kroeber understands the question as a form of statement, and calls attention to other stylistic devices of Qoheleth: sectional indicators (וְשַׁבְתִּי, אֲנִי אָמַרְתִּי, וְאֶרְאֶה, יָדַעְתִּי, רָאִיתִי, וּפָנִיתִי אֲנִי לִרְאוֹת), preference for participles, absence of vav consecutive, and so forth.

[12]This applies to all attempts to explain the structure in terms of logical sequence: H. L. Ginsberg, "The Structure and Contents of the Book of Koheleth," VTSup 3 (1955) 138-49; and redaction, as well as structural analysis or new criticism: A. Wright, "The Riddle of the Sphinx: The Structure of the Book of Qoheleth," *CBQ* 30 (1968): 313-34.

[13]Galling, "Das Rätsel der Zeit im Urteil Kohelets (Koh 3: 1-15)," 2, thinks of four sections, vv. 1-8, 9-11, 12-13, and 14-15.

[14]Birth-death-war-peace (3:2a and 3:8b).

that effect life or death, namely war and peace. Between these two, birth and death, take place all that characterizes human existence: planting and uprooting (weeds?), killing and healing, tearing down and rebuilding, weeping and laughing, mourning and exulting, buying and selling,[15] making love and remaining continent, seeking and losing, retaining and discarding, tearing and mending, keeping silence and speaking, loving and hating.

The form of the didactic poem in 3:2-8 is closest to onomastica, or lists; it has its nearest biblical parallel in Job 38–41, but resembles encyclopedic lists from Egyptian and Mesopotamian wisdom literature.[16] A pedagogic device, such lists seem originally to have been a means of ordering the world so that one could make sense of his environment, but served admirably to teach the young scribe what could be known about a particular topic. The subject matter of onomastica is generally related to nature, hence the descriptive term "Naturweisheit."[17] The emphasis in Eccl 3:2-8 is upon human activity. The form of 3:10-15 is that of the so-called royal testament or confession; a more appropriate term is autobiographical narrative.[18] The genre is typical of the Egyptian instructions, in which the Pharaoh or his vizier (counselor) advises his son as to the correct behavior before gods and men. But it is also found in Proverbs (7:6-27; 24:30-34). This counsel represents the lifetime

---

[15]The meaning of 3:5a is disputed. On the basis of 1 Kgs 3:25 and Isa 5:2a, it has been argued that the allusions are to heaping up rocks during war to make a field uncultivable and to clearing away stones so as to plant something. But the contrasts so understood are not easily related. The Midrash Qoheleth Rabba interpreted the verse as a veiled reference to sexuality, hence in synonymous parallelism with 5:2b. This view rests on a pun between אֲבָנִים and בָּנִים, and necessitates an emendation. Neither the popular saying in Jer 2:27 ("You are my father" (to a tree); "You have given me birth" (to a stone)) nor the statement by John the Baptist that God is able to raise up children of Abraham from these stones (Matt 3:9) supports such an interpretation. It may be noted, however, that Ovid knew a tradition according to which the two survivors in the Mesopotamian flood narrative engendered offspring by throwing stones over their shoulders (see W. G. Lambert, *Babylonian Wisdom Literature* [1960] 93). A third possibility has been suggested by Galling, who takes as his point of departure the insight of O. Eissfeldt ("Der Beutel der Lebendigen," BZAW [Phil. hist. Klasse, Bd. 105, 1960]) that Yahweh was thought of as keeping a record of the devout in a bag. Since small stones in a bag have been found at Nuzi, constituting the means by which a shepherd kept an accurate account of his sheep and goats, Galling argues that the metaphor is an allusion to profits and losses, hence the business of buying and selling ("Das Rätsel der Zeit im Urteil Kohelets [Koh 3:1-15]," 10-12). We follow Galling, although with reservation.

[16]See G. von Rad, "Hiob 38 und die altägyptische Weisheit," VTSup 3 (1955) 293-301.

[17]H. Richter, "Die Naturweisheit des Alten Testaments in Buche Hiob," ZAW 70 (1958): 1-20.

[18]R. N. Whybray, *The Succession Narrative*, SBT (1968) 72-76. For a discussion of the literary genres in wisdom literature, see the author's contribution to *The Old Testament and Form Criticism*, ed. J. H. Hayes (1974).

achievement of the scribe, the vast accumulation of rich experience. Hence the "I have seen" and "I know" carry the authority of office and experience, and consequently are not to be taken lightly.[19] Qoheleth has juxtaposed onomastica, the cumulative information about human experience, and autobiographical narrative, the fruit of a lifetime of study. The latter makes the point that all human striving is futile, yes, even the desire to know, since God has concealed vital knowledge from man. The mood, then, is one of tragic pessimism.[20] This skepticism as to man's ability to know is heightened by the partial knowledge permitted him, namely that God does not act to insure the principle of retribution. The old idea of צְדָקָה has given way to cold fear as the central stance. No longer can man know that he is צַדִּיק; now salvation (life), if it comes, is a gift.[21]

The reason for Qoheleth's skepticism is expressed in 3:11, which has been a *Walpurgisnachts-Traum* for all commentators.[22] This nightmare of interpretation does not derive simply from the presence of the much-discussed הָעֹלָם, but from the total sentiment of the verse. On the face of it 3:11 appears to be an elaboration of the pessimistic observation in 3:10, which is milder by far than 1:13b. The business (הָעִנְיָן) is the frustrating search for הָעֹלָם, to be discussed later. Just as 3:11 is integrally related to 3:10, it is also closely joined to 3:12-15, which gives the conclusions arising from the reflection on the nature of things, as well as the reasons for those deductions. Analysis of 3:11, then, should provide the key to the entire unit. Anticipating the discussion to follow, 3:11 raises the basic issues under discussion in wisdom literature today: (1) creation, (2) order, (3) enigma, (4) sovereignty, and (5) totality.

II.

The verse opens with an affirmation of the goodness of creation undoubtedly reminiscent of Gen. 1, where the creative work is repeatedly described as טֹוב. However, the key terms in the Priestly narrative of creation are passed over in favor of a vocabulary that is less theological in tone: אֶת־הַכֹּל עָשָׂה יָפֶה. Instead of the comprehensive "heavens and earth," Qoheleth employs an abstract הַכֹּל, a favorite antithesis of חֵלֶק. The reversal of word order serves to emphasize the object of עָשָׂה: everything he has made beautiful. The use of עָשָׂה instead of

---

[19]See my *Prophetic Conflict*. BZAW 124 (1971) 116-23 ("'esâ and dābār: The Problem of Authority/Certitude in Wisdom and Prophetic Literature").

[20]H. W. Hertzberg, *Der Prediger*, KAT (1963) 230, uses this phrase with reference to the mood of Gen 1–4 which Qoheleth has in mind.

[21]Gese, "Die Krisis der Weisheit bei Koheleth," 139-51.

[22]This quotation is taken from Kroeber, *Der Prediger*, 31, who is citing H. Graetz, *Kohelet oder der Salomonische Prediger* (1871) 3: The interpretation of Qoheleth in 2,000 years "ist ein formlicher exegetischer Walpurgisnachts-Traum."

בְּרָא accords with the author's revolutionary stance, and suggests that the strange form in 12:1 (בּוֹרְאֶיךָ) is more correctly understood as a derivative of the root בְּרָא, "to dig, cut."[23] The word would then be a double entendre for grave and cistern (wife; cf. Prov 5:15-19), hence a fitting climax to Qoheleth's positive counsel set over against the warning of approaching death. The use of יָפֶה rather than טוֹב is occasioned by the context, which allows a descriptive adjective of beauty but which renders one of goodness either contradictory or banal. Perhaps the use of וְלַעֲשׂוֹת טוֹב in 3:12 is a conscious attempt at the transformation of theological vocabulary, for here the טוֹב in 3:12 is completely neutral, has been emptied of all ethical content. In this regard it is noteworthy that 5:18 (17) uses both טוֹב and יָפֶה in a neutral sense of fitting or appropriate.

The statement that God has made everything beautiful is the fruit of experience; its truth no wise man would deny. Only the "fool" totally devoid of aesthetic appreciation could fail to perceive the grandeur of the created order, a beauty so moving that it elicited from the lips of the *"rationalistic"* sages hymns of praise to the Creator. This much even Qoheleth could affirm: God has made everything beautiful. Nevertheless, the affirmation stands under a cloud of qualifications. The introductory verse within the second section of the unit under discussion gives little hint of the negative tenor of what follows, but merely registers the experiential nature of the conclusion (3:10). Perhaps the verse should be read in the light of 1:13, where the adjective רָע modifies the "business" that God has given man. If this is correct, 3:10 already suggests that what follows is far from an ecstatic hymnic declaration. In any case, the rest of the verse, together with 3:12-15, qualify the affirmation to such an extent that one cannot claim that it provided any solace to Qoheleth's tragic pessimistic spirit. Historical existence is for him a living *in tormentis*.[24]

One of the reasons for the skepticism is Qoheleth's recognition that הַכֹּל is denied him. Only a חֵלֶק is *granted him*, and even that is a direct *gift* of God.[25] But Qoheleth could abide this reality if there were proof that the dispenser of the portion were graciously disposed toward his creatures. However, the evidence of experience suggested to Qoheleth that God was neither favorably nor unfavorably

---

[23]P. Humbert, "Emploi et portée du verbe bara' (créer) dans l'Ancien Testament," *TZ* 3 (1947): 402.

[24]Galling, "Das Rätsel der Zeit im Urteil Kohelets (Koh. 3:1-15)," 1, writes that Qoheleth is the first in the Old Testament to discover the historicality of man as *in tormentis* and to treat it thematically, thus constituting a "crisis of enlightenment in Israel." Galling denies that 3:11 refers to the creation of the world (2), taking it as an allusion to a favorable moment for action that brings it to culmination.

[25]The root נתן occurs throughout the book of Qoheleth; it emphasizes the fact that salvation is no longer automatic, the result of standing in צְדָקָה. "Für ihn muss das Heil ein direkt an den Menschen gerichtetes Geschenk Gottes sein"—Gese, "Die Krisis der Weisheit bei Koheleth," 151.

disposed toward man, but rather completely indifferent (9:1). "God is in heaven and you are on earth": here we see the key to Qoheleth's pathos as well as to his life style. Inasmuch as God is the distant unknowable ruler and guarantor of the universe, man should strive to remain outside his focus of attention. But such existence is devoid of ultimate meaning, since it is concerned with transitory things, hence the descriptive adjective רָע. Once again Qoheleth has used a word fraught with theological content, but in a thoroughly neutral manner. Indeed, the same "neutralization" is evident in חֵלֶק, so important in Israelite thought as the portion of divine blessing.

How different Qoheleth's affirmation that "God has made all things beautiful" is from Sir 39:16! In a hymnic setting Sirach proclaims that "the works of God, *all of them*, are good" (מַעֲשֵׂי־אֵל כֻּלָּם טוֹבִים). Indeed Sirach admonishes his hearers to sing a hymn of praise to bless the Lord for all his works (39:14b), and suggests the appropriateness of affirming that all the works of God are good. Verse 17 implies, however, that a substantial number of doubters existed in Sirach's day too, a theme to which we shall return. This intrusion of polemics into hymnic literature must not blind us to the significance of such praise to the sages, a point "marvelously" overdone by Gerhard von Rad in his recent *Weisheit in Israel*.[26] The study of the wonders of creation generated a feeling of awe as well as of appreciation, most appropriately expressed in hymnody. Hence the sage frequently gave voice to songs of praise once he reached the frontiers of human knowledge. The impact of such praises lies behind Qoheleth's grudging (?) admission that God has made everything beautiful. For Qoheleth, though, this was nothing about which to sing.

The use of הַכֹּל means that adversity as well as prosperity are adjudged beautiful. To this theme Qoheleth returns in 7:13-14, here in a clearly negative mood. The rhetorical question, "Who can make straight what he has made crooked?" implies that something has gone awry with the work of God (as it is specifically stated in 7:29). At the same time it calls attention to man's inability to undo what God has established for eternity. Both prosperity and adversity are God's doing, and man cannot probe into the future (7:14), that is, he cannot distinguish whether something is good or bad in prospect. Just as in 3:11, so also in 7:14, the knowledge of a good creation provides no comfort to one who finds himself in adversity. Once again comparison with Sirach is instructive. In 39:16-35, a majestic broken hymn on the way nature itself reinforces the principle of retribution,[27] the emphasis is placed on polarities that are apparently contradictory, but in reality are means of ensuring that morality is rewarded and wickedness punished. Sirach appears to be unaware of the contradiction to his affirmation that all God's works are good when he concedes that bad things were created *from the beginning* for sin-

---

[26](1971) 211-16 and passim.

[27]This theme is developed in "midrash form" by the author of Wisd.

ners (cf. Prov 16:4). He does, however, recognize that good and bad things are in the eye of the beholder ("To the holy his ways are straight, just as they are obstacles to the wicked," v. 24). The indifferent universe of Qoheleth is replaced by one that is passionately involved in human affairs, and this conviction, like Qoheleth's, is said to be the result of experience ("Therefore from the beginning I have been convinced, and have thought this out and left it in writing: The works of the Lord are all good, and he will supply every need in its hour," vv. 32-33). Here speaks a *preacher* indeed, with his admonition to sing praise and bless Yahweh's name (v. 35); but it is not from this platform that the *Prediger* (Qoheleth) utters his voice.

Man's inability to comprehend the mystery of creation, mentioned in Eccl 7:14, is taken up again in 11:5, a passage of uncertain meaning. The protasis seems to refer to two mysteries, the workings of the wind and the growth of a foetus (cf. John 3:8). The apodosis presents no difficulty; it denies that man knows the work of God who made הַכֹּל. The usefulness of such mysteries in addressing the problem of theodicy was quickly perceived; the argument of 2 Esd 4 is heavily fraught with rhetorical questions dealing with the limits of human cognition. The context of Qoheleth's observation results in no diminution of pathos, even though 11:5 is set within several observations about business ventures. For Qoheleth there was no separation beween theology and ethics.

This tendency of creation faith to appear in wholly unexpected places, as well as in hymns celebrating the wonders of nature, would appear to corroborate the conclusion of several scholars that wisdom literature is grounded in creation faith.[28] In light of these frequent assertions, one might expect to find numerous references to creation in wisdom literature. Such is not the case, except in Sirach, who cannot stand as normative for wisdom. In Proverbs the creation theme rarely appears save in the general allusion to man's Maker (14:31; 16:4, 11; 17:5; 20:12; 22:2). In reality one cannot speak of creation faith in Proverbs. Even the reference to the creation of wisdom at the beginning of Yahweh's work subordinates creation theology to חָכְמָה speculation. The picture is somewhat different in Job, although the near absence of creation phraseology in the hymnic chapters 5 and 9, which are transparently coined from the same traditions as the doxologies of Amos (4:13; 5:8-9; 9:5-6), is remarkable.[29] Other passages recall the general creaturehood of man as emphasized in Proverbs (Job 4:17; 10:8-11; 31:15; 32:22; 35:10; 36:3). Still others stress the majesty of him who stretched out the heavens hard as molten mirror (9:8; 26:7; 37:18; cf. 38:4-11) and conquered chaos (26:7-14; 40:15-24). The subordina-

---

[28]W. Zimmerli, "Ort und Grenze der Weisheit im Rahmen der alttestamentlichen Theologie," *SPOA* 121-36 (esp. 135-36); C. Westermann, "Weisheit im Sprichwort," *Schalom: Studien zur Glaube und Geschichte Israels. A. Jepsen Festschrift* (1971) 82-83.

[29]See the author's discussion of these similarities in "The Influence of the Wise upon Amos," *ZAW*, 79 (1967), 49-50.

tion of creation to wisdom occurs in Sirach too (1:4, 9; 24:9), as do the general references to man's Maker (4:6; 7:30; 10:12; 15:14; 32:13; 33:13; 38:15; 39:5). But the praise of God for his creative works reaches a new height with Sirach (11:4; 16:26-30; 17:1-20; 18:1-7; 33:15; 39:21-35; 42:15–43:33). Even farm labor and medicines[30] are said to have been created by God (7:15, 38:4). In short, creation theology plays a minor role in early Proverbs, a slightly greater role in Job, and a significant one in Sirach. In this regard Qoheleth is closer to Proverbs than to his near contemporary Sirach.

The real point of the statement that wisdom literature is grounded in creation theology does not have to do with frequency of occurrence, but rather with the nature of authority.[31] Whereas the rest of the Old Testament, particularly the legal and prophetic traditions, appeals to the authority of a spoken word, revelation, that is, wisdom literature grounds its counsel in the nature of reality, or more correctly, in the original decrees of creation. The sages did not understand history in the way the prophets, priests and historians interpreted it,[32] namely as the arena within which God worked to bring about his plans for a covenant people. Neither redemptive nor retributive historical events play a role in their thoughts, which was much more concerned with the individual than the nation. This does not mean that the sage was

---

[30]J. Marböck, *Weisheit im Wandel* (1971) 154-60, recognizes the great significance of Sirach's discussion of the physician. See also von Rad, *Weisheit in Israel*, 325-29, for the impact of the collapse of the belief that sickness was indicative of rebellion against the Creator.

[31]So Zimmerli, "Ort und Grenze der Weisheit im Rahmen der alttestamentlichen Theologie," 129-34. Westermann, "Weisheit im Sprichwort," 73-85 (esp. 75-78), argues that *Mahnspruch* is secondary to *Aussagespruch*, indeed that the earliest proverbs had no need of imperatives and admonitions, since "to know was to act." The last observation is open to serious question: knowledge did not necessarily compel action, as the numerous disputations within the Old Testament and ancient Near Eastern literature prove.

[32]See von Rad, *Weisheit in Israel*, 337-63, and H. J. Hermisson, "Weisheit und Geschichte," in *Probleme biblischer Theologie. Festschrift G. von Rad*, ed. H. W. Wolff (1971) 136-54. The latter article is a good example of the kind of reasoning the author criticized in "Method in Determining Wisdom Influence upon 'Historical' Literature," *JBL* 88 (1969): 129-42. The mere labeling of opposing views does not render one's own position more cogent; the example from 1 Kgs 13, which Hermisson criticizes as "superficial" (148), was chosen precisely to *demonstrate* the superficiality of many claims of wisdom influence upon "historical" literature, and was written "tongue-in-cheek." Perhaps the warning was not entirely without fruit, for Hermisson frequently feels the necessity to add disclaimers (140, 141, 143n.11, 147-48, 151, 153n.21). Certainly one would agree with him that wisdom is not the only supposition of the succession narrative (148). It is difficult for me to imagine Israelite culture as one in which only *one segment* (the wise) recognized and discussed: (1) the ill consequences of pride and value of humility, (2) the importance of the appropriate word for a given occasion, (3) the act-consequence schema, (4) the psychology of man (old age), and (5) great *individuals* (the *king!* and his family) through whom the deity worked to accomplish his purpose.

bereft of normative "words"; on the contrary, the original creative deed established an order that remained normative for all time.[33] But the existence of such an order, which some scholars have called horizontal revelation,[34] is a theological construct.[35] The primordial message of God for his creatures is available to man through the use of his reason. Furthermore, the universe itself is not silent but rings forth with praise of the Creator. Hence the importance of the hearing ear, the fruit of diligent study at the seat of learning. And should man be unable to grasp the message of the universe, God has provided him with another witness, Dame Wisdom. No latecomer she, Lady Wisdom existed in the beginning before creation. Since she was present when the original decrees were pronounced, her message carries the urgency of life or death, and her love of man explains the evangelistic fervor. Unfortunately Qoheleth did not share this view of the universe and Wisdom; for him the world had become silent, had lost its dialogical character. Hence not a word is spoken about Dame Wisdom; the cold, indifferent universe has no place for her.[36]

When the sage grounded his counsel on the way things are, he was doing more than providing a basis for conduct in authoritative fashion. He was proclaiming his faith in the fundamental order that sustains the universe, the principle that rewards virtue and punishes vice. Indeed one gets the impression that creation faith functions more within the context of "retribution" than ethical motivation per se. In order to affirm justice in the world despite appearances to the contrary, it was essential that the wise man believe in creation rather than chaos. Purpose, intention, goal were mandatory; the belief in creation assured $\tau\acute{\epsilon}\lambda o\varsigma$. In essence then, creation faith undergirds the wise man's belief in order, to which we now turn.

III.

"He has made everything beautiful *in its time*" (בְּעִתּוֹ). Here is the first effort at qualifying the beauty of the created order. Such an observation arises from the existence of polarities in human experience, one of which is designated as good or beneficial, the other as evil or harmful. The first subsection of the major unit under consideration is devoted to the naming of fourteen such antitheses (3:2-8). It is possible that Qoheleth makes use of a poem that was neutral in tone (as in 1:4-7), and by placing it in the present context has changed its import decisively. Its

---

[33]H. H. Schmid, *Gerechtigkeit als Weltordnung* (1968) and *Wesen und Geschichte der Weisheit*, BZAW 101 (1966).

[34]Above all, J. C. Rylaarsdam, *Revelation in Jewish Wisdom Literature* (1946).

[35]For opposing views see H. D. Preuss, "Erwägungen zum theologischen Ort alttestamentlicher Weisheitsliteratur," *EvT* 30 (1970): 396-406 and von Rad, *Weisheit in Israel*, 102-31.

[36]Von Rad, *Weisheit in Israel*, 226, 300, contrasts the Israelite idea of Wisdom who "addresses man" and the Egyptian concept of Maat.

negative impact is enhanced by the concluding rhetorical question ("What gain has the worker from his toil?" v. 10). "For everything there is a season (זְמָן), and a time (עֵת) for every matter under heaven" (3:1). The meaning of עֵת is something like "occasion for" or "possibility for"; the verse observes that there is a right time and a wrong time for everything, a theme that frequently appears in wisdom literature. This idea dominates the book of Sirach, the Greek text of which uses the pregnant καιρός about sixty times.[37]

The form of 3:1-9 is that of didactic poetry, with the kernel of the poem drawing upon onomastica-like material. The poem is a work of art, especially in its use of chiasmus and paranomasia. Besides the example of chiasmus mentioned in the preceding discussion of structure, there is a fine specimen in 3:8 (love-hate, war-peace). The paranomasia appears in 3:4b (סְפוֹד־רְקוֹד), perhaps also in 3:3b and 3:4a (לִבְנוֹת־לִבְכּוֹת).[38] The point of the poem in its present setting cannot be an affirmation that one should seek to act at the appropriate time, for Qoheleth observes that man cannot know that vital fact. Rather it laments the predetermined monotony of all human affairs, the fact that the veil of secrecy hangs over everything that happens. Implicit in the poem is the recognition that man can do only one of these antitheses at a time, but he cannot know which to choose at any given עֵת. In 3:17 the conviction that God has appointed a time for every matter is set within a context of the theodicy question, in a sense resolving the issue. The fact that Qoheleth relentlessly continues his attack on divine justice suggests a secondary origin for this verse, unless one is willing to assume that Qoheleth, like Sirach and some maxims in the book of Proverbs, was attempting to hold together antithetic viewpoints to achieve totality.[39] In 9:12 Qoheleth returns to the idea that man does not know his time, and concludes that his fate (מִקְרֶה) is one with that of the beasts (he will be snared at an evil time; cf. 3:18-21).

How does Qoheleth's use of the idea of an appropriate time for everything compare with that of other wisdom texts? It has been observed that "In essence the goal of wisdom instruction was the recognition of the right time, the right place and the right degree of human conduct."[40] Put another way, the distinctive feature of wisdom thinking is order. The sages believed that God had established "fixed decrees" comparable with natural law by which the universe was sustained. In addition God was the guarantor of this order, punishing or rewarding human conduct so as to assure the survival of the universe itself. This idea Israel borrowed from her neighbors; both in Egyptian and Mesopotamian literature order was essential to the

---

[37]This number is taken from von Rad, *Weisheit in Israel*, 322.

[38]D. G. Wildeboer, *Der Prediger*, KHAT (1898) 131.

[39]Gordis, *Koheleth, the Man and His World*, passim, suggests another alternative, namely, the use of quotations.

[40]H. H. Schmid, *Wesen und Geschichte der Weisheit*, 190.

sages.[41] Man's task, accordingly, was to discern the order of the world by means of examined experience. Once a hidden secret was opened to him, the sage coined it in a proverb, thus achieving a degree of mastery over the world. The accumulation of discoveries as to the nature of this order was transmitted from generation to generation, each time being tested by new experience. For no word was final; each proverb was subject to confirmation or disconfirmation. Cosmic and ethical order was explored, so that man might learn how to behave toward God and his fellowmen. This effort to discover hidden decrees, while utilitarian in character, was far more than the attempt to discern what is good for man.[42] In essence it was a discovery of and participation in the ordering of the world, that is, the prevention of a return to chaos. For this reason righteousness involved God, man, and creation itself. Thus an urgency in the proverbial literature is comprehensible; so too is the scornful attitude expressed toward the "fool." If a mastery of the appropriate time, place and degree of conduct is essential to the order of the universe, an impulse to dogma and systematization is built into wisdom thinking.[43]

This "dogma," usually referred to in German scholarship as the *Tun-Ergehen-Zusammenhang*,[44] and in English literature as Act-Consequence or Cause-Effect Principle, is likewise a constituent factor in wisdom literature, but by no means exclusively so.[45] A result of the belief in purpose and order, the retribution schema was not merely a grounding of ethical teaching; that is, it did not emerge simply to provide motivation for conduct. Although it has been argued that the principle of order became independent of God and constituted a "law" to which even Yahweh was subject,[46] this thesis is difficult, if not impossible, to support textually.[47] The existence of the book of Job indicates, nevertheless, that some people were willing to entertain such notions. In a sense Job's defense stands or falls on the principle

---

[41]Ibid., 33-36, 85-140.

[42]Such an anthropocentric emphasis is central to the vastly important article by Zimmerli entitled "Zur Struktur der alttestamentlichen Weisheit," *ZAW* 51 (1933): 177-204.

[43]Preuss, "Erwägungen zum theologischen Ort alttestamentlicher Weisheitsliteratur," 397-98.

[44]K. Koch, ed., *Um das Prinzip der Vergeltung in Religion und Recht des Alten Testament*, WF 125 (1972). von Rad, *Weisheit in Israel*, 385, writes that it is more appropriate to speak of a dogmatic preoccupation of interpreters! One can only respond that the texts justify such preoccupation.

[45]This point has been emphasized by the author in "Popular Questioning of the Justice of God in Ancient Israel," *ZAW* 82 (1970): 382-84, and by von Rad, *Weisheit in Israel*, 252-53.

[46]Preuss, "Erwägungen zum theologischen Ort alttestamentlicher Weisheitsliteratur," 398.

[47]Gese, *Lehre und Wirklchkeit in der Alten Weisheit* (1958) 45-50, and von Rad, *Weisheit in Israel*, 131-48.

of retribution that he has rejected, and the author's point is that God is free to act in a way that is disconsonant with the "law" of individual retribution.[48]

The fact that a "dogma" about reward and punishment arose is illustrative of the optimism with which the sage viewed both the world and his ability to understand the divine mysteries. While the wise man readily conceded that there was a limit to his knowledge, this bit of humility does not negate the existence of the belief in individual retribution. Of course, the sages were aware of a breach in the wall, but succeeded remarkably well in plugging the hole even after the breach had widened to a chasm under the ruthless attacks of Job and Qoheleth. We are now in a position to answer the question about Qoheleth's use of the idea of the right time as compared with that of other wisdom texts. In a word, Qoheleth has theologized the ancient teaching:[49] by joining the idea of the appropriate time to a theological determinism, Qoheleth has limited man and in a sense God also. There is no individual retribution, and man cannot know what the appropriate deed is for any moment. Indeed, man is unable even to distinguish good and bad (or perhaps shades of good). "Say not, 'Why were the former days better than these?' For it is not from wisdom that you ask this" (7:10). If this verse is understood in light of Sir 36:1-17, especially v. 6 ("Show signs anew, and work further wonders; make thy hand and thy right arm glorious"), its relevance to the theodicy question is readily discernible. Even if one does not use Sirach's text as a key to the postulating of an audience for whom this word of Qoheleth was intended, the observation is clearly an attack against the way things are, that is, against God who is responsible for the current state of affairs.

The simple formula, "Say not" is used preeminently in contexts dealing with the justice of God. Even where the denial of the principle of retribution is missing, as in Prov 20:22 and 24:29, the problem under discussion is integrally related to divine justice. This ancient formula, in use as early as the Egyptian Instruction of Amen-em-ope, was taken up by Sirach with enthusiasm. Almost without exception the contexts are theodicial in character; in nearly every instance Sirach is fighting against those who deny the principle of rewards for the good man and are arrogantly boasting that they sin with impunity.

> Do not say, "Who will have power over me?" for the Lord will surely punish you. Do not say, "I sinned, and what happened to me?" for the Lord is slow to anger. Do not be so confident of atonement that you add sin to sin. Do not say, "His mercy is great, he will forgive the multitude of my sins," for both mercy and wrath are with him, and his anger rests on sinners.   (5:3-6)

---

[48]For additional discussion see my "Popular Questioning of the Justice of God in Ancient Israel," 380-95.

[49]Von Rad, *Weisheit in Israel*, 188.

Similar warnings are given throughout the text of Sirach. "Do not say, 'He will consider the multitude of my gifts, and when I make an offering to the Most High God he will accept it'" (7:9). "Do not say, 'Because of the Lord I left the right way'; for he will not do what he hates. Do not say, 'It was he who led me astray' for he has no need for a sinful man" (15:11-12). "Do not say, 'I shall be hidden from the Lord, and who from on high will remember me?' Among so many people I shall not be known, for what is my soul in the boundless creation? . . . Like a tempest which no one can see, so most of his works are concealed. Who will announce his acts of justice? Or who will await them? For the covenant is far off'" (16:17, 21-22). To these may be added a variant, "No one can say." In all three instances the subject matter is like that under discussion. "No one can say, 'What is this?' 'Why is that?' for in God's time all things will be sought after" (cf. Eccl 3:15). "No one can say, 'What is this?' 'Why is that?' for everything has been created for its use" (39:21). "And no one can say, 'This is worse than that', for all things will prove good in their season" (39:34).

These polemical texts throw considerable light upon the sociotheological situation in which Sirach functioned as a teacher in the בֵּת־מִדְרָשׁ. Such prohibitives indicate that the skeptic has always harassed the sage who hoped against hope that somewhere, somehow inequity would disappear so that justice would shine with the brilliance of midday. The numerous references to the justice of God, many of which are so stated as to reveal the challenge resting behind them, witness to the difficulty of affirming the principle of retribution. One way of maintaining it was to claim that God sees everything that takes place. Accordingly there is a wealth of literature that lays stress upon the clarity of God's vision. No victim of nearsightedness or inattention, he scans the entire horizon and keeps an accurate record of man's deeds, whether good or bad. By the time of Sirach and Bar., epithets had arisen to emphasize God's full knowledge (חֹזֶה כֹּל, Sir 15:18; ὁ εἰδὼς τὰ πάντα, Bar 3:32),[50] each reminding the Israelite that he sins at his own peril or that his virtue does not escape notice.

The principle of retribution was challenged from the other side too. Not only were there doubters who questioned the justice of God on the basis of their experience; there were also men who believed that the deity was capable of overlooking or forgiving misconduct. Whether any of the sages prior to Sirach belonged to the ranks of these who questioned the "dogma" of retribution in favor of a merciful God is a disputed question. The text from Proverbs that is sometimes quoted in this connection is ambiguous; it may refer to human forgiveness (28:13). In Job 11:6 Zophar argues that God exacts of Job *less* than his guilt deserves, but this is still a long way from divine mercy as celebrated in Old Testament literature outside the wisdom corpus. Much closer are Job 10:12 and 12:4, which refer to God

---

[50]Fichtner, *Die altorientalische Weisheit in ihrer israelitisch-jüdischen Ausprägung*, 106-17.

as the source of the steadfast love and the one who responded to Job's prayer at an earlier period of his life. Such recollection of a bygone vital religious experience by one who has now discovered that God is his personal antagonist is all the more impressive, and points to an oversight of much critical scholarship.[51] Perhaps Sirach has preserved a genuine aspect of wisdom, for it was indeed a "tiny step"[52] from hymns about the divine mysteries concealed in nature to the uttering of fervent prayers. This close relationship of hymn and prayer is also evident in Wisd., where a distinction between the two is sometimes impossible (11:23–12:2). It is noteworthy that some intertestamental literature seeks to combine divine justice and mercy (Tob 3:2). How, then, does Qoheleth fit into the picture that has evolved from this discussion? For him there is no divine compassion. But neither is there divine justice. Such absolutization of the limited experience of one man is in tension with Qoheleth's thesis that God has put הָעֹלָם in man's heart. . . a discussion of this difficult text is our immediate task.

IV.

"Also he has put eternity(?) into man's mind" (גַּם אֶת־הָעֹלָם נָתַן בְּלִבָּם). The beauty of everything in its own time is not the final word Qoheleth has to say. By nature man is endowed with a compulsive drive not only to appreciate the beauty of creation on the aesthetic level, but also to know its character and meaning so as to gain self-certainty, security and happiness. Whence comes this ceaseless tug to know what holds the world together and to use this knowledge for one's well being? Does Qoheleth view such restlessness of the soul as a gift or curse? The answer to this question depends upon the meaning of הָעֹלָם. If we dare to enter this well known playground of fantasy, it is with full knowledge that the meaning of this obscure הָעֹלָם "is far off, and deep, very deep, who can find it out?" (Eccl 7:24).

In the history of Qoheleth research, four basic solutions to the meaning of this word have inevitably suggested themselves:[53] (1) eternity, (2) world, (3) course of the world, and (4) knowledge or ignorance. The first three attempt to understand the

---

[51]See Fichtner's summary, ibid., 110. The proverbs that demand love of one's enemy (Prov 20:22; 24:17-18, 29; 25:21-22) may throw light on the problem under discussion. If God did not forgive even his devotees, how could he demand forgiveness of them, or at the very least, compassion? For extra-Israelite parallels see Merikare 112, 119; Anii 300; Amen-em-ope 22:1-8; and Babyl. Prov 21–26.

[52]Von Rad, *Weisheit in Israel*, 389.

[53]For a summary of current research see F. Ellermeier, *Qohelet* (967) 309-22 and O. Loretz, *Qohelet und der Alte Orient* (1964) 281-85.

MT as a defective form of עוֹלָם, whereas the fourth substitutes different vowels. The LXX translator of Qoheleth renders the phrase as follows: καί γε σὺν τὸν αἰῶνα ἔδωκεν. This reading is in accord with the meaning of עָלָם in rabbinic literature where a distinction is made between this world (עוֹלָם הַזֶּה) and the world to come (עוֹלָם הַבָּא). The usual objection to this understanding of the term in Qoheleth carries little weight, specifically that הָעֹלָם never bears such an abstract meaning in the rest of the Old Testament. It is well known that Qoheleth's vocabulary and syntax are unique within the Hebrew canon. Nevertheless, it is significant that Qoheleth uses עָלָם in its usual Old Testament sense in 1:4, 10; 2:16; 3:14; 9:6. More cogent is the argument against such an interpretation of הָעֹלָם from context; if eternity is meant, why the remorseful 3:11bβ? The special endowment of eternity, whatever that means, would have been cause for jubilation, not sorrow. How far Qoheleth is from a belief in man's innate endowment of eternity can be seen in his almost flippant rhetorical question dismissing the new idea of resurrection ("Who knows whether the spirit [breath] of man goes upward and the spirit of the beast goes down to the earth?" 3:21). Others have suggested that הָעֹלָם means a desire for eternity;[54] amid the restless changes of temporality man has a notion of eternity. Unlike the animals man is conscious of the passing of time; the meaning of הָעֹלָם would thus approximate that of צֶלֶם in Gen. 1:26.[55] But Eccl 3:18-22 makes the point that the fate of man and beast is the same, hence the sting in the heart must be something else. Incidentally, it is remarkable that the sages refused to make use of the idea of the image of God, which does not occur until Sirach. The reason for this refusal to take up such a concept may lie in wisdom's experiential character, which prefers analogies that surface from human experience rather than from speculation about the unseen.

The Vulgate reads *mundum tradidit disputationi eorum* at Eccl 3:11, and Jerome's commentary conveys the same idea: *saeculum didit in corda eorum.* Following this lead some scholars use such phrases as "love of the world," "*Weltsinn,*" or "*Welt.*"[56] Inasmuch as עָלָם in the Old Testament always has a temporal meaning, others argue that Qoheleth uses the term to refer to a period of time, particularly to the remotest age.[57] The emphasis would then be upon the knowledge that the world is running its course, passing away, and with it man too. The defective writing of הָעֹלָם has led others to suggest that the root is עלם, to

---

[54]F. Delitzsch. The quotation is taken from Ellermeier, *Qohelet*, 311.

[55]Zimmerli, *Der Prediger*, 172, writes that Qoheleth cannot accept the exaltation of man in Gen 1:26 and Ps 8, so he substitutes הָעֹלָם. Wildeboer, *Der Prediger*, 133, also relates Gen 1:26 to Eccl 3:10, remarking that the influence of childhood education is manifest.

[56]Gordis, *Koheleth, the Man and His World*, 231, and Kroeber, *Der Prediger*, 85, 116.

[57]Loretz, *Qohelet und der Alte Orient*, 284-85.

conceal.[58] A meaning such as ignorance is then given to the form. But the same consonants can be read in a different manner, namely "knowledge," although this meaning does not suit the context. Among the many emendations that have been offered one is worthy of consideration: הֶעָמָל (toil).

The meaning of הָעֹלָם is further complicated by the following בְּלִבָּם. Despite the attractiveness of K. Galling's[59] emendation to בּוֹ or לוֹ, the loss of which is credibly explained as the result of dittography and metathesis (מִבְּלִי to לְבָם), we cannot go this route. The acknowledged logical coherence is no cogent argument, and the dismissal of 1 Kgs 10:24 and Jer 31:33 (cf. Ps 119:11) as irrevelant for the understanding of Eccl 3:11 on the grounds that nowhere else is הָעֹלָם said to be placed in man's heart is unsatisfactory. The בְּלִבָּם must refer to mankind in 3:10, also in the plural (לִבְנֵי הָאָדָם). But Galling is correct that the meaning of Eccl 3:11 must be temporal; God has given man a life that is characterized by transitoriness, yet man tries to find out the future. The desire to calculate, to seek after what is yet to be in such manner as to secure oneself for whatever befalls him—this is God's gift. Yet man's tendency to strive for permanence, to assure the survival of his name, is destined to fail. So, too, is every inquiry about past and future events, even if man is so created that he must ask about his moment under the sun.

Whatever the meaning of הָעֹלָם may be, the context emphasizes man's inability to discover it. With this judgment as to man's limitations of knowledge we have arrived at a significant theme in wisdom literature. The idea is expressed beautifully in Prov 25:2 ("It is the glory of God to conceal things (הַסְתֵּר), but the glory of kings is to search things out"). The unchecked optimism is strikingly different from Qoheleth's lament; perhaps the tradition that Solomon was a sage par excellence (or at least a patron of the wise men) stands behind this optimism. Here was a king who, according to the tradition, was granted special insight so that his wisdom surpassed that of non-Israelites. Similarly Hezekiah was a sponsor of the wise men, and may have sat for this portrait. The task facing both kings, and others whose connection with the sages is not known, was to search out the mysteries that God had concealed.

The limits of human wisdom are recalled in isolated proverbs (Prov 16:1, 9; 19:21; 20:24; 21:30, 27:1), hymns (Job 5:9; 28:20-23), and "school questions" (catechisms; so Prov 30:2-4; Job 11:7-12). Thus Qoheleth stands in a long tradition when recognizing that the divine mysteries hidden in the world cannot be grasped. This ignorance is not due to laziness, for Qoheleth has determined to be wise. Despite his efforts, however, he succeeds only in discovering the profundity of what is being

---

[58]M. Dahood, "Canaanite-Phoenician Influence in Qoheleth," *Bib* 33 (1952): 206 (darkness, ignorance, noting Ugaritic *glm*).

[59]"Das Rätsel der Zeit im Urteil Kohelets (Koh 3:1-15)," 4-5.

sought ("But it was far from me. That which is, is far off, and deep, very deep; who can find it out?" Eccl 7:23b-24).

One thing Qoheleth does discover is that the order of the world is in disarray (3:16–4:3), that there is no relationship between one's being and his welfare. The position of old wisdom, that a man's external affairs correctly mirror his inner character, is rejected. Qoheleth knows that the wicked reap the harvest of the innocent, and vice versa (9:11-12). Inasmuch as one cannot count on reward for virtue or punishment for vice, what is good for man is to enjoy himself, for even that ability is a gift of God. This is man's lot: walking under a mysterious closed universe, never certain before any possibility, step by step dependent upon God's free gift, ever ready to bear the riddle and stress of life.[60] What this means is spelled out in 3:16–4:3.

This uncertainty about the future was difficult to accept. The result was an attempt to gain some means of making contact with the unknown. Divination was essential to the Babylonian sages.[61] But what about the Israelite wise man? It has been argued that the Joseph narrative and Daniel are wisdom in orientation;[62] if true, this would provide proof that divination played a decisive role in Israelite wisdom too. Particularly significant to this thesis is the interpretation of dreams, for it was assumed that a dream was one of the many legitimate means of revelation. Accordingly, Joseph was not only an important recipent of dreams, but also a valuable and skilled interpreter of royal dreams. Likewise Daniel was able to narrate and explain the meaning of King Nebuchadnezzar's dream that even the wisest Babylonian counselors could not do. There is little if any justification for seeing these texts as even remotely related to wisdom literature, for the differences are far too numerous to be ignored. In any case dream interpretation as recorded in the Old Testament did not threaten divine sovereignty, for it was Yahweh who enabled the wise man to read the contours of divine plans for the future. Divination as such was ruled out, chiefly because of God's freedom to act as he chose. In this regard Qoheleth is representative of Israelite wisdom: "For in many dreams . . . is also vanity" (5:7 [6]).

V.

We come now to "der Pfeil des Geistes zerbricht."[63] The desire to know the hidden mysteries of God is denied any fulfillment: "Yet so that he cannot find out what God has done" (‎מִבְּלִי אֲשֶׁר לֹא־יִמְצָא הָאָדָם אֶת־הַמַּעֲשֶׂה אֲשֶׁר־‎

---

[60]Zimmerli, *Der Prediger*, 174.

[61]Lambert, *Babylonian Wisdom Literature*, 1.

[62]For criticism of this view, see the author's essay, "Method in Determining Wisdom Influence upon 'Historical' Literature," 135-37.

[63]Kroeber, *Der Prediger*, 135.

עָשָׂה הָאֱלֹהִים). Whatever it is that God has placed in man's mind will do him no good, for God (not Yahweh) has made him incapable of discovering it. Here we are approaching the demonic; this text is not far from others in the ancient Near East describing a god's jealousy lest human creatures achieve a status or power that threatens the deity, or from those accounts of a divine test with a stacked deck of cards. In both cases man is made aware of "possibilities" that are not really open to him, and all his striving is הֲבֵל הֲבָלִים.

The way to this viewpoint was prepared in Israel by the book of Job, the framework of which depicts just such a test in complete disregard for the well-being of the servant who for the moment becomes a target for divine arrows. What is at stake in the poetry, however, is the vital issue of God's freedom over against the principle of retribution. While there is provided no solution to the problem of theodicy, at least the freedom of God is proclaimed powerfully. Even the divine speeches of sublime irrelevance may be expressive of God's freedom; so free is he that he does not feel compelled to answer Job's Promethean challenge. Rather God permits nature itself to speak in his behalf.[64] The frequent claim of Job that "God must" is totally ignored; no principle is allowed to rob God of his freedom to act. The result, as Job finally realized, is that man is completely at the mercy of God, and his only alternative is to put his hand to his mouth and repent in dust and ashes. But at least there is hope that the prior relationship will now be restored, and that the last word is not of mortal man cowering before his Maker in terror.

For Qoheleth there can be no talk about a vital prayer relationship with God.[65] On the contrary, the idea of the fear of God has reverted to the numinous of bygone eras. For the other sages the fear of the Lord is the beginning of wisdom; it is the Israelite equivalent of our term "religion." For Qoheleth it signifies cold terror; the fear of the Lord means that one is in mortal danger when dealing with God, who interferes in human affairs only at the point of judgment. Such a sense of the word is evident in 3:14; 5:7[6]; and 8:13, perhaps elsewhere. Thus "only fear of the invisible God remains, and every feeling of relationship and of trust in his character known to the devout is missing."[66] A great gulf separates man from God; "the knowledge of this distance is the key to the understanding of the book of Qoheleth."[67] Ancient Israel, too, had recognized a gulf between man and God, but had believed that the distance was spanned by a Lord who was active in the lives of his people. "Bei K. dagegen bleibt nur Furcht vor der Unbegreiflichkeit Gottes übrig und es fehlt jedes Gefühl der Verbundenheit und des Vetrauens";[68] this fear arises

---

[64]Von Rad, *Weisheit in Israel*, 291, quoting Karl Barth.
[65]Hertzberg, *Der Prediger*, 226.
[66]J. Hempel, *Gott und Mensch im Alten Testament*, BWANT 38 (1936) 25.
[67]Hertzberg, *Der Prediger*, 108.
[68]Hempel, *Gott und Mensch im Alten Testament*, 25.

from the sense of "littleness and unworthiness over against the overpowering, invisible and holy, before whom one must quake and tremble."[69]

Now it is possible for the fear of God to provide the basis for a vital relationship with God and to form the foundation for ethical conduct. Can that be the case with Qoheleth? Unfortunately the answer is negative; nowhere does Qoheleth suggest that יְרֵאת־אֱלֹהִים had a positive aspect. On the contrary, the fear of God does not control his life in any significant manner; it does, however, temper his conduct to a degree. Inasmuch as one cannot perceive the absolute difference between good and evil, it is dangerous to choose one life style to the exclusion of another. This is the source of the moderate "hedonism," which seeks to encompass the best of everything, that is, to embrace the totality (הַכֹּל).

VI.

The secret with which God has endowed man in such a way as to render it useless save as a sting makes it impossible for mortal man to comprehend the entirety. From A to Z (birth to death), that is forbidden him (מֵרֹאשׁ וְעַד־סוֹף). Still it is clear to him that *in its time* everything is beautiful, and that includes all polarities. Since all knowledge is partial, there can be no absolutes, no certainties. This also goes for traditional virtues; they have lost their power to compel and to sustain faith. All that remains is a cautious open-armed attempt to enjoy one's lot without grudging the whole, which is in God's hands.

Qoheleth has even coined a stylistic device to express his desire to hold in creative tension each half of a polarity. This device is comparable to our "both . . . and." Twice in 3:11 this so-called "Zwar-aber-Aussage"[70] manifests itself. Both the גַּם and the מִבְּלִי are devices that break the sentence; the author wishes to say that apparent contradictions are true. In most instances the positive assertion represents traditional wisdom, whereas the correction of the statement arises from Qoheleth's experience. In this manner Qoheleth remains true to the dialogical character of wisdom, for he refuses to accept something if it does not accord with his own experience.

The content of Qoheleth's thought is also ambiguous. In the interest of totality he combines an openness to the world and conservatism, faith and skepticism, denial of new ideas and receptivity to various streams of thought.[71] But his openness is different from that of the Israelite sage who felt remarkably at home in the world, and whose openness was to the benevolent God to whom the battle belonged (Prov 21:31). Rather his is a willingness to listen to the unheard of, or the seldom voiced,

---

[69]Ibid., 4.

[70]Zimmerli, *Der Prediger*, 220.

[71]Kroeber, *Der Prediger*, 6.

viewpoints within Israel and from afar. On the other hand, he remains conservative, completely unwilling to take the step of nihilism to which his logic impels him. His retention of Yahwistic faith, while certainly on the outer fringe, is a remarkable inconsequence;[72] perhaps W. Zimmerli is right that the Old Testament religious man may rebel, may indeed rear himself up against suffering and injustice throughout the world, but it does not occur to him to deny his God.[73]

The faith that Qoheleth voices is a strange blend of caution and extreme rebellion. It has been said that wisdom literature has less as its intention the creating of luck than the avoidance of misfortune, hence that "in erster Linie will sie Vorsicht sein."[74] In this regard Qoheleth certainly advises against any action that would bring misfortune down upon one's head, and even concedes that the light is sweet. On the other hand, his teaching borders on heresy. While he may advise against following Job in struggling with one who is stronger than the challenger, at the same time he swims alone against the powerful stream of the whole "wisdom establishment." In so doing he calls the sages back to the limits of their knowledge, and thus remains true to ancient Yahwism—and ancient wisdom.[75] The nearly flippant "Who knows?" stands as a strong reminder of God's freedom and man's creatureliness, warns against any and all systems that seek to explain the whole of reality, and forces man to accept life as it is granted him without anxious thoughts about the future.

This grasping after comprehensiveness has led J. G. Herder to see in Qoheleth a Faust-like conflict between two souls;[76] perhaps the analogy from H. Hesse's *Steppenwolf* would be better, for the idea of a thousand souls within the breast more accurately portrays the desire for הכל so important to Qoheleth. In this respect

---

[72]Von Rad, *Theologie des Alten Testament*, 1 (1957) 457.

[73]*Die Weisheit des Predigers Salomo* (1936) 29.

[74]Kroeber, *Der Prediger*, 12.

[75]Gese, "Die Krisis der Weisheit bei Koheleth," 139-51, esp. 150-51.

[76]See Kroeber, *Der Prediger*, 31. He refers to Herder, *Briefe, das Studium der Theologie betreffend*, ed. J. G. Muller (1808) 135ff. Qoheleth's fondness for looking at both sides of an issue has been discussed recently by Ernest Horton, Jr., "Koheleth's Concept of Opposites," *Numen* 19 (1972): 1-21. Horton isolates four principles employed by Qoheleth in dealing with opposites: (1) preference, (2) both-and, (3) cancellation, and (4) neither-nor. Unlike the Taoists who look for hidden meanings and attempt to connect opposites, Qoheleth is said to be content with mere description of polarities; he also differs from Taoists, according to Horton, in his preference for everyday concretizations over abstractions (10), in his positive attitude toward sex over against the Taoist's complementary view of the male-female polarities (12), and in his negative assessment of man's ability to change things as opposed to the Taoist's optimism (12-13). Horton also notes the vast differences between Aristotle and Qoheleth, concluding that the latter is like Semitic literature in hedonism, but unlike it in the concept of opposites (15-19).

alone Sirach was an excellent disciple of Qoheleth,[77] for the principle of comprehensiveness plays a dominant role in his thought. Even the fundamental polarity, life and death, so significant to Qoheleth, has left an indelible mark upon Sirach's thought, both in his frequent struggles with those who deny the concept of retribution and in his almost matter-of-fact observation that the ancient sentence is written, "You must die" (14:17; cf. 8:7; 38:22). Qoheleth, too, was sadly aware of that sentence, for the spectre of death looms large over all he writes (some have said, "the smell of the tomb!"). Inasmuch as no one has any word about when and how death takes him, man and beast are alike, and nonexistence preferable to life in certain cases, since there are relative grades of life. Here alone do we hear a sage conclude, "So I hated life" (2:17a). The reason for this startling observation, it would appear, one can discover in Eccl 3:11. "He has made everything beautiful in its time; also he has put eternity into man's mind, yet so that he cannot find out what God has done from the beginning to the end."

Before attempting to draw this discussion to a close, a few words about 3:12-15 are necessary, inasmuch as they draw the practical consequences of divine secrecy and provide further reflection upon the work of God. Since the mystery of life is hidden, man should enjoy life as much as possible, but (גַּם is adversative here as in 5:18[19]) ever mindful that even the "bit of healthy animal life which comes with the years of vigor"[78] is a gift of God. Just as in Gen. 1:7 there is a note of gloom in the background arising from the fact that man's breath is a gift and can be withdrawn at any moment, so here the negative aspect must not be overlooked. Again Qoheleth returns to the crucial term, this time clearly in a temporal sense; what God does endures forever (לְעוֹלָם), and *nothing can alter it* (cf. Sir 18:6). Here Qoheleth uses an ancient formula[79] known to us from Egypt as well as Dt. 4:2; 13:1 [12:32]; and Jer 26:2. As a final comment about divine determinism Qoheleth varies the disciplinary theory of suffering to suggest that the permanence of divine activity has as its purpose the instilling of fear in human beings. The monotony of such determinism strikes Qoheleth as ludicrous; this must be the explanation for the strange metaphor of God searching in circles (וְהָאֱלֹהִים יְבַקֵּשׁ אֶת־נִרְדָּף) for what he has already seen once (cf. Sir 39:17).

VII.

There is a sense in which every generation is in conflict with the understanding of reality as proclaimed by a previous age; wisdom literature welcomed such validation or disconfirmation of its claims inasmuch as it refused to incapsulate the

---

[77]A discussion of the principle of comprehensiveness can be found in Marböck, *Weisheit im Wandel*, 152-54.

[78]G. A. Barton, *Ecclesiastes*, ICC (1908) 102.

[79]W. Hermann, "Zu Kohelet 3,14," *WZ* 3 (1953/1954): 163-65.

quintessence of moral conduct as the answer to every situation. This refusal bore witness to the sage's humility, for only God could speak the last word. The danger of the resulting moral relativism is illustrated by Qoheleth, who has lost the optimism of bygone ages and whose view of man's incapacity is truly revolutionary. For him cruel reality has shattered the moral universe, leaving chaos. Unlike Job who waged a gigantic Jacob-like struggle for God's blessing, Qoheleth was so impressed with the inability of man to discover the true nature of reality that he shrugged his shoulders and became a lonely man, no longer in dialogue with the world.[80] Unable to draw strength and courage from a vital relationship with God, who seems not to have been a "You" to him, Qoheleth can only say: "whether it is love or hate man does not know" (9:1). Here stands secular man;[81] one is tempted also to say, "Here one confronts gallows humor."[82]

We hear Qoheleth admonish us to enjoy youth *for* we grow old; to enjoy toil *yet* it is sorry business; to enjoy the *woman* whom we love *but* there is not one in a thousand(!); to eat, drink, and wear festive garments *yet* sorrow, fasting, and mourning are better; to pursue knowledge *but* it only increases sorrow; to embrace life, *yet* like the sword of Damocles the ancient sentence, "You must die," hangs over us. We also know that all these observations stand under the shadow of Qoheleth's plaintive cry, "So I hated life," and haunting query, "Who knows what is good for man?" (6:12). How then can one derive from such "laughter" the necessary insight to justify the term "gallows humor"? Surely it is not to be found in Qoheleth's passive ethics,[83] the strict obedience and total submission to an indifferent

---

[80]Von Rad, *Weisheit in Israel*, 300, notes the loss of dialogue with God and the world.

[81]A. Lauha, "Die Krise des religiösen Glaubens bei Koheleth," VTSup 3 (1955) 183-91, particularly 188-91.

[82]Hertzberg, *Der Prediger*, 237.

[83]Pedersen, "Scepticisme israélite," 322, 361, characterizes Qoheleth's ethics negatively as resignation and positively as prudence. Hertzberg, *Der Prediger*, 225, also writes of Qoheleth's ethics as passive. We follow Pedersen and Hertzberg, despite the recent defense of Qoheleth's ethics as positive, optimistic, possessing the nerve of life by G. von Rad, *Weisheit in Israel*, 298-99, R. B. Y. Scott, *The Way of Wisdom* (1971) 184-87. The following facts are decisive in our understanding of Qoheleth's ethics: (1) the positive counsel of Qoheleth hangs precariously between the initial blanket denial of any gain to pleasure and the final allegory of the approaching night that cancels all so-called profit; (2) the primary datum of religious experience, the freedom of God to draw near to man or to withdraw from him in silence, and its corollary, man's inability to hide from the Hidden God (see L. Perlitt, "Die Verborgenheit Gottes," *Probleme biblischer Theologie*, 367-82, esp. 367, 373) find expression in Qoheleth's lament that man cannot penetrate the darkness of mystery and his admonition that man should guard his lips lest he incur guilt, i.e., that he should fear God (see now M. Palfy, "Allgemein-menschliche Beziehungen der Furcht im Alten Testament," *Schalom: Studien zu Glaube und Geschichte Israels*, 23-27, for a discussion of the redemptive aspect of the fear of God characteristic of the rest of the Old Testament; "So ist Gottesfurcht immer eine Gabe der Liebe Gottes: eine Heilsgabe als göttliche Forderung zum wahren Dienen Gottes, des

God devoid of compassion, forgiveness, and redemption. If contact with Transcendence is made neither in the counsel nor in the despair of Qoheleth, where does he become a "lonely man of faith"?[84] The insight of K. Miskotte is on the right track: Qoheleth's grasping of *Life* is Yahweh's way of holding his own in expectation.[85] The key word for us is "way" which we understand in the sense of *path*; hence we conclude that Qoheleth stands as a haunting reminder to all humanity, believers and unbelievers, that there is no certainty except that of the ancient decree, "You must die."[86] Reflecting upon the consequent existence *in tormentis*, we, too, sooner or later find ourselves where Qoheleth was,[87] for who can really say whether we encounter divine caprice or compassion, or indeed nothing? This much we know (Qoheleth would have said יָדַעְתִּי): only he who has ever recognized the claims of the eternal gospel (dread, *Angst*) upon his life is open to the possibility of a temporal gospel (forgiveness, love). But if and when we cannot affirm the latter,

---

Herrn," 26); (3) this Hidden God is clearly conceded to be Judge of all the living, even if one who is slack in carrying out his responsibilities, as evidenced by the sorry state of humanity (there is folly in high places, and none to comfort the victims of such high handedness; man's lot is painful by day and vexatious by night; no women can be trusted and precious few men); (4) although this arbitrary Judge makes no effort to right the wrongs that have ripped open the social fabric and crushed the soul of a people, He is not a tyrant, for He gives to man the pleasures of youth (food, drink, sexuality), which are to be seized with gusto; (5) but even this nectar is bittersweet, since the Hidden God holds man accountable for these good things which last but a moment even for those fortunate enough to have sufficient power to enjoy them; and (6) Death, the final decree from the aching Void, comes to one and all, erasing in its wake the memory of former pleasures. In no case is the occasional polemical defense of divine justice, which would remove some of the sting from these conclusions, to be attributed to Qoheleth.

[84]The phrase is taken from J. B. Solovietchek's article by that title in *Tradition* 7 (1965): 5-67.

[85]*When the Gods Are Silent* (1967) 453.

[86]Scarcely enough time for the ink to dry passed between the composition of these words and the arrival of a telegram to Heidelberg, where I was on sabbatical, with the entirely unexpected news of Phil's death. Three years of working beside him have deepened the friendship of student days and enlarged its scope to dimensions other than the purely scholarly one. His death, then, is a great personal loss; it has been a privilege to know him, one for which I am truly thankful.

[87]This alone provides an adequate explanation for the strange power of Qoheleth to attract believers and humanists and to evoke vastly different responses even among the former. To illustrate, Qoheleth has been called (1) the most shocking messianic prophecy in the Old Testament, Hertzberg, *Der Prediger*, 238; (2) the sage who taught Israel the proper fear of God and thus called her back to genuine monistic Yahwism, Gese, "Die Krisis der Weisheit bei Kohelet," 150-51; (3) the secular compromiser as opposed to Job, the *homo religiosus*, Lauha, "Die Krise des religiösen Glaubens bei Kohelet," 188-91; and (4) the crown of faith, Miskotte, *When the Gods are Silent*, 450.

yes, have even shrugged our shoulders ("who knows?") and become utterly lonely, Qoheleth beckons to us and we walk together in the sweet light (11:7) of companionship (4:10) on the way toward becoming lonely men of faith[88] in a silent universe.[89]

---

[88]Does Galling envision an openness to divine encounter when he asks if Qoheleth alludes to Job's silence, *which is an act of faith*, "Das Rätsel der Zeit im Urteil Kohelets (Koh 3:1-15)," 15? We refer to something entirely different from traditional faith; rather it is a life under divine silence and indifference, but in faithful comradeship.

[89]The poignant cry of Job in MacLeish's *J.B.* that "[God] does not love. He is," would have been understood by Qoheleth. Would he also have comprehended Sarah's response: "But we do. That's the wonder"?

37 (1979)

The Shadow of Death in Qoheleth

A striking inconsistency in Job's attitude toward death prompted Samuel Terrien to write at length about "Fear and Fascination of Death" in *Job: Poet of Existence*.[1] In his view, Job went through three stages in his flirtation with death, while being tossed about between the fear and fascination of death. In 3:19 Job passed *from hatred of life to love of death*, as if in total agreement with Sophocles: "Not to be born is the most to be desired; but having seen the light, the next best thing is to go whence one came as soon as may be" (*Oedipus at Colonus*, 1225-28). A decisive change occurred in 6:8-13, where the earlier wish to escape gave way to *strong desire to remain faithful to a God of love*. At this stage Job went after death "not because he hated life, but because he feared, through the disintegration of his personality, the weakening of his will to trust."[2] In 7:1-21 Job no longer pursued death as solace or safeguard; instead, *fear of death replaced its fascination*.

This pilgrimage from a death wish that sprang from hatred of life, to a desire for death as a preventive of unfaithfulness to God, and ultimately to terror before death's power suffices to explain why at one moment Job calls for strangulation (Job 7: 15), and complains of life's brevity at another (10:18-20). In Job's plaint about his brief stay on earth, Terrien found evidence that the suffering hero was slowly being reconciled to existence.[3]

Terrien's analysis of Job's fear and fascination of death throbs with existential pathos and theological profundity. The former reaches a high point in an observation about life's supreme irony: faith that does not know despair prevents one from forcing the riddle of self and existence; but despair kills faith, and, when carried to

---

[1](Indianapolis and New York: Bobbs-Merrill, 1957) 40-65.
[2]*Job: Poet of Existence*, 55-56 (with tenses altered for stylistic reasons).
[3]Ibid., 61.

the extreme, may bring self-extermination.[4] Accordingly, death is taken with utmost seriousness—as worse than a hellish life, and the closing of a wound rather than the opening of a gate. The latter imagery connects with a theological observation that in unfaith "life is not worth living, for it is not the vestibule to heaven."[5] Job, who saw the futility of death, perceived the revelatory potential of creation. Still, in the presence of his friends, he faced nothingness, and even dared to suggest that in the scandal of Job's death, God would behold the void. In effect, Job "risked theological death in order to confront life in the raw."[6] As a reward, in Terrien's judgment, "God's lonely man is received into the society of God."[7]

In my study of Qoheleth I have encountered the same ambiguity about life and death that Terrien found in Job.[8] On the one hand, Qoheleth writes that he hates life, and views death as something to be desired, particularly because it affords rest. On the other hand, he thinks the living have hope, albeit a qualified one. Consequently, he chases life with abandon. A study of this ambivalence in Qoheleth seems an appropriate tribute to one whose scholarship I have long admired and whose friendship I cherish.

So I Hated Life

The starting point for a consideration of Qoheleth's attltude toward death must surely be his shocking conclusion to a series of experiments: "So I hated life because the work that is done under the sun is burdensome to me; for everything

---

[4]Ibid., 41. Cf. Ernest Becker's observation that "the irony of man's condition is that the deepest need is to be free of the anxiety of death and annihilation; but it is life itself which awakens it, and so we must shrink from being fully alive" (*The Denial of Death* [New York: Free Press, 1973] 66). Becker points out that we can "use anxiety as an eternal spring for growth into new dimensions of thought and trust" (92).

[5]The dominant O.T. view of death as final occurs in its stark form in 2 Sam 14:14 ("For we shall surely die, and like water that is spilled on the ground that cannot be gathered up . . . "). To this view may be compared the interesting exchange between Aqhat and Anat (*ANET* 151).

[6]Terrien, *Job: Poet of Existence*, 18. Curiously, the O.T. has provided two terms for the opposite of Job's risk, namely the evasion of life's full intensity (the Jonah syndrome) and tranquilizing oneself with trivia so as to live normal lives (Philistinism).

[7]Terrien, *Job: Poet of Existence*, 239. I do not intend to assess the validity of Terrien's analysis, but to use it as a clue for a similar study of Qoheleth. For further treatment, see Walter L. Michel, "Death in Job," *Dialog* 11 (1972): 183-89, and his Ph.D. diss. entitled "The Ugaritic Texts and the Mythological Expressions in the Book of Job (including a New Translation of and Philological Notes on the Book of Job)" (University of Wisconsin, 1970).

[8]Fundamental differences between Job and Qoheleth grow out of their contrasting views of divine activity. For Job, death possessed the power to prevent his vindication and threatened a loss of trust in God, whereas Qoheleth needed no divine commendation, and completely lacks trust in a benevolent creator.

is empty and a chasing after wind" (2:17).[9] Having boasted that he had surpassed all royal predecessors in Jerusalem at acquiring wisdom (1:12-18), Qoheleth put that knowledge, painful as it was, to the test of experience (2:1-11). In each instance he raised a serious question about various answers to life's meaning. The cumulative negative verdicts forced him to ponder the value of wisdom. Noting that one fate strikes sage and fool, Qoheleth concluded that wisdom enjoys only relative advantage over folly. He reflected on approaching death, together with the resultant obliteration of all memory of his life, and pressed forward into radical denial of life's essential goodness.

Qoheleth's journey to this vantage point was a lonely one, while crowds thronged the road that led to wholesale endorsement of life as the highest good. On this well-trodden highway sages walked alongside prophets and priests, for all three believed that God usually rewarded virtue with long life, health and prosperity. The same theme punctuates their messages, whether spoken by a representative of priestly, prophetic, or sapiential thought.

> Lo, I have set before you today life and the good, death and the evil. . . . This day I call heaven and earth to witness against you. Life and death I have set before you, blessing and curse. Therefore, choose life so that you and your progeny can live.   (Deut 30:15, 19)

> For thus says the Lord to the house of Israel,
>   "Seek me and live. . . .
> Seek good, and not evil,
>   that you may live. . . .
> Hate evil, love good,
>   and establish justice in the gate.
> Perhaps the Lord, God of hosts,
>   will have compassion on the remnant of Joseph."   (Amos 5:4, 14a, 15)

> Long life is in her right hand,
>   wealth and honor in her left. . . .
> Come, eat my bread
>   and drink the wine I have mixed.
> Leave folly, and live.
>   Then walk in the path of understanding.   (Prov 3:16; 9:5-6)

With one voice those who traveled the main road identified life with the good, and looked upon death as an appropriate cipher for the evil. While an occasional

---

[9]Unless otherwise specified, translations are the author's. On τόποι and themes in Qoheleth, see esp. Oswald Loretz, *Qoheleth und der Alte Orient* (Freiburg: Herder, 1964) 196-212, 218-300.

prophet grew weary of life because of his special burden,[10] and others down on their luck glanced coquettishly at death,[11] the overwhelming majority seems to have equated life with the greatest good. Even those who dared to take their own life chose death because of an unbearable shame[12] or as an expression of supreme loyalty to a fallen king.[13]

At the same time that death connoted the evil that everyone sought to avoid, it also stood for the moment of transition from this world to Sheol, the land of the fathers. So long as that passage from one world into another came at the end of a long, full life, it caused no special anxiety. Just as Israelites harvested grain in season, God gathered his harvest and laid it safely away in a barn (Job 5:26). In such instances death hardly caused a wringing of the hands in despair. Furthermore, as long as corporate solidarity was the dominant mode of thinking, even an early death was amenable to belief in divine favor.[14]

For Qoheleth, too many examples of premature death canceled life's advantages. Admittedly, he can speak of death in nearly neutral terms: "A generation goes, and a generation comes; but the earth remains forever" (1:4); "a time to be born and a time to die, a time to plant and a time to pull up what was planted" (3:2). Still, we must ask whether such sayings have been affected by the stench of the tomb that H. Wheeler Robinson identified in Qoheleth.[15] Certainly the hyperbolic observation that "the woman whose heart is snares and nets and whose hands are fetters is more bitter than death" (7:26a) gives little, if any, support to a neutral understanding of death. For Qoheleth, death possesses a full measure of existential Angst.[16]

---

[10]Elijah, Jeremiah, Jonah.

[11]Samson, Tobit, Joanna.

[12]Ahithophel.

[13]Saul's armorbearer.

[14]L. H. Silberman, "Death in the Hebrew Bible and Apocalyptic Literature," *Perspectives on Death*, ed. L. O. Mills (Nashville: Abingdon Press, 1969) 26.

[15]*Inspiration and Revelation in the Old Testament* (Oxford: Clarendon, 1946) 258. The fact that Qoheleth "reaches its climax in an eloquent but sombre picture of death" lends credibility to Robinson's observation. Gerhard von Rad, *Wisdom in Israel* (Nashville and New York: Abingdon, 1972) 228, writes: "Behind the problem of the future, there lies for Koheleth the still more difficult question of death which casts its shadow over every meaningful interpretation of life. Whenever Koheleth speaks of fate (מִקְרֶה), death is always envisaged at the same time." But von Rad insists that Qoheleth's zest for life must not be confused with that which "as often settles in the shadow of despair" (231).

[16]L. R. Bailey, "Death as a Theological Problem in the Old Testament," *Pastoral Psychology* 22 (1971): 20-32, emphasizes a more positive or neutral attitude toward death, suggesting that Israelites had a minimum of anxiety over death. He writes: "And this lack of sustained, systematic, thematic treatment suggests that death did not hold the terror for the Israelites that it does for us" (p. 22). Bailey concludes that in general the Old Testament view is death accepting as opposed to death denying or defying (25). Qoheleth "diverges in this respect, as in others, from the true tradition of Israel" (R. Martin-Achard, *From Death to Life*

For that reason he pronounces the day of death better than the day of birth (7:1) and makes the startling declaration that it is "better to go to the house of mourning than to frequent the house of feasting, since it is the end of everyone, and the living should reflect upon it" (7:2). Pondering the moment of approaching death reminded Qoheleth of toil's futility, since its fruits will enrich his survivor, who may be a fool. Further reflection upon the injustice of hard-earned possessions falling into the hands of one who did not labor for them evoked feelings of despair.[17] Small wonder he concludes: "Sorrow is better than laughter, for in sadness of countenance a heart is glad; the heart of the wise is in a house of sorrow, and the heart of fools is in a house of gladness" (7:4).

Let it be noted that Qoheleth's despair arose in large measure from a powerful conviction that life ought to be embraced wholeheartedly. Hatred of life and a concomitant flirtation with death signal Qoheleth's fundamental opposition to injustice. Life devoid of equity, both human and divine, is hollow mockery. In such situations, death's lure can hardly be resisted.

The Dead Find Rest

Death as rest from oppression functions as a powerful metaphor in Qoheleth's thought. Persuaded that comfort could not be found in the face of oppressors in whom power resides, he reasoned that the dead were more fortunate than the living since they are no longer subject to cruelty, and have come into a measure of rest. Better than the dead or the living, he conjectured, is the one who has never been, for (s)he has not beheld evil deeds (4:1-3). In this brief observation Qoheleth pauses twice to focus attention upon a lack of comfort for the tears of the oppressed, unless one should render the final word of verse one by מְנַחֵם ("vindicator").[18] Similarly, he joins together chiastically all the oppressions that are done under the sun with the evil work that occurs under the sun (4:1, 3), and thus testifies to the impact of social injustice upon his thoughts about life and death.[19]

[London: Oliver & Boyd, 1960] 7).

[17]George Barton, *The Book of Ecclesiastes*, ICC (Edinburgh: T.&T. Clark, 1908) 82, writes: "The fact that death buries the wise and the foolish in the same oblivion, makes Qoheleth pronounce great wisdom vanity, in spite of the fact that he has just seen in wisdom the advantages of reality." Barton remarks that literary expression of Qoheleth's pessimism permitted him to continue to enjoy life (93).

[18]The iteration of מְנַחֵם functions rhetorically (Barton, *The Book of Ecclesiastes*, 114). On the sense of מְנַקֵּם, see G. E. Mendenhall, *The Tenth Generation* (Baltimore and London: Johns Hopkins University Press, 1973) 69-104.

[19]Barton, *The Book of Ecclesiastes*, 114, comments that "the deep emotion which the tears of the oppressed excited in Qoheleth is evidence of his profound sympathies with the lower classes." R. Gordis makes a similar observation about 2:16 and 4:1, in which "the cynic's pose of studied indifference falls away and the impassioned spirit of Koheleth, the idealistic seeker of truth and justice, is revealed" (*Koheleth—The Man and His World* [New

In yet another passage Qoheleth moved from an obvious injustice, this time of divine origin, to question the value of life as opposed to an aborted birth (6:1-6).[20] In this instance one who had acquired life's goods, consisting of wealth, possessions, and honor, lacked either the ability or the time to enjoy them, so that a stranger devoured them. This misfortune prompted Qoheleth to conjecture that a person who begat a hundred children and lived many years, but failed to enjoy the good and lacked a burial was less fortunate than the stillborn.

For in vanity it [the stillborn] comes and in darkness it departs,
　　and in darkness its name is covered;
moreover, it has not seen the sun and has not known (anything);
　　(yet) it has rest rather than he.　　　　　　　　　　　　　　　　(6:4-5)

In these two texts (Qoh 4:1-3 and 6:1-6) Qoheleth seems to take a wholly positive view of death in certain circumstances. The first generalizes from an experience of common misery: since wickedness thrives on every hand, death—nay, nonexistence—is better than life. Presumably, Qoheleth assumes that the innocent individual cannot throw off an oppressive yoke, and in the absence of hope, life becomes intolerable. The second text has a wholly different starting point. It recognizes that appearances often deceive, for in some instances persons who seem to be objects of divine favor bear a hidden burden. Long life does not always constitute a blessing. Sometimes a person may live to a ripe old age without having possessed the power to enjoy life at all.[21] Furthermore, an absence of proper burial[22] cancels any advantages of longevity. Consequently, no one can be assured of either, and lacking both, one becomes less fortunate than an aborted birth. At least a stillborn child has no memory of unfulfilled desires while living in luxury's lap.

But Qoheleth knows that such judgments apply only to specific circumstances. Elsewhere he allows views to surface that qualify such an endorsement of death and

---

York: Schocken, 1951] 223). On this text, see also the remarks by Rudi Kroeber, *Der Prediger*, SQAW 13 (Berlin: Akademie, 1963) 137.

[20]R. Gordis, *Koheleth—The Man and His World*, 257, observes: "There is a distinctly modern implication here of the essential loneliness of the individual personality." Gordis recognizes the rhetorical power of 6:6, which begins with a protasis and ends with a question to which only a negative answer applies (259-60).

[21]The closer one comes to death, "cumulative quantitative weakness arrives at a qualitative difference" (Silberman, "Death in the Hebrew Bible and Apocalyptic Literature," 23). It follows that life in some circumstances is a form of death (cf. Lloyd Bailey's similar remarks about inauthentic existence as a form of death; "Death as a Theological Problem in the Old Testament," 29), and that one can even speak of "stages of dying" (H. W. Wolff, *Anthropology of the Old Testament* [Philadelphia: Fortress Press, 1974] 100-13).

[22]K. Galling, *Der Prediger*, HAT 18 (Tübingen: Mohr [Siebeck], 1969) 104, concludes that the allusion to a proper burial implies that the numerous sons mentioned in 6:3 were impious.

nonexistence. For example, in 7:16-17 he warns against extreme virtue and vice, and supports the counsel with two rhetorical questions: "Why should you destroy yourself?" (7:16); "Why should you die prematurely?" (7:17). Inasmuch as no one possesses power over the day of death (8:8),[23] or knowledge about the appropriate time of any significant event (3:11),[24] (s)he cannot embrace death with open arms.

Furthermore, the debilitating effects of approaching death—with its darkness (Qoh 12:2, 3b)—hardly recommend the days of death's darkness to anyone. Such is the powerful message of the final poetic allegory (12:1-8). In my view, Qoheleth suggests the correct perspective from which to interpret the somber description of death's encroachment upon one's waning years. He urges enjoyment tempered by a sobering remembrance that days of darkness will far outnumber the longest life under the sun (11:8).

Do such qualifications imply that Qoheleth did not really conceive of death as better than life? Was he led to extreme formulations that he sought to soften in further observations about death? On the surface, at least, it would seem so, for did not Qoheleth observe that a living dog has an advantage over a dead lion?

The Living Have Hope

The context within which the supposedly positive view of life occurs bristles with polemic (8:16–9:6). Qoheleth determined to know wisdom and to perceive the expenditure of energy on earth, since sleep eludes the seeker both *by day* and by night. But God's work also escapes the eager searcher, though a sage may claim that he has actually found it. Qoheleth's boldness can hardly be missed: "But even if the wise man claims to know, he is not able to find out" (8:17b).

Still searching, Qoheleth reflected upon the fact that the righteous and wise, together with their deeds, reside in God's powerful hand, but no one knows whether God's disposition toward humans is love or hate.[25] One thing looms before them

---

[23]W. Zimmerli, "The Place and Limit of the Wisdom in the Framework of the Old Testament Theology," *SJT* 17 (1964): 156 (*Studies in Ancient Israelite Wisdom*, ed. J. L. Crenshaw [New York: Ktav, 1976] 324) writes that Qoheleth encountered the reality of the creator more clearly than any other Israelite sage. He adds: "In a manner hitherto unheard of in the Old Testament, Ecclesiastes sees death as the power that takes away the power of the whole creation and even of man's Wisdom. The fact that every man's hour of death is incalculable gives full evidence of God's majesty and freedom."

[24]On Qoheleth's view that God has concealed vital knowledge from humans, see the author's essay entitled "The Eternal Gospel (Eccles 3:11)," in *Essays in Old Testament Ethics*, ed. J. L. Crenshaw and J. T. Willis [New York: Ktav, 1974] 23-55). Von Rad, *Wisdom in Israel*, 234, remarks that "Koheleth . . . experiences the hiddenness of the future as one of the heaviest burdens of life."

[25]H. W. Hertzberg, *Der Prediger*, KAT 17 (Gütersloh: Mohn, 1963) 176, writes that "nicht einmal über sein eigenes Ich ist er völlig Herr!" Qoheleth's denial that moral or religious virtues alter one's fixed fate strikes Hertzberg as a revolutionary idea in the O.T. (177).

with absolute certainty: a single fate befalls righteous and unrighteous, clean and unclean, sacrificer and nonsacrificer, good and bad, swearer and the one who disdains oaths.[26] One fate puts an end to everything that is done under the sun; furthermore, human hearts are filled with evil and madness. Such is the evil Qoheleth spied out—a madness that death stills.[27]

Nevertheless, whoever is chosen among the living has hope, "for the living know that they will die, but the dead know nothing, and have no more reward, since their memory is forgotten" (9:5).[28] In addition, "their love, their hatred, their passion have already perished, and they no longer have a portion in anything that is accomplished on earth" (9:6).

To prove his point that the living have a modicum of hope, Qoheleth cites a familiar aphorism: "A living dog is better than a dead lion" (9:4b). Because of its amazing prowess as a hunter, the lion was early recognized as an apt metaphor for royalty (Gen 49:9, Hos 13:7). The lowly cur, restricted to a life of scavenging on the perimeters of human existence, functioned as a term of opprobrium. The epithet "dog" was hurled in the faces of male prostitutes, who belonged, in the speaker's opinion, outside the domain of human beings (Deut 23:18-19). The term also became a means of self-abnegation,[29] particularly in the presence of nobility (1 Sam 24:14). One text even has a person shrink from a prophetic description of his role in a *coup d'etat* with the words: "What is your servant, who is but a dog, that he should do this great thing?" (2 Kings 8: 13, RSV).

Precisely what Qoheleth means by this aphorism remains uncertain.[30] One thing does present itself as a reasonable conclusion: knowledge that one must die seems to constitute no real advantage.[31] For that reason, Qoheleth's citation of a familiar

---

[26]The final pair in this series of opposites reverses the order from positive to negative terms, perhaps to avoid closing on a negative note (Gordis, *Koheleth—The Man and his World*, 301). Qoheleth's exceptional stylistic powers dictate the use of *lamed* to govern the first three pairs and a coordinate construction of *kaph* for the last two pairs (Gordis, ibid.).

[27]"Die letzten Worte bilden absichtlich einem fragmentarischen Satz, der jah abbricht, wie das Leben" (Wildeboer). "The final words—and then off to the dead—form a consciously fragmentary sentence that breaks off like life itself." The translation of Wildeboer's striking observation is taken from Gordis, *Koheleth—The Man and His World*, 301.

[28]Hertzberg, *Der Prediger*, 178, perceives the sarcastic irony in 9:5. The living have practically nothing, and the dead have less than nothing. The verse has a particularly impressive use of paronomasia (שָׂכָר and זִכְרָם).

[29]George W. Coats, "Self-Abasement and Insult Formulas," *JBL* 89 (1970): 14-26.

[30]I have suggested elsewhere that this clever aphorism may have functioned as a defense for remarriage by a woman whose second husband came from a lower social class ("Riddle," IDBSup, 749).

[31]W. Zimmerli, *Man and His Hope in the Old Testament* (London: SCM, 1971) 21. Barton, *The Book of Ecclesiastes*, 160, misses the irony in Qoheleth's statement. He writes: "To have power to perceive that one must die is to be greater than the dead, who have no

saying hardly justifies a claim that he actually thought life was characterized by hope. Can one really say hope, which consists of knowledge that one must die, gives the living much advantage over the dead? At least those who have entered the land of darkness have sloughed off every vestige of passion and do not participate any longer in human madness.

It follows that Qoheleth's polemic against excessive claims to knowledge continues in the citation of a sapiential dictum.[32] The saying is quoted "tongue-in-cheek," and thus demands that one bestow upon it a certain ironical twist if (s)he wishes to recover Qoheleth's true intention. The hope that belongs to the living scarcely provides grounds for exultation.

The living would indeed have hope if they could depend upon God to grant life after death. Unfortunately, one returns just as (s)he came: naked (5:14). In his hand rests nothing of all that his toil accumulated, so what profit was it to have labored and spent many days burdened by life's heavy toll? (5:15-16). Man and beast share the same fate: both return to dust (3:18-20). But Qoheleth shrinks from the impact of this conclusion. Accordingly, he qualifies his scepticism by clothing it in the form of a rhetorical question: "Who knows whether man's breath ascends and animals' breath descends?" (3:21). Nevertheless, Qoheleth's "hideous caricature"[33] of the idea of God's testing his creatures (3:18) leaves little, if any, doubt about his own answer to the question. A God who tests mankind to show them that they are but beasts cannot be expected to separate the two in death. For at that very moment chance reigns.

> The race is not to the swift, nor the battle to the strong, nor bread to the wise, nor riches to the intelligent, nor favor to the men of skill; but time and chance[34] happen to them all. (9:11, RSV)

The divine hunter's snare suddenly falls, and silence ensues.

Elsewhere Qoheleth distinguishes between dust, which returns to the earth, and breath, which returns to God who gave it (12:7). Surely here resides some foundation upon which to build an abiding hope. On the contrary, for Qoheleth goes on to sum up the meaning of the allegory on old age and death: "The emptiest emptiness, says Qoheleth, everything is empty" (12:8). One cannot imagine such a conclusion

---

knowledge." Accordingly, "the dead are denied participation in the only world of which Qoheleth knows, this to his mind makes the pathos of death a tragedy."

[32]On Qoheleth's citation of popular wisdom, see above all Gordis, *Koheleth—the Man and His World*, passim, and H. P. Müller, "Wie Sprach Qohälät von Gott?," *VT* 18 (1968): 507-21.

[33]The language is taken from von Rad, *Wisdom in Israel*, 202n.10.

[34]Since the only other use of פֶּגַע (1 Kgs 5:18 MT) qualifies it with an adjective רָע, the translation "chance" (RSV, NEB, AT [Chicago Bible]) seems more appropriate than "mischance" (JB), or "a time of calamity" (NSB) which ignores the *waw* and alters the syntax.

if the allusion to breath's return to God contained the slightest grounds for hope. In truth, divine support of life has vanished for Qoheleth.[35]

Now if death affords rest for the weary, and the living possess no *real* advantage over the dead, while in certain circumstances the stillborn or nonexistent enjoys a superior status, suicide offers a compelling alternative to further living.[36] Its lure would seem irresistible for one who hates life and falls into despair's vice-like grip. The marvel is that Qoheleth shuns this easy resolution of his misery in favor of another powerful answer.

> Go, eat your bread in joy,
> and drink your wine with a glad heart,
> for God has already approved your behavior.
> Let your clothing be white at all times,
> and do not lack oil upon your head.
> Enjoy life with the woman whom you love
> all the days of your empty life
> that he has given you under the sun—
> all your empty days. . . .
> for there is no work, thought, knowledge, or wisdom
> in Sheol, to which you are going.   (9:7-9a, 10b)[37]

The twofold repetition of "all the days of your empty life,"[38] together with the final sobering thought about human destiny, prove that Qoheleth has not forgotten the lessons forced upon him by death's ominous shadow. But neither has he allowed that threatening presence to rob him of fleeting pleasure, which he even dares to sanction by divine approval. One can only wonder about the source of this knowl-

---

[35]Von Rad, *Wisdom in Israel*, 305 ("The fact of ultimate death first finds expression as a real intellectual problem in the teachings at the point where faith in Yahweh's support of life begins to disappear"). Von Rad describes Qoheleth's quest as an attempt to answer the question of man's lot (salvation) without any confidence in life (235).

[36]Outside Israel, pessimists openly endorse suicide ("A Dispute over Suicide," *ANET* 405-407. "The Dialogue of Pessimism," *ANET* 600-601). For some strange reason, Israel's skeptical tradition stops short of that radical decision. Was it because of a strong conviction that life belongs to Yahweh? A. F. Key, "The Concept of Death in Early Israelite Religion," *JBR* 32 (1964): 247, sums up Israel's attitude toward death as follows: "Thus, while death was accepted, it was accepted only passively. It was not something to be sought. It is only in the depths of despair that death is ever requested, and suicide is a very infrequent occurrence."

[37]M. Jastrow, *A Gentle Cynic* (Philadelphia and London: Lippincott, 1919) 137, observes that "Koheleth may talk about hating life . . . but he does not really think this," for the real Koheleth reveals himself in the opposite sentiment ("Light is sweet . . . " 11:7) and in his advice to eat, drink, and be merry. For advice similar to Qoheleth's, see Siduri's counsel to Gilgamesh (*ANET* 90).

[38]With slight variation.

edge that God has granted approval before the act, particularly when the information comes from a person sceptical of similar claims.[39] Not only does Qoheleth deny that a sage actually discovers truth, but he also remarks in another place that the common fate that befalls sage and fool cancels any advantage of wisdom (2:13-14).[40] Despite the fact that a fool walks around in darkness, while a wise person possesses eyes, both stumble over the same obstacle: chance. As a result, Qoheleth questions his own aspirations to sagacity, and reflects upon the fact that he will die just like a fool (2:15-16). As a consequence, he hates life, because of the burdensome character of what is done under the sun. Nevertheless, he considers the sun's light sweet.[41] We have now returned to our initial observation about Qoheleth's hatred of life, and thus have come full circle. That circuitous route we have traversed has underscored a movement of thought similar to the one noted by Professor Terrien in Job. For Qoheleth it went from enthusiastic endorsement of life to flirtation with death as rest, from sheer pleasure over light's sweetness to hatred of life under certain circumstances. Truly, Qoheleth did not succumb to despair without a fight.

Death in Proverbs and Sirach

In vain do we search canonical proverbs for this ambiguity towards death that characterizes Job and Qoheleth. Only one brief aphorism (14:13) approaches the spirit of Qoheleth's praise of mourning: "Even in laughter the heart is sad, and the end of joy is grief" (RSV).[42] Still, the author of this enigmatic text remains outside the tent within which Job and Qoheleth reside.

Death in Proverbs invariably wears the robe of bitterest foe. Men and women shun it with one accord, for nothing commends death to anyone. Those who please God escape Sheol and Abaddon's ravenous appetite, for God rewards them with riches and length of days.[43] Righteousness and the fear of the Lord prolong life; wickedness shortens it. Whereas a virtuous person may fall seven times and rise again each time, the lamp of a wicked person will be extinguished. The adulteress' feet go down to death, and the adulterer proceeds to die like an ox. No one who goes to a loose woman's house regains life, but those who visit Dame Wisdom obtain long life, riches and honor. Indeed, Wisdom is a tree of life, bestowing happiness upon those who pick her fruit. Similarly, the teaching of the wise is a

---

[39]Perhaps 2:24-26 throws light on this text. "Apart from God, who can enjoy anything?" implies that God approves whatever we do, or we would not be able to accomplish it.

[40]Contrast, however, 7:11-12.

[41]K. H. Miskotte, *When the Gods are Silent* (New York: Harper & Row. 1967) 450-60, emphasizes the importance and sweetness of light to Qoheleth.

[42]The translation is conjectural.

[43]The threat of death thus undergirds morality (Key, "The Concept of Death in Early Israelite Religion," 246).

fountain of life, enabling one to escape death's snares. The wicked, on the other hand, fall into a pit and all hope perishes. Such are the prevailing sentiments regarding death in the canonical proverbs.[44]

The situation is altogether different in Sirach. Here ambiguity occurs once again, although with slight variations. On the one hand, Ben Sira views death as God's instrument of punishment. Accordingly, this teacher frequently appeals to his students to reflect upon their death as a means of avoiding sin (7:36; 28:6).[45] Convinced that God has presented everyone with a choice between life and death, Ben Sira urges each person to choose wisely (15:16). Since death functions punitively, it follows that things go well for the godly one at death (1:13). Having entered the world as a result of woman's sin, death has become universal (25:24). Inasmuch as none can escape death's summons, Ben Sira manages to treat the subject half humorously. Thus he quotes an epitaph: "Remember my doom, for yours is like it: yesterday it was mine, and today it is yours" (38:22). Of course "all living beings become old like a garment, for the decree from of old is, 'You must surely die'" (14:17).

Although Ben Sira conceives of death as a punishment for sin, he also recognizes that some things are worse than death.

> Death is better than a miserable life,
>   and eternal rest than chronic sickness.   (30:17 RSV)

> My son, do not lead the life of a beggar;
>   it is better to die than to beg.   (40:28 RSV)

> Of three things my heart is afraid,
>   and of a fourth I am frightened:
> The slander of a city, the gathering of a mob,
>   and false accusation—all these are worse than death.   (26:5 RSV)

Such an understanding of reality led Ben Sira to welcome death in certain instances. He pleads for the shedding of tears in behalf of the dead who lack light, but he also encourages weeping for the fool who lacks intelligence. Actually, Ben Sira contends, one needs to weep less bitterly for the dead who have obtained rest, than for the fool, over whom mourning lasts for a lifetime (22:11).

In a single passage Ben Sira articulates the complexity of his view of death (41:1-4). Here he addresses death and laments its bitterness to one who lives at peace among his possessions, but he also concedes that death is entirely welcome to one who is in poverty, ill health, and advancing years. In a surprising conclusion,

---

[44]For these references, see Prov 2:16-19; 3:1-2, 16, 18; 5:5; 7:22-23; 10:2, 27; 11:7; 13:14; 24:16, 20; 27:20.

[45]On Ben Sira's use of a debate form, see my article entitled "The Problem of Theodicy in Sirach: On Human Bondage," *JBL* 94 (1975): 48-51.

Ben Sira advises against fearing death since it is the Lord's decree for everyone, and asks: "How can you reject the good pleasure of the Most High?" Curiously, Ben Sira moves in this rhetorical question to an equation of death and divine intention, which hardly harmonizes with his belief that death results from sin.[46]

Conclusion

To recapitulate, death for the authors of Proverbs functions in a wholly negative manner, while its ambiguity pervades the thinking of Job, Qoheleth, and Sirach. For Proverbs life signifies God's blessing, death, his curse. The universe is calculable, and God, trustworthy. He rewards virtue, and punishes vice. The sage secures his existence by observing nature and human behavior, as well as by appropriating inherited traditions. Man's ultimate limit, premature death, is controllable. Consequently, anyone who embraces death belongs to the company of evildoers. In Job a decisive change takes place. Because of a collapse in the principle of retribution, life itself assumes the form of a curse. No longer proof of divine favor, length of days merely prolongs human misery for one whose God has become a personal enemy. In such circumstances, death appears as a welcome friend, especially since it prevents loss of integrity that a weakened mind and body make likely. Qoheleth, too, refused to view life as God's gift for virtue. As a result, he shared Job's divided mind about death. Ben Sira attempted to salvage the view of Proverbs, although nuanced quite differently. For him death constituted punishment for sin, but it also hung over everyone's head as a divine decree. In addition, Ben Sira endorsed Job and Qoheleth's view that in certain instances death was preferable to life.[47] In the final resort, both Ben Sira and Qoheleth stopped short of Job's bold metaphor for death. Neither dared to use terms of endearment when addressing worms ("my mother and sister," Job 17:14b), although Ben Sira did remark that at death everyone comes into an inheritance of maggots and worms (10:11; cf. 19:3).[48] Truly, all three thinkers believed that "Quand on meurt, c'est pour longtemps."[49]

---

[46]Possibly, Ben Sira means that the *time* of death is determined by God's good pleasure. The author of Wisdom of Solomon views death as God's means of preventing righteous persons from going astray, and measures life qualitatively rather than quantitatively (4:7-15).

[47]*In certain instances!* Still, this falls far short of the sentiment expressed at the conclusion of "The Dialogue of Pessimism": "Then what is good? To have my neck and yours broken and to be thrown into the river" (*ANET* 601).

[48]While Job's remark contains bitter irony, Qoheleth's and Ben Sira's expression constitutes a parody on sacral language. God's gift to his people, her inheritance, is the privilege of being devoured by worms that dwell in the promised land. Stated differently, in Sheol "maggots and worms are the true sovereigns" (Wolff, *Anthropology of the Old Testament*, 103).

[49]This title of a popular French song is taken from Terrien, *Job: Poet of Existence*, 130.

38 (1995)

The Perils of Specializing in Wisdom: What I Have Learned from Thirty Years of Teaching

In a recent movie on HBO, *Almost an Angel*, Paul Hogan comments on the close relationship between "wise" and "weird." A moment's reflection confirms the accuracy of this insight, for contemporary society no longer values traditional wisdom and considers its champions representatives of a bygone era, like dinosaurs. Having become relics from the past, we count on our vast fund of proverbial lore to prepare for every circumstance, but even this priceless legacy does not always work. Sometimes, yes, as when my younger son and I were first in line for the next available tennis court but were bumped by two young Vanderbilt women who lied about how long they had been waiting, prompting me to quote a Sumerian proverb in parting: "In court the word of a beautiful woman carries the day." At other times, no. Random events in our lives compel us to acknowledge utter helplessness in the face of disease, human perversity, and the unknown, indeed the unknowable. Faced with any one of countless anomalies of existence, we search in vain, like Job's three friends—yes, and the other two disputants, Elihu and the poet's God—for an appropriate word that will illumine the dark night of the soul forced on us by yet another enigma.

As a specialist in wisdom, I have endured the usual jokes by colleagues—and worse, the expectation that I actually excel in arcane knowledge, the "how-to" sort of wisdom associated with the adjective חָכָם in the Hebrew Bible. My few attempts to "program" a VCR, to repair something mechanical, and to install a storm door suffice to disqualify me as a transmitter of the kind of knowledge that makes culture possible, to paraphrase Ben Sira.

Ancient Understandings of Wisdom

How much more vulnerable am I when one considers the richer meaning of חָכָם, "knowing and doing the right thing." Merely acquiring a huge sum of information does not make one wise, for learned scoundrels like Jonadab, who advised Amnon about the best way to seduce his sister Tamar, understand the power inherent to knowledge. The genuine sage goes beyond knowledge to wisdom, which expresses itself in ethical behavior. The natural assumption, therefore, that specialists in wisdom are moral giants imposes an enormous burden. Ancient sages felt the burden too; that sense of living under a heavy weight is the subject of this address. Both teachers and students in the ancient world, whether in an informal setting at home or in structured education, reflected frequently on the heightened expectations of their interaction.

Additional pressure came from above, the conviction that sagacity and piety embraced one another. The argument seems simple enough. The creator ordained that a principle of order, right dealing, or justice would determine human destiny, indeed the very continued existence of the universe itself. Living in accord with this principle brought generous dividends, specifically life and prosperity, while defying it resulted in disaster. Such reasoning soon gave birth to personal piety, and a calculating moral conscience eventuated in a sense of utter dependence on divine grace, ending in fatalism.

Four cardinal virtues gradually forged their way into the public arena: timing, eloquence, integrity, and restraint. Truly wise persons needed to know when to venture an opinion, how to express it most effectively, how to sort out truth from falsehood, and how to resist the temptation to browbeat an opponent. They had to master every passion—above all, lust, pride, and anger. Those who lacked these virtues fell into the unenviable category of the "heated person" (the "hothead"), whereas individuals possessing the requisite virtues belonged to the "silent." Biblical sages varied the description, calling the former "fools" or "sinners," while identifying the latter as "wise" or "pious."

Not everyone welcomed the challenge presented by this understanding of reality, a worldview with a moral imperative built into the universe itself. From the young came extraordinary resistance. Youthful passion evoked persistent warnings against pursuit of sexual pleasure with prostitutes, other men's wives, and "holy women." Inordinate desire for beer and wine also produced fervent pleas to consider the consequences of such behavior. The wish to possess independent means, whether an early inheritance or adequate silver and gold to support a lavish lifestyle, prompted some young men to become highway robbers or to demand their inheritance before the father's death, and thus warnings about such ill-fated behavior came into being. Moreover, the lure of adventure enticed the brave and the foolhardy to join the military, envisioning the promise of travel, loot, and obliging women.

In two texts, *The Instruction of Ani* from Egypt and the Sumerian *Instruction of Sube'awilum*, the boys actually respond to their fathers' teaching. Khonshotep emphasizes the difficulty of reaching such moral heights as already attained by Ani, thus conceding the moral inferiority of youth. The father dismisses his son's reasoning as specious, insisting that virtually anyone can be taught and appealing to the domestication of wild animals and the mastering of Egyptian by Nubians and Syrians. The other text consists of conventional teaching, largely in prohibitions, and an unnamed son's pessimistic response. Both instances challenge the common assumption today that loss of nerve accompanies advancing years and prefigures one's demise. In this ancient text robust youth seems overwhelmed by the moral demands imposed by society and its authority figures. Perhaps the harsh disciplinary measures in the ancient world went a long way toward instilling pessimism in recipients of frequent beatings. Expressions like the Egyptian remark that "a student's ear is on his back" imply that real learning takes place only as a result of relentless whipping, an attitude also present in biblical wisdom literature. Interestingly, Egyptian teachers praise students less often than blaming them, while the opposite emphasis occurs in the Bible. This difference in pedagogical perspective may explain the curious absence of riddles in Egyptian wisdom, as well as their presence in Israelite instruction. Playful teasing fits more readily in situations eliciting a teacher's smile than in those governed by a scowl.

Naturally, students differed in their resistance to learning, and these gradations gave rise to distinct vocabulary designating types of learners. They range from naive or innocent persons, the uninformed and inexperienced, to unscrupulous mockers and malicious troublemakers. In contrast to these challenging students stands the perfect match between teacher and student, to which Egyptian sages attributed a hearing ear. The final section of the *Instruction of Ptahhotep* develops this notion with typical audial puns, reinforcing the importance of sound in sapiential literature.

To some degree, the difference in authority between teacher and student exacerbated the learning process, whether familial or professional. The generational gap, largely disappearing in modern theological education, and the ancient appreciation for the aged left the young in a corner just biding their time until they, too, joined the exalted ranks. Even the nomenclature for teacher and student—"father" and "son"—emphasized this gulf between an authoritative instructor and a submissive recipient of another's largesse. The situation differs little in the rare instances of maternal instruction, once in Mesopotamia and once in the Bible, for the Queen of Massa in the latter instance speaks to Prince Lemuel with full authority, moral and official.

In short, the teachings speak with a single voice of parental or professional authority, punctuated only twice by youthful protest. The inevitable conflict between the generations remains largely suppressed, although the nature of the teachers' criticism of their students provides a window into the underlying resentment that led to objectionable conduct. Israelite teachers placed a premium on diligence, perhaps because of socioeconomic factors. People with modest means could easily fall into poverty if they failed to apply themselves to the tasks at hand, hence the numerous biblical maxims about laziness. In Egypt a different situation existed, and professional students faced other dangers, particularly avarice and greed, expressing themselves in a temptation to show preference for wealthy litigants. For this reason, strife between generations expressed itself differently in the two countries, probably in Mesopotamia also, where instruction was altogether professional as in Egypt.

One theme typifies this generational struggle—delayed gratification. At last enjoying the fruits of their labors and basking in long-postponed delights, teachers urged youngsters to imitate them by waiting patiently until they have earned such pleasures. Young people, never known for patience, saw life passing them by and despaired of ever harvesting their fields. The sober conclusions of Qoheleth and Papyrus Insinger, reinforced by popular erotic poetry such as Song of Songs and the Harper Songs, shifted the burden of proof to those authority figures urging austerity for the present. The survival of a worldview hung in the balances, for a single generation could cancel the gains of all who preceded it.

Astonishingly, these teachers did not offer a comprehensive program leading to success. At most they gave general advice about broad subjects, with a few exceptions. Even these specific warnings—avoid the foreign woman, drunkenness, and laziness—lack detail, as the extensive debate about the meaning of "foreign" demonstrates. Professional instructions became considerably more specific, but even they frequently upheld general virtues and conveyed a worldview rather than concentrating on individual ethical choices. Sapiential instruction may resemble the "untying of knots" or even the "tying of knots"—negatively the unraveling of intricate secrets about the world and its inhabitants, or positively the painstaking interweaving of disparate realities to show intimate connections between previously unrelated things—but such navigation in the semantic sea undoubtedly encountered rough waters.

Ben Sira attached ambiguity to another term for wisdom whose basic meaning is "discipline." He writes: "Like her name, wisdom does not disclose herself to many" (6:22). The obvious pun on the similarity between the Hebrew words for "discipline" (מוּסָר) and "fetters" (מוֹסֵר) conceals a more fundamental insight into the intrinsic barriers to knowledge encountered by every aspiring student. She seems at first a hard taskmaster, distant and harsh, mocking all efforts at gaining access to her abode. Her yoke chafes the tender skin, and her whip stings deeper than the surface rashes they inflict. Thoughts of her as a lover carry the unwelcome pathos associated with unrequited love—until, that is, she transforms herself before the successful student and eagerly advances to embrace him.

Thus far תַּחְבֻּלוֹת and מוּסָר, but what of חָכְמָה? Despite W. F. Albright's conjecture of a Canaanite goddess of wisdom,[1] the noun occurs only twice in Donner/Röllig's collection of West Semitic inscriptions,[2] both times with that for righteousness (*sdq[h]*). Azitawadda from Karatepe in Anatolia (8th–7th c.) recalls that every king treated him as a father because of his righteousness, wisdom, and goodness of heart. Similarly, Zenjirli (8th c.) boasts that because of his wisdom and righteousness he grasped the hem of the robe of the Assyrian king. The well-known

---

[1]"Some Canaanite-Phoenician Sources of Hebrew Wisdom," *SVT* 3 (1955): 1-15.

[2]H. Donner-W. Röllig, *Kanaanäische und Aramäiche Inschriften*, I–III (Wiesbaden: Otto Harrassowitz, 1964, 1966, 1968).

association of wisdom with kingship grew out of society's anxiety over leadership and ever-present abuse of power. By claiming to possess wisdom, rulers acknowledged their subjects' uneasiness, and when ordinary citizens alluded to royal wisdom they lifted up an ideal toward which they hoped their king would aspire.

The noun חָכְמָה attracted other expressions, chiefly to complete parallel poetic stichs. Thus "understanding," "knowledge," "teaching," and "counsel" joined the earlier terms for "steering" and "discipline," but another expression, "folly," vied for dominance. The biblical personification of wisdom and folly went far beyond the poetic attribution of personal qualities to abstract nouns such as righteousness and truth, who, according to a psalmist, kissed one another. Mythic features, together with divine characteristics, combined to produce wisdom as understood in Proverbs 8, Sirach 24, and Wisdom of Solomon 7. Elements from the description of the sex goddess Ashtart/Isis and the Egyptian *Ma'at* have merged to create an attractive divine emissary who assisted in creation and eventually came to expression among Israelites as the Mosaic legislation or as a divine hypostasis. The sensual appeal of her rival, folly, lured young students, capturing them through the power of speech. Like wisdom, folly also prepared a feast for guests, but her *pièce de résistance* consisted of erotic delight, aptly described in the words "Stolen water is sweet, and bread eaten in secret is pleasant" (Prov 9:17). The failure of Egyptian sages to portray folly in this way seems like a squandered opportunity, but the goddess Maat never addressed young men in the manner employed by Isis aretalogies and biblical personifications of wisdom and folly. The closest Egyptians came to such personification implied divine reflection, expressed by *Hu* and *Sia* ("thought" and "meditation").

Modern Interpretations of Ancient Wisdom

Like those who pursued wisdom long ago, modern interpreters encounter extraordinary resistance, above all in determining the parameters of the search. The current scene amounts to a methodological nightmare, one conjured up by a mixture of the general and the specific. Paying lip service to my warning that appeared in print more than twenty-five years ago,[3] most critics fail to grasp its full import as they further defuse the distinctiveness of biblical wisdom by enlarging its corpus with an appetite resembling Sheol's. Every attempt to isolate the semantic field of wisdom, an endeavor going back to J. Schmidt's study of sapiential stylistics in 1936[4] long before publications by R. N. Whybray[5] or Nili Shupak,[6] founders on the

---

[3]"Method in Determining Wisdom Influence upon 'Historical' Literature," *JBL* 88 (1969): 129-42.

[4]*Studien zur Stilistik der alttestamentlichen Spruchliteratur*, AA 13/1 (Münster, 1936).

[5]*The Intellectual Tradition in the Old Testament*, BZAW 135 (Berlin and New York: Walter de Gruyter, 1974).

irrefutable fact that all societal groups employ cognitive language. The presence of expressions such as intelligent or clever, hearing and understanding, implies nothing about the influence of a specific professional group on the rest of the community. E. W. Heaton's recent examination of the school tradition in the Old Testament[7] attributes virtually everything in the Bible to the sages, making Shupak's study of semantic fields of wisdom in Egypt and the Bible appear far more circumspect.

Every analysis of this kind makes an assumption that language accurately reflects the social situation it describes. Things become complicated the moment one ponders the ambiguity of language. For example, although the Hebrew verb לָמַד, "to teach," certainly belongs to the context of education, its application to heifers reveals a much wider use. The fact that neither the adjective חָכָם nor the noun חָכְמָה occurs with respect to David's counselors Ahithophel and Cushai raises doubt about their affiliation with professional חֲכָמִים. Furthermore, despite a personal desire to follow Claudia V. Camp in recognizing wider feminine representation in ancient wisdom,[8] I think the adjective attributed to the women of Tekoa and Abel belongs to general use and consequently does not link them with a professional group of sages.

This quest to discover semantic parallels from two different cultures comes up against far greater obstacles. Shupak's conclusions, although modest, evolve from correct intuitions, and she refuses to overlook decisive differences. The impact of Maat on the book of Proverbs affects the description of personified wisdom, contributing the idea of righteousness as the foundation of the throne and the image of wisdom holding in her hands righteousness and life. Still, no parallel exists in biblical wisdom to a divine being that ensures the order of the universe. The closest resemblance between Maat and wisdom is the role of subordinate preexistent associate at creation, the source of divine pleasure. Moreover, the oft-cited onomastica from Egypt and Mesopotamia differ markedly from the only biblical text compared to them in some textbooks on wisdom, namely the divine speeches in the book of Job. Onomastica comprise neither encyclopedic nor nature wisdom, as Michael V. Fox has recognized,[9] and the obscure allusion in 1 Kgs 4:32-33 to Solomon's proverbs and songs probably refers to fables.

Although Egyptian scribes recognized a specific genre for teaching, *sebayit*, they employed the term so widely that it loses evidentiary value for identifying wisdom literature. It occurs with a whole range of literary types, suggesting that the

---

[6]*Where Can Wisdom Be Found?* OBO 130 (Fribourg and Göttingen: University Press and Vandenhoeck & Ruprecht, 1993).

[7]*The School Tradition of the Old Testament* (Oxford: Clarendon Press, 1994).

[8]*Wisdom and the Feminine in the Book of Proverbs* (Sheffield: Almond, 1985) and "The Wise Women of 2 Samuel: A Role Model for Women in Early Israel," *CBQ* 43 (1981): 14-29.

[9]"Egyptian Onomastica and Biblical Wisdom," *VT* 36 (1986): 302-10.

essential connection was the "academy." No biblical equivalent exists. Conversely, Israelite sages and Mesopotamian teachers used "my son" in direct address, but this vocative form appears only once in Egyptian instructions despite explicit statements in some texts that a father gave the teaching to his son.

Now if modern interpreters cannot rely on precise vocabulary and terms for genre, what enables them to render judgments about the scope of the wisdom corpus? Similar texts from Egypt and Mesopotamia? Yes, and no. The argument actually becomes circular; nonbiblicists took over the biblical category, wisdom, to describe similar texts, and then biblical scholars used those ancient Near Eastern texts to delimit the wisdom corpus. W. G. Lambert's caveat that Babylonian wisdom is essentially "magic"[10] states the problem exactly, for one searches in vain for similar omen texts in biblical wisdom. Egyptian omen texts exist, but they differ notably from instruction literature or scribal texts. The negative confession in Job 31 resembles a variant of such magical texts, further complicating a difficult book. Mesopotamian parallels place it squarely within speculative wisdom about innocent suffering, but Egyptian instructions virtually ignore this type of wisdom, the only exception being a brief section in *The Admonitions of Ipuwer*, which resembles biblical apocalyptic. One can therefore appreciate Claus Westermann's insistence that the book of Job belongs to the category of lament,[11] but restricting the category of wisdom to proverbs seems shortsighted, particularly when Qoheleth unites the two kinds of wisdom.

The division among specialists in biblical wisdom could hardly be sharper, with two groups struggling for dominance. Representing the perspective of *belles lettres* or high literature, Whybray and Heaton reach opposite conclusions. Whereas the former denies the existence of a class of wise teachers, חֲכָמִים, and posits an intellectual tradition of landed aristocracy, the latter thinks Israelite sages operated influential schools that either composed or shaped, while preserving, almost the entire Hebrew Bible. The prophets Amos and Isaiah studied at a school in Jerusalem, Heaton conjectures, and the Deuteronomist was also educated in a wisdom school. This "academy" had a counterpart in religious education, a "seminary" for training priests like Ezra. Heaton does not hesitate to dismiss as rubbish certain undesirable features of Deuteronomy and Proverbs, for he thinks warlike animosity against Canaanites and mythic attributions to wisdom could not have come from academicians.

The largely negative conclusions of my examination of evidence for schools in ancient Israel have been reinforced by two recent investigations, David W. Jamieson-Drake's archaeological study of cultural artifacts and administrative public

---

[10]*Babylonian Wisdom Literature* (Oxford: Clarendon Press, 1960) 1.

[11]*Der Aufbau des Buches Hiob*, CTHM 6 (Stuttgart: Calwer Verlag, 1977). ET: *The Structure of the Book of Job* (Philadelphia: Fortress Press, 1981).

works in Judah,[12] and Stuart Weeks' exhaustive analysis of abecedaries and drawings[13] that André Lemaire used to posit extensive educational settings in Israel.[14] Several sites at which abecedaries turned up could under no stretch of the imagination have served as schools: Khirbet El'Qom was a tomb; Nahal Michmash was accessible only by a rope ladder; Kuntillet Ajrud had a tiny bench room in a remote desert site on top of a steep hill; Lachish yielded graffiti; Izbet Sartah was roughly two miles from Aphek, with a population of about a hundred people. The sample from Arad seems decorative, that from Aroer too brief—the letters קר, perhaps part of a name; the use of limestone for the Gezer calendar is strange, for wood or clay were much more serviceable for exercises in writing. Moreover, the variation in the order of פ and ע at Kuntillet Ajrud rules out a student copying a teacher's script, and the syntax of אָמַר does not accord with that of conventional letter writing. Only the three consecutive letters of the Hebrew alphabet from Qadesh-Barnea, זחט, together with instruction in hieratic numerals and measures, point to schooling, but these may attest to a scribal guild.[15]

The other arguments for Israelite schools fare no better, as Friedemann Golka has demonstrated.[16] The biblical evidence, overwhelmingly negative, makes the silence resound all the more. Parallels from Egypt, Mesopotamia, and Ugarit lose their value when one considers the essential differences: advanced administrative governments with widespread imperial connections as opposed to an emerging state; complex systems of writing versus a simple alphabet; a developed priestly caste associated with rich temples over against family guilds.

Not every biblical critic takes high literature as the standard for wisdom. Westermann[17] and Golka[18] have recently mined African proverbs in search of clues for interpreting Israel's proverbial sayings. For them, the folk proverb constitutes the basic wisdom saying, and the similarities between biblical folk sayings and African proverbs suggests an early preexilic origin for most of the sayings in the book of Proverbs. Even maxims about kings do not require court origins, in their view, for African folk sayings often refer to chiefs. These African proverbs are secular, like

---

[12]*Scribes and Schools in Monarchic-Judah: A Socio-Archaeological Approach* (Sheffield: JSOT Press, 1991).

[13]*Early Israelite Wisdom*, OThM (Oxford; Clarendon Press, 1994).

[14]*Les Écoles et la formation de la Bible dans l'ancien Israël*, OBO 39 (Fribourg and Göttingen: University Press and Vandenhoeck & Ruprecht, 1981).

[15]See Weeks, *Early Israelite Wisdom*, 137-53, and James L. Crenshaw, "Education in Ancient Israel," *JBL* 104 (1985): 601-15.

[16]"Die israelitische Weisheitsschule oder 'Des Kaisers neue Kleider'," *VT* 33 (1983): 257-70. ET in *The Leopard's Spots* (Edinburgh: T. & T. Clark, 1993) 4-15.

[17]"Weisheit im Sprichwort," *Schalom*, ed. Karl-Heinz Bernhardt (Stuttgart: Calwer Verlag, 1971) and *Wurzeln der Weisheit* (Göttingen: Vandenhoeck & Ruprecht, 1990). ET: *Roots of Wisdom* (Louisville: Westminster/John Knox, 1995).

[18]*The Leopard's Spots.*

many biblical aphorisms, suggesting that pietists may have reworked biblical proverbs.

Anyone who rejects the hypothesis of schools must explain how learning took place in Israel. Rather than assuming that formal schools existed throughout the land, why not believe that education ordinarily occurred in family guilds specializing in crafts of various kinds? Most of this instruction demanded little or no literacy; emphasis naturally fell on oral transmission of information, primarily aimed at moral formation. Sometimes in the ancient world listening was equated with learning, but at other times it seems to have preceded learning. Sensual imagery associates learning with eating, whether a biblical scroll or a sheet of papyrus. As late as the early second century, Ben Sira spoke of the importance of listening to intelligent persons converse, as if this dialogical approach to education were the norm. That emphasis on hearing rather than writing or reading stands out in biblical wisdom, where the absence of instruction to read a text—the verb כָּתַב appears only a half dozen times—contrasts with the numerous references to writing in Egyptian scribal texts. Nevertheless, some people could write in ancient Israel, as inscriptions, sherds, and seals attest. One need not think of just any jubilant worker spontaneously incising a message in stone on successfully completing the Siloam tunnel. That inscription was probably incised by someone especially commissioned by King Hezekiah; analogy with the origin of the inscription of Mesha, king of Moab, readily comes to mind. The protests of the soldier near Lachish that no one ever hired a scribe for him may fall into the category of protesting too much, like the Assyrian kings who boast about literary skill, oblivious to its virtual nonexistence.

Two verbs indicate that Israelites distinguished between elementary and advanced learning: חָקַר and בָּקַשׁ.[19] These verbs refer to probing deeply into a matter and searching for its hidden secrets. Furthermore, sages held in high esteem those students who went beyond the mere preservation of traditional insights, adding their unique interpretations. Warnings in Egyptian wisdom against adding anything while copying a text and in Sirach against exceeding one's assignment imply that teachers recognized certain dangers in granting such freedom to students.

Modern specialists in wisdom also provoke ideological attacks from theologians who emphasize its pagan character, by which is meant an absence of specifically Yahwistic features and the abundance of ideas and expressions shared with extrabiblical texts from the ancient Near East. Horst Dietrich Preuss seizes the notion of an alien corpus and condemns it for the universal teachings it transmits, ideas grounded

---

[19]Job 28:27 may allude to four distinct stages in education, each indicated by a different verb: (1) רָאָה, "to observe"; (2) סָפַר, "to express"; (3) כוּן, "to establish"; and (4) חָקַר, "to probe." Students observe nature and human beings, watching for insights that apply more broadly; they articulate that insight and discuss it with intelligent persons; they form hypotheses; and they test their accuracy through intensive analysis.

in a theology of creation.[20] Resisting the very thing that made wisdom literature theologically viable in the modern world, he opts for the scandal of particularity, one based on a narrow understanding of divine activity in the world.

Leo G. Perdue has grasped the enormous theological potential in the ancient Near Eastern understanding of creation as a mythic conflict that elicited constant refinement and examining of traditional views.[21] Such perceptive reading of the text of Job enables one to relate the cult more closely with wisdom, inasmuch as dramatic representations of epic struggles may have communicated that vital message more effectively than otherwise would have been possible.

Besides being the unwilling target for guardians of the faith as they perceive it, specialists in wisdom also fall into the category of agnostics, necessarily so. We simply do not know the sociological setting within which sages did their work. In all probability, the central place of instruction was the family, and the curriculum consisted of folk proverbs, the product of long observation. At what point the shift to formal education occurred remains a mystery. The reference to Hezekiah's men transmitting written texts teases the imagination, although doing little more than that. Similarly, Ben Sira's cryptic invitation to those who wish to study in his house of interpretation raises the possibility that he presided over an official school, but the expression בְּתֵ־מִדְרָשׁ does not entirely rule out informal instruction within the family setting. The language may indeed be metaphoric, like the invitation in the book of Proverbs to acquire an education for money. The later Wisdom of Solomon describes a Greek curriculum in some detail and offers an extensive "midrash" on biblical history without specifying a single name—on the assumption that readers knew the biblical characters sufficiently well to recognize them from mere allusions.

A Redeeming Feature of Ancient Wisdom

Enduring this limit on what we can know and suffering the scorn of religious enthusiasts would be intolerable but for one thing, the element of surprise. Ordinarily, interpreters see exactly what they look for; examine recent commentaries on Qoheleth if you doubt this statement. Was he an optimist or a pessimist? The answer depends on how one reads the seven injunctions to enjoy life, whether as enthusiastic liberation or desperate grasping after something in an absurd universe. The refrains describing reality as utterly futile settle the issue for me, despite the arguments by Whybray[22] and Graham Ogden.[23] What makes interpreters disagree on

---

[20]"Die Gottesbild der älteren Weisheit Israels," *SVT* 23 (1972): 117-45; "Erwägungen zum theologischen Ort alttestamentlicher Weisheitsliteratur," *EvTh* 30 (1970): 393-417; and "Alttestamentliche Weisheit in Christlicher Theologie," *BETL* 33 (1974): 165-81.

[21]*Wisdom and Creation* (Nashville: Abingdon Press, 1994).

[22]"Qoheleth, Preacher of Joy." *JSOT* 23 (1982): 87-98.

[23]*Qoheleth* (Sheffield: JSOT Press, 1987).

such fundamental issues if not the worldview one imposes on the text from the outside?

On rare occasions we see things for which nothing has prepared us. For example, who would have expected to discover a Sumerian and an Egyptian text that attributes pessimism to vibrant youth? What about the ancient instruction, addressed to a child barely weaned from his mother's breast, that contains a sharp warning against committing adultery? Who could ever have anticipated the exquisite prayer nestled within the skeptical sayings of Agur in Prov 30:1-14, or for that matter, the vindictive and apocalyptic one in Sirach 36? Does an agnostic/atheist pray, and does a teacher like Ben Sira hate Israel's enemies and expect divine deliverance? How can one make any sense of the two divine speeches in Job 38–41? By what means did someone smuggle into a wisdom poem two theophanies, the one reported by an awestruck Eliphaz and the subsequent double-barreled barrage that silenced Job? Does present revelation belong within wisdom literature? By what standard of logic did ancient editors justify the epilogues to the books of Job and Qoheleth, divesting both of their essential thrust? Who would ever have thought that Egyptian instructions would introduce the idea of charismatic wisdom? By what hidden and twisted path can one travel from wisdom literature prior to Sirach, arriving at a poem praising Israelite ancestral heroes? The surprises always force scholars to reexamine the evidence; perhaps we have missed something essential to a correct understanding of the data.

During high school days my debate coach and Latin teacher taught me the three keys to successful public speaking: "Stand up, speak up, shut up." For some time I puzzled over the absence of what Greek rhetoricians called ἦθος, integrity. Why did Miss Annie Boggs leave that indispensable ingredient out? Perhaps the answer lies in the fact that in bygone years integrity was taken for granted. Sadly, that time has vanished. For that matter, so have the presuppositions of ancient wisdom, and we can only hope that by listening, searching, and probing the unknown we shall some day recover them.

Key Hebrew Terms and Expressions

Subjects

Urgent Advice and Probing Questions.
Collected Writings on Old Testament Wisdom.
   by James L. Crenshaw.

Mercer University Press, 6316 Peake Road, Macon, Georgia 31210-3960.
Isbn 0-86554-483-2. Catalog and warehouse pick number: MUP/H379.
Camera-ready pages composed by Mercer University Press on a Gateway 2000,
   via WordPerfect dos 5.1 and wpwin 5.1/5.2, and printed on a LaserMaster 1000.
Text font: TimesNewRomanPS, plus ATECH Hebrew and Greek.
   Display font: Helvetica. Cover titles: Peignot Demi.
Printed and bound by Braun-Brumfield Inc., Ann Arbor MI 48106.
Printed via offset lithography on 50# Natural Smooth, 500 ppi.
Smyth sewn and cased into Kivar 7 Performa cloth, printed black plus PMS 504c,
   with polyester film lamination over binder's boards,
      and with headbands and matching endleaves.
                                          [October 1995]

THEOLOGICAL SEMINARY
NEW YORK